Maya Apocalypse

FELICITAS D. GOODMAN

Maya Apocalypse

Seventeen Years with the Women of a Yucatan Village

INDIANA UNIVERSITY PRESS

Bloomington and Indianapolis

This book is a publication of

Indiana University Press
601 North Morton Street
Bloomington, IN 47404-3797 USA

http://iupress.indiana.edu

Telephone orders   800-842-6796
Fax orders   812-855-7931
Orders by e-mail   iuporder@indiana.edu

The paper used in this publication meets the minimum
requirements of American National Standard for Information
Sciences—Permanence of Paper for Printed Library
Materials, ANSI Z39.48-1984.

Manufactured in the United States of America

Library of Congress Cataloging-in-Publication Data

Goodman, Felicitas D.
    Maya apocalypse : seventeen years with the women of a
Yucatan village / Felicitas D. Goodman.
        p.   cm.
    Includes bibliographical references and index.
    ISBN 0-253-33908-1 (alk. paper)
    1. Iglesia Apostólica de la Fe en Cristo Jesús—History. 2. Yucatán
(Mexico : State)—Church history—20th century. 3. Pentecostalism—
Mexico—Yucatán (State)—History—20th century 4. Millennialism—
Mexico—Yucatán (State)—History—20th century. 5. Maya women—
Religious life—Mexico—Yucatán (State)—History—20th century.
I. Title
    BX7990.I4 G66 2001
    306.6'8994'097265—dc21
                                                  2001016796

    1   2   3   4   5   06   05   04   03   02   01

For Dona Eus

Contents

Preliminary Remarks

My initial interest in a Pentecostal congregation came about by way of the back door, so to speak. What was dancing in my head, as they were in the heads of many fellow graduate students in anthropology in the 1960s, were vague dreams of doing fieldwork on who-knows-what exotic topic with some totally unknown tribe living in a faraway mysterious place, in Tibet perhaps, or on the banks of the Congo, or on some palm-dotted forgotten island in the Pacific Ocean. In the course of time, none of those dreams ever approached the possible. Instead, serendipitously, things began to happen close by. In ethnographic publications I ran across repeated references to an odd kind of speech that people uttered when they were "possessed." Unintelligible gibberish, one observer termed it (he had observed this behavior on an island in Melanesia). Unintelligible speech, spoken while possessed? Memories of childhood Bible classes eventually provided the answer to the question of where I had heard about something similar before. This had to be the same phenomenon as the "unknown tongues" that the Apostles spoke when they were filled with the Holy Spirit! So this strange speech behavior had a generalized human dimension; it was not tied to one particular culture! I was off to a running start. For a paper to be given in a seminar in anthropological linguistics, conducted by Dr. Erika Bourguignon, I chose the topic of "glossolalia," the generic term for the phenomenon. Bourguignon supplied me with sound tapes of such speech, the very first I ever heard. I was totally captivated—never mind that the speech did not derive from a mysterious, faraway island in the Pacific, but rather from various Pentecostal denominations located in the pedestrian, "close-by" Ohio, Texas, the Caribbean—for I soon realized how rich this raw material was that I was now allowed to analyze. In these soundtracks from four different Pentecostal congregations, there stretched horizons far wider and more mysterious than any Pacific voyage could ever encompass. The material eventually allowed me to develop my first working hypothesis of this non-ordinary speech behavior, namely, that its striking accent and intonation pattern, as well as certain phonetic features, did not constitute traits of a different kind of natural language at all, which was the received opinion. Rather, these features expressed bodily changes a person underwent during a trance, accompanying or possibly facilitating the religious experience.

Observations in various Pentecostal congregations in this country confirmed my initial working hypothesis. However, the speakers on Bourguignon's tapes, as well as those I had observed in the American Midwest, all had English as their mother tongue. To test the validity of my theories, I needed to hear glossolalia uttered by people speaking some other language. So I went on to do fieldwork with Spanish-speaking Pentecostals in Mexico City. What I saw and recorded there in the modest little Apostolic (Pentecostal) temple in the summer of 1968 did indeed demonstrate the validity of my initial supposition: the syllables uttered during speaking in tongues were different, but the accent and intonation pattern, as well as certain phonetic features, were the same. They seemed biologically fixed.

The work in Mexico City with Spanish speakers suggested the next question, namely: What would speaking in tongues be like if the speaker's mother tongue was not an Indo-European language such as English or Spanish, but instead non–Indo-European, a so-called "exotic" language, for instance, Maya? Would the same neurophysiologically prefigured patterns that I was by now so familiar with appear in that instance too? My curiosity took me to the Maya speakers of Yucatan the following summer and to the discovery of the affirmative answer to this question.

It was also in Yucatan that I started doing participant observation with two families, especially the women, about the intertwining of ordinary tasks and sacred concerns. There was the taking care of babies and doing the daily laundry, making tortillas and raising chickens and turkeys and pigs by day; and in the evenings, there was the walking to the small mud-and-wattle temple of the Iglesia Apostolica de la Fe en Cristo Jesus, to be there when the Holy Spirit came calling.

It is a fact of participant observation that one is never done. Each season ends up pregnant with the questions for the next one. It was logical that I should return in 1970, but then I was caught up in the dizzying whirl of a millenarian outbreak, complete with expectations of the end of the world. When no trumpets sounded to announce the first day of the glorious millennium and the world continued its humdrum existence on September 2, 1970, I understandably had to find out during still another fieldwork season how the congregation had coped with the failed prophecy. And of course, I needed to know what happened after that. Suddenly, it was nineteen years later. In November 1988, yet another trip was canceled by the news that Eustaquia S.[1] had died. Eus was my wise teacher, consultant, and most loving Maya Indian sister-mother. Since then, I have not been back. To her, this account is reverently dedicated.

That Eus should be foremost in my mind here is understandable. But I also owe a debt of gratitude to my teachers in graduate school, especially to Erika Bourguignon, who first introduced me to the topic of the trance states; Robert K. Dentan, who opened my eyes to a different way of looking at religious behavior; and Michael Little, who insisted on rigor during my initial bungling attempts at understanding the religious trance as a neurophysiological phenomenon. I am grateful to Robert W. Blair and Refugio Vermont-Salas of the Department of Anthropology at the University of Chicago for their dedicated labor in putting together the voluminous textbook on spoken Yucatecan Maya that was of such help to me. The Denison University Research Foundation helped finance a number of my excursions to Yucatan. I hope in addition that this story will be a monument to my many friends and helpers in the Apostolic congregation of that sprawling Maya village in northern Yucatan (which I am calling Utzpak, "Beautiful Walls"), and particularly to Eus's family, who so generously shared their life and their experiences with me. The account of these nearly two decades is a composite of my fieldwork reports, shared with Erika Bourguignon while I was still a graduate student (until 1971) and, later, my personal diaries and correspondence with Eus's family (particularly her husband, Nohoch Felix, and her youngest daughter, Nina), as well as tape-recordings of worship services, interviews, and personal accounts.

A word needs to be said here about my title. The first part, "Maya Apocalypse," refers to the main topic, namely the convoluted evolution of the ecstatic trance experience in a Pentecostal congregation. The second part, "Seventeen Years with the Women of a Yucatan Village," requires some comment. Anthropological fieldwork usually centers on the activity of the men. Even if the report is written by a woman, this male-centeredness often predominates. Alone as a woman in the Latin American world, however, I soon realized that my survival depended on an alliance with the women. Consequently, male activity, no matter how dramatic, soon appeared in my field notes filtered, as it were, through the eyes of the women. More and more my account became a woman's book.

Pronunciation Guide

a—as in father

e—as in ember

i—as in in

o—as in orchid

u—as in tuition

double vowels are long

x—as in shoe

c—as in cat

k—is the same, except glottalized (see below)

ʔ is a consonant called a glottal stop; it is formed as a catch in the throat; it sounds like the difference between "Johnny yearns" and "Johnny ʔearns." In Yucatecan place names, "Tz" is pronounced like the last two consonants in "cats." "Dz" is the same as "Tz," but is followed by a glottal stop.

Introduction

The present study is intended as an anthropologically oriented contribution to the investigation of the Pentecostal movement. Pentecostalism is a Protestant evangelical movement. Its roots are to be found in the Reformation tradition, in the evangelical and holiness movements of the nineteenth century, and in the spiritual awakenings of the beginning of the twentieth century. Pentecostals differ from mainstream denominations by insisting on the reality of the experience of the (adult) baptism by the Holy Spirit and by the conviction that the gifts of the Holy Spirit, such as speaking in tongues, prophecy, divine healing, and exorcism, are the norm for Christian church life. They emphasize eschatology and the Second Coming of Christ and exhibit an exuberance of worship not found in the traditional congregations. The conflict between the Pentecostal religious style and that of the established denominations involves the contrast between an experience-oriented worship and a principally theologically informed religiosity. While soon splitting into a number of branches, the Pentecostal movement spread rapidly in the English-speaking world (see Nichol 1966), and in the second decade of the twentieth century it began its march southward into Latin America.

Soon, however, sociologists began noting a certain ephemeral quality about these congregations. After some years, for example, speaking in tongues, originally the main attraction, was being dropped by some congregations, initiating a return of the group to "orthodoxy," that is, reverting from the experiential to the theological style of worship. On the community level, such perceived attrition usually results in the instituting of an aggressive missionizing. As for the individual, the waning of the capacity of speaking in tongues results in much painful soul-searching as the believer attempts to discover the reason for what is perceived as the withdrawal of the Holy Spirit.

The question suggests itself whether such an evolution is an occasional happenstance, possibly the result of certain social constellations, or whether it represents the workings of the surface manifestation of certain biological processes, such as the Swiss psychiatrist Th. Spoerri (1969) stipulated decades ago, when he suggested that after prolonged ecstatic experiences involved in speaking in tongues, "the brain heals itself."

The lore of the various congregations that I came to know during fieldwork both in Mexico City and in the Yucatan provided no clear answer. I encountered references to the Holy Spirit unaccountably leaving some members but by no means all of them. The comment usually involved the "delicate" nature of the Holy Spirit, that is, easily offended, but no suggestion of the nature of the offense. However, the puzzling impermanent nature of these congregations persisted.

I eventually realized that the question concerning the reasons why some congregations persisted and other dissolved or lost their ecstatic behavior altogether could only be answered by engaging in a study carried on over a number of years, beginning close to the congregation's inception and lasting till its possible dissolution or transformation into a traditional fundamentalist group.

The group I eventually chose for this study was the Maya village Apostolic congregation in Yucatan, familiar to me since 1969. It provided the material for my dissertation (published in 1974 in Goodman et al., *Trance, Healing and Hallucination*), which I have incorporated in this report.

I observed the congregation until 1986, making yearly visits and filling in the gaps by correspondence. My visits ended with the death of my "Eus," Eustaquia S., my principal consultant and dear friend. At that time, the congregation was still a solid, viable group, its ecstatic experiences part of their worship service. By contrast, a local Pentecostal congregation had long since dissolved. Its young minister had agonized. Two young girls had experienced demon possession. Their uncle, not a minister or even an experienced preacher, had bungled their exorcism, and they scandalized the village in the course of it by stripping naked in public. The Apostolic congregation, however, despite a number of severe crises, persisted over the nearly two decades of observation. The reasons for this remarkable resilience are manifold. In the main, they involve the following factors:

1. Luis L.

Foremost, there is the minister Luis L., in appearance resembling an American Plains Indian, and a wrought-iron master by trade. These ornate iron window and door grates are an important article of manufacture in Merida, introduced by the Spanish conquerors. A fluent Maya speaker with several years of high school, Luis was a charismatic preacher, a passable guitarist, and, most important, a gifted organizer. He eventually led a revolt against the exploitative administration of the Apostolic Church, seceded from the national organization, and founded his own Maya organization of Apostolic congregations. It eventually consisted of more than twenty congregations. His ministers were allowed to keep the offerings as their remuneration. If one of them could not make ends meet, he paid him a salary out of his own pocket. His missionizing efforts centered in the village, but he also had congregations in the urban centers, in Merida, Chetumal, and Campeche.

2. Recruitment

In Mexico City, recruitment of converts happens principally by public preaching on streetcorners or in parks. The prospects tend to be of the lowest social stratum, at least according to the perception of the church administration. As Bishop Gaxiola of the Apostolic Church of the Faith in Jesus Christ of Mexico stated during an interview in Mexico City in 1968, "As to our converts, we take them from the gutter." As Eus, my principal consultant would say, "We have no such gutters." The members of Apostolic temple I came to know in Mexico City— the washerwomen, shoeshine boys, cobblers, and professional soldiers—were not from the gutter either. Our village congregation also included manual laborers, but they provided only supplemental cash income, for all householders grew their own corn and most of them owned their own homestead and, in many cases, also a ranch.

As to recruitment in Yucatecan Utzpak, as in other Maya villages, public sermons such as in Mexico City do not attract any prospects. There is a dignity, a stateliness, a built-in perception of the right way to do things that determines the manner in which missionizing can be done. And this right way is by invitation. If you accept, fine. If you don't, you are not asked again. And if the occasion is considered to be of some importance, the invitation is most properly issued to a member of one's extended family. The congregation in Utzpak started when Don Fulgencio C. was invited to hear a sermon of the evangelist Oscar Hill in the house of relatives. He, in turn, invited relatives to a sermon in his house. During the millennial uprising in the congregation in 1970, there was great anxiety about the unconverted. On the first of September of that year, when according to the prophecies the world would end, they would all die. So the men of the congregation went to the neighboring villages to preach to the unconverted of their kin. As a result of this predilection, as shown by my genealogical charts, the congregation consisted mainly of members of three extended families. In the course of time, the net became even denser and more resilient because of intermarriage.

What they eventually created was a three-generation replica of the larger village. When, a decade later, the preacher Pedro No? "gave" his congregation to the parent organization, the latter did not gain additional individual members, it gained two large extended families. The members were referred to as such—"the No?" or "the Balam."

3. Ecstatic Trance Behavior

The Bible mentions a number of "gifts of the Holy Spirit" (I Corinthians 12:4–11). All of these have a precondition of instituting a neurophysiological change termed the ecstatic trance. Among those mentioned, the "discerning of the souls" and "interpretation" (of glossolalia) are not usually engaged in in our congregation. "Divination" occurs rather often. However, speaking in tongues is of central importance. Every service features an "altar call," the proper occasion for this "gift of the Holy Spirit." The doctrine that a single "baptism by the Holy Spirit" is sufficient for admission to heaven is not a part of the lore of the congregation. Instead, people listen for it during the altar call and comment on its quality. Much speaking in tongues also occurs during (adult) baptism at the seashore. Apparently recognizing the important role that speaking in tongues plays in keeping the enthusiasm of the congregation alive, Luis L. organizes numerous revival meetings lasting three to four days, often in Utzpak. At those occasions, he drives the crowds assembled into speaking in tongues with his fiery rhetoric. When he became acquainted with a trance dance that stimulated trance behavior and that a number of evangelical groups became interested in, he immediately began introducing the innovation into his congregations.

Over the years, such activities in no way diminished.

4. The Role of the Women

On the peninsula of Yucatan, the women have been traders surely since pre-Columbian times. Using the long traditional *booch,* the scarf, as a tumpline, they are even today the ones who circulate merchandise and produce, walking many miles over narrow paths to the numerous isolated villages. Much of what they trade—bananas and other fruit, coffee, piglets, and chickens—they grow themselves in their *solar,* the large area of the homestead surrounding their houses. In fact, women own the plants and the small livestock on the *solar.* What the family does not consume is their personal income, theirs to dispose of as they please. If the husband tries to rob his wife of it, she has the right to leave him, and often does. The cottage industries, mainly involving hammocks and dressmaking, are also run by women; only the marketing is usually done by the men. In the section of Utzpak where the Apostolic temple is located, the mill, two flourishing haberdasheries, and two of the four grocery stores are owned by women.

That such strong economically powerful women would not easily bend their necks into the biblically mandated yoke could be anticipated. In the early days of the fledgling congregation (1969–1970), the minister was from Campeche, an urbanite, comfortable with the Spanish tradition that women were subordinate, they had to obey. He organized the "Dorcas," a women's organization. Then he felt within his rights to use their accumulated membership dues as his petty cash. As was to be expected, he ran headlong into the opposition of the women. Eus, a highly intelligent Maya peasant woman, narrow lipped and with the profile of a Toltec priest, told him politely but firmly that he had to keep his hands out of their savings in the powdered-milk box. Angrily, he countered that both she and her fellow Dorcas had a compact with Satan. It impressed them not at all. He continued his petty pilfering when no one was looking, but it was a contest that later ministers wisely stayed away from.

In other respects, however, the women quickly understood how to recruit this new church into their own service in the war of the sexes. You had to be married *de registro*, legally, that is, if you wanted to be baptized and become a member of the congregation. The bridegroom pays all expenses of the wedding—the food, the wedding dress, and even the bride's undergarments and shoes. Marriage gave them a better hold on their men than simply living together in the aboriginal way. "Adulterers do not enter into heaven." The onus of adultery also provided them with the opportunity, which they fully exploited, of breaking their men of their predilection, of ancient Maya origin, of entering into a double alliance—that is, taking a second wife, often in the same village. It was a custom that the Catholic Church had fought against for hundreds of years.

On the other hand, a few of the married *hermanas* had "friends." In those happy, pre-AIDS times, the tolerant comment of those in the know was usually "they probably enjoy it."

During the services in the temple, women always outnumber men, often ten to one. They are not allowed to step up on the rostrum, conduct services, or preach, but often use the "testimony" format to deliver mini-sermons. Just like the men, they can and often do present "special hymns" in front of the congregation, a coveted privilege. They often speak in tongues and prophecies. When Luis L. introduced a special dance as an efficient new strategy for inducing speaking in tongues, they were enthusiastic and almost the only participants. And when, in 1985, a girl whose aunt was a member of the congregation experienced a life-threatening, dangerous, protracted episode of demonic possession, it was Wilma, daughter of Eus, who took over the priestly role of the exorcist, successfully freeing the girl. The minister at the time refused to even help her for fear that the girl's demon might possess him instead.

Fieldwork

"All theory is gray," says the German poet Goethe in one of his aphorisms, freely translated, "Embrace instead the golden glow of life's green tree." The ethnographic section of this report concerns the golden glow of life's green tree, of which the Introduction is merely a reflection, a distillate. What I tried to do by participant observation was to collect as much of everyday life as was meaningful to me as the observer—"vacuum-cleaner anthropology," as Professor Erika Bourguignon, my venerated dissertation advisor and friend, dubbed it. I always obtained permission for my intrusion, but I was, of course, an intruder. "The man called Bee," the Yanomamo Indians called their ethnographer, Napoleon Chagnon, a pesky, busy, irritating fly, getting into everyone's face. In the course of time they got used to me. "So you are back?" Or a good-natured "*Hach poloctal* [You've gotten fat.]" Some developed a genuine affection for me—Rodolfa the beekeeper and, of course, Eus and all her numerous family—and they knew how much I appreciated that.

What resulted was, to use Clifford Geertz's felicitous phrase, a thick description. It is the world seen through the eyes of the women, rarely given much space in traditional ethnographies. It is also post-modern in the sense that the effect of the ethnographer on the group studied is balanced by proper consideration of the relations of the ethnographer to the group and its environment.

And so, *coten whaye shect?abah.* Come in and sit down.

Maya Apocalypse

1. The Context

Yucatan: Geography and Habitat

The village I call Utzpak is located in the northern part of the Yucatan Peninsula, east of Motul and about thirty miles south of the seacoast. It was once part of the classical Maya settlement area. There is a road about 1 kilometer long and straight as an arrow that leads from the outskirts of the village to a series of six small limestone structures, still standing upright under the centuries-old load of vegetation; the Utzpak boys like to play in the ancient chambers.

The Peninsula is a limestone shelf covered with low scrub vegetation, fast-growing softwood trees, and thorny vines left over after the destruction of the rain forest. The rainwater cannot form rivers or lakes because it percolates down through the limestone and accumulates in underground caverns and wells, which are called cenotes (from the Maya *tsꞌenoot*). The water of the cenotes appears dark green and oily, and there are haunting stories of people falling in and drowning or committing suicide. You cannot dig a well; you need to blast it, and as one walks down a village street, one occasionally hears a shout —"*Bomba!*"—warning the passersby to take cover against falling stone fragments. The performance of a popular song is also regularly interrupted by the same shout, and "*bomba*" in this case is a joke inserted into the melody.

"Stone is the mother of Yucatan," Eus says. She puts a handful of slaked lime into the water in which the corn is soaked that is to be ground into a yellow, fragrant *masa* at the mill on the morrow. Rotted limestone is the *sascab*, the white earth that forms the cement-like smooth layer that lines her wooden washtub. Her animals drink water from an eroded depression; no need to buy any troughs. She builds a coop for a brooding hen from a few flat fragments. The staves of her oval home are anchored in piles of limestone. Her garden wall, about 4 feet high, is constructed the same way—flat limestone slabs piled on top of each other, held in place without mortar, held simply by their weight. It looks artless but is not. "What do you call a really disgusting person?" I ask. "*Puerco* [pig]," she says. "No, no, that's Spanish. How about in Maya?" I expect an obscenity, of course, but what she says, laughing, I cannot find in my vocabulary list—something like a "crooked cradle"—and I don't understand the image until she demonstrates it. As the stones are piled on top of each other, the lower stone needs to be slightly convex, while the one that goes on top needs to be a bit concave, or they will slip. A wall containing a stone of the wrong shape, a "crooked cradle," could easily collapse. I note in passing how *puerco* refers to a personality trait while being called a crooked cradle indicates deficiency in community relations. Actually, crooked cradles are rare; the walls are very stable and because of the irregular protrusions one can climb a garden wall almost as if it had steps. At night, stray dogs will do that to invade the open kitchen house, knock down a *lec* [large gourd], and devour the dry tortillas stored in it.

The humus layer covering the limestone outcroppings is not continuous, so a plough is useless. Fertile crumbs of soil accumulate instead in small depressions leached into the limestone. As a sensitive extension of his hand, Eus's husband, Nohoch Felix ("old" Felix senior, as against "Chan" [small] Felix, Felix junior), uses his planting stick, or dibble, and gently probes the soil until he feels a depression deep enough to allow a few seeds of corn to grow, or some *shpelum* [black beans].

History of the Yucatan

Politically, the Yucatan Peninsula is part of the Republic of Mexico, the largest of the Mesoamerican states. Its territory is occupied by a profusion of Indian groups belonging to a large number of different tribes and representing numerous distinct language families. This patchwork quilt, however, assumes a strictly homogeneous Maya hue on the Yucatan Peninsula.

On the eve of the conquest by the Spaniards, the Yucatan Peninsula was divided into a number of centralized states and loose confederations of towns. Although it was not effectively conquered until 1545, its discovery preceded the conquest of Tenochtitlan and the empire of Montezuma:

> In 1511, a Spanish ship on its way from Panama to Santo Domingo was blown off its course and shipwrecked off the southern coast of Yucatan. Only two men who finally reached the mainland in a small boat survived, Geronimo de Aguilar and Gonzalo Guerrero. . . . Although [these two men] came to Yucatan as refugees rather than as conquerors, they may have unconsciously paved the way for the eventual conquest of the Peninsula, for (prior to 1527) the population of the Peninsula was devastated by a series of epidemics that were probably of European origin. It is likely that they were introduced by Spaniards like Aguilar and Gerrero, who had been shipwrecked off the coast of the Peninsula.
>
> The Spaniard who is credited with discovering Yucatan is Francisco Hernandez de Cordova. (Bricker 1981, 13)

Despite devastating population losses due to European diseases and prolonged warfare against the Spanish, the Maya peasant persisted. Through history, he resisted the Spanish overlord and later the Mexican state, which became independent of the Spanish Crown in 1821, with one bloody uprising after another. The memory of each earlier revolt fed the succeeding one. At the beginning of the Caste War in the 1840s, the name of Jacinto Canek, leader of the 1761 revolt, was written on the walls of houses as a revolutionary slogan (Reed 1964, 44).

1761: Cisteil

CANEK

The Maya Indians proclaimed the independence of Yucatan and announced the forthcoming independence of America.

Jacinto Uc, who made trumpets sound by caressing the leaves of trees, crowned himself king. Canek, "black snake," is his chosen name. The king of Yucatan tied around his neck the mantle of Our Lady of the Conception and harangued the other Indians. They rolled grains of corn on the ground and sang the war chant. The prophets, the men with warm breasts enlightened by the gods, said that he who died fighting would reawaken. Canek said that he was not king for love of power, that power craves more and more power, and that when the jug is full the water spills out. He said that he was king against the power of the powerful and announced the end of serfdom and of whipping posts and of Indians lining up to kiss the master's hand.

In Cisteil and other villages the echoes multiplied, words became screams; and monks and captains rolled in blood.

1761: Merida

FRAGMENTS

After much killing, they took him prisoner. Saint Joseph was the patron saint of this colonial victory. They accused Canek of scourging Christ and of stuffing Christ's mouth with grass. He was convicted. He was to be broken alive with iron bars in the main square of Merida.

Canek entered the square on muleback, his face almost hidden by an enormous paper crown. On the crown his infamy was spelled out: "Risen against God and against the King."

They chopped him up bit by bit, without permitting him the relief of death, worse than an animal's fate in a slaughterhouse; then they threw the fragments of him into the bonfire. A prolonged ovation punctuated the ceremony. Beneath the ovation, it was whispered that the serfs would put ground glass in the masters' bread.

In the second decade of the twentieth century, the Maya peasants, once more fighting for land in the Mexican revolution, sang a song from the Caste

War, the chorus of which was remembered by Reina, my first hostess in Utzpak, in the early 1970s:

> *Yucatecos libres*
> *Marchan al oriente*
> *Alli quitar los malos*
> *Estos como blanca gente. Chicochin . . .*
> (Free Yucatecans are marching to the east,
> there to expel the bad ones, those white people.)

Yucatan Today

A strong undercurrent of separateness from the Republic continues to pervade life in Yucatan. This is emphasized by the important role that the Maya language plays in public and private life, especially in the villages. However, in the northern villages, a large number of Spanish loan words are mixed in with Maya, and "Our Maya is not good, you have to go south, to Quintana Roo, for really beautiful Maya" is a frequently heard remark. Eus, my dear friend and principal consultant, was very conscious of her perfect command of Maya and made expansive fun of those women who would carelessly sprinkle their Maya with Spanish. "They don't even notice it," she would say ruefully.

In Merida, the capital of Yucatan (Eus called it "Ho?," its old Maya name), the urbanites speak Spanish, the language of prestige, although many of them also have Maya as their mother tongue. Reina, who had dreams of leaving the village to live in Merida, insisted on speaking Spanish the first summer that I lived in her house, and I did not hear her speak Maya until the second season I was there. Spanish is used in all official business and public transactions, including church services. Street and radio advertising does use Maya, in competition for the villagers' cash. However, instruction in the Maya language, which until the early 1960s was compulsory in the teachers' training schools, has been abolished. Wilma, one of Eus's daughters, sent her children to the Utzpak grade school. One of her sons did very poorly, and one day we (Eus, Wilma, five of her older children, and I) all marched to the school together to speak with the principal and to protest what Wilma thought was deliberate mistreatment of her son. The principal just shrugged. "He is obstinate and not particularly intelligent," he said. "He won't say a word in school." Wilma was furious afterward. "Oscar is not dumb," she said. "He would do all right if they spoke Maya to him. But they have these *wachos,* these outsiders, coming in to teach here, and they don't know any Maya."

The Pentecostal Movement

The majority of Yucatecans are Catholic. However, the Catholic Church has kept aloof from the everyday life of the people everywhere in Mexico since the Mexican Revolution. (To change that situation, according to newspaper reports, a "pastoral action" meeting was convened in Mexico City in the fall of 1969 to "acquaint the Catholic Church with the social realities of Mexican life.") Indifference to the Catholic Church was evident in Utzpak. Few people attended mass in the cavernous Catholic Church, built by Indian slave labor in the eighteenth century—not even on feast days. This situation left the field wide open to Protestant missionizing. In addition, state and church are separated according to the Mexican constitution. Thus, there is no legal basis for the state authorities to interfere with Protestant proselytizing.[1] In fact, as Pablo A. Deiros points out,

> Evangelical Christianity has become both a religious and a political power
> in Latin America. In terms of religious affiliation, the recent growth of
> "evangelical" groups (a broad term including also fundamentalist and
> Pentecostal churches) has been phenomenal. In all of Latin America, there
> are 481 million people, of whom sixty million now belong to evangelical
> churches. (1992, 144)

And David Stoll relates, "One bishop in Brazil has warned that Latin America is turning Protestant faster than Central Europe did in the sixteenth century" (1990, xiv).

The Latin American evangelical movement is divided into three broad categories: mainline Protestantism, Evangelical Protestantism, and Pentecostal Protestantism. Of the three, Pentecostalism is the fastest-growing Christian movement of the region. As Stoll remarks, "by the 1960s, both kinds of Protestantism had clearly been overtaken by a third, Pentecostalism. Two-thirds of Latin American Protestants were Pentecostals and that proportion was increasing to three-quarters by the 1980s" (1990, 101). What was true in the 1980s was visible as early as the 1960s, when Christian Lalive d'Epinay (1969) spoke of the spread of Pentecostalism as the "Pentecostal explosion."

The question is: What gave Pentecostalism its edge? Deiros suggests that the popularity of Pentecostalism "is attributable, in part, to its adherents' characteristic attitude of constant testimony and religious militancy that translates into a zeal for winning souls" (1992, 151). However, other Protestant missionizing, for instance that of the Mormons or of Jehovah's Witnesses, shares this same zeal for winning souls, so this does not really account for the Pentecostal success. Deiros states further that "apart from their distinctive understanding of the doctrine of the Holy Spirit, Pentecostals share the doctrinal and ethical convictions and, more important, the abiding sense of the meaning and necessity of a personal experience of redemption, of their non-Pentecostal evangelical counterparts" (ibid., 151). Stoll points to the ability of the Pentecostals to "organize relatively stable, expanding structures, with a definite capacity for adapting to changing conditions" (1990, 318). This statement has clearly been unchecked against fieldwork reports resulting from participant observation.

The essays assembled by Martin and Mullen (1984) cite a number of examples of the propensity of Pentecostal congregations to dissolve and to return to "orthodoxy." However, as is clear from these reports, for every Pentecostal congregation that dissolves, another new one springs up around the corner, thus leaving the statistics intact. So there is obviously another factor involved in the success of Pentecostalism. What could that factor be? Deiros speaks simply of a "distinctive understanding of the doctrine of the Holy Spirit" and of a "personal experience of redemption" as being specific to the Pentecostal congregations, without clarifying either how the understanding is distinctive or how such a personal experience might come about. Stoll is more outspoken: "Like spiritism, [Pentecostalism] appeals to the magical proclivities of the population. But unlike spiritism, which encourages amoral clientalistic relations with a plethora of deities, Pentecostalism places authority in a single godhead, creates universal ethical standards, and promotes individual responsibility" (1990, 318).

What both men allude to, without any clear idea of all that is involved, is the fact that Pentecostalism, unlike the other Protestant movements, facilitates access to the religious trance, to the ecstatic experience involved in speaking in tongues. This is what is hiding behind Deiros's "personal experience," and the desperate need of all humans to undergo a religious trance is manifest in the "magical proclivities of the population" Stoll points to. It is easy to spot the pejorative meaning of his remark: "proclivity," according to Webster, is "a strong inherent inclination toward something objectionable." It is truly curious to see two authors of the 1990s still frozen in the attitudes of the 1950s, when the pathology model used to "explain" the ecstatic trance constituted the received wisdom, and persons speaking in tongues were described as schizophrenics, hysterics, or epileptics (Sargant 1975). So what about the religious trance and the ecstatic experience, the presence of which Deiros so coyly disguises and Stoll finds so objectionable?

This kind of trance is one of a number of altered states of consciousness of which humans are capable because it is part of their genetic endowment. Put simply, a perceiving individual, under everyday, ordinary circumstances, might say, "I open my eyes and in front of me I see a tree." However, the same person, under radically changed circumstances, having recourse to a qualitatively modified type of perception, might then say, "I close my eyes and I see a spirit." Such changes, as a matter of course, are internal to the individual; they concern his/her state of consciousness. In other words, it is a modification in the state of consciousness of the individual that in one instance makes it possible for him/her to perceive a tree and in the other instance to see a spirit, or, in other words, to turn the ordinary state of consciousness into an altered one. The question is, how is such a modification of consciousness brought about?

Since no society has ever been known to be without religion, and statistical research has indicated that the overwhelming majority of societies engage in trance behavior during religious rituals (Bourguignon 1973), it is logical that various techniques for achieving this altered state of consciousness should be familiar to religious practitioners around the world. The most popular of these techniques involve rhythmic stimulation. Dramatic changes are instituted in response to this strategy. The rate of the heartbeat increases; the blood pressure drops; in the blood serum, adrenaline, noradrenalin, and cortisol diminish; and the brain begins to release a peptide, the beta endorphin. This compound is the body's own opiate and is what produces the infinite joy associated with ecstasy. The electric activity of the brain also changes; high-amplitude and low-frequency theta waves appear in EEGs produced by alternating current, while at the same time the brain begins to act like a battery and produces an enormous increase in its negative potential, as seen in direct-current EEGs.[2] All of these changes are instituted on cue; that is, when the rhythmic activity— the drumming, clapping, singing, and so forth—starts, and the systems of the body involved in the trance return to previous conditions when the stimulation stops. In other words, the trance behavior is under control, which distinguishes it from psychotic phenomena, where such control cannot be exercised. The trance experience awards the practitioner not only temporary euphoria but also long-term dissolution of stress-related tension. People who have to do without this experience—for example, modern city dwellers—tend to suffer from ecstasy deprivation along with a related propensity for psychosomatic illnesses and various addictive behaviors. Most important, however, the religious trance converts religion from a matter of belief—of faith, of "holding to be true"—to a matter of experience. In other words, it is the biological entryway to the realm where the spirits dwell.

While all humans are capable of experiencing a religious trance, not all communities utilize it in the same manner. Humans, as we know, have a propensity for adapting physical capabilities to cultural ends. All humans can sing, for instance, but not everybody sings operatic arias. The same selective adaptation also happens with the religious trance. Depending on the type of society in question, the trance is used for different types of experiences.[3] The hunter-gatherers use it as a vehicle for spirit journeys. But the people with whom Christianity originated were not hunters; they were cultivators, agriculturalists. Cultivators the world over do not go on spirit journeys; they use the religious trance instead for possession.[4] What is experienced during a possession is the opening of the body so that a spirit being can enter it and use it for its own purposes. In the case of Pentecostalism, the possessing alien being is the Holy Spirit, the Spirit of God, part of the Trinity. This is what constitutes what Deiros terms Pentecostalism's "distinctive understanding of the doctrine of the Holy Spirit." To be sure, the Holy Spirit never has anything specific to say with its semantically vacuous syllables, nothing that bears any relevance to life in ordinary reality. It is also easily offended, sometimes staying away for reasons that are difficult to discern. What is certain, and what is stated over and over again when people "testify," is that the presence of the Holy Spirit (*el mora en mi*—"it takes up its abode in me") brings with it overwhelming rapture and awards hope, joy, and health.

A young deacon of the Apostolic congregation in Mexico City, where I did fieldwork in 1968, summarized the experience this way: "My body becomes a tabernacle and then the Holy Spirit enters." He continued, "and then the Holy Spirit takes hold of my tongue." This taking hold of one's tongue refers to "speaking in tongues," or, in linguistic terms, "glossolalia."

According to Pentecostal dogma, speaking in tongues constitutes the baptism by the Holy Spirit, without which one cannot enter into heaven. It indicates to the congregation that the supplicant has been sealed by the seal of the Lord and has been given the promise of salvation. The literature about this kind of religious trance behavior has never been particularly ample. In and before the 1960s, Cutten's work was often quoted as one of the early attempts at describing the behavior in Christian churches from a psychological and historical perspective. In the late 1960s and early 1970s linguists began to revisit the topic (Jaquith 1970; Samarin 1968). Despite the prominence of the Pentecostal movement in Latin America (and around the world for that matter), where speaking in tongues is of central concern, scientific interest in the phenomenon seems to have disappeared completely by the 1990s. This may be the reason why modern authors, who do survey research and not fieldwork, may have missed it. Stoll gives it only passing mention, and there is no entry for it at all in the voluminous tome about fundamentalism edited by Marty and Appleby (1991).

As pointed out before, speaking in tongues is an act of vocalization, of uttering sounds while the person is in the religious trance.[5] The syllables uttered are empty of semantic content, although Pentecostals believe that what they say is a language that could be understood if someone who spoke it was present. This theory is called xenoglossia. However, the syllables produced do not conform to the characteristics of a natural language as defined by modern linguistics. The confusion dissolves if we define speaking in tongues not as language but as communication. In this sense, it is communication between the Holy Spirit and the speaker, and between the speaker and the congregation.

Speaking in tongues is not one single behavior but rather a behavioral complex. First of all, the supplicants learn to go into trance with the help of the strong rhythmic stimulation provided by the congregation in the form of music, clapping, punctuated shouting, and singing. This removes them from the awareness of ordinary reality. While I was filming, for instance, they no longer reacted to strong light, heat, or manipulation. I observed that they no longer reacted to the flashbulb of my camera or heat from a 1,000-watt movie light I used at very close range during filming in the small Utzpak temple. In another instance, I observed that a woman in the Utzpak congregation did not feel it when her small daughter unzipped her dress in the back. The trance experience is not vacuous, however; it is only that the supplicants' experiences are not perceivable to the observer. They may feel feverish, they may note pressure on their chest, or they may feel that they are floating. Some report seeing a bright light. The observer, for his/her part, will often detect that the supplicant is physically agitated. There may be exaggerated perspiration and salivation. Tears may flow, the face is flushed, there is rigidity, or one sees shivering, shaking, twitching, or even jumping. The term "hyperarousal" can properly be employed to describe this agitated state.

After supplicants learn to go into trance, they learn to utter sounds: there is vocalization. Some people, especially those who acquire the behavior spontaneously, learn both the trance and the vocalization simultaneously. The trance now acts as a substratum to this speech, producing or generating a number of its features. One of these is its strong rhythmic quality, a regular alternation of consonants and vowels that evinces all the hallmarks of involuntary bodily functions such as heartbeat or breathing. Another feature, a very mysterious one, is a characteristic intonation pattern: there is an onset of a unit utterance (like a sentence in ordinary speech) in the medium range of the speaker; then it rises to a peak at the end of the first third of the curve, and this is perceivable as being louder or simply much faster. Finally, the voice of the speaker drops, but this drop is usually much lower than that at the end of a declarative sentence in English. A curve of a unit utterance registered by the level recorder in the phonetics lab clearly shows this pattern (Figure 1). This complex pattern cannot be mimicked in ordinary consciousness, thus obviating the contention sometimes heard that the behavior is "faked"; however, the longer a person has been speaking in tongues, the less pronounced these patterns become.

After falling silent, many supplicants do not instantly become aware of ordinary reality. They might appear confused; their speech seems slow before they return fully to ordinary consciousness. Once this happens, they remember very little of their actions during the trance. In particular, they cannot judge how long they spoke in tongues. They may not even be sure that they uttered anything at all, and if they are, they cannot repeat their utterance. Characteristically, however, once they are in trance again, their utterance is the same.

Pentecostalism in the Yucatan

In summary, then, the appeal of the Pentecostal movement, with its many branches, derives from the fact that it makes available the trance experience and legitimates its enjoyment. In Mexico, the Pentecostal movement is represented by a number of different branches. The one that concerns us here is the Apostolic denomination. It was started in Mexico in 1914 by Mexicans who had become acquainted with this new religious style in the United States (Gaxiola 1970). The church authorities maintain, however, that the Apostolic Church of Mexico is independent of any American involvement. It is organized into twelve districts, with its headquarters, under a bishop president, in Mexico City. In 1964, it had over 1,000 ministers, and the movement was represented in all sections of the country.

In 1949, proselytizing began in what was at that time termed the southeastern district: the states of Tabasco, Yucatan, Oaxaca, and Chiapas and the southern part of Veracruz. Although in this manner Yucatan was nominally included, actual missionizing did not begin there until 1959, when an evangelist named Oscar Gill (or Hill; he signed his name either way) from the Guadalajara Apostolic congregation began evangelizing there. By 1970, there were eighteen established congregations (fourteen in villages and four in urban areas) in what is presently termed the southeastern district (Yucatan; Campeche; Quintana Roo, a part of Veracruz; and the eastern section of Tabasco). This district, like all the others, is headed by a bishop. Its central offices are in Villahermosa. Half the offerings collected at the local level go there. In turn, the elders representing the bishop's office make regular visits to the various sections. There are three sections: 1) Quintana Roo, Campeche, and Yucatan; 2) Tabasco (consisting of five subsections); and 3) part of Veracruz. Each section is headed by a representative or supervisor appointed by the bishop.

The bishop's office convenes a yearly meeting of ministers. It is also in charge of holding a yearly Biblical Institute, at which new candidates for the ministry are trained and those already in office are given advanced instruction. Training on the most advanced level takes place in the permanent Biblical Institute at Tepic, Nayarit; this institute is run by the national organization.

The sections also have their own meetings at regular yearly intervals. At these meetings, new ministers are inducted into office and decisions are made concerning the placement of ministers and the reassignment of others to different congregations. Members of the local congregations are free to attend these meetings and often do. Evangelizing campaigns may be organized at the meetings, but more often such efforts are left to the initiative of the congregations.

The Apostolic missionizing effort was facilitated by inexpensive bus transport along Yucatan's paved highways. In the 1970s, for instance, all the villages that had active congregations, including Utzpak, were along these highways—Temax, Dziuche, Limones, Cafetal, Bacalar, Nicolas Bravo, Jesus Gonzales Ortega, Cenotillo, Calkini, San Antonio Sakachen, Tizimin, Cuarenta y Dos, and Campos. Efforts at missionizing in Tibilom, where Eus and her family lived before coming to Utzpak and which is accessible only by jungle path, were consistently warded off. Holkah, the neighboring community, was on the paved highway and had a Pentecostal congregation, but when the minister and some of the members of his church wanted to hold a service in Tibilom, they were driven off with violence. The Apostolics also tried to get a toehold in Tibilom. In September of 1970, three ministers and several *hermanos* ("brothers," i.e., members) went there to hold a service. Upon arrival, they were met and evicted by a spectacular show of force—church bells ringing, fireworks popping, knives and guns openly displayed. However, one of the ministers, Chan Felix, the son of Eus, was a native of Tibilom, and his sister, Wilma, still lived there at the time. She threatened to knife anyone who might touch her younger brother. So an agreement was worked out that he would be tolerated, but no one else. To make sure of his position, Chan Felix secured official permission for his evangelizing from the provincial authorities in Sotuta. In January of 1971, however, the villagers once more prevented him from holding services, and his sister was threatened with arson. Things changed when in 1973 electricity was introduced and the bus company extended its services to the village. Simultaneously, there was a sudden increase in the membership of the Apostolic congregation.

The Village of Utzpak

The community of Utzpak lies along one of the highways that radiates outward into the Peninsula from Merida. This highway had reached the village in 1961. At the time I started fieldwork there, in 1969, it ended at the outskirts of the settlement and was in the process of being extended. This highway is also the main street of the village, which opens to a large village square; the plaza, having tall live oak trees and benches; the Catholic Church; and the town hall. The owner of one of the large cattle ranches has a spacious home near the plaza, but he and his family are rarely there. This home is rectangular, is constructed of limestone and mortar (called *mamposteria*), and has a roof of corrugated tar paper. About 10 percent of the 1,080 homes of the village[6] are of this design; these homes usually also have electricity. They belong to the urbanized minority; the men wear *catrin*—that is, Western-type slacks and shirts—as well as shoes. The women favor Western-type dresses, and their children stay in school beyond the second grade. The other 90 percent of the homes have the traditional oval shape, are thatched with palm fronds, are constructed of mud and wattle, and have a dirt floor. These homes are known to have been built this way for several thousand years. The village has six mills where the soaked corn is ground into *masa* for the daily tortillas, a movie theater, a children's clinic, a permanent market hall, eleven stores, and six taverns. It also has a six-grade primary school with nine state-paid and six federally paid teachers. There are two policemen, both part-time employees of the community. Misconduct (usually fighting) is punished by one to fifteen days of community service. Cases of assault or murder are taken to Merida. The municipal president acts as judge and mediator in civil suits. In 1969, there were twice as many radios as there were homes, about twenty-five television sets, and forty-two motor vehicles.

Utzpak is situated just outside the so-called *henequen* belt, where this fiber is produced in monoculture, with all the misery that dependence on the world market and its fluctuating prices brings to the Third World. Eus and I were coming home from a trip to Merida, and an elderly peasant woman was sitting next to us on the bus, her embroidered folk dress, the *ʔipil*, a dirty gray. When we got off, I made a disparaging remark about the woman's dirty *ʔipil*. Eus's face turned stern, clearly disapproving of my hasty judgment. "She comes from Temax," she said. "The men there don't work on the ranches. They cut *henequen* and work in the *desfibradoras* [*henequen*-processing plants]. They make so little, she does not have any money for soap." Work on the *henequen* ranches outside the *henequen* belt is looked down upon, and only about 10 percent of the Utzpak men sought employment there in the 1960s.

The population of Utzpak (5,232 in 1969) is predominantly agricultural, and its peasant character is accentuated by the dress of the people. Most of the women and about half the men still wear the native costume. This consists, for the men, of white cotton pants and jacket—only the oldest men still wear the traditional unpleated kilt on top of their pants—and *alpargatas* (sandals), nowadays usually made of rubber tires. Some of the younger men alternate between the informal peasant garb and the more formal city attire. The women wear an embroidered, loosely fitting dress over an underskirt edged in eyelet embroidery, and an obligatory shawl, the *rebozo*. A woman dressed this way is called a *mestiza*. The word "*indio*" is used only in a derogatory sense. "*Es tu genio indio* [It is your Indian disposition]," Reina shouts at her husband, Santiago, when she is really furious at him. A woman either *anda de vestido,* that is, she wears (walks in) a dress, or *anda de ʔipil,* wears a folk costume. For women, the way they dress is a clear expression of worldview and social orientation: with unswerving consistency Eus, consciously peasant, wears an *ʔipil,* while Reina, the incipient urbanite, wears a dress. In other words, unlike the men, the women are always consistent in the way they dress. But whether in dress or in *ʔipil,* women are all interested in embroidery. An embroidery pattern for an *ʔipil* brought in from another village is immediately examined and sometimes copied for sale, although villages and even certain women have their own characteristic patterns which are recognized as such. Only women embroider, but men and women share equally in the weaving of the hammocks.

Most of the householders of Utzpak have their own corn plantings, their *col* (the Mexican word *milpa* is preferred by many authors). Utzpak is surrounded by *ejido* holdings, a federally administered program providing land from the haciendas, the large landholdings divided in the 1920s after the Mexican Revolution, for the rural population. A *col* can only be utilized for about three years. The land is worked by slash-and-burn cultivation, where the plot is burned over by very small, controlled fires, and the ashes fertilize the soil. The first year's harvest is good, provided the rains arrive on time at the end of May. The next year gives a medium yield, and the third year is often hardly worth the work put into it. Then the land has to lie fallow for about twenty years, and the householder needs to go to the administrative office in the village where, for a few pesos, he is assigned another piece of land to work. Utzpak seems to have enough *ejido* land to satisfy demands, which is not the case with many other villages, and the cattle ranchers, who still own many thousands of acres, are jealously guarding their holdings. A cattle rancher I briefly met in Mexico City, with extensive holdings in northern Yucatan, maintained that he would shoot on sight any man who would try to plant a *milpa* on his land. If getting a plot to work does not seem to be a problem in Utzpak, the price of seeds is. The Banco Agrario de Yucatan offers credit at 4 percent interest, but the peasants, unfamiliar with Euro-American money management, want neither to borrow nor to pay back debts. These attitudes are reinforced by recurrent charges of mismanagement against the Bank's branch offices in the villages. For example, according to newspaper reports, in January of 1971, five employees of the branch offices in two Maya villages were savagely beaten with *henequen* ropes for mismanagement and were then forced to leave the communities barefoot over paths deliberately strewn with stones and thorns. The story, including the part about the condition of the paths, may have been embroidered somewhat, given the traditional enmity of the urbanites against the villagers. In Yucatan, as I should know from wearing open sandals, all paths are naturally strewn with thorns and stones.

The *col* is not only a source of subsistence. It is also a sacred place, and U Yum coli, the lords or grandfathers of the cornfield, are given food offerings, the *hanli col,* so that they will watch over the plantings. Reina told that her father-in-law (an important member of the Apostolic congregation) regularly took *hanli col* to his corn garden. "If you do that," she said, "and somebody wants to steal a watermelon, he will be paralyzed. He won't be able to move until he puts that melon down."

Most of the protein needs of the households used to be provided by hunting. Game, especially deer, but also peccary, various large rodents, and armadillo, used to be so plentiful that when in the 1940s there was no corn harvest for two consecutive years because of a drought, Nohoch Felix kept the family going just by hunting. "We got very tired eating meat all the time," Eus said. Due to overpopulation and the demands of the tourist industry, there was very little game left by the late 1980s.

In order to earn cash for seeds and other necessities, Nohoch Felix and the other men used to work on the large ranches (this was true when I first started doing fieldwork in Utzpak in 1969), sowing, weeding, and harvesting the corn and the beans. The ranchers would send large rickety trucks to pick up the workers in the mornings and bring them back in the evenings, and there was much joking and shouting as they rumbled through the main street. The wages were very low, but still, it was cash. But then, in the early 1970s, the government tried to force the ranchers to pay a more equitable minimum wage, and they stopped growing corn and concentrated exclusively on cattle. For the approximately 240 ranches surrounding Utzpak, some quite large, many small, with a total of 38,075 cattle in 1969, this represented no hardship; meat brought a good price. But the action threw the peasants out of work and had them scrambling to find alternative employment. Yucatan used to be famous for its honey and wax, but few people have the requisite knowledge anymore. In the congregation, there was only one beekeeper.

Much petty cash is earned by the women. When Eus was younger, she made some money sewing shorts and shirts. Then the treadle sewing machine that she had inherited from her mother broke and could not be repaired. So she switched to gardening. As was true of most homesteads in Utzpak, her property was surrounded by several acres of land, the *solar.* Eus had regular crops of cilantro for sale, but principally she grew flowering bushes and fruit trees. For planters, she would pick up rusty tin cans discarded along the highway and would patiently nurse the small seedlings along for years, with Nohoch Felix adding his skill of grafting. Many of the tall avocado, lime, *anona*, orange, and other fruit trees growing in Utzpak today came from Eus's nursery.

Reina's husband, Santiago, although a local boy, refused to do ranch work, not even on his father's ranch. "He is looking for what is soft," Eus said. Having no skills at all, he would do hauling with a *companero*, collect bottles from the dump and wash them for sale, or hunt for deer when there was a local fiesta and sell deer-meat tacos. Reina, coming from the *henequen* belt, had none of Eus's skills, but she knew how to read and write, which often helped her illiterate husband in his various jobs. For a while there was a representative of the government in the village who distributed cotton thread to the women for weaving hammocks. But she paid very little for the finished body of the hammock, and standing next to the upright loom all day gave Reina severe muscle pains in her back and shoulders. So she switched to raising pigs. These pigs, small, wiry, and efficient scavengers, practically raised themselves on the garbage in the streets and brought a good price. But then the municipal government forbade the free roaming of the pigs because they were picking up trichinosis from the contaminated offal, and there was little for them to eat in Reina's barren *solar*. She tried keeping them on corn gruel instead, but that was too expensive. The government offered to pay the householders for raising a large hybrid breed of pigs, but, as Reina pointed out, the sties the government demanded had to be constructed of cement and few people could afford that. "The pigs are supposed to live better than we do," she complained, and besides, the wells did not contain enough water for scrubbing the sties down all the time.

The Apostolic Congregation

In 1969, there were only about 300 Protestants in Utzpak. The oldest Protestant congregation was Presbyterian, and there were also Baptists and Pentecostals in the village. During my first stay in Utzpak, one of the former ministers of the Apostolic congregation there gave me the following account of its history:

> *Brief History of the Apostolic Church of the Faith in Jesus Christ, Utzpak, Yucatan. Written by Hermano Luis L., Pastor*

> When the missionary of Hermano Oscar Hill was in the city of Merida, he was visited by Senor Fulgencio C., who, because he was interested in the things of God, invited Hermano Hill to come and visit him in the place of his residence, which was located in the pretty community of Utzpak. Hermano Hill accepted this invitation

with great pleasure, and after a considerable time, he succeeded with the help of God in having a group of people accept the Word of God. After receiving instruction, these persons were baptized in the name of Jesus Christ, on the thirteenth day of July of the year 1960. From that time on, the work kept growing, thanks to our Lord.

The mission time of Hermano Hill having been completed, he had to leave the field, and the responsibility passed on to Hermano Juan L., initiated deacon of the church in Merida. He stayed in Utzpak only a brief time, for at a convention it was decided to transfer him to the city of Villahermosa, Tabasco, as evangelist. The church in Utzpak was entrusted to Hermano Santiago M., who stayed with the congregation for the duration of a year.

As the result of the decision of another convention, the small church of Utzpak then passed on to the care of another deacon, Hermano Luis P., who after a short time had to abandon the work.

After that, the care of the church of Utzpak remained in the hands of Hermano Luis L. and the said Hermano carried this responsibility for a year and a half.

The next person in charge, or rather the pastor, was Hermano Felix S., who for about two years came to serve the Lord in this small congregation, which God chose to bless during his stay. The latter on two occasions left for the city of Villahermosa to continue with his theological studies, and during the second stay, he was replaced in Utzpak by Hermano Barrera.

The church of Utzpak has passed through many struggles, but until now God has supported it with the power of His protection, and in the midst of the storm, He has made it flourish. This church has carried the precious seed on to other communities, such as the city of Temax and the village of Cansahcab, and with the help of God, will carry it on to other communities as well. We are, therefore, begging those who may come to read these lines to direct their supplication to the Almighty, asking Him to send His bountiful blessings to this church.

This brief history was assembled with good will, and we are giving it as a gift to Hermana Felicitas D. Goodman, as a token of our affection, wishing that God may bless her and that one day she may surrender to Him and thus obtain eternal life.

Her brother in Christ, Luis L.,

Pastor of the church in Merida, Yucatan

I could not know at the time, and apparently Hermano Luis L. was unaware of it also, that Don Fulgencio went to Merida in 1960 in order to invite an evangelist to Utzpak. He had previously already been converted by someone else, as told in the following excerpt from my diary:

DIARY ENTRY, JANUARY 13, 1985

My last day. Eus washes my warm underwear, kills and prepares a chicken for today and tomorrow. I watch by the hearth so the cats do not rob the chicken pieces while they are toasting over the charcoal. There is no *monte* [scrub vegetation] anymore for charcoal, but Eus makes her own.

We go to the service the last time, say good-by to Rodolfa and Old Candil, and see Marci, the girl who had been possessed, and her mother, go to the altar to register their intention to be baptized.

Sleep only four hours, wake up about two A.M. with diarrhea. We catch the bus out at 6:15. I stand until Temax, get a seat, fall asleep. During what seems to be an interval between two periods of sleep, I clearly hear fragments of a sermon: . . . Nuestro Senor Jesus Cristo, . . . gracias a Dios . . . , and other equally characteristic snatches, delivered in a bright voice. Must be the radio in the bus, I muse, remembering that about fifteen years ago Luis L. had occasionally talked about his plans of preaching on radio. I even see the sunlight and occasional green slipping by the bus window, and some advertisement that I screen out as a matter of habit. I settle into deeper relaxation and suddenly I "see," bathed in very faint pink light, a lovely little tree with a silver stem and pointed purple leaves that are silver on their reverse side. The leaves are slightly curled and in one of them, very obviously, there is a silver bead, like a perfect dewdrop, caught in the depression of the leaf, close to the stem.

Later, as we lug my baggage to Eus's brother's house for temporary storage, I ask her about that radio program in the bus. She swears that there was absolutely nothing of the kind going on, she did not sleep a wink, there was no radio going, no music, and certainly no sermon—absolutely nothing. "In your dream you were in heaven," she suggests. I find nothing attractive in the idea of a heaven where I have to listen to yet another fundamentalist sermon and finally abandon the attempt to understand why she heard nothing. Instead, I keep remembering the glowing, transparent, unearthly beauty of the little tree and feel deeply grateful that I had the privilege of seeing it.

We have several hours to kill until I leave for the airport, so Eus decides to visit her friend, Dona Ugulina, who is recovering from a fractured hip at her son's house nearby. This Don Felipe V. is a carpenter, very much an urbanite, but still a member of the Presbyterian congregation in Utzpak. When during our conversation I mention that I want to write a book about the Utzpak Apostolic congregation, he becomes interested. Did I know who had originally converted Don Fulgencio? No, not Hermano Hill. Had I never heard of Don Rich, of Ricardo May of Xbek? Of the man who lived and died like a beggar and was buried like a king? No, Eus says, she has never heard of him either, it must have been before her time. She and her family did not move to Utzpak until 1959. So Don Felipe puts down his newspaper and tells the story of Don Rich, and that is how I know the identity of the radiant silver bead that I have seen.

It seems that Don Rich was working as a ranch hand. Then something happened; he became seriously ill, perhaps there had been an accident. He could no longer walk and was confined to his hammock for almost twenty years. Then he started reading the Bible. Suddenly, he experienced a miracle and was able to rise from his hammock. He continued to read the Bible on the sly, until one day he forgot to hide it. His family found it and asked why he had been hiding it. "I thought it might offend you," he said. "Not at all," they said. So he started talking about all the wonders that he had come to know through reading it, which no one had ever told him about. "The Church has forgotten the Bible," he said. And that became his theme, "*La biblia olvidada*"—the forgotten Bible.

Eventually Don Rich drifted into Utzpak, where he had some relatives. He arrived with nothing to his name, no money, nothing. His hair was matted, his clothes were torn. He wore an old jacket, and in its pocket was the Bible. That was all. He never founded a church. Instead, he talked to everyone who would listen, attacking Catholicism and affirming the forgotten Bible. This is how Don Felipe came to know him. He talked to Don Rich's family, saying, "You should help him; after all, he is your uncle." But all they did was offer him an unoccupied house in exchange for taking care of their pigs. But Don Rich refused that, saying that his job was to preach. So he lived in an abandoned shed, and Don Felipe got him some money for food from the Presbyterian congregation.

He preached all over Utzpak, and many people came to listen and to learn about the Bible. The most prominent among them was Don Fulgencio, who was converted by him. Eventually, however, Don Rich became ill. No one came to his shed except for some boys, and he was afraid they would steal from him, so he never sent them out for any food but instead chased them away. He ate only tortillas and jalapeno peppers and had only dogs for company.

When Don Rich died in 1958, the shed was full of excrement and blood. He was laid to rest, as was customary, in a temporary grave; it was the biggest funeral Utzpak had seen for many years. Everyone came. But, three years later, when it became time for his bones to be cleaned, there was no family ossuary to receive them. They were thrown on the trash pile at the cemetery.

At that time, Don Fulgencio was still a member of the Presbyterian church. Soon after the death of Don Rich, Don Fulgencio had a dispute with the Presbyterians over the wedding of his daughter. Her groom did not belong to the congregation, so they would not marry her in the church. Don Fulgencio was very bitter about that. That was when his daughter told him about Hermano Hill, and this is why Don Fulgencio then went to Merida and invited Hermano Hill to come and preach in Utzpak.

2. 1969

Arrival in the Yucatan

In the summer of 1968, I did extensive fieldwork in an Apostolic congregation in Mexico City. The pastor of the congregation, Rev. Domingo Torres, had no problems with accepting my role as a scientific observer and had been helpful in every way. I had reason to believe that he would be interested in knowing that I had written an article prominently featuring the observations at his temple—the article was eventually published in the *Journal for the Scientific Study of Religion* as well as in the Swiss journal *Confinia Psychiatrica* (Goodman 1969a and b)—and I also wanted to request his permission to mention him and his congregation by name. I used this opportunity to ask him for the address of an Apostolic congregation either in Yucatan or in Guatemala so that I could continue my research, this time with Maya speakers for whom Spanish was the second language. In February 1969, I received an answer from Rev. Torres asking in turn for my permission to translate the above-mentioned article into Spanish for one of the publications of his church. He then continued:

> I can now finally also give you the address of our church in Merida. . . . The name of the pastor in question is Luis L. . . . He is a young friend of mine and I believe that he will help you in every way possible. I do not believe that you could carry out the project you envision in Merida. However, I was told that not far from the city there is a place called Utzpak[1] where most of the people speak Maya. We have a small church there, where I believe you could do your research. I cannot give you any address because I assume that the village is small and for that reason I suppose it apparently does not have any named streets. The Merida pastor will help you in every way possible. I will today also write to him about this matter.

Subsequently, I wrote to the Merida pastor, and indeed, his much-anticipated answer arrived the following month. He would be glad to be helpful; he would also ask the *hermano* (Pastor Chan Felix) in charge of the temple in the said village to aid my work. Would I please communicate to him the date of my arrival, for he needed to travel to Nayarit within the next four months, and he would want to be in Merida when I arrived.

I wrote to both of them enthusiastically but received no answer from either. I was later told in Utzpak that, indeed, a puzzling letter had been received, but by that time, Pastor Chan Felix had left for the Bible School in Tepic, Nayarit.

The letter was given to a Dona Eus, his mother, but she did not know how to read and, eventually, it got lost. Having received no answer from Merida, I assumed that the pastor was too busy and that he would have written if there had been any difficulty with meeting me. With this optimistic conclusion, I flew to Mexico City in June 1969 to do some visiting and there sent telegrams to both pastors announcing my arrival time as the 22nd of June. There was no problem with sending a message to Merida, of course, but I was told that Utzpak had no telegraph office. My telegram would be transmitted to Motul, and from there it would be taken by regular mail service to Utzpak. Not surprisingly, nobody in Utzpak ever professed to having seen it.

The bus trip to Merida lasts twenty-two hours. The hungrier, thirstier, and sweatier I get, the more my feelings of certainty evaporate. If no one is at the bus station, I think defiantly, I will find my way to that mythical village all by myself. I have been to Yucatan briefly before, so what is the big deal?

But when I alight in the new, gleaming, ultramodern bus terminal in Merida, there is Pastor Luis L., a slender, dark, handsome man, quick to smile, looking for a Senora Goodman. He brings a young *hermano* from his congregation, who is entrusted with my bags, and single file we walk for what seems forever along narrow cobblestone streets, finally arriving at his mother's home, a dilapidated building with a tall, creaky wooden door. Looking around, I am reminded of what dwellings in Rome might have looked like after the collapse of the Empire: the poor people taking over the fancy residences, the high-ceilinged rooms with decaying walls, makeshift partitions covered with cobwebs and dust, and chickens wandering in and out, one hen brooding in a box in the corner on top of assorted junk.

Peregrina, the pastor's mother, slender like her son, her dark face deeply etched with lines of worry, offers me a bath. I am given a small tin tub of water, a towel, and a *jicara,* half of a gourd that grows on trees (*Crescentia cujete L.*), which is an all-purpose ladle. I am guided to a niche in the garden wall that is protected by a wooden frame with plastic thrown over it. Not having been initiated into the proper ritual of a Yucatecan bath, where you soap down first and then splash the water over you, I leave the water in the tub, to the consternation of my hostess. I cannot convince her that I have really taken a bath.

After lunch, during which Luis L. plays hymns (very well indeed) on the guitar, we go back to the bus station. No, not to Utzpak yet. We will stop in Temax for a service at the house of the minister there and stay overnight. The new minister of Utzpak, an Hermano Barrera, will also join us.

The rickety bus is loaded beyond capacity, as though all of Yucatan is on the move. A radio is blaring; it is hot and humid. Thatched oval houses, whitewashed rock garden walls, enormous colonial churches, and ruined shells of 100-year-old administrative buildings glide by while we carry on a conversation on free will, predestination, theodicy. It seems oddly out of place in a bus filled with women loaded down with shopping bags and babies and men in ragged work clothes carrying machetes or vintage hunting rifles. When the bus stops at the larger communities such as Motul, boys, some no more than 10 years old, invade the bus, offering tacos, cookies, and Popsicles for sale.

Finally in Temax, we walk to the home of the *hermano* where the service is to be held this evening. Stepping through the gate, I realize that this is not a European-style village home with a small garden, as I had unconsciously expected. Rather, it comes from an entirely different settlement pattern—a large integrated homestead and yet part of a village—known to have existed in this form for 4,000 years or more (see Hammond 1991), a cultural form stubbornly retained over the millennia. There is the spacious oval main house, constructed of mud and wattle on a low limestone foundation wall. This house has a dirt floor, a high roof thatched with palm fronds, and as its only furniture numerous hammocks strung on the two crossbeams. There is another smaller house of the same design for the adolescent boys; and there is a kitchen house with the rods of the wattle inches apart to allow the smoke of the cooking fire to escape. It contains the hearth, an elevated stone platform, where a fire is burning between three stones, cooking the beans for the evening meal in a blackened pot suspended from a tripod. There is also a bath house and a well and some chicken coops; in the back there is the "patio," a spot by the garden wall set aside for a latrine, strewn with corn cobs. There are orange trees, lime trees, *nance* trees, *anona* trees, and one large avocado tree and small scattered plots with cilantro, tomatoes, and chile. In and around all of this there are dogs barking, chickens and pigeons pecking, turkeys with chicks strutting by, a pensive cat on a tree stump, a hog rooting in a puddle, and a multitude of children trying to teach a young parrot to say "*Paz de Cristo* [peace of Christ]," the obligatory greeting of the Apostolics.

Then there are the adults. The father, looking like Sitting Bull, has just arrived home from work on a ranch. The mother and her two daughters, all in *ʔipiles,* are busy making tortillas. The younger daughter gave birth to her third child two weeks ago. She complains of pains in her stomach and back, but when I offer her some aspirin, she refuses because she has just taken some "hot" medicine and the two might conflict.

We are joined by the new pastor of Utzpak, Barrera, rather fat, fair, wearing sunglasses, accompanied by two teenage "evangelists." The men want to go see about some land for a temple and ask if I want to go along. I refuse, saying that I would rather stay with the women. Everybody is happy; I am apparently now considered a more proper person, dispelling some of the suspicion that I have aroused by being a woman alone. The younger daughter had actually asked me if I was Luis L.'s wife, apparently this being the only way in which she could account for me.

It takes quite a while before the men come back, so we women spend the time talking. We have a lot in common—cooking, washing clothes, giving birth, nursing the sick. The adolescent boys of the family stand around respectfully, listening in. The son-in-law and father of the newborn arrives, bringing wood in a tumpline for the evening fire. He is the minister of the Temax congregation and wants to know exactly where I come from. So I draw a map of the United States in the dust of the yard, then one of Europe. You see, that tiny spot, that is Hungary. It seems unreal. The boys attach my hammock to one of the beams. I bought it in Acapulco; it is colorful but has thick strands and looks narrow next to the ample thin-threaded ones of the family. They say mine is pretty, but I, not having tried it yet, suggest that it is probably uncomfortable and only good for cheating tourists. They like that. As if proving my point, when I sit in it, it suddenly stretches to the floor, spilling me. Now we really have fun with my "rubber" *hamaca,* and there is much less strangeness between us. I am dispatched to the bath house, and the son-in-law puts a bucket of water in front of me together with a *jicara.* In the meantime, I have made some inquiries concerning this "bath," and so I make sure that in the proper manner I use up all the water this time. We eat, tortillas and beans, and I am given a hard-boiled egg.

By the time the *hermanos* return, it has turned dark. The women go to set up chairs in the yard for the service while the men sit in the hammocks, singing hymns. Behind her curtain of flour sacks, the young mother has just finished nursing her infant. She changes it on her lap, sitting in the hammock, then takes another diaper and swaddles it so tightly that nothing but its tiny face shows. She starts retching and vomiting, and her mother goes to attend to her.

Finally, we go out into the yard. The small table of the family serves as altar. It is covered with an embroidered tablecloth and there is a plastic dish for the offerings and two greenhouse plants for decoration. A Coleman lamp on a high limestone wall casts a cold, indifferent light on the scene.

The congregation consists of about twelve women, six men, and a few children, and more people keep coming. Luis L. conducts the service and gives the sermon. He says that before the Spanish came, the Maya worshiped idols. The Catholics brought a little doll with a pretty face and a well-painted mouth, but all that actually happened was that people passed from an ugly idol to a pretty one. He extols the gifts of the Holy Spirit. Then he introduces me, having rehearsed beforehand how to pronounce Columbus, Ohio, and asks me to say something. There I stand, under the flowering oleanders in front of a thatched

Maya house, in front of women in their ʔipiles, *rebozos* covering their heads, some young, some old, and some even very old. They look at me impassively, neither smiling nor frowning. I don't see the men farther back in the shadows. I try to recall how such requests are handled in the temple in Mexico City and attempt to follow the same format. I say that I bring greetings from the Apostolic churches in the United States, and especially from Hermano Torres in the capital. I tell how tired the world is of war and other evils and how it needs to hear of miracles, such as the miraculous gift of tongues. I say that I have come to learn from them so that I can go back and tell about it. Some of the women nod and there is a single "*Gloria a Dios, Aleluya*" from a male voice, but other than that, no "*Amen,*" no "*Gracias a Dios,*" nothing. When I ask Luis L. later whether he felt that the congregation understood me, he says he thinks so, but nobody said anything because I was a stranger, although he had reassured them that they did not need to be afraid of me just because I was white.

Luis L. continues the service, speaking about the Holy Spirit and straight fundamentalism, and his speech is very far removed from the sophistication of our conversation in the bus. He then turns to practical matters: how to acquire the 1,500 pesos needed for a plot of ground for the temple. "You, Hermana Teresa," he starts out, "you for instance have four hens . . ." "*Pues mira,*" she sighs, "they have all died on me." Appreciative giggles from the other women. "Well, you then, Hermana Trinidad?" "I have only two, one for my husband, one for me." Some more giggles.

He tries another avenue. "The men could donate one day of work. That would bring 20 pesos each." A male voice comments, "More likely 8 pesos." "A woman could go to her neighbor and wash a dozen [pieces of laundry] for 5 pesos." "The price is 2 pesos," a very old woman comments.

Finally, he gives up. "*Pues,*" he says, "ask and ye shall be given. The Lord will provide." The offerings of the evening, we hear later, amounted to 102 pesos, about eight dollars.

The service concludes with another hymn. We say good-by to each other with limp handshakes. "*Dios le bendiga,*" they say—"may God bless you."

In the house, the young mother has vomited again. Luis L.; the Utzpak minister, Barrera; and a number of other men go in and by the light of a small candle stump crowd around her. She sits in her hammock, the swaddled infant in her lap. Luis L. places his hands on her head and prays with great emphasis. Others pray along, each with his own petition. Luis L. goes into glossolalia, and so does Barrera. Their syllables are different from those I had heard in Mexico City, but the familiar cadence is unmistakable. I long for my tape-recorder, but it is out of reach. The next morning the young mother is much better, but I hear no comment that it is the prayer that has healed her.

The Village: Settling In

Luis L. had maintained that there would be no problem finding lodging for me in Utzpak, but things look different when we get there. The hotel has no rooms available; the manager of the clothing store and owner of the hotel, eyeing me suspiciously, maintain that they are all rented out to the engineers working on the extension of the highway. Hermana Reina, a small, delicate woman to whom Luis L. introduces me, has a spacious, one-room *mamposteria* house and hooks for an extra hammock, but that spot is apparently reserved for her brother-in-law. He could perhaps sleep in the kitchen shed, but I have visions of him coming in to look for something in the nondescript piles of clothes along the wall, and me in an abbreviated nightgown. We finally locate a small unoccupied *mamposteria* house with a well, catty-corner and almost across the street from Reina's, with a dirt floor but without a brother-in-law. When we go to pay the rent, I remember how reprehensible I thought it was that Ford Motor Company, with all its money, paid its Mexican workers only the miserable local wages. So I offer to pay a bit more than what the owners ask for. I never thought that, eventually, I would sympathize with Ford. When we came to know each other better, Reina told me every day, whenever my landlady defaulted on yet another promise, that this resulted from my overpaying. In fact, in a manner not quite clear to me, it seems that even the fact that the roadbed in my street is of irregular rock outcroppings and has no facing like the highway is in some way due to my carelessness in this business deal. At least she does not blame the presence of the mouse-size tropical cockroaches in my new home on the same flawed judgment. The walls, as usual, are not plastered and offer a perfect haven for these flying monsters that come tumbling out of every crevice when I start unpacking. I am glad no one hears me screaming. The first night I spend in my house, I switch on the flashlight whenever their characteristic low chirring noise wakes me to see whether one of them has landed in my hammock. I never did get used to these giant cockroaches in all the time I spent in Yucatan. No matter how much I tried to be nonchalant about yet another one of those tanks in insect clothing appearing in front of me, glaring across the orange I was eating or sitting on my hammock, I went into hysterics.

Reina offers me some *atole* for lunch and we spend the afternoon in her house visiting. She has an eleven-month-old daughter named Lupita. "I didn't get pregnant for three years," she says, "and I was desperate. Wouldn't I ever get to wash any children's clothes?" Her friends told her that she was lucky because they all had more than one child and had to work very hard. But she envied them; it was as if someone were repeatedly dealing her a physical blow making her barren. "Santiago, my husband, was also getting very discouraged with me. I suggested that we could adopt a child. There are always people who have more children than they can feed and are glad to give you one, but he said that he could not love a child properly that was not his own. Besides, his friends were making fun of him because he could not get his wife pregnant. Finally, Dona Res, the *yerbera* [herbalist] across the street treated me with only hot medicine, and then I finally conceived." When her water broke late during her pregnancy, Dona Tomasita, the neighborhood midwife, told her that her time had come and she should take a bath. So she did—she even washed her hair— and Tomasita tied a rope to a beam in the ceiling. She was to hold on to that and, sitting in the hammock, she was to push. There was a lot of pain, but the baby wouldn't emerge, and Tomasita was afraid that both she and the baby would die. So Santiago rented one of the two local cabs and took her to a physician in Merida. He operated on her and Lupita was born early the next morning, but then he simply put them out on the street. She was in no condition to travel, so in their extremity, they went to Luis L.'s house and his mother took care of her for a whole week. Peregrina kept all the doors open, not like in Utzpak, where all the doors are closed after delivery. She let her eat everything, feeding her not only food having the property of being "hot," such as tortillas, the custom in Utzpak, but also nutritious "cold" foods.

Santiago comes home from the market; he takes his shirt off and relaxes in his hammock. It begins to rain. After a while he decides to take a bath, not in the cemented corner of the house cordoned off by a short curtain and a drain hole that allows the bath water to run off into an underground natural cavern, but out in the rain. He strips to his shorts, takes Lupita on his arm, and Reina opens the rain trough. He squats and the child laughs as he splashes water on her from all sides, while Reina watches them, rocking in her hammock. Then Lupita starts objecting, probably beginning to feel cold. So Reina takes over, rinses her with tepid water from her hearth in the kitchen shed, dries her carefully, and powders her all over. The child smiles without uttering a sound and grabs the powder box to play with.

A service is scheduled this evening in the Apostolic temple. It is only three houses down from Reina's, but she does not come with me. Her father-in-law, Don Eduardo, is an important member of the congregation, but neither she nor her husband attends the services regularly, and they do not speak in tongues. "Santiago likes his beer too much," she laughs. And she often prefers to sleep instead of going to the service. "The devil has you by one foot," she quotes Luis L. as warning her. So I go alone.

The service is to begin at seven this evening and, being very curious, I arrive some time before to look around. The temple is a small, rectangular, mud-and-wattle building with a corrugated tar-paper roof and cement floor. The interior of the temple resembles the one in Mexico City, the whitewashed walls and some twisted ribbons of faded red crepe paper strung at ceiling height barely disguising the crumpled ugliness of the roof. There are window openings and wooden shutters, but no windows; after all, we are south of the Tropic of Cancer. The evening breeze wafts in pleasantly, giving some relief after the suffocating heat of the day.

The podium is raised almost 2 feet. On the left, two steps lead up to it, and in the center, at the place of the rostrum, it arches forward. The middle of the rostrum is decorated with a half sun, painted in blue with red rays. A white cloth hangs down in front of it with "*Dios es Amor*" [God is love] embroidered on it and under it a very large border, three yellow-and-brown baskets filled with flowers stitched in *ʔipil* style. On either side of the rostrum there are brown plastic vases filled with pleasing arrangements of greens and flowers. Posters with biblical sayings are tacked on the wall behind the rostrum. In front of it at floor level there is a small table with a dish for the offerings, and to the right of it a musical instrument unknown to me. I learn later that it is called a *marimbol;* it is a homemade wooden box about 1 foot by 1 foot by 1½ feet, which has holes on its side. On top, metal strips are nailed down. During the service, a man straddles the box and plucks these strips to accompany the singing.

The congregation sits on wooden folding chairs, and there are some narrow benches for the children. People are beginning to assemble; a few men in the white peasant garb, women in *ʔipiles* or tight-fitting dresses, their heads covered with the *rebozo* or a mantilla. I am of course also wearing a mantilla and, as required, no jewelry. The wristwatch does not count. There is animated conversation among the women, all in Maya. I am sitting in the first row on the women's side, on the left. My tape-recorder is adjusted, my notes about the temple completed. I turn toward the entrance to see who else is coming. A boy enters, about 8 years of age. He carries bunches of aromatic herbs. Behind him comes a slender woman bearing flowers, in *ʔipil* and *rebozo,* and with her entry the atmosphere in the church is transformed. "The first wife of King Hunyg was Lady Chuvy Tzut . . ." or something like that, it says in the *Annals of the Cakchiquels* (Raynaud, Asturias, and Mendoza 1946). I wondered when I read that what such a Maya lady might be like. Now, here is the lady. She is not really taller than the other women of the congregation, about 5 feet or a little less, but her slenderness and, above all, her bearing make her appear taller. While the other women in the temple have round faces, hers is an elongated oval. She has large eyes, a delicately hooked nose, and fine lips, reminiscent of the faces of the nobles in the paintings of the ancient pyramids of Bonampak.

She goes to the altar and kneels to pray. Then she takes the herbs from the boy and arranges them in the two vases, along with her flowers. She turns back toward us and sits down, one chair away from me. The ʔipil that makes the other women appear bulky flows down on her in graceful folds. She talks to the women behind me and they call her Hermana Eus. Her Maya seems precise, every glottal stop clear, not like the more "washed-out" dialect of Utzpak. Unceremoniously, she asks me a few questions in Spanish, my name, where I am from, why I am here, and renders my answers into Maya for the women behind me. Then she sits on a chair near me.

Reina had told me that Barrera had taken his pregnant wife to Campeche, their home, so she could be assisted by her mother and grandmother during delivery. In his place, the two young evangelists I met in Temax conduct the service, which follows the same outline that I am familiar with from Mexico City. One of them, Joaquin, starts the service, which is conducted in Spanish. By now the congregation has increased to nine women and six men. He announces the hymn, then there is a prayer and he passes the lead to his companion Teofilo, who calls for testimonies. One man rises. I ask the women behind me for his name: he is Antonio. I would come to know him well, Antonio with his dark eyes, color of the cenotes, a slight man, ranch hand and weekend barber, whose visions a scant year later would set off the millenarian upheaval. He uses the opportunity for delivering a mini-sermon. Another man gets up. "Isauro," whispers Eus; the following year he is one of the leaders of the millenarian events. He gives a biblical quotation. Joaquin is next; he says word for word what I have heard him recite in Temax, with the same irritating pomposity, "*Yo tambien me pongo a pied esta noche para decir gracias a Dios por la vida que me dio . . .* [I too rise this evening to give thanks to God for the life he has given me]." Then he asks the congregation to pray for his mother, who still refuses to be converted.

There is another hymn, then Joaquin hits the little bell on the rostrum, the signal for the altar call. He has to reach up; only ministers and pastors are allowed to step on the podium, and certainly no women. The congregation rises and goes to the podium, and expectantly, I turn on my tape-recorder because this is when speaking in tongues takes place. No luck. My notes are less than charitable. "That insufferable Joaquin goes on shouting his prayer so loudly I can hear nothing else. I wish he would catch a very bad cold or break something or other." "Nothing serious, of course," I add repentantly, "just enough to keep him out of circulation."

Time for individual hymns. Members of the congregation have handed Teofilo little pieces of paper with their names on them, and he now calls on each one in turn to sing while he accompanies them on his guitar. Epi, a tall man with a morose face, the one to be shaken most tragically when prophecy fails, is the first one, then comes Joaquin. "Gosh," I write, "not him!" He performs, as I feared, wildly off key from the first to the last note. Antonio is next, then a wrinkled-face elderly man in gleaming white. "My husband," Eus nods.

All through the subsequent service, I am more fascinated by Eus than by what goes on. With Joaquin in charge of so much of it, "with little inspiration and even less intelligence," this lapse can, I hope, be forgiven. My notes have a tendency to go like this: "Hermano Joaquin has great trouble reading the biblical passage. The Lady Eus is about to go to sleep. Hermano Teofilo is holding the bible like a waiter balancing a tray. She has slender dark arms, very high forehead, slender feet. *Corito* and offerings. Her *ʔipil* is beautiful. Hermano Antonio's sermon does not get off first base. There is an enormous cockroach on the rostrum, watching the proceedings. . . ."

Antonio's sermon concerns sin. Illness is a punishment for sin. All diversions—dancing, smoking, and drinking—are of Satan. To support this statement, he quotes, so it seems, the entire New Testament. Finally we get to the concluding prayer and hymn. I go home discouraged because there has been no glossolalia worth recording, and I wonder whether maybe I have come to the wrong place. But there usually is a service every evening except on Fridays, and two on Sunday, so I decide not to give up hope as yet.

If the glossolalia performance is disappointing to date, at least things are looking up as far as my home situation is concerned. In the neighborhood bakery, I discover the European-style delectable white roll called *frances* here, introduced a century ago by the bakers of Queen Charlotte, wife of the ill-fated Hapsburg monarch Maximilian. Luis L. did purchase a kerosene stove for me in Merida, as he had promised, and sent it down. With the help of Reina, Santiago, and about fifteen neighborhood children, who always took a lively interest in everything I did, we assemble it and it actually works. I am able to cook oatmeal, that ambrosia of suffering field workers, with milk from powder. It stops my diarrhea, and despite the dirt floor, total lack of sanitation, absence of electricity, and constant profuse perspiration, I feel positively rejuvenated. Luis L. also sends me a typewriter on loan. It works mainly by persuasion, but it is better than having to write everything by hand. And when I am over at Reina's, Eus comes by. Later that day, she visits me at my place. I learn that she is 63 years old and had nine children, eight of them living. "I must have enjoyed giving birth to children," she laughs, "having so many of them." Then her face clouds over. "That little boy of mine, he was well in the morning, then he had a fever, and by evening, he was dead." She wants to know about customs in my church. What does *luterano* mean? It is derived from Martin Luther, the name of the man who hundreds of years ago founded our denomination. This is confusing: "So you worship San Martin?" Later I show her my Chicago Maya textbook. She never learned to read because when she was a child during the

Mexican Revolution; the teachers all fled to the cities, where it was safer than out in the villages. But she has fun correcting my pronunciation of some passages I read to her. "*Bish a beel?* [How is your road?]," meaning, "Hi, how are you?," and the obligatory answer, "*Maalob* [Good]," and its equally obligatory continuation, "*Baashca waʔalic?* [What do you say?]." "*Mishbaʔa* [Nothing]." On the basis of this modest sample, from then on she delights in telling everyone that I am making great progress in learning Maya. As I am to find out, she is remarkably language conscious, telling of her pleasure of listening to foreign-language broadcasts over her radio just to hear what all those foreign languages sound like.

Joaquin and Teofilo skip the Wednesday service, no reason given, and announce one for 7 o'clock on Thursday, June 26. But when Reina and I arrive at the temple, the door is still locked. So, we go back to her house to lie down, I in the guest hammock, she in hers with little Lupita. I wish I had had someone like Reina to teach me about nursing babies. I was warned to keep my baby to a strict schedule or I would do it irreparable harm. Suckle it punctually only every four hours, no matter how much milk soaked my clothes and whether the baby cried or not. And how mine cried and fussed. Lupita never seems to cry, and she is chubby, healthy, and content. Reina nurses her when she is thirsty, or tired, or just maybe embarrassed. Reina carries her on her hip everywhere she goes and nurses her whenever and wherever. She is also agile—she either crawls the way toddlers all do around here, on her little fanny and slapping the floor rhythmically with her hands, right, left, right, left—or she walks at her mother's hand. She also likes to sit by her mother on a low stool when Reina works for two hours straight every day making tortillas. She has no toys, but everything is a toy for her, a little glob of *masa* [the yellow corn mush of which the tortillas are made], leaves, flowers, stones. She will also sit patiently on the tiled floor of her grandfather's house next door, playing with old keys, sticks, whatever he gives her. She eats a mush of black beans, *colado,* that is, passed through a sieve, then plays with her food, and if things get too messy, as when she stirs the puddle of her own urine with her pudgy little hand, Reina simply says, "*Es un desastre, mi Lupita,*" and washes her. When Lupita finally gets tired, her mother rocks her to sleep in the soft, ample hammock.

As all babies around here, Lupita wears no diapers. When she lies in her hammock, a soft rag is placed under her buttocks. Out of her hammock, she wears a panty, not like little boys, who run around naked. If Lupita urinates into her panties, her mother says, "*Ya urinaste . . .*" and changes her. Wet panties are not always washed (frequently they are simply placed on the low thatched roof to dry), but Lupita has no diaper rash. On a later occasion, I asked Reina about toilet training. Did she try to teach Lupita to let her know about the onset of a bowel movement? "Of course not," she said indignantly.

"She is much too little to understand. When she is bigger, I will tell her what to do. In the meantime, when she is dirty, I clean her or give her a bath and change her clothes."

We fall asleep in the comfortable darkness and are awakened by the bright, precise voice of Eus. "*Ola, Reina . . .* " It is 8:30 P.M., and the service has just begun. From the plaza, about five long blocks away, there sounds the background music of a free film, advertising Princesa soap. Maybe for that reason, or because Barrera is still in Campeche, attendance at the service is very low. In addition to myself and Reina, only Eus, five men, and a young mother with a 3-year-old at her feet asleep on the cement floor and an infant at her breast that kept sucking noisily all through the service attend, along with Joaquin and Teofilo.

I always wait anxiously for the altar call—I absolutely have to get some more glossolalia on my tape—but the men remain motionless; only Joaquin starts speaking in tongues. It sounds very much like Barrera, who I had heard in Temax, and I am wondering whether they come from the same congregation in Campeche. After the usual prayers and hymns and hymn solos, the congregation reads the 23rd Psalm in unison, and once more, Antonio gives the sermon. He has the congregation read biblical passages, then tells how he was tempted to go to dances, but with the Lord's help, he did not succumb. I wish I knew why dancing is considered so dangerous for the soul, coming as it does right after *cine* [picture shows] in the list of sins—*cine, baile, tomar, fumar* [movies, dancing, drinking, smoking]—that is habitually recited. And how he could read very little before and learned it by studying the Bible. He calls on various men to read some biblical passages that he has chosen and that fit into his sermon, but barely. Eus, who is sitting next to me, is taking a catnap. I keep wondering what brought her to this congregation.

Enter Hermano Barrera

Since there is no service on Friday, I go to visit with Eus. Her home is quite far, along the highway past the cemetery. She has a traditional oval Maya house, mud and wattle, dirt floor, palm-frond and *sacate* [grass] thatch. "After the conquest," comments the translator of the Popul Vuh, the Quiche Maya chronicle, "their kings and princes lived in utter misery, in small huts, their wives making tortillas." She is out by the wash trough, set up on a wooden stand under some trees, but when she sees me, she hurries in, drying her soapy hands on her apron. As we walk through the house, I barely see her husband in the semi-darkness hastily buttoning on a loose jacket. I am ushered through the kitchen shed, very close to the main house. "There is still another room," Eus comments. We get to this third house, which has larger door openings and a cement floor. It is sparkling clean. Barrera has just arrived back from Campeche and is relaxing in the hammock. Eus presents the old man to me, who has followed us in. He is her husband whom I have seen in the temple, but I still do not catch his name. He has green eyes, but his facial features, especially his long earlobes, remind me of pictures of the last Nohoch Taat, the "Old Father" of the Maya Cruzoob, the Brothers of the Talking Cross, who played such an important role in the Caste War of Yucatan during the last century, when the Maya peasants nearly drove the Mexicans out of their Maya homeland. We sit down and Eus remains standing, leaning against the door frame.

The conversation soon turns to speaking in tongues. It is obviously the subject of paramount interest. Who has already received the gift of the Holy Spirit? Who has prayed for it and how long? Barrera tells that in his home congregation in Campeche, a man and his wife have just now received the gift while he was there. They had prayed for it for three years. The first indication that it would happen came at an ordinary service. The woman said that she felt very hot and the man that he noted a tremendous pressure on his chest, as if he were compressed from both sides. But they did not continue praying and it passed. They told Barrera about it and he said, "Let us pray." So they prayed for the manifestation to come, and soon the woman began speaking in tongues. The man only uttered a few words, but they were in an unknown language. During the next service he could control himself no longer, and he began shouting and calling out. "It is enormous how the power shakes some people, and you wonder why the body has to go through this tremendous experience," Barrera muses. This couple has a sister living with them, and she is terribly unhappy because she has not yet received the Holy Spirit. Her sister tells her how it feels; that she did not know where she was, she had no sensation of treading the ground. So this sister came to him for consolation. He told her that the Holy Spirit wants to create a new, celestial being in her and for that to happen all sorts of material must be available in her, such as love and charity. Also, he told her, she needs to die internally before this creation of a new being can take place. She went away with a new understanding, for she now knew that apparently the Holy Spirit simply thought that she was not ready yet.

On the other hand, in Tabasco, Barrera says, some men are *endemoniados*, possessed by demons, so they go about killing people. A dance is not considered a successful affair unless at least two men have been killed. It seems that the demons simply will not give way to the Holy Spirit. There was one man who had killed eight men until he was finally converted, and he is now a preacher. Even preachers might get killed in Tabasco, and a preacher never knows when it might be his turn. All he can do is pray. "In Jalisco," he continues, "the Holy Spirit possessed three men and three women, and they began to tear their clothes from their bodies, right there in front of the congregation.

What a situation for a pastor! He began beating them with his belt, and they suddenly knew who they were and started grabbing for their clothes."

Barrera then talks about himself for a while. He had severe sinusitis, needed several operations, and took to drink. He would drink a large bottle of *aguardiente* every day. But when he became converted, his health was immediately restored, and he never drinks any more.

Answering my question about his own speaking in tongues, he says it took him two years of prayer before he ever received this gift of the Holy Spirit. Both Luis L., he says, and Joaquin, who lived in his house, received it before they were even baptized. He asks me, how about you? No, I have not spoken in tongues. *Pues,* he would like me to receive the gift, too, and says he will pray for me anytime I am ready. I take the opportunity to ask for his permission to tape and film during the service, as I had done in the temple in Mexico City. He has no objections. After all, he says, if the Lord does not want me to do it, there will be nothing on the tapes and films. It has happened before.

Later during this fieldwork season, I had an opportunity to record Barrera's conversion story, which provided more details than the above conversation:

> I left home when I was 14 years old. I was disobedient, very rebellious, and would have none of the discipline of my home. I was working in Campeche, doing this and that, and it was there that I heard a boy singing that hymn that you now also know quite well, which begins, "*Mas alla del sol, mas alla del sol, tengo un hogar, bellow hogar, mas alla del sol . . .* " [Beyond the sun, I have a home, a beautiful home]. The boy's name was Canshoc, and I very much wanted his friendship, and I wanted him to teach me that hymn. We did become friends, and he was the first one to tell me about the gospel. It made a tremendous impression on me. When I first realized that everything in the Bible was God's word and true, I spent days crying over my own fate and how I was going to perdition. After a while, though, we separated, and I forgot about God. I started on a bad life, with smoking, and drinking, and drugs, and women, well just everything that you can imagine. When I met Canshoc again, about a year and a half later, we were so far apart, we couldn't even greet each other any more. I was married, and then I met Luis L., a minister of this church. He was a salesman for the same house for which I was collecting agent. By this time I was heartily sick of myself; I was drinking a bottle of *aguardiente* every day; I had an incurable illness [sinusitis], for which I had been operated on twice; *pues,* I was a mess. Luis L. started talking to me of the gospel and I finally asked him how I could change my life. "Kneel down there at the altar and

humble yourself." "There is no altar here," I said. "There is an altar anywhere a man kneels down and confesses his sins to God." *Pues,* I figured I would try it, and I would make God a proposition. I said, "All right, Lord, help me to stop drinking and smoking, and I'll serve you." And I humbled myself, and confessed my sins to the Lord, and asked for his forgiveness, and the Lord worked his miracle on me. It wasn't that I told myself that I would not smoke or drink; I didn't want to anymore. I would go to taverns to collect and there would be beer and *aguardiente,* and it just didn't represent any temptation for me. And the Lord made me healthy. Things went well for a while, but after a time, a person may become weak. You become, we might say, cold. One day, the family of my wife gave a fiesta. They are rich, you see. My father was very rich, too, from cattle trading. Then he started gambling away his money. He was always accompanied by two *pistoleros,* bodyguards. He lived at night and slept in the day-time, until he died of an embolism. One of my brothers let me have a house when I was married, but when I became converted they threw me out in the street. I had intended to stay away, but I got so weak that I went to their fiesta just to smell the tobacco. I thought, I wouldn't smoke, just smell it again. The men of the family started taunting me, saying why wouldn't I stay and have a real binge, some-thing lasting for a week, for this is how they do things. I said, all right, I'll do it. Then I don't know how or why, but Juan L. came to the door, and I went to open it, and we started talking, and instead of a week's binge, we went to pray. However, I still was not firm enough. Man is weak. Also, I was unhappy because my wife refused to be converted. That is a great burden to bear. There came a friend, and he led me into some illegal activity. In the course of it, I lost everything, my equipment, my truck, *pues,* everything I owned, and I was left with a pile of debts. But with God's help, I soon accumulated the several thousand pesos that I owed. God is truly powerful. I de-livered myself up to the Lord to be his slave for all my life, and he has given me his mercy. Finally also my wife became converted.

After I was baptized, I prayed for the Holy Spirit long and hard but did not receive it. There was one time when I cried and cried, and I was bathed in perspiration, and I saw a light, but I did not receive the gift of tongues; it was my companion who did. But the next time it was also given to me. It is a lovely experience the first time, something you can hardly describe; there was a pressure on my chest, I felt as if I was being lifted up bodily, and my tongue felt swollen. At first, it is not possible to control the manifestation in any way, and it is such a pleasure. *Pues,* the flesh is weak, and man is what he is; you want to have it all the time. But prayer is also to edify others, and when you speak in tongues, no one present can understand you. So, after a while I learned to contain myself to a certain extent and also use ordinary-language prayer. The gift of tongues is a true benediction of the Lord.[2]

The service on the evening of the 28th of June is the first one conducted by Barrera in Utzpak. There are eight men present, five women with infants, and lots of children. I note a total absence of boys above about 8 years of age. Barrera opens the service, and after the hymn and the prayer he passes the lead of the service to Joaquin, who calls for testimonies. These are all given by men, mostly quotations from the Bible, always mentioning also chapter and verse. Barrera is the only exception. He takes the opportunity to tell how happy he is to be back in Utzpak. The congregation intones a special *corito* which accompanies the giving of the offering. One by one, first the men then the women go up to the small table in front of the rostrum and deposit a coin or a bill. Some make change. After another hymn, the congregation intones the special *corito* that signals the start of the altar call, "*Fuego, fuego, fuego es que quiero, damelo, damelo, Senor . . .*" [Fire, fire, it is fire that I desire, give it to me, oh Lord]! I wonder if this is only a biblical metaphor for the power of the Holy Spirit or whether it is also a reference to the perception of heat that goes along with the trance. Barrera is in charge again and hits the bell for the congregation to come to the podium. He handles that bell like a field marshal his baton. Bell: "Remain standing at your places!" Bell: "Stand up in reverence to the Word of the Lord!" Bell, bell: "Some of you are going to sleep. This is not the time to go to sleep!"

During the altar call, Joaquin once more is much too loud. Although I hear only him, some of the other men must also have spoken in tongues. The trance tends to be accompanied by profuse perspiration, and they come back to their seats wiping their faces.

This is the evening featuring the men's organization, the Senores Cristianos, and after the individual hymns offered by Epi, Joaquin, Antonio, and Eus's husband, seven of the men assemble in a row in front of the podium facing us and sing a hymn. They read a biblical passage in unison, then follow it up by a second hymn. "This was offered in the praise of the Lord," Eus's husband says. Then they turn to the right with what looks like military precision, walk toward the back, and go to their individual seats to sit down. Antonio takes over and calls for a *corito,* another one of those lively, short, and melodious hymns that I really like. This one is "Triumfara," and Eus's husband (I now hear he is called Nohoch Felix) accompanies it on the *marimbol.* He sits on it, his right hand plucking the *lamellas* between his legs, his left hand manipulating the single *lamella* on the extreme left side, producing a pleasant, highly rhythmical twang of varying pitch.

After a brief sermon by Antonio and another *corito*, Barrera steps to the rostrum. The man, I discover, has a fast, effective, and enthusiastic preaching style, a real evangelist, and very much aware of his audience. He peppers his sermon with Maya words: "There sits a man in his *chan casita* [small house], doing nothing for the salvation of his soul, just counting his *taakin* [money]"; or: "You can't put new wine into an old *chu?* [container]." There are also frequent references to *cacasmak,* which I don't understand. When I ask Eus later, she says Barrera doesn't really know much Maya, and what I heard should actually be pronounced *kasaan maac* [bad man], that is, Satan. His presentation is so lively that not even Eus goes to sleep. He bases his sermon on I Corinthians 15: 50–54:

> This is what I mean, brothers: flesh and blood cannot inherit the kingdom of God; no more can corruption inherit incorruption. Now I am going to tell you a mystery. Not all of us shall fall asleep, but all of us are to be changed in an instant, in a twinkling of an eye, at the sound of the last trumpet. The trumpet will sound and the dead will be raised incorruptible, and we shall be changed. This corruptible body must be clothed with incorruptibility, this mortal body with immortality, then will the saying of scripture be fulfilled: "Death is swallowed up in victory."

Barrera tells how Juan L., the brother of Luis L. converted him in Chetumal, and how Luis L. kept telling him that if he continued on his present path, "You, Hermano, will go *derechito al infierno* [straight to hell]." He repeats the stories he had told us earlier about people speaking in tongues in Campeche. By the medium of speaking in tongues, the Holy Spirit gives us the certainty about our salvation.

It was quite late when the service concluded, and solicitously Barrera orders Joaquin and Teofilo to accompany me home so that I will not get lost in the darkness. He had been to my place earlier with his two evangelists to see if I needed anything. Together, they had shortened the legs of my table, and so in return I bought a combination screwdriver and flashlight that Barrera had for sale. Not having any electricity, I drew the line at the flaming pink plastic chandelier of Japanese manufacture, though. I could not see much future for that in Utzpak. Anyway, most people, myself included, had no electric light. Its advertisement, printed on thin cardboard, could be put to good use, however. I had noted at Eus's house that it took the place of a missing door panel. Maybe that was what Barrera should market.

Since the young men tarry, I think I ought to make a little conversation, and so I ask whether they too will be going to study at the Instituto Biblico in Tepic. They both say no and the conversation turns to other things. But apparently the inquiry stings them because they come back to it and set out to prove to me that worldly knowledge will only deter them from seeking the salvation of their souls. The Holy Spirit will enlighten them and teach them all they need to know. Joaquin has no schooling at all and learned to read from the Bible, Teofilo had two years of primary school. The Bible is in a very real sense their only contact with the world of thought. Upon my question whether the Holy Spirit will tell different things to different people, they answer in the affirmative. But my next suggestion—that if they could find out what it says to other people, that might help them to preach better and more wisely—is unacceptable. Other people are of no interest. How about God? After all, he is infinitely wise and perfect, I say; did they know all about him? Some hesitation. Maybe if they learn something about the marvelous world that he created, about the plants, the animals, the stars, won't they understand a little more of that perfection? How about the marvel of a grasshopper? They become very angry at the poor grasshopper. No, they aver, they do not need to know anything about grasshoppers. God created the world only so men would have something to eat, to subsist, and besides, all this will soon pass anyway. They keep quoting the Bible to me and are not at all deterred by the fact that they cannot give chapter and verse when I challenge them to tell me exactly where it says in Genesis that all things were only created for man to eat. That I ask such questions simply shows, they feel, that my mind is cluttered with worldly things and thus cannot grasp the matters of the soul. So much for Theology 101.

Different visitors come by in the next few days. A young man brings a brief manual for an ohm meter. Could I translate it into Spanish for him? I am puzzled because those gadgets usually come with a translation, but I translate it for him, of course without charge. When afterward he does not leave right away, I ask him if he could, as a counter favor, go and buy me, for my money, a new battery for my pocket radio, which he does. I don't see him again. Santiago appears, without Reina this time. He doesn't seem to have any particular reason for coming, just sits there in my hammock. This irks me, for I understand that even in a family situation, a man does not knowingly sit in the hammock of an unattached woman. He goes on swinging, stretching, and laughing without any discernible reason. He shows off his manliness by pulling a tick off his arm and burning it with a match, again laughing, and all in all he seems to be waiting for something, I don't know what. I finally get tired of him. I ask him if he would please spray my house against insects, and then he can take the Flit can with him and spray his own house too. I would in the meantime go and visit with his wife. As he takes hold of the spray can, his face is a study in hurt perplexity.

And then there are the women. Two questions always come up during such visits: "How come my husband is not with me?" and, "Am I not afraid to sleep alone in the house?" I am aware that, as anywhere in Latin America, telling them that I am divorced would be unwise, so I emphasize that I have four children; that I had to come alone because my husband had to work, just like theirs; and that I want to write a book about the *hermanas* at the Apostolic temple. A large picture of a man on my wall would be useful, but I only have a printed one of Franz Boas in one of my textbooks, and it is much too small. Besides, the cockroaches would eat it. What are they afraid of, I ask? Are there bad people? No, there are no bad people. Of the *cucarachas* then, as I am? Laughter. Then of what? *Pues,* there are things around, things walking about maybe, or moving in the shadows, *y eso si asusta a uno* [and that does frighten you].

More and more I get the impression that I am causing a great deal of discomfort, a disturbance in the natural order of things, and for some, it becomes too acute to bear:

Yesterday, two teenage girls came visiting. One of them, Adi, I already know. She often comes with one or the other of her siblings to talk about the weather, about the free *cine* [movie], or just to look around. The other is a stranger to me. She seems tense, terribly ill at ease. I ask the usual questions: Does she have brothers and sisters? No, and her mother is dead, she keeps house for her father. All the while she keeps wandering around looking. She has a cut on her foot, so I give her some boiled water to wash it and put a Band-Aid on it. The cut is healed, but I go along with the game. She starts asking in a hurried, aggressive tone. Do I know that there are rattlesnakes? Yes, but not here in town. Tarantulas, scorpions? Yes. Then why am I not afraid? I ask her instead, "What are you afraid of?" *Pues,* there are things that give one—a Maya word that I do not know—*susto* [fear], that is. Maybe so, I admit, but I have not been *asustada* yet. And where is my husband? Oh, for Franz Boas! He is working, I say, and cannot be with me. She leaves without even the customary "*Bueno!*" Soon she, Adi, and another teenage cousin come back. They have tattered old songbooks in their hands, comic-book format, with popular melodies from grade-B movies. The girl thrusts one at me. Do I understand these? Of course I do, the songs are in Spanish, aren't they? She says she likes to sing. Really? Why doesn't she sing for me? We could make it a television show. (There are sets in several homes in the village.) I announce, "Here are three senoritas to present their selection of popular songs." She begins, and Adi and the other girl join in. They sing a popular plaint about a man who says that his wife has left him, but the *cura* [priest] says that a divorce is sin. She may go to live with anyone she wants to, but he will not give her a divorce, for that is a sin. I am familiar with it; it is often sung by itinerant performers in the Mexico City buses. I clap and ask for another song. They start a rapid one which I do not know. The girl starts wiggling à la go-go. Do I dance, she asks? I laugh, "Not like that." She seems to get more and more excited, and I cannot account for it. Once more she starts on the divorce song, and I begin to note where the three of them giggle and nudge each other. "Divorce, you can go where you want, the *cura* says it's a sin . . . " The message is becoming quite clear. They think I have run away from my husband, am living here sinfully alone but won't admit it.

I get up as they continue giggling. "Well, senoritas," I say, "I have to make a visit. I have the feeling that you still have some questions to ask me. What is it you'd like to know?" They are astounded. Us? Why, nothing, nothing at all. At that point, one of the girls pulls at the end of my tied belt. I laugh, lightly slap her hand, and say, "*Bueno . . .* " They giggle and turn to go.

It was not until near the end of that first fieldwork season that I learned from Eus the true meaning of this adventure and of the comportment of everybody around. Our conversation concerning this matter starts out with my asking her whether adultery and fornication, which are attacked so frequently in the sermons, actually represent a problem. Emphatically, Eus confirms it. For instance, she says, there are women without husbands, widows, deserted wives, who have no livelihood. They will rent their house out to anyone for any purpose. Chan Felix told his father, and he in turn told me, that one woman said that for 10 pesos, no; but for 50, even a dog could have her house for a night or a day. She would then leave, sometimes even going to Merida, in order not to be in the way.

Close to her place, Eus continues, there is a house which was rented by a woman who came from Merida every weekend. When Eus would go to the service on Saturdays, she could see the men coming, on bicycles or even in cars. She shakes her head. "How can those women ever stand it?" she asks rhetorically. Once she saw a girl she did not know, and so she asked her who she was looking for. The girl said that she wanted to find Don O., the local procurer. With her usual astuteness, Eus had no problems ferreting out the details. It turned out that the girl was 16 years old. She had been married, but her husband mistreated her, so she ran away. She had heard that working for Don O. was good, and she knew from experience that she would make enough money to live on.

So this is the image I had inadvertently presented! The cognitive dissonance of my neighbors resulted from the fact that I seemed like a prostitute but then did not do what prostitutes did.

Barrera Goes to Work

On Sunday the *matutin* [morning] service begins at 6:00. I oversleep and get there at 7:00, just as Barrera begins his sermon. I count seven men and three women. He had suggested previously that people should fast before coming and had perhaps run into opposition, because he expands on it being better to eat spiritually than in body. Then he turns to the manifestation of the Holy Spirit. Before he himself had the manifestation of speaking in tongues, he was full of doubts. Maybe what people said was true, maybe it was not. But after he himself had spoken in tongues, he had no more doubts. There is a hymn, accompanied by Nohoch Felix on the *marimbol.* I note that Eus affectionately calls him "*nohoch,*" old or senior.

There is an altar call after the sermon and a hymn. This time, I hear a lot of glossolalia, and the men also move while in trance. Epi, his face never losing its morose expression, bends his upper body up and down while on his knees. Barrera rocks back and forth on palms and knees. Joaquin, also in glossolalia, puts his hands behind his neck, then releases them and holds one hand slightly upward. After the altar call, Barrera talks again, once more about speaking in tongues. "If you feel like shouting, shout," he says. "That is noisy, but we have the service in the daytime for this reason."

Without any transition, the *matutin* goes over into the Prayer Service for the Manifestation of the Holy Spirit. Barrera gives exact orders.[3] Those who desire to receive the Holy Spirit are instructed to kneel in a row next to the podium. Those that have already received it are to kneel behind them. He points to the exact positions to be occupied. Anyone who wishes to receive the Holy Spirit is to repeat "*sellame, sellame, sellame* [seal me]," nothing else. When they feel that their language is changing, they should not get scared and stop and just cry, like some people. For it is the change in language that constitutes the manifestation of the Holy Spirit. They should continue, for now it is God who speaks through them, and no one knows in what language. Those who have already experienced the manifestation before are to say nothing else but "*sellalos, sellalos, sellalos* [seal them]." If they want to say something else in prayer, they should resist it. If, however, their language should change, they should obey and let the Holy Spirit take over.

Barrera has not assigned any place to the women. Slowly, Eus goes up to the altar, closes the shutters of the window and kneels down, beside her the woman with her babe in her arms. There is a prayer for glossolalia when everyone says whatever comes to mind, very loudly. Then the "*sellame, sellame*" and "*sellalos, sellalos*" takes over at an accelerating pace.

At this point, I start filming, and the tape-recorder is running too. The men who had undergone the experience before keep going into glossolalia, then reverting back to "*sellalos.*" There is a tendency for those in trance to scoot a bit closer to each other. The various glossolalia utterances have discernible peaks and drops, in some instances, then pass into prayer in ordinary speech. Finally, the activity abates, and the men wipe their faces. Recovery is instantaneous, except for Nohoch Felix, who sits on the *marimbol* once more, his arms still shaking slightly. A *corito* is intoned, then Barrera starts talking again, with a pale, perfectly calm face and an even voice. He says that if any of those present would like to pray in their own home, in private, rather than at the service, he will be glad to come to them. Then he asks, did those praying for the manifestation feel anything special? Antonio and Nohoch Felix answer in the affirmative. He suggests that they go on praying. They should continually say "*sellame,*" and if their tongue refuses to say this Spanish word any more, then they should let it happen, even if it comes out stuttering—God often speaks through people in that way. Nohoch Felix cannot formulate exactly what he feels, but he knows it was something.

Barrera calls for a hymn, then once more orders the same arrangement as before. The two men proficient in glossolalia, Epi and another rather young man, as well as Barrera and Joaquin, quickly pass from "*sellalos*" into speaking in tongues. Epi's experience is particularly striking. He keeps repeating certain prayerful motions and his tears are flowing; there is some salivation and a tremendous amount of perspiration. Of the beginners, Nohoch Felix is once more in trance, his arms shaking. Antonio is clapping and his "*sellame*" gradually turns into a low, compressed, extended shout, strange for a man who has a rather high tenor voice and in ordinary speech has the prominent, pronounced glottalization of stops of the native Maya speaker. Nohoch Felix is now on palms and knees. I cannot hear his glossolalia, but Barrera is next to him, putting his hands on his head, then bending down and listening. In between, he lapses into glossolalia himself, with slightly upturned face, his eyes closed, perspiration thick on his forehead. The noise level is deafening. And yet there are islands of quietude. Isauro, Santiago, and Don Eduardo, his father, are praying in a low voice, kneeling side by side. Before kneeling down, Don Eduardo spreads a freshly ironed handkerchief on the floor under his immaculate white pants. Reina wanders in and out, Lupita in her arms or at her breast. Eus stands absolutely motionless at the podium.

Finally, Joaquin gets up. The praying becomes very quiet. Antonio, who is still on his knees, clapping like an automaton, stops when Joaquin lightly taps his back. Everyone is dripping with perspiration. Eus goes to her seat; so do Isauro, Santiago, and Don Eduardo. Joaquin and Epi pass into glossolalia once more. Barrera gets up and rings the bell. The glossolalia stops instantly. All go to their seats, wiping their faces. Eus opens the window shutters and Barrera asks everybody to sit down.

Barrera is pale, his usual color, very calm and commonplace. He asks for testimonials about the experience of the Holy Spirit. Antonio comes forward and faces the congregation. In general terms, he speaks of his happiness to have had the rapture, *el gozo,* of the Lord. Then Nohoch Felix steps up and also speaks of his great joy, but when Barrera asks him whether he thinks that he has had the manifestation of the Holy Spirit, he hesitates and says that he is not sure. Barrera becomes impatient: "Of course he has had it, I myself have heard it, I don't know why he now doesn't want to admit it. He has had a very strong manifestation, his language has changed, and that is precisely what this is about." Warming to the subject, he then continues, "Some people keep saying that they have not as yet had the manifestation of the Holy Spirit, when in fact they did undergo it. I remember two sisters in Chetumal who maintained the same thing. The sign is the change in language, and when that happens, that is it. I don't know what else they expected. You feel heat, pressure, you think you are here no longer, and your language changes." Alvio, who did not receive the manifestation, comes forward. He felt nothing, he says. Barrera thinks that perhaps he has a hard heart and needs more prayer.

Very ceremoniously now, Barrera records in his notebook that on Sunday, June 29, 1969, the Hermano (Nohoch) Felix C. C. and the Hermano Antonio J. P. were baptized by the Holy Spirit. He then announces that Sunday afternoon will be dedicated to prayer and a meeting of the men's society. Those who intend to fast all day may stay with him in the temple. Only Santiago and Don Eduardo go home to eat; all the other men stay on.

When I come back for the evening service, Barrera is absent. The men ask me if I can sing some *coritos* in English. Not being a churchgoer back home, I admit that I cannot and see my prestige visibly dropping. So I ask if they would like to hear themselves on the tape-recorder, which is a new gadget for them. Everybody perks up. A few days ago Eus had me show her how it works, and while I adjust it for replay, she explains about it in Maya. We spend half an hour listening to the various singers. There is amusement at mistakes and personal quirks. They instantly recognize themselves and everybody else. Suddenly we turn, and there sits Barrera. We smile at each other guiltily, like children caught at a forbidden game. At a later occasion, by the way, the reaction to the soundtrack was quite different. I was at Eus's place, and Nohoch Felix came from the bush, the *monte,* with the firewood he had cut for the day, carrying it in a tumpline across his forehead. He wanted to hear how yesterday's *coritos* and hymns sounded in the tape-recorder. In playing them back for him, I advanced over a section containing the glossolalia of himself and of Alvio, a man who had recently received the gift. Barrera came from his room and stopped to listen. When I got to the glossolalia section, Barrera called out, startled, "What is that?" Nohoch Felix had no idea either, and so instead of amplifying, I thought it better to advance rapidly. Now, the fidelity of the recorder is quite good, and these people immediately recognize each other's voices, even if there is only a word or so audible. Not even Barrera, who did not seem ever to go into a very deep trance, recognized either himself, or the glossolalia of the others, although he had testified to having heard the glossolalias of both Nohoch Felix and Alvio.

The service this evening is preceded by the Escuela Dominical, the Bible School. After a hymn, a prayer, and a *corito*, Barrera has the congregation read from the first Epistle of Paul to Timothy 2: 8–15:

> It is my wish, then, that in every place the men shall offer prayers with blameless hands held aloft, and be free from anger and dissension. Similarly, the women must deport themselves properly. They should dress modestly and quietly, and not be decked out in fancy hairstyles, gold ornaments, pearls, or costly clothing; rather, as becomes women who profess to be religious, their adornment should be good deeds. A woman must learn in silence and be completely submissive. I do not permit a woman to act as teacher, or in any way to have authority over a man; she must be quiet. For Adam was created first, Eve afterward. Moreover, it was not Adam who was deceived, but the woman. It was she who was both led astray and fell into sin. She will be saved through childbearing, provided she continues in faith and love and holiness—her chastity being taken for granted.

Although other biblical passages are read subsequently, from the Epistle of Peter, from the Proverbs; Barrera chooses to elaborate on the Timothy text in his sermon and preaches about the family. "In many countries," he says, "men and women are considered equal. That causes divorces. Satan separates the man from the woman if the woman thinks that she is equal to the man. Men should be prudent with their wives; the wife should not be beaten or scolded harshly. The woman should live in the fear of the Lord. She should obey her husband, into whose possession she has surrendered herself. There are even some horrible homes where the man does the laundry, the cleaning, and cooking. That must not happen to us. His home is the poor working man's refuge. If the woman is restless, he should provide her with a female companion. If in a home the woman becomes the head of the family, the family perishes. The woman is weak and has to get her orders from the man. He should teach her hymns, talk to her about God, keep her occupied."

Subsequently, Barrera instructs the men about how to hold the Bible when they appear as a group: "You carry it with you, then at this point in the hymn, you hold it aloft, like so. Don't forget." He then has them rehearse how to read in unison the biblical passage chosen for the evening.

In the following pause, Eus comes in, carrying a foot-long object. It is the skeletal lower jaw of a horse, with all its teeth still in place except the last one on either side, that Nohoch Felix found in the *monte* and painted green. "Listen," Eus smiles as she holds it up and knocks against it with her right fist, "It sounds like many people clapping, *masima?* [Isn't it so?]" In the upcoming service, she uses it as a rattle to accompany the hymns, and my description of subsequent services usually contains the notation, "And Eus on the jaws."

While the congregation assembles, Joaquin kneels at the extreme left of the podium, Epi at the extreme right. Eus nudges me, "Epi is speaking in tongues. It is a miracle, *masima?*" I can get quite close with my microphone; it is so rare that I can catch an individual glossolalia utterance, the only soundtrack suitable for analysis. Antonio, at an imploring glance from me, obligingly stops plucking his guitar. Joaquin continues praying, but I try to screen him out. In glossolalia, his ordinarily conceited face softens to that of a child. I should remember that when I get so exasperated with him.

The service begins with a hymn, as usual, and it is an enthusiastic celebration. Barrera has his guitar; Eus's grandson, Jose, Wilma's son, who lives with his grandparents, has a rattle in each hand; Nohoch Felix works the *marimbol;* and Eus uses her horse jaw by turning its front teeth toward her chest with her right hand and knocking against it with her loosely curled left fist. During the altar call, Epi once more speaks in tongues and does not react to Barrera's bell signaling the end of the prayer. Not until the third stanza of the following *corito* does he come out of trance. Nohoch Felix seems to be elated that he is now among those baptized by the Holy Spirit, calling out a "*Gracias a Dios!*" or an "*Aleluya!*" much more often than before. When Barrera asks for special hymns to be presented individually to the congregation, he is the first one to hand his slip of paper with his name on it up to the rostrum with what might for that elderly gentleman actually be called a swagger.

JULY 1, 1969, EVENING SERVICE

Barrera had announced that this would be a service to found a women's organization, called the Dorcas. There are seven women present and five men. Despite the occasion and the larger number of women present, only the men give testimonies, reciting something from the Bible or requesting the prayer of the *hermanos* so that members of their family will be converted too. The women remain totally passive.

It is very hot and Eus, who is next to me, has made a loop of a section of her long *rebozo,* fanning herself with it. We are standing, singing a *corito.* A big cockroach flies by. Nonchalantly, Eus slams it down with her *rebozo* loop. Then, aware of the incongruity of the situation, she turns to smile at me.

After the introductory section of the service, Barrera asks for volunteers to become members of the Dorcas. Six women line up in front of the podium, including Eus. Barrera lectures them. They are enjoined to attend all services. Of course, they cannot serve the Lord like the Apostles did, but there are many womanly tasks they can do, such as inviting neighbor women and woman friends to the service, or offering to carry one of their babies if needed. "If one of your friends says, 'I can't go,' you are to say, 'Come on, I'll carry one of your children, so let's go.'" He announces that as Dorcas, they will have to pay a peso a week as a membership fee to Eus, who will be the treasurer. She will save the money so they will be able to buy new corrugated tar paper for the roof. Later he will also appoint a president and a secretary. Eus has that special blank expression that is her mask that she wears when she does not want anyone to guess what she is thinking. She tells me afterward that she is the treasurer of the church already, since before the time that Barrera arrived. So what is he talking about?

More from the Home Front

Big shock: Santiago comes with Lupita on his arm, saying that his wife died last night. When I look at him uncomprehendingly, he repeats it in Maya, "*Tu ciimi.*" And where is she now? At home. It suddenly dawns on me what is happening. Where have I read that in some places people say that they are dying when they become sick? I cautiously probe: What seems to be wrong? *Pues*, her stomach, perhaps something she ate. Would they like to have some pills? Santiago approves. *Haa*, that's right, maybe the ones that cured Joaquin. So we go to his house together, he with Lupita, I armed with a sulfa preparation and Kao-Con. I take care of Reina and, with a sigh of relief, Santiago hands Lupita to her mother and vanishes into the world of men.

Later, when he returns, I ask Reina and Santiago about the interdiction of the dance, which still puzzles me. It is not the dance itself, Santiago maintains, it is the gay music, which the *hermanos* say is of the devil, and also because they don't want people to have a good time, *que se divierten*. As I know from the teenagers, however, the village dance is not an innocent "good time." On Monday evening, for instance, there was a dance at the local tavern. They had a five-piece band, "Los Corsaros," playing electrical instruments that reverberated from horizon to horizon. Adi came by the next afternoon, looking uncombed and tired. She had not gotten home until five in the morning and was full of gossip of who was with whom and which boy fought with which other boy. Then Adi's younger cousin also dropped in. Her mother made her come home at two. She does not let her drink, but Adi does drink. At such dances, she says, the men get some girls drunk and then do not bring them back home until the next morning. All this "sinful" activity is then probably subsumed under "*baile*," as the *hermanos* see it.

In the evening, Eus and Nohoch Felix come to visit. The latter is still elated because of the attention of the Holy Spirit to him and wants to hear the hymns on tape. Eus laughs. She is obviously not impressed by the less-than-perfect musical achievements immortalized on the tape. "Whatever do you want that for?" she asks. I explain that what I am really interested in is the manifestation of the Holy Spirit, but the hymns provide me with some of the atmosphere. Now that I know that it gives people pleasure to hear themselves, I will record even more of them than before. My honesty satisfies her.

Sore throat. Everything is sticky with humidity after last night's rain. After all, this is the rainy season, which usually starts at the end of May but is late this year. When I used the word for summer the other day, Eus asked what exactly did I mean? I suddenly realized that dividing the year into four seasons does not make any sense here, where there are only two: the dry season and the rainy one. Two of my tapes stick. I think it is the humidity, so I heat some of my charcoal on Reina's *comal*, the metal plate for baking tortillas, trying to turn it into "activated" charcoal. It actually works, somewhat. I fix some *guanayaba* with lemon and sugar to help my sore throat because by itself this fruit has little taste. It helps my throat, but I remember too late that it can have a laxative effect. Back to Kao-Con. I pick up a short board from the floor left by a previous tenant to lay my books on, because the cardboard box I had used has collapsed from the moisture. I find a dead scorpion under it and a very much alive tremendous black spider. I do not rest very well either, for my touristy hammock of rather thick nylon twine is extremely uncomfortable. Reina is going to make me one of four strands, which is a measurement of width. The edge will have a pattern of *tablitas,* small rectangles. There are also designs of pine trees and little dogs running, but she likes the rectangles best. To think that I had never even noticed that the hammock edge had a pattern. At the upright loom, it will take her a week. I will pay 40 pesos for the material of fine boiled cotton thread and 40 pesos for the labor. Mindful of my unpardonable mistake concerning the rent, I make very sure that Reina thinks this is a fair and equitable price and that I do not pay more than what is customary locally.

In trying to identify a neighbor woman whom I said had visited me, Reina refers to her as a *mestiza.* I cannot see any difference between her and Reina, either in dress or in physical type. Neither looks like a mixed-breed, the way we use the term mestizo, but rather both look very "Indian" to me. I ask "How do you tell who is a *mestiza* and who is an *india?*" Reina gets very upset. To call a woman an *india* is an insult. Her sister-in-law has called her *una india* many times, and she does it because she hates Reina on account of her Indian surname, which is *Cab?* [honey]. Her sister-in-law thinks she is better than Reina because her surname is Zepeda Balaam. The "Balaam" part of that name is

Indian too, meaning priest, I interject. *Pues,* her sister-in-law doesn't know that. Every time she passes her in the street, she calls her *india* and even worse things. And when she didn't conceive, she called her *mula* [mule] to her face, suggesting that she did not conceive because she was sleeping with another man. Finally, when Reina became *enferma con esa,* pregnant with this child, she called her big-bellied and even maintained that the child was not by her brother, Santiago, but by another man. Her sister-in-law's husband recently bought a house in another part of Utzpak, so they don't see each other very often any more. But that sister-in-law is still extremely envious of Lupita, although she has several children of her own. And what does Santiago say to all of this? He says that Reina should pay no attention to his sister.

A very old, bent, and toothless woman in ?*ipil* comes to my door. She is selling some embroidery, the strips that go around the neck and the edge of a ?*ipil.* I invite her in and have her sit in my hammock. She is a widow; her husband died eight months ago, leaving her nothing to live on. She has only one daughter with several children who can do little for her beyond giving her an occasional tortilla or a few beans. When her husband lived, she always had good things to eat, even meat sometimes. It is hard to go without eating. This is not a sobbing complaint, merely a statement—that's how the world is. Her husband used to work on an *henequen* ranch, and the widow of an *henequen* worker gets 5 pesos a week. But her husband quit that work some years before he died, and therefore she is not entitled to anything. She was given the embroidery to sell on commission, since she cannot work as a washerwoman any more. She broke her right arm and the bone is not knitting. I buy one of her sets and give her 2 pesos more for a "bite" (beefsteak), just for her, I admonish her. In the market she can get a nice slice of freshly slaughtered beef for that. I hope Reina does not find out. The woman is from a neighboring village and outside the gossip network. When old people come to the door or to the garden wall and call out "*caridad* [charity]," the proper alms are 20 centavos.

At noon, Eus comes for me. One of her friends, Dona Tomasa, had a cataract operation and therefore cannot go to church. She would like to hear the hymns on the tape-recorder. Dona Tomasa is the grandmother of Chucha, my landlady. Some of the family live and work in Merida. I imagine that is how they are able to afford the operation. She is very happy because as a result of it she can now distinguish the houses on the corner.

A number of women and children gather around to hear the hymns. The house is *mamposteria,* with high walls and tiled floor; a small ornate chest of Cortez vintage, called a *baul,* is propped up in the corner on artfully carved legs. Except for the hammocks and a few chairs, there is no other furniture. I tell Chucha, my landlady, that I would like to borrow a chair; my guests have no place to sit. She says "*Haa*," the chesty, deep-throated Maya "Yes, indeed," but it is obvious that she does not mean it. It is my fault. Reina warned me not to pay the second month's rent in advance.

Eus and I go shopping at the market hall. As we walk down the highway, we hear the cadenced strains of a prayer for rain coming from behind a house, which I had heard a number of times back in the United States during lectures on Maya rituals. Eus notes my interest. "They are doing a prayer to their gods," she remarks. There is none of the derision reserved for Catholics for "worshipping idols." The market hall is close to the plaza. The government had it built for the village some years ago, but in comparison to the local markets in Mexico City, there is very little to buy. Even apples and wilted pieces of cabbage, strangers to the tropics, are rarely offered. I get one onion, two tomatoes, and a paper bag of rolled oats. I add two soft drinks for Eus and myself and a few cookies that are sold by the piece. We want to return to my house but are caught and drenched by a sudden downpour and flee to Reina's. When I tell about the plight of the old woman from whom I bought the embroidery, Eus and Reina point out that many people living in Utzpak are not originally from here. There is some land for *col* available around the village; that is why they come. On the *henequen* ranches they get to work at most two days a week, making 20 pesos. No one can support a family on that. And yet here, "they" will not let those outsiders have a parcel of *ejido* land to grow corn on. "They" keep it all to themselves, and the people go hungry. "And if you have to buy the corn, how are you going to buy the beans?" This is a standing comment. Nobody seems to have a clear idea, though, who "they" are. However, even for the locals life is hard. Women often try to sell things to make ends meet, but what are you going to sell?

On the other hand, Eus says, life is better now than it used to be. There is no war. In 1917, some uniformed men came to Libre Union, the place were she was born. They said that their lieutenant would come later, but that was a lie. They were merely out to rob the people. Her father, an itinerant merchant, sent her mother to the *monte* with the children. Her mother took cornmeal and sugar along and made some gruel for them, but the food soon ran out and they were very hungry. Back in the village, the soldiers locked the men up in jail and demanded money. Eus's father gave them what cash he had and so was spared, but the other men were killed. Then they went on a rampage. They started burning down all the houses. In one house, they killed two men, then a boy of 14, then two more in the kitchen house. Only their white bones were left and some putrid flesh. "Burned human flesh has a special smell to it," she recalled. "You never forget it." Then the soldiers surprised some men on the highway and cut them to pieces with their machetes as though they were pigs and scattered their remains; here a piece of finger, there a head. She saw that herself. In Yucatan, this sort of killing went on much longer than in Mexico; in many regions until 1924.

We talk about having children. I have had four. That is not too bad, Eus thinks, but her nine were too many, and so were the twenty-three that her father sired with two wives. One should not have more children than one can feed or that the mother can take care of. "In your country," Eus turns to me, "what do women do in order not to have so many children?" I talk about our kinds of birth control, the pill, the diaphragm, but it turns out that I do not tell them anything they do not already know. "That is how the women in Merida do it." But is it true that the pill makes one sick? It agrees with me, I say, but I have heard of cases where women cannot tolerate it. Anyway, Reina suggests, those pills are probably too expensive for them. As I find out later, there actually is possibly also a native system of contraception available. Eus and I were talking about men, and Eus maintained that Yucatecan men were extremely violent. The word "macho" is not used here. As an example, she told about a "bad woman" that she knew, whom her neighbors hated. They kept robbing her hens and damaging her plants. One time four drunk men grabbed her. They held her arms and legs and raped her, all four of them. They also shoved a pop bottle up into her vagina. "This is what that woman told me," Eus avers. "She was so sick, she had to stay in her hammock for three months." I neglect at the time to ask who a "bad" woman is, and Eus does not elaborate, probably assuming that I know. It seems that a "bad" woman in these Maya villages is one who knows about certain teas which will supposedly make a woman temporarily barren, and the men hate her for this knowledge.

I was looking for eggs in the market hall, but there were none, nor did they have any in the two grocery stores we passed on the way home. So in the evening Eus brought me four that she had for sale. How come there are none to be had in Utzpak? I ask. It seems that some time ago all the hens around here died, victims of *la mortandad,* the dying. But she fed her ten hens sulfa pills and poured oil down their beaks, and they all survived. Mindful of her remark that women have few things to sell, I ask her if she would sell me one of her hens; I would love to eat some chicken.

Next day, Eus brings the chicken, all plucked and clean. Of course there is a limit to how many chickens I can consume, and in casting about for what else I might be able to buy from her, I ask if she would "sell" me some Maya lessons. She catches on immediately. I should come to her house, she suggests; she has time available in the mornings, say from about 9:00 to 11:00. She goes home to do her daily laundry while I take my chicken over to Reina's house and start chicken *paprikas* on Reina's hearth. I also peel a potato, taking care to impress

Reina and Eus with the neat spiral of peeling I am creating with my paring knife. They peel potatoes, I thought quite awkwardly, by hacking small bits of peeling off and away from themselves with their big machete. Eus shakes her head. "She gets her potato peeled," she remarks to Reina, "but she sure does it all wrong."

I never cease to admire the Yucatecan hearth, though. Instead of the high, wasteful pile of wood that I consume when I cook for a picnic outside, they have three stones of equal size placed on the hearth with gaps in between. The slabs of wood are about 3 feet long and are gradually pushed through the gaps toward the center where the fire burns. That way the fire can easily be regulated and requires a minimum of firewood.

While my chicken simmers, I swing in Reina's guest hammock and watch her working at her loom. We talk about the temple. Her father-in-law, Don Eduardo, has been *apostolico* for years, she says. Before she knew Santiago, the Apostolics used to hold their services in his house. He owned a large plot where his house stood, and he ceded a piece to the Apostolics to build a temple on. The *hermanos* constructed the temple themselves, cutting the wood in the *monte,* piling the limestones for a foundation, tying the roof. All this happened long before Reina moved from Temax to Utzpak.

Was I married the Catholic way, she wants to know? No, was she? No, only in a civil ceremony. Her father wanted her to marry in the Catholic church, but Don Eduardo would have none of it. He told Santiago that if he married her in a Catholic ceremony, he would have to pay for it himself. However, if she and Santiago would dispense with the Catholic ceremony, Don Eduardo would give them money and also a building lot, and he would have a house built for them. So Santiago came and told her, and they decided that on a certain weekend, he would come and visit her in Temax as always, but instead of leaving at nine that evening, as he usually did, he would have a taxi ready on the next corner and would wait for her. She waited until everyone in her parental home was asleep. Then she took two dresses and slipped out of the house. Only one of her sisters-in-law saw her, but she said nothing because if she had called out, she might possibly have been blamed for Reina eloping. Together, she and Santiago drove to Utzpak. His father paid for the taxi, and they spent the night together. The next morning, Don Eduardo and his wife went to see Reina's father to talk things over. He was very angry, saying that she was his only daughter, that all he ever wanted was that she be married in church. But now that she had left, there was nothing he could do about it.

Santiago and Reina were married in a civil ceremony, and immediately after the wedding, building was started on their house, as Santiago's father had promised. So they now have a *mamposteria* house, and by local standards it is quite nicely furnished, tending more toward urban than rural appearance. She has two chairs, two taborets, and a small bench. In the shower corner, one sits on a log hollowed out to fit the contours of one's posterior. King Tut can be seen sitting on a comfortable throne shaped in the same Maya way to fit his contours, but since his times the West has forgotten how to make a truly comfortable chair. She has a table and also a *coqueta,* a combination of chest of drawers, wardrobe, and small shelf with a mirror. Two sticks are wedged into the corners for hanging up clothes. And of course there are the hammocks, suspended from S-hooks that fit into heavy iron plates inserted into the wall. The hammocks, as everywhere, are bed and cradle, love seat when two people sit in it on opposite sides, couch, and easy chair.

Reina's kitchen is a lightly built wattle structure which leans against the back wall of the house. It has a *huano* [palm-frond] thatch, the gaps of which are used for storage and sometimes to hide money. Very few staples are kept in storage, which makes good sense in view of the moisture, the cockroaches, the rats, and the mice. Reina keeps black beans, coffee, rice, and oatmeal in small quantities; cooking oil; salt that is always runny; and some yellowish-gray sugar. She says the white sugar is exported to the United States. She also has soap powder (Fab) and bluing for her wash and a flat iron that she heats up on the *comal.*

In addition to the hearth, there is a low, three-legged, very solid round table, on which Reina forms the tortillas on a recycled piece of plastic packaging, cleans a fish, or plucks an occasional chicken. She has three buckets and a chamber pot; three aluminum cooking pots; a square metal canister for soaking the corn for tortillas; a *lec,* which is a large thick-walled gourd to keep the tortillas warm; three soup spoons; a paring knife; two soup plates; a number of *jicaras* (in Maya, *luuch*), light, made from very tough tree-gourds that are cut in half; a kerosene lamp; a palm-leaf broom that is gentle to the dirt floor; and, of course, the ever-present machete.

The well is on Don Eduardo's section. Tiny transparent shells float in the water, still building the limestone shelf that is Yucatan. Santiago's bicycle is also kept in the yard. The patio is in the back of the yard under some trees, marked with a downed tree trunk that has thorns coming out of every bark fold. Thus, one cannot lean on it when defecating, but it does not prevent the pigs and turkeys from entering the enclosure and contesting for one's fresh excrement. Later, when I move in with Reina, it seems to me that they are always lying in wait, especially for me.

Two weeks after her wedding, Reina went back to see her father. He was still angry, but he did not beat her, and since then he has become reconciled to her civil ceremony. Eloping is actually the cheapest and easiest way to get married, she says, and very popular. But sometimes, she adds wistfully, she does have a dream where she is attired as a bride. She has a long white dress on, she wears a bridal crown, a veil, and Santiago and lots of people are waiting for her. Then again, she is dressed the same way, but instead of Santiago, a strange man is waiting for her.

Now her father has come down with multiple sclerosis, and his four sons are taking care of him and of Reina's mother. One supplies the tortillas, the other one the beans; that is how it is done. When her mother gets very upset about her father's condition, she says that maybe he has been bewitched. His sons have taken him to various physicians in Merida, but they say that there is no cure. Perhaps they could perform a brain operation on him, but there is no guarantee that it would help. So his sons decided against it. Many times, she says, doctors merely want to use the poor people to experiment on them, but they don't really help.

On July 3, 1969, a Thursday, there is an evening service for, as Barrera announces, "special intents." Apparently, he means healing. In *Is Latin America Turning Protestant?*, David Stoll has only bad things to say about the faith healers in the Pentecostal churches: "The most notorious figures in pentecostalism," he writes, "were its faith healers. The more money you give to the Lord's work as represented by his humble servant here tonight, healers taught, the more the Lord will bless you in the form of restoring your health, reconciling your family, and bestowing you with wealth" (1990, 49). That was not at all what happened in Utzpak, where faith healing had nothing to do with collecting offerings or acquiring wealth or restoring harmony within the family. The ritual was only about healing, and it was not an outsider who provided the service; as had been the case also in Temax when I first arrived, it was the preacher and the members of the congregation themselves who prayed for the sick, usually in tongues.

At this service, for instance, Barrera has the congregation come to the podium after a *corito* to pray for a sick infant, whose mother carries it with her. She had shown it to Eus before the service, and Eus passed her hand over its forehead. Yes, the child does have a fever, she confirmed. Under the lead of Barrera, the entire small congregation, three men and four women, is beginning to pray for it. Barrera puts his hand firmly on the infant's forehead, then envelops its head with his two hands, pressing lightly. The infant begins to whimper, then cries weakly. Barrera goes in and out of glossolalia. Joaquin is also in glossolalia, then Epi too, and Antonio doubles over on his knees, but I cannot hear him. Barrera now prays in ordinary language, his one hand still on the child's head, the other one raised high. Then he lets the prayer die down. He goes to the rostrum and sounds the bell, which terminates the prayer. When the people are back at their seats, he admonishes them that if they are praying for a particular sick person, they should concentrate all their thoughts, all their prayer, and all their words on that person and not let their thoughts wander.

"Prayer for the sick is very powerful," Reina says, "but you cannot rely on it entirely. Some people have too much faith. When Hermano Juan L. was pastor here, his infant daughter was very sick with diarrhea. Instead of taking her to the local children's clinic, they continued praying over her and she died."

After another hymn, there is a second altar call, the one for speaking in tongues. There are five men at the podium now (some stragglers usually come in later) and two other women alongside the mother, who never left her spot. The baby hangs limply on her shoulder. The only woman who is not at the podium is the wife of Antonio, who also came in late. She sits in the back row on the women's side, looking very dark, an Indian madonna in her colorful *?ipil,* her *rebozo* on her head, a baby flat on her lap, a tiny girl at her knees.

I take some notes on the kinetic patterns during glossolalia. All the men are as motionless as the women when they pray in ordinary language; the shaking, bending, and hand movements apparently do not start until they are in trance. Barrera, who is kneeling, has his hands on his knees, and in this position he bends rapidly up and down. When he rises, his glossolalia stops. Epi and Antonio are doubling over, but only Epi's glossolalia is audible.

Once more, Barrera places his hands on the baby's head, praying loudly. Gradually, the communal prayer dies down. After another *corito,* there is a Bible reading. Barrera and the congregation alternately read a verse each through an entire chapter. Barrera's sermon is about the joys of heaven. Won't it be beautiful, he says, when the Lord will say, look here, Hermano Antonio, here is your place, and the one over there, that one has been prepared for Hermano Epi. Other people meantime, like the Catholics, will have their choice of cauldron size. Television is to be avoided because it keeps people from praying and occupies them with the matters of the world. The same goes for dances. If anybody wants to go to the movies, let him pray for an hour first and then see if he still wants to go.

At the conclusion of the service, Barrera asks that there be a prayer offered for Epi's wife, who is sick. There are now eight men kneeling at the podium in a quiet, unemotional healing prayer.

After the prayer, I tell Barrera how moist the recent rains have left my floor. As a result I have gotten a cold and I seem to have a temperature. My left leg started hurting as I walked today. With Joaquin and Eus in tow, he comes to look things over. Maybe one could dry the floor out with a layer of *sascab,* "white earth." But after sizing up the situation, he says that *sascab* will not help because apparently the house was built over a cave. I think he is right. I remember that recently when my floor was briefly flooded, the water that drained in swirled through a number of rat holes. I was hoping that it would drown the one brazen rat that had stolen my meat from my pot that I had suspended from a horizontal wire. Yucatecan rats must be tightrope walkers. When the cave fills up, he says, water enters the house and there is nothing anyone can do about that. He suggests that tomorrow I should immediately go and find another house. Hermana Eus could go with me to see about a refund on the rent that I have already paid.

Apparently, this is not all that we are going to talk about. He sits in my hammock which I offer to him, swinging a little, and then asks why I want to go to Temax. Two days ago, I explain, I had asked Joaquin to please find out from the mother of the household we had visited there when it would be convenient for me to come and pay a brief visit. He goes there regularly to help with the services. It seems that Joaquin had apparently misunderstood, telling the poor woman that I wanted to speak Maya with her and that I was on my way back to the States and intended to say good-by. Joaquin is not very bright. I explain that I had asked Luis L.'s advice about this, that all I wanted to do was to take a few items, some sugar, oats, milk powder, as a present. After all, they had taken me in, a total stranger, a white woman, and had shared their food and their home with me. Did he think that this was not the appropriate thing to do? He hesitates. Actually, of course, they are *gente humilde* [humble people], that is, lower class. I can see that he thinks that I am not. So this is not exactly the right thing to do. When I am apparently deaf in that ear, he continues that besides they are not even at home except on Wednesdays and Fridays. Great, I say, that was exactly what Joaquin was supposed to find out. "All right," he says, "so perhaps you can go. . . ." Then over my head, to Eus: "You can leave with the 12:30 bus, and there is a bus coming back at five. That will be the easiest way to do it." Eus nods to me as if to say, right, that's how we'll do it. Obviously, the situation is cut from the same cloth as Barrera's sermon. The congregation, as he seems to see it, is a "household," and he is the head of it. I am one of the household's women, and a restless one at that, who needs a female companion, and Eus is tapped for the role. In this manner, my appearance as a single woman without male protection as well as the threat I thereby represent to the natural order is eliminated. It also prevents me from running around on the landscape and continuing my aberrant behavior. St. Paul would be pleased.

Obediently, I take my lodging problem to Reina the next morning. She suggests that perhaps I can rent Don Eduardo's house, for he is in Merida for a medical treatment of his gums. Anyway, I should bring my things over to her house in the afternoon and she will put them into Don Eduardo's house. And I should spend the night at her place. Gratefully, I accept her offer, although I continue to work on my fieldnotes in my house.

To my amazement, after just one dry night, my runny nose, my sore throat, my headache, and the pain in my leg are all gone. The only problem I have left is the fact that some of my stuff is now in Don Eduardo's house and out of my reach. I do long for my toothbrush. I recall that I also have some moisturizing cream. Wouldn't it be nice to be needing that again? The reason Don Eduardo's house is off limits is because Santiago's older unmarried brother is sleeping there. Therefore I cannot enter, and in the absence of Santiago, Reina cannot go there either to get my things. "He is single, so I cannot pass through the house when he is there," Reina says. She feels sorry for him. He should get married, she thinks, for a bachelor does not have it easy. There is no food waiting for him when he comes home from work. He has to start his beans himself, then he has to go buy his tortillas. When he gets wet at work, no one is there to light the fire for him so he can have a warm bath. Actually, this brother-in-law is quite a thorn in Reina's side. He gets drunk regularly on weekends, and when he is drunk, she says, he is a *cochino* [a pig]. "But after all, he has no family to take care of, so what else is there for him to do?" Not until he leaves for work are we able to fetch my bag, and curiously I look around in Don Eduardo's house. It has a beautifully tiled floor, but no furniture except for a lovely carved *baul* on delicate legs in one corner.

The avoidance pattern between men and women, it seems, is not only observed with someone as obviously taboo as a brother-in-law but is clearly in place also in neighborhood interaction. In fact, I am beginning to figure out the details of why I am getting this we-women-together-in-a-harem feeling around here. As I watch life up and down the street (and so much goes on in the open air), I note how the men seem consciously to project an image of separateness and of toughness. They come home from their *col* or the ranches perspiring, ragged shirts open, gun slung over their shoulder, swaggering. This is not my interpretation of signals that I perhaps do not understand. Not just Eus and Reina but women quite generally see their men as violent. They suffer from their weekly drunken binges because when they are drunk, they get abusive. According to Eus, Nohoch Felix did not beat her when he came home drunk, but only because she would make no comment. "After all, if he beat me, I would leave, and then, forced by necessity, I would have to come back two days later. That would have been very embarrassing in front of the neighbors." Her oldest daughter, who makes her home in Merida, is not married to the man she lives with, and he beats her regularly, even when he is not drunk. For that reason, Eus never goes to visit her.

Reina asks me if my husband ever beats me or takes my earnings away. Most of the women's earnings here come from their husbandry on the large *solares*, actually an extended home garden, where they raise and thus own the pigs and the hens and the turkeys, and where they harvest the eggs, the fruit, and the seedlings. They dispose of these goods usually by sending their own or their neighbors' children on selling errands. The children get a small share of the profits. Eus tells of a neighbor who used to make it a habit of taking these earnings away from his wife. She finally left him to live in Merida, taking the two youngest children with her. The three older ones are with their grandmother now.

I never hear any banter between men and women going on from house to house or jokes called out across the street. Among women that is done all the time. Eus and I walk down the street, and Eus shares her *rebozo* with me because the sun is mercilessly hot. One of the old women in front of a house along the street, her *ʔipil* hitched up into the band of her half-slip underneath, as is done for work, calls out to us in Maya. Eus translates, laughing. "She is mean," she says. "I should not share my *rebozo* with you, you should tan until you are as *boosh* [as black] as we are." There is laughter from several other houses too, with the added spice that nobody is quite sure how much Maya I really understand.

While we are in the temple, the men come over to me, talking about the recording of the hymns or asking about the price of the tape-recorder or of the camera; however, I see no conversation among men and women there, either. Only when shopping in a store run by a man is this interdiction void, as it is absent also within the homestead, where women talk freely with male guests. And of course there is the propositioning. Eus tells of walking down the highway toward her home; a man caught up with her and said he wanted to have sex with her. She answered that there was no reason for him to come to her, after all, his mother was living just down the street. "*Tsʔooci,*" she grins; finished, that was the end of that.

It also seems that intimate conversation is more likely to occur among women than between married couples. I observe that Eus and Reina tell each other more of the small details of daily life than Eus tells to Nohoch Felix or Reina to Santiago. Beyond that there is a caressing or touching pattern among women that struck me from the start. In Temax, I was stretched out in my hammock, exhausted from the long bus ride from Mexico City and all that activity in Temax. My foot was sticking out of the hammock because you tend to lie somewhat diagonally, and as the mother of the house passed by, she took my foot into her hand, stroked it, squeezed it a little, and said how soft and white it was. This need for and satisfaction from physical contact between women can be seen all over. Old women will walk down the street hand in hand. All women upon meeting me would take my left arm, caress it, and gently stroke it. I was walking down the highway toward Eus's place and overtook two girls, Turkish towels on their heads, the substitute for a *rebozo* among women in dress rather than in *ʔipil.* We exchanged the customary "*Buenas,*" and although I knew neither one of them, one of the girls started stroking my left arm, saying that I should also get a towel so that I would not tan too much. The behavior is as formalized as our handshake or our complex rules about not shaking someone's hand. Eus is visibly startled when I put my arm around her shoulder, but never if I follow the pattern involving the left arm.

With Don Eduardo still in Merida, we cannot decide where I should eventually stay, so I go to Eus for another Maya lesson. Actually, I admit to myself that it is not merely the Maya lesson that attracts me. I had not realized how oppressive Reina's yard was until I saw Eus's the first time I arrived for a lesson. Except for the back section around the patio, Reina's is denuded of vegetation by her pigs. There are only some *guanaba* bushes left and a shade tree where she does her laundry. Eus's yard is separated from her barnyard by an *albarrada* (a whitewashed wall made of fragments of limestone) and, by contrast, is lush with orange bushes and an orange and a *zaramuyo* tree and tall, slender papaya trees swaying in the wind. There is a spreading bougainvillea promiscuously dropping its light purple blossoms, potted flowers and seedlings everywhere, and a clump of sugar cane, its yellow contrasting with an edge of green grass. When I remark about it, Eus mentions that she had seen a picture of trimmed grass like that in a magazine, and since then has kept her grass cut with her scissors, trying to achieve the same effect. "*Hats?uts, masima?* [Pretty, isn't it?]" she beams. In the years to come, I never tire of photographing Eus's yard over and over again. It is enchanting to sit with her in the shade of the orange tree, surrounded by all that tropical glory.

As for my Maya lesson, the previous day I had asked her to tell me something about herself on tape, and I had started to transcribe it. It proves a useful way to start learning with someone who has never done any teaching before. In fact, she continually amazes me. During my first lesson with her, we simply checked my transcription, and she helped me with the words in the text that I did not know. Today, we do the same thing, but she asks me questions. Very skillfully, she keeps coming back to similar questions until I can answer all of them correctly. And she makes plans about what questions we will be working with on Monday.

Our conversation turns to clothes. With interest, she looks through my dresses. Why have I brought so few? At home I must surely have many more. I tell her about the embroidery I bought from the old widow; I want her to sew me an *?ipil*. She has a treadle machine she inherited from her mother, and I overhear that out of flour sacks she has sewed shorts for Santiago at 2.50 pesos apiece. She starts immediately, taking some twine to measure the length for the material we will need to buy. "We'll make it short, just below your knees; that will look nice." I do not bring up the topic, but privately wonder whether an *?ipil* at a fashionable length would not be unacceptably frivolous, *mundano* [of the world]. It certainly would have been in the Hungarian convent school back home. What about St. Paul's injunction about women dressing modestly? Or was religion part of "the men's world" as far as the women were concerned?

So I ask her to tell about her conversion in Spanish, thinking that it might provide some answers, and with her permission, I tape it:

> I have a friend called Dona Valuch. She is the wife of Hermano Goyo. About ten years ago she invited me to attend some services the *hermanos* were holding in her house. I had been a Catholic before, but there is no certainty with the Catholics. Catholics don't believe in God, they believe in the statues of saints, that they can do miracles. But in Merida, I have seen how they make these statues. They make them from *sascab,* and then they paint them. After that, the *cura* blesses them, and already they can do miracles. Once there was no rain, and Nohoch Felix was about to lose his harvest. So I went to Tizimin to pray to the famous Tres Reyes, the Three Kings there. I bought a big candle for 3 pesos, and every morning for a week I went there, carrying the big candle, and prayed three Salvos [popular for "Salve," a prayer in honor of the Virgin Mary] as I had promised, and listened to the mass. Then I went home, but a few days later I came back for the second week. This is how they tell you to do it: you have to come for three weeks. But when I got home the second time, Nohoch Felix's harvest was already lost for the sun, and so I never went back for a third week, for it was clear that those Kings could not perform miracles.
>
> At first, I went alone to the services in Dona Valuch's house, and took only Nina along [her youngest daughter, 9 years old at the time]. Nohoch Felix would say, "*Co?osh,* let's go to the movies." But I would answer, "You go alone, you just give me the money for my ticket." And with that I would go to the service and contribute it in the offering.
>
> One evening it was very dark, so Nohoch Felix took me to Dona Valuch's house with a flashlight. I said, "Why don't you come in?" So he did, and from then on, he did not go to the *cine* any more, but only to the services. He would still smoke, and if I objected he would go out to the *solar* to do it. I said, "From me you can hide, but from Jesus you cannot." So he stopped and that cured his asthma. Eventually, he also stopped drinking.
>
> What the priest says does not give one certainty. With the *apostolicos,* there is certainty because the Holy Spirit manifests itself.

Later on in the conversation, she also adds another important point. At the services in the temple, she says, there is always excitement. You know everyone and hear what they were doing. People sing new hymns, and there are visitors and sometimes even a minister of a different congregation. At the Catholic church, things are always the same, very boring.

When the opportunity presents itself, I also record what Nohoch Felix has to say about his conversion. It seems that while he was supposedly at the movies, he was actually already trying to find out something about this new kind of service:

> The *hermanos* were holding some services in the house of Hermano Goyo and, going for a walk, I would stop on the corner to hear what they were saying. I kept doing this for a long time. Finally they asked me, "Are you always just going to stand at the corner listening?" So I started going to the services, and I also went to the services in the house of Don Fulgencio. And everything they said became fixed in my mind. Finally, I decide to become converted. I say to myself, "What I have done, I have done. It is already behind me. Maybe Christ will accept me. I am going to follow him, and I'll see where that will take me. I'll follow him, I don't know where to." Then the *hermanos* said, "You will have to get legally married. Whoever is not married will not be accepted by Christ." When I hear this, I immediately say, "*Pues*, let's go do it." And the *hermanos* came, and they held a wedding service, and we killed turkeys for tacos, and we served everybody Pepsi-Cola. Before I was converted, things were quite different. We served Habanero [a hard liquor] and beer on the day *de mi Santo* [name's day], and what expenses we had! And these drunkards that we would invite, we would serve them one day, and then they'd come back the following day to be served again. With the *hermanos*, it is not like that. What you spend, you spend, and that's it.
>
> I was baptized about three years ago. They baptized us together, five of us, there at Santa Clara. The spot where they hold the baptism is about a league away from Santa Clara, following the highway. It is beautiful, there at the seashore; there is a beach, you can go, and go, and go, and there are many coconut trees. When the baptism is over, the people come to eat, and they take their *chan almuerzo* [little lunch] under the trees, lots of people, lots of souls, very nice.
>
> Before I was converted, I belonged to the Catholic Church. I was very devout; I took boxes of votive candles to the church. The *cura* would say, "Come, my little sons, I will free you of your sins. Come on such and such a day, at seven or at six, early in the morning." So he would promise to free us of our sins, and he a bigger sinner than

we are. [He laughs.] This showed me that of these *curas* none gave any certainty. They suck everything from their thumb. Another thing I didn't like was the matter of the images that they say we should adore. They are not as holy as they maintain. The Holy One is sitting up there on his celestial throne; nobody knows him, nobody can reach up to him. They make them of stone, of cardboard, of gypsum, in all sorts of forms, but they have no intestines whatever, they have no blood at all, they are not the work of Christ. We are the ones that are his work, for no matter where we get scratched, no matter with what, we bleed, even from our fingers.

After the baptism, my life certainly changed. Before, I would leave home with 25 pesos or 20, and when I would come back, I would not even have 5 centavos left. Now when I go out, I leave with 5 pesos, and I come back with 4.50 or 3.50. Also, I am happy, for we always go singing happy songs, and there I am in the church, very gay; I grab my guitar, and all sounds so full of joy.

I have even been baptized by the Holy Spirit now. You were there. I have spoken in other tongues, not in Spanish, and every word seems to come out upside down, and you ask yourself, What might that be? For they are words that you don't understand, and yet they keep coming. And when the Holy Spirit comes, it feels as if my head is swelling up, but real big, and then it becomes small once more, I don't know how, and this feeling reaches into the legs and the middle of the back. It grabs you, and you feel the Lord's power; there is nothing like it, and nothing will stop it. So this is all the matter that I have done.

In addition to the story, there was a linguistic quirk that kept intriguing me as I was working on the transcription, namely how Nohoch Felix tended always to go from the larger unit to the smaller one: come at seven or at six, I took 25 pesos or 20, I'd come back with 4.50 or maybe 3.50. It seems a generally used stylistic convention. The local clothing store, La Elegancia, advertises a sale of garments going from 200 pesos to 150. It is as if they are all still building pyramids, putting down the wide base and going upward in ever-narrowing layers.

Beyond this linguistic oddity, I cannot of course help noting once more, as I had already done during fieldwork in Mexico City (see Goodman 1972b), how conversion stories as a genre generally conform to a certain cross-culturally observed pattern. As the *Handbook of Religious Conversion*[4] puts it, in the majority of modern Christian conversions there is "a conscious, deliberate decision based on either the consideration of normal life experiences which seem to have given life new perspective, or the affective impact of an experience" (Maloney and Southard 1992, 153). Clearly, the pivotal matter for Barrera, Eus, and Nohoch Felix, the unshakable core of what they had gone through, was precisely the "affective impact of an experience," which is as close as the authors of that chapter in the *Handbook of Religious Conversion* managed to get to the heart of the matter, the ecstatic trance. Lewis E. Rambo gets a bit closer when he points out that "conversion requires the intervention of God to deliver me from the captivity that I perceive ensnaring me" (1993, xii). Pentecostalism goes one step farther, however. The *apostolicos* that I came to know derived their unshakable certainty from their trance experience. That was what convinced them in the most personal way, namely in their bodies, of the reality, of the very presence of the Holy Spirit, of a divine being.

As far as another feature usually reported of conversion stories is concerned (namely the one reported by St. Paul, "before I was . . . and now I am the opposite"), that appears to be, at least in the cases that I am familiar with, exclusively a male concern. All of the men seem to obey a "flip-flop" rule, emphasizing a radical "before-and-after" structure of the experience. Eus, however, does not speak of it, and I will quote statements of women later on who equally simply do not report it. For the women, apparently, the conversion is not the traumatic shock that it is for the men, who are shaken to their roots. Rather, it is like a special thread that they happen to pick up along the way and then delight in weaving smoothly into the tapestry of their lives. By the way, Nohoch Felix did not bother to note that it was actually not he, but his wife Eus, who first developed an interest in the Apostolic services. Stories by men to be quoted later tend to share this omission of the role of the wives or mothers.

On the afternoon of July 8, 1969, we have a premature cyclone. At first it is merely an oversize thunderstorm, and with satisfaction I observe how Reina's high cement threshold is holding back the water while the street outside is flooding. Meanwhile, in the back, Reina's kitchen shed is beginning to look like Noah's ark. I rush back to my house, worried about my notes, and arrive just as the water begins to gurgle up from the numerous rat holes in my floor as if from a dozen broken pipes. Within literally minutes, I am in 3 inches of water. Reina and Santiago come to the rescue, and through the knee-deep mud and slime, we carry the remainder of my belongings to Don Eduardo's house. Reina comes with half a bucket of very hot water and makes me stick my feet into it "so you won't get any rheumatism." Then, in the midst of the storm, Don Eduardo arrives to share the excitement.

With his permission, Reina's household is now basically moved to his house next door, and the rest of the day is filled with emergency measures. We cannot cook; Reina's hearth is under water and my kerosene stove is out of commission. We share what cold cooked food we have and take a talcum bath, since we cannot heat any water. When it gets dark, we all take to our hammocks: first against the wall the brother-in-law, who seems to try to shrink into the masonry; next to him Don Eduardo; then Santiago; and then Reina with Lupita; then I, behind a discrete partition of two blankets on a string. Outside, the rain has stopped and there is a riotous concert of the *muuch,* the giant frogs of the region. A few *hermanos* seem to have reached the temple and I detect the strands of a hymn above the frog symphony. "How did you get to the temple?" I ask Barrera the following day. "Mostly swimming," he said.

Within two days, the effects of the cyclone are practically gone. The floodwater has percolated through the limestone into the womb of the underground caverns, and the houses are beginning to dry out. Mine, however, continues to be uninhabitable, so my move to Reina's house is final. Thus, now I am also quite naturally a part of the evening socializing at her corner, which had been interrupted by the cyclone. Everyone has had a bath; the children run around in clean clothes, their wet hair plastered to their heads. Adolescent girls come by selling *vaporcitos,* steamed cornmeal dumplings with modest traces of meat in them, wrapped in banana leaves. We women sit on the curb; Lupita nurses. Dona Tomasita ambles over and sits on Reina's threshold. She kids me about my wearing an *ʔipil,* saying she wanted to see who the pretty mestiza was. Another woman from further down the street, walking along with her small daughter at her breast, stops to talk to Reina and stays when I get her a chair. Her husband is a lumberjack and is rarely home, so she lives here with her mother. Boys drive hoops down the street, actually discarded bicycle tires. Then the light turns to orange, soaking the walls and the thatched roofs, and suddenly it is dark. Eus and Nohoch Felix thread their way over the stones, Eus in a brilliantly embroidered *ʔipil,* done in shiny red and green thread, her hair in a heavy knot, held in place by a loose comb, a bunch of flowers in her hand. "They walk in beauty," Columbus wrote home, even if not about the Maya. It is time to go to church.

Quite subtly now, by moving in with Reina, I am thought of as part of a family and no longer a woman alone, a situation that had not only been disturbing to the neighborhood, but, judging by the aggressiveness of the teenagers, possibly not without risk. With this move, I become more than just part of the corner scene. Also, the visiting patterns change instantly. The young evangelists are now clearly subject to a very strictly observed avoidance pattern. There are no more theological discussions, and especially Teofilo is painfully embarrassed if I direct anything more at him than the formal "*Paz de Cristo.*" For those neighbor women from farther down the street, who had come by so often, I am now not only uninteresting but also visibly a member of the Apostolic Church and thus to be shunned. They do not even come by anymore to have their children's ugly sores treated with my antibiotic ointment. With some women, Eus has the same experience. "We are not liked here," she says. "There is a woman who lives near me and she never speaks to me. She does not see me in the Catholic church, so she turns her nose up at me." I do not see the teenagers anymore, either. I miss their casual talk—anthropologists live on gossip—but I especially miss the children. They had, so to speak, declared me their pet. Sometimes there were as many as ten in the house, watching me type or just squatting on the threshold like little birds. Also, they were a useful source of information. "And Dona Reyes, how many children does she have?" They always knew. Most useful for me, they had definite insect categories, which I quickly adopted. When a new insect came along—and in the rainy season that was an hourly occurrence—I would ask whichever kid came along, "*Pica, o no pica?* [Does it sting or doesn't it?]," and structured my reaction accordingly, from indifference to shameless aggression. But Reina is very much impressed by the work that I have to do and keeps them away. Only one of the older ones, an orphan girl named Caduch, is not intimidated and keeps coming, although less frequently. One day she comes and explains that her grandmother needs 5 pesos, and if I can help her out, she can do my washing for me until the 5 pesos are used up. So I give her the money for her *chiich* [grandmother], but she lingers to chat a little. Later in the rainy season, her mother's relatives come and take her with them to another village, and I am sorry to see her go.

The greatest reversal, however, takes place in the case of Santiago. Whether anyone of his family is present or not, he is now neutral to brotherly, even solicitous in a paterfamilias sort of way. And he never again swings in my hammock.

So things are really back to comfortable normalcy, and I cannot explain why that first day back in Reina's house after the cyclone is so miserable for me. Maybe it is the floor. Don Eduardo's floor is tiled, and Reina's is a dirt floor and harbors within itself all the memories of rats, cockroaches, spiders, bugs, mud, and slime, ready to beset me. But then again, a day later I actually no longer resent that floor. Anyway, this day starts out strangely. My psychological upset actually began the evening before. Inexplicably, I felt irritated by the fact that the sun kept setting at the same time every evening. Wasn't the day supposed to be getting shorter by now? Then at the start of the service, I was going to open up the small flap of the tape-recorder and unexpectedly no longer knew how to do it, finally asking Eus for help. Later, when I lay in my hammock in Reina's place, facing the open window, I felt like I was falling, ever falling into a dark eternity; then, terrified, I was floating alone in an inky bottomless sea. This morning, I started talking to Reina in Hungarian, and no matter how hard I worked at it, I could for a while think neither of Spanish nor of English. As I try to put it all together later, I think this was a delayed culture-shock reaction, but somehow it had the texture of a changed state of consciousness, and within another hour, it dissolved and never came back.

The next night I am left alone in the house. At one in the morning there is a knock on the door. A house door has no locks, but when the occasion warrants it, a short pole is leaned against it from the inside [*troncar*], and I had been instructed to put it in place. It is Reina with Lupita wrapped in her faded blanket, a hammock over her arm. "Let's you and I go to the kitchen to sleep," Santiago had told her. Then when she was fast asleep, he left. "*El cabron* [the s.o.b.]," she says angrily. "Where do men go when they leave like that? No doubt to *cine, baile*, and who knows, doing their *porquerias*, their dirty things." Actually, a few days before, she had remarked that she did not particularly enjoy lovemaking. "I am cold that way," she said. "Once or twice a month, that is enough for me." So perhaps Santiago had reason to go elsewhere.

There is an evening service the following day, attendance seven women, five men, and many children. In his sermon, Barrera emphasizes that people should not worry about the future, for Christ's Second Coming is close at hand. It is the first time he has talked about the topic of the Second Coming, and I have no way of knowing that this is not a simple formulaic statement but will increasingly assume a frightening reality the following year.

Nothing more about this service except that I am beginning to record how Barrera induces his own glossolalia. Clapping serves this purpose; also certain trigger words and postures bring it on, such as kneeling with his hands on his thighs and then rocking. None of these strategies, however, is absolutely effective. Today, for instance, he rocks on his knees, hands on thighs, but no glossolalia follows. He adds clapping and glossolalia ensues. Then he throws up his arms and the glossolalia is lost.

The following afternoon, Eus and I go to Temax. Eus primps like a young girl. Her definition of *mundano* obviously does not preclude a carefully ironed festive ʔipil, fragrant talcum for her face and neck (of which I also get a generous portion), a pretty hanky, a nice pocketbook, and the perfume "Madera del Oriente," which her daughter Nina sent her from Mexico City, where she works as a housemaid.

In Temax, we find Roberta, the young mother, and her infant quite well. Roberta is beautiful with her ample body and young, round face, set off by shimmering earrings. When she suckles her son, he is practically smothered by her soft, big breast. After nursing she swaddles him—this is done until the baby reaches the age of three months—in a large, embroidered white cloth in such a way that he is placed diagonally on the cloth, one corner covers his head, the opposite corner is pulled over his feet, and the right and left corners are slung around his body and around his legs, so he ends up a straight little mummy.

In one end of her hammock, she forms a depression in which he sleeps as in a little cocoon. She then goes out to the *solar* to continue her daily laundry, while in the house, as we converse, various members of the family make the baby in the hammock swing every time they pass by.

During the conversation, Eus likes to show off my Maya. "*Masima,* Hermana? [Isn't that so, Hermana?]," and I am supposed to catch the ball. With my Level 101 knowledge, that is not always easy. My interest in Maya gives rise to a conversation between Eus and the father of the household. He says that his son, husband of Roberta and minister of the local Apostolic temple, reads the biblical text in Spanish but then preaches in Maya. That way, the old man says, people can hear the *Maya legitimo,* the true and correct Maya, and from there "the fight can be carried outward." Eus agrees. When she goes shopping, she says, she simply expects that people will understand Maya. She will say, "*Conten taabliya, conten p?aak* [I am buying a round cake of chocolate, I am buying some tomatoes]," and of course, they do understand her.

When I get home that evening, Reina receives me with the news that the Americans are maintaining that they landed on the moon. She has seen it on television down the street. I had previously overheard people asking each other in Don Antonio's general store whether the Americans had made it to the moon yet. So the landing must actually have taken place now. However, Reina is not impressed. Anybody could pretend to have done something like that, she says, simply by playacting, making a film. So maybe it is true, maybe it is not. I am taken aback. Clearly, Reina and I do not agree on what we would accept as proof about an event having taken place. Is a film actually sufficient proof? She is also worried. If indeed it did happen, people should not do such things, for wouldn't that mean that man wanted to be more than God, walking on the moon? It is bound to bring trouble, a drought, sickness, war, something like that. In the temple, on the other hand, the event causes only a passing ripple: it is another bit of worldliness, that landing on the moon, nothing but some more *mundano* stuff. The "big" story is still that the other day Paula, the mother of Pedrito, the infant stricken with polio, finally spoke in tongues.

I am out of a number of items that I could buy better in Merida, and I also need to go to the bank, so I am asking around how I might take a trip there. Utzpak is at the end of the line, so to speak; the highway stops shortly after it breaks through the eastern edge of the village. To get to Merida, *ti Ho?* [one can take the bus], which starts out at the Utzpak plaza, in front of the municipal building, at 5:30 A.M. Or one can reserve passage on one of the two private limousines, which leave at 6:00 A.M. and return about 5:00 in the afternoon. When Reina's family hears my plan, even Don Eduardo, who usually pays no attention to female concerns, makes it a point to tell me that I should choose the limousine, although it is more expensive than a bus ticket, because that way I would be taken directly to the door of Hermano Luis L.'s house, and he and his mother would take care of me. Without further consultation, he and Reina send Santiago to book passage for me with "El Negro," the driver of one of these coaches. "El Negro" is not the driver's real name: in the village all men, but no women, have a nickname that everyone knows and uses, but never to their face.

These limousine drivers, by the way, fulfill other functions as well. They carry messages, deliver packages, mail letters, buy medicine. On this particular morning, there is Paula, asking El Negro to have a prescription for her Pedrito filled. It will cost 80 pesos, she sighs.

The trip in the ancient, rickety Dodge, built for eight and always carrying more—on the return trip, there were sixteen of us and one pet parrot—is a demonstration of "we men togetherness." I am studiously and carefully ignored. The conversation is exclusively in Maya. To my amazement, I can follow the gist of it. At one point a passenger makes the remark that there are not enough eggs in Utzpak. Eggs being synonymous with "balls," he has a hard time making clear through the ensuing laughter that he thinks the ranchers should send eggs to Utzpak for sale. Pedrito, a hunchback, is picked up at his door, a very, very tiny man, only about a foot and a half tall. He is carrying an oversize briefcase, like any *hombre de negocios* [businessman], and he is treated with exquisite tenderness. In Merida, he has his own permanent beggar's place.

The male passengers in the limousine are whistled at and shouted to and kidded as we pass through the village, but not once, and I keep checking and rechecking my impressions, is a woman accorded the same attention. When we pick up an elderly lady, also at her door, she and I are ignored together. On the way home, one of the passengers is a little boy, about 5 years old. His mother sits with us on the seats behind the driver, but he is taken by the men to join them in front, and there is horseplay with him all the way home. When his sister, about a year younger, tries to horn in on the game, she is ignored. I think this is where the violence of the men that the women complain so much about may have its source. Men seem irresistibly drawn to little boys; they slap them, pinch them, and tease them every which way, until the boys "blow up," which is rewarded with laughter and approval and helps to lower their flashpoint. I saw no such patterns in Mexico City. As Eus related, her son, Enrique, used to love to fight, even as a very little boy. The men would give him 5 centavos, and he would fight any boy they would point out. As an adult, he continued the same way. Once he had a fight with a man in a tavern, who then lay in wait for him. When Enrique passed by, he shot at him. "He was a devil of a man," Eus said, "but he did not manage to kill Enrique. He only wounded him in the abdomen. In the hospital, it took seven stitches to close the wound. Enrique finally moved from Tibolom, our home, and now lives near Campeche, *al monte*. He works his *col* and he hunts wild boars [peccary]."

In Merida, I am taken care of, guided, and guarded as a member of the family. I am accompanied to the bank and on my shopping errands. I am fed, and a bath is prepared. During the prayer before the brunch, Peregrina goes into a beautiful glossolalia, three complete utterances, each with its own peak, and I feel like crying because I do not have my tape-recorder with me. In passing, I note how relative one's impressions are. When, upon arrival, I first saw Peregrina's home, it seemed so terribly, pitifully poor. This time I felt, so help me, in the lap of luxury.

At home in Utzpak, in the meantime, the men have been busy all day fixing the roof of the temple. Insects and humidity are very hard on wooden structures. "The repair is really urgent," I overheard Luis saying the other day. "One strong wind, and the roof falls on our heads. And won't our neighbors enjoy that!" They had been to the *monte* and cut poles, had taken down the old roof, and had peeled and tied the fresh poles in place with lianas. Nohoch Felix and Epi were near the ridgepole, waiting for the corrugated tar paper as I filmed, with Joaquin knocking holes into pop-bottle caps and threading wire through them. They were used in an ingenious way to hold the paper to the poles without it tearing out.

After all that activity, the evening service has a desultory quality about it. When I arrive, there are only four men present. Joaquin tries to get a discussion going. His needle is stuck on the "only one God, not three" theme, usually a favorite subject of discussion, but Alvio, Isauro, and Antonio are too tired for theological niceties. They go to the front and start practicing a hymn, leaving Joaquin to preach to admiring Gregoria, Isauro's wife, and a bunch of small children. Under Barrera's guidance, the service then takes its usual course, except everything is in slow motion. Clearly, physical tiredness is not conducive to trance and glossolalia. Barrera tries rocking on his knees, but only a brief phrase results. He goes to clapping, but that does not help either. "*Halleluja*" triggers a brief utterance, but there is no sustained manifestation. Joaquin, ordinarily such a facile glossolalist, has similar problems.

Making a Joyful Noise

Diary entry. Sunday morning. I am up early and dress. But before I have a chance to light my stove, which is still moist due to last night's heavy rain, Eus knocks. "*Co?osh*, Hermana. [Let's go.]" I hastily swallow a raw egg, then grab my equipment and we leave.

In the church, Eus kneels at the podium. The last conscious memory I have of the episode to follow is that of thinking, "At home when I was a child, we were taught a little prayer before we sat down in church." Then, someplace in the church, I do not remember where, I leaned against something, I do not know what. I saw light, but then again, I was surrounded by light, or perhaps not, because the light was in me, and I was the light. In this light I saw words in black outline—or were they just letters?—descending upside down as if on a waterfall of light. And at the same time, I was full of gaiety as if my entire being were resounding with silver bells. Never before had I ever felt this kind of luminous, ethereal, delightful happiness.

I recovered with the thought, "Now I finally know what joy is." I still don't remember where this was in the church. I don't remember seeing Eus get back from the podium. And in my field notes, I simply start recording, "Sunday morning. The service is already in progress . . ."

Paula has brought her little Pedrito to be prayed over at this Sunday service. Eus whispers to me that the baby has no strength in his legs at all, not in his arms either. The medicines that the physicians in Merida have prescribed for him do not help. Antonio and Old Candil, who always puts on old-fashioned gold-rimmed glasses when it comes to reading the Bible, and Barrera are praying for the child. Candil is in glossolalia, kneeling, palms on the floor, head down. Occasionally, he grabs the edge of the podium. Barrera alternates between encircling the child's head with both his hands, occasionally pressing it lightly, with prayer intermixed with glossolalia, and putting one hand on the child's head while raising his other hand high. Gradually, the prayer dies down and the men go to their seats; Paula with her baby in arms continues kneeling at the podium.

More people are beginning to come in. Barrera officially starts the service with his usual greeting, then follows the hymn, prayer in place, another hymn, testimony by Antonio, and then the *corito*, "*Fuego, fuego . . .*" [Lord, give me fire, fire, fire is what I want. . . .] During the latter part of the *corito*, the congregation begins to approach the podium. There is a hierarchy now, with those who have already received the gift of the Holy Spirit kneeling closest to it as a place of prestige: Candil, Nohoch Felix, Antonio. Isauro kneels about 3 feet behind them: he has not as yet spoken in tongues. Barrera kneels on the podium, behind the rostrum. On the women's side, Eus kneels beside Paula with her sick child. No one seems to be bothered by my walking around, filming.

Barrera remarked once that the person who has the gift of tongues needs to use it in working for the Lord. He does it admirably, having near-perfect control over the behavior. Apparently, he has certain words with which he performs the switch into the light trance state, such as "*obra*." He calls out "*Obra, obra, Senor* [Lord, work your miracle]," and then proceeds in glossolalia. Un-

derstandably, the control is not perfect. Occasionally a slip occurs, a glossolalia phrase breaks before it is completed as he gets up from his crouched position, and he reverts to ordinary language. On one occasion, later on this day,
Barrera is in the midst of his sermon. In context, he uses the word "*obra.*" A
brief, awkward pause ensues, then he says, "*Bendito sea Dios* [Blessed be the
Lord]," which fits just about anywhere, and continues his sermon.

Barrera approaches Paula with her baby. He goes down on his knees but
does not succeed in going into glossolalia. Finally, he manages, but it is only a
very brief utterance. He "takes it over" to the child but loses it almost immediately.

The prayer ends. All leave the podium and Barrera steps behind the rostrum.
It continues to amaze me how quickly a glossolalist recovers. A moment ago,
there was a flushed face, tense muscles, profuse perspiration. Now there is a
pale face for Barrera, his light complexion more visible than for the others,
perspiration gone, face calm, all movements relaxed.

Bible reading in unison, the same text three times. "You have not learned to
pray much," Barrera scolds the congregation. After all, the *matutin* is for prayer,
one hour of prayer, a pause, another hour of prayer. There is an altar call. In
the ensuing pause, Antonio approaches Barrera. He tells him that he cannot
participate in the rest of the services this Sunday because he has a job as a barber. Barrera admonishes him by saying that people who stop praying become
"cold," "*asi se enfria uno.*" Antonio is obviously crestfallen but leaves anyway.
Eus walks about in the temple, chatting with the other women. Alvio brings his
4-year-old daughter to me. She sings *coritos* so nicely at home, he'd like her to
sing for me so that afterward she can be heard on the recorder. But the child
is too shy.

I make use of the brief pause to slip out to powder myself next door; I am
itchy with perspiration. But I discover to my dismay that my talcum is in Don
Eduardo's house. I tiptoe in, hoping that the brother-in-law is asleep. I had
heard him stumble home at daybreak, belching hugely. He is in his hammock,
and while usually he does not look at me, he is now glowering at me, ready to
pounce like a cat at a mouse, and very softly going "pssss, pssss." I pretend not
to hear him, grab my talcum, and flee to Reina's shower.

I get back to the temple in time for the beginning of the prayer for the manifestation of the Holy Spirit. Barrera's instructions are the same as on previous
occasions. If you feel something supernatural, he says, don't resist it, for that
is the Holy Spirit. Repeat "*sellame, sellame,*" until your tongue gets tired. To my
surprise, he now gives direct instructions also to the women: if they get tired
kneeling, they should stand; they should not return to their seats but rather go
back to kneeling.

Barrera instructs Alvio and Isauro, who have not as yet spoken in tongues, to kneel directly next to the podium. Nohoch Felix, Candil, and Epi are to kneel behind them. They should leave enough room between them so he can pass. There is a tendency, as I observed before, for those kneeling to draw closer together during this prayer.

To the hymn "Santo Espiritu descende" [Come and descend, Holy Spirit], people take their places. Very soon, Alvio goes into trance and subsequent glossolalia. Despite his dark complexion, his flush is quite visible. He is totally oblivious to the fact that I have the camera and later the microphone trained on him, the latter often very close to his face. He is kneeling, palms on floor, shaking, there is tremendous perspiration, even on the back of his hands; some small quantity of clear salivation in front of him forms a puddle on the cement floor. Barrera's glossolalia level is steadily dropping. Finally, the session ends.

Barrera asks if anybody felt anything and Alvio comes to the front. Facing the congregation, he says that he did, and he thinks that maybe he also had a change of language, but he does not know—after fifteen minutes of tremendous vocalization! Barrera, who had been passing from one supplicant to the other, confirms that indeed Alvio has spoken in tongues. So has his wife, Gregoria. She herself is not certain, she says that she felt something, "*gozo* [rapture]," I hear her say later, rather bemusedly, to the other women, but she does not know for sure if her language changed. Again, Barrera confirms the fact. I did not hear her clearly enough, but I am sure that she was in trance. At one point, she broke out in profuse perspiration, and about the same time, one of her little daughters, a child desperate for the attention of her mother, who was nursing a 1-year-old, went up to her and unzipped her dress from behind. Catching my glance, she then zipped the dress back up again, and her mother never even flinched.

I am observing Epi. During the last prayer, he does not get up to kneel at the podium. Instead he stays in his seat, for his 4-year-old son has gone to sleep on his lap. He goes into glossolalia, but his trance is light. He rocks back and forth, never losing hold of his son. I had seen the two together before. Even very small boys prefer to stick to their fathers, no matter what the latter might be doing, and are never shooed away. Epi was kneeling at that time and embracing his son, who was standing next to him. He was in considerable trance, uttering continuous glossolalia and rocking back and forth, all the while maintaining enough control so that he never pressed the little boy too tightly.

Once more, Barrera repeats his instructions. Only Isauro is now without the baptism by the Holy Spirit. Barrera orders him to the podium, and the four others who are already speaking in tongues are ranged in a semicircle behind him. Enthusiastically, the congregation intones, "*Fuego, fuego . . .*" and all efforts are concentrated on Isauro. He is a straight-backed, dignified man, more Spanish than Indian in appearance, who has sold his small herd of cattle so he would not have to go out to his ranch to take care of it and instead could be close to the temple at all times. Epi goes into glossolalia, but he is exhausted and his pitch is lower than before. Alvio is back in glossolalia, also at a lower pitch. Suddenly Epi recovers, goes very high, then drops fast and reverts to "*sellalos, sellalos . . .*" With Joaquin and his shouting out of the picture (he is in Temax, conducting the Sunday service there), I also hear Candil's utterance clearly for the first time. It is a very fast, high tremolo of alternating pitch, a ululating often produced by beginning speakers. Nohoch Felix, who never vocalizes very loudly, has the same kind of soundtrack. Gregoria is still perspiring; Epi is back in glossolalia. However, the general level is beginning to drop, and soon everyone is back in ordinary language, and people begin wiping their faces. A group of neighborhood children, who had crowded into the open side door to watch the goings-on, begins to melt away, and people return to their seats.

Barrera calls Isauro to the front. Yes, he did feel something, as if he were being compressed inside, but as to his language, he felt only a small change. This was all that Gregoria had reported and Barrera had accepted it as satisfactory. However, with the men, Barrera is jacking up his requirements. He tells Isauro that he should pray more, and when the Holy Spirit wants to speak, he should say what the Spirit wants him to say.

Then, once more there is the brief, impressive ceremony of entering the new names into the book. "Hoy, domingo, el 27 de julio 1969 se bautiso con el Espiritu Santo Hermano Alvio E. and Hermana Gregoria C."

After a short pause, Bible School begins. In his thorough way, Barrera quickly discovers that his congregation has very little idea of what it is he is talking about. At one point, he is totally exasperated. "Apparently, for you this is only words, words. . . . I will have to come with a dictionary, and we will talk about every important word separately, such as *bendicion* or *santidad*." Things get worse. "*Fornicar,* now that is forbidden, it is a very big sin. It is a mortal sin. So what is *fornicar?*" Nobody has any idea. In the same context, and *concupiscencia del ojo* [concupiscence of the eye]? He fairly spits it out. Of course, he is losing on two fronts. Aside from the women, whose Spanish is minimal anyway, this is not the vocabulary of the market that the men are conversant in. And besides, what they want is to experience the Holy Spirit and so acquire that all-important ticket to heaven. As Joaquin had maintained, if there was anything they were supposed to know, the Holy Spirit would tell them. No need for homework. They stare back at him, faces blank. He tries a different tack, taking count of how many Bibles are around. There are eight men present with six Bibles, and seventeen women with three copies. He assigns biblical passages to be learned by heart and makes sure that the assignments are taken home in writing. I supply the notepaper.

Finally, after six-and-a-half hours, we are dismissed. I feel positively heroic with only one raw egg in my stomach and nothing more.

The evening service is preceded by a meeting of the Dorcas, chaired by Barrera. He talks once more about their task of raising money for church purposes. The officers, who serve for one year, will get to go to the regional meetings of the church. He names Rodolfa, a slight and lively woman, pretty but with very few teeth, to be president. She is Candil's second wife; his first wife left him. She does not know how to write, and that is all right for a president, but for a secretary, there is need for a woman who does. She will be in charge of the minutes and of correspondence. Barrera will teach her how to do everything. It turns out that Gregoria can write. Her usually pale, soft madonna oval of a face with pronounced Mongolian eyes is flushed. What a day! She has been baptized by the Holy Spirit, now everyone will know that she can write, and she has been named secretary of the Dorcas. What matter if the organization has only six members, three of them officers?

I am wondering what is going to happen to Barrera's Latin American all-male world, in which in his perception the women are supposed to be concerned with nothing but tots and tortillas, once he empowers them in the congregation in this manner. As an urbanite, he seems totally unaware that in the Maya village world, into which his missionizing zeal has thrust him, men and women are separate but equal, in a delicately poised balance. There is on the men's side an obvious anxiety that this equilibrium is being disturbed. Only the men offer hymns as a personal performance, only the men give testimony. "The chief anxiety of these Maya men concerns order," I wrote to Erika Bourguignon at the time, but I could not quite place it. As soon as the women feel safe to enter into these attractive activities, and surely contrary to Barrera's expectation, the men noisily approve, with repeated shouts of "*Halleluja!*" and "*Gracias a Dios!*" The discomfiture of imbalance is beginning to dissolve. Barrera is astute enough to detect that something is going on, but he thinks that the men disapprove of the increased participation of the women. However, there is nothing he can do about it. He is tied to the regulations of the Church; he has to start the organization of the Dorcas. So he tries to minimize the significance of the emergence of the women, emphasizing their subordination. They are cute, *chan* [little], working for the *chan cosa* [cause], they are *chan secretaria, chan presidente,* collecting *chan taakin* [money], and in a supreme effort, even a reduplication, in both Maya and Spanish, they are *chan mujercitas* [little, little women]. But he has sown the wind, and he cannot foresee the fruit of the storm it will eventually yield.

During the evening service, for the first time, three women rise during testimony time. Rodolfa recites a biblical passage with chapter and verse, just like the men. She must have prepared carefully, with help, since she cannot read. Eus volunteers to sing a hymn to the glory of God, and Gregoria tells of her gratefulness for having received the baptism by the Holy Spirit. Enthusiastic shouts of "*Aleluya,*" and "*Gloria a Dios*" reward them from the men's side. When I first came and found not a single woman in the temple who had had a glossolalia experience, I asked Reina about it. She maintained that sort of thing was extremely rare for women, and she personally never knew a female glossolalist. Now, with Gregoria's success to spur them on, other women may well follow suit.

The day before, Eus had received a letter from her son Chan Felix, which she asked me to read to her. The ministers do receive a stipend while in training at the Tepic, Nayarit, Biblical Institute, but it is only 400 pesos per month, and he is in dire need of cash. Eus passed the letter on to Luis, and all day long he had been soliciting help for "your former minister," Felix S. People have deposited envelopes with donations on the rostrum, and instead of simply reporting the result of the collection, Luis now makes it a dramatic occasion. Ceremoniously, he opens each envelope, names the sum, and keeps adding up the amount. It turns out to be 28.50 pesos (about $2.50 U. S.). One man comes up to the podium and makes it an even 30 pesos.

More and more during subsequent services, two concerns of Barrera's stand in the foreground. As more people begin speaking in tongues, he feels that it is becoming increasingly urgent to perform a baptism by water. Barrera warns of the danger that only persons baptized by the Holy Spirit might incur. Since the body has not yet been washed clean of sin, the Spirit is working on an old body, and this old body cannot support the Holy Spirit. In the meantime, he warns the men not to drink, not to call each other foul names, and to get married. Less than 30 percent of the married couples in Utzpak are formally married, he says, and to live with each other without official sanction, at least in a civil ceremony, is *fornicar,* a mortal sin. Actually, the underlying attack is directed not only against the Indian form of marriage, where two young people simply set up housekeeping together, but principally against the men taking a second wife. The Catholic Church has fought against this Maya custom ever since the conquest, without success. Eus would occasionally point out a woman as we walked the streets of Utzpak as the second wife of so-and-so. Later on, when defection from the Apostolic congregation became more frequent, the reason given was often committing *un pecado mortal,* a mortal sin, euphemistic for taking a second wife.

As to Barrera's second concern, as he keeps explaining, if the Second Coming were to take place right now, even those who had been baptized by the Holy

Spirit but not also by water would be lost. And there are many signs warning that Christ's Second Coming is close at hand. The mere fact that so many people are now speaking in tongues is a clear indication. He asks rhetorically "When has so much speaking in tongues occurred before the present series?" No one can remember. "*Ya hace tiempo* [It has been a while]," somebody volunteers.

Meanwhile, the services continue with increased female participation. During the segment when the congregation is enjoined to offer hymns to praise the Lord, three school-age girls volunteer for the first time. As they stand there in front of the podium, singing timidly, one keeps knotting her mantilla more and more tightly around her middle. After the offering of the Senores Cristianos, the Dorcas are called to the front for the first time. They come forward hesitantly. While the fathers hold the screaming babies, the Dorcas perform valiantly.

Visiting

Luis L., from Merida, is here on a ministerial visit. During the altar call, I observe how he induces his glossolalia. He has his guitar with him, and as he kneels down, he keeps hold of the instrument. While he prays, he grabs it with both hands and, exerting a great deal of pressure, he goes into glossolalia. As he lets go of it, holding it only with one hand, he lapses into ordinary language. During the next altar call, there is a variation of this same strategy. He lifts his right arm in prayer, then puts both hands on the neck of the guitar and glossolalia follows. Then he takes his left hand off the guitar and lapses into ordinary language. Once more, he grabs the guitar with both hands, but with his energy level apparently exhausted, no more glossolalia follows. He wipes his eyes and continues praying in ordinary language.

Paula is here with sick Pedrito and with her husband. She had asked the congregation for prayers so that her husband would also be converted, and today he has come along, mainly apparently because Pedrito will be presented to the congregation. Barrera formally requests Luis L. to present Pedrito.

In a brief sermon, Luis L. explains that the Apostolic Church does not baptize infants, since they are without sin. Also, there is no *comadre* and *compadre*, baptismal sponsors, the entire congregation assuming this role. Then he takes the little boy, gravely calling him "Hermano Pedro," and prays over him. He goes into glossolalia, handling the child much like he had his guitar, pressing his legs and stretching them, but clearly with enough control, for the child only whimpers and no pressure marks are left on his pale small limbs. A white-haired man and an equally elderly woman, the child's grandparents, stand behind the kneeling parents. The grandfather kisses the child, which is returned to his mother.

In his sermon, Luis L. tries to impress on the congregation that it needs to support its minister financially. Does anybody tithe like the Bible demands? They are honest enough to say no. I am not surprised. Where would the money come from? While I hear no stories about anyone going hungry (the government maintains the price of tortillas at a set low level), cash is extremely hard to come by. The ranches pay poorly, the Temax *henequen* plants even less, and what agricultural surplus there is has no convenient market. Luis and Joaquin, both city men, are physically unable to do the hard labor on the ranches, and they have no *solar* to grow food of their own, even if they knew how. As mentioned before, they try to make a living by selling relatively expensive junk from Japan and Hong Kong, introduced via Belize, but there are no customers. To make their financial situation even more precarious, half of the slim offerings must be surrendered to the district headquarters of the Apostolic Church in Villahermosa.

Luis L. has been pastor in Utzpak before and of course knows the situation. So he does not press the point of tithing any further. The service ends with another prayer for Pedrito.

Eus and I go visit some *hermanas,* something that Eus loves to do. We start out at seven in the morning to beat the heat of the day. Reception is friendly everywhere, but in contrast to the practice of the German and Hungarian peasants I know so well, we are not offered anything to eat or to drink. We are always invited into the house though; hammocks that during the day are tied into a neat bundle and suspended from the beams are let down and we are asked to sit. When Eus sits down, she has an elegant way to fit into the weave, like an eighteenth-century lady into a chaise lounge. Her freshly ironed ʔ*ipil* settles in soft folds, her hand rests on the back edge of the hammock. By comparison, I awkwardly squat in the middle (if I am lucky). The conversations are always entirely in Maya. Eus tells proudly of the big book which I have for studying the language, *le masawal tʔaana* [this Indian tongue], and occasionally I am given the chance to display that I have already learned a little. My nicest sentence is something like "*sansamaal umpʔit maas* [every day a little more]," which always brings pleased laughter. All of them want their picture taken. Eus had anticipated that and had suggested that I take the camera. We get home about one; I am simply limp from the burning heat. "*Hach chʔococ cʔiin* [It is a very hot day]," is the Maya sentence I shall remember forever. We said it several hundred times that day.

I am working on refining my understanding of the gender bar. It seems the married men will talk with me if their wives are present, or in church, or if their own mother is present, that is, if there is an initial relationship between me and a female member of their household. The unmarried men will not have contact with me under any circumstance.

I experience one rather funny exception. Eus and I were in Don Antonio's general store. Don Antonio reads the newspaper and always asks questions about the United States, such as do I know Jacqueline Kennedy? How come I don't? Yesterday, there was a very old man in the store, his one eyelid drooping, bending over a cane. He said to Eus that I was pretty and that if he were 40 and still had his money, he would not let me go back to the States. Then, turning to me, he asked whether I would not want to take him with me; after all, he was a good risk, since he was already old. When we left, he blew me a kiss, and the entire store hugely enjoyed the little intermezzo. His extreme old age, I imagine, probably excused him from the generally operating avoidance. Eus told me the following story about him: he used to be very rich, selling cattle in Merida. His wife died and he remarried, taking a very young girl. He bought her everything, a house in Merida, clothes, jewels. However, she soon acquired a lover, who would fetch her in the evening at nine, returning her home in the morning at four. If her husband then came to her hammock, she would say, "*Cochino*, get away from me, you stink. Why don't you go and take a bath?" Now he has nothing; his sons of his former marriage give him his food as a gift, and even the house he lives in here in Utzpak belongs to his second wife, who may at any time decide to throw him out.

More Services

Noticeably in the subsequent weeks, my notes taken during the services reflect the increasing role the women have begun to assume. Simultaneously, the glossolalia of the men begins to shed the ululating pattern of the beginner and settles into a pronounced syllable inventory. All this is demonstrated by the following description of an evening service.

July 19, 1969

Starting attendance four men, five women, and eight children. During testimony time, Gregoria now always speaks up also. She asks for the prayer of the congregation for her parents and siblings to be converted.

Attendance begins to increase. There is an altar call. When hymns are asked for that will glorify God, Gregoria volunteers. She is fourth after Paulino, a recent new member, Candil, and Nohoch Felix. She has an infant on one arm, holds the hymnal with the other hand, and cannot carry a tune, but her performance earns her numerous "*Amens*" and "*Gracias a Dios.*" The baby keeps pulling her large white mantilla off, and she finally resolutely piles it on top of her head and finishes her presentation. Paula comes in with little Pedrito and, as usual, kneels in front of the podium with the baby slumped weakly on her shoulder.

Isauro asks for a special offering for Barrera, who needs to go to Campeche. So the delivery of his wife's baby must be imminent. It is the measure of his popularity that this time the small plastic dish holds not coins but only bills, and I see two 10-peso ones in addition to mine.

Barrera goes into glossolalia during the altar call. I note that those speakers who are no longer at the level of the high ululating form of the beginners but now have a segmented inventory, consonant-vowel, consonant-vowel—such as Epi and of course Barrera—produce more or less the same syllables, but they are quite different from those I heard in the Mexico City congregation: *ʔa-i-a, ʔa-i-a,* or *ʔaria, ʔaria.* In other words, something like their own glossolalia dialect is beginning to emerge. The "*ʔaria*" variant is especially remarkable, because in Maya, there is no trilled "r," and when the Maya speakers in the ordinary state of consciousness use Spanish, they either drop this phone or they produce a glottal fricative. So that phonetic rule does not carry over into the glossolalia. What does carry over is the person's manner of speaking. Barrera has a fast delivery and an exact, clipped way of enunciating; Epi drags his words, speaking as if he has a big, round dumpling in his mouth. Such differences also appear in the glossolalia, although not when a person is still in the high-energy ululating mode.

I am also curious about what exactly triggers Barrera's glossolalia, which he uses liberally throughout the service, not merely during the altar call, and I make a special note of it during the following Sunday service. All observations are of course embedded into the rich social fabric of the congregation.

SUNDAY, JULY 20, 1969

When I get to the temple at six in the morning, the service has not begun yet. Barrera is talking to a man who has not attended services for a long time and has decided to come back. Such returns are happening frequently now that Barrera has taken over. Reina told me that when Chan Felix was still minister, the congregation would often consist of only Don Eduardo and Eus. Chan Felix, Reina said, did not know how to preach. Nor would he ever report on how much money was collected, who might come to visit, or what was going on in other congregations. People want to know those things, she says. That is how Barrera is different.

Barrera, Isauro, and the new man finally go to the podium to kneel and pray. Barrera places his hands on the podium, goes into glossolalia, then lifts his hands high, and the glossolalia stops.

Finally, Barrera rings for the service to begin. There are four men and four women present. Throughout the subsequent service I keep observing what triggering mechanisms Barrera uses to induce his glossolalia. There is no doubt about the effectiveness of his rocking on his knees with his hands on his thighs, but I am worried about his trigger words, which I had pinpointed earlier. The observation seems to be valid, but there are too many words. Right now, it is "*misericordia.*" I wonder if he uses some kind of breath control, but I am not sure.

After a *corito* and prayer, Barrera introduces an *hermano* from Chetumal, Jose D. S., a native of Utzpak, who has come to visit the congregation. I hear from Reina later that this Jose D. S. is the son of the leading Catholic layman here in the village, and his conversion was quite a sensation. "What attracted him?" I ask. "He just liked the Apostolics better," she shrugs. From Eus I hear that he brought more merchandise for Barrera and Joaquin to sell, imported through Chetumal. During the service, he announces a gift of 69 pesos from the *hermanos* in Chetumal for improvement on the church, and in presenting it, he makes it an even 70 pesos. With his wife coming back soon with two small sons and a newborn, Barrera needs to move out of the house at Eus's place and into the *casa pastoral.* It is separated from the temple by a high limestone wall and has a leaky roof. This gift will take care of the necessary repairs. He asks for a *corito* and a prayer for the offering so that the givers may receive multiple compensation for their gift. It sounds like he has a catch in his throat, and without any motion or trigger word, the glossolalia ensues. Perhaps this is the mechanism I am looking for: certain contexts, often but not always stereo-typically connected with particular words, produce the excitement, an arousal that in turn leads to the light trance and the glossolalia. In the present case, the excitement generated by the generous gift from friends, taking a big worry off his mind, is already present, and nothing else is needed.

Prayer for receiving the Holy Spirit. Barrera gives instructions as before. "Don't think of any problem you may have, think only of your contact with God." Over by the men's side, Jose D. S. has joined those who have already received the Holy Spirit. I overheard the men quizzing him before the service. Yes, he tells them, he has been baptized by both water and by the Holy Spirit. When he goes into glossolalia, he grabs hold of his right elbow behind his back with his left hand. Even under ordinary circumstances he prefers the use of his left hand to that of his right, and he rocks lightly back and forth. There is some clear salivation. His pulse (syllable) inventory is reminiscent of that of Luis L. and of Luis's mother in Merida. So here is evidence of another glossolalia dia-lect. His body language also differs from that of the locals. He lightly knocks his heels together while kneeling and in glossolalia, and he sometimes has his hands on his hips, pointing toward the back.

During this period, Alvio and Candil are both in glossolalia, and now Paula joins them. She has left Pedrito with the other women, and her glossolalia has the haunting ululating pitch of the beginners that seems to take them to the very edge of the state. I have her on tape, and with my microphone in my blouse pocket, I begin filming her. Up to now I have never stepped up on the podium, but I simply cannot catch enough of her in the extremely confined space between the other women, the podium, and the wall. Counting on the fact that by now everybody is used to me and takes my somewhat out-of-the-ordinary activities for granted, I push through. But as I pass, the baby of the woman kneeling next to Paula grabs my microphone wire and won't let go. I decide to risk it anyway. I step up on the podium, kneel down, and start searching for Paula's face in the viewfinder, but in the subdued light, I cannot locate it. This is a bad time to remember Barrera's opinion that if the Lord does not want me to catch anything on my film, there won't be anything. I just hope that the heavenly and apparently male administration does not choose this occasion to express its displeasure over my getting on the podium, that exclusively male preserve. Finally, in what seems a very long time, I get the baby untangled from the wire, and Paula's tense, tear-streaked face appears in the camera. Barrera passes me without taking note, and nothing is said about my infraction later.

Paula keeps up her high, rapid glossolalia. Barrera rings, and Paula stops and goes over into sobbing. She returns to her seat, wiping her face. When Barrera later calls her to the front, she says that she is grateful that she felt the rapture of the Lord.

After a pause of about ten minutes, the Escuela Dominical begins. Barrera has ambitions. He wants his congregation to learn and fully understand the Acts. Then he starts speaking of the history of the Apostolic Church in Mexico and specifically in Yucatan. But his audience has problems with the vocabulary. "What is *testigo* [witness]?," he probes, then carefully explains it. Half an hour later only one person remembers what it means. And then there are the place names. Where was the gospel preached to the gentiles? On the road to what city did Paul go blind? No one knows. Like Sisyphus, Barrera is never done. Maybe to console himself, he does a head count, down to babes in arms. There are twenty-seven women and eleven men present.

For the noon hour, the congregation is invited to a service of thanksgiving for the first harvest at Apolinario Ch.'s house. He is not yet a member of the church; he does not even attend the services. But he lives among Apostolics, and privately I assume that this service, which he clearly considers necessary for the continued success of his *col*, will cost him less than the equivalent Catholic one. I ask Eus whether I should go. We have six-and-a-half hours of service behind us, the heat is unbearable, and the way to Apolinario's house is a good half hour. But Eus is a fabulous trouper and will not brook weakness.

"You may be able to take pictures of the people drinking *atole*," she says. My flagging spirits are raised to their appropriate level. I go.

If it were not so abominably hot, I would even enjoy this long walk. The streets are not European village alleys. They are wide avenues, bordered by three-foot-high whitewashed *albarradas* and wildflowers blooming among the limestone outcroppings of the narrow, winding path in the middle. Oval houses with palm-frond roofs peek out above the *albarradas* or open up to the street. Pigs root among the rocks; a rooster pursues an unwilling hen. Occasionally, we meet a woman on an errand. "*Paseando?*" she asks [Taking a walk?]. "*Haa,*" we answer, "*paseando.*" It makes me feel right at home. In Hungary, as well as in the Swabian villages of southwestern Germany, the casual greeting is also that of naming the activity the other person appears to be engaged in.

We are now almost *al monte* [at the bush], at the outskirts of the village; Apolinario's house is the last one. It is the usual oval mud-and-wattle structure with a *huano* roof, called *casa de paja* [straw house] around here. There are people in and about, some of the congregation, others strangers to us, neighbors of the family come out of curiosity. A table is placed in the shade in front of the house, covered with a blue oilcloth with a flower pattern. Two large bunches of flowers in plastic containers flank a dish containing corn on the cob covered with a carefully embroidered cloth. It looks like a ritual offering.

Barrera conducts a very appealing brief service, as is customary for such an *accion de gracia* [ritual of thanksgiving]; no propaganda for his church, only an invitation to those present to attend the services. There are hymns, a *corito*, and prayer, during which Barrera utters a brief glossolalia, then he has the couple kneel, praying for them and their small son with a brief laying on of hands. After the service, everyone is served corn on the cob, including the cobs from the dish, and *atole* in a *luuch*. As Eus had foreseen, everyone is delighted that I take pictures. There are no fees charged and no offering taken. At 2:30 P.M., we amble homeward, lugging chairs and the piles of hymnals.

The evening's service is preceded by a meeting of the Dorcas. Barrera drills them on procedure and feels the interest of his women slipping. "Now we are just learning," he reassures them. "Later we will have many important things to do." The women nod indifferently.

Jose D. S. begins the service. His is a faster pace than Barrera's; he drives the singing, and later he has everyone consecutively and rapidly recite a biblical quotation with chapter and verse. When he calls on Eus and me, Barrera says protectively, "*Ellas no saben* [They can't do that]." I wonder how much of this is the style of Juan L. and Luis L. The Chetumal congregation is that of Juan L., and Jose even kneels down the same way that Juan L. does.

There are eleven men and eight women at the first altar call. Barrera and Jose go into very loud glossolalia, also Nohoch Felix.

Special hymns are offered, one of them by two 12-year-old girls. I recall seeing one of them, a pretty thing with large eyes and sensuous lips, carrying a heavy bundle of wood in a tumpline down the street while protecting her complexion with a flowery umbrella.

While Jose is standing behind the table in front of the rostrum, I am again struck by the way this man prefers using his left hand and how awkwardly he holds his right arm, almost as if it were paralyzed. Reina told me, in fact, that in the village he was nicknamed "El Mocho," the cripple. However, here is a curious thing: twice I observed that when he has a slight, clear salivation during a trance, he wipes it off with his right hand.

Paula has come in with Pedrito and kneels at length at the podium. Barrera takes over from Jose, there is a prayer, then Barrera hands the document of presentation of Pedrito to Paula and her husband. They kneel in front of the rostrum, and he prays for them with a laying on of hands.

In his sermon, it is back to fire and brimstone. In hell, people burn eternally, but they will not be consumed. So punishment will go on forever and ever. He warns about the temptations of the world—drinking, smoking, dancing, picture shows, other women—and has some new items to add: television, for the concupiscence of the eye can be aroused just as easily by a television picture, or even by *el box*, the popular boxing matches. Once more, he explicates the extreme danger incurred by people who have not as yet been baptized by water and asks those who would like to be baptized to come to the front. The baptism is going to be at the beginning of August. Four men—among them Paula's husband—and nine women approach the podium. Barrera writes a list. In the ensuing prayer, Barrera, Luis, Epi, Nohoch Felix, and Jose are in glossolalia, the latter standing and again grabbing his right elbow in the back with his left hand. He fades into ordinary language with "*Halleluja.*"

Barrera then announces that in his absence, Hermano Jose D. S. and Hermano Joaquin C. will be in charge of the services. He has them kneel, lifts one hand, and, holding his Bible in the other, he performs a laying on of hands. He prays, and at the word *poder* [power] he goes into glossolalia.

After church, Eus usually walks me to Reina's house, where we briefly talk about the next day. Then she walks back to the temple and with Nohoch Felix and her 8-year-old grandson Jose, they walk home. This evening, in the uncertain light of the moon—our streetlights have been out since the last big rain—she looks back toward the temple, straining to see. She says a hurried "*Ma?alob*, Hermana," and leaves. Next day she tells me that a man who had been waiting in front of the temple, supposedly for one of the girls, had grabbed hold of Jose. This is what she saw from our corner. By the time she got there, he had thrown the child to the ground. Jose could not say why. "Why do you think it happened?" I ask. She shrugs. "That man is that way. He has a demon in him."

It is demon season also for poor Reina. Tearfully, she charged yesterday that Santiago's sister's daughter had stolen 16 pesos from her. It seems that she keeps her spare money hidden in the *huano* roof of her kitchen shack. This child, she claims, has always stolen money from her if by chance she left it on the table. This time she must have observed her as she took a peso from its hiding place. The girl's younger brother maintained that he saw his sister climb up and hunt for something in the *huano*, but he did not see her take anything out. The whole neighborhood hears Reina crying and complaining. Later, her brother-in-law, the husband of Santiago's sister, comes to pay the money back. He does not think that his child has taken anything, but he wants *amistad* [friendship] within the family. Reina accepts the offer, but he has only a 20-peso bill, and so under cover she sends the young son of her neighbor, who sometimes does shopping for me, to ask me for the 4 pesos she needs to make change. Then there is another tearful episode, the reason for which I hear later from Eus. It seems that Santiago's brother, the normally silent brother-in-law, has so insulted Reina that she even threatened to go to the *presidente*, the head of the municipality, to complain about him.

As to the theft of money, Eus says that the entire family of Santiago is that way. She knows for a fact that Santiago's mother, now deceased, used to grab and cook the chickens of the neighbors if they happened to stray into her yard and the neighbor was not looking. Some time ago, the then treasurer of the Apostolic Church here, a girl of 28, absconded with the church money with Santiago's youngest brother, who was 17 at the time. It was not difficult; the money was kept behind the rostrum in a powdered-milk can. Members of the congregation found a letter of hers directed to the boy, very mushy. She must have copied it from one of those *cuentos* [romance comic books], says Eus. They went to Merida, where they are now living together, and the money was never returned.

On Saturday morning, the pleasing noises of the awakening village—cocks crowing, turkeys gobbling, pigs grunting, the *nixtamal* [corn] mill putt-putting—is interrupted by the sound of the church bell, but as if the bell were cracked and were being hit hard and yet hesitantly. "It is the *doble* [the double]," Reina says. "Someone has died." The Catholic church has a large and a small bell, and when a Catholic person dies, they hit the two bells simultaneously. She scurries to keep Lupita in the house so she will not by chance see the coffin, should it be carried by.

Later, I heard that Utzpak's leading man of the PRI, the governing party of Mexico, died quite suddenly of a heart attack. Eus and I are in Don Antonio's store buying some ropes for hanging a hammock when we see the door of the house across the street open and a group of women emerge, bearing candles and flowers. One of the women is sobbing loudly. Then a large group of men follow, six of them carrying the coffin. The coffin is a wooden box, narrower at the foot end, festooned in gray. At the head end, the festooning forms an elevated cross. "When an *hermano* dies," Eus remarks as we are watching the procession wending its way toward the church on the plaza, "hardly anybody cries, and there are no candles. After all, we know where he is going, and so there is no reason to cry. Although, of course, no one can be absolutely certain that he has done everything right. Only God knows." Then she adds, laughing, "For the Catholics, it's easier. Remember what Hermano Barrera said last Sunday? A Catholic can sin all his life, and then, when the final hour comes, he calls the priest. And the priest says, here, pay me 40 pesos for the mass, and off to heaven you go." She shakes her head admiringly, "I wonder where the *hermano* always gets those things he says."

Two years later, Eus tells me, the bones are excavated and cleaned and are then placed into an individual or a family ossuary. You save space that way. "*Y en tu pais?* [And in your land?]" Many of our conversations go that way. On an earlier occasion, she told that it was thought around here that people in the United States bathed only once a week, not every day like the Maya people do, and that they ate horse meat, but she did not think that was true. When I explain about our burial practices, she comments that we must have vast cemeteries and a lot of land to waste. Her home is next to the cemetery, and some people are afraid to pass by it, but that is because they do not really believe in God. If a person is dead, she says, he is dead, and he does not come back. Once, though, she had a dream. Two women (she uses "*coolelo?ob*" [Maya ladies]) were crossing the road and went into the cemetery. She could not see their faces because they had their *rebozos* tightly wrapped around their head, and the dream made her very uneasy.

The Tuesday evening's service is *patronizado,* sponsored by the Senores Cristianos. During testimony time, an elderly man, Gregorio A., speaks up. He is the husband of Eus's friend Dona Valuch and he says that he is happy to be with the *hermanos* once more. Eus says that he changed and went from the Apostolics to the Pentecostals. The principal doctrinal difference is that the Pentecostals see the Trinity as three beings, while the Apostolics hold that the Trinity represents three names for the same divine entity. The Pentecostals have a small, half-finished church in the *barrio* [section] north of here. Four months ago, a young man came from Cansahcab to missionize in this small church. He knew no one in Utzpak, and three men grabbed him; two held him and the third one kept hitting him in the chest and stomach until he started vomiting blood. They left him lying in the street. Later, he crawled to a nearby house and asked for help. He was taken to a sanitarium in Merida and has since recovered, but the local Pentecostal congregation has practically dissolved. That is why Gregorio came back. Eus heard that every two weeks somebody holds a service at the Pentecostal temple, but there is not much attendance. She worries about Chan Felix, who also goes on missionizing trips, but he tells her that in the first place he knows how to fight and thus can defend himself, and besides, he knows a lot of people, and a person who is known in a municipality is protected simply by that fact.

In his sermon, Jose D. S. reassures the congregation about speaking in tongues. They should not be frightened by it, for when the Holy Spirit enters the person, the evil animals possessing a person (such as those mentioned in the New Testament) will have to leave.

During the service, I have a hard time sitting still. Although I had promised myself not to do it again, I once more lean against the wall while recording glossolalia and a number of ants start crawling around on my legs under my skirt. While this is merely annoying—they are not fire ants—what awaits me on the door of Reina's house afterward is downright frightening. I had never seen any live tarantulas before, and there are two spiders the size of soup plates lazily crawling around on Reina's door. When Eus sees my panic—these hairy, brown monsters are obviously preventing me from opening the door—she sends her grandson to climb over the *albarrada* and get my bottle of kerosene. Calmly, she douses them and throws a burning match on them, setting them on fire. They run around like little piles of fire and die with a small "pop," leaving an evil stench and a blackened shell behind. The execution makes me sad; maybe I just should have disregarded them.

Reina wants to wean Lupita, but Lupita does not want to be weaned. She also refuses to drink milk from a bottle. There is no fresh milk—I need to recall that this is a culture without native dairy herds—but the PRI distributes powdered whole milk for free to its members. I ask if PAN, the second party in Mexico which, however, has never been in power, also does something equivalent, but Reina says that there are no PANistas around, besides, the PANistas are *los contrarios* [the opposition], so one should not have anything to do with them, although she has no idea of what exactly they are against.

Last night before the service we sat on the curb and Lupita crawled on my lap, fumbling at my dress to reach my breast. There was considerable laughter from Reina; the midwife, old Tomasita; and Raquel from across the street. "So," Tomasita said, "you want something white?" Once more Reina tried to offer the bottle, but without success. Lupita would have to go to bed hungry, she threatened. I was at the service, so I did not witness the continuation of the contest, but during the night, Lupita cried, and I could hear her contented sucking. This morning the battle is still on. Reina has painted her breast with the bluing used for washing, something done generally during weaning. I find the breast looks ghastly; so does Lupita, who steadfastly refuses to suck, but with equal persistence also refuses the bottle. By noon, when I get home from Eus,

Lupita has emerged victorious. No more painted breasts, and she is happily back with her *chuuch*.

Reina wants to wean Lupita because she is almost a year old and it is the thing to do, but nursing, she says, does not prevent another pregnancy. Most women can conceive while nursing. She started menstruating two months after delivery and soon was back on a monthly schedule. Thus there is usually not much time between weaning and the arrival of the next child. Lupita is lucky that Reina is not pregnant yet, for with the arrival of the next one, the older child is pushed out of the lap of the mother. I see no malnutrition as a result; the children drink black bean broth in the morning or chocolate beaten into hot water in tall, slender, hand-carved wooden chocolate vessels. This, by the way, is also what many adults still do for breakfast. "Did you drink yet?" means Have you had breakfast yet? Chocolate comes from Central America, and the Maya word *chocwa* is the root of our word. But the deprivation of the older child is psychological, as is demonstrated on our corner. For instance, the lumberjack's wife has three children. The oldest is a boy, about 5, then comes another boy, about 3, and a girl, 15 months old. When the mother comes by in the evening to chat, the scene always evolves the same way. The little girl demands her *chuuch*. The mother sits down on the curb and begins to nurse her. The 3-year-old tugs at her, pushes her, and rubs against her, only to be repulsed with angry words and threats. Finally, he runs away.

Another neighbor has a 3-year-old girl and a 14-month-old boy. The boy still nurses. The little girl, called Lucy, will not stay home. Always at mealtime, we see the mother walking down the street, trying to find her daughter. Lucy refuses to play with her little brother and often wanders quite far, entering houses where there are children and playing there. Another drama of the same nature is played out in the temple, where Gregoria has a 3-year-old daughter and a baby girl about 11 months old. For the 3-year-old, the temple is the convenient place for protest. As soon as the youngest starts nursing, she starts screaming. She usually manages to get her mother to take the youngest to Alvio, then she goes to sleep in her mother's arms, the proper order of the world restored.

More Visiting

I love our frequent sallies "to go see *hermanas*." Eus knows everything about everybody, knee-deep gossip, an anthropologist's heaven.

After passing briefly by the very neat mud-and-wattle house of Alvio and Gregoria, we go toward Epi's house and on the way pass the former home of Paulino. He sold it some time ago. It seems that one day he came home from hunting earlier than expected, and as he was showering, the neighbor came to the door, calling to his wife that it was time to have their chocolate together.

Paulino went for him with his shotgun but did not catch him. He then sold his house and divorced his wife. Today, however, they are back together again. "He should have been used to this sort of thing," Eus remarked wryly. "She did the same thing to him when they were still living out on his ranch."

Then there is Ester's home. Her husband Chucho buys and sells livestock, so they are well-to-do, and she has a *mamposteria* house with a roofed-over terrace attached to it that serves as kitchen, laundry room, and shower. Conveniently, her well is right next to it. She rarely comes to the services at the temple; her husband is very jealous. He will not let her attend Hermano G.'s services either. He is the local Baptist missionary, an American. Sometimes after his services, which are attended only by a few old women, he invites his converts to have a *refresco* [soft drink] with him and takes them for a ride in his car. Chucho will not allow his wife to go by car with another man and have a *refresco* with him.

Finally, we arrive at Epi's house. Epi is at home, relaxing in his hammock, with his baby daughter in his arms. His son is at his mother's skirt. We settle down to a comfortable conversation and I have a chance to ask him about his conversion. This is a summary of his story.

> Epi first married when he was 14 years old; that is, he went to live with a 16-year-old girl. He could not marry her legally, because for that you have to be 15 years old. By this girl, he had a son, but he left her and married his present wife in a Catholic ceremony when he was 19. He is 24 years old now. He used to be a heavy drinker, sleeping it off in the street, and he enjoyed playing cards all night, often losing his entire earnings. His mother made him attend the services of the Catholic Church, but he went only rarely. Occasionally, he also attended the services of the Presbyterians, but they made no impression on him. After all, they go to the movies, to dances, so obviously their doctrine "cannot be the truth." He kept feeling *ese temor* [this fear]. Once he saw how Luis L. and Candil went to pray for a sick old man who has since died. He listened to them pray as he was standing on the street corner. When Luis L. came out of the house, he started talking to him. Many other conversations followed, and he began attending the Apostolic services regularly. Luis L. instructed the congregation about not fighting, not insulting others, and if they had a second woman, to leave her. He was baptized by water, and from then on felt great fear even if he only thought of going to a dance or to play pool. A month later, he also received the gift of the Holy Spirit and now, as a clear expression of the male before-and-after conversion rule, he no longer feels afraid any more.

We finally arrive at Paula's home. It is a disconcertingly messy traditional house. Hammocks hang every which way, the dirt floor is not swept, and over to one side there is a baby crib full of dirty laundry. She has no kitchen house. Instead, the stones of her hearth are placed outside near an orange bush, with the ashes blowing about. There is no shady spot for doing the laundry. Her children are the first really unkempt ones I have seen. Clearly they do not get the customary daily bath; they have grimy arms and unwashed bottoms. It is close to nine in the morning, but Paula is not making any tortillas, and she is scolding Rosa, her oldest daughter, because she has forgotten to put the beans on the fire. Her husband works for a local *ranchero* who has seven ranches. He pays him only 12 pesos a day, but often gives the *cura* 500 pesos for three masses. Paula was married at 14. She now has eight children; Pedrito is her youngest. This is Paula's story:

> As a child she once saw a saint. People said that he performed miracles and that he was so alive that he even moved his feet. She went up to him; he was standing practically buried in flowers. So she put her hands through the flowers and found his feet cold and rigid; they were made of gypsum. The *cura* also said that when he blessed the water, it became sacred, but he did not really change the water; it was well water just as it was before. He acted as though he were a *yerbero* [an herbalist] who turns herbs into medicine.
>
> Despite these disappointments, she still used to attend the Catholic services as a girl, but she never understood what the priest said in the mass, for it was all in Latin. She did not worry about sinning because they were told that you could always confess what you had done and then things would be right again. So she continued going to movies and dances. Pedrito became ill with polio when he was only two months old. People said that a baptism would cure the sick, so she had him baptized in the Catholic Church, but it was not true, for it did not cure Pedrito.
>
> When she was first married, she also attended Hermano G.'s Baptist services, but it was actually her father, Don Fulgencio, who first introduced her and his other children to the gospel. Now, however, she is sure that he once more has a demon in his heart. He keeps talking about religion, but he curses at people and he does not really believe in anything. Actually, she thinks people do not understand that the Bible is the true and exact word of God. Therefore, you have to teach them little by little. You should not do like Hermano V. in Temax, who goes up to people and tells them that they must change their ways and be baptized or they will go straight to hell and eternal

damnation. No wonder the men at the plaza beat up on him. They taunt him, saying, "What about the Holy Spirit? Does it walk down the street? Do you see it? Does it come into your temple?" They don't understand that the Holy Spirit is a spirit and enters the heart.

Things were different with Chan Felix. He would come by sometimes and merely talk to the children. But she did not want to listen to him and would close the door when she saw him coming. But then Pedrito got worse, so one day she finally decided to ask him to pray over her child. Chan Felix had his guitar with him, and he told her that she would have to kneel down and cover her head and pray with him. After the prayer, he sang a hymn. This touched her heart and she started praying too and attending the services in the temple. But when in the temple, she always felt like crying. She also worried so much about Pedrito catching cold on the way to church or in the church, or about him getting sicker, so many times she did not attend.

The night before she received the Holy Spirit she dreamt that she should fast and then the Holy Spirit would come. And that was the way it happened. Now she no longer worries about Pedrito getting sicker; she takes him to church whenever there is a service, and she does not cover him so tightly anymore either. He has not gotten sicker, and even his fever is less.

Eus has little charity when it comes to messy houses and voices her disapproval after we leave with a few well-chosen words that Paula would not want to hear. "She buys her tortillas," she says, "so she has too much time to run around." It brings to her mind how things were when her own children were small. She used to get up early in the morning, clean her house, grind the soaked corn into *masa* on her hand mill, do her laundry, and she always took care of her children. When she was pregnant, she would eat eggs. She nursed each child for a year, but when they began biting too much, she would wean them. Now, however, her children hardly ever write, or when they come to visit, they expect her to wash their clothes for them and to feed them, and they neither give her money for food nor bring her any presents. "If my children feel no affection for me, what do I care?" she shrugs, but she says it several times. When Chan Felix comes home, though, she feeds him and washes for him and gives him money that his father knows nothing about. "He is my son, after all," she says. But then, as if that were not enough justification, she adds, "He works for the Lord, so of course I help him." Are your other sons also *apostolicos*, I ask? She shakes her head, and there is a note of deep sorrow. "They will not leave the world," she says. "They go to dances, to the *cine*, they have several women. So of course when Judgment Day comes, they will be on the other side, and that hurts."

Does she hear from her daughter Nina? No, not even Nina, who works in Mexico City, writes much anymore, although she always felt very close to her. "Once, a few months ago, Nina wrote that she would come home soon and bring me a son-in-law. I had Nohoch Felix write her a letter saying that I had no son-in-law. I knew that she was not married, and I didn't want to see the man she was living with."

It brings up the topic of how to raise girls. "Some mothers are careless," she says. "When a boy comes to call on their daughter, they let him stay in the house with the girl while they go off to the *nixtamal* mill with their *huuch* [bucket of soaked corn]. Mothers end up with grandchildren very fast that way." She never allowed that sort of thing. She would send her daughter off to the mill, and if the boy wanted to go along, that was all right. "*Si, yo soy mala,*" she laughs [I am bad].

"So Don Fulgencio is Paula's father?" I ask after a proper pause. "*Ma ta wila?* [Didn't you see that when they presented Pedrito?]" she asks back. "I saw him only from the back," I defend myself, and she shakes her head. It is hard to get a good grade from Eus. Then, she says that Don Fulgencio first joined the Baptists, then the Pentecostals, and then the Presbyterians. To the Baptists he only belonged for six months. She repeats what Paula said, "He has a demon in his heart and does not really believe anything." It was said about him that when he was a bullfighter, he would not evoke God when facing a bull. Instead, always in Maya, he would call out, "*Compadre Diablo,* help me," and he would then throw himself in front of the bull and fell the animal. Amusingly, I discover, bullfighting in Maya is called *pay vacash* [playing with cows]. He was not overly conscientious about money, it seems. Don Fulgencio, Don F., and Don J. used to be in charge of the Baptist treasury. They kept borrowing money from the treasury, but finally it was all spent, with Don J. owing the largest amount. Then a man who already had three wives took away his daughter. In shame, Don. J. left Utzpak and the money was never returned.

Don Fulgencio kept inviting Eus to the Pentecostal services, which were being held in his house. "We never take up any collection," he would say. But she retorted, "If you take up no collection, how are you going to build a church? Are you always going to have the services in your house? How are you going to buy a Coleman lamp, and how are you going to pay for the kerosene? The offerings are needed for a proper church."

Don Fulgencio, white-haired and bent, with the intense eyes of a zealot, had spoken to me in church and said that he would like to come and talk with me. On the afternoon of our visit with Paula, he indeed did come to Eus's place, his extreme old age apparently obviating the avoidance rule. He talked at length about himself. He used to be a *torero,* very much caught up in the matters of the world. But then he found Christ. He heard Oscar Hill preach, and he has been going to various churches. Did I think that the world was going to come to an end? Yes, I say, some day it will. *Pues,* at the place where he works, the men say that it was not going to happen, although it is clearly stated in the Bible. Was it really true that his daughter received the Holy Spirit? Yes, I was there when it happened and heard her speaking in tongues. *Pues,* many people contend that they did, but when Oscar Hill was here evangelizing, during all his time, only one person received the Holy Spirit. Did I want to hear some Maya hymns? Yes, very much. He sings the well-known one about Christ dying on the cross that I already have on tape from Eus. I record it anyway, to please him. I ask him whether he would not like to sing something for me from his *torero* days? He cannot recall any songs and finally maintains that it is a sin to remember the things of the world.

When I get to Eus's house the next day for my Maya lesson, some men are constructing an *albarrada,* a wall to separate Eus's land from the narrow section along the highway, which belongs to someone else. The men are talking very loudly. "The fatherland needs sons," one says. "Don Fulgencio and his preachings about chastity—how can we be chaste and also produce sons?" Don Fulgencio does seem to get around.

When Eus and I leave, I to check my mail, Eus to take her corn to the mill, Eus stops to talk to the owner of the plot, who is helping with the work, telling him that his *albarrada* is cutting into her land. The man gets very angry. "I know your kind of people. Those of your religion are all alike, take what you can get. You are taking away one meter and a half of my land. That is not Christian. It is bad testimony." That really stings Eus. An extremely lively interchange in Maya follows, with Eus never losing her half smile and the man getting angrier all the time. I catch only that she suggests that when Nohoch Felix comes home, he will get out the documents and new measurements can be taken, and there is no need to offend people about their religion. This is not about religion, she says, it is about justice. "And he a Presbyterian," she says indignantly, as we walk down the highway toward the mill. Then, savoring her triumph, she adds, "I may not know much Spanish, but in Maya, I know all the right words." I noticed in passing that in speaking about the measurements, she used Spanish number words throughout. It is a sad commentary on the destruction of the sophisticated Maya culture by the Spanish conqueror that all that is left of the number words in village usage is *umpʔe, caapʔe, oshpʔe* (or *untul, caatul, oshtul* if referring to animate objects), one, two, three. Gone is the sophisticated mathematical knowledge reflected, for instance, in Maya astronomy, whose charts correctly predicted eclipses of the moon and even of the sun for thousands of years before and after the conquest.

An evening service with Jose D. S. He could not, of course, help noticing the prominent role the women were beginning to play in the Utzpak congregation, so to an attendance of five men and eleven women he preached about the place of women. Woman was not formed from the foot of man, which would have made her less than he was, or from his head, which would have made her his master, but from his rib, which rendered her neither more nor less than a man. However, man was still her master. A woman wearing short hair, a man's shirt, and pants cannot enter into heaven. For, according to the Bible, a woman must be dressed decently.

As to the Holy Spirit, he continues, the Bible teaches that it confers many gifts, not only that of speaking in tongues. In the Chetumal congregation there is Jose G., who has the gift of work. He is a tailor, and he can sew pants very fast and well. Of the money he makes, he gives three-quarters to the church. His wife always cleans the church. She cannot stand even the smallest bit of dirt on the church floor. And then there is a man who has the gift of prophecy and of the correct inspiration about the Bible. He is called Don Victor. He fasted for four days, and finally God spoke to him. He did not even know how to read and write at the time, but now he knows the Bible by heart, including chapter and verse.

While we are working on Maya the next day, Jose D. S. comes in with Joaquin. Eus had earlier unburdened herself concerning Joaquin, who was still staying with her while Barrera was in Campeche. Eus has an immaculate bucket for drinking water from the well and another one with rainwater for household tasks. So what does Joaquin do? He washes his face in the drinking water. When he drinks coffee, he leaves a residue in the *luuch*, which she then has to scrub with Fab to get it clean again. In the evening, he takes his shower so late that he needs light, so he burns her candle. With Barrera gone, Joaquin does not go on the selling rounds, as he is supposed to. When Chan Felix has no money, he goes out and works on a ranch, but Joaquin can do no such labor. She asked him how he made a living at home, but all he said was that he got up early every morning; he did not say what sort of work he did. Barrera told her that he was a *vago*, an unemployed drifter.

Joaquin has a personal feud going on with Eus's grandson Jose. Jose climbs up into the rafters to fetch a box stored there, and Joaquin says, "He is climbing around up there like a monkey. It looks to me like he has a monkey's face." Now Eus is not always happy with little Jose either. The other day he had red welts over his back and chest. "I beat him with a rope," Eus explains. "He is a *bandido* [He runs around]." He was supposed to watch the chickens and the dog, but when she came home he was nowhere to be seen. But this does not mean that she will let Joaquin call Jose a monkey. "Who has a monkey's face around here is you," she retorts. Today Joaquin has it in for Jose again. The child is mean, he tells Jose D. S., and should learn some kindness and humility. His remark gets to the wrong address. The minister tells him to go to the main house and pray to God for some love and humility, that the child is young and does not know what he is doing. That fits right in with how Eus sees things. Joaquin shouts loudly when he prays, she says, and brags to everybody about how much he fasts. He could certainly do with some more prayer. Joaquin tells her, "Hermana, I never hear you pray." She does not let that pass without an indignant comment. "I am there in my hammock praying," she counters, "and God can hear me. He does not need to be shouted at. I may not be able to read, but I hear the *hermanos* telling about what is in the Bible, and there is talk there about people who stand on streetcorners and pray loudly. But the Lord wants you to do it quietly in your room."

The visit gives me a chance to ask Jose D. S. about how he became converted. Once more, we see the before-and-after rule operating and, as in the case of Nohoch Felix and Paula, it is apparently the woman who takes the initiative when it comes to joining the new sect.

It seems that Jose's wife started going to the Apostolic services, and he would say many evil things to her, such as she would learn how to do sorcery there. She kept on going anyway. One day he shouted at her as she was leaving and he was ready to throw a shoe at her. As she closed the door, he saw a stone flying at him. He thought it would hit him, but instead it started turning around on the floor like a top. It gave him the shivers, and he decided to go see what sort of service his wife was attending. That night when they returned, the stone was gone. He continued going to the Apostolic services and liked what he saw, so he stuck with it. He started speaking in tongues even before his baptism with water. He liked the Apostolics better than the Baptists, where he was baptized before. The Baptists preach without any enthusiasm, he says.

They do not go out to evangelize either. "We go out all the time, talking to the souls," he says. And with the *sabatistas,* the Seventh-Day Adventists, anybody can get up and preach. A person might be a member for scarcely a month and already he stands up there preaching. With the baptism, you should feel like a different person. But he did not feel any different after the baptism with the Baptists or after the rebaptism with the Catholics. So Juan L. said, "Back to the water with you." And he did feel a different man after that baptism. Before, he often wanted to die, but now he does not think of death anymore. He studies the Bible a lot. Before he goes to work, during his noon break, and after work and the evening meal, he is always occupied with his Bible. He is happy with the power that the Holy Spirit gives. For instance, he can fast from 5 o'clock on Thursday evening until Friday noon, and he does not even feel thirsty.

Interval in Merida

I knew from frequent announcements of Barrera that there would be a special week of "nothing but praying for the Holy Spirit" beginning in Merida the first weekend in August. I was hoping to do a lot of recording, so I asked Eus to come to Merida with me, and we had El Negro take us to the Apostolic Church in the Colonia Esperanza. Eus said that we could stay with Hermano Goyo Duarte, who had a small house built of stone across from the temple grounds, but it had a *huano* roof and a kitchen shed behind it, just like out in the country. Hermano Goyo's wife, Cornelia, Eus said, was deaf. She did beautiful embroidery; Eus thought I might want to buy a set of embroidered pieces for an ?*ipil* from her.

When we enter, we find only Hermano Goyo at home, relaxing in his coarse, *henequen*-rope hammock, a man near 80 with white hair, a deeply lined dark face, and very long earlobes. He speaks a cultured, sophisticated Spanish—he rolls his r's, which most Maya speakers do not do, and his voice is deep and resonant. Eus tells him about me, and although he does not feel well—he caught cold working in the *henequen* fields—he is stimulated to tell about his life.

It seems that he was born on a ranch, and since he did not want to be a slave like his father, he fled to the nearby town of Ticul. He was a mere boy at the time, knew no Spanish, and could neither read nor write. In 1908, when he was 18, he became acquainted with the Presbyterians, who had just begun missionizing in Yucatan. He learned to read and began studying the Bible. Soon he became one of the helpers of the new congregation, but the people of the town banded together and attacked the Presbyterians, and he had to flee for his life. He was drafted and was a soldier all through the Mexican Revolution. After the Revolution, he continued in the Presbyterian church, but ten years ago Oscar Hill came to Merida, and through him he became acquainted with the Apostolic faith. He was baptized together with his wife. The baptismal certificate, signed by Oscar Hill, hangs on his wall, together with a picture of the Virgin of Guadalupe, a photograph of his wife, and a Mexican flag cut out of a newspaper.

Soon, however, there was a conflict with Oscar Hill. Although he, Goyo, was a deacon of the new church and had received the Holy Spirit soon after his baptism, Oscar Hill tended to disregard his advice and even refused to tell him about the finances of the church.

He had hoped to become a minister in the church, but in the mean-time, Juan L. had become converted, and he was sent to the Biblical Institute instead of Goyo. Despite all these disappointments, Goyo continued in the Apostolic Church, although, he says, "It is my impression that people have very little understanding of the gospel. They didn't have it when I was young, and they don't now. Besides, I don't really like the preaching style of those *muchachos* like Luis L. and the others. They shout too much!" However, about a year ago, he became interested in the Baha'i movement, which has a center in Merida. He goes to their study meetings and has bought some of their publications. Enthusiastically, he tells of the Baha'i dream, which is also his, of one church for all mankind, in which all faiths can live in harmony together, as Jesus wants it.

I should like to interject here that most of the time I would turn the tape-recorder on only when people telling about their conversion came to the story proper, and then I would strip the account, as it were, editing it to its bare bones for expediency. That, however, is not really how telling is done in Maya country. People take their time; the linearity and directness that we prize so highly are not important, and there is an inimitable flavor to their story that is difficult to reproduce. With Hermano Goyo, however, I kept my tape-recorder on continuously as the old man was speaking, and so caught a precious instance of the art of storytelling, Yucatecan style, on the wing, as it were.

The Baha'i? *Pues,* I became a member recently, not a long time ago, maybe two months. Maybe it is written in my membership card. No, it isn't. But in this prayer book, maybe. That *hermana* gave it to me as a present. I bought all their large books. Here, this is her writing. It says, "To my friend Gregorio Duarte Gonzales with all my affection, At the Baha'i Center, *et nah Ho?* [at the city of Merida]." I don't think she put the date when they gave it to me. Yes, here it is, the first of June, 1969.

Q: How did you become interested in Baha'i?

It was because of something I was told by an *hermano.* He said that, "Hermano," he said, "there are some American women, there is also an American man, but mainly they are women, and I wish you could see how amiable they are. And they have meetings at a place, it is called, I believe, the Center of Baha'i." He did not know where this establishment was, he only knew this much, that it was over there in the 64th District, close to a filling station, before you got to the police. You got to the corner of the filling station, and then there was another filling station. There it was, between those two filling stations. So I went to look for it. I'll see.

About three in the afternoon, I went and walked about that place. I did that twice, but nobody. I encountered nobody. But I was very interested. So I approached the gentleman at the filling station, and I asked this question. I asked if there were people in that house. And he says, yes, definitely there are. But perhaps they go out in the afternoon, maybe to do some shopping. Aha! Would you, Sir, perhaps know at what time they have a meeting? They do have meetings, don't they? Yes, well, they do have meetings almost every evening, he says. *Bueno.*

So I had this idea that I would write them a letter and I would send it to them. I wrote the letter and I put on the envelope simply Centro Baha'i. I said that I had already come by twice in order to obtain information about what the Center represented, that I encountered no one at their center. Therefore, I conceived this idea to send them this letter because I should like to have an interview with you to find out whether what they were doing was really of interest to me so that we might do the work of the Lord.

Bueno. I took that letter and I placed it into the house. I don't know when they found it, who knows when, maybe when they swept that place. They had no mailbox, so I let it drop in the center of the house, up on the landing, that is where it fell. Perhaps the *hermano* found it, that *senor,* or perhaps one of the *hermanas.* You knew them? No, I don't believe so. There are many of them, they are divided into many nations, many towns. His wife, she speaks Spanish well, I believe she is a teacher, the other one is a *senorita,* but very pretty, they call her Susanna. Perhaps they were in the process of moving, I don't know, or perhaps they simply did not feel like answering my letter, nothing came. There are only the two of us here, I go to work early, we are working far away, so I have to leave at four in the morning, my poor wife has to get up at three to fix my breakfast. When the mailman comes, my wife is perhaps out shopping, and I have a lock on my door, so where should he put the letter? So I talked to him, and I said, it is an opportunity for me, for quite a while I have been trying to get in touch with that *senor,* I don't know his name, and the mailman said, he says, "Man, Senor Gregorio," he says, "here is your letter, I couldn't deliver it because no one was home." The reason is that there are only two of us in the house, my wife goes shopping, I go to my work. So he gave it to me; there were several pages.

Pues, then I went to that place and I told that *senor* that this was an opportunity for me, that for quite a while I had been looking for the opportunity to discuss this matter with him, that I don't know what they called it, is it a doctrine? Surely it must be a doctrine and not a sect in its form. And he says, "Right, it is not a sect, it is getting established everywhere in the world, not only here, almost in every nation, over there in Africa, there are about 30 million there, and they enter a country in groups to make known this doctrine. Here the activities are very laborious, the people are involved in their entertainment. For this reason, we don't make much propaganda in the cities, such as here in Merida. Of course, the time will come that they need to convert, when they will have nowhere else to go. So where will they go? They will have to submit eventually. For this reason we are going into the villages." Their tactics are good, they proceed like the army. In order to defeat the adversary, they occupy the strategic localities to trap the enemy. They are working in villages such as Chabecal, Dzibilchaltun, Conchen, Pazacal, I don't know in which other villages.

About eight days ago, we were taking our leave after the meeting, and two *hermanas* came in whom I had already met. And one of them said, "We are just coming from Chapa." And I say, "You are coming from Chapa? Hay, Hermana, Chapa is close to my home-town, you must have gone through Ticul, Ticul is my hometown. So when are you going to give me the opportunity to go with you? I have some friends in Chapa, some evangelical *hermanos.* Those are the ones that should really come to know this doctrine, because it is difficult to convert people who do not know the gospel because they have no light of a religion whatsoever." And there were these *hermanas,* they went to San Salvador, and . . .

We leave our bags at Hermano Goyo's place and walk over to Luis L.'s new temple. Before it was built, they used to have the services in Peregrina's house. It is a relatively large building of cement block. There is a well-placed covered walkway and a number of live oak trees for shade. The first person we encounter is Teofilo, Joaquin's erstwhile sidekick. He tells us that because he is from the country and has never lived in a city, the *hermanos* have decided that he should spend some time in Merida to become more *civilizado.* A tall man with wavy hair and Indian eyes that contrast with his light skin introduces himself as Manuel H., the pastor who has taken over from Barrera, while the latter is at the Biblical Institute in Tepic, Nayarit. Neither he nor Teofilo know anything about when the weeklong prayer for the Holy Spirit is to start. So Eus and I decide to make it a holiday. We walk to the center of town, buy a soft drink and some *pan dulce* [sweet bread], pastry of absolutely Viennese quality, and sit on a bench. It is the purest pleasure to go on an excursion with Eus. She has the capacity to enjoy everything like a very young girl.

An elderly man comes up to us and greets Eus most respectfully. It seems he knows her entire family. When Eus introduces me and says that I also understand Maya, he says that he is very proud of being a Maya and speaks Maya with anybody who can understand it. "*Soy muy Mayero* [I am very much a Maya]," he says. He ridicules the people who come to the city and then pretend that they speak only Spanish. I now know enough active Maya to carry on a light chat about health and the weather, and although we revert to Spanish after the first pleasantries, I do not feel a stranger. I would hate to have Eus say about me, as she does about Joaquin, "*Ma tu naatic mishba?a* [He (she) understands nothing]" with that special tone of contempt of hers.

To mark the special occasion, I insist on hiring a horse-drawn cab for the way to Luis L.'s house. "The streetcar is cheaper," Eus points out, "and probably safer," but I will have my ride. On the uneven pavement of 20th Street the narrow and very high carriage tilts dangerously, but we do get to our destination safely, heaven only knows how.

Peregrina opens the door, says a hurried welcome, and throws a mantilla over my head. A prayer is in progress and we are expected to join in. A girl is kneeling with her back to us at the rocker in one corner, a portly woman is kneeling at the bench, and Peregrina is close to me. For a woman in her sixties, she has a strong and slender body, in contrast to her aged face. A strand of white hair hangs down over her face from under her white mantilla. Soon she is in glossolalia. Her body rocks up and down, and as the intonation peaks she stretches out her arms and her hands flutter very rapidly back and forth. I have my tape-recorder open; in kneeling down I happened to put it on the chair next to me. Unexpectedly, Peregrina begins singing with the pulses of her utterance. For the first time, I can record singing in trance. The girl at the rocker, obviously also in trance, sings a similar melody. Then the pitch of both women drop, and Peregrina reverts to ordinary language. From her prayer I understand that someone has given her a gift of money needed for the work of God, and she was expressing her gratitude for that. To my consternation, I hear her also praying for me, saying that I have come to Yucatan to receive the Holy Spirit and am now living with them in poverty and humility so that later I can go back to preach to thousands of souls. In sudden anguish I wonder whether perhaps her pastor son, Luis L., has misinformed her about the purpose of my stay, about my role as an observer, or whether it is her own imagination that is running away with her. Anyway, my joyful holiday mood dissolves as I suddenly see unanticipated trouble ahead with my fieldwork situation.

The prayers completed, Peregrina takes time to once more welcome Eus and myself. Eus has brought eggs and some limes as a present, and I follow Peregrina into her dimly lit narrow kitchen where she begins to prepare lunch. I relish intimate kitchen conversations. Besides, I am hoping that I might be able to defuse the situation that she has created. As she begins pressing black beans through a colander, a lengthy task, I ask her to tell me something about her conversion. I have the impression that traces of her trance still carry over; there is an intensity to her voice that tears at and invades me. God spoke to her in a dream, she says.[5] This was during a night in December 1959, and he told her that she would become ill but would recover. She was also told that her son Juan would convert to Jesus soon after his twenty-first birthday, and about problems in her sister's family, and that she herself would speak to many thousands of souls. God also commanded her to throw out the idols she was keeping in her house, those statues of saints and of the Virgin of Guadalupe. All the while she continued seeing a light which sent out many rays and a big Bible with a cross behind it. "After that," she said, "God gave me a sign, and I saw white angels, and white horses going by, and his flag, very, very white."

Three or four days later, she was seized by violent trembling. Her whole body was shaking and she was able to walk only by holding on to the walls. Her worried sons took her to the hospital, and there she had a second vision. "I saw an enormous book, which was the Holy Bible, attached above the door of the hospital." However, the examination at the hospital revealed no illness and she was sent home. There she became stiff, and she laid in her hammock not moving and not responding for three days. When she finally woke up, her sons brought Oscar Hill to her and he talked to her about the gospel. He prayed for her and invited her to the services of the Apostolic congregation. Her husband kept saying, "What are they doing for you at those services?" "Nothing but praying for me," she would answer. Soon her trembling stopped. Not quite a month later, and even before the baptism with water, she received the gift of the Holy Spirit. "I prayed for it," she said, "and then I felt the heat, the heat of the Lord, it reached up to my neck, and I saw a great light, it was like one of those very large streetlamps, and I began to weep. And then I started speaking in tongues, and I prayed and prayed."[6]

"Was it your son Luis L. who became converted?" I asked. "No, it was Juan L., and he became converted a few months after his twenty-first birthday, just like the Lord foretold. And there was big trouble in my sister's family. Both of her daughters became pregnant out of wedlock, the youngest at only 13."

"It is sad," she continued, as she was beating some eggs. "People become converted, and pretty soon, they leave their religion." Of the people with whom she was baptized, she is the only one who speaks in tongues anymore. "The reason why some people who speak in tongues later lose this capacity together with the Holy Spirit is that maybe they go and drink a glass of beer, or they go to a novena, the Catholic prayer ritual for the dead, of a relative, thinking that after all, the pastor does not see it. Of course, the Holy Spirit knows, and it can only live in a clean house." There is no opportunity for me to mention my own discomfort with their concerns about the status of my soul.

The evening service takes place in the house of Hermana Licha, a member of Luis L.'s congregation, a slender, elegantly dressed young woman with a delicate, narrow face. Manuel H., whom we met in the morning, is in charge of the service. He says that Luis L. cannot come because he and some other *hermanos* are at the house of an Hermana Paula, who is in death agony. Much was made later of this event, and when a year later I ran into Pastor Manuel once more, he told me the details about that prayer for the dying woman.

It seems that after the service in Licha's house, he joined the other *hermanos* at the bedside of Paula. He found that her extremities were cold, and her perspiration felt sticky. She did not react to the prayers of the *hermanos* present. The physician had left, saying that there was nothing more he could do. In the words of Manuel, "We prayed for a few hours, then left to rest and returned at sunrise. There were only a few *hermanos* left with the dying woman in her hammock. Their faith had become very weak. 'We prayed and prayed,' they said, 'but God has not heard us.' Again we started praying, and continued for half an hour. Nothing. Finally I said, 'Lord, I am not worthy to place my hand on her, but perhaps you will choose to act through me.' So I put my fingers very lightly on her forehead, saying, 'May the Holy Spirit work on you.' Not five minutes later she began to speak. She is still living, taking care of her six children."[7]

When I return to the service at Licha's house, I am surprised that the congregation is no larger than the one in Utzpak; twelve women and five men, and only five children. The reason might be that this service does not take place in the temple. Licha's oldest daughter, a very pretty teenager in a fashionable flowery dress, plays the guitar, quite proficiently. During testimony time, an old man tells of a dream in which he saw many *hermanos* enjoying themselves in a big, beautiful garden. Some of them he knew, but many he did not recognize. Peregrina gives thanks for the 100 pesos she received. She will be able to buy chairs for the *casa pastoral*. During the altar call, both Peregrina and also Licha are in glossolalia. Once more, I hear Peregrina's beautiful trance song. Licha holds her left hand high and lightly clenched, then she goes into glossolalia— the ululating, high-energy form—as she is sitting on her heels, her body bent forward, palms on the floor.

After the service, Licha invites Eus and me into her kitchen to a *sopa de novio* [bridegroom's soup], actually a vegetable salad in mayonnaise. "It will do you no harm," she assures us when we hesitate—mayonnaise in this heat?—"it has been refrigerated." While we eat, she talks about herself. She works in an office, her husband is Chinese, he speaks English and works as a tourist guide. She used to be the kind of wife who absolutely and without objection obeyed her husband because that was the way she was brought up. She started to attend the Apostolic services in secret, inventing all sorts of reasons for going out. When she heard others in glossolalia, she did not quite believe that it was the Holy Spirit speaking and not the person. When it happened to her, it was like *un trago*, an intoxicating drink. When she had to address a group of women to speak about the Apostolic faith for the first time, she was terribly worried. Then the Holy Spirit took over. She felt it coming, and then she heard herself speak, and the people said *"Amen,"* and *"Aleluya,"* and *"Gracias a Dios,"* but she had no control over her own speaking, nor did she know what she was saying.

One evening, her husband was furious with her because she was getting ready to go to the service. But this time, instead of being submissive, she threw his supper dishes at him. "Only the Lord could have given me the strength to do that," she laughed. He was flabbergasted and gave her no more trouble. Now they live pretty much apart. She has her life, he has his. Outwardly, they stay married because of the children; her youngest daughter is only 10.

The following day is a Sunday, and since I do not think that it is important for me to go to the Escuela Dominical, we take the bus to Chich'en Itza. Although her birthplace, Libre Union, is only 10 kilometers from Chich'en, Eus has never been there. Great fun. I film her admiring the creations of her ancestors. *"Hach meya,"* she keeps saying, so much work. One thing worries her though: Was this extensive site built before or after the Flood? At one point, I film her tracing the outline of a priest with a profile that could be hers. When I take a picture of the sacred well, a woman in ʔipil wants to charge me for photographing her. Eus forbids me to pay her. "You were taking a picture of the landscape," she argues. "Besides, she is not dying of hunger. *Es muy viva* [She is very impertinent]."

Eus is indefatigable, climbing up and down the ninety-one steps of the pyramid and the many ladders, totally fearless, which I cannot say for myself. When a guide overhears us speaking Maya, with Eus naming for me the various implements, such as *shʔuun kuul* for the round shields in the ball court, he gives us a special tour around the Warriors' Castle. An American asks Eus to pose in her colorful Sunday ʔipil. We have fun telling each other that we do this without charging anything. When he asks her to write her name in his book, I do it for her under the pretext that she did not understand his English request.

"I hear people tell," she recounts, "that there is an underground passage between Chich'en and Ushmal. At one time, a rope connected the sky and the earth, then the Lords did their evil deeds and cut the rope. It lies petrified in that passageway. That is what I heard."

We are back at Goyo's place in time to take our bath, change, and walk over to the temple for the evening service. Luis L.'s new temple is quite spacious inside; the walls are whitewashed and the floor is cement. The podium has a wooden railing on both sides of the rostrum. There is an amplifier for the electric guitar played by Luis L. to the left of the rostrum, and a boy uses two polished sticks for a resounding rhythm accent. Unfortunately, without any curtains the large hall has a frightful echo that wreaks havoc with my tape-recorder. Barrera opens the service, to an attendance of four men, thirteen women, no babies, no small children playing catch in the back or sleeping on the floor as they do in Utzpak. He is here from Campeche to participate in the weeklong prayer for the Holy Spirit; his wife has not yet given birth. In the first testimony of the evening, a woman tells that the physician had completely given up on Hermana Paula last night, he could not detect her pulse anymore. However, *gracias a Dios,* after much prayer, she woke up, a real miracle of the Lord.

Later in the service, Barrera passes to Luis L., here from Tepic for the occasion, who asks for a special offering for Pastor Felix S., who is soon to leave the Biblical Institute in Tepic and needs money for the trip home. Eus's face remains immobile, as though the request concerns a stranger, but she gives 5 pesos, a large sum for her. Luis L. then officially opens the week's campaign for the manifestation of the Holy Spirit. The baptism by water and by the Holy Spirit are both needed to enter into heaven, he argues. You would not want to ask for it when it was too late, would you? There is an altar call. Two women so crippled that they cannot kneel are helped to chairs in front of the rostrum. Peregrina comes to me and asks whether I would also like to pray for the baptism of the Holy Spirit. Not only for doctrinal reasons, but also afraid that an intense trance experience would interfere with my ability to continue observing the goings-on, I refuse, saying that it is not time for me as yet, that I have other tasks to fulfill for the Lord. I say it with a pleading smile, but that is lost on her. Her face hardens and she goes to the rostrum without another word.

By now there are twenty women and thirteen men kneeling at the podium, but there is none of the careful preparation and strategic positioning that makes Barrera's trance induction so successful. Here, the activity is more or less haphazard, so a great deal of effort needs to be expanded for a relatively low return. I wish I could sufficiently convey the complex activities on such an occasion. What must seem to the casual observer like a disturbed anthill upon careful scrutiny actually dissolves into a number of structured scenes. Peregrina is kneeling at the women's side and very quickly goes into glossolalia. Luis L. claps furiously next to Manuel H., who first claps and then bends down so deeply that his head nearly touches the floor. His hands are on the floor also, but with his thumbs bent rigidly up and toward the back. He may be in glossolalia, but I cannot hear it. Luis L. goes over to a woman, places his hand on her head, and shakes it lightly. This shaking is done in such a way that the pastor takes hold from both sides of the head of a supplicant and, applying some pressure, shakes it with small, rapid, rather jerky movements.

Laying on hands, Luis L. now proceeds first to one of the crippled women, then to the other one, then, beginning to clap again, he passes on to a man, then to a boy about 10 years old, behind whom he kneels down. He rises and passes on to another man, then to two more boys, shaking their heads. Judging from her movements, one of the girls is now in glossolalia, but I can hear only a few fragments; everything is obliterated by the echo. Eus has gone to kneel at the altar, and Luis L. gently places his hand on her head. She rises, standing still and relaxed in the midst of all the movement about her.

I am seeking out Barrera. He has gone to the boy, shaking his head and laying on hands. Meanwhile Manuel H. is working with a tall, light-skinned man, kneeling down beside him, then also shaking his head. Luis L. now stands next to Manuel H., clapping, while Manuel jumps up and down, also clapping, and keeps shouting, "*Sellalo, sellalo!*" and "*Gloria Cristo.*" He is in and out of glossolalia. Luis L. is back with one of the crippled women, while Barrera has his hand on the shoulder of yet another man while raising his right hand. His eyes are tightly closed, his face beady with heavy perspiration, his glossolalia loud and fast. Luis L. passes to yet another man, while Manuel H. is still occupied with his former subject.

I move closer to Peregrina and can hear how her glossolalia has faded into ordinary language. Also, Manuel H., Luis L., and Barrera have now relinquished their trance utterance. People begin to wander away from the podium. Peregrina, her hands on her back, is leaning against the wall, praying. The bell rings, and Luis L. concludes the service. Afterward, I walk up to Peregrina. I explain to her that it is a sacrifice on my part to postpone seeking the Holy Spirit, but that I must complete my work first. She shakes her head, her face grim. "You could be speaking to thousands of souls," she says and turns away.

Eus and I walk out into the yard. The sun has set and the air is cool and fragrant. Licha and her daughters have prepared iced *horchata*, a pleasantly sweet drink, not from almonds as the Spanish did it, but the cheaper popular variant of rolled oats in water. I make a small contribution and get some for us. I tell Licha that Peregrina is unhappy with me and why. I do it in terms that I assume would be intelligible to her as a professional woman, namely concerning my work as an observer, which an intense trance experience would interfere with. I do not touch on the fact that speaking in tongues would for me also involve accepting the fundamentalist doctrines of Pentecostalism, which I am unwilling to do. This was a point I was never able to touch on, even with Eus, although it made me feel dishonest. Licha puts her arm around my shoulder. "Don't worry," she says. "Let us hope that soon you will be done with your work and then you can seek the Holy Spirit."

For the night, we once more sling our hammock around old Goyo's hospitable beam. Overnight visitors always bring their own hammocks, and Eus has brought a matrimonial, a hammock wide enough to accommodate a married couple. One person lies at the head end, the other at the foot end of the hammock, and the knotless weave forms a stiff ridge separating the sleepers.

For a while, we swing gently back and forth, listening to the high whine of the mosquitoes, hoping they will not find us. Then Eus, who was born with eyes on the back of her head and must have picked up my quandary, starts talking quietly. "I cannot fast and pray for long periods like the *hermanos*," she says. "I don't think that I'll receive the Holy Spirit. It says in the Bible that if you don't receive it, you cannot enter into heaven. Hermano Luis del V. thinks that some people receive it in their last hour, when they are very sick in their hammock and ready to go. Perhaps God will send it to me then. But I don't worry about that. Maybe I can stand at the door." "*Amen*, Hermana," I say. I would not mind standing there with her. I fall asleep, at peace. Obviously, not everything has to be told.

Originally, I had intended to stay in Merida for the entire week and be present at all the various prayers for the Holy Spirit, but the echo in the temple was so disturbing that I decided to return to Utzpak with Eus. A visitor from Merida told later that at the end of that week two men and five women had received the Holy Spirit, to my mind a meager harvest at best. A man, she said, started somersaulting all through the temple. The people drew back in fear as he began hitting wildly about him and kept shouting. He just went on, although he bumped into the chairs several times. It was truly supernatural, she thought. As to herself, she suddenly had the impression that she was all alone as she was praying, and that the other women around her were being lifted up and out of sight except for the one kneeling very close to her. Apparently, no mention was made of my conflict with Peregrina, or Eus, who hears everything, would have known.

Back in Utzpak

El Negro picks us up in Merida, and as I am getting out at Reina's house, the *doble* is sounding once more, this time for a 20-year-old woman, married nine months and pregnant for five. "*Bonita, gorda* [Pretty, fat]," says Dona Tomasita. A friend of Reina's comes by and shows a photograph of the deceased, and she is just that, with an oval Indian face, round cheeks, ample double chin. At our corner in the evening, the women are unanimous in their criticism. They say that the hepatitis that killed her could have been cured. Her husband's family had cattle, they could have sold a steer. But they were *egoista* and took her only to the physician in Temax for treatment. Her own family did not even know that she was sick, or they would have taken her to a physician in Merida. "What good is all that talk now," Reina interjects, "she is dead." But Dona Raquel says that her husband has not detached himself from her; he can't let go of her and cries and cries. A week later, Eus and I go to the cemetery because I want to see her grave. We go to the small house in the section for the recently dead, where the bones are cleaned for permanent burial. There is a cardboard Fab box with bones and a skull. "Look," Eus says with a short laugh, turning the skull, "he still has some hair left on him." At the temporary burial site, there is a wreath of yellowed leaves and white roses and in the middle, a *lima china,* a sweet orange. "It must have been her husband who brought her something to eat," I remark. "He really loved her, didn't he?" Eus will not let me get away with my romantic notions. "*Ma? tech* [Not to you, i.e., that's what you think]," she says. "He spent last night with his lover down the street."

At testimony time during the next evening service, conducted by Jose D. S., Joaquin says that when he went to Temax on Monday to conduct a service there, he had a fever and his eyes hurt very badly, but now, after praying, he is feeling "*completamente bien* [very well], *gracias a Dios.*" Well, maybe, but he had also swallowed some of my aspirin shortly before the service.

When Jose D. S. prays in tongues, he always moves the same way, but no one picks his motion pattern up from him. Unlike the syllable inventory that eventually becomes like a group dialect, the movements seem to be fixed individually. I kept noting in our congregation (and I also observed this in Merida) that while the young girl I saw in Peregrina's house mirrored Peregrina's trance song, she did not raise her arms or show the characteristic hand flutter of Peregrina.

In his sermon, Jose mentioned that he was persecuted a great deal for his religion, even insulted and told that he was not a man. Eus said that Jose went to visit one of his sisters, and it was a good thing he was not there when Jose came, for he would have thrown him out when he said that.

The following day at noon, Don Fulgencio comes to Reina's house to invite me to this evening's thanksgiving service at his home. It is to dedicate his *chan casita de oracion,* his small chapel that he has built next to his house. He would also like me to tape some of the hymns that his daughter-in-law can sing in Maya. "She sings very beautifully," he says. "When I first heard her sing, I said to my son, 'I hope you will marry her because then we can hear these lovely hymns all day long.'" Unfortunately, I have very little tape left, so I cannot tape any additional hymns. Maybe I can buy more tape, he suggests, and then I should come to his house, but not in the evenings or on weekends because his son does not like this religion and would object.

Don Fulgencio's *chan casita de oracion* is a square mud-and-wattle room, about 5 by 5 meters. The Coleman lamp borrowed from the temple burns in the middle. More and more people come crowding in. I count six men, twelve women, and the unbelievable number of thirty-five children. Eus is right, some family planning is urgently needed, or Yucatan will run out of food.

Eus and I start out with her grandson Jose and with Joaquin, who had offered to put my bag on his bicycle. It is always very heavy with my tape-recorder, camera, flashlight, and notebook. He will take a different route, he said, easier for his bicycle, and we will meet at Don Fulgencio's place, where he is going to open the service. But he does not show up, and Eus is ready to fly off the handle. We go in search of him. By some sixth sense, she spies him in Paula's well-lit house where, in return for who-knows-what inducement, he is engaged in praying for Pedrito. My bag with its expensive contents is still on his bicycle out in the street. Resolutely, Eus takes it. Let him look for it. In the pitch darkness of a cloudy night, without streetlights? She shrugs.

On the way back to Don Fulgencio's house, I ask how a person who has received the Holy Spirit can act the way he does. "He does not have the Holy Spirit," she retorts. "The devil is in his heart. I tell him so and then he gets very angry. 'Hermana,' he says, 'how can you say such a thing?' I tell him, 'It must be so. Look at how you are acting with other people. You said about Hermano Jose "This man is always criticizing me. He tells the *hermanos* in the temple that I sleep late and that I don't work. *Me esta cabronando este hombre* [He is a pain in the ass]. *Chinga este hombre* [He is a mother f——]." Those are insults.' Then he says 'I said no such thing.' When of course I heard it, and so did my grandson Jose."

Back in Don Fulgencio's chapel, Jose D. S. is running out of patience with Joaquin, whose absence is holding up the proceedings. He repeats the stories about Joaquin's laziness, saying that indeed, he is not working for God.

Don Fulgencio uses the opportunity for some friendly chatting. He looks handsome in his white shirt, his taut, dark face happy for the festive occasion. "Hermana," he says to me, "when I was a *torero*, it was nothing but drinking, marijuana, and love affairs. But all that is over since I have known Christ." Then I hear him talk to Don Eduardo in the back. "Do you believe, Hermano Eduardo, that the world is coming to an end?"

With Joaquin still absent, Isauro finally opens the service. Don Fulgencio stands in front, facing us, his arms raised in benediction. Here is a man who would dearly like to be the priest himself and for whom this chapel is the first step toward realizing that dream. Finally, he sits down without having said anything. After the usual round of hymns, prayer, *coritos*, and testimony, Jose takes over. Before he embarks on his sermon, he announces that Hermano Fulgencio C. wants to make a promise to Jesus in prayer, and he asks everyone to pray for him while he is making this promise. Don Fulgencio and his wife kneel down at the table that serves as the altar, the stooped old woman crying. He starts out with an invocation, but at that moment Joaquin shows up, and when it comes to the promise Fulgencio wants to make, the devil, who must definitely be leagued with Joaquin, makes the latter shout so loudly that none of us can hear a single solitary word of the much-anticipated *promesa*.

In his sermon, Jose drones on endlessly about why the *sabatistas* are wrong to celebrate the Saturday instead of the Sunday. To bolster his argument, he reads interminable passages from the Bible. Others are obviously as bored as I am. In front of me, Paula's oldest daughter Rosa and Candil's wife Rodolfa compare the rubber bands of various colors they are wearing on their wrists. Jewelry is forbidden, so boyfriends give these bands instead. Black is the most expensive and thus the gift of a true *novio*. Finally, Jose has exhausted the topic of the *sabatistas* and turns to some prophecies from the Apocalypse, at which his audience perks up notably. There will be a number of plagues, he says, and only if a person is baptized in the name of one God, not of three, will he live to participate in the millennium.

After the service we are asked to wait, and we are served *ʔisʔum,* an *atole* made from fresh young corn. It is pleasantly sweet, but has a slight touch of acidity, a sign of fermentation, and during the night it gives me the worst diarrhea of my trip. While we drink it, Jose and I talk about some biblical passages, still about the aberration of the *sabatistas.* He is so shocked because apparently some friends have just invited him to a service with that sect. To make his point, he loans me a sheet of paper with writing on it so I can study up on this point. The following morning, I see upon reading it that its author is that same Don Victor, the member of the Chetumal congregation that Jose had mentioned in one of his sermons. I am struck by the orderly composition, the logical arrangement of the quotations, the use of red ink for emphasis, and a sophisticated comparison between the old and the more recent translation of the texts, all witness to a truly extraordinary mind, much committed to theological speculation.

During the next service, Jose announces that Paula has invited the congregation for a service at her house upon the occasion of Pedrito's first birthday. We should not forget to bring some small present. Before the service, I saw Don Fulgencio, who came to borrow the Coleman lamp of the temple for the occasion. He said that he knew that Paula had received the Holy Spirit, but now she is assailed by doubts because Pedrito has a fever again. "People of little faith," he said as he trooped off to buy kerosene for the lamp.

The following day, we walk to Paula's place. She has set up a table in her house, on it a bunch of flowers in a plastic container, surrounded by gifts, some pastry, Nestlé's canned milk, and a few tiny wrapped packages. I count sixteen women and six men. I cannot count the children—they wander in and out—but there are many. Pedrito is in the arms of one of his sisters. Jose D. S. opens the service with a request for a prayer for Pedrito. The child cries, so Paula takes him. During the prayer we all stand, men and women mixed; there is no room to kneel. It is beautiful, all those dark faces against the background of the mud wall, their eyes closed, praying. During testimony time, Paula speaks of her conversion in Maya. When Don Fulgencio invited me, he said "Paulita will speak in Maya tonight so you can learn it." Later, after the prayer with glosso-lalia from Jose D. S. and Nohoch Felix, the women crowd around Paula with Pedrito, and some of them hand him 1-peso bills. The child grabs them and smiles, his head bent to one side, his right arm nearly without control, his pale motionless legs dangling down his mother's side.

The following day a horsefly stings me, making my right leg swell up. It itches frightfully and makes me miserable all night. Reina also sleeps poorly. She dreams that she had a new baby boy. He was small, naked, and beautiful. "It must have been the *atole* I drank late last night," she muses. "That is heavy food and can give you nightmares." It is a special night for dreams, for at Eus's place, Joaquin dreams that he smoked and later committed some other trans-gression that he did not specify. In his dream, one of the *hermanos* informed him that now there was no redemption possible for him. When we are alone, Eus once more remembers her dream of the two ladies. She saw them coming to the cemetery seemingly from nowhere, and when she asked one of them where she was going, she answered, "Nowhere in particular." "Now I am a little afraid to go past the cemetery," she confesses, "but you are the only one to whom I am saying this."

We use the morning to go visit Alvio. Eus made the arrangements in the temple the other day, when I overheard her tell Alvio exactly what kind of in-formation I am looking for. Alvio is a terribly fast talker; I soon gave up try-ing to transcribe what he said. But, fundamentally, he says that he used to go to no church and he could neither read nor write. He and a friend worked together on a ranch, and this friend had a Bible with him. With the help of his friend, he learned to read, using the Bible as a text. One night he had a vision of God, the way he looked in some pictures in the Catholic church, telling him to become converted. Then he moved to Utzpak with his family and almost forgot about his vision. He was busy selling and buying for his sister, who had a prosperous clothing store in town. She had a lot of money and spent a large portion of it on doctors, who told her that there was nothing wrong with her. He, Alvio, made good money too, but his children kept getting sick, and he spent most of his income on doctor bills. Finally, a few months ago, at the urging of his wife, Gregoria, he started attending the Apostolic services with her. Now, instead of going to the physician they pray over their children, and they get well. He stopped going to the movies and to dances and also decided to stop working so hard at business dealings, which absorbed a lot of thought. Instead, he started working on the ranch again, making just enough money to live on. He spends the rest of the time learning to read the Bible. His wife can read better than he, and she is helping him, and after having already received the Holy Spirit, they will both be baptized together this August. At one point, Gregoria joins our conversation. She likes to go out and "talk to the souls," she says, that is, to evangelize, but never to strangers, only to relatives. This concentration on relatives seems to be a general tendency, also for the men, which helps to explain why my records show that recruiting spreads almost exclusively along family lines, and why the congregation represents, in the main, only three extended families. In fact, the Presbyterian church also spread in the same manner, apparently. Tomasita, the midwife, has been a member for thirty years, she says. All her descendents are members there also, but she volunteers the interesting detail that her sons bring their wives to the church, while her daughters do not recruit their husbands.

At noon, I sit in Reina's kitchen to chat. She is making tortillas. Lupita is sitting on a footstool, playing with a glob of *masa*. It is a relaxed occasion, and I learn a lot during these conversations. So I have my questions ready. Why, I ask, do people leave the Church after having been baptized? Reina thinks that it is because they love their diversions. People should be certain that they are truly ready to leave the world behind. However, I notice that she is not as jolly and attentive as usual. Rather, she seems to be listening to noises coming from the direction of Don Eduardo's house. Suddenly, she jumps up and runs toward the *albarrada* separating the two properties. Then she comes rushing back, shouting, "Hermana, help, help, Santiago and Jorge are fighting!" I run back with her, and it is a frightening scene. There is Santiago on top of his brother, apparently trying to choke him, bobbing up and down, alternately grunting and screaming. Santiago's brother is a puny fellow who spends most of his money on drink instead of on beans, while Santiago, although smaller than I, has a heavy build and bulging muscles. I cannot see myself tugging at him as Reina does, so I go back to the kitchen, where Lupita and the tortillas have been left without supervision. I pick up the child, who is used to me, so she thinks it is a picnic, and turn the tortillas on the *comal*. The screaming fight goes on outside, and Reina brushes past me, shouting that she is going to call the police. I walk out after her. By Raquel's house several neighbor women have gathered, all looking interested and worried, but no one makes any motion to interfere. When I return to the kitchen and stuff the tortillas into the *lek* to keep them warm, the screaming dies down, and soon Santiago comes in, buttoning his shirt. Where is Dona Reina? She got frightened and went for the police. Why would she want to do that? After all, he wasn't doing anything. He had merely threatened his brother with words, telling him to keep away from "*ese senora*," he says, "and then I put my hand into his face like this (spreading his fingers) and I pushed him, so he would understand." Then he held him down because his brother had hit him with a piece of wood. That brother of his was always bothering them, insulting Reina when Santiago was not around.

At this point, Reina comes back. Jorge is trying to escape. They encounter him as he walks around the corner, and the police take him in. Santiago relates that he had gone to his father's house to shave with his father's safety razor and to relax. Then Jorge came in from gathering wood and started screaming at him for having opened Don Eduardo's house. "He has no business telling me what to do. The house is not his, it belongs to our father. He is the only one who can tell us what to do." Jorge then grabbed a piece of wood, and Santiago held him down. He wrestled the wood away from him. When Jorge went for a stone, he had to continue holding him down. He wasn't going to do anything to him. "You could have killed him," Reina says angrily. "How can brothers fight like that?" "If the police come, I am not going," Santiago insists. But Reina is adamant. "Of course you'll go. You tell them what went on, and when your father comes home, I'll tell him and he can go to the police and settle matters."

Three men come to the door, taller and stronger than average. One of them, wearing a policeman's cap, remains stationed in front of the door. The other two come in. One squats on the threshold; the other one, very dark, middle-aged, talks calmly to Santiago. "It is not punishment," he assures Santiago. "We just want to clear things up." Santiago leaves without protest.

Now it is women's day. From across the street, Raquel comes in to get the details. "I wanted everything to look very nice, I didn't want the *hermana* to know anything about all of these problems," I hear Reina complaining. Dona Juana, an elderly woman from down the street who does not usually sit on the corner with us, comes in to ask for some water. Supposedly, her well rope tore, but of course she joins the discussion. "What a good thing they now have five *calabosos* [cells] so the prisoners can't get into each other's hair any more," she says. Everyone laughs. The midwife's son comes to the door. He is a bachelor, quite elderly, and not too shy even when I am around. "Jorge is quite quarrel-some, isn't he?" he ventures. "People say he even threw the *hermana* out of the house." Reina sets the record straight. Then she sends the neighbor's boy to the prison in the municipal building with a soft drink for Santiago. "It is hot in there," she says solicitously.

After a long while, Don Eduardo arrives on horseback with a load of freshly cut hay. Reina will tell him, she says, after he has had his bath and eaten his noonday meal. He might get sick otherwise. I suspect she wants the men to stew for a while, for she actually waits for another three whole hours so Don Eduardo can take his nap. Then she tells him. Another half hour later we watch the old man in his immaculate white peasant's garb and new sombrero slowly making his way down the street toward the plaza. "What did he say?" I ask. "He said he would have beaten them both, had he been here. The first one that starts another fight will be thrown out into the street."

Shortly before it is time to leave for church, Eus's grandson comes in. "The *hermanos* have arrived." "What *hermanos?*" "Hermano Barrera and Hermano Felix, Chan Felix." It is a wonderful surprise. All week there had been rumors about Luis del V. coming back. No one knew exactly, and Jose D. S., who was expected back in Chetumal, was sitting on pins and needles. Chan Felix was actually not expected until a week later. I was very curious about him for many reasons. After all, his was the first name I knew in Utzpak, he was Eus's son, and his name kept coming up whenever there was talk about "how things at the temple used to be." We all step outside, and in the rapidly darkening evening, there comes Eus with her son. I can only see that he is tall. The introductions are not completed yet when here comes Santiago, released from prison and looking very surly. He would probably have given Reina a bad time, but Chan Felix picks up Lupita, who immediately takes to him, and asks friendly questions, which effectively defuses the situation. Reina tells me later that the police fined each of the brothers 11.50 pesos or one day of work. Santiago elected the fine, Jorge the day of work, and he was seen on Monday sweeping the plaza.

At the church, we are met by Barrera. His wife gave birth to a boy on August 1, 1969, and in Merida, seven people received the Holy Spirit. "*Que benediction!* [What a blessing!]," Barrera beams.

By the light in the temple I can see that Chan Felix has his mother's long-limbed handsomeness, and as the evening progresses, it becomes clear that he also has her cool intelligence and control. But what is most outstanding about him is his smooth, rich singing voice. I decided then and there that I was going to use some of that mellow singing as a background for the film I was planning about Utzpak and the congregation, which indeed I later did. Even his guitar-playing is a far cry from Barrera's well-intentioned but tedious strumming. On the other hand, Reina is right. He certainly is no inspired preacher. What we hear from him is clear, well-thought-out exegesis, exceedingly boring. During the altar call, I try to catch some of his glossolalia, but it is either too low or he does not go into it at all. That is quite unusual because visitors are wont to be practiced trancers who are in control of their glossolalia as far as anyone can be and tend to give the host congregation a good sampling.

After Chan Felix's sermon, Barrera takes over. He repeats the often-heard warning that those who have received the Holy Spirit before having been baptized with water are in grave danger. They are old wine pouches scarred with scratches from tobacco, drinking, fornication, and adultery, which must be washed away by the water of baptism or the pouch will tear. A dance, a glass of beer, a *chan mujercita*, and pronto, they can no longer speak in tongues. The baptism will take place on Monday at the seaport of Santa Clara. They will be baptized in the name of the only God, not in the name of the three, as done by the Pentecostals. It is for this reason that the Pentecostals bear no proper fruit. Not having been baptized correctly, they have no new body.

Barrera then announces that Jose D. S. will leave for Chetumal on the morrow and asks for a special offering for his bus ticket. Jose is asked to come forward so the congregation can pray for him. He kneels in front of the rostrum, the other men at some distance behind him, or they stand at their seats. Barrera lays on hands. Afterward, Jose speaks. He will continue on the path of God until the end of his life, and he will go on evangelizing. He thanks the congregation for the offering, which is almost enough to take him to Chetumal. Barrera takes over, saying that he was there when Jose first received the Holy Spirit, and what a joy to see him come this far, so that he can even preach now. He passes to Chan Felix, who says simply and with understanding that it is getting late, people should go home and rest and be there tomorrow early for the Sunday *matutin*. He then asks for the sick to come forward so that they can be prayed for. Eus goes to the podium and kneels down next to Anita, a very old one-eyed woman who goes begging when she has no washing to do; her daughter Ana; and Gregoria. Very lightly, Chan Felix lays his hands on his mother's head. He and Barrera then pass on to the others present—Paula's husband, some other women—and to Alvio and his little girl.

Chan Felix's visit is the topic of conversation for several days at our corner. "What a beautiful voice," Reina keeps saying. And according to Tomasita, who attended the Presbyterian services not far from the temple, the *hermanos* of that church were going to invite Chan Felix to sing for them, as they used to before he left for Tepic. "And do you remember how he kept weeping and weeping when he first received the manifestation of the Holy Spirit?" Reina recalls. "Everyone was worried he would never stop!" "Reina is right," Eus later confirms the story. "He wept and wept."

Soon after the baptism on the seashore to be described below, I took the opportunity to ask Chan Felix about his conversion. His account had the same cool, formalistic quality about it that I noted when I heard him preach for the first time. And of the many men whose conversion stories I recorded, he was the only one who made no mention of the wrenching before-and-after experience usually so typical of the male accounts:

> My former life was taken up by all the matters and diversions of the world and the pleasures everyone else enjoys. I never even consid-

ered that there might exist a God whom one should serve. It was my mother who was the first to hear the gospel, and she began to invite us, her children, that they should also come and attend services with her. But I paid no attention to her and continued my life as I had done before. It was years later that I started listening to sermons about the gospel. It made no particular impression on me, but I continued anyway, and especially one preacher began getting me interested. It was Juan L., who came from Merida and is now the pastor of the congregation in Chetumal. He was young and was really struggling here in this village, living the life of an evangelist. He finally got me to accept our Lord Jesus Christ, and he taught me his words.

(Eus, who had been listening in as Chan Felix was talking, commented later, "Actually, it was I who first invited Juan L. to hold a service in our house. My sons Felix, Enrique, and Erme were sitting in the back and listened. They swore later that the sermon of the minister had been full of innuendoes directed exclusively against them." Eus thought this highly amusing.)

After some months, actually two months, some leading men of the Southwestern District came here and conducted a baptism. It was about eight years ago. So on December 26, 1962, I was baptized. But actually, I never had any intentions at all to work in the field of the Lord. Then God was merciful. I was completely illiterate, I could neither read nor write, but a year after I was baptized, through the good offices of the Hermano Eucadio J. L., who was the supervising bishop of the Southwestern District at the time, I was invited to Merida to learn to read and write. It was there that I became enthusiastic about the idea of becoming a preacher and I was instructed in everything concerning the work of the Lord, the development of which we are seeing today in a manner never anticipated before. So it has been five years now since I started to testify to the power of the Lord which is capable of changing the hearts of people. It has been a blessing for me and a satisfaction to be able to serve the Lord Jesus Christ.

(Q: And when did you receive the manifestation of the Holy Spirit?)

That happened when I was initiated as a preacher in the Apostolic Church, which I can state has been five-and-a-half years ago. The minister here was the Hermano Santiago M. T., who at present works in the congregation of Ciudad de Gutierres Gomez.

(Q: Do you remember what it was like the first time?)

Indeed, I do remember. It happened when we were not praying

specifically for the Holy Spirit, when I received the Holy Spirit. It was just an ordinary prayer. I had the desire always to seek the matters of God with all my heart, and I earnestly prayed that he show me his power. And I began to plead that he might manifest his power in me so that I might feel this gift, this power that he promised by his Holy Spirit. What it feels like, I cannot explain, it cannot be expressed in a concrete manner. Then, as I was praying in this manner, I could feel that God was manifesting his power in me. I could do nothing but weep and speak, and as God was manifesting his power, I paid no attention to what I was saying. I was beginning to speak, but it was not in the true sense of the word the language that I possess or am familiar with, but rather a speech which God manifested in me and which I could not comprehend. Afterward, I was told that God had indeed manifested himself in me and that he kept his word that he would give his Holy Spirit to everyone. And that was all, and from that time on I can control myself, so that when I want to speak in tongues, I do it, and when I do not want to, I can stop myself.

I also ask Chan Felix about the often-mentioned Biblical Institute in Tepic, Nayarit. He explains that the Southeastern Section of the Apostolic Church is divided into several sectors. Utzpak, Chetumal, and Merida form one sector, and they together provide each student of the Institute with 400 pesos for two months' worth of living expenses. The Institute has no physical plant; classes are held in a private home. Originally, there were six students registered for the course he just completed, but one dropped out. The subjects taught are reading and grammar, world history and world geography, the literature of the Bible, and how to evangelize. The teachers are several ministers sent from the district headquarters in Villahermosa and two female teachers. Classes run from 8 A.M. to 1 P.M. and 3 P.M. to 7 P.M., every day except Sunday.

Much of the proceedings of the Sunday service on August 3, 1969, are dominated by the baptism planned for the following Monday. In the pause between the *matutin* and the prayer for the Holy Spirit there is a special session for the baptismal candidates. Chairs are placed close to the altar, and the candidates are asked to sit there. Those present are Alvio and his wife Gregoria, Isauro and his wife Juanita, and Epi's shy and unassuming wife Neri. Paula arrives later and reports regretfully that Pedrito has a temperature again and that her husband now has doubts and probably won't want to be baptized. Paulino has developed an eye infection and probably will not be able to come either.

Chan Felix sits down in front of the group and once more explains the important points of the upcoming ritual. He knows, he says, that three of them have already received the Holy Spirit, but without the baptism by water they are fragile old vessels, unable to retain the new wine represented by the Holy Spirit. He reads from the Constitution of the Apostolic Church, which stipulates that baptism must be performed by immersion. It represents death, he explains. Sins must be confessed to God, and after the baptism, the person is incapable of sinning anymore and a new life begins. If afterward we sin, we condemn ourselves. Baptism is in the name of Jesus Christ only. This was how the Apostles performed it. They knew that the three names were of one God only, namely, of Jesus Christ. It must be done "in the name of Christ," and not "in the names of . . . " St. Peter was the first one who did it in this way. This was how it was done in this church because it was the only correct way. If it is done differently, the baptism is invalid. Before the Apostles received the Holy Spirit in the first Pentecost, they did not understand this point.

Everyone, he continues, must believe in Christ's resurrection and the spiritual body of the just, as well as in eternal life. The just will go to the right place, not to the eternal fire. The candidates must also believe that God can heal us, and this is why the church has the prayer for the sick. Everyone baptized must leave worldly amusements behind and live in sanctity. They must not eat the blood of animals, although it may taste good, for it is the life of the animal. And they may not eat the meat of animals choked to death. All this is forbidden by the word of God. They should attend all services and be sure to tithe.

All candidates are asked to kneel and to raise their hands and Chan Felix lays on hands and prays, but without glossolalia.

There is also an announcement that we are to assemble at the temple at 5:00 tomorrow morning—the truck will leave at 6:00—and that the bus ride would cost 5 pesos. Those who are going to be baptized will, of course, have to fast, and as many of the others as want to.

In the ensuing pause Eus asks me how baptism is done in our church. She is shocked when she hears that we baptize infants. "But Hermana," she exclaims, "that is contrary to the Bible. If you are baptized only that way, you are not going to enter into heaven." Then, she adds, very sadly, "How are we going to meet that way?"

During the prayer for the Holy Spirit that follows the instruction of the baptismal candidates, it is obvious how the prospect of the upcoming baptism has fired up the enthusiasm of Barrera and Chan Felix. For the first time in Utzpak, I see them use a technique of "driving," as I had termed it in the Mexico City congregation, where I had initially observed it. Much more emphatically than usual, Barrera employs its first step, the shaking of the candidate's head, on Gregoria's sister Elide. She has her 9-month-old infant in her arms during this prayer, while her 3-year-old daughter climbs up on the podium in an effort to get her attention. Impatiently, Barrera sends the child away, then once more places his hand on Elide's head, lightly shaking it. Elide does not react, so he turns to Isauro's wife Juanita, who kneels next to her, apparently in glossolalia for the first time. At that moment, she lapses into ordinary speech, but then goes back into tongues, very high, going higher. Then, she leans over on the podium and wipes her face with a slow, absent movement. Barrera is in glossolalia himself now and shakes her head, driving her higher, as if his intention were to intensify her trance to the utmost of her capacity. She is so deeply in trance that she does not notice that her mantilla has slipped off her head. Barrera picks it up and replaces it. He goes over to Goyo. The man is trembling and rocking on his knees. Barrera drives him using his own glossolalia, shouting it almost into his ear, punctuating its rhythm with an up-and-down motion of his fist. Goyo has his hands resting on the podium, his arms shaking, his face distorted. Noting that Juanita's glossolalia is less energetic, Barrera returns to her and tries to drive her higher, but without success. She goes higher, but without moving. Then she once more begins to rock. Chan Felix tries to drive Elide, but her little girl, determined to get her attention, throws herself on the floor and starts screaming. One of the young girls takes her out of the temple, but Elide's attention has been disrupted. Finally, Barrera rings the bell. The trances are so deep that not everyone reacts, and Barrera has to ring a second time. He calls Juanita and Elide to the front. Yes, Juanita has felt her language change. With obvious satisfaction, he announces that yes indeed, Juanita has received the Holy Spirit. How about Elide? She felt almost like a change of language, but not quite. He asks Goyo, who is back at his seat, what he felt. All he knows is that he wanted to cry. Addressing also Don Eduardo, who sits next to him, Barrera warns them, "You both are old and tired. You may die tomorrow, and you should be prepared. You should come to the services more often, fast and pray, for Christ is coming soon, and you must be ready."

After the Bible School, Eus asks, "What are you going to eat?" It is a standing question both from her and from Reina, and entirely justified, because quite often I end up with nothing but oatmeal. The black beans, the local mainstay, make me sick. By six in the morning, the freshly slaughtered pork is sold out on the market, and in the afternoon, the time when beef is available is quite indefinite. Tomasita usually comes back reporting that nothing but *shiich*, sinewy meat and skin, is left. The neighbor boy sometimes tries to find me some eggs, but more often than not the *mortandad* has once more wiped out the hens. This morning, however, I am in luck. Reina found a slice of pork for me on the market, and I can cook some rice with it and eat a tomato and a tortilla from Reina. It is a constant wonder of Reina that I am satisfied with only one tortilla, when she needs twelve to get full. It makes me ache that the reason for my continence is the simple fact that I eat as much meat as they share between the four of them.

In the afternoon, I walk to Eus's house. By the time I get there, I am wet with perspiration, for I cannot get used to walking and moving slowly, as one reasonably should in the tropics. "You walk like a boy," an 8-year-old girl tells me, who sometimes comes to Reina's house to sell me *vaporcitos*. Her father is paralyzed as a result of a hunting accident, and her mother tries to provide for the family by preparing corn on the cob and other items for sale.

At Eus's house, Eus is busy cooking. Barrera is sweating at the upright loom, weaving a hammock for his older son, who is going to be evicted from his mother's hammock by the new arrival. In the village, both men and women weave the hammocks, but Barrera is a city man, ignorant of the skill, and now has to learn it from Eus. Nohoch Felix is relaxing in a hammock suspended in the shade between two orange trees nearby, his sombrero shading his eyes, watching Barrera and offering well-meaning suggestions on how he should pass from one row to the next. "The boy does not need a very wide one," he consoles him.

The weather is unusually hot and oppressive and the mood mellow for the evening service. Even the children are quiet. Alvio's young daughter comes sneaking up to me and puts her small hand in mine as we listen to the special hymns. Barrera is sitting on the *marimbol,* and when Antonio intones the hymn about the beautiful home beyond the sun, his 5-year-old daughter stands shyly next to Barrera. He puts his arm around her and blows on her, a wonderful way to cool a perspiring child in the heat of night, then lets her sit next to him. Epi sings, "Grande gozo" [Great rapture], and then Joaquin follows with "En la villa" [In the village]. By that time, the child is asleep in Barrera's arm, her heart-shaped face very dark against his white shirt, the large bright flowers embroidered on her ʔipil moving gently with her quiet breath. Finally, Barrera has to resume directing the service and hands his charge back to her father.

After the conclusion of the service, Elide goes up to Luis and asks him something. In response, Barrera calls for a prayer "to help with the special problem of Hermana Elide." Apparently, Elide needs help in deciding whether to defy her husband's interdiction, for the prayer takes place, and afterward Barrera announces that Elide will come along tomorrow and be baptized.

The Baptism on the Seashore

AUGUST 4, 1969

Reina and I get up at 3:30 A.M. We prepare some food to take along—*frances,* fried meat, and jalapeno (courtesy of the anthropologist)—and Santiago goes to buy soft drinks. I ready my movie camera, and as people start arriving in front of the temple, I begin taking a few pictures. The children get into the act, calling my attention to the rooting pigs and the courting tom turkeys in the street. The conversation turns around Elide. Her husband abuses her and is against her getting baptized. Things are going to be tough for her. But she insists that she wants to be baptized with her sister Gregoria.

We wait and wait. Dona Juanita comes by to chat. She is hunting for her turkeys, as she does every morning. They are toms and there are many hens in the various *solares*. Will the weather hold, she wonders? Look at all those clouds! On the other hand, some rain would be good. Then she repeats what by now has become accepted dogma in the village. "We are having such a drought because those men went to the moon. And those new illnesses that people are coming down with, it is clear that they come from the moon too."

Chan Felix comes on his bicycle. The brakes on the truck he rented are not working. The owner is trying to fix them, but who knows when he'll get done? "So why didn't he fix them last night?" asks Reina, practical as always. People shrug their shoulders and wait. I expect the congregation to pray for a solution, but that does not happen. What is man's job is left to man; God is only in charge of miracles.

Eus's grandson Jose has been running around, gathering information. "Hermana," he calls to me, "they've found a new truck." Others nod. That's right. Another truck is on its way. Nobody has left the stretch of the street that I can overlook, and neither Chan Felix nor Barrera are visible, but those standing around me have picked up signals that usually pass me by. This sort of strange message transmission happens all the time. Santiago will rush out of the house and down the street. "My mother has come with my turkeys," Reina explains. How does she know? She just does. It may have been a brief call passing down the street, together with the noise of the daily bus from Merida briefly braking on the highway. Or that for a fleeting moment people oriented themselves in a certain direction. Who knows? Anyway, Jose is right. Soon both preachers come around the corner; a panel truck inches across the outcroppings of limestone, tilting this way and that, and stops in front of the temple. Benches and collapsible chairs are loaded on, and the children begin scrambling on board. Paula with Pedrito gets to sit in the cabin next to the driver. Jose has put himself in charge of my camera bag; a neighbor boy, whose trip I financed and who is along for the ride, carries my other bag. "Don't let him get into deep water," his mother calls to me. The women are helped on next with their babies. Eus is made comfortable on a chair; Elide is next to her, her face taut with fear and doubt. I sit on a pile of chairs next to Gregoria. For the men there is standing room only. They pull their sombreros deep into their faces to keep them from blowing off. It is 7:30 A.M. when we finally pull out, and the sun is burning hot. We women put towels on our heads for protection and try to shield the children that keep squirming in and out. Joaquin has the temple's guitar but soon gives up playing it for lack of space. Instead he starts singing, hymn after hymn after *corito,* and I forgive him some of his failings, for everyone sings along enthusiastically, and I can see his usefulness. "*Andamos muy alegre* [We are going along most joyfully]," Nohoch Felix nods brightly.

In Temax, we halt for a little while. There has been talk that a member of the Temax congregation would also be baptized, but no one shows up. As we pull out, some of the men in front of the tavern shout obscenities. It is in Maya, and Eus looks at me to see if I understand. I do, and we both laugh. The laurel trees along the highway hang so low that we are brushed by the branches. More laughter. We pass through Cansahcab. We are to meet Luis L. here with his party from Merida, but they are not there. The truck stops at a *tortilleria,* and some of the fathers get off to buy tortillas. When the Merida party still does not show, we drive on. Soon we turn into a bumpy, narrow country road. "I used to come this way when I was working on the ranch," Alvio shouts at me over the roar of the ancient engine. "There is a narrow valley nearby with a small river flowing toward the sea. It has lots of fine fish, since few people know about it. It is very beautiful."

As we draw nearer to the coast, there are small dead trees and tall cacti. Then some coconut trees appear, and a few houses near the seashore, and the truck stops. We have arrived at Santa Clara. With baskets, bags, and babies we walk toward the shore and soon are ankle deep in sand. The sky is clouded over; there is an occasional drop of rain. We stop at a shelter constructed of poles with a palm-frond roof and deposit our loads. From her large *henequen* basket, Eus pulls some sheets and, with the help of Gregoria and Neri, she converts the shelter into a square tent by tying the corners of the sheets to the poles. Over to one side Jose and some other boys are enjoying their first swim. Reina has Lupita splashing close to the shore in the warm ocean water.

Now some of the people are beginning to crowd around Chan Felix, Luis L., and Elide. The latter stands very still, her dark face expressionless, her eyes big with terror. Chan Felix is talking to her as I get there. Salvation is a personal matter, he is saying; it concerns no one but her alone. If she has confessed her sins to God, "we are disposed to baptize you." She just stands there, mute, suckling her infant. Juanita, Neri, Paula, and Gregoria go to the shelter to change, and after they emerge dressed in old clothes, kerchiefs on their heads, the men go in to put on old pants and shirts. There are Alvio; Paulino, whose eye has healed in time; and, to our surprise, also Paula's husband Artemio. They line up before Chan Felix, who repeats once more that baptism represents dying. After it comes the new life, a service to God. The baptism will be carried out the same way as the Apostles did it, by immersion; first the women, then the men. He reads a section from Matthew. With the baptism, the person becomes a member of the Church. If he does not keep the promises he has made to God, there is no pardon, only judgment. These promises have been made before God and the witnesses present. He then makes them kneel and repeats the warnings as before. Everyone joins in the subsequent prayer, then rises. The women join hands; Chan Felix takes Gregoria's, who is first in line, and slowly they begin walking out into the water, while on the shore, the rest of the congregation is singing a hymn with Luis L. playing the guitar. The words are lost in the rushing of the wind on the water, with which the melody joins into a single pulsing chorus.

Slowly, I walk after them, filming. I am fully clothed; my bathing suit would clearly be inappropriate, but luckily the water is very warm. A few raindrops fall on the lens of my camera. Jose and his friend splash around me, self-appointed bodyguards, chasing away the local boys, who are playing with a board and have come close, curious about the unusual goings-on. Soon I am in the water up to my belt. Chan Felix has halted his group further out; they are praying, with only fragments of the hymn sung on the shore wafting by on the wind. I cannot hear him repeating the baptismal formula, but in measured succession, one woman after the other is submerged, her hands folded in prayer. Then begins the slow walk back toward the shore. Luis L. begins to intone a different hymn; I hear "Soy bautisado . . . " [I have been baptized] when I get the same feeling as when something that concerns us is being signaled down the street. I look up and see that a row of people, seven in all, is progressing toward us along the edge of the water. A shout goes up: Luis L. and the hermanos from Merida! In the alternating cloudy gray and sunlight, I recognize Luis L., followed by Manuel H., Teofil, Hermana Licha, and three other women of the Merida congregation. They join the Utzpak group, and more powerfully than before we hear the triumphant hymn, "Soy bautisado . . . ," as Chan Felix and his new church members slowly approach the shore.

The baptized women go into the shelter of sheets and change into dry clothes. Somehow in the crowd, I have lost sight of Elide. Elsa, a middle-aged woman of the Merida congregation, who in her long ?ipil walks with the noncorporeal grace of a nun and talks with a soft, gay voice, is also going to be baptized today. She vanishes into the shelter and reappears in a faded cotton dress. Closely behind her, in the wet clothes discarded by her sister Gregoria, comes Elide, her face rigid with tension. Somewhere in the back of the crowd, her baby is crying, but she does not turn her head. Elsa holds her hand and they walk into the water with Chan Felix, when once more, Elide turns back. She strips a ring from her finger, the only piece of jewelry she is wearing, and hands it to Gregoria, who is close behind her on the shore. Her face relaxes, and with measured steps, she wades into the waves with Chan Felix and Elsa.

Once more, the baptism proceeds as before, then the men's turn follows. The chorus is louder now, reinforced by Licha and Luis L.'s strong voices. Off and on, there is a light shower of rain. My arm is getting tired from holding the camera in all sorts of awkward positions. I go to the shelter to change films. When I get back to the shore, Eus touches my arm, "Look, Paula is crying." Paula is standing up to her knees in the water, tears running down her face, head bent, praying in glossolalia. On the shore, in front of the tight group of *hermanos,* Artemio kneels, his hands and face pressed into the sand. Slowly he gets up, takes Pedrito from the arms of his oldest daughter, and wades into the water to Paula. Paula immerses the baby in the sea, and she and Artemio pray in loud and urgent supplication. The water, after all, has washed away the sins of the people. Perhaps now it can also wash away Pedrito's paralysis. With a corner of her *?ipil,* Eus, who has followed the couple, keeps wiping the water from the pale little face. On the shore, the men have joined in the prayer. Most of them are in glossolalia now. At one point, just as Luis L.'s powerful voice rises above that of the others and he lifts his hands high in supplication, the sun comes out, as if his wordless plea has rent the very clouds asunder.

All prayers said and all hymns sung, we finally get to the *chan almuerzo* [little repast] under the palm-frond roof that Nohoch Felix had so zestfully antici-pated yesterday. Food is shared freely all around. I end up with a slice of can-taloupe from Licha and Isua, a tortilla made of fresh corn from Eus, and Lupita on my lap, while the neighbor boy munches on one of my sandwiches. My skirt is nearly dry when Lupita thoroughly wets it. "*Ya te orinaste,*" laughs her mother, as she takes her from me so I can once more wade into the ocean to rinse myself off. Paula goes around to everybody, telling glowingly how Pedrito moved his feet in the water. Elide suckles her baby, and Alvio scolds Gregoria because she did not come immediately after being baptized to give her infant its *chuuch* [nurse it]. I let Nohoch Felix use up my last few feet of film. Santiago asks Luis L., "Is there permission to bathe?" but he is rebuked with a stern, "No, there is not. This is a sacred occasion. Why spoil it?" I want to feel sorry for him, but Reina tells me later in confidence that he had already gone swimming during the baptism, with the driver.

There is another, more ample, shower, and we wait until it is over before we get into the truck.

Everybody is in high excitement on the way home except Gregoria, who complains about her husband's criticism to everyone who wants to listen. Soon, however, she is drowned out by the singing. Chan Felix has the guitar, and he starts one hymn on the heels of the next one with everyone joining in. When he gets tired, Luis L. asks for the instrument. He sits high above us on the roof of the driver's cabin and shouts down to us, "Sing, Hermanos, this is how the children of God are known!" He sings and sings, the strumming of his guitar hardly audible over the roar of the engine, white teeth flashing, black eyes over aquiline nose brilliant in his dark face, wiry hair standing straight up in the wind, a prophet in the glory of intoxication. When he finally hands the guitar back down again, two strings are torn. The lead passes on to Licha, who has a high, metallic voice and inexhaustible enthusiasm. Singing, clapping, laughing, we finally stop once more at the door of the temple. It is nearly 4 o'clock. I have the pardonable urge to change into dry clothes and crawl into my hammock, but a service has been announced. "The time of slavery is over," somebody shouts, eliciting general laughter. "We don't have to go to work if we don't want to." And we all file into the church.

Elide usually sits in the back of the temple somewhere, but today she takes a seat beside Eus in the first row, her face serene. Barrera opens the service and when in the course of it he asks for testimonies, Paula stands up and comes to the front. For ten days, she says, her son refused to eat and had a fever; today he started eating again and his temperature was normal. Her husband was baptized with her; God granted her everything she asked for. She offers the hymn, "*Yo tengo una corona en el cielo . . .* " [I have a crown in heaven], and then she continues: walking from the shore toward the truck she heard many hymns, but they were not sung by the *hermanos.* Rather, it seemed to her, they were being sung in a very large cathedral.

Later, after the altar call, Barrera gives a brief sermon. "You are all happy, aren't you?" he asks rhetorically. "Well, I am sure that the angels are also having a fiesta today. If there is rejoicing in heaven over one sinner, just imagine how much there is today over eight!" He presents Luis L. formally to the congregation as a visitor, and we are asked to stand up to greet him. All other visitors are asked to come to the front, and we stand up once more to greet them collectively as well. Everyone included, there are fifteen men and eighteen women crowded into the small temple. Because of their high rank as ministers, Luis L. and Manuel H., as well as Chan Felix, stay on the podium, seated on chairs; the others go back to their seats. Chan Felix reports that the truck that took us to Santa Clara cost less than the one they had originally rented, and so 25 pesos are left for the church treasury.

After the special hymns presented by some of our congregation and all the guests from Merida, he passes the conduction of the service on to Luis L.

"*Gozaos* [Enjoy yourselves]," he says, employing the stately Spanish plural of the Bible, "enjoy yourselves. Today, God is happy. Although he lives thousands of miles away, he sends his greetings to the congregation in Utzpak. *Yo soy muy contento con Dios* [I am very well satisfied with the Lord]."

After some more hymns and prayers, Luis L. addresses those newly baptized. If they do not keep the promises they have given today, the Church will erase their names from the membership rolls, but their names will also be erased from the book of life. He directs them to come to the podium. Saying something different to each one, he hands out the baptismal certificate, then he has them kneel. There is a common prayer, and he lays on hands. Then they are dismissed, with the congregation intoning, "*Recibimos* . . . [We have received]." It is now past 6 o'clock, and most of the babies are screaming, despite all the *chuuch* offered. But there is still another sermon by Luis L.

There are thousands or maybe hundreds of Christian movements, he starts out, his voice bouncing off the rafters without a trace of exhaustion, but only one, theirs, teaches the true word of Christ. The other people are only creatures of God; they are not his children. "The baptism of the Holy Spirit is the wings that the Lord has given us, so that one day we can present ourselves with our seal of guarantee, and the Lord will say to us, 'Faithful servant, you were faithful with little, I will now put you in charge of much.' Yes, Hermanos, it is not jewelry that is the guarantee of salvation, not many clothes, not much knowledge, no, no, no! What is the guarantee of salvation is the Holy Spirit and the baptism. Having these two things and leading a Christian life, you, Hermana, need not worry about whether there is anything to eat, or what clothes to wear, for one day you will have eternal life with the Lord. . . . If the husband is opposed to his wife going to church, she will have to give him love and forgive him, but she will still have to go to church. If a person loves his brother or his sister, he will bring them to church. Also, the members of the church need to work diligently, for then they can contribute to God's work. Maybe that way, by next year, the present humble house of straw can be replaced by a beautiful one built of stone." And they will also be able to tithe more amply. After all, a father manages to keep his son in good clothes and to provide him with everything he needs. A congregation should be able to do no less for its pastor.

Chan Felix takes over from him and asks for donations so the guests from Merida can go and buy supper, and for Luis L., who needs to return to the Biblical Institute in Tepic. After another prayer, the service finally ends. It has lasted nearly four hours.

Elsa and another *hermana* from Merida take their bath at Reina's place, and we chat a little before they go to eat. Why didn't Reina also get baptized? I expect her stock answer, "*Pues* . . . *todavia estamos pensando* . . . [Well, we are still thinking about it]," which is so useful for warding off unwanted inquiry, but instead she says, "How nice it was that Gregoria and her husband were baptized at the same time. That way they leave the world together." But Santiago loves his beer and his diversions, and if she joins the church alone, he would live his life apart and leave her behind.

When the *hermanas* leave, Reina and I decide to unfurl our hammocks and go to sleep. Santiago is out somewhere. There is a knock on the door which we have already closed with a pole leaned against it. We admit Valentin, the young pastor from Temax, and his wife. They wanted to present their baby son to the congregation and were distressed that the service was in the afternoon and not in the evening, as they had understood. They cannot return home tonight; the last bus has left, so Reina invites them to hang their hammock and spend the night with us. Valentin is a gifted artist. There is a drawing by him in the temple of Baby Moses floating down the Nile in a wooden trough like the ones used in Utzpak for storing clothes. I also bought one from him which he called "Awakening," with a biblical quotation and a stylized rendition of the Yucatecan landscape, trees trailing lianas and a deer with a weight problem in front. After all, this is the land "of the pheasant and the deer." When he hears that I am shortly going to return to Mexico City, he asks me to request some books for him from the bishop's office. He already has *The Christian Home* and *Heroes of the Old Testament,* but he would also like to get Maclovio Gaxiola's *Theology,* his *Homiletics for Preachers,* and if at all possible, the New Testament in Maya. When the young mother nurses her baby, we notice that he has an umbilical hernia. Reina thinks that the little boy has a hernia because when his mother was pregnant "a sickness entered her body." Eus later gave the same explanation, adding, however, that the young woman probably also let the little boy cry too much instead of nursing him on demand.

The Last Week

Rodolfa had promised to come and visit me in the afternoon of the day after the baptism. She, too, wanted to tell me about her conversion, she said. But then she did not show up, she said because of the rain. "How come?" Eus scoffs at her when we bump into her in front of the temple in the evening. "You said you'd come at three and the rain did not start till five." To which Rodolfa just shrugs her shoulder and smiles. It looks like the service will start late, so we go back to Reina's and I record her story.

> I used to be a Catholic but never understood anything of the services
> in the Catholic Church. I heard about the *hermanos,* and Juan L.
> spoke to me about the gospel and invited us to come to Merida and
> attend the services. I went alone with my mother-in-law and we took
> the little ones. Candil would say, "Where are you women going?
> Don't you have anything to do?" But we continued going anyway.
> Candil enjoyed the things of the world; he drank, he smoked, he was
> *muy parrandista* [out for fun]. Finally he couldn't stand it any
> longer; he was curious to see what the services were like, and he
> accompanied us. He would not show himself openly, just stayed in
> the dark, in the back, his cigarettes in his pocket. He kept coming
> and gradually realized that this religion was the right thing. He
> stopped smoking and left the other things of the world behind.

(Q: What do you like about the *apostolicos*?)

What I like best about the services are the prayers. I also like Juan L. He is much gentler than Luis L. and has more patience.

(Q: Does your mother-in-law still attend the services?)

She does not come very often any more. She says she has to keep her daughter company, who likes the things of the world. Also, her daughter's husband does not like to attend church either. Now they have a soft drink stand, and so they don't come to the services for that reason. Also, they would rather read *cuentos* than the Bible.

The first thing that Eus says when she comes to fetch me to go to church the following evening is, "Hermano Juan arrived this afternoon." "Juan who?" "Juan L., Hermano Luis L.'s brother. He came to tell Chan Felix that he is being sent to Cozumel this Sunday to evangelize." Juan L. had been pastor in Utzpak some years previously and his name had been cropping up all summer, but I had never met him. So this news was quite a surprise.

At the church, Barrera introduced me to him. He closely resembles his brother Luis L. and is quite tall for a Yucatecan, so that when we speak he is at eye level with me (I am 5'2"); he is very dark complected and has the same aquiline nose and flashing smile, the same passionate manner of speaking as his brother, except he seems a bit more muted, as though in the nine years since Oscar Hill first won him for his cause some of the luster had worn off.

For the first time at this service the Dorcas are in charge of actually sponsoring the proceedings. Gregoria opens, and after the first hymn it is she who issues the altar call. Juan L., kneeling at the podium, is soon in glossolalia. When he has his hands on his knees and is rocking back and forth, he speaks in tongues; when he puts his hands on the edge of the podium, he lapses into ordinary language. Since he has a strong voice, I get an impression of his vocalization, although not enough of his syllable inventory, for as usual, to my chagrin, Joaquin keeps shouting as though, as Eus says, God were deaf.

It would now have been Rodolfa's turn to call for testimonies, but she plays hooky, so without blinking an eye, Gregoria does it in her stead. Then, with the *corito* "*Esta muy alto . . .*" [It is very high], Juanita, Isauro's wife, takes over, calls for special hymns, and passes to Eus, who takes charge of announcing the collection of offerings and of the subsequent prayer. Everything proceeds so smoothly, one would think that the women had been taking care of this part of the service forever.

Chan Felix introduces Juan L. to the congregation as an evangelist of the Church and also the pastor of the Chetumal congregation and, he says, he will now deliver the sermon.

Juan L.'s sermon is not well organized, but it is effective because of the enthusiasm with which it is delivered and because it touches on all manner of issues important to the congregation. "The Holy Spirit," he says, "is manifesting its power everywhere. Praying in Campeche on Thursday, two *hermanos* received the Holy Spirit, a husband and wife, and in Chetumal on the same day four *hermanas*, among them a young girl, the daughter of our *hermano* Jose D. S. On the same day the Lord touched also another *hermana*, Magdalena M., with his seal. This *hermana* is the younger sister of Hermana Elsa, who was baptized in Santa Clara, and they started speaking in tongues simultaneously, one in Chetumal, the other on the seashore. What a portentous and marvelous manifestation of the Lord Jesus! Here and in Merida, in Campeche and in Tabasco, and in all of Mexico and Central America, and in all of America, and all over the world, God is pouring out his Holy Spirit. . . . This was the promise of the Lord, 'I shall be with you, and I shall be in you. . . .'" He proceeds with the scriptural arguments for "one God only, not three" and continues, somewhat irrationally, with a description of the Chetumal temple. It is of "material," cement blocks; it is large for a small city, but it is intended for a big God, and it has room for many hundreds of people, "for we want to do something great for a great God." He skips to the missionizing effort. On the island of Cozumel, where Chan Felix is going to go as an evangelist, there are six homes where Jesus has been accepted. Five *hermanos* have been baptized, and four have received the Holy Spirit. Chan Felix will be the fisherman of souls on that island. On September 24, 1969, there will be a meeting of pastors to decide where each one of them will go in order best to serve the missionizing effort in Yucatan, which brings to mind the ever-worrisome financial problem and a plea for more generous tithing. The pastor, after all, he argues, gets to keep only half of the offering. "We don't often get to eat meat, but we do at least need tortillas and beans to live." There is no reaction from the congregation of only four men and seven women.

He calls for a reading of the Scripture and a prayer, then continues, speaking of his own conversion. On May 8, 1961, he received the Holy Spirit at 8 o'clock in the evening. "All of a sudden I sang, and I spoke in Greek, and Latin, and Chinese, and other languages that I had never heard." This is the well-known claim of "xenoglossia," speaking in "other tongues" that could be understood if someone were to be present who knew them. As he admitted in a conversation later, neither he, nor his mother or her maid, who heard him, knew any of these languages. But he knew anyway what they were.

The service passes on to Chan Felix, who asks for a special offering for Juan L. so he can return to Chetumal, He tells that they are hoping to buy an additional plot of land from Don Eduardo so that the congregation can build a fitting temple. After a final prayer we are dismissed. Some of the men and the pastors stay on, and I hear them singing as I fall asleep in my hammock.

Wilma, one of Eus's daughters, lives in the village of Tibolom (the name means "at the mileage marker") and sends a message that she needs some medicine for her newborn baby. The request is carried from her village by shoppers to the market in the capital, where Eus's brother has a stand, and relayed to Eus by returning Utzpak travelers. So, on August 6, 1969, Eus and I take the bus to Merida.

I board the bus at the plaza, and one of the teenagers that used to visit me regularly when I was living in Chucha's house is also a passenger. But when I greet her, she ostentatiously ignores me. I tell Eus when she gets in at her corner past the cemetery. "They now know that you belong to us," she nods. It happens to her in Utzpak all the time. For Wilma in Tibilom it is worse. She wanted to have an Apostolic service at her home but received threats that if she did so, her neighbors would set fire to her house. How about her husband Ruben? He used to be opposed to the gospel but has started to change his mind somewhat and is beginning to read the Bible. However, Wilma's mother-in-law has gotten mad and won't talk to her. "So Gregoria decided to ignore her. Now her mother-in-law is crying because Gregoria won't talk to her." Eus finds all that hilarious.

In Merida, we buy the medicine, an antibiotic, in a large pharmacy. No prescription is needed; you merely tell the pharmacist, who sits at a table in front, what you want and maybe what for, and you get it. Then we board one of the crowded streetcars to the central market and take our purchase to the stall of Don Agapito, a small, slender, gray-haired man with twinkling eyes and a friendly smile. He is affluent by local standards; he sells dry goods and some fruit at his small stall. Eus says that he has even been able to build his own house of cement blocks in a suburb, the Colonia Mercedes Barrera. When we get to his stall, his wife, Dona Sylvia, only about 4 feet tall, like so many of the village women, with beautiful, large eyes, a trader like her husband, has just brought him some beans in a small enamel pot and tortillas in an embroidered cloth. He sits eating it on a small stool, while the three of them exchange a large volume of gossip in rapid-fire Maya, of which I catch almost nothing. He is expecting some callers from Tibolom, he says, so he will be able to send the medicine to Wilma when they come by.

We take another streetcar—it is amazing to me how Eus gets around although she cannot read. We go to Peregrina and encounter Pastor Manuel H. He has heard about the baptism on the seashore, and we chat about the experience of the Holy Spirit. "When I received it, it was during a prayer service for the Holy Spirit. I felt as if I was no longer stepping on the earth, although I was kneeling. I felt like a rain was coming down on me, on my neck, my shoulders, and penetrating my chest. Then I felt how my language changed. I tried to speak in Spanish, but I couldn't."

AUGUST 7, 1969

"Don Eduardo has sold the plot up to *medio pozo* [half the well] to the *hermanos*," Reina tells me first thing this morning. "The plot has quite a history," she says, and enjoys laying it all out. It seems that it was supposed to be for Santiago's sister, the one that was always so mean to her. But she didn't want it. She said that it was too small and by the time she put down her *albarrada*, there would be no room for her animals. So she found a plot for a home elsewhere in Utzpak, and Don Eduardo gave her the money for it as her share of the inheritance. Don Eduardo had hoped that if his daughter bought that land and lived on it he could stay with her, because as a widower he felt quite lonely. But his daughter maintained that with her children, she simply had not enough space for her father to move in.

Then a woman bought Don Eduardo's plot. She was known to be very bad, a thief, they said. No neighbor could get along with her. Secretly, Don Eduardo had apparently hoped that this woman would consent to live with him. But Santiago was very unhappy about these plans of his father. "One evil woman has left," Reina quoted him as saying, meaning his own mother, "why get a worse one in her place?" But she said that Don Eduardo was ugly and she was afraid of him, and after all, "*Porque quiero burro?* [Why would I want a donkey?]" meaning, why would I want a relationship only for material advantage? And she demanded her money back. So now the church bought the plot for 1,500 pesos. "Where did they get the money?" I ask, for it could not possibly have been accumulated by tithing. "Hermana Licha, she makes good money as a secretary in an office in Merida, and she will buy it and then give it to the church as a gift. She paid 500 pesos down; the rest will be paid when the documents have been made out." Now, according to Reina, Don Eduardo says that he will also give Santiago his share of his inheritance and sign the plot where their house stands over to him, and also the house. Don Eduardo also hopes to sell his ranch. He says that he is tired and has a backache and a stomachache nearly all the time. He is hoping to get 20,000 pesos for it. Then maybe he will move to Merida.

When I get back from Maya lessons with Eus, Reina has visitors—Dona Felipa (the older sister of Don Eduardo) and her husband, who live in Merida. Felipa is a tiny old woman who walks with a cane. About ten years ago her eyes hurt and a friend gave her some medicine for it. It blinded her completely. Her husband, hawk-nosed and thin as a rail, is stone deaf. They have several sons with whom they live in turn. For cash, Felipa *anda de caridad* [goes begging].

Reina and Santiago treat the old couple with exquisite courtesy. The old man sits on Reina's taboret, and Santiago calls to him, "*Culen huaye* [Sit over here]," offering him the front half of his hammock, which is more comfortable. Reina helps Felipa take a bath. Later, Don Eduardo comes over to chat with his sister. After he leaves, I have a chance to talk with her. She says she likes *esta santa religion,* meaning the Apostolic faith, but cannot attend the services in Merida because she does not have the strength to sit through an entire service. Off and on for the past nine years, she has attended the services ever since this new religion came to Yucatan. There was a story in the newspapers that a woman had spoken with Christ. Did I believe that? I am cautious. "There are many things we cannot judge." "*Yo no hach lo creo* [I don't really believe it]," she says categorically. She is unhappy about being blind because it deprives her of many activities that she used to enjoy, such as making tortillas, for instance. She has learned to form them just by touch, but she cannot bake them on the hot *comal.*

She feels sorry for her *hermanito* [her little, i.e., younger, brother], Don Eduardo, because he has no wife. But then, she shrugs, what can he do? *Es su suerte* [It is his fate]. And too bad that his oldest son has no woman either. But then, he drinks too much. Again she shrugs. *Es su suerte.* This attitude marks a fundamental difference between the *apostolicos* and the world around them. Never once have I ever heard anyone in the Apostolic Church say *es su suerte.* The Holy Spirit changes things. Humans are not subject to *su suerte.*

At the service on the 7th of August, an invitation is announced for an evening service the next day at Alvio's house. It is to begin at six, but that simply means that is the approximate time when the men will start carrying the chairs to Alvio's house, who lives about half an hour's walk from the church. Eus, who has well-grounded reservations about anything starting on time, does not come to fetch me until past seven. I have often wondered how she knows the time. Without being aware of it, she must be watching the sun because no one in her family has a watch, and there is no clock at the plaza striking the time. She frequently checks her intuition with me though, and "Hermana, *baash oora?* [What is the time?]" was one of the first phrases I learned from her.

We walk to Alvio's house and are ushered in to sit in the hammocks, where some of the babies have already been put to sleep. The women start talking about the embroidery on my new *ʔipil,* the one done by the wife of Hermano Goyo in Merida, tracing the unfamiliar design with their fingers. I remember the first time this happened. I was sitting in church and one of the teenagers sitting in the row behind me was poking along the lines of the cross-stitch arc embroidered on my *ʔipil,* totally oblivious to the fact that I was inside. That time, I was secretly annoyed about the uninvited intrusion. Now I am proud of the intimacy it seems to express.

Still no service. While Eus gossips with the other women, I start to play Hungarian and German finger games with the children. Finally, Chan Felix gets tired of waiting and starts, with Barrera and Joaquin nowhere in sight. It seems that they had wanted to use the daylight hours to continue working on the roof of the *casa pastoral,* because Barrera is anxious to bring his family back from Campeche.

The service is being held in the courtyard. We are surrounded by a high *albarrada,* the chairs are set out in irregular rows, and a Coleman lamp illuminates the scene. It also attracts insects and I swallow hard as I see an enormous cockroach crawling around in a leisurely manner on Chan Felix's white shirt collar. His sermon is based on Hebrews 2:14, with its exhortation to faithfulness. The manifestation of the Holy Spirit shows that God is real, and with it we reach salvation. And salvation must be the most important concern in life.

The service is nearly over when Barrera and Joaquin finally show up with the church's guitar. After finishing their work, they went and took their bath—after all, nobody expects them to come to church unbathed.

I am in a quandary about how to catch up with typing my field notes before leaving, for I am badly behind. The daylight hours are simply too short and Reina has no electricity in her house; neither does anybody else I know. Only the rich do, who, as we sometimes glimpse through an open window, have tiled floors, plastered walls, caned chairs and benches, a wardrobe in the corner, and a lightbulb hanging from the ceiling, but they do not come to the temple. So I hit on the idea to ask Chan Felix and Barrera if I can type in the church for one night. I assume that I will be alone, but since Chan Felix is home, there is no room for Barrera and Joaquin in Eus's small house, and they have decided to sleep in the temple. When I arrive with my typewriter and other necessities, I find that they are making ready to go to bed. Joaquin, who possesses no hammock, pushes two benches together and folds a shirt for a pillow. The structural poles are too far apart in the temple for suspending a hammock, so Barrera makes similar arrangements, then comes to me, a rubber band and a piece of newspaper in hand. "Do you ever kill spiders?" he inquires. "Not if I can help it." "*Pues,* here you have to. Many of them are poisonous." He calls me to the front door of the church, where the outside light has attracted an army of insects. A number of spiders have collected to enjoy the feast. "That one there," he says, "is gray and innocent looking, but it jumps and has a vicious bite. Then there is this one, it has beige, rather portly legs and a big mouth in the center of its body. Beware, that one is really bad, and it can grow much bigger. There are quite a number of them in the church. Then that one." He points to a monstrosity, it looks like a collage of a giant bedbug and a scorpion. "That has a bite almost as bad as a viper. Of course, there are also the tarantulas, and the black widows, and more. But not to worry. If you injure a spider even on one leg, it will die. I always go hunting for some before I turn in," he says cheerfully. "I am not very good at it, but I usually manage to hit a few." He is right. His paper wad and rubber band artillery consistently misfires. Then he goes to his bench and soon, after a loud and sincere prayer, he is snoring, while I sit at my typewriter under the only lightbulb, surrounded by aggressively whirring insects and all the many hungry and poisonous spiders that he has scared up. It takes all my dedication and a teeth-gritting effort of self-control, plus the conviction that Reina will know exactly at what time I beat my retreat, that keeps me at my task. She is almost as good at telling time without the aid of modern technology as Eus is.

At exactly 12 o'clock, I hear a rhythmical, heavy breathing, starting from the direction of the *casa pastoral.* Childhood memories of my grandmother's ghost stories drive me into a furious sweat before I figure out that it must be Don Eduardo's horse looking for a midnight snack. But the worst is still to come. I am getting hungry, and Eus has left me a small pot with *is?um,* an *atole* made from fresh corn. It tastes a bit sour, but I think nothing of it until I start reacting with a violent diarrhea. That does it. Reina or no Reina, I pack my papers. It is about three in the morning, and braving tarantulas, snakes, centipedes, and whatever else may be crawling around this time of the night on the patio, I flee *hal pach* [the back way] to the safety of Reina's house and chamber pot, where there are probably just as many poisonous spiders as in the church, but at least I never see them.

August 9, 1969

I have been here for nearly three months and have never yet been to a *ts?onoot* [cenote], a well eroded by the water into the soft limestone. It is like going to Rome and not seeing the pope. During the second week of my stay here, the *cura,* the Catholic priest of the village, invited me to go on a drive with him and see one, but I declined the invitation, because Eus and I were going to go to Temax that day. I suggested that he come by again the following week, but he never came back. As I discovered since then, an invitation once refused is not repeated. So Eus offers to take me to see one, and Nohoch Felix and Chan Felix decide to go along for the ride.

At five in the morning they knock at my door, and after a long bus ride we get off in the middle of nowhere, leave the highway and turn into a jungle path. During the Caste War the Maya peasants herded their Mexican captives along such hidden paths. Few survived the walk, and their shadows are haunting the thickets. I see huge iguanas on the trees and orchids growing from the branches. At one point we hear a strange rustling noise, and in front of me Eus hitches up her *?ipil* and, looking for all the world like a giant grasshopper, jumps 2 feet in the air across something that looks like a brown brook of hustling insect bodies, about a foot and a half wide. I don't hesitate to follow suit, and then am told that it is a battalion of army ants that is crossing our path. "When we were living on the ranch," Eus says, "we always listened for the rustling of army ants. They would often come at night, but we would hear them anyway and flee. After they pass, the house is completely clean, not a scorpion or cockroach left. They eat them all."

The cenote, called Bella Vista, is beautiful, larger than the sacred well at Chichen Itza. The air is cool, the water is green and oily looking, a few trees nod at its rim, and it appears strangely dark and foreboding. It is not fenced in, and I am very careful about how close I go, because its rim looks eroded and brittle. It worries me how my companions squat so nonchalantly at its very edge. After all, Nohoch Felix is the one who loves to tell stories about people falling in and drowning. But Eus says those are usually suicides.

The return bus lets us off at the edge of the village, and we walk through a part of Utzpak that I am unfamiliar with. We come by the Pentecostal church, without a roof and deserted. It reminded me of an Apostolic temple that Don Fulgencio once started on his own land, long before he built his *chan casita de oracion,* which is also in ruins now. It was never finished because Don Fulgencio started quarreling with the *hermanos.* I ask Chan Felix what he thinks the reason is for what I see as a tendency of the *apostolicos* to fraction, for I have heard that Hermano Goyo, Dona Valuch's husband, also has particularized ideas. It is rumored that he is starting to build his own prayer house too. Chan Felix denies that any theological conflict is involved. "It is just that Don Fulgencio wants a Fulgencio Temple, and Hermano Goyo a Goyo Temple. The crux of the matter is that at the temple, we demand tithing. They don't want to tithe because they think that a pastor ought to work with his hands as does everybody else and not enjoy what they consider a soft life of idleness. So they want to go it alone. Who loses in the end is Don Fulgencio and Hermano Goyo." "Hermana Valuch," Eus adds, "thinks the same way. She is convinced that tithing is wrong, and she doesn't come to the services very often anymore."

"Here at this spot," Eus reminisces as we turn another corner, "we once came by, Hermana Valuch and I, and some of the other *hermanas* who had attended a service in her house, and a woman came out the door, I don't remember her name, and she called us *brujas* [witches], and she put her right hand on her left upper arm and patted it a little like this, which meant that she was going to beat us. They say that from that time on she has not been able to move her left arm. *Pues,* that is what they say. They even say that the family called a physician the same evening, but he could do nothing for her."

I spend the day packing, and we have a scary time in the afternoon because Santiago had gone to Motul, Don Eduardo was not at home either, and Jorge was apparently getting drunk in the tavern down the main street. Dona Juanita came by to say that she had seen him drinking glass after glass. Then Dona Raquel from across the street called a warning that he was approaching. Reina leaned the pole against the door, and we did not even go out on the patio, but used the chamber pot in the house. She kept her ear cocked to the noises in the street. "He is coming," she said. And then with a relieved sigh, "Now he has passed the house." Even Lupita perceived her mother's anxiety and did not utter a sound. Finally, Reina slipped out and after prolonged reconnaissance she came back with the intelligence that he had gone to sleep. But she was not really at ease until Don Eduardo came home from the ranch, and only then did she take the pole away from the door to let the fresh air in. She says that when I am gone, she will go to sleep in Raquel's house if Santiago is gone for the night.

The reason why Santiago had gone to Motul was to sell bottles. That was his latest business venture. The beginning of July, he and his *companero,* his friend and business partner, went to Motul to the fiesta to sell tacos. He described at length how good they were, deer meat with little pieces of orange and *epasota* [saltwort] and cilantro. But the fiesta was not well attended, people had no money, and they hardly made enough money to cover expenses. Then he went to the *monte* to cut firewood for sale. "What I make, we eat," he said after that episode. "There is never enough left over to invest." So now he collects bottles from various households, paying a few centavos for each. The whole household assembles under the laurel tree and washes bottles, Don Eduardo included. "He doesn't want to work on the ranch," explains Reina, "he is looking for soft work." "She is embarrassed about me," laughs Santiago. To me, it does not look soft at all as he comes in, perspiration running down his face, smarting under the load of a sack full of old, dirty bottles. "If only the *bracero* program would still be operating," he sighs. "That was good, you spent a year in the United States, made some money and then you came back and had your savings to start a nice business." Then he turns to me. "Can't you pass the two of us, my *companero* and me, across the border as your laborers? We would find some work, and in a few months, we would be back." I try to explain why that is not workable, besides being illegal, and Don Eduardo just laughs about his harebrained idea, but I can see that Santiago puts my refusal down to a lack of good will.

When it gets dark and Santiago is still not back, we take to our hammocks and chat. Reina takes my leaving very hard. She won't wear the new slip I gave her; she'll save it as a keepsake, she maintains. Besides, she is afraid that Lupita will get sick after I leave since she has taken so to me. Finally, she falls asleep and the noises of the night take over. A giant frog croaks off and on outside; inside the mice rustle on the table. I recognize the whirring of the flying cockroaches and take in the chewing, scuttling, scratching, and swooshing of assorted other wildlife, and above it all, the whine of the hungry mosquitoes. "Some sting," I shrug as I go to sleep, "but most don't do anything."

The evening service on the following, my last, day is well attended; there are eight men and ten women. I see Paula with her husband and Pedrito, and also Don Fulgencio. Barrera preaches about the need to attend church regularly. If you cannot live according to the Word of God, do not go through with the baptism, because the devil will really be gleeful about a person who is unable to keep his promises to God and thus will be condemned. In conclusion, he asks the congregation to pray for me so that I may receive the Holy Spirit too, and also that I may be able to come and visit them again. He then passes to Chan Felix.

Chan Felix announces what everyone already knows, that he will be going to Cozumel and that Barrera will be the minister of the Utzpak church. He asks the congregation to cooperate with him, for he has a difficult task, taking care also of the congregations in Temax and Cansahcab. He then presents Elide's two little girls to the congregation, praying for both of them. It is a rational, well-composed prayer, but without a single glossolalia phrase, and all of a sudden that does not seem right to me.

He then asks for the sick to come to the front so that they can be prayed over and continues by suggesting that the congregation pray for me, my work, and my trip home. After a concluding prayer, the women come to say good-by to me, one after the other, and they are very formal about it, shaking my hand with the customary limp touch and saying, "*Dios le bendiga,*" and some repeat that other formula, a plaint that I have heard so much during these last few days, "*Ya nos acostumbramos . . . ,* [We have gotten used to you and now you off and go away]," and Eus stands beside me and keeps saying that in two years I will be back. In the meantime, the men are at their seats, just standing there, not coming forward, until I understand that for this formal occasion the strict separation and the "place of the woman" once more becomes operative. So I go over to the men's side and shake hands with each one of them, and now it is I who says, "*Dios le bendiga.*" And it seems as if each one of the faces, so open to me all this summer, are somehow closing. I have my new ʔipil on; I am deeply tanned, so that I look almost as brown as everybody else around here; I have my mantilla on my head; and everyone calls me "Hermana Felicitas"; and yet once more I feel relegated to the place on the outside, to the role of the white woman that people should not be afraid of, although she is white, but they still are.

Eus says, for the last time, "*Coosh,* Hermana [Come on, let's go]," and I answer, "*Coosh tuun* [Let us go, then]," and together with Nohoch Felix, we walk out into the street. I want to say, look, over there is the evening star, *ec,* we have laughed so much about my not being able to pronounce a glottalized "k" at the end of a word, and now I know how to do it, but I can't. We stop at Reina's corner, and Nohoch Felix keeps shaking my hand, his Spanish, never very firm, turning more and more into Maya. Then, Eus takes me into her arms and says something very involved in Maya, of which I understand only, "*Hats²uts* [Very pretty]," and "*Wa cushano²on* [If we live to see it, i.e., your return]," for I am crying into her *rebozo*. A last *abrazo* and they turn, and in the moonlight, they start walking down the street, over the boulders, and they do not turn back.

Reina with Lupita, Raquel with her son, and Don Eduardo with my heaviest bag take me to the bus in the morning. I try to open the window, but it is stuck, and by the time it finally yields, everyone is gone. Utzpak puts on its face of stranger and in a few minutes, the last oval house with its white *albarrada* drops out of sight.

In Merida, I leave my bags at the bus station and take the city bus to the Apostolic temple. Sunday school is in progress. Luis L.'s talent for organizing is evident. He has the congregation divided into small groups, each one practicing the text from the book of Acts about the Pentecost and the gift of tongues. When they leave, the children come out as a group first, and when they see me, they shout in unison, "*Paz de Cristo,* Hermana."

After a meal in Licha's house she, Luis L., and I relax in the hammocks before I have to go catch the bus. "I think actually that the Holy Spirit can manifest itself in a person without there being a gift of tongues," Luis L. muses. "That was how it happened to me."

> I used to live like everyone else, sinning. Especially, I liked to go to dances. My brother, Juan, used to talk about the gospel, but I wasn't really interested. Then my father died, and there was a special memorial service. I went, not to hear the gospel, but only out of courtesy to my mother and my brother. I liked the singing, but all the rest of the service didn't really impress me. However, I did go again next Sunday, more out of boredom than interest. The week went by, I went again, and another, and already I liked the service better. I didn't particularly pray for the baptism of the Holy Spirit. I saw my mother receive the Holy Spirit [with a smile, he imitates her characteristic fluttering hand movement], and it frightened me. There was an altar call, and just so that I would not feel out of place, I went up to the altar with the others. All of a sudden I felt myself to be the greatest sinner in all the world. I started praying in a very loud voice, asking for forgiveness, and suddenly I became aware that I was standing there before the altar, all alone, and I was puzzled.
>
> Another week went by and a friend came by and said, "Let's go dancing." So I took my bath, and I said, "*Pues*—let's go." For a while, we stood across from the dance hall, looking. Finally, my friend said, "Why don't we go in?" So we crossed the street to go in, when all of a sudden I heard a voice. Very clearly it said, "*No entras aqui, no es tu*

lugar [Don't enter here, this is not the place where you belong]," and again, "*No entras aqui, no es tu lugar.*" This was the turning point for me. From then on, I started going to the services regularly. I was baptized, and a few weeks later I also received the gift of tongues. So you see, I think that I really received the baptism by the Holy Spirit at that time when I understood that I was a sinner. So it must be possible to be baptized by the Holy Spirit even without speaking in tongues. But for the church, for the congregation, the gift of tongues is the outward sign. This is how the congregation knows that the Holy Spirit baptized the person. The other kind of baptism only God knows. After speaking in tongues, the person remains with joy and with the hope that God will keep his promise of salvation.

Licha's daughter, a student at the University of Yucatan, and her little sister accompanied me to the bus station and waited until the bus left. Its door closed, and all of a sudden, I was alone.

Discussion

My initial motivation for going to Yucatan to do fieldwork there with a Pentecostal congregation had to do with a question of theory. My analysis of glossolalia soundtracks of English and Spanish speakers indicated the presence of an impressive suprasegmental feature, superimposed, that is, on the syllable inventory. While the syllables varied from congregation to congregation, this suprasegmental pattern remained always the same. It consisted of a special, rigidly regular rhythm and an intonation pattern, the curve of which rose to a peak at the end of its first third and dropped down during the second and the third part. This pattern was independent of variations in the syllables themselves. I speculated that it had other than linguistic origins and was possibly due to changes in the body that people underwent during an ecstatic trance experience. If this was so, then the pattern would also be detectable if the speakers had an "exotic," that is, a non–Indo-European language as their mother tongue. The Maya of Yucatan was such an exotic language.

My observations in the Apostolic congregation of Utzpak, a Maya village in northern Yucatan, confirmed this assumption. However, the three months of participant observation provided numerous additional insights, fleshing out the bare outline of the behavior that I had gained during the three months of visiting and recording I had done in Mexico City.

The foregoing report, in addition to its human dimension, gives the details of these observations. I should like briefly to recapitulate what I learned in that village congregation with respect to the behavior of speaking in tongues.

Quite generally, apparently, humans are capable spontaneously to institute the physical change here termed ecstatic trance, which is the substrate for the speech behavior of glossolalia. It can thus appear spontaneously, as happened to me. What is utilized in ritual context is the fact that it is a learned, and thus a teachable, behavior. In other congregations, both in Yucatan and elsewhere, the principal method of instruction is quite haphazard: if the expectation of "change of language, which is the sign," and the desire for the experience are well enough anchored; if rhythmic stimulation is offered; and if there are others present who are experienced in the behavior, the switch into it is going to happen—one of these days. What made the situation in Utzpak special was the fact that Barrera did not leave matters to chance. Rather, he had those who were already proficient kneel around those desiring the experience. This "radiation" was extremely effective, resulting not only in parishioners acquiring the behavior much faster than, for example, in Merida during the week's prayer for the Holy Spirit, but also in a rapid growth of the congregation itself. The strategy was not, however, imitated in other congregations. Barrera did not advertise it and other ministers remained unaware of the possibility. In fact, Barrera did not realize the utility of his method either, and instead considered the rapid growth in the number of glossolalia speakers in his congregation to be a sign that the Second Coming was finally imminent.

The instituting of the ecstatic trance tended to precede the glossolalia. Physical exertion seemed to prevent its occurrence. It was expressed in heat, perspiration, trembling, rapid heart rate, and the flow of tears, as well as in kinetic behavior that was individually different. Some men raised their arms. One woman would clutch the end of her mantilla, another one would have a characteristic hand flutter. The visionary experiences reported were quite simple, the appearance of light, of being pelted by rain, of others being snatched away, of "no longer being here." The central point was the fact that speaking in tongues was the entrance ticket to salvation and heaven, and it demonstrated the factual presence of the Holy Spirit. "That gives us certainty," was an often-heard assertion.

Despite the considerable arousal, however, this particular trance seemed to be unstable. Everyone in the congregation could cite examples of someone no longer speaking in tongues. Going to a dance, drinking a beer, or having an affair was usually cited as the reason. To counter the problem, ministers apparently developed elaborate and individually different techniques for calling forth the glossolalia and assuming control over it, but eventually it seemed to slip away anyway, as in the case of Chan Felix.

As to the glossolalia utterances themselves, novices, both men and women, initially tended to utter a very high and prolonged "ululating" pattern. It soon passed over into a segmented, that is, syllabic form. The phonetic inventory of the syllables, however, had different rules than Maya. For instance, in glossolalia, these village parishioners often employed the rolled "r," which did not exist in Maya, so that Maya speakers when using Spanish tended to substitute an uvular fricative (like the French "r"). To my surprise, the syllables that began to emerge were not at all like the ʔ*aria,* ʔ*aria,* ʔ*aria* of Barrera and his assistant, Joaquin. Rather, unlike the individualistic kinetic pattern, the congregation began to develop its own glossolalia dialect and this despite the fact that in tape-recorded form, they did not recognize their own glossolalia. In other words, perception while in trance did not carry over into perception during the ordinary state of consciousness. In all cases, however, the glossolalia recorded in the Yucatecan congregation showed the same rhythmic pattern and (and this is very important) the identical intonation curve as recorded everywhere else.

3. 1970

Return to Yucatan[1]

Although during my first stay in Utzpak I was able to answer my pressing questions concerning the nature of glossolalia, I soon decided that I would return. Reports in the literature about such congregations were more in the nature of a snapshot—a stay of half a year or less, usually. I intended instead to do a long-time study about the life history of such a community. I also wanted to do some more filming. Besides, as a European, I loved village life, and I relished the idea of spending more time with Eus, whose friendship I increasingly treasured. I promised her that I would try to return in 1971.

The reason for the two-year delay was mainly financial. I would need time to save enough money for another field trip. But thanks to a generous grant from my employer, Denison University, I was able to return a year earlier, and this time in style, by plane. I had received some letters during the intervening time: one from Reina with thanks for the pictures I had sent, with kisses from Lupita—"she now knows how to give kisses to Mama and Papi"; and one from Eus, written by Nohoch Felix, asking about the name of the ointment that had healed the sore on her leg, because one of her nieces also needed it. I had shopped for presents and, thanks to Denison, I had a 100-dollar movie light for taking pictures inside the temple and a large Sony tape-recorder, heavy, but of much better quality than the one I had used in 1969.

On July 2, 1970, after a beautiful, quiet flight off the coast of Yucatan, we touch down at the Merida airport, tiny after the one in Mexico City. As I walk toward the airport buildings, I see Eus waving from the roof. The passageway to the arrival area seems endless. The familiar soft, warm, humid, fragrant tropical air streams in through the window openings, and at the end, beyond the door, there leans Eus, small and girl-like slender. It is a curious distortion. I remember her from last year as tall and imposing. "*Paz de Cristo,* Hermana," she beams. Licha and her stepson are waiting with a cab in front. Eus later tells everyone how tiny the plane was up in the sky, and how it got bigger and bigger, and with me inside!

We go to Peregrina's house. She complains of rheumatism and wants to know what we do for that in the United States. In Merida, they only sell aspirin with caffeine, which she says does not help her, so I give her a bottle with 100 pills from my supply. She likes the material for a dress I brought her. Her son, Pastor Luis L., is still in California, where he went after completing his course in Tepic, Nayarit. I have brought the film I put together during the winter about the congregation and the baptism on the seashore and am looking forward to showing it to the congregation. I had written to Licha about that, asking if we could rent a projector in Merida. Licha did nothing about it but hopes she will be able to find one. And Peregrina hopes to get Luis L.'s typewriter back from the girl who wanted to buy it but could not pay for it. So things are getting off to a slow start. I feel my enthusiasm wilting when Peregrina says, "*Y fijense nomas* [and just imagine], in your village of all places, an *hermano*, his name is Tono, he had a vision of the devil, and he is now preaching all over about that vision." I perk up, although I do not know what to make of it. Who is Tono? And a demonic vision? I file the intelligence away. I could not know that I had just heard the first blast of the apocalyptic trumpet.

We need to go and eat, and since Eus has promised her brother to bring me to the market when I return, that is where we go. We bring some *frances* stuffed with *cochinito pibil* [piglet baked in an earth oven]. Eus says it is not piglet, that would be too expensive, but rather *wetch* [armadillo]; but whatever it is, it is spicy and delicious. Don Agapito and his wife greet me like a long-lost relative and quickly start to tease me in Maya to see whether I have forgotten anything. I receive a passing grade—after all, I had worked on it during the winter—and they share a sweet *pozole* with us. Afterward, we go back to Peregrina's house.

For a while, I watch Peregrina's niece embroider an *ʔipil*. She came to Merida to learn dressmaking. The technique she uses is truly remarkable. She has threaded the treadle machine with a white bobbin and the top thread is colored silk. The material, which has a pattern of flowers drawn in pencil, is stretched into an embroidery hoop. Then she starts the machine and with quick hand motions shoves the hoop back and forth, creating the flower design. Then she changes the thread, choosing a different color, and goes over the design again. It is more like painting than embroidering. She lets me try, but of course I make a total mess of it. She consoles me, saying that she has practiced the technique since she was a small girl. No wonder I cannot match that. So I go to join Eus, who is relaxing in her hammock, and pass the time gossiping until we have to leave to catch the bus.

The day after I left in August, Eus tells me, she came down with a high fever; nothing would help, no home remedy, not even the aspirin of which I had left her a good supply. Then Chan Felix came back from Merida the following day because he had forgotten some of his papers that he wanted to take with him to Cozumel. He was alarmed about her condition and got the doctor. He pumped her full of shots and more pills, but she could not eat. She finally forced herself to eat just one tortilla, then two, then three, *con trabajo* [with effort], nursing herself back to health, but it took more than two weeks. "People said I got sick because you left." She laughs it off, but Peregrina, who has been listening in, remarks "*Pues,* why not? It could be."

Reina has a new baby daughter; Eus does not know her name. Don Eduardo threw his older son Jorge out of the house because he was annoying Don Eduardo's new wife. "He told his son he didn't even want to see his shadow again." Don Eduardo got married? Who is the woman? *Pues, una pagana* [a pagan, read Catholic]. He gave Jorge 2,000 pesos, that was all. Santiago got the same, although Reina had waited on the old man hand and foot for four years, cooking, washing, ironing for him. "He allowed them to stay in their house until they build their own, but what can they build," Eus wonders, "after paying for their lot? At most a *chan jacalucho* [a little hut] with a tar-paper roof." Don Eduardo's first wife had to starve so he could buy land. The new one is a spendthrift, all she wants to drink is milk and chocomilk, and she keeps buying a whole kilo of meat at a time, and the two of them never go to church anymore.

And who is that Tono who had a vision of the devil? "You know him. Remember, the barber, Hermano Antonio?" Of course, I do remember him—a small man with deep-seated eyes, about 25 or so, and a strong Maya accent in his Spanish—and his wife, who looked as if she had just stepped out of a Maya stele, speaking no Spanish at all. She rarely came to the services. Antonio, however, attended regularly and occasionally brought his three little girls to church. According to Eus, he became a Presbyterian a few years ago, then he passed on to the Baptists, to Jehovah's Witnesses, and the Pentecostals, before he ended up with the Apostolics. "He must enjoy bathing," Eus quips. When last year I had asked him about his baptism, he eagerly said that he had been, both by the Spirit and by water. "Now all I need is tithing to be saved."

"One day," Eus says, "Antonio was praying in the temple, and he suddenly saw many devils with horns who wanted to grab him. He ran out of the temple and collapsed outside. Since then he has the capacity to see who is truly saved. A person who only pretends to be converted appears to him with a completely black face. Then he saw the devil again, and he landed on the roof of the Catholic church on the plaza."

Peregrina and her niece join us, and there is joking in Spanish and in Maya about how big the horns of the devils might have been that frightened Hermano Antonio. "Peregrina says that he preaches outside of Utzpak," I say. "*Haa,*" Eus nods, "but that is because his wife has many lovers, and he can no longer stand it."

The remark explains something I remembered from last year. Toward the end of my stay, Antonio came to see me at Reina's house. He described how beautiful his house was, surrounded by trees, and wouldn't I go and visit his wife? I suggested it to Eus, but she kept postponing it, and at the time I was not sure why. Now I knew. She would not even visit her oldest daughter in Merida because she suspected her of prostitution.

We bathe, eat what is left of our armadillo sandwich, and at four, as it is getting cooler, we take the bus to Utzpak. We even have the same driver as last year. Once more we rattle and roar down the narrow highway, with the thorny, bare, and brown jungle; regimented rows of *henequen* fields and white-washed *albarradas* rush by. Occasionally we slow down for scrawny cows, humped Brahman cattle, horses, kids, dogs, and trucks loaded high with bundles of *henequen* to be processed into fiber. The latter we pass with just inches to spare.

Reina's new baby is asleep in her hammock, a tiny bundle of which I could not see much, for it is past seven in the evening and dark. Her name is Cilia, the name of Santiago's mother, who was apparently being rehabilitated in view of the scandalous chocomilk consumption of the new wife. I am to be *comadre*, sponsor, for her *hetsmec* ritual, whatever that is. We unpack my gifts by the light of a candle that throws its shadow on a new oilcloth on the table. Santiago is happy with his own safety razor; he has still been borrowing his father's. Lupita is taller than last year, but not heavier. As I try her crisp U.S. dresses on her, she invests me with my new kinship position: I am her *chichi* (Spanish corruption of the Maya *chiich*, grandmother). I get an updated version of the sad tale of Don Eduardo's doings. He even quarreled with the *hermanos*, demanding that they complete the *albarrada* separating the church property from his plot. Santiago's mother had to cook for the whole family for 3 pesos a day, Reina recalls, but the new wife spends money all around and wants to drink nothing but milk and chocomilk.

Eus arrives with her 19-year-old daughter Nina, who recently returned from Mexico City, Eus's youngest child, slender and with a gentle voice like her brother Chan Felix. Nina was recently baptized by the Holy Spirit and also by water, Eus beams. When she teases that Nina likes movies, the girl corrects her mother, "did like." The entry of Nina is one of those fortunate happenstances that fieldworkers are sometimes blessed with. Her observations provide access to a younger generation of women in the congregation than Eus has connections with, and who play a pivotal role in the apocalyptic events to follow.

I am tired from the trip and long for my new hammock that I bought from Eus, but it does not seem right to skip church, with Eus calling her familiar, "*Coosh*, Hermana," at the door and Nina looking expectantly for me to come along.

Changes in the Temple

The temple is still a familiar building, but the interior has been spruced up. New paper streamers replace the old torn ones under the rafters, four faded purple plastic candelabras tinkle vacantly from the ceiling, and the single light-bulb is clothed in a white Chinese paper lantern. Baby Moses is no longer floating on the waters. Instead, there is a new drawing by Valentin, of the Cross and the Sword dominating the round earth, drawn into a triangle and surrounded by roses. The entire "physical plant," while more stimulating to the senses, seems also somehow harsher than last year.

The podium looks different, too. An American congregation has donated a public address system to the congregation, which I piously hope will break down soon, for it is much too powerful for the small temple, and also a record-player. To accommodate the latter, and the amplifier, a second small table has been placed on the podium, but in such a way that now the two tables, one to the right and one to the left of podium, are like a barricade along its entire edge, a barrier between Barrera and the congregation. The impression of sepa-ration is heightened by the fact that when we enter, Barrera is kneeling on the podium to pray but, in contrast to last year, his back is to the congregation and he is resting his elbows on the box that contains the church documents.

The congregation is more numerous than before. We start out with eleven men and fourteen women, and, of course, uncounted restless children. There are those among the adults whom I do not know yet, several of the men, and among the women, Lucrecia, Barrera's wife, light-skinned like her husband and still nursing her new baby boy. In passing I note with relief that Joaquin is nowhere in sight. I hear later that he used to hold the services in Cansahcab but preached so poorly that the *hermanos* would get up in the middle of the ser-vice and leave one by one. Finally, there was no congregation left. Barrera ap-parently did not care. According to Nina, he did not check up on Joaquin. He did not go to Cansahcab, either, to talk to the *hermanos,* although he could easily have reached the village by bicycle. Instead, he believed everything that Joaquin said, namely that the *hermanos* there were all sinners who did not want to be saved. Finally, Joaquin was sent to Chetumal. Barrera preferred to stay at home in Utzpak. "He does nothing but sleep," Nina said. "In the mornings, he does not get up until eight, and then at noon, he sleeps again. And then he complains that he cannot sleep at night." He never sweeps the temple and does not change the water for the flowers.

Barrera accompanies the opening hymn on his guitar, but it is now a rattling electric one. And Eus no longer performs on the jaws. I see them later on her trash heap. As the service continues, it seems that Barrera is taking everything at a faster clip than last year, as if he is restless, or impatient, and he keeps shouting into the microphone as though he is addressing the entire quarter. During the altar call Epi, such an impressive glossolalist last year, apparently has trouble breaking into vocalization. There seems to be a deterioration of his energy level. At least that is how I interpret his new kinetic pattern. I have ob-served repeatedly that when people have problems getting into trance, they move a lot. Epi shoves his hands back and forth, parallel to the floor, and keeps shaking his head furiously, all the while apparently trying to speak in tongues but not making it. Then he doubles up, presses his arms against his ribcage, and finally accomplishes it. His utterance is a long one, but occasionally it is mixed with Spanish phrases, "*Gracias a Dios,*" and finally, "*Oh Dios mio,*" again to my mind, and according to my observations of similar behavior in the Mexico City temple, a sign that his trance experience is getting weaker. In a man as plagued by *ese temor* [this fear], such signs of loss of contact with the Holy Spirit are likely to cause a great deal of anxiety. When he sits down, he breathes heavily, pulls out a handkerchief, and wipes his forehead.

The service is sponsored by the Dorcas, and Nina and Lucrecia are now in leading roles. When the women line up to sing their special hymn, I see that Alvio's wife Gregoria is visibly pregnant.

Barrera's sermon is shorter than usual and different in tone. No trace of the good humor of last year and the jocular use of Maya phrases. "Dust will turn to dust," he thunders. "The works of men do not last. Let us pray for the young, for the flesh is strongest in them. The flesh is the enemy of Jesus, the flesh does not love the matters of God." Turning to the offering, he admonishes the congregation that God wants sacrifices. "Of course, if you have nothing, what will you give? But those that have should give abundantly." In other words, the tithing situation is probably as discouraging as ever. To my surprise, the ritual of offering has been totally revamped. We no longer go to the front casually to put our coins into the plastic dish on the table; rather, Nina and Rodolfa pass from row to row collecting the money, as it is done in the Catholic Church, then kneel with their dishes in their hands on either side of the table in front of the altar until the prayer for the offerings is completed.

At the conclusion of the service, Barrera asks for the sick to come to the altar so they can be prayed over. But only the physically ill should come, he says. This injunction is also new. Only four men and two women answer the call, and the congregation prays for them in their seats. Barrera returns to kneel at the box against the wall, and only Epi stands next to them, saying a very long prayer in ordinary language, but with his hands trembling.

When I return to Reina's house, everyone is asleep. Instead of the candle, the kerosene lamp is burning low on the table, Reina has unfurled my hammock, spread my curtain that shields me from the family—or them from me—and the window is open. As I gaze into the starry night from my hammock, I hear no whining of the mosquitoes and no threatening whir of my nemeses, the cockroaches. I am wondering whether last year I suffered from an oversize paranoia with respect to the insect visitation of the Peninsula or whether this year my perception is blurred by romantic euphoria.

Because of my relative affluence, I have decided against my diet of mostly oatmeal and have asked Eus on the way home whether, for proper compensation, she would be willing to cook for me. I figure that if I have one well-cooked meal at noon, I can cope more easily with the vagaries of the local food supply. In the evenings, I can make do with *frances* and a soft drink, or even nothing. As she so often does, she surprises me with how much she has already observed about what foods I can safely eat. She knows that I cannot tolerate black beans, or even corn on the cob (perhaps because the shell of the kernels is too hard), and she picks up my problem that I seem to need more protein than she is used to having. Actually, it is as if I had never left; our relationship has that quality of endurance about it.

So the next morning I walk to her house. I find her edging a new half-slip with the eyelet embroidery I brought her. These half-slips are about six inches longer than the *ʔipil,* and with all the women sewing their own, there is a large variety of eyelet embroidery for sale at the local clothing store. In Columbus, I found only one rather skimpy product, but Eus maintains she liked it, finding it *pim* [finer] than the local merchandise. We do some Maya, mainly eliciting new vocabulary. It amazes me how completely male oriented my Chicago textbook is, despite the fact that occasionally the authors, two men, do bring field-recorded conversations with women. However, they are not about topics of interest to us. Most of the words concerning the home, the children, cooking, washing, sewing, giving birth, and nursing are missing. So are the names of flowers, plants, birds, all of the things that intimately shape the world of women. I wonder if the authors are even aware of this strong male bias. Most probably not. When we are doing some kinship terms, another curious observation comes to light. I ask about "my son," and she gives "*in hijo.*" "Why do you use the Spanish word here?" I want to know. She is a little embarrassed. "People don't use the Maya word because it is not nice." "What is it?" "*In wish.*" "*Wish*" means "urine" or "to urinate." So perhaps two older terms, one possibly signifying "my issue" and the other "urine," had collapsed into one. In a community of exclusively Maya speakers that would cause no problem, but with outsiders listening in, that was another matter. I had read about similar linguistic avoidances before, again in culture contact, as when Thai students came to the United States and no longer used certain Thai words that might sound obscene to English-speakers. But I had not seen any reference to Maya in that context.[2]

I am beginning to have an abominable headache, and Eus lets down a hammock and makes me rest while she fixes lunch. She brings me a *luuch* with water to drink. It is boiled, she says, *bei paala,* like you do it for children. Who cares? I am scared of amoebas. Clouds begin to boil up above the edge of the *albarrada,* and in heavy drops it starts to rain. Eus is happy. She tells how from January to May there was no rain at all. That was normal, of course; it was *la seca* [the dry period]. But it should have ended and the rains should have started at the end of May, around the feast day of San Isidro, who is responsible for the moisture. But here it is July, and still no rain. So there is no beef to buy; the cattle stay skinny, having nothing but dry pasture to graze on. Sometimes there would be a little sprinkle, *ump?e chan shtoosa,* but it would not amount to anything. This one is really the first good rain, and much too late.

I ask about various members of the congregation. She says that Don Fulgencio hardly ever comes to the temple any more. No services are being held in his *chan casita de oracion* either; some members of his family sleep there now. There has been a wedding—Enrico M. married one of the Chan girls. He is a recent convert. "He came to the services only to look for a girl. They know that our girls are virgins. That is why they come. Now he no longer attends church any more," is Eus's comment. Paula is pregnant again; the baby, her ninth, is due next month. Poor little Pedrito can move his arms and hands, but not his legs. He is paralyzed from the hips down. "When the new baby comes, what will become of him?" Eus muses. "He will be neglected for sure." Paula's husband works on the ranch; he has no money for seed and has only been able to clear a few *mecates* (1/25 of a hectare) for his own sowing.

"Did Hermano Barrera tell you that he sold your camera?" No, I have not had a chance to talk with him as yet, except for exchanging a brief greeting. Worried about his inability to make a living in Utzpak, I had given him a Polaroid camera before leaving last year. I thought that perhaps he could make some money for his growing family by taking pictures around here. After all, people always like to be photographed. He was enthusiastic about the idea. Men, he theorized, would probably rather pay for a picture of themselves than for an extra piece of meat. The agreement had been that he would eventually save enough from his earnings that he would be able to reimburse me for the camera. He then wrote that he had miscalculated the price for the prints, not charging enough to make a profit. He found that he would have to charge more for the prints than the people could afford. Should he send me the camera? I answered that he should keep it and give it to me when I returned. Actually, Eus says, he did not work very hard at the project. She saw him take pictures only at one baptism, and he took all sorts of shots, not merely of people. Then he needed money, so he sold the camera and bought a piglet. They were going to feed it, and when it got big, they were going to sell it and pay for the camera that way. However, his wife became ill. Her milk collected in her breasts, making them hard and painful. Dona Res, the *yerbera,* the herbal healer from across the street, treated her with a mixture of lime, lime juice, and fresh herbs, Eus did not know which herbs. The cure was successful, but Lucrecia was to eat good food, so they killed the piglet. Eus laughs, "So now they have neither camera nor piglet." I could imagine how the congregation enjoyed that story. "And Barrera brought an infant back to life. *Tu ciimi* [It had died]," she said. That was all she knew about that.

Nina joins our conversation at this point. "You heard about Hermano Antonio?" I nod. "*Pues,* I also had a vision of a demon." Encouraged by my interest, she tells how on June 14, 1970, the day before her baptism, she was resting in her hammock. "You know, the Devil is very keen on getting people before they are baptized." She saw a man as if behind a glass, in ordinary working clothes, barefoot, floating above the ground. His face was that of an ordinary person, but no one that she knew. "*Gloria a Dios,*" she greeted him. He answered in Maya saying, "*Ma diosu,* [Glory, but not to God], *ten, ten* [to me, to me]." This was how she knew that it was the Devil. So she said to herself, "In the name of God, I am going to see who that man is!" But when she opened her eyes, he was gone.

Not to be outdone, Eus also had a story to add. It had to do with the death of Don Vicente, one of the earliest of Oscar Hill's converts in Utzpak. Everybody remembered his death, which occurred in 1966, she said, because by the instructions he gave on his deathbed, he flouted the burial customs of the community:

He said there should be no food served after he died, for the dead do not eat. He cried, saying that he would die at 2 o'clock. The *hermanos* who were with him stopped praying at two, and he died. His Catholic daughter came to light candles for him, but his son Valentin, who was an *hermano,* put them out. She became so angry she did not come to the funeral. There was not even a wake for Don Vicente. The *hermanos* who were with him slept till morning.

I had heard the story of Don Vicente's death the year before, but now Eus adds a detail that is new to me. "The reason Don Vicente cried on his deathbed was that he was afraid that the Devil might come for him. He kept begging Hermano Felipe, who was the minister at the time, to stay with him and pray, for he was afraid of the Devil. People who are about to die are often afraid that the Devil might come for them."

"The Demon is all around," Nina asserts, warming to the topic. "Not even small children are spared." To my surprise, the familiar acting up that I had observed last year as a result of children being pushed out of their mother's lap because, I thought, of nursing a new sibling, was now also evidence being marshaled to demonstrate demonic presence. Alvio's younger son, Nina relates, kept crying in church. When they took the child home, he slept. It was obvious that the Devil possessed the body of the child. The same thing happened also with Barrera's older son. He threw himself on the ground, screaming, pawing the earth, even eating it. On their way home from Temax in the bus, he cried and would not stop, although there was absolutely nothing wrong with him. They prayed over him for an hour, then the child stopped crying and was fine. Isauro's younger child kept crying as soon as the service began. When Juanita took him home, there was nothing wrong, and the boy went to sleep. Next day, the same thing happened. In that case also, prayer helped, and the problem did not return.

"What you need to say in that case," Nina asserts, "is *Satanas, en el nombre de Jesucristo yo te reprendo* [Satan, in the name of the Lord, I banish you]."

The Devil will then leave the body of the child, the child will start sleeping, and all will be well. He may, however, come back. With Barrera's second son, for instance, it took seven months before the Devil finally gave up.

I remember, by the way, that Reina had no such possession theory about screaming infants. "*Es su genio* [It is their character]," she said. She used the same expression also about Santiago. When he insisted on annoying her, she shouted at him, "*Tu me cayes mal ahoy* [You are aggravating me today], *es tu genio indio* [it is your Indian character]," and then for greater emphasis, she repeated it in Maya, "*a maasewal genio.*"

When I get home that evening, there is greeting all around on our corner. All are accounted for: Raquel, the neighbor from across the street; Tomasita, the midwife; the lumberjack's wife; and even Dona Juanita from down the street come by. They all remark about my new dress, *color de pavo* [peacock blue]. I don't understand why that is important until Reina tells that two nights before I arrived she dreamt that I wore a dress of exactly that color. Reina has also heard about the resurrection of the infant. "A real miracle," she nods.

As I settle in, I understand that I have been subject neither to undue paranoia nor uncalled-for euphoria. I have simply never experienced a dry Yucatan. With yesterday's rain, things are back to normal again. My clothes are soggy—Santiago's roof is a sieve on my side—and we have to explore each corner in turn to discover which one is the driest for my baggage. That night the cockroaches flutter their heavy wings, and the mosquitoes find a way to get at my delicious blood through the mesh of my hammock. "You must understand," Eus teased in the afternoon, making a *chʔuup, chʔuup* noise with her lips, "they are tired of brown, and don't get white very often."

Before the evening service, Lucrecia comes by with her older son to introduce herself. She is a slender young woman with a regular, mobile face, quick and nervous movements, clearly very intelligent. The child has open sores on his nose, lips, cheeks, forehead, and arm. I found last year that my broad-spectrum antibiotic ointment cured these sores, so I give Lucrecia a tube of it and tell her how to use it. She is also from Campeche, just like Barrera, but at home they spoke only Maya. Spanish is her second language. As I have the opportunity to hear many times later, her glossolalia is identical to that of Barrera's, although Barrera knows no Maya, supporting my contention that the glossolalia is independent of a person's mother tongue.

The evening service of July 4, 1970, is sponsored by Los Juveniles, the young people, three girls and four boys, another surprising innovation. Rosa, Paula's daughter, who has blossomed into a teenager, opens the service. The temple seems crowded; I count fourteen men and an equal number of women. The picture bears out what I had already heard from Eus, that many more people had been baptized. "He baptizes them in a hurry," Eus complains, "only to fill the church. I listened to the gospel for a long time before I ever thought about baptism. And those girls, they kneel down and already they speak in tongues. *Nada mas asi lo hacen* [Maybe they are pretending]. That is what I believe." When I press her on this matter, she makes an interesting observation. A familiar experience of many subjects learning glossolalia, as I mentioned before, is the fact that initially they enter only into the trance proper; that is, they experience the neurophysiological changes; they feel hot, there is a sensation of floating or pressure on the rib cage. The speech behavior is then added later, it "floats," as it were, on the physical change. Eus now maintains that if this happens, that is, if the girls report that they feel hot and feel something "supernatural" without also speaking in tongues, that means that Satan is trying to enter their body. That is, there is an immediate danger of demonic possession. Of course there is also the opposite case. Eus says, "Once a boy came to the service, Reinaldo C. In that service, he immediately began speaking in tongues. Then he never came back. How can that be the Holy Spirit? It has to be Satan."

I think her disparaging remark about the girls refers to four *hermanas,* 14 to 16 years old, whom Nina has told me about. They learned speaking in tongues shortly after having been baptized, one on August 31, 1969, two on September 7, 1969, and one on October 3, 1969. Eus remembered the dates of those baptisms. As I had occasion to observe later, these girls were also making a practice of a delayed return from the trance, joining Lucrecia and Juanita. It interfered with the structure of the service (which Eus of course immediately picked up), by which previously the various parts—testimony time, singing, sermons, and prayers—had been strictly separated.

Barrera's Ambitions and the Second Coming

After the service, while I sit on a chair in front of the podium, I have an extensive conversation with Barrera. Eus, who has slept through most of the service, has long ago left with Nohoch Felix. I have brought Barrera two packs of Polaroid film, and I am mildly curious about how he is going to wiggle out of the matter. As I expect, there is no mention of the piglet. Instead, he says that the camera is in Chetumal and repeats the problem with the price of the prints. What does he owe me for the camera and film packs? I tell him, nothing, instead he can pray for me when he is so inclined. He remains in perfect control. "*Dios le paga* [May God pay you]."

We go on to a variety of topics, skipping here and there. Antonio's wife is a prostitute, he contends, and the Holy Spirit told Antonio to leave her if she did not mend her ways. She was instructed about the Holy Spirit and five times she was prepared to be baptized, but she never went through with it. Recently, she decided to accompany Antonio on his missionary work anyway.

Life is so poor in Utzpak that evangelists sent from the outside are never able to make it. They would rather go to the towns. He, too, would like to return to Campeche: "*Me empuja ese deseo* [I am prompted by this desire]." He likes Utzpak, but his yearning for Campeche is getting overwhelming. After all, Isauro can take over here, or Chan Felix. Even though the congregation is larger now, the offerings are still not enough to pay expenses. It is hard to fast on Sundays if there is so little to eat on weekdays. "*Pero, que vamos hacer,*" he sighs [What can we do]? *Si morimos, por Cristo morimos* [We die for Christ]."

He turns to Antonio's visions. It is clear that the Second Coming is close at hand; that is why Antonio is given those visions. The Holy Spirit is also manifesting itself increasingly in other ways. Besides Antonio having the gift of revelations, Don Victor of Chetumal has the gift of prophecy, and Epi has the gift of healing. The way that is manifested is that Epi has this overwhelming urge continually to pray for the healing of the sick.

What seems clear to me from our conversation is that Barrera is apparently using Antonio's visions as a springboard for his own dreams of a conquest of sorts of Yucatan. "The whole Peninsula should be evangelized!" he says. He even has concrete ideas of how to accomplish that. Money is no object; God will provide. The Holy Spirit has told Antonio that the *hermanos* should go out and evangelize, so what he is planning is that five men from the present congregation should fan out over the Peninsula, doing just that. "We must concentrate on the capitals of the Peninsula," he intones enthusiastically. Some will go to Campeche; they can earn money by washing cars, repairing shoes, or working in a *taconeria* [making tacos]. The men from here are satisfied to work just a little, only enough to have something to eat, and then they could use the rest of their time to evangelize. "Imagine, Hermana," he exclaims, "there are 700,000 people in Campeche. What prospects!" Things are difficult in Merida, though; they can probably not go there because the congregation consists mostly of women, "and thus there are problems."

Here in Utzpak, he and the other *hermanos* visit almost every house to invite people to the services. Some come, others do not; it is up to God. He gives the impression that the growth of the congregation during the time I was gone is due solely to their evangelizing effort. However, judging from what I found last year, I am convinced that there is also another contributing factor, one that Barrera as an urbanite does not recognize, and that is the role that kin relationships play in the recruiting efforts. With the help of Eus and Nina, I later compile a list of newly baptized members, noting who is related to whom, and find that out of twenty-four, only two are not members of the three extended families that I have identified the year before. I recall that Robert Redfield, in his much-quoted work about the folk culture of Yucatan (1941), maintained that the Maya had a very limited kinship range. Maybe he did not look in the right direction.

The following afternoon, I go over to the church with my tape-recorder. I want to record Barrera's version of the details of Antonio's visions. When I arrive, he is talking with a man who has apparently been brought by one of the new members of the congregation and who is sitting by, listening. The man is quizzing Barrera about healing with the help of the Holy Spirit, and Barrera tells him that just a month ago, a mother came to him with her infant who had bronchitis, and nothing would help. She brought the child to him as the last resort because the physician concluded that the little boy was dying. He held him in his arms and prayed for him for over an hour. It was astounding to see how the baby, rigid and cold when first placed into his arms, became warm and started breathing normally as he was praying. *Gracias a Dios,* the baby continues well to this day. The visitor seems unconvinced. He proposes that there is a condition called cyanosis, in which a baby would also appear near death, but then the condition improves spontaneously and might not return. Barrera counters that in this case, God had worked his wonders, because bronchitis was different from cyanosis, and that the child had been very ill but had recovered as a result of his prayers and now continues in good health and that, indeed, the child had been quite dead. I found subsequently that everyone knew the story, and the resuscitated baby was pointed out to me repeatedly as "the infant that Hermano Barrera brought back to life."[3]

After the visitors leave, I ask Barrera about Antonio's visions. Barrera gets out a formal statement, which he has written on the basis of what Antonio told him, containing some fascinating details. It seems that in early May, Antonio told the *hermanos* that he did not know what was happening to him, but unless he prayed ten or maybe eight times a day, he did not feel well. These prayers concerned "the conversion of his family," that is, his wife.

Suddenly, during a prayer for the sick in a private home, God took his head away, that is, he could not feel his head for several minutes, although he touched, pressed, and stroked it. He thought this strange, stopped praying, and went outside. About 20 meters from the house, he fell down, as if pushed, in a dead faint. From then on, he felt that evil forces were pursuing him. A few days later he was in his home, and about 4 o'clock in the morning he woke up and, with his eyes wide open, saw demons surrounding him, trying to destroy him. He started off for the church, but two corners away from home, he fell down in another faint, flecks of foam coming from his mouth. His family fetched Barrera, who came with several *hermanos* and started praying for him. After several hours, Antonio was freed of this sickness and asked for continued prayers, since he had to suffer in this manner because God wanted to give him something very precious.

On the following Sunday, May 17, 1970, Antonio fasted, as was the custom in the church, and after several periods of prayer in the temple, he got up and said in a loud voice, "Hermanos, be watchful, for it is important that we prepare ourselves." He then told about the vision he just had, where God showed him several candles as if in the process of being extinguished, and a voice (that of the Holy Spirit) told him that this was the condition of the Apostolic Church. It was urgent that the *hermanos* go out and evangelize, for Christ's coming was close at hand.

After that, every time he prayed, God gave him this warning. What was he waiting for? Why had he not left yet to go and preach to the people?

On June 3, 1970, there was a meeting of pastors and their aides in Villahermosa, Tabasco, and at that meeting God gave Antonio a miraculous gift, that of "distinguishing the souls." The bishop of the Southeastern District of the Apostolic Church was present, and he showed to the *hermanos* in the Bible that such a gift of the Holy Spirit was indeed mentioned there (I Corinthians 12:10). This meant that Antonio saw on the forehead of truly believing *hermanos* a brilliantly glowing shield, the faces of other *hermanos* appeared natural, and still others had frighteningly black foreheads. Later, in various Catholic churches in Merida, where Antonio accompanied him to distribute Apostolic leaflets, Antonio saw the priests appearing in diabolical shapes or having the head of a devil. When he had such a vision, he felt that something exceedingly hot entered him, he began shivering and trembling, his heart started beating at an enormous rate, and perspiration poured from his body. Afterward, it appeared as if nothing at all had happened to him, except that he was very thirsty.

The Apostolic Church authorities sent Antonio to evangelize in San Antonio Sacachchen, which was the only community available at the time. From there he was to go on to Calkini. However, he once more quarreled with his wife about her lovers and therefore, before moving to Calkini, on June 20, he came with his family to consult with Barrera in Utzpak. His family spent the night in the *casa pastoral,* and he and Barrera hung their hammocks in the church. At about 3 o'clock in the morning he woke up Barrera because he felt a terrifying force surrounding him. He maintained that this force came because he had not been sleeping. Rather, he had gone out to relieve himself and after coming back, he had lain awake. Then he saw a vision. God showed him a ribbon with a woman on it, also a blank ribbon, and a pair of scissors. Barrera later helped him interpret the vision as meaning that there were two ways in which God was going to have the *hermanos* work for the Church. One was the material plane, but that contained the trap of the woman, that is, of adultery, which was a mortal sin. The other ribbon represented the spiritual plane, such as preaching, evangelizing, which brought no material rewards. The scissors could be used to cut off either ribbon.

A Sunday Service

The following day, July 5, 1970, is my first Sunday in Utzpak since I got back. Service is announced for 6:30 A.M., and Barrera and Isauro are wearing black ties with their white shirts, very dignified. The *matutin* starts out with five men and only two women, and later the number of the men increases to eight. Barrera's first sermon seems clearly directed toward the men he is hoping to send out to evangelize. They do not need any *sabiduria* [sophisticated knowledge]; all they require is an earnestness to seek the things of God. After all, the Apostles were humble men, and they received the ministry as a gift from God. They would also be awarded other gifts of the Holy Spirit. There is an *hermano* in Tizimin; he is extremely humble, he hardly has enough clothes to cover himself, and he walks barefoot. But he has the miraculous gift of healing. One day a man was bitten by a *cuatro narices* [a very poisonous snake], and his foot became enormously swollen. Then this *hermano* prayed over him, and he was cured.

Barrera then announces that there will be a whole hour of prayer for the Holy Spirit, with the express purpose of asking for the gift of evangelizing. In praying, they should say that even if they are *necio* [dim-witted], the Holy Spirit should still award them this particular gift. Barrera is so agitated he can hardly contain himself, and instead of having perfect control over his glossolalia, as he had last year, he lapses into it before he even kneels down. Yet while in 1969 his utterances had been so fast that I could hardly transcribe them, and his episodes were lengthy and frequent, his utterances now are slower and occur less often.

While the adults are praying, Barrera's eldest son, Luisito, barely 3, intones his own little singsong, his bright child's voice chiming audibly above the din: "*Me pega mi mama, me pega mi papa, es borracho mi papa* [My mother beats me, my father beats me . . . my father is drunk]." I do not imagine that his ditty is true—he is probably just trying to get their attention—but Eus and I look at each other in shared amusement. However, perhaps this is the sort of behavior that Nina has classed as demonically inspired.

Finally there is a pause, fully two hours later. The ranks of the women have increased to seven. While everyone relaxes, Isauro's wife Juanita starts reading aloud from a devotional pamphlet. I have brought prints of some of the pictures I took last year and Eus competently takes over distributing them, which is a bit complicated because most of them show several people on the same print and everyone is to receive one.

During the subsequent prayer for the Holy Spirit, Barrera follows the same strategy as last year, with those already speaking in tongues kneeling behind those seeking the manifestation. Two teenagers, a boy and a girl called Anita and Mariano, a trim young peasant who is new to me, are among the supplicants. When Barrera sounds the bell, Gregoria continues speaking in tongues, and Anita pays no attention either. She is rocking on her knees, her body bowed low, sobbing and vocalizing, on and on, even after the second bell signal. Eus whispers that Anita is one of Old Candil's daughters; she is married and she is desperate because she still has no child. I imagine that in her case she is perhaps still inexperienced in speaking in tongues and for this reason she has not picked up on the signal of the bell, but how come Gregoria does not either? She had no problems with that last year. And how about the teenagers? I do not realize until later that the women's odd behavior is a harbinger of the general ritual disintegration that is about to take place. There is no questioning, either, of those who had spoken in tongues, as had been Barrera's custom last year.

During Sunday school, Barrera takes his topic from a pamphlet distributed by the church administration. This is "The Day of the Pastor." The pastor is the friend of everyone in the congregation. Everyone can come to him for advice. A woman might think that she does not want to ask the pastor for advice because he is a man. But she should think of him rather as a brother and a helper. After all, she should remember that the pastor thinks least of *estas suciedades* [those filthy things] such as sex.

He then continues with another sore topic, also treated in the pamphlet, namely that the congregation has the obligation of supporting the pastor in a manner befitting his station. He becomes very agitated at that point. Everyone is getting extremely tired, but, as if he wants to take revenge on the congregation for not supporting him properly, he makes us stand through an exceptionally long reading of a biblical text, which is not usually done. It is getting hot, and we are all perspiring and swaying on our feet, but he commands, "Don't sit down!" then continues scathingly, "We already have rheumatism, it won't go away from sitting, so we might as well stand for the glory of God." Outside, the giant frogs are still serenading riotously, and I get through all that standing by watching one of their young offspring try to climb the wall behind the altar. The boys, the 3- and 4-year-olds, are as intrigued with the frog's antics as I am, pleased that it finally makes it up to two feet on the wall and then disappears into a crack, while the little girls do not pay any attention at all to the baby frog's doings.

In the afternoon, there are meetings of the *secciones,* the three church organizations, and the evening service is well attended; there are sixteen women and twelve men and, of course, a host of children. During the offering of the individual hymns, Barrera and Isauro present one together. Barrera is obviously grooming Isauro to assume his place once he is allowed by the Church authorities to return to Campeche, which he apparently so desperately wants.

Later during the service, Isauro takes over. He speaks about the heavy load the pastor has to bear as the spiritual guide of the congregation, about Barrera's merits, and that the *secciones* want to express their appreciation to him. Then the representative of each group—Nohoch Felix for the Senores Cristianos, Gregoria for the Dorcas, and a boy called Win for the Juveniles—each hand Barrera a gift. The gifts are wrapped in U.S. fashion, tissue paper and red ribbons with bows. Barrera accepts the packages unsmilingly. Eus says under her breath that the presents are pants, a shirt, and shoes. She knows because Nina has done the shopping in Temax. Eus is not pleased; they spent the offerings for these gifts, when the church has so many other more urgent needs. Even the electric bill has been allowed to accumulate. Such things were not done when Chan Felix was pastor here. She is convinced that the church will never prosper that way.

A Trip to Merida

The following Monday, Eus and I go to Merida. I have discovered that Eus needs glasses—she has great difficulty sewing without them—so I make an appointment for her for late afternoon that day with the ophthalmologist who three years ago operated on her left eye for a cataract. I need a movie light (my expensive one refuses to function) and also a Super 8 projector, which Licha has not been able to find. There are other items, too; sandals for Dona Raquel and especially a *pavellon,* a mosquito net, for me. The last one is Eus's suggestion. When the topic first came up, I described to her what I had seen in the movies, gossamer fabric hanging in rich folds from the ceiling and enveloping a pair in a passionate embrace, *tu meecoob,* on a bed with deep, luxurious pillows. We laughed about the scene until we both had tears in our eyes. She assures me the Yucatecan *pavellon* is quite different, something like a very thin fabric box supported by two slender rods or sticks and tied to the *munecas* [dolls, reinforced loops or ends of the hammock].

In Merida, we are hit by a tremendous downpour, and soon wade in knee-high water because the sewers overflow, being obviously too small to accommodate such huge quantities of rain. As always when we go to Merida, we stop at Peregrina's house first and to our surprise encounter Barrera. It seemed that he had an urgent phone call from Antonio to say that his wife was sick. She is pregnant again and recently they had to walk more than 12 kilometers, and now she is having some pain.

After getting Eus's glasses, we go to spend the night at her brother's house. The mosquitoes are not as fierce there as in the center of town with its dense population and open patios, but our pleasure is diminished by the old couple, who share the room with us, snoring all through the night. I never expected that such very small people could snore so ferociously. It was useful, though, that we went there, because one of Don Agapito's sons was in Los Angeles and had left his typewriter at home, which I was allowed to rent. Don Agapito resembled his sister, slender and relatively tall, about five feet. He and I have fun playing around with words; he is quite knowledgeable about both Maya and Spanish. He can tell which Maya words seem modern, which other words come from classical times, and which are Spanish loan words. Eus's sister-in-law, Dona Sylvia, is so small she could conceivably walk under my outstretched arm. In Utzpak, there are many representatives of this bloodline, and when such a *chaparrita* [small one], as Eus calls them, goes to the mill to have her soaked corn ground for *masa,* they have to put a chair for her next to the *masa* container so she can reach it. The men of the same bloodline are not much taller, and they do not seem to have any neck at all. One of the drivers of the Utzpak bus is one of them, and he has the hardest time reaching the pedals. Dona Sylvia is quite heavy, though, and a real trader, very sharp; she knows the price of everything and how much profit one can expect with each item. I had seen her only once last year, and at that time she acted aloof and distant. But since then, the ointment I sent, upon Eus's request, had cured an eczema on her daughter's knee. We have an animated conversation in the kitchen, all about her youngest son, who was so heavy when she gave birth to him that he almost killed her at delivery and who was very good in school; and about her daughter, who was sewing in Los Angeles. They are not paying her very much because she is doing it illegally, but it is still more than she could make in Merida. All the while she is preparing the chicken Eus contributed and is making the tortillas from corn she had brought in from Tibolom, their home village. Those tortillas had a most delicious, flower-like fragrance, which wafted from one end to the other of the two-room house. She is wearing gold-colored earrings, the traditional half-moon design, and a gold necklace with a pendant of the Virgin Mary on it—not the Virgin of Guadalupe, but the one "of the roses" —and in the bedroom there is a low table with statues of saints and a votive candle burning in front of them, but she does not seem to have any problem with Eus not being a Catholic. Before we leave the next morning, she asks if she can borrow a few hundred pesos from me. Her daughter was going to send her some money from Los Angeles but had to pay several other bills first. She needs to buy the merchandise people had ordered and which she wants to deliver in Tibolom. Of course I oblige, and the upshot of it is that we are all going to go to Tibolom together, Eus to visit her two daughters who live there, and Nina and I just for the ride. We will take the bus, then change to a small truck that makes regular runs to the village, and for the way back, we will rent some horses. Seeing my less-than-enthusiastic reaction to the latter plan, Dona Sylvia assures me that she knows of a very tame and gentle horse for me.

The rest of our shopping is also successful; I even find a *luuch* [half-gourd] in the market that I want to use for splashing myself when bathing, as Eus does. Reina has given me a powdered-milk can for the purpose, but I am a purist. Besides, the can has sharp edges. The renting of the projector, however, turns out to be extremely difficult. We walk up and down countless narrow cobble-stone streets, where only our superior intelligence and remarkable agility save us from being killed by the fast-moving traffic. Searching for the projector takes the often-encountered pattern of "he does not have one, but heard from a cousin . . . who knows a man . . . who has a friend . . . who has a son. . . . who might be inclined. . . ." I finally locate a store owner who is willing to let me have his small projector if I pay the entire price, of which he will refund a portion if and when I return it. We do not find a *pavellon*. I am later able to buy it locally at Dona Bartola's, and Eus and Raquel from across the street break some straight branches off one of Raquel's trees and mount it for me. I have been getting severe headaches from lack of sleep. I am afraid that I might not wake up if something alien and horrible drops into my hammock. The first night in my cheesecloth box and out of reach of all the creepy-crawlies is delicious beyond compare.

The only thing that aggravates me in Merida is the condescending attitude of the clerks toward Eus. It is not the polite "*usted*" and "*senora*," the way the city women, myself included, are addressed, but rather the familiar and in this context actually insulting "*tu*," and "*mamita*," as though they are not sure whether she has the money to buy the items she wants, such as plastic shoes for herself and a pair of panties. The matter doesn't upset Eus, though; she reacts with a stony neutrality, which seems to come on automatically.

We Women Together

A few days later, I am working on a Maya lesson with Eus when Santiago comes through the gate hole of the *albarrada*, all dressed up in dark pants and white shirt. I overhear conversation between him and Reina; he is tired of local trading and wants to do something else, maybe get cheap merchandise in Chetumal and sell it high in Utzpak. What he has been doing is to buy a sack of corn and then sell it in small quantities to the householders. But last year's harvest was poor, so instead of eating their own, people had to buy the corn for the daily tortillas. For that reason corn is more expensive this year than last, costing 4 pesos for the *almud* (a dry measure, 1.76 liters), and this year's harvest is not going to be available until much later. He even started selling corn on an installment plan, and still people owe him money. Reina keeps pointing out that at this rate, the money they have received from his father will soon be gone, and although they have bought a plot of land, there is no house on it yet. She keeps nagging Santiago to go to work on his father's ranch, or at least erect an *albarrada,* plant trees, blast for a well on their land. Santiago does not show much enthusiasm for any of these strenuous activities. Besides, he says, the price of corn is not his fault. But Reina threatens that if things do not change, she will go visit her mother in Temax; she will stay away for a week, a month, and maybe she will never come back. Santiago has his counterproposal ready. In the free harbor of Chetumal, everything is cheap. He will buy merchandise such as fly poison, blouses and shirts, cuts of material for pants, and cheese, and then sell it for much more money in Utzpak. So this morning in Eus's yard, after the customary pleasantries, he comes to the purpose of his visit: a number of his customers did not pay him. But he needs to go to Chetumal today to buy, so could I perhaps help him out with 200 pesos? I oblige, and he leaves with uncharacteristic haste.

A few minutes later Reina arrives with a whole retinue. Baby Cilia on her arm, Lupita at her hand, and Raquel's son and daughter. She sits down on a chair Eus brings out and fans herself furiously, pretending to be awfully hot, but it is quite obvious that she has been crying. She is going to visit her mother in Temax, she says, and would I feed her hens and turkeys for her? We chat for a little while, both Eus and I strenuously avoiding any questions. Fifteen minutes before the bus is scheduled to stop at Eus's corner, she leaves. Ten seconds later Raquel's boy comes running back. Could I lend Reina 20 pesos? She is going to sell one of her turkeys next week, then she will pay me back. So I dive for my pocketbook once more. Actually, I am glad that Reina can go and visit her mother. Even when Santiago is not away on business, her evenings are lonely. She sits in her hammock, plays with Lupita, and nurses or cleans the baby while Santiago is out somewhere drinking beer with his friends, *en la calle* [having fun in the street].

But I am now left with the problem of who is going to sleep in the house with me, it not being proper to be alone at night. Eus suggests that I ask Lucrecia, since Barrera is still in Merida, but Lucrecia has already made other plans. Usually, she would ask one of the young girls in the congregation to stay with her, but this time she is going to spend the night with Hermana Teresa, a young woman who has recently joined the congregation. What is she afraid of? Men, she admits. I finally ask old Tomasita, the midwife. She is a widow, living with her single, middle-aged son, and she says she will come.

Since there is no electricity in Reina's house, I go to the temple in the afternoon to try out the projector I have brought from Merida. It is a miserable little contraption, but it is all there was. I have to cut my expensive film in half because the motor of the projector is too weak to transport a full reel. The news about my plan to try the film has spread, so I have lots of company in addition to Eus. There is Lucrecia, and Isauro's wife Juanita, and a number of teenage girls, very much "us women" company. Eus brings a sheet, and with everybody's help we spread it between two rafters. I project a few scenes against it, with everyone laughing and shouting as they recognize those that appear, although they are somewhat distorted due to the circumstances.

And then, of course, there is the gossip. Have I seen Don Eduardo's wife yet? They say that her first husband died, her second one left her because she was lazy. All she ever wants to do is to eat and spend lots of money on medicines. Him marrying a Catholic! Now he no longer comes to the services anymore because of her. Of course, that means that he is lost; he gave up all chances for his salvation. He is ashamed, didn't you see that when the *hermanos* passed by his house to go to the service, his double, tall house door was locked? And he always turns his radio on loudly when there is a service. And he quarrels with the *hermanos* about the *albarrada.* Now he no longer talks to anyone. Barrera did the right thing to read him out of the congregation: once an *hermano,* now an *hermano* no longer, that was how he put it! Eus, a longtime friend of the old man, does not think that was right. "I wonder if Barrera has the authority to do that?" she says. The Catholics are just as strict, Lucrecia counters. Didn't she remember Jaber? How his mother asked him what he would do if he got sick and there was no one in the family to care for him? So he quit coming to the temple. "And Pedro," Juanita adds. "After he became baptized, he started praying before eating like we do, and his mother told him that there would be no food when he got done." "And so now he only takes his bath at home and sleeps there," Nina told, "and he eats where he can." "And Sundays he spends with us," Lucrecia says.

When we are alone, Eus tells me more details about the excommunication of Don Eduardo. It seems that Barrera was supposed to take a document about the church property that Don Eduardo had ceded to the congregation to be notarized in Merida and then come back with it. But Barrera did not bring it back, and Eus did not know what the complications were. So Don Eduardo called him *ladron* [rascal or thief], and Barrera formulated an answer in writing and read it to the congregation during a church service. He said nothing about all the good things Don Eduardo had done for the congregation, like years ago giving free land to the temple. Instead, he accused him of adultery and fornication, and then came that formula about Don Eduardo having been an *hermano*, but now was *hermano* no longer. Such an action had never been taken before. Had Don Eduardo been in church that day, it might have come to blows. He told Eus that if Barrera left he would come back, but not before. It is obvious that Eus strongly disapproves of all that has happened. If there is a conflict, she said, people will simply stop coming. That is what Don Eduardo has been doing. He has not been to the services for quite a while because he was courting Dona Andrea at the time, going to Temax on Saturday mornings and coming back Sunday evenings, and of course it was anybody's guess what he was doing in Temax overnight.

When later during this fieldwork season I was working through the baptismal records of the Church stored in Merida, I came across an entry that illustrated the points made by Eus. Gregorio D., popularly called Hermano Goyito in the Utzpak congregation, was reported as having "*salido de la iglesia por su voluntad protestando en contra de la doctrina y criticandola* [left the Church voluntarily, rejecting the doctrine and criticizing it]." I had talked with Goyito in 1969, and he told me that he had had a quarrel with Oscar Hill about the latter's arbitrary use of the funds of the congregation and that he certainly did not renounce his membership, but rather Oscar Hill tried to kick him out. The congregation never took cognizance of Goyito's expulsion, and when Oscar Hill left the scene, Goyito returned to the temple. And at a service in Merida, I heard Luis L. ask for a special offering for him because he was in a Merida hospital recovering from an operation.

There is no evening service, so Tomasita and I are able to hit the hammocks right after sundown. It is still pretty early, so we have a fine conversation. It is such a pleasure to swing gently in the hammock and just talk. Tomasita is past 70. She delivered Reina's second baby, charging only 20 pesos because Reina had so little money. Actually, the local charge was 40 pesos for girls and 50 pesos for boys. Soon, Reina came in for a bit of raking over the coals. It did not mean that you accepted Jesus if you merely sang hymns while you worked like Reina did. Reina and Santiago did not believe in God. They had taken Lupita to be baptized in the Catholic Church to please Reina's mother. They would surely do the same thing with little Cilia. They kept saying that they were *apostolicos*, but they never attended any church services. By contrast, she had been a Presbyterian for the past thirty-five years, and the church down the street was like home. She hardly ever missed any services. When she sang a lovely hymn, she was not just parroting it like Reina. Her heart would fill with a great joy, and she felt wide and happy. When she was a young mother, she would put her little girls to bed, Raquel and her sister Lupe, and then she would teach them to sing hymns.

After using the chamber pot, Tomasita returns to the subject of Reina. They would surely go through with the *hetsmec* of Cilia with me as the *madrona* because that meant a gift a money, although Cilia was still too young for the ritual. She was going to be only two months old at the end of July. What exactly is this *hetsmec*? I ask, for Reina has not mentioned it again. It is actually "*hets-meek*," to hug a child (*meek*) straddled on your hip. It is supposed to assure that the child's legs will grow straight. Then some object is placed in the child's hands, such as perhaps a piece of cloth with a needle and thread in it if it is a girl, which will mean that she will grow up to enjoy sewing or embroidering.

The next morning, Raquel comes to check if I have fed the chickens and the turkeys. Then she gets the *candela* [the kitchen fire] going and shows me how to prepare a soft-boiled egg, Yucatecan style. You put the egg into a tin can, pour boiling water on it and wait a little while. You take it out and knock a small hole into it on the rough limestone wall and drink it, sucking it through the hole. Had I heard that Barrera had problems with the municipal authorities? No, not really. What problems? It seems that Dona Juanita, who lived on the other side of the temple, went to the *presidente*, the magistrate, and complained about the noise the services were making. The *presidente* warned Barrera to hold services earlier so as not to cause any disturbance.

"*Mira no mas* [Well, what do you know]," Raquel says suddenly. "Here comes Don Eduardo's *gorda* [his fat one]." Then she introduces her as Dona Andrea. Dona Andrea is indeed fat, wobbly, and endowed with a tremendous belly, but with a pleasant face. She gets right to the point with a number of rapid-fire questions. Where is Reina? In Temax. Who is taking care of the poultry? I am. Did Santiago order Reina to go visit her mother in Temax? I don't know. How long is she going to stay? I don't know. Did Santiago go to Chetumal? He did. She stops to catch her breath, perhaps satisfied with the results of the interrogation, then complains about her rheumatism and asks if I have any American medicine against that. I give her some aspirin and tell her that it is now also available in Merida in the large pharmacies. We part as friends, and she invites me to come and visit her when I have the time.

So this is the woman for whose sake Don Eduardo left the church? And the gossip about him was right, he really did act like a person banished. He no longer talked to me either, although before we had long conversations, about what marriage was like in other places and whether men have the right to several wives. He laughed uproariously when I mentioned that in some villages in Mexico, the men married sisters because that way there was no jealousy about the man. "*Tu haahil, hermana?* [Really?]" But when I saw him by the well in the yard the other morning, he laughed and answered with "*Amen*" when I said, "*Paz de Cristo,*" but that was all.

When I pass his house on my way to the grocery store later in the afternoon, Dona Andrea waves for me to come in and sit for a while. "Where is Don Eduardo?" I ask. "*Esta de purga*" is her excuse; he has taken a laxative to rid himself of intestinal parasites, so he cannot socialize.

I do not want to leave the chickens and the turkeys alone too long, so the next day, Eus comes by to see how I am doing. She has gotten news from Chan Felix. Things are not going well on the island of Cozumel. In fact, there had been five other *hermanos* there before he had arrived to try to start a congregation, and they had all failed and returned to the Peninsula. He has not been able to hold a real service there yet, either. Prices are terribly high. He does not think that he wants to stay. Maybe it is because there are so many tourists there. In other places, when Chan Felix would run out of money, he would go to the *monte* and cut some firewood for sale. But you cannot do that on Cozumel. He sent word that maybe he would go to Bacalar. The minister there is a mason; he would like to learn that trade. "As a minister, you cannot work on a ranch, where you have to stay away all week. The minister has to hold four services during the week." And the offerings were never enough to support a family. After all, Chan Felix was not like Juan L., who went from congregation to congregation preaching and then taking up a collection in each one under the pretext of "for Hermano Juan's trip," "pressing out the people and pocketing the money."

"Barrera says that when he goes back to Campeche, Chan Felix might take over for him." Eus does not think so. When Chan Felix was pastor in Utzpak, he was not popular. "I hear people say that if Chan Felix came back, they would stop coming to the services. Maybe people don't want a minister from their own village." Valentin was not popular in Temax, his hometown, either, and his congregation remained small. They had a plot for a temple, but there was no money to build a temple on it. They had only gotten as far as the foundations. "So what will happen when Barrera goes back to Campeche?" Eus does not think that will happen anytime soon. Barrera has friends in Campeche who keep telling him that he should come back, that there is work to be had, and he would like to go and evangelize there. But the church administration will not let him go because the congregation is growing here and is producing an income. "Barrera said that Isauro was another one who might take over for him." Eus does not think much of that either. "People are already gossiping about him, saying that he was baptized only a year ago, and now he is already preaching. That is presumptuous, they say."

As we are waiting for the evening service to begin, I start filming the crawling babies. I was surprised to see that other babies crawl the same way Lupita did. They fold one of their legs, either the right or the left, under their buttocks, and then heave themselves forward by slapping the ground rhythmically, right, left, right left. Perhaps it is because of being raised in a hammock that this pattern got established. None of them go on all fours as mine did. And although none of them can walk yet, they squat securely, suspending their little bodies in perfect balance between their legs.

With Barrera still absent, Isauro is in charge of the subsequent service, and his brother opens it. Attendance is high; eight men and nine women. During the altar call, Isauro's wife, Juanita, goes into glossolalia, then does not obey the bell signal but continues trembling, shaking, and sobbing and speaking in tongues way into the next hymn. So here is still another woman not following the accepted pattern. Is it in defiance of Barrera? Her recovery, though, when it comes, is as before. She lapses into ordinary speech, collects her 1-year-old, who has crawled close to the podium, and calmly goes back to her seat. Her face shows no trace of weeping, not even her eyes.

Barrera had given me a list of all those who have received the Holy Spirit since I had left. To my great surprise, Eus was among them. When I asked her about it, she said that last October she had not been well. She had fasted and was feeling so weak that in church she had stayed on her chair rather than kneeling. She had prayed and suddenly she was even more tired, and yet at the same time she was strong enough to go up to the altar, kneel down, and pray. Barrera declared that she had spoken in tongues, and that this was the way people felt afterward. She attached no great importance to the matter. She could remember nothing, but Barrera said that it happened, so it had to be true. Something that needed to be accomplished had been accomplished, that was all.

There is no service on the evening of July 10, 1970, and I want to retire early, but Eus, that slave driver, comes with Nina. They argue that there are three members of the congregation who have electric light, Paula, Mariano, and Valuch. Let's go and do some filming. So we do. At Paula's house, we see Pedrito. He seems to be paralyzed except for his left arm. When he reaches out to shake hands with me, his limp little fingers feel hot. He seems to be immersed in perpetual fever, and the medicine the family bought did not help.

I am always impressed with Mariano and his wife, whom we visit next. They are exquisitely neat personally; so are their two little girls in their beautiful ?ipiles. Their house matches their appearance. It is the traditional mud-and-wattle structure, but instead of the staves merely being placed vertically into the limestone foundation, theirs are reinforced by a handsome horizontal weave. Their corn bin, yard, and household objects are all in perfect order. "They like to work," Eus says approvingly. The oval house is small inside and crowded with visiting *hermanos*, so filming is difficult, but it is appreciated anyway.

By the time we leave, it is much too dark, and so we do not make it to Valuch's house, which at any rate was much too far, at the edge of the village in the north. Besides, I want to be home when Tomasita comes to spend the night. However, she is not there yet when we arrive. So Eus and I go to Raquel's house, but no one answers our knock. Eus is sure that someone of the family will show up later, so she leaves. I am ready for my hammock when Tomasito appears with her grandson San, a friendly 12-year-old. San will sleep in the house with me; she cannot come because they have just had a death in the family. One of her sons had taken his wife to Merida to give birth in a clinic. She was delivered of a little girl. They were on their way home three days later when in the bus the baby came down with a very high fever. Before they could make it to the clinic, the baby was dead, having turned quite blue. The physician said that he could not account for the death of the infant. "There is a bird," Eus explains later, "it is larger than a buzzard, and when it passes overhead, it causes evil things to happen, like the death of a small child."

The following day, I go to Eus's for a while, and when I return, Reina is back. Cilia has come down with diarrhea in Temax; she does not know what might have caused it. Her excrement has turned green, so the illness might have been caused by *mal ojo* [the evil eye]. She tried to cure it by washing the baby's hands and her fontanella with a decoction of aris and ruda, which was what you did in such cases, but it did not help. So she thought that perhaps the cause lay in *viento de agua* [water wind], which required the same treatment. However, little Cilia got worse, so eventually she took the baby to the local physician who prescribed a sulfa suspension and some drops, and that did make her better. We are still talking about it when Raquel comes to see Reina and the baby cries and produces another green stool. Raquel suggests that the drops and the suspension are probably intended to cure white diarrhea, not the green one. So we troop over to Dona Res, the *yerbera* across the street, and she gives Reina some herbs. She calls them *shpetetum*. She is to boil them in water, then bathe the child in the concoction, and while she is still moist, swaddle her and not dry her until an hour later. The baby emerges from the treatment swathed in the limp leaves of the herb, and no more diarrhea. But she immediately drops off to sleep again and can hardly be roused to nurse. That is worrisome, of course. When I look at the box in which the drops came, I find them to contain phenobarbital. Since the child seems to be all right, I suggest that Reina leave the drops out, and soon little Cilia is back to normal. So between the three of us, the physician, the *yerbera*, and "we women together," the baby got over her first diarrhea.

Visit to Temax

In the afternoon, we go to Temax to visit with Valentin's family. I want to invite them to see my film that evening and to take my presents for Valentin —a Bible in Spanish, the Acts in Maya (which was all I could find in Mexico City), and, as a special surprise, a box of high-quality water colors and a large pad of the right kind of paper. He asks what he can do for me in return. Almost thoughtlessly, I say that he could pray for me. It is a formula used extensively in such situations, also by the Catholics, and the answer is usually noncommittal, like Barrera's "*Dios le paga*" or the Maya "*Maalob tuun, Dios bootic tech* [Well then, may God pay you]." So I am startled when in response, Valentin calls the family to prayer, the women cover their heads, and there is a lengthy, very kind and sincere supplication for the well-being of myself and all my progeny.

Valentin and his mother-in-law Carolina then take us to see the start of the temple on their plot. Their roof is nearly completed, as is the foundation and a podium, all of limestone and cemented together with *sascab*, white earth, and not indented as in Utzpak, but straight across. The side walls are slightly curved, and the whole structure gives the impression of being a magnified and ennobled Maya house. There is something of a straightforward awe and reverence about the structure, such as one felt in the courtyard at classical Uxmal. Carolina picks some blooming branches from a bush in the yard of the church and hands the bunch to Valentin, who places it into the rafters above the altar. Nothing is said about it.

Eus wants to do some shopping for soap and coffee at the Temax Conasupo, a government-run store where prices are lower than in privately owned establishments. Utzpak has no Conasupo. Valentin has gone home, and so Carolina is not inhibited by his presence. She complains to Eus in great detail about their *compadre*, his father, who still will not be baptized. He gets drunk off and on, has his friends in the street, and has not yet married his wife legally.

As we approached the Conasupo, we see some burning cans being thrown out into the street. I think they are firecrackers, but much more astutely, Eus and Carolina know at a glance what is happening. "Look, the Canton is burning!" And indeed, several men are throwing gasoline cans out of the Canton, the store of El Chino (the Chinese merchant), obviously so that they will not explode. Soon a crowd of the curious gather around, all men; the church bells are tolling, but there is no police, no fire engine, only the three or four employees of El Chino's household working frantically to contain the flames. Nor is the reaction a result of El Chino being a stranger. He has married a Temax girl, and his son attended the University in Mexico City and is the local physician.

Still, no one helps. The employees begin throwing sand on the burning gasoline, lugging buckets of water from goodness knows what well, while the flames scoot up the walls, lick at the doors, and consume the merchandise on the shelves. All the while the crowd of men enjoy the spectacle from a safe distance, standing around or sitting on the benches of the plaza and calling out in general merriment that I should film them, not the fire. Eus is furious. In Maya and very loudly she scolds that it is a scandal that so many men are just standing around and doing absolutely nothing to help someone in need. Exasperated, she turns to Carolina. "If I were a man," she says, "I'd have everyone in a bucket brigade in no time." I do not doubt it. But the men simply shrug. A woman cannot command the men.

"There comes the owner," says Carolina. He looks like everyone else, dark pants, light shirt, a blue cap. Gesticulating angrily, he shouts at the lookers-on, telling them to go packing if they do not want to help and calling for his gun so he can shoot himself. The crowd merely withdraws a few steps and continues watching.

Since there is nothing we can do to help the poor shop owner, Eus begins paying attention to my filming. She starts pointing out the most dramatic angles and calls my attention to the roof, where the men are fighting a losing battle against the flames that are threatening to engulf it. A Pepsi-Cola truck turns into the plaza with merry band music playing over its loudspeaker. Suddenly the tune breaks, and a male voice, obviously aghast, calls out "*Maachis!*" the Maya euphemism for *Madre*, Mother of God, an often-used expletive.

Finally, the flames die down in the face of the truly heroic effort of the few firefighters. They actually succeed in preventing the fire from reaching the gasoline station in the same building, which would have caused a tremendous explosion. "*Otsil maac* [Poor man,]" I remark to Eus as we board the bus. "*Baash otsil maac?* [What poor man?]" she counters. "He has piles of money in the bank, many heads of cattle, and the local bar and the movie theater also belong to him. He will make up for his losses in no time." And indeed, back in Utzpak, there are already rumors circulating in the evening that for the film of the day, he charges double for the ticket and even demands payment for the children, who usually get in free.

In the bus, we bump into Barrera, also on his way home. He had stayed in Merida and did not go all the way to Calkini, from where Antonio had called him. It would have been too expensive, he charges. "About time he got home instead of spending money in Merida," Eus remarks under her breath. The intelligence on the corner has been that Lucrecia was out of cash for corn and beans as early as last Friday. He did not know how Antonio's wife was—he did not seem to care either—but he had heard that in Chetumal four more people had received the Holy Spirit and five had done so in Bacalar. Truly these were signs that the Second Coming was fast approaching. We heard later that Antonio's wife had a miscarriage in Calkini.

Showing of the Film

All of Valentin's family arrive from Temax on time for the evening service and the showing of the film. They bring a beautiful big rooster for me. They had wanted to invite me to eat, but they did not know how I prepared the meat, so they thought they would leave it to me. The fowl is a big sacrifice and I feel terrible about it, but a gift has to be reciprocated or all honor will be lost.

Valentin's son, whom I had seen as a tiny newborn last year, is now a handsome little boy. When the family hears about my interest in infants crawling, they suggest that we go to the church before the beginning of the service so I can film him. So we all walk over and Valentin coaxes his son into a beautiful long crawl across the smooth cement church floor.

The service is sponsored by Los Juveniles. In his sermon, Barrera repeats what he had told us on the bus about the Holy Spirit being received by people in Chetumal and in Bacalar, indicating that Christ will soon come. Also, a week ago a bright light appeared in the sky over Chetumal; many people saw it. No one knew what it was, but obviously this was a time of signs and miracles. The question was whether many people could still be converted and saved before Christ's coming. There might not be enough time, and large numbers would go to eternal perdition. "They are going to go to hell, Hermanos," he shouts, "and in hell, there is nothing but burning sulfur, which causes terrible torment and pain forever."

During the subsequent altar call, Juanita once more does not pick up on the bell signal that marks the end of the ritual and the terminating of the trance. Pressing one hand into the palm of the other, she has the corner of her black lace mantilla firmly caught in her clenched fist. And she is joined by Lucrecia, who also prolongs her speaking in tongues much beyond the bell tone.

As the service progresses, more and more people crowd in, neighbors in addition to members whom we have not seen for quite a while, all coming to see the film. With Eus's help we drape her sheet over the edge of the back wall. I test the light; all systems are go. I thread the film, all is ready, and then the projector refuses to work. What are we going to do?, I whisper to Barrera. Undaunted, he goes and fetches a screwdriver and expertly takes the contraption apart. Diagnosis: nothing wrong inside. "*Muy corriente,*" he murmurs [A very cheaply made thing]. "Maybe it needs lubricating oil," is my suggestion, based on years of experience with obstreperous technology. There is of course no lubricating oil around, but Barrera has the solution. He fetches his Vaseline hair dressing, and low and behold, one drop into the right spot, and the little motor starts spinning along, enveloped in violet-scented fumes.

Before I switch on the film, Barrera points out to the audience that this is not one of those films that you see in the movie houses, the viewing of which is a grievous sin. Rather, this film concerns important events of the congregation and thus is pleasing to God. But if anyone is worried, he is, of course, free to leave. No one moves. So I present it, without soundtrack, which I do not have, and in three parts, which is all the small reels can handle. Scenes of the baptism by the seashore, which I thought were especially impressive, are viewed in silence, but loud laughter and the calling out of names greets the scenes in the street. When it is over, the women who have seen the small one I had taken of Eus visiting Chichen Itza, which I had used to test the projector, call for that one also. Do they really want to see it? General assent. While it is running, I hear a woman saying "*Artista, artista* [Actress]," rather loudly in the back, especially when Eus appears, but I pay no attention because I am too occupied with keeping the reels running and wiping the perspiration off my face. I talk with Eus about it the following day; she says that some women are now teasing her that way, and not in a friendly manner, either. "They are jealous," she shrugs.

Sunday Services with a Difference

JULY 12, 1970

Punctually at 6:00 A.M., I go to the temple door, but no one is around. The only noise is Don Eduardo's radio going full blast. I go back to Reina's place and do some typing, and when an hour and a half later there is still no hymn to be heard, I check again. There are now seven men and no women. Barrera is outside talking with Valentin, who has stayed over for the Sunday services. Finally, past eight, with only three women but twelve men, Barrera begins the service. After the various introductory rituals, there is a brief homily by Barrera about the fact that Christians always had the problem that they did not esteem spiritual values sufficiently. Not riches, not knowledge, not the "filth" are important, only the Word of God.

For his sermon, he chooses Matthew 24:30–31, which he also assigns as a text to be learned by heart:

> Then the sign of the Son of Man will appear in the sky, and "all the clans of earth will strike their breasts" as they see "the Son of Man coming on the clouds of heaven" with power and great glory. He will dispatch his angels

"with a mighty trumpet blast, and they will assemble his chosen from the four winds, from one end of the heavens to the other."

In his sermon, Barrera speaks about the Devil having very little time left to do his evil deeds, so he will try everything to reach his goal of parting people from God. Of course, the Adversary knows which person is especially pious and will concentrate his efforts on him, and he will naturally try to rise within the Apostolic congregations, which are all very close to God. In Veracruz, there was a man who had the same gift as Hermano Antonio:

> He could see what others could not see, namely whether a person entering the temple was a true believer or not and an *hermano*. A visitor came to visit this congregation in Veracruz, and he entered with "*Paz de Cristo*," but the *hermano* who had this gift immediately recognized him as Satan himself and told him, "What do you want here? Why are you trying to deceive us? Get out of here!" The man got very angry and started cursing in the vilest way, showing that in effect he was what the true believer had taken him for.

For the prayer for the Holy Spirit, Barrera gives no instructions at all. Gone is the strategy that had been so successful last year, and which I had seen him use just a little while ago, where the supplicants were ringed by those already proficient in speaking in tongues. Neither does Barrera come down among those praying for the manifestation to place his hands on their heads or to listen for changes in their language. Instead, they are left to their own devices while Barrera, behind his barricade of tables, prays at the box at the back wall.

At the conclusion of the prayer, Barrera asks, almost indifferently, whether anyone has felt *alguna bendicion* [any blessing]. No one comes forward. I recall a scene from the previous week, where a teenage boy kept sobbing and bending forward on his knees rapidly over and over again. I clearly heard him go into the initial *ʔuʔuʔu* that marked the beginner's glossolalia. It took him a long time before he returned to ordinary consciousness, yet not once did Barrera approach him. And because the boy had no recollection of what had happened to him, he did not come forward either, nor did he receive the coveted official recognition of his experience.

The subject for the Escuela Dominical is Isaiah and his times. Barrera assigns a text from Isaiah, and there is much good-natured laughter when those he calls upon to recite it falter. Barrera, however, gets very impatient. He then calls on Isauro and three other *hermanos* to explain the four sections of the text in the church pamphlet about the times of Isaiah. The four men with their limited reading capacity stumble through the passage with its stilted Spanish and abstruse vocabulary, then give an exegesis that concerns not the times of the prophet, about whom they know even less than Barrera, but some personal thoughts about the vanity of the world. Incomprehensibly, Barrera is not even listening. Ensconced behind his barrier, he seems busy with some accounts.

When Isauro, the last one of the four, is done, Barrera finally emerges and begins quizzing his hapless students about the three kings that ruled during Isaiah's lifetime, about their respective vices and punishments. As could be expected, he cannot even elicit their names. Barrera becomes quite indignant. The men especially, he says, would at first hearing easily remember all sorts of filthy things—gossip, jokes, curse words, they would know them all. But God's things must also be remembered. He threatens dire punishment but does not spell out what kind. Even mild-mannered Nohoch Felix, who is home from working on the ranch, later remarks indignantly that Barrera expects too much, that he should call on the young people for recitation, they still have a head for learning. As for him, he could certainly not remember the strange names of those kings.

In the afternoon, I attend the meeting of the Dorcas. Joaquina, a new member this year, is the treasurer. She is the sister-in-law of Isauro and much talked about because she keeps getting pregnant, but she has a history of stillbirths: the child comes out legs first and dies, but she refuses to have it by cesarian section. She no longer comes to the sessions of the Dorcas because she is so upset that the money from the milk-powder can is always missing. One day, she was quoted as saying, she opened the can and there was a note in it, "Borrowed 100 pesos." It was not even signed. So Eus, who is sub-treasurer this year, gives the report about how much money there is, how much they had earned from the *talento*—that is, selling tacos they had prepared as an offering and sold during the pauses between services—and how much they owed for dues. The *hermanas* pay up, a peso a week, some in advance, but most of them are four or more weeks in arrears. There is no work for the men. The highway construction, which had kept them going for a while, has stopped, and not even the women can find any work, such as doing washing. Barrera needs money; he is no longer selling any Chetumal merchandise, perhaps for lack of customers. That is possibly why he keeps taking the money from the Dorcas' can. Eus does not think that that is any excuse. She is angry and says privately, "I may not be able to read, but I can definitely remember what everybody pays or owes. One time I get the milk can and it is empty. So who emptied it? I say something about the can being empty. So afterward in the service Barrera says the Devil likes it when money comes in, but not when it goes out. That was clearly meant for me."

After the meetings of the *secciones,* we are all invited to a service in Old Candil's house. There are more and more of these private services lately, often even in addition to the weekday evening services; they are popular perhaps because some of the relaxed familiarity and the old fervor tend to reappear. This one is to be *una accion de gracia* [a thanksgiving service], because Old Candil's broken rib has finally healed. After an accident in which he fell off his horse, his family took him to a *cura huesos* [bone healer], and he had healed quite well and eagerly started working his *col* again. Although he was a tailor by trade, the only work truly worthy of a man, he felt, was working in his corn garden. As a result, his rib started hurting once more, and he had no money to go to the hospital. However, with the prayer of the *hermanos,* things were really getting better now. The family is also hoping for a prayer for one of Candil and Rodolfa's daughters, who is deaf in one ear and now also has a sore throat. Eus says that the girl is deaf because Rodolfa hits her children on the head when they annoy her. She even did that to her younger sisters, who together with their mother shared Rodolfa's household. She, Eus, never hit her children hard, only pinched them if they were really acting up. I remember the welts on her grandson Jose's back, but of course I mind my manners.

Epi and Barrera speak in tongues, especially when Floriano, one of the recently baptized young men, asks to be prayed over. After the service, we are served a watermelon drink, crushed watermelon in ice water. "*Que puercos* [What pigs]," Nohoch Felix complains afterward. "They did not even wash the glasses when they passed them to other people."

During testimony time of the evening service that day, Pedro relates that he used to be a lumberjack and smoke great quantities of marijuana. When he came to know the gospel, he quit, backsliding only once, five months after his conversion.

At home, Reina's mother has come for a visit. She has brought an invitation to a wedding in Dzoncahuich. The son of one of Reina's brothers is getting married. She has brought along two young grandsons, who are playing with Lupita in her hammock. They twist and turn and roll without the slightest danger of ever falling out. Then they begin playing a word game: "*tuuch* [belly button]," they shriek, "*tuuch*," poking each other and laughing, and then "*chiich* [grandmother]," "*chiich*," over and over again. When they get too rambunctious, Reina threatens to call the *sapo* [toad], and it will come to eat them.

The Trip to Tibolom

JULY 13, 1970

The day after feasting on the Temax rooster, Eus and I board the bus to Merida, the first leg of our trip to Tibolom. Eus considers it her home village, although she was born in Libre Union. But she and her family were driven from Libre Union by the Revolution and moved to Tibolom, farther into the bush. We go to the central market to leave our bags with Don Agapito and to our surprise encounter one of Eus's younger sons, Armin. He is muscular, very dark skinned, and quite tall. Eus laughs when she sees how his stature startles me. "In your country," she remarks, "everybody is as tall as Armin, *masima*? Isn't it strange for you that here everyone is so small?" She is right, of course. During this second visit, I have difficulties reconciling my memory of people with their actual stature. I had remembered them all much taller, especially her.

Armin is a skilled mason, but he has no money to buy tools. Besides, there is very little construction going on, and so work is scarce. He and his friends took to the road and bummed around the Peninsula, doing occasional work when they could find it. Armin decided to let his hair grow down to his shoulders as he had seen it in American magazines and also grew a very heavy beard. In Campeche, he was thrown in jail because the police thought he was from Cuba, and he had no ID card to prove otherwise. "Didn't you speak to them in Maya?" I ask. "After all, no Cuban knows any Maya." But that had never occurred to him. The police cut his hair and his mustache and beard and kept him locked up for two weeks. He said that they treated their prisoners well, giving them enough to eat, and even allowed the *apostolicos* of Campeche to hold religious services in jail. When he got out, there was a street fight at which he and his friends "happened to be present." So the police picked them up again and kept them locked up for another two weeks. Armin and Nina have not seen each other for two years, so it is decided that he will also come along to Tibolom.

In the evening, we attend a service at the house of Enrique, one of Eus's older sons. After his shoot-out with a neighbor in Tibolom (which had cost the man some length of his intestines) and spending some time in the *monte* growing corn and hunting peccaries, he decided to move to Merida and work in the market selling fingernail polish and shaving lotion. Eus is unhappy that he still has not legally married his wife, but she can understand the reason. The woman was married before, and they simply do not have the 400 pesos to pay for her divorce.

Enrique is a slender, small man, gentle-looking like his father. It is hard for me to imagine that he could be aggressive or violent. But I recall that when I was waiting for the city trolley in Merida, there was a young man in front of me, well-dressed, well-groomed, with a quiet, pleasant face. The wind agitated his loose shirt and under it, quite visible, there was the handle of a vicious-looking knife stuck into his belt.

The service at Enrique's house is conducted by Luis L. He seems little changed by his year of study in Tepic, and in his sermon, he retains his folksy style. There is no crowd of worshippers, merely Enrique and his family, some neighbors and friends, and the pastor's mother Peregrina, who never misses one of her son's services. There is no glossolalia.

We spend the night at Don Agapito's house. Eus has brought hammocks for herself, Nina, and me. Armin sleeps on a *petate* [mat] on the floor. For a while, we women talk in the kitchen. Sylvia wants to go to Tibolom not only to sell and barter but also to check up on the several head of cattle she has grazing there. Recently somebody, apparently wielding a machete, had severely injured her *novina,* a cow that had not calved yet. And the bull of her niece was even killed. Nobody knew who did it or even why. "*Son puercos,*" Eus says, "they are pigs," the usual epithet for aggressive, violent men.

After Eus and Sylvia go to bed, Don Agapito and I still sit in the kitchen until almost midnight, talking about the Caste War (1849 to approximately 1912), about his grandfather's trading trips through the jungle, and about how he had walked many times from Yaxcabah to Tibolom and all the way to Bacalar and Belize. He would even encounter the Indians, those that were fighting the Ladinos in the jungle, because the line between them ran close to Tibolom. We also talk about the increasing poverty, how the soil is so tired that instead of three harvests it gives only one, and about *henequen* politics. It seems that the governor of Yucatan attempted to force the *henequen* ranchers to increase the pay of the men to 28 pesos a day. They did so for a few days, then some of them returned to the previous 10-pesos-a-day schedule, while others suspended production entirely. "There is not much of a market for *henequen* rope anyway these days; the nylon rope is crowding it out of the market." He confirms what I heard from an old man in Utzpak whom I knew from last year, not a member of the congregation, that the cattle ranchers had occupied certain outlying areas where there was still some land reserve, so that no *col* could be planted there.

I settle into my hammock when there is a knock on the door. It is one of Don Agapito's nephews who also wants to go to Tibolom, with the news that the truck that was going to take us there has broken down. "Don't worry," says Don Agapito, "you can go as far as Holcah and rent horses there."

We get up at four the next morning to catch the first bus going into town and to the bus depot. In addition to our own baggage, we are loaded down with bunches of bananas and twenty bags of wheat flour Dona Sylvia wants to take to "Bolom" (she leaves off the "ti" of Tibolom, which simply means "at" [the milestone] and is dropped when speaking Maya).

The bus to Holcah is one of those old, rickety ones started with a screwdriver and held together with baling wire. But it runs, and the tickets are cheap. To load the freight the bus is carrying, the driver's helper unlocks the back door but then closes it with "this door is not for getting off." The men, most of them going to work with all manner of bundles, mock him, laughing, and it gets to be like a singsong, "*No es para salir, no es para salir. . . .*" A large number of them want to get off at Holcah. The driver stops once, at the entrance to the community, then whizzes all the way through, not responding to the frantic calls and pounding on the bus wall, until he is past the last house. It is an overwhelming task to collect all of our bundles and the suitcases; we only manage because of Armin's unusual strength and height, or we would have arrived in Bolom sans hammocks, sans ʔipiles, sans chickens, and horrors, sans Dona Sylvia's merchandise. One of the men is not so lucky. When he searches for his bundle among those thrown out of the bus for his companions, his is missing. He pounds on the side of the bus, but it drives off. We see him run after it, and although it does slow down at a construction site down the road, he loses the race.

Since, as we know, there is no truck going to Tibolom, Armin tries to get horses for us, but they have all left for work. So, there is nothing for it but to walk the two *leguas* (about 10 kilometers). It is still rather cool, and with the green trees of the jungle looming ahead, I have expectations inspired by memories of gaily marching along the path through a rustling German forest, maybe the Spessard, singing happy hiking songs. I am confused and imprudent enough to communicate these fantasies to Eus.

The first few kilometers are not too bad. Eus met up with an old Maya gentleman while we waited for horses whom she knows because he was the minister of the local Pentecostal church. He is going to his ranch with his son, also a minister, and his grandson, who is going to experience his very first day working on the *col*. It sounds like a much-anticipated initiation. Without much ado, he heaves one of our heavy suitcases on his back and carries it all the way to his place, a distance of about 4 kilometers.

After he leaves, the loads have to be redistributed, and I am entrusted with a bundle of flour bags. Eus fashions a tumpline from her *rebozo*, her scarf; I am not allowed to use mine because it is new and of high quality. She places the flour sacks into its fold and loads me with it. In about ten minutes, the cursed things assume the weight of salt. "How about those songs?" Eus taunts. So here I am, tumpline across my forehead, the goods of a Maya trader on my back, singing, "*Wohlauf, die Luft geht frisch und rein, wer lange sitzt, muss rosten*" [Let's start, the air is fresh and clean, who spends his life sitting will rust] and many more. Meanwhile, I try to overlook the fact that there is no stonier piece of real estate in the world than the Yucatan Peninsula, and most of those stones are clearly spread on that path from Holcah to Tibolom. I am wearing open sandals—walking shoes are impossible in this heat—and my feet start swelling. We are bitten by horseflies and beset by mosquitoes. Armin, who is in the lead, kills a small rattlesnake. Obviously, the Spessard was never like this.

After another 2 or 3 endless kilometers, Eus takes pity on me. She gives me the *sabucan* [a large shopping bag] with the box of bananas to carry, and she takes over the flour bags. Gaily she reminisces about how she used to trek from the ranch to Tibolom with a baby tied into her *rebozo,* a load on her head, and a *sabucan* in each hand.

Sylvia announces that we are halfway there. Eus agrees, but I have no idea how they know; something about a particular tree, but they all look the same to me. I am hoping that we might now take a rest, but on we go. I am getting terribly thirsty, and providentially, about 2 kilometers outside Tibolom, we encounter a road construction crew. One of the men offers us some water from his large bottle gourd. I drink too, uttering a silent prayer against amoebas. The water tastes sweet and cool. Nina gets out some leaflets printed by the Apostolic Church, and Eus announces gravely, "Now comes more water, the water of life." With an unsmiling face, Nina distributes the leaflets. All the men accept them; one even sits down on his wheelbarrow and begins reading it. We say our "*Dios bootic,*" Sylvia parts with some of her bananas as a return gift, and we move on.

Finally, we get to the edge of the village and rest, in order, I discover, to make ourselves presentable. Eus lets her long hair down and rebraids it; so does Sylvia and Nina. I comb my short strands, and then we march in, in a leisurely fashion, as though we do 10-kilometer marches every day of the week.

Curiously, I look around. Tibolom seems very much like Utzpak, except there are no electric poles. Other than that, it has the same wide streets and mixture of traditional and *mamposteria* houses, the surface of the roads alternating between limestone outcroppings and mud. There are the rutting pigs and the skinny dogs and everywhere the whitewashed *albarradas.* And there are the women walking about, most of them in *ʔipil,* not as many dresses as in Utzpak. The vast Catholic church is a picturesque ruin, with one small section of it roofed over for services. The municipal building is a similar ruin; apparently only a corner section of it is in use. The plaza is much wider than the one in Utzpak, but only part of it is cleared of weeds. It must have had an extensive elevated section at one time. Most of it has collapsed, but around the church it is still intact, with steps leading up to its highest part.

At the *nixtamal* mill (not driven by electricity, as in Utzpak, but by a steam generator), we encounter Eus's daughter Wilma. She is strikingly beautiful, with her mother's profile, but more delicate, her face smooth, and with heavy, long black hair that she wears in a loose knot held in place by a comb. Eus must have looked like that when she was a young woman. She is surprised to see us because she had heard that the truck had broken down and so she did not expect us. Together we go to her homestead, which originally was Eus and Nohoch Felix's. They gave it to Wilma because Nohoch Felix had a quarrel with the most important rancher in the area and so no one would hire him anymore. That was why they moved to Utzpak.

Wilma's courtyard is much larger than Eus's in Utzpak, cool and shady.

Fondly, Eus pats all the trees that she had planted, admiring how much bigger they have gotten, and pointing out the well that was blasted for her and No-hoch Felix. In a private aside, she sighs how neglected everything looks, the doors of the two houses hanging loose, parts of the palm-frond roof in tatters. Then she adds, "But what can Wilma do? She has six children, there is not enough food to give her strength, and her husband, Ruben, is gone all week to work on the ranch."

Eus gives one of the children some money for eggs, and I send my friend Jose, Wilma's oldest, who has greeted me with a shy smile, to buy soft drinks for everyone. Wilma and Consuelo, her oldest daughter, make tortillas. Eus and I also provide the food for supper. Food, I found, was ordinarily only offered on ceremonial occasions, such as at the services in the private homes that we attended in Utzpak or at a wedding.

I am curious about the chapel that has been built into the church ruin, and so Eus takes me there. The priest is present, I am told, because there will be a wedding on the morrow, at which he is going to say mass, and also he is going to baptize five children. I introduce myself, and we exchange pleasantries. He is an American, Father Robert, and we chat for a bit while people crowd around to hear English spoken. It is generally held that Maya and English are very similar. After all, I am told, there is the English word "miss," and there is also the same Maya word "*miis.*" Never mind that the latter means "broom," or "to sweep." When, after our conversation, I turn to our audience and ask whether they have understood anything, they admit laughingly that they have not. The reason is, they say, because we are talking too fast.

The *cura,* Father Robert, has lived in Sotuta, the neighboring town and bish-opric, for nine years. He speaks Spanish well, and to the delight of his congre-gation, he also knows some Maya. He is aware of the linguistic work done by Professor McQuown of the University of Chicago, whose students wrote the textbook I am using. Last year, Father Robert became paralyzed on his left side, and he went to the States for treatment. It was not a stroke, and instead of recovering in the U.S., he became very ill due to the change in food and climate. When he returned, he became sick once more and was just convalescing now. He has his own jeep, so I ask him whether he can take us to Sotuta with him, where we could catch a bus to Merida. While we are talking, Nina distributes some more of her little pamphlets, and all but the Father's driver accepts them. Later in the evening, he celebrates mass and preaches a sermon, which Nina goes to hear. She comes home quite amazed. The *cura's* organist had repeated the sermon in Maya, and it had all been very biblical. Maybe he had tried hard-er, she says, because she was there.

With Wilma in the evening, the conversation quickly turns to Apostolic missionizing. There is no Apostolic church in Tibolom, nor is there a Pentecostal one. When the minister who helped us carry our suitcase on the way here came to evangelize, the truck that carried him as well as some members of his congregation was shot at. Since then, he has not come back to Tibolom. Instead, Wilma occasionally goes to Holcah to attend the Pentecostal service there. Eus approves. "All this talk about the Trinity," she shrugs, "is really not all that important. Actually the two churches are very similar." Both women assert that half of Tibolom already "believes in the gospel," and many are studying the New Testament. Wilma says that a man who was attending the catechism classes at the Catholic church even took Jose with him to sing some hymns for the children. Jose has a lovely boy's soprano voice and knows many hymns by heart. Since then, the children gave him a hard time, taunting him with "*chan ministro* [little minister]." One time Wilma entered the Catholic church. There was a padre substituting for Father Robert, and she was curious about him, but a man told her, "Get out of here! You are evangelical." She retorted, "Did you make this church? If you did, then you can tell me to get out. Otherwise, I stay." And loudly, so everyone could hear her, she added that she did not think that the statues of saints could do miracles.

We spend the night all crowded into Wilma's main house. Her second building is in such poor condition that no one can sleep there. It is not a pleasant occasion. All the children, even Jose, who is now 10, urinate on the dirt floor when they have to get up at night instead of using a chamber pot, to the disgust of Eus, who would not tolerate such behavior even from much smaller children. The corner used for showering is marked off by a ring of soil. Eus said that she used to excavate it every week and spread *sascab* in the depression to make it feel clean. Wilma does not do that, and since the children urinate there also, it is a pretty disgusting spot. Yet we have to bathe in order to stay well. "I don't understand some of my children," Eus sighs.

The following morning we go to visit a neighbor to pick up a strip of embroidery Eus ordered for an ʔipil. We chat, in Maya of course, about her married daughter, about the baby that keeps getting ill, and spontaneously, the woman grabs my left arm and caresses it in a way very similar to what I had observed in Utzpak, except with a little more emphasis on the hand. It seems like a dialect variation of the Utzpak greeting pattern among women.

This is the day of the wedding, and, of course, much of the conversation is about that. The young people who are to be married had to wait for two years for this day. It seems that the groom's mother was against the match and spread the rumor that the bride was pregnant. In the end, time proved the mother-in-law wrong. As I knew also from Utzpak, the precondition for a legitimate marriage, and even for a common-law one, is that the bride has to be a virgin. If during the wedding night the man finds her to be otherwise, he has the right to send the girl back to her mother. Reina told about how the local tavern owner had a daughter who "liked to keep company with the men in the cantina." If a girl was *de carrera,* had a bad reputation, then no one would marry her. This girl fell in love with a boy and was now four months pregnant. She begged him to marry her, even if only by common law, that is by running away with her, but he refused, and now he has a girlfriend who is an untouched "senorita." According to Reina, the men say that that is the only way in which they can be sure that the child is theirs. "If the woman will give in to one man, she will give in to another one too," is the generally accepted opinion.

Socorro, Eus's other daughter, who also lives in Tibolom, comes to see us just as we are grabbing a tortilla before going to the plaza to see the wedding. Socorro, plain and green-eyed like her father, is quite affluent. Her husband buys and sells cattle, and Socorro is an expert gardener who often receives prizes for her produce at competitions in Merida. She and Wilma decide that we have enough time, and that I need to be made pretty, that is, to be dressed "correctly" before going to the wedding. The two women make me unpack my best *ʔipil,* which I have brought along at Eus's prompting "just in case," the one embroidered in vivid color, executed in *alta seda* [high silk], and Wilma loans me one of her half-slips with eyelet embroidery, a necessary complement to the *ʔipil.* Wilma heats up her small flatiron on her *comal* and irons my wrinkled *ʔipil* on her kitchen table, a very laborious procedure. Then I almost put it on wrong, scandalizing Eus and Nina, who are watching, and my two helpers. I was not aware that the middle crease has to be folded inward in front in order to be correct. After inquiring whether jewelry is permitted in my church at home, Socorro takes off her double gold necklace with the medallion of the Virgin and drapes it around my neck. She also loans me her earrings, long ones with a green stone. After adding my shiny, new, and very long *rebozo,* crossing it on my chest, they all nod, satisfied with the result: *una mestiza elegante.* I am struck by the infinite care, almost reverence, with which each piece is handled, unfolded, smoothed out. Reina, who wears only dresses, never shows this attitude toward her clothes.

We go on to the plaza because the wedding is going to take place in the Catholic church. I do a lot of filming when we get there. Some of the wedding party wears the latest Mexico City fashion, others are decked out in gorgeous three-tiered *ʔipiles.* For some reason that is not made clear to me, the bride decides that she wants no pictures, and there are some tense moments after the mass when the wedding party stands on the plaza, exuding resentment. Eus, Wilma, Nina, and some local friends stand over on the other side forming an equally tight knot, waiting to see what will happen. I go on filming, alternately concentrating on a noisy gaggle of turkeys and the wedding party—the juxtaposition seems quite appropriate—and on a boy who climbs up on a dangerously wobbly high ladder in order to ring the church bell.

Finally, the wedding party's anger apparently dissolves and they proceed to the groom's house. The groom's family must be well off to put on such an elaborate wedding, for in Yucatan, as everywhere in Mexico also, the groom's family is responsible for all the costs of the wedding, including the bride's gown and shoes. That is one reason why many young men choose not to go through with an official wedding. The families simply cannot bear the expense.

Given the obvious previous animosity, I am surprised when "my" group calmly follows the wedding party to the groom's house, obeying Eus, who says that for sure I will want to film the preparation of the food for the guests. When we get there, Eus begins expertly directing everyone how to act naturally and telling them not to stare into the camera. By the time I have filmed the ladies making tortillas, and even one of them heaving a giant glob of *masa,* we are the best of friends. Eus has obviously gauged the change of mood correctly, because soon the groom's father comes over to invite us to the wedding meal. I am about to feel touched by the man's generosity, when Eus informs me that this invitation has come in return for some prints of the wedding pictures they are expecting. It makes me feel awful because I have not taken any photographs, I have only filmed. What to do? Refusing the food now would be impossibly awkward. We all walk over to where the guests are seated on benches, and I eat, hoping that my bad conscience will not cause me any indigestion. As it turns out, the delectable quality of the food quickly overcomes my moral reservations. We have roast turkey meat wrapped into tortillas, and bean broth with meat dumplings made with eggs, and we drink soft drinks. The men and the women, by the way, are strictly separated at this festive occasion. Only one very old man, quite drunk, breaks the taboo and comes over to me to tell me something obscure about Genesis. Eus quickly puts a stop to it, telling the venerable elder that I have work to do and cannot chat. To make the point, I start filming the young people. The girls wear either dresses or ?ipil and are sitting on the benches with their mothers, waiting to be asked to dance. The young men are standing around, gathering up their courage. The recorded music blasting over a loudspeaker is popular Mexican with a smattering of U.S. tunes, among them "Jingle Bells."

For a few moments the *cura* drops by. He cannot stay to eat, he says; he has to visit a sick parishioner. He does not create much of a stir. I do get to ask him about the trip to Sotuta the following morning, and he nods that it would be all right and that we should be at the church at nine.

Armin has decided to walk back to Holcah, and only we women—Sylvia, Eus, Nina, and I—go in the *cura's* jeep. The *cura* sits next to the driver, wearing a baseball cap, and we have the back seat, folding our legs as best we can, draping ourselves around the boxes, bags, and suitcases, ours and his. Nina hugs the piglet that Eus has bought in Tibolom, which she wants to raise for sale. It is no mean task for Nina; the malicious little beast keeps squirming, wiggling, and screaming all the way to Sotuta.

The jeep has no windshield, there are of course no seat belts, and the driver is absolutely mad, taking the curves of the bumpy jungle path as though it were the course of the Indy 500. "*Kʔasaan maak* [crazy man]," Eus breathes angrily. We do, by divine grace, eventually make it to Sotuta all in one piece, and the *cura* even invites us into his spacious house. It is quite luxurious, with upholstered chairs and the pinnacle of luxury, a flush toilet. We are offered iced soft drinks, and while Eus dozes in her chair, the *cura* speaks about the work of the Church in Yucatan. We are soon joined by a young American couple in jeans and shirt. They are here as representatives of the "Papal Action for Latin America." Their work, something like that of the Peace Corps, is financed by various U.S. dioceses. They both know Spanish—the young man has a B.A. in Spanish from a university in Pennsylvania—but our conversation is carried on in English. No, they do not think that they need to have any training in anthropology to do their work here, for all they want to do is to help the people and sow the Word of God. The girl had been in Sotuta before, when she worked for three years as a mission aide and ran a small boarding house for boys attending school here away from home. She was surprised that the natives could actually be taught to do good work, for she had managed to train only two women to take over the boarding house when she had to leave. They have now been here only for a short time, and they have already been able to put together a group willing to help each other, for example repairing each other's houses, and the women were very happy that she was able to teach them how to sew *ʔipiles*. Too bad that the art of making those pretty garments was getting lost, she pined. Before coming to Sotuta, they had had a six-week-long culture course in Washington, so they knew all about the Maya. It seemed that the Maya of old were almost as good as the Christians. Even in Sotuta, apparently, old people were being cared for. Yucatan used to be a real paradise where no one stole, murdered, or even cheated. Recently, however, there was quite a bit of migration to the Peninsula from Mexico, and this was clearly to be blamed for the moral degradation to be observed today. They are going to start a credit union with income they would realize from the sale of used clothing collected in the States. The church, the *cura* adds, should become a center for community activity, based on the three T's: Time, Talent, Treasure. These three T's are what the individual receives from God, and therefore, naturally, part of the gain should be returned to the Church. Shades of Barrera.

We take the bus to Merida from Sotuta, still burdened by the protesting piglet. In the Merida bus station, the women distribute the luggage between them, and the piglet with an end of twine tied to its back leg is entrusted to me. I am still wearing my *ʔipil grande* with its embroidery of *alta seda*, and it must have been some sight to see me dragging the squealing little monster down the populous streets of Merida from the bus station to the market and then from the market to the local bus for the trip to Dona Sylvia's house. I try to stare the starers down, and am only hoping that no casual U.S. visitor who might by chance know me is witness to my extremity.

Poor piggy, really. The driver of the Utzpak bus demands that it be stored in the baggage compartment below. It must have been hot down there and perhaps also lacking in oxygen, for when we land in Utzpak, the pitiable animal is near expiring, and lives only two more days, dashing Eus's hopes for a profitable venture. She butchers and smokes it. Nohoch Felix will have none of it, calling it *basura* [garbage], but she lets me have a bite, and it is tender and delicious.

Back Home Again

As I catch up on the local news at our gossip corner, I find that the affairs of Don Eduardo and his *gorda* continue to be in the public eye. "Don Eduardo will not allow anyone of the congregation to give welcoming presents to Dona Andrea," Raquel reports. And Reina says that when there is a service, he will not let his wife get water from the well or do the washing in the yard. When the *hermanos* gather for a service, he sits in front of his house, turning his back on them and singing a hymn.

While we were gone, the Devil made also a public appearance. As Reina had heard:

> Last weekend the Devil appeared in the Utzpak *calaboso.* There was a prisoner there, and the Devil appeared to him and said, "*Buenos dias, caballero,* would you like me to get you out of here?" The man started shouting, but when the people got there, he had already taken off most of his clothes in preparation for killing himself. The Devil vanished; they saw only his tail. It looked like the tail of a steer.

In the temple before the next service, the Devil in the *calaboso* was also the topic of conversation. After all, that was nothing new; the Devil had been seen in the prison three years ago, too. At that time, a man committed suicide by hanging himself with a belt as a result. The same thing happened with the brother of Hermano Peregrino, Candil volunteered. He had beaten his wife over the head with a slab of wood, and when he saw her on the floor bleeding, he thought he had killed her. In prison after being arrested, he saw the Devil and he hung himself by using his pants as a rope.

On July 17, 1970, there is a private service in Mariano's house. For a private service, attendance is unusually high, ten women and twelve men. We are seated in the yard, we women concentrated in the front, the men in the back and on the sides. The children are made to squat on a fallen tree, which calms them down somewhat, all except Barrera's son, Luisito. His father bribes him with 20 centavos, but he is soon acting up again, and his mother takes him to the back by his ear.

Barrera's sermon concerns the story of Sodom and Gomorrah. In Tabasco, he says, people say that you have to eat the pineapple peeled; that is, you have to call a spade a spade. So that is what he is going to do. Those two cities were destroyed because there was homosexuality by both sexes. He goes to great lengths to describe what happens to those kind of sinners in hell. The generally somber tone is later lightened a bit when, while introducing the prayer to the sick he tells that Hermano G., the Texan Baptist missionary well known in Utzpak, was once asked to pray for a sick person. When he found out that the man had a contagious disease, he said that he would pray for him at home. That caused general merriment. Then he adds that if a person gets well as a result of the prayer, that is for Jesus. If he does not, that is for Jesus as well.

At the Sunday service, as has become customary this year, each of the three societies—the Senores Cristianos, the Dorcas, and the Juveniles—presents a special hymn. It is remarkable how these groups have increased since last year, the men's to fourteen, the married women's to eleven, and the young people's to seven girls and seven boys.

In his sermon, Barrera pushes on with the apocalyptic theme to a jammed audience of twenty men and twenty-one women. The horses of the apocalypse bring sickness, hunger, and other plagues. God would not send them if he loved only a man's body. Rather, he sees only man's inside. Humans are supposed to have problems. There is much illness, the soil is exhausted, all the prophecies of tribulations are coming true—all for the purpose of bringing man closer to God. Everything will get much worse, so that man will have to repent and find God.

The mood is oppressive also at Reina's house. She and Santiago have been to Dzonkahuich to the wedding. It was very fancy, Reina says. Her nephew, the groom, was 17—he was the caretaker of one of his father's ranches—and the bride was 16. Her brother was the supervisor of the work on the *ejido* land of the village and made good money, and so he could afford the 400 pesos for the wedding mass. The high point, to Reina's mind, was that the *madrina* and *padrino,* the baptismal sponsors of the groom, came all the way from Merida and brought the wedding rings. But instead of coming to the wedding and enjoying all the good food, even turkey, Santiago spent the day in the *cantina* and by evening was quite drunk. "I found him," she says triumphantly, "and he was so drunk that I was able to grab all his money. I don't know how he will get home. Maybe walking." I think that unlikely; it is more than 20 kilometers, but when Santiago finally shows up, he is very mad indeed.

The reason he even had some money was because he had brought quite a bit of merchandise from Chetumal and, despite the depressed economy of the village, had been able to sell some. He had hung all the shirts and pieces of material that he had bought on the wire which was stretched across the house and served to dry towels and baby clothes and dresses when it rained outside or simply to save things from the cockroaches and especially the black mold that immediately ruined everything stored in an unventilated container. This was the manner in which such merchandise was also displayed in the clothing stores, and it was obvious that he was seeing himself as the master of a vast stock of precious goods, *un hombre de negocios* [a businessman].

The Trip to Chetumal and the Chetumal Cooperative Church Compound

On July 20, 1970, I go to Eus's place early because we want to take the bus to Chetumal. Hermano Jose has invited us several times to come and see his congregation. I am hoping to get a look at the church archives, which I am told are kept in Chetumal. I have discussed the plans with Reina and have the feeling that Santiago, who is beginning to run low on merchandise, will ask me to do some shopping for him at the free port. I hate shopping, even for myself, and I do not relish the idea of doing it for him. I think I am pretty safe after his debacle at Dzonkahuich. But at 11:30 A.M., shortly before the bus leaves, he appears at Eus's place with a list and 450 pesos. I really want to refuse, but Eus accepts for both of us.

In Merida, we change to the night bus for Chetumal and arrive there at 3:30 in the morning, expecting to be received by Jose. But he is nowhere in sight. The night is humid and warm, but the station is small and uncomfortable, so we decide to take a cab to the address that Jose has given us. We could have walked. The cabby takes us only two blocks down the road, and leaves us in front of what appears in the darkness to be a wooden shed, its windows shuttered and its door locked. No one answers our knock. There is another shed beside that one; it appears to be merely a shelter, a palm-frond roof supported by four corner posts. The outline of a hammock appears barely visible next to the far post. I am getting uneasy, but undaunted, Eus walks closer and calls out, "*Ola?*" There is a sleepy response from a male voice. We are at the right spot. The shelter turns out to be occupied by five *hermanos,* among them Chan Felix, whose assignment in Bacalar is not to start until tomorrow. The plan had been that Jose would come from his home and wake up Chan Felix, who was then going to pick us up at the station. But the night before, the service did not end until 11 o'clock, and everyone overslept. A groggy Juan L. emerges from somewhere and helps us hang our hammocks, Eus's in the large kitchen next to the wooden house, which turns out to be the temple, and mine in a small adjacent room.

So this is how we arrive at what to my surprise turns out to be a cooperative church compound. As I discover in the morning, there is in the wooden building adjacent to the large room that serves as the church; a large, immaculate kitchen; a living room; and another room that serves as private room, office, and storeroom for Juan L. There is a third, smaller building, which houses two showers and two separate toilets, all with running water. Much of the area is cemented over. The roofed-over open shelter serves as bedroom, living room, recreation room, and storeroom for merchandise for the *hermanos* belonging to the compound. The compound has its own water tank and is enclosed by a high fence. The master of it all is Juan L., who is also the supervisor of the Apostolic congregations of Quintana Roo, where Chetumal is located, as well as of Campeche and of Yucatan. All these congregations are part of the Seccion Sureste, the southeastern section of the Apostolic Church. He is subordinate to the bishop of that section, who at the time was Sabino Lopez Palma, who had offices in Villahermosa. Unfortunately, as I find out, the church archives are not in Chetumal. They are stored in Merida, and I will have to ask Luis L., Juan's brother, if I can study them there.

As I understand from looking around and making a nuisance of myself by asking a lot of questions, the compound's economic activities are also headed by Juan L. He "owns," that is, he is the head representative of, a plastics firm. Obviously, he also has the highest income. The *hermanos* go out from house to house selling plastic goods, mainly dishes, on an installment plan. They are allowed to keep the down payment, and the income from the installment plan, in addition to paying for the merchandise, goes in part to the church and to pay Juan L.'s and Jose's salary. The housekeeping is done by the wife of an *hermano* who at present is preaching in Tizimin. She has a 5-year-old daughter and a 2-year-old son. Jose is in charge of collecting the installments. Other congregations have found a different solution for economic cooperation, says Chan Felix. In Campeche, they have what we might call a credit union. The *hermanos* earn the money; they put it all in one account, and the interest is apportioned between them and the expenses "for the work of the Lord."

The *hermanos* working for Juan L. at the time are two I do not know, plus Nicolas of Utzpak, the brother of Cecilia, who has a stand on the main street of Utzpak renting out *cuentos* and occasionally comes to the services, and

Joaquin's brother. And there is the perennial freeloader, Joaquin himself. He had been out selling with Nicolas and injured his foot in the spokes of the back wheel of Nicolas's motorcycle. So Nicolas had to pay for his hospital bill, and Juan L. came up with money for his food. His foot was almost healed when the same accident occurred again. "I put it in there," he shrugs when I ask what happened. "That," Chan Felix kids, "means that you did it on purpose." The semantic analysis is lost on Joaquin, but not of course on Eus, who finds it highly amusing. In the meantime, Joaquin is lolling in his hammock, nursing his bandaged foot and waiting for the day, as Eus says, when he can put it into the spokes again.

The next morning a little after six, I wake up to the sound of loud prayer. I recognize Juan L.'s voice. He is alternating between glossolalia and ordinary speech. There is only a thin plank wall separating the church from my room; it is as if I am sitting in the church too, and I curse myself for not bringing my tape-recorder. From the sound of it, people are entering, praying, and then leaving, presumably for work.

Later, Chan Felix accompanies his mother and me on that infernal shopping errand for Santiago. We eat breakfast in a restaurant, but Chan Felix refuses my invitation. He is fasting and will not even take water. A jukebox is going full blast, intoning a Mexican love song. Chan Felix comments that such matters as love should be a private matter between a man and a woman and should not be expressed publicly. Mainly, however, the inspiration for artistic activity, such as the composition and singing of songs, should result only from religious inspiration. Do all *hermanos* think so, I ask? This is how it should be, he insists. Pastors make poor consultants.

Nicolas has loaned me his tape-recorder, so I feel complete again. Eus and I go to the evening service, and for the first time I am able to see the inside of the church of this compound. The principal decorations of the rather roomy temple consist of Christmas baubles. Some red balls are suspended from the ceiling above the congregation, and balls and golden stars hang above the area serving as an altar, which is not elevated. Instead, it is set off by a balustrade. The latter is decorated with Christmas lights, which keep blinking on and off during the entire service. All the girls and most of the women wear not a tri-angular mantilla like in Utzpak, but a flowery, transparent white scarf, which they call a *chalina*, very pretty; it is almost like a folk costume.

At the beginning of the service there are fourteen women and nine men. Juan L. plays an electric guitar and conducts the entire service with military precision. Getting up for the Bible readings, collecting the offering, and comments of "*Amen, Aleluya*" all are performed with well-drilled accuracy. I miss the children, but Chan Felix has called them to the palm-frond shed, where he has them singing, praying, and, indeed, listening. The testimonies contain much personal information—a son sick, a wife in the hospital, a husband refusing to be converted—details not usually mentioned in Utzpak, since everybody knows them anyway. Jose asks for prayers for me so I will promptly receive the Holy Spirit and for Eus's well-being.

During the altar call, there is tremendous shouting; everybody prays much louder than in Utzpak. Jose's kinetic pattern, which I had observed during his visit to Utzpak the previous year, has changed. Instead of folding his hands behind his back and bending forward and back while kneeling, he now lifts both arms and remains rigidly upright. Then he lets one arm drop, weaving lightly around his own axis. Two other men close to him, both also kneeling, are in intense glossolalia, one jumping up and down on his knees—I am never quite sure how the men do that, but they do not get up first—and the other one rocking back and forth. The motion pattern is not individual, but rather characteristic of this congregation as a whole. I see a woman kneeling in the aisle doing the same thing. Jose then lifts both arms up again and rubs his hands together with hands and fingers perfectly straight, a common gesture among Yucatecan men when their hands are cold or wet. But his palms hardly touch. The two men I have been observing are still rocking on their knees, although with their trunks now parallel to the floor. Jose rises, but in the second aisle a boy has the same motion pattern while in glossolalia. Jose's 16-year-old daughter, his oldest, also speaks in tongues, twitching her whole body back and forth.

Juan L.'s sermon reminds me of Barrera's. He has a loud voice and a fast, intense delivery; he refers to factors in the life of his audience without expanding too much on them; needless to say, there is the imminence of the Second Coming and the urgency of the need for both kinds of baptism. Speaking to an urban congregation, he also demonstrates his sophistication, describing heaven as having air conditioning, giving the date and place of publication of the version of the Bible he is using, and telling what the language of Jesus is. Some of the same features characterized Barrera's popular sermons too. So when Eus says that "people don't want a minister from their own village," she is perhaps speaking of this urban style. I once overheard Candil and Isauro remarking about an obviously rural visiting minister who had come to preach in Utzpak as talking too slowly and being repetitious, but mainly not knowing anything.

After the service, the *hermanos* belonging to the compound have themselves a bull session in the palm-frond shelter, and their voices are clearly audible in my small room. Just before I doze off, I hear Joaquin's voice. He gleefully describes an incident, which he either witnessed or read about, in which a Protestant minister asked a *cura* some questions, and when the *cura* did not know the answer, he knocked him down. There is laughter; nobody puts Joaquin in his place, and I am struck once more by the casual acceptance of violence that the women keep pointing out. There is a prayer marking the end of the session. It is past midnight.

At half past five the next morning, I wake up to the familiar phrasing of glossolalia from the other side of my board wall. I start recording it, but when at 8 o'clock it is still going on, I decide to call it quits, when one man's glossolalia passes over into trance song, interspersed with the spoken form. When I go over into the temple to see whose glossolalia that is, I discover, to my surprise, that it is Joaquin's. His glossolalia is of a much lower pitch than last year, also slower, and then it is elaborated by his trance singing.

There are four men present at this morning session, among them Juan L. He is kneeling next to a chair with his arms resting on it, and he is also speaking in tongues. An *hermano* I do not know now also breaks into a trance song. It is much more complex than that of Joaquin but bears no resemblance to the hymns, *coritos,* or even the popular music blaring from jukeboxes and radios all over this quarter of the city. I cannot hear much resemblance to Peregrina's trance song either, which I heard once more in Merida. It seems to me, however, that all three trance-based behaviors, speaking in tongues, body motion, and singing, have this in common, that they seem to weaken over time, but at a different rate. The glossolalia is apparently the most stable, then comes the singing, and the kinetic manifestations are the least resistant to change.

Unexpectedly, Joaquin's trance song breaks off. He passes into the spoken utterance, briefly regains his song, then returns to ordinary language with, "*Aleluya, la sangre de Cristo tiene poder* [The blood of Christ has power]."

In the afternoon, Eus and I go on an excursion to Bacalar. Eus wants to see the congregation that Chan Felix is slated to take over, and he comes along. Eus and I go for a walk along the shore of the lovely inland lagoon that Bacalar is known for and collect tiny shells in the murky and tepid water. The *hermana* we visit has seven children. Her husband used to work on highway construction, but that work stopped. There is some tourism in Bacalar because of the lagoon, but it provides scant employment, and hunger is always around the corner. Their home is constructed of cardboard and poles with a tar-paper roof.

We go to an afternoon Apostolic service with her. The temple is built the same way as her home, except it has boards instead of cardboard for walls. Its only decoration is some plastic flowers strung along the edge of the roofline. The attendance is fourteen men and thirteen women and is further swelled by Manuel H. and three *hermanos* who come to visit the congregation from Cuarenta y Dos, a village not far from Bacalar. Here again the girls and some of the women are wearing the *chalina.* Manuel introduces Chan Felix as a visitor. Apparently the congregation is quite rural, so that when Chan Felix in turn introduces his mother, he says that she is "*muy Maya,*" and he also is "*puro*

Maya." Then he asks her to say something to the congregation in Maya, which she does with aplomb, giving a well-thought-out mini-sermon and earning enthusiastic "*Amens*" and "*Aleluyas.*"

Manuel's sermon is very slow and very boring. There is the usual pitch for baptism, and five women and two men indicate their desire to be baptized. During the altar call, our hostess goes into glossolalia. She has her sick child in her arms, her youngest, and it keeps squirming and crying, but eventually it goes to sleep, gently rocked by the rhythmical tremors of its mother's trance.

We want to return from Bacalar to Chetumal by catching the Valladolid bus on the highway, but it never comes, although we wait until 1 o'clock in the morning. Chan Felix finally finds a taxi and we share the fare among the ten of us who crowd into the vehicle.

Before we leave for Merida the following day, Juan L. and I have a long conversation. He wants to know about xenoglossia. Do I think that when people speak in tongues they use a foreign language, one that they do not know? I tell him that I have never had the opportunity to record any such event. He insists that if God wanted to give someone an important message, he could certainly use a person at the service by making him speak in an unknown tongue, one that he would not be able to speak under ordinary circumstances. We agree that miracles are certainly possible and part as friends.

Home Again

Back in Utzpak, Santiago does not seem to appreciate the merchandise we have bought him, or rather the effort involved, and Eus is angry because he gives her no present for doing the shopping for him, which would have been the proper thing to do. Reina tells that she has heard from Barrera's wife that Barrera has written a letter to Juan L. as the supervisor of the Apostolic Church of the District saying that he wants to leave Utzpak. Lucrecia is all for it. She wants to wean her young son with the help of her mother in Campeche. Besides, she has her family there.

At the evening service of July 23, 1970, I observe a curious little scene, characteristic of Barrera's prevailing mood. Barrera is behind his barricade, obviously preoccupied. Isauro and Candil come up to him to ask about which hymn he wants for the opening. He shrugs his shoulders. "I don't care. Choose for yourselves." The men are obviously confused and hurt. In his sermon, he threatens that if God sees that a person does not try to accept him, God will kill him.

During the prayer for the sick, a considerable number of the congregation pray for them in tongues, and the prayer assumes an unusual air of heightened tension, almost abandonment. Alvio is very loud, Juanita is sobbing, Lucrecia is on her knees rocking, alternately speaking and weeping, her shoulders shaking. The younger Candil is shouting out a fluid glossolalia utterance, Mariano is standing, his arms extending upward, alternately folding his hands and rubbing them together to the rhythm of his utterance. Several young girls, Rosa and Angela among them, speak in tongues fast and long, and practically nobody responds to Barrera's bell signal.

As to the private services, one follows on the heels of the other. One is held on the later afternoon of July 24, 1970, in the home of Agostin V., a recently baptized *hermano*. His *mamposteria* house is quite small; it has a tar-paper roof, a dirt floor, an upright frame for weaving hammocks, and a radio in a box nailed to the wall. There are quantities of children about, and some of them have a bad heat rash. The mothers lay them on their laps, pull up their clothes, and, rubbing and scratching them, they blow on them to give them some relief. The air is very stuffy, so the men stay outside, enjoying the cool breeze, and Barrera leans against the *albarrada*, cleaning his fingernails. In effect, only the women are inside when Isauro opens the service. But when it comes time for the sermon, Barrera demands that everyone come inside. He is on his favorite theme; the world is full of evil, all manner of sins, adultery, idolatry, drinking, dances. Passionately he shouts, "I will be so happy when Christ comes and all is destroyed."

In the evening of the same day, there is still another private service, this time in Teresa's house. She is also one of the recently baptized ones; her husband Chucho deals cattle and is so affluent that they even have electricity in their *mamposteria* house. So the *hermanos* drag all their electrical equipment along, a walk of half an hour, their loudspeaker, amplifier, and electrical guitar. They construct a veritable spider's web of extension cords to connect it all, and since there is no place to put the amplifier, they suspend it above the side door. Conditions are especially trying during this service; twenty-six women with their children crowded into the small house, the men squeezed in and out, and in the intense heat the stench of urine from the nearby patio competes with the stench inside of our perspiration. And the electrically amplified sound nearly blasts the tar paper off the roof.

Barrera preaches about the foolish and the wise virgins. Even the foolish virgins believed in God, but they did not surrender themselves to Christ and did not believe in the Second Coming. Jesus will come when we least expect him. There are many people with "filthy theories" who do not believe that, but he hopes that all the visitors are prudent virgins. With a laugh, Nina says later that the Catholics say that when Christ comes, they will be saved and the *evangelicos* are the ones who will burn.

Driving toward a Peak

Things start up slowly on this Sunday morning. In his yard, now separated from the church property by a new *albarrada* that was completed yesterday, Don Eduardo is singing a hymn, very loudly, "*Orar sin cesar, venceremos* . . . [If we pray incessantly, we will be victorious]." No one is there to hear him—although it is 6 o'clock, when the service is to start—except Isauro, who is sweeping the temple. By 7 o'clock, there are four men and a girl, then others start straggling in. Mariano comes to kneel in front of the altar, praying, but seems to have problems with speaking in tongues. Barrera is sitting up on the platform, studying a church pamphlet. Then he climbs down and goes to the back to talk to Isauro about the filth of the world and about the tribulations soon to be experienced by the Church. A teenage girl comes in with a small boy on her arms. "This is the boy," she says to me, "who died many times. He turned purple, and then Barrera prayed over him, and now he is well and growing beautifully."

During the introductory service, Barrera makes us stand through the entire reading of chapters 5, 7, 9, and 10 of Revelation, up to the section about the mighty angel with the scroll:

> Then the angel whom I saw standing on the sea and on the land raised his
> right hand to heaven and took an oath by the One who lives forever and
> ever, who created heaven and earth and sea along with everything in them:
> "There shall be no more delay. When the time comes for the seventh angel
> to blow his trumpet, the mysterious plan of God, which he announced to
> his servants the prophets, shall be accomplished in full."

At the conclusion of the service, Barrera announces that there will be a small conference with "the leaders" of the church. There are seven men and ten women present. No one leaves, so apparently they all assume they are leaders. Barrera talks about the Russians and about the United States. They will soon be fighting the Third World War. Then, he says, they will all converge on Israel. In the meantime, Mexico will not be a bed of roses, either. After all these wars, everything will be destroyed except for the (Apostolic) Church.

During the subsequent altar call, it is quite clear that carrying the speaking in tongues way beyond bell signal has by now become a pattern. It takes so much time, however, that there is no intermission before the start of the Service for the Holy Spirit. This time, Barrera resumes his earlier strategy, arranging those who have already acquired the manifestation behind those still praying for it. Some of the women of the latter group immediately achieve glossolalia, and so does Mariano, with a curious, very fast staccato pattern, a kind of stutter, apparently equivalent to the ˀuˀuˀuˀu or *bubububu* of female novices. Simultaneously, his previous impressive hand and arm motions are reduced into a mere rocking movement with outstretched arms, as though all his energy is now absorbed by this important new step.

After the prayer for the Holy Spirit, Barrera asks the customary question about whether anybody has felt anything. The mother of the resuscitated baby tells of her rapture and breaks into tears, a clear indication that she has achieved the initial trance step. But since she has not spoken, it does not count. The next woman, whom I do not know, hesitates to answer, and Barrera encourages her to speak in Maya—"I understand more than last year." Eus's comment later is, "He knows more than he admits. This is how many people act." But then the woman elects to talk in halting Spanish, saying that she felt nothing. Mariano reports that he heard his language change but he could understand nothing.

During Sunday school session, Barrera keeps us standing through all of chapters 14 through 19 of Revelation, and when the congregation shows obvious signs of tiredness in the rising heat, he commands that we should stand for the glory of God and reread the entire text once more from the more recent translation. It takes more than half an hour. I am still trying to concentrate though, disregarding the pain in my legs that are still swollen from the walk to Tibolom. It is small consolation that Reina thinks that now they are pretty, "fat." And as I am listening for the second time to how the beast was captured along with the false prophet and both were hurled down alive into the burning sulfur, I keep wondering: What is he trying to accomplish? Reestablish discipline, emphasize his authority? Break down resistance?

At noon, during the session of the Dorcas, I am struck by how well the women have learned the procedure of such meetings as envisioned by the church. Gregoria reads the minutes of last Sunday's session; they have used the exact form dictated by Barrera last year. Each one of the members, in alphabetical order, is called on to recite a Bible verse. The dues are collected, the hymns are sung, and the prayers spoken, all without a hitch. Barrera has made the round of the meetings, giving a talk first to the Senores. As Eus knows from Nohoch Felix, he does not talk about money there. Probably, she thinks, because regrettably they do not pay attention to what happens to the church's money. Old Candil still owes the church 500 pesos that he borrowed because Rodolfa was sick, and that was during the time when Chan Felix was the minister.

After talking to the Juveniles, Barrera comes to us women. And it is quite obvious that what he is issuing is a declaration of war.

Although preaching is forbidden to women, he starts out, they have already accomplished a great deal in the church. They are allowed to sponsor and, thus, lead services, they can go out and evangelize, they are allowed to fast and pray for the sick. Thus, the women of the church are continually occupied with matters pleasing to God. However, a house would fall if a support was taken out. All three organizations have to work together; otherwise the work will collapse. The important point is, however—and here he waves a small booklet containing the Constitution of the Apostolic Church of Mexico—that all three organizations of the Church work with the approbation of the minister. He has absolute say over everything. He can use the money coming from the offerings whichever way he sees fit, for God put him into the position he holds. He cites an example from Campeche. The minister there sent an evangelist to Sacabchen and gave him a flat 500 pesos for his expenses for one month. Barrera thought that was excessive, and he told the minister so. The minister argued with him for a while, and when Barrera continued to voice his objections, the minister suggested that they pray. During this prayer, due to the grace of God, Barrera understood that the minister was right.

Of the offerings, 50 percent was supposed to go to the minister for expenses of the church, such as electricity. Also, the minister should not starve to death. The older members of the congregation, such as the Dorcas, should explain all this to the newer ones, so they will not get any wrong ideas. This September, there will be a meeting of the organization of the Juveniles in Coahuitla, and it will require 800 pesos for the person sent to represent Utzpak. They would all have to work very hard to get that money together. Every Dorca who is an officeholder serves for one year, and the harder she works, the greater will be her crown in heaven.

Eus and I are sitting side by side, and all through his presentation he seems to be speaking at her, or at me, or at both of us; it is hard to tell.

He calls for a prayer to conclude the session. As is the custom, everyone says whatever his or her inspiration dictates, with the voices usually blending in a chorus. However, Barrera's prayer is excessively loud, so we can all hear that he is asking God to forgive the *hermanas* if they have thoughts that are not "in accordance with reality." "Please, God, forgive them," he repeats.

Eus and I go shopping in the afternoon, and Eus indignantly repeats all her various charges against Barrera's financial dealings, how Barrera took 50 percent of the offerings, not 25 percent as was the custom at Chan Felix's time, and then helped himself to whatever he wanted. Eus says that she will tell Juan L. about the finances of the church if she has a chance.

Returning to her home, we encounter Nina, who reports that at the meeting of the Juveniles, Barrera has said materially the same thing that he told the Dorcas, continually pounding the Constitution of the Apostolic Church and making it very clear that he is the sole master of anything and everything. She is good at weaving hammocks, so she and the other young people decided how they would use the money they earn with various projects. She would weave a very wide hammock to sell for the church. So she was given 60 pesos for *canamo* [boiled cotton thread for hammock-weaving] out of the church's funds, and she bought *canamo* of many different colors. Such colorful hammocks sell in Chetumal or Campeche for as much as 140 pesos, a nice profit for the church. The hammock was not even half finished when Barrera came by, and seeing the remaining *canamo,* he gathered it all up saying, "*Sea Ud. gente conmigo* [Be nice to me], and I will also be nice to you." And he made himself a fine new hammock, leaving the Juveniles with a narrow one that brought no profit to the church. He should go out and work like other men do, was Nina's comment.

For some reason, perhaps because the two women are so angry, our conversation drifts to the topic of witchcraft. Witchcraft is all around, they say. Some time ago a woman, she was called Agripa and came from Saye, was thrown into a cenote to drown because she was a witch. She bewitched a young man. He found a candle in his hat, that was how she had done it, and he became very ill, but he did not die. There were also witches in Tibolom; that was the reason why so many people there became ill of an incurable disease. The witch there became ill herself, maybe God punished her that way. There was a woman here in Utzpak who accused Eus of witchcraft. "I will beat you," she said to Eus, patting her left upper arm, which was the gesture that always accompanied such threats. But then she died in Merida two months later. And then there was Dona Ugulina, who knew how to do *treinta-y-tres,* "33." She even had a book about it. Its performance caused an incurable illness. A woman asked Dona Ugulina to perform it against a thief who made off with her blanket. She did not know that it had been her own son until his hand began to dry up. But then it was too late. There was no way in which the curse could be withdrawn. He pleaded that he was innocent, but if that was so, "33" would have been ineffective against him. There was no medicine for it, and he died.

Eus finally came up with the comic relief. Dona Ugulina, who was a good friend of hers, had a favorite water pitcher, she told. One day it was gone from the table in her front room that was always open to the street, as was the custom. Dona Ugulina let it be known that she knew how to do "33," and the following day, quite miraculously, her pitcher reappeared on her table.

At the evening service of July 26, 1970, there is a great deal of glossolalia. Epi is more energetic than before; he apparently does not need the kinetic pattern I saw earlier to propel himself into speaking in tongues, which returns to the impressive level of last year. Simultaneously, however, he no longer plays a dominant role in the prayer for the sick. That is taken over by Mariano and Alvio. Barrera announces that on Monday he will go to see Antonio again, for he is weak and alone. Eus raises her eyebrows. What does he mean, "again?" Last time, when supposedly he went to visit Antonio, he never linked up with him. Antonio wanted to come back to Utzpak, but as we all knew, there were problems for him here, for his wife still had not been converted. He asked for a special offering for Antonio. Recently there has been much more paper money in the bowls than before, when my offering was often the only bill.

JULY 27, 1970

The morning's news is that Barrera has taken his wife with him on his trip. Reina saw her dressed up in her good clothes. Normally her kitchen things and her table are out in the yard under a palm-frond roof where she cooks, but now she has stored it all in the *casa pastoral*. This means, Reina conjectures, that Lucrecia intends to stay away for a while.

Later in the day the news spreads along the road that Antonio has just returned, but he did have a chance to talk with Barrera in Merida. I see him later at the evening service held in Rodolfa's house for her birthday. His face seems less youthful, puffy, and his eyes tired. As I watch him, a small black moth settles on his forehead, above his left eyebrow, as though Satan has applied his bat's seal there as he was passing by. He is greeted by various *hermanos,* but there is no awe. He has brought his wife with him; she is heavy with child, so dark and beautiful. Later in the service, which is conducted by Chan Felix in the absence of Barrera, Antonio is formally greeted as a visitor. Rodolfa is clearly pleased with all these important goings-on for her birthday. There is a birthday hymn and a prayer for her, then Chan Felix directs her to speak. She expresses her gratitude for having reached the age of 35 and asks the congregation to continue praying for her. After the conclusion of the service, we are served a dessert that looks and tastes like tinted laundry starch. I have no idea why it causes a furious diarrhea the next morning.

JULY 28, 1970

Eus and I go shopping in the morning. With her, that is always also visiting time, for while some women pass us with a brief *"Paseando?"* [Going for a walk?], others stop to tell their news. *"Ola, vecina* [neighbor]," Eus stops to talk with a small, worn-looking woman with a harelip. We get a review of her recent life. How her husband was hit by lightning, which paralyzed him, so he could no longer work. She had nothing to eat for her two little girls, so she went begging. People gave her clothes for her children. Then she found a job. It was wonderful. She earned 10 pesos a day by raising and lowering the red flag on the highway to Tizimin, where construction was going on.

It is story time also at Payi's store, all in Maya this time, where we stop to buy soft drinks. While we are drinking them, a plump woman in a pretty *ʔipil* comes in to do some shopping. Eus tells me later that she knows this woman because her husband used to be a Presbyterian minister. Besides, her adopted daughter is the niece of Joaquina's husband. What Eus apparently does not know is that her husband used to get drunk regularly every Sunday. One Sunday, he participated in a brawl in the tavern, wounding a man so badly that he lost an eye. He was sentenced to five years in prison. His wife sold everything they owned and with the 5,000 pesos realized that way, she paid all sorts of fines in Merida and her husband was released from prison after a month. But now he still got drunk every Sunday. The physician gave him some pills to cure him of his desire for alcohol, but he insists on swallowing them whole, so they pass through him. He won't allow his wife to grind them up and put them into his food or drink. Every day, she now lights a candle before the picture of St. Martin, but it does no good. Eus's blunt remark is that you do not pray with candles. Instead, she should come to the temple and bring her husband with her. He could be cured there.

When we get home, Isauro comes by with Antonio to say good-by to Chan Felix, who is leaving that afternoon for Bacalar. It is customary on such occasions for the women to leave the men alone in the main house. So Eus is soaping her wash at the *batea* [wash trough], Nina is busying herself with making some lemonade, and I am typing, all three of us pretending not to be interested. So I am actually startled when Chan Felix comes out of the house and invites the three of us to a prayer. It is something of a surprise that it is not Chan Felix, who outranks both men in the church hierarchy, but Antonio who is in charge of this brief ritual, directing us to kneel and praying more loudly than the others for each one of us in turn, and of course, also for my eventual and hopefully speedy conversion.

In the afternoon, Nina takes me to see Joaquina's house. The walk would be the last lighthearted occasion of this fieldwork season. Joaquina's house is a feast for the eye, a lovely example of a completely traditional oval Maya mud-and-wattle structure—the wattle woven through horizontally and daubed with brown mud—and a palm-frond roof in perfect repair. Inside the house, there is the *candela* nestled into its north arc, a thick bundle of the two-foot-long firewood next to it, a sepia-colored earth floor, and bundles of hammocks hanging from the crossbeams. Joaquina is sitting outside in the shade of a tall *nance* tree next to the low round table everyone uses for making tortillas. She has a bundle of lush, freshly picked banana leaves next to her and a large brown *lek* with cornmeal filling for preparing *vaporcitos*. It is to be her talent to be sold during the pauses of today's evening service.

JULY 28, 1970, EVENING SERVICE

Barrera has returned from his trip and presides over the service, which is sponsored by the Dorcas. Joaquina opens, then passes to Juanita. During the testimonies, Pedro announces that for a long time he has been wanting to go and evangelize. He was unhappy with his family, so he was divorced, and now he definitely has decided that he will go to Santa Cruz to serve as an evangelist.

There is a *corito* and then an altar call. Barrera has left one of the two tables that he usually employs to form his barricade down in front of the rostrum, and I start filming him. I want to record his kinetic pattern but have not been able to do it because he is always praying in the back. But he moves very little, so I stop recording. When Juanita rings for the end of the altar call, he rises and goes to the rostrum. Angrily, and using my full name, he says, "Hermana Felicitas D. Goodman, I must ask you not to use your light during the prayer. It does something to me, I don't know what." I am understandably startled. It had been with his express permission that I was filming during the services. Nina says later that that had been a sign that he "was not praying right," for if you pray in the right way, you do not notice such things. No such conflict has ever arisen between the minister and myself, and the congregation is hushed and disturbed.

The service takes its usual course. The Dorcas offer a hymn and Joaquina passes to Teresa, who calls for the offering. Joaqina and Rodolfa collect the money in the new ritual manner.

Teresa passes to Barrera. Looking up from his Bible during the reading of the text, he says imperiously, "Don't sleep, and do as I say; those that can, have to stand." He then informs the congregation, "I had to go on a brief trip for a necessity, but God has already brought me back to glorify his name." Adding to the tension already prevailing in the congregation at this point, Barrera then announces that tomorrow, Wednesday, there will be a meeting of all the men of the congregation; later he limits it to all the men who have been baptized. The women will be informed by their men about what is discussed.

In his sermon, Barrera talks about the parable of the watchman: the watchman was the man who was responsible for what happened to the people in the city. The same is true today—we all have the responsibility for what happens to the other people when Christ comes again. He then continues:

> Now I want you to pay very close attention. Recently, this past Sunday that is, the Holy Spirit manifested its power to an *hermano* in Chetumal, to Hermano Jose. You all know Jose. He is a native of Utzpak. This Sunday, then, he started praying, and the power of the Holy Spirit manifested itself and showed him many churches. These churches, however, were terribly dirty. The people who entered them found themselves surrounded by spiderwebs, well, the churches were in complete disarray, dirty, and wormeaten, and that is where the people were. And the *hermano* asked the same power that gave him the vision, and he asked, "What manner of thing is

this?" And the answer came, "These poor people think that they are truly in a well-ordered church, but just look, all around them they have only disorder." And in truth, there was not a bit of purity around them, much less an immaculate church. And immediately the same voice told him, "They are expecting you to talk to them and give them the message. Why don't you enter into these homes, into these synagogues, in order to make them all clean? Christ will soon come and you people, what are you doing?"

And this *hermano*, this Hermano Jose, as he rose, felt something like an attack of trembling in his body, and he started talking to Hermano Juan L. and the other *hermanos* who were in that place, and immediately our Hermano Juan L. went to Tizimin to talk to our Hermano Gilberto there because he has this wish that we all have, to do something for the honor of Jesus Christ.

Barrera then reminds the congregation that Antonio's vision is also an announcement by the Lord that the Second Coming is imminent. "Everybody is our neighbor," he says, "and we need to help all to be saved before it is too late."

The excitement generated by the news of Jose's vision is immediately evident in the congregation's subsequent glossolalia behavior. Whereas ordinarily the period following the sermon is one of quiet, of relaxation, there is now a renewed burst of glossolalia, made more impressive by the fact that one of the men is now also caught in the pattern of delayed return.

During the prayer for the sick, there is a great deal of glossolalia. Dolores, a 16-year-old, is rocking and sobbing. Antonio is very loud. Mariano's utterance is still an improbably rapid stutter. He cannot pick up on the bell signal and continues with his glossolalia. Finally, he recovers, rubs his hands over his face, presses his fingers over his temples, then sits down, hands before his face.

On the next day, July 29, 1970, at close to six in the evening, the brothers Juan L. and Luis L. arrive together on a powerful new motorcycle. They park it by Reina's house and Barrera comes in to say "*Paz de Cristo.*" He tells me that there is no such thing as a church archive in Merida, only some letters and a baptismal record that I am welcome to see when I come to visit. Then Juan and Luis go to the temple and closet themselves with Barrera. Soon the *hermanos* of the congregation begin assembling, and, occasionally, very loud prayer and glossolalia are audible from behind the closed doors.

Evening service. The service takes place in the home of Venustiano, a recently baptized man. The only men present are Isauro, his brother Ernesto, and old Don Fulgencio, whom we have not seen for a while. The service is opened by Ernesto, who then passes to Isauro. The latter announces that Luis L. and Juan L. have arrived and that plans are at present being made for the work of the Lord; that is why the *hermanos* are absent. "If you can," Isauro says, "you should pray all night. We don't know when Christ will manifest himself. He is trying to give us some message, this is what he is at present using the bodies of the *hermanos* in the temple."

For his biblical text, Isauro chooses that perennial favorite, the first Pentecost in the Acts. In his remarks, he refers to Jose's vision, and there is a feeling of presence, of urgency, which readily communicates itself. Besides, it has rained and it is beastly hot and humid, which adds to the tension. Isauro then continues:

> This night may be like any other night for other people, but for us, it is different. We know that the Second Coming is very close, although the nonbelievers still don't give it credence. The first Pentecost was not a fiesta with dances, picture shows, or bullfights, things of the world. It was an invisible fiesta, and this is why so many still don't believe. This is not simply a manifestation of the Holy Spirit, as we have all experienced it before, this is the promise we have all been waiting for so long. New gifts of the Holy Spirit are being received at this moment in the temple: some *hermanos* are giving an interpretation of the tongues, and many more will begin doing that, now that the Second Coming is so much closer. The same Holy Spirit working on the *hermanos* has also let it be known that not all the people will accept God. However, God does not want the death of a single sinner.

At this point Isauro, an unusually dignified, quiet man with a great deal of composure, breaks into tears, bends over his Bible, and says between sobs, "Let us pray." He kneels down. Almost instantly Rosa, Joaquina, and Gregoria, and then also Juanita and Teresa—all the women present who have already received the Holy Spirit—go into glossolalia, except for Nina and Eus. Rosa kneels on the dirt floor, rocking on her knees; the others are standing.

Isauro continues with his sermon. There are always neighbors crowding in the doorways at these services in private homes, and Isauro now turns to them, admonishing them not to speak ill about what they have seen. They are not familiar with the manifestation of the Lord, and if they speak ill of what they have seen, they might go to eternal perdition. While he speaks, Rosa, bending very low, continues her sobbing, high-intensity glossolalia.

"Messages are now expected from Christ," Isauro says, "about how to go on, how he wants the work to be continued." At this moment, the women once more go into very loud glossolalia. Rosa still continues—she has been in glossolalia for seven minutes by now—as does Gregoria, with her sleeping infant on her arms.

Finally Rosa stands up, after more than ten minutes of glossolalia. "If some of the *hermanas*," Isauro continues, "want to get together in someone's house to pray through the night, that will be the right thing to do. Or people can also pray alone, of course." The service concludes with the usual invitation to the sharing of food, "*Dice la hermana que esperomos un momento* [The *hermana* says we should wait a moment]."

While we are waiting for the food, Isauro announces, "Let us pray for the sick child of this *hermana*," pointing to Paula, who had come in with Pedrito on her arm, "for although we know that the Second Coming is now going to be very soon, let us in the meantime pray that this child will get well." Rosa, who is the sister of Pedrito, goes into glossolalia again, while Gregoria finally passes from her glossolalia into the usual pattern of exhaustion, "*oh s—s—s oh s—s—s,*" and then saying, "*Obra, o Jesus* [Work your miracles, oh Jesus]."

Isauro then tells Gregoria and Teresa, who are giving rapt attention, "Pray, then rest, keep vigil, pray again." The women are wide-eyed and distracted. Then Isauro and the other men leave to join those in the temple. Despite all these events, the women still pass out the cooked sweet rice, which emphasizes the ritual character of this food exchange.

It strikes me that for the first time there is mention in this service of the view that some of the *hermanos* are interpreting what other *hermanos* are saying in tongues. It is quite a surprise. Although mentioned in the Bible as a gift of the Holy Spirit, interpretation is not a behavior that occurs generally in the Apostolic churches in Mexico. When, in 1968, I asked the then bishop of the Church, Manuel Gaxiola, in an interview in Mexico City about this point, he said that he was against the practice because people tended to say anything that they happened to think of. Its use therefore in translating messages relating to the Second Coming represented a true innovation in Utzpak.

Outside, after eating, Rodolfa and her sisters and daughters gather around Eus. The topic: Barrera's outburst against my taking pictures with a floodlight in church. Eus had been saying all along that somebody else must have been complaining about it in addition to Barrera not being able to pray properly. Rodolfa puts her arm around my shoulder. "When are you coming back?" Next year, or maybe in two years. "Two years? That is too long. Come back next year. By that time, there will be another pastor." The conversation disintegrates into a general gossip session, with Barrera the target, how he made such poor use of my camera by taking a few pictures at only one baptism after I left. Then Rodolfa said that she had overheard Mila, the granddaughter of Anita, complaining that *shnuuk* [old, but in a disparaging sense] Hermana Felicitas filmed her too while she was praying. So, she says, that meant that she had not kept her eyes closed while praying, which is highly improper. Besides, as Eus points out, she had no business complaining, for I always gave her grandmother Anita large alms when she came begging. Anita had no adult sons to take care of her, only two that died in infancy. She was left with only one daughter. "So she has no one to help her," says Eus. "If her daughter gives her something to eat in the morning, she eats; if she doesn't, she goes hungry."

Back home at Reina's place, we can still hear loud praying from the temple. My impulse is to sneak into the temple courtyard with my tape-recorder and do some eavesdropping, but then I think better of it: what food for gossip if somebody saw me, which was sure to happen. During the night, though, I wake up several times with glossolalia in my ears.

In the morning, the haunting impression of last night's service continues to be with me. There is still prayer going on in the temple. I recall feeling this way in Berlin on the eve of the outbreak of World War II: Something big and terrifying is approaching. I am actually taken aback to find that life around me is still going on as always. Santiago leaves to look for work. In the next yard, I can hear Don Eduardo loudly scolding Dona Andrea for buying two small chickens for 7 pesos each. "*Hach coʔo, hach coʔo!* [Very expensive!]" he keeps shouting. Little Cilia is cooing in her hammock. Reina is out looking for Lupita, who is now an independent adventuress, off by herself to see her grandfather, to see Dona Raquel, or to see Dona Rach. Dona Rach's daughter comes by and says that at past midnight she still cannot sleep because of the racket of the *hermanos*. Reina has come back with Lupita and suggests that Dona Juanita probably *la entro la bilis* [had a gall-bladder attack], that is, became furious over all the commotion in the temple. "Why were they praying all night anyway?" I explain about the Second Coming. Reina: "It is because so many people still will not believe. They call the *hermanos locos* [crazy]. So Jose had the same sort of thing like Antonio?" "That is what they say." Reina: "They say that Antonio has a power. He can see who is a true believer."

Since Nohoch Felix is out at the ranch working, Eus and I have no man to inform us about what exactly has transpired during the night, which will later be remembered by the congregation as the night when Satan began his attack and by the larger community as the time when the madness struck the congregation. But Eus has been out shopping early and has encountered her friend Valuch, whose husband Goyo was at the church all night. It seems that during the night, the *hermanos* had been praying for guidance about who was to go out to evangelize. It was agreed that Epi, Isauro, Antonio, Alvio, Ernesto, and Goyo were to go out to preach. Goyo, however, did not think that he should go, since he did not know enough about the gospel. During the night, however, according to Valuch, Antonio listened to Goyo speaking in tongues and interpreted it as saying, "The Devil is already coming, spreading his wings, you are only for things of this world." Then Goyo started praying in tongues again, and Antonio listened to him and said, "You must go, preach the word of God."

It was also decided that those *hermanos* who would not go to evangelize would give 10 pesos per week to an *hermana* whose husband was out evangelizing. Those *hermanas* whose husband would be "in the field," were to stay with the families where the husbands were still present. Eus's comment was that Nohoch Felix made 50 pesos at most per week; that was barely enough for two days' food, so how could he contribute? The *hermanos* were also trying to come up with 200 pesos for Dito, a recently converted *hermano,* so he could legally marry his wife, without which he could not go out to spread God's word.

We are still talking in front of Reina's house when Nina comes back from an errand. She tells that early in the morning Antonio had wanted to hang himself with his belt. The *hermanos* who were with him saw two angels behind him, one with a sword, the other one with a whip. "He has the Spirit of God," is Nina's comment, "that is why el Demonio wants to kill him." She also says that some of the women actually prayed through the night, first in Gregoria's house and then in Teresa's. In addition to Gregoria and Teresa, the group included Mila, Rosa, Juana, and Joaquina. They formed what began to appear like an inner circle, *hach consagradas* [very dedicated], Eus calls them, while Eus, Nina, and myself seem to be an outer group. Valuch also considers herself part of the latter. The way she knows that, Eus quotes her as saying, is that "when Barrera sees Teresa or Gregoria, he lifts his eyebrows. When he sees me, he doesn't."

I have been talking with Reina about having to leave soon, so she decides in the midst of all these goings-on to have the *hetsmec* ceremony for little Cilia. Having inquired from Tomasita what the duties of a *hetsmec comadre* are, I have paid for her registration at the magistrate's office *sacar su nombre* [to obtain her name], and I bought a frilly little dress from Dona Bartola, the local clothing store. With Santiago as a witness, Reina places tiny, plump Cilia in my arms, and to the delight of her parents she obliges with a broad smile and a gentle cooing. In turn, Reina makes her hold my sewing kit, which is small enough for her tiny fingers, my pen, the copy book where Reina enters the installments due to Santiago, and a 10-peso bill from me. That way, Cilia is going to enjoy sewing, going to school, and earning some money. Santiago disappears at this juncture. It is women's stuff, he says, but also he probably does not want to be reminded that he still owes me 200 pesos. Then Reina places Cilia on my hip for her first experience of being carried straddled that way. Eus comes later in the company of Nina and jokes that out on the ranch there was no one to do the *hetsmec* ritual for Nina, and that is why she is not walking right. Nina, also kidding, immediately demonstrates that there is nothing wrong with her walking.

At noon, Luis L. and Juan L. leave on their supernatural errand, speeding away on their motorcycle to spread the word to other congregations about the messages of the Holy Spirit and the imminence of the Second Coming.

Later, there is some commotion at the church, and I go over to see what is going on. A number of *hermanas* are standing around at the entrance, mainly the in-group. We chat a bit about the weather and then see Antonio emerging from the church, his face pudgy and his eyes tired. In his appearance there is little of the young peasant of a few nights ago. He is wearing dark pants and a buttoned-down shirt, a ballpoint pen in his shirt pocket. He says that he has come for three months, since his wife is expecting. At this point, Ernesto arrives, and when I ask if a service is going to be held now, he says that it is to be a meeting for married couples only. "*Adelante* [Let's go]," says Antonio, and all go in, while I walk back home.

At this service, I hear in the evening, the official announcement was made about the men who were going to go "into the field" and about the arrangements for the families to be left behind.

July 30, 1970, Evening Service

If I expected merely another service that evening, I was utterly wrong. For events suddenly surged to a climax. In fact, the congregation experienced visions, demonic possession, exorcism, grossly prolonged and unmanageable ecstatic trance, and spontaneous acquisition of glossolalia. In an atmosphere of utter panic, all those uncommitted were exhorted to become baptized, and these passionate pleas were coupled with strident attacks on those who still hung back. In the view of the street, it was this evening when the madness truly started.

At the outset, there are sixteen men and nineteen women, as well as many children. In the course of the service many more people crowd in, until the small church fairly bursts at the seams. Somehow, this overcrowding amplifies everything that is to take place this evening. Isauro opens the service, which is to be dedicated to evangelizing. Barrera is kneeling at the box by the back wall, praying. Isauro's first prayer concerns the souls that are approaching, that is, people who are beginning to show an interest in being converted. After a hymn, Isauro calls for testimonies. Antonio rises, and with closed eyes he gives thanks for the manifestations that are being received. Then Chan Candelario jumps to his feet, says a few words about God's grace and then, hyperventilating, literally pumping air, his right hand stretched out stiffly before him, he goes into glossolalia; his face suddenly flushes, his eyes open up wide, he shouts very loudly. Antonio joins him with the same movement, then Alvio, then almost everybody jumps up, especially at the men's and the juvenile sections, where they can hear what Chan Candelario is saying. There is a tremendous burst of prayer. Roberta also goes into glossolalia. Chan Candelario continues with his vocalization and is still very tense; he starts shouting again, and I am unable to distinguish whether he is now speaking in tongues or in ordinary language.

When a modicum of quiet is restored, Isauro says that Chan Candelario has just seen Christ, a very rare vision, not given to all. Gregoria gets up and, shouting to be heard in the noise, suggests that there should be a prayer for those who will go to evangelize. Pedro joins in this petition, saying that he and Alvio will go to Merida tomorrow and from there to Cenotillo. Alvio gets up: "Let us all say good-by in a special prayer." Isauro comments that all these special petitions can be taken care of in front of the altar. He calls for the *corito* "*Orar sin cesar*" [Pray without pause], and the people come forward crowding around the platform, while Barrera still prays at his box. They go into glossolalia with outstretched arms, Alvio perspiring profusely. Rosa is shaking, screaming, and sobbing at the altar, doubled over. Dolores, another teenager, has a similar sobbing pattern. Epi is shouting out a prayer, still in ordinary language. His little daughter is screaming. Paula has started praying in glossolalia, and now Epi is in trance too, with a glossolalia very much like his high-energy pattern of last year, without any kinetics whatever. Rosa continues at the altar, and when Isauro rings the bell she cannot react. Gregoria's tears still flow profusely. Juanita does not react either. Angela's glossolalia is a very high ʔaiʔaiʔai, and it also continues. A dog wanders in and sniffs at a dead cockroach on the floor, but no one pays attention to it, though such an occurrence usually produces an instant indignant reaction.

It is customary to go on with the service and to proceed to the next section, even though some may still be in glossolalia. Isauro tries to get hold of the situation in this way. He calls for special hymns, and the first one to come forward is Alfredo. He begins, but he is hardly audible above the very intense glossolalia of Rosa and Angela, who are both of the same age. Neither reacts to the fact that a special hymn is being offered. Angela begins alternating between ordinary language and glossolalia phrases, while Rosa reverts to more varied syllables, indicating that in both girls the intensity of the trance is diminishing. Barrera, still kneeling and with his left hand on his hip, continues praying with his back to us. Alfredo's singing still cannot be heard. Antonio is sitting beside Chan Candelario in the front row of the men, shaking him by the neck and patting him on his back. Chan Candelario finally stops shouting. There is a puddle of saliva in front of Angela, who is back in glossolalia. Rosa is still in. Barrera turns and throws a glance at her but then continues with his prayer. Angela's dress is soaked with perspiration. Teresa, Gregoria, and Joaquina are also back in glossolalia. Rosa and Angela are rocking back and forth on their knees. Angela's mantilla slips from her head, but no one makes a motion to adjust it. Finally, she does it herself while still in the glossolalia pattern. The children sitting next to Angela watch her intently.

Chan Candelario has calmed down; he sits with eyes closed, his head slightly leaning back. Angela has returned to consciousness and is praying in ordinary language, but she continues rocking on her knees and then goes back into glossolalia. Rosa is still in trance. This goes on although Alfredo has now completed his hymn and Pedro and Ernesto are offering theirs. Once more regaining conscious control, Angela wipes her eyes, as does Rosa also; but only for a brief moment, then she is back in glossolalia. There may be others; I am concentrating on the main actors, and there is a tremendous din accompanying all these activities. Barrera is still kneeling at the box; once more Angela wipes her eyes; Rosa is sobbing and rocking, her glossolalia now at the *s—s—s—s* level of near-exhaustion. Angela has gotten up and has gone back to her seat, but Rosa continues with *s—s—s—s*.

A *corito* is called for the offering and it is collected while Rosa briefly regains consciousness, only to lapse once more, even more strongly, into the glossolalia pattern. Chan Candelario offers a special hymn, and Rosa's kinetic pattern becomes very energetic: her elbows are trembling, and she repeatedly throws her body to one side and to another; her rich pulse inventory is audible in the pause before the general prayer is started. Holding her head very rigid, she closes and opens her hands and continues to rock on her knees. At his box, still kneeling, Luis lifts his arms in supplication. Rosa slips back into the *s—s—s—s* pattern.

Isauro passes to Barrera, while Rosa, having lost most of her vocalization capacity, sighs rhythmically *ʔohhh, ʔohhh*. Barrera, at the rostrum now, announces the biblical text to be read from the Acts, but since Rosa continues, he puts his hand on her head, bending down to her. Instead of calming her, this sends her into a brief but very steep recovery of the trance level, after which she has trouble swallowing; shaken by the rhythm of the trance, she struggles with the accumulating saliva, obviously with very tight throat muscles.

Paula, large with child, is now beside her daughter, trying to get her to come out of the trance. Barrera does not get to read the biblical passage, for over on the men's side another scene is developing. Mariano is holding his arms high with his characteristic weaving pattern and utters his very fast staccato glossolalia, his eyes tightly shut, facing Pedro and Chan Candelario. Antonio leans over toward Mariano, as if trying to understand what he is saying. Rosa still cannot swallow. Paula has her hand on her daughter's shoulder. Rosa is sighing, "*Si, Dios mio, si, no puedo* . . . [Yes, Lord, yes, I cannot]." Pedro meanwhile is interpreting Mariano's glossolalia to him, while Antonio explains something quietly to Chan Candelario. This is in part conjecture about what I see: we cannot hear what is being said over the deafening welter of sounds with everyone praying very loudly, although just minutes ago Barrera had asked for a silent prayer. Paula has begun to fan Rosa, who is back to a sighing pattern, still in trance. She is handed a glass of water for her daughter, who cannot swallow it. Chan Candelario asks for a prayer and requests that the congregation make way for Rosa, who is led, or rather lifted, away from the altar, to the first chair of the center row of the juvenile section, directly next to Eus's and my chair. Eus begins to fan her, but she cannot sit; rather her head rests on the top edge of the back of her chair and her legs are stretched out, resting on the front edge of the seat. Paula joins Eus in fanning the girl, while another cup of water is handed toward the front.

Suddenly, there is an uproar close to Rosa, on the men's side, where Antonio has gone down on his knees. Barrera is by his side almost instantly, pressing Antonio's head between his hands and shouting first in glossolalia, then in ordinary speech. From the latter we understand that Antonio has all of a sudden been possessed by the Devil. He quickly recovers and tells Barrera that the Devil has gone out into the street: "Let's go see him!" And he leads Barrera out through the men's side, with most of the adult men behind them. A tremendous upsurge of glossolalia is audible from the outside, sending Rosa back into a recovery of the trance level as she lies diagonally on the chair, her head rigidly back, her hands still and hard-looking. When she starts speaking in trance, first in ordinary language, then in glossolalia, Gregoria begins sobbing and also goes into trance, as do all the other women around her. Rosa's two small brothers and three sisters, who are sitting on the children's bench beside me, are sobbing in real distress. Isauro comes over to Rosa, in glossolalia, his eyes tightly closed, then he goes back to the table in front of the rostrum. Nina sinks down on her knees beside Rosa; in glossolalia, she collapses on her elbows and stays in that posture—very rigid, her hands as still as a Dresden figurine's—all through the rest of the service, only slightly rocking occasionally. Dolores is also in very high glossolalia, getting quite hoarse. Santiago has appeared in the back, a rare guest at the services, attracted by all the commotion, especially by the one in the street, as I hear the next day. Paula cries over Rosa and tells her small children to leave, but none of them obeys. Some more water is passed down. Rosa begins to sob out names—Mila, then the husband of Reyes—which are eagerly listened for and passed on down toward the back of the church, as being a revelation of the Holy Spirit about those of deficient devotion. Barrera comes back from the street, goes up to her and, putting his hands on her head, tells her to control herself. When she keeps repeating the same phrases over and over again, he says, "*Ya lo diste* [You've already said that], *ya lo diste.*" Her chest is heaving. He continues in a soothing but loud voice, "*Sí, hija, sí, hija* [Yes, daughter]," while lightly shaking her head. Dolores, two rows back, screams out a glossolalia very much modeled on Rosa's, but without names. "God will use you," Barrera says to Rosa, "yes, he will. I know [about Reye's husband, that is, who is considered *muy rebelde* (very obstinate) in matters of the Lord, preferring Hermano G.'s Baptist services to those of the Apostolics]. I know already. Give her water." Then he repeats, "*Si, hija, si . . .*"

This scene is overcut by another, in which Chan Candelario, Isauro, Alfredo, and Alvio bend over Gaspar, a heavyset elderly man in a blue shirt. Antonio tries to hear him, shakes his head, then draws closer to listen in. Paula and Barrera take Rosa outside and to the rear, into the *casa pastoral*. Nina comments the next day, "Rosa was sick because being possessed by the Holy Spirit is intoxicating." Paula's children are still crying in front. Barrera comes back in and places his hand on Gaspar's head in recognition of his glossolalia. Dolores is still in a sobbing glossolalia, and Mila is kneeling in front with Antonio, who prays over her in a strange, very drawn-out manner, "*Si, Dios mio, manifiestate* [Yes, my Lord, manifest yourself]," very different from his usual speaking voice. Dolores is still in glossolalia, and Barrera is up behind the rostrum, trying to get hold of the congregation, whose attention is being thrown hither and thither by all the different goings-on. He warns the visitors not to think that what they are seeing is anything sad; it is a most joyous occasion, and they should not be confounded by science, which speaks against the manifestation of God and his reality. The Devil has been defeated. Many people have come to the services for a long time without surrendering themselves. There is no more time, for from yesterday afternoon until this morning at three, the Holy Spirit has distributed its gifts, here, in the church of Utzpak. There is loud glossolalia by Mila, Angela, and Dolores. Barrera continues: he has to say all the words that God is giving him to say. His face is flushed, contorted; off and on there are tears. All of a sudden, he too comes up with names. "And you, Eustaquia, and Nina, and the husband of Reyes, and Cruz, wife of Antonio, you all, you must consecrate yourself to Him or perish. I am pushed by a power to say these things, these are not my words," he shouts into the microphone of the public address system. "The Devil is now defeated, give in to God!"

"And you, Hermana Felicitas," he continues, his face even more contorted in a mask of crying, his lips trembling, "if you don't surrender to God, you will most certainly die!" Then he passes into glossolalia, confirming my impression that he has been in trance all along. It has clearly lowered his inhibition, leading him to hurl imprecations against those keeping aloof for one reason or another. Eus wipes her eyes with the corner of her *rebozo*, but her face betrays no emotion.

"Let us pray," commands Barrera in a quieter voice. Eus and I stand side by side, and she nods to me: here we are together, the condemned. Nina, in deep trance, continues kneeling at her mother's feet. Over on the men's side, I see Gregorio, Luis L.'s brother-in-law, a tall and strong man by local standards, surveying the scene with an amused smile. Nina told the following day that Rosa was now also talking like Antonio, with authority. She saw Gregorio smile about what the *hermanos* were doing, and she said, "There is Satan, and he should leave."

Gaspar is embracing Antonio, who can hardly hold up under his bear hug. Both are shaking together to the rhythm of their glossolalia. Barrera has knelt down behind the rostrum. Mariano is in front of it, extending his weaving arms upward, rubbing his hands together and uttering such a rapid glossolalia that on the tape later it sounds as if there were a mechanical failure in the recorder. Eus has taken off her glasses and is wiping her tears off.

Antonio, who has begun making the rounds to get people to declare that they want to be baptized, is now at my seat. He bends over me, his spittle and sweat dribbling on the paper of my open notebook. He exhorts me to get baptized. I say that I have already been baptized. "How? By immersion or by a little bit of water on your head?" "By a little water." He is saddened. "But that is not sufficient, my daughter," he says, breathing heavily. There is some rattled-off quotation about Jonah in the stomach of the whale and then the question, "Have you at least already repented?" "Oh, yes." "Then why not get baptized tomorrow?" "I'll have to wait for my husband, and when he also repents, we will be baptized together." He straightens out, his hand still on my head, and shouts out a joyous "*Aleluya!*" Barrera rings his bell. Behind me, Dolores is in glossolalia; so is Juanita, who is hanging on to her chair rather than sitting on it.

Barrera is urging anyone who has not been baptized to do it now; this is the last opportunity, there will be no other. People start coming forward to the altar. Alvio is standing close to where I sit, inviting everyone to come and volunteer to be baptized. "Come one, come all, Christ will promptly arrive, there is no time to lose . . . " like a ticket vendor for the show of the bearded lady. Eight women and nine men come forward to the altar. Barrera is crying into the microphone. "The first time I ever saw Barrera crying," Eus comments later. Children are screaming; Teresa is sobbing. Nina is still in trance. Alvio, Chan Candelario, and Epi are kneeling behind those who want to be baptized, praying for them, while Mila is at the altar, shouting glossolalia.

Someone, perhaps an irate neighbor, is knocking. Mariano sends one of the young men to investigate. There is more knocking. The prayer becomes noticeably more subdued. Mila, however, is still in glossolalia, every bit a copy of Rosa's. Antonio continues hunting for baptismal prospects. He is concentrating on a woman in the back. Barrera is on his knees behind the rostrum. I see Eus's lips moving in prayer. Nina is in the same posture as before, but no glossolalia is audible. Antonio is praising the Lord because he has found another candidate for the baptism. Dolores has lost level in her glossolalia, going into a *t—t—t* pattern. Antonio has passed on to still another baptismal prospect, rocking on his heels as he talks and prays. Then he goes to Gregorio, Luis L.'s brother-in-law, but soon gives up on him.

Barrera rises and rings, saying, "Hermanos, listen for a moment," but no one pays attention. Antonio has come to the front, now praying loudly for the conversion of his wife. There is a woman in front of the altar who is praying loudly, "So many times I've had the opportunity to be baptized and never made use of it. Oh Lord, I want to be baptized now . . . " She is Elide's daughter, known to a number of people as a prostitute. Barrera points to her; Alvio and Mariano kneel down on either side of her. She has gone into trance, and now the two men drive her into glossolalia by shouting their own utterances at her in their prayer.

Once more Barrera rings but cannot get hold of the congregation. Chan Candelario is praying loudly, his baby in his arms. Antonio is now by a girl behind me. The girl gives her consent to be baptized, and Antonio shouts out his gratitude. He is very loud. At this point it is he who is really the master of the congregation, not Barrera, who is still trying to command attention by ringing his bell. There is a moment's silence, like a breath pause, and then Agosto, our usually impassive guitarist, throws up his arms and, weaving back and forth on his feet, eyes tightly closed, head slightly back, also goes into glossolalia. Mariano comes and puts his hand under his head; Epi is behind him, also Chan Candelario and Alfredo. Barrera comes down from the platform and goes into glossolalia. Antonio, on his relentless quest, has now approached yet another woman in the rear of the church.

Two more women come to the front and want to be baptized. They are on their knees, praying loudly, while Mariano stands facing them, his eyes tightly closed, uttering his easily recognizable rapid glossolalia. Barrera has gone back up on the platform and announces that all day tomorrow there will be *doctrina*, that is, instruction about the baptism, for those who have come forward to the altar. In the back, there is still some sobbing. Antonio has gone on to Pedro, while Barrera is once more whipping up the passion for the baptism. I catch a glimpse of him as his calculating, shrewd glance sweeps over the congregation. It is now 10:30 P.M. Antonio comes marching down the aisle between the men's and the juvenile section, his trunk slanting slightly forward, his right arm stiffly up in something like a Roman salute, his legs stiff at the knees. With one finger, very rigidly, he points to the microphone, which Barrera relinquishes, and with mounting excitement, he begins shouting into it, face flushed, eyes first half closed then torn open as if by an outside agency, perspiration dripping from his forehead: "Jehovah is with us. . . . Jehovah has said, 6 o'clock tomorrow morning. He who forgets is not with Jehovah."

Barrera takes the microphone: "This is Jehovah's message for tomorrow."

After the benediction I pack up to go, and Barrera steps up behind me. "There is so little time," he says pleadingly, "you must get baptized now." I put my hand on his, "Thank you for all your caring, Hermano." Then Eus and I climb over Nina, who is still rigid and prostrate, and leave.

I thought Eus would go on home, but she only accompanies me to borrow a handkerchief and then goes back to the temple to attend to Nina.

The next morning, July 31, 1970, even Santiago is still impressed by last night's events. "What a beautiful service," he comments. "So many people, and all possessed by the Holy Spirit." "The Holy Spirit should take hold of you, too," Reina counters uncharitably, "of your head, I mean." She is still mad at him because he had Eus and me procure merchandise in Chetumal, which is now practically unsellable because of the delay of the harvest due to too little rain. Santiago pays no attention to her. "Maybe next year, when you come back," he says, "the two of us will also have been baptized."

The street is alive with new intelligence. "There was shouting in the church all night," complains Dona Juanita. Nina comes by from the market and confirms it. She heard at the market that the *hermanos* prayed all night. They also kept vigil over Antonio to prevent him from committing suicide. He stayed in the *casa pastoral*, sitting or kneeling on a sheet of plastic and praying. And so that the *hermanos* would at all times know whether he was trying to leave or whether he moved suspiciously, they tied a cowbell to him. The interpretation of Antonio's attempts at suicide are that Antonio was possessed by the Spirit of God, and the Devil could not tolerate that and therefore tried to get him to kill himself, depriving the Holy Spirit, as it were, of a human abode.

At one point, Reina hears, Mariano and Antonio saw a big wheel turning very fast, and Jesus too, far away. Nina corrects her, "No, Antonio had the vision, and Mariano interpreted it for him. Antonio saw a big wheel of many colors, and there was a person in the center of it, and that was Jesus."

Nina had been told that Barrera had attacked her by name and that Rosa had also mentioned her. She asks me to play the scene back to her on tape and listens carefully but merely nods and does not comment. Eus thinks Barrera's reference to me is funny, and during the day, which I spend at her house, I get to hear it several times as a teasing taunt, "Hermana Felicitas, if you . . ."

The evening service of July 31 is announced as a preparation for those to be baptized the following day. Generally, the previous day's excitement has abated, but looking back, it seems clear to me that it actually marks the next phase in the evolution of the apocalyptic events.

Ernesto opens the service. He is noticeably hoarse, as is Chan Candelario, to whom he passes later on. During the second altar call, Gregoria goes into a lengthy glossolalia, which continues into the special hymns. Rosa, Dolores,

Angela, and Nina are all speaking in tongues, but they keep it under considerable control. Barrera, in his sermon, reports that there are fourteen candidates who want to be baptized, but that Satan is already working on some of them, trying to dissuade them from getting baptized, attacking them this morning and this afternoon too. However, we should remember that we may not have another opportunity. "What is easier," he asks, "to serve Jesus or burn forever?"

He reads off the names of those who have already indicated their desire to be baptized. If there is anyone else, would they please come forward, so they can be given a brief instruction and can join tomorrow's baptism.

Mariano's wife Raquel holds up her hand. Lorenzo praises her resolve and asks her to sit down in the front of the juvenile section, which has been cleared for the baptismal candidates. "He who becomes baptized," Barrera tells her, "can forever stay in the presence of Jehovah. In the water, one dies; there are no more dances, no more sin, for the dead do not sin." He has her read several biblical passages aloud, which she does with assurance and considerable facility.

At this point, there are loud voices from the *casa pastoral*; we hear the exorcistic formula, "*Yo te reprendo* [I expel you]," and a great shout of various glossolalia utterances. The effect is singularly dramatic and is not lost on the congregation. In the course of the evening, several groups make very impressive use of this possibility of a counterpoint, of glossolalia utterances in the *casa pastoral* answering those in the temple. The *hermanos* come back. "Do not be frightened," Barrera tells the congregation, referring to a demonic possession that has apparently just been taking place, "eventually we will all be tried, every one of us." Antonio kneels down at the altar. What occurs next is a fast-moving, highly dramatic scene of the Devil possessing Antonio; with a voice quite different from that of Antonio's ordinary voice, he is demanding Raquel. Isauro comes in from the *casa pastoral*, his eyes closed, weaving uncertainly as he walks, speaking in tongues. He places his hand on Antonio's head. Mariano follows, putting his hand on Antonio's temple. Barrera calls for a prayer, while Antonio, that is, the Devil, continues demanding Raquel. Rosa and Dolores are in glossolalia, as is Barrera, still behind the rostrum; he is very hoarse. Chan Candelario comes in and joins the prayer. Isauro regains consciousness, but Juanita and Gregoria are now in trance. Another act of the temple's mystery play ends with the defeat of Satan, who is exorcised from Antonio because of the power of the prayer in tongues used against him. Antonio, freed of the Demon, rises, goes back to his seat, and sits down. Barrera, administering a final blow to the mighty Adversary, comes down from the platform still speaking in tongues, but as he reaches Antonio, he lapses into ordinary speech, as does Antonio, indicating that the Devil has departed. Clearly, however, their stiff movements show that both are still in trance.

The Devil, though, does not yet concede defeat, and suddenly he is back. Antonio jumps up and with his voice once more that of the Demon, demands Raquel. Barrera takes over the negotiations. Shouting angrily, he tells the Demon that he cannot have Raquel, that she is a good, Christian woman who wants the baptism, this *alimento* [food]. This exchange is repeated with only a slight variation, Barrera telling the Demon that he must leave, and, apparently satisfied that he has been obeyed, he goes back to the rostrum. Barrera has not carried the fight on alone. Chan Candelario has also been there, uttering a very loud glossolalia, and Juanita, Gregoria, Dolores, and Rosa have been producing a torrent of trance utterances. Antonio has his fists pressed against his forehead. They are jutting outward, so that they look like horns. Chan Candelario continues in glossolalia, very loudly. Barrera remains at the rostrum, praying quietly and giving the impression that the battle has finally been won.

Victory is intimated now by Antonio, who gets up from his seat, steps up to Barrera, and points to the microphone, which Barrera hands to him.

"Let the service continue. Jehovah, the Lord of hosts, is with you," Antonio says, giving us to understand that once more the Devil has been expelled. He then goes on:

"My wife's heart is simple, but she loves me to destroy me. However, one must not love father, mother, wife or son more than God. Jesus loves us; the Holy Spirit is proof of that. My wife is afraid that if she comes into the temple, she might receive the Holy Spirit. Her mother knows Satan too. The two of them are surrounded by thousands and thousands of spirits.[4] Those cannot enter here; they are out there in the *monte*, they belong there. If they were to enter here, Jesus would destroy them."

Antonio's outstretched hand slowly forms a fist. "For the baptism," he proclaims, "people have to be sepulchred, as Jesus was for three days in the earth. All those who still want to be baptized should come to the altar, so they can be prayed over." With his eyes closed, he points to the front of the altar. Nine women, all young, heed the call, as well as four young men. Antonio, with his eyes still closed, hands the microphone back to Barrera. After the prayer, he takes the microphone once more and, now staring wide-eyed, he says, "For the second time, the Lord has used us." He then returns the microphone to Barrera.

At this point Barrera resumes control over the proceedings. He announces that all those who want to be baptized should be at the church tomorrow at six: there will be a truck to take everybody who wants to go out to Santa Clara. He calls for a hymn. While the singing is going on—it is the hymn "Mi buen salvador" [My kind Savior]—Ernesto comes in, in the same kind of rigid, almost frozen posture as his brother Isauro had exhibited before him. In fact, at first I take him for Isauro. He is leading two women, neither of whom I recognize as they pass me with their backs turned. There is something in the atmosphere, however, that has suddenly changed. I cannot pinpoint it, something different in the way Mariano (another member of the congregation) walks behind those two women as they approach the altar and kneel down, his arms held high and his hands weaving in and out, and in the special way he places his hand on the head of the woman on the left. He is followed by Chan Candelario, who stops close to where I am sitting, and I am startled as he starts hyperventilating, pumping air through his nose in rapid, deep inhalations, which sends him instantly into glossolalia. Gregoria goes into glossolalia. Barrera comes down from behind the rostrum and also starts praying for the woman kneeling on the left, placing his hands on her head and shaking it. Epi rises from his seat and joins him, praying loudly, "*Sellala, sellala* . . . [Seal her, seal her]!" She moves slightly to the right, and with a start, I realize who it is who has occasioned all this attention: Cruz, the wife of Antonio!

Rosa goes into intense glossolalia. What almost gets lost in the shuffle is that the woman with Cruz is Porfiria, the mother of Old Candil, who has never been keen on getting baptized, and in surprise, her son, usually a very quiet man, lets go with a loud glossolalia utterance. Ernesto gets up, and Barrera talks quietly with him and Mariano while the glossolalia and the prayers are still going on. They leave, and soon loud voices are audible in prayer and glossolalia from the *casa pastoral.* Presently Gregoria and some other *hermanas* join the men, so that we have the bright cadences of the glossolalia accompanying the tense events in the church, without the latter being disrupted. Cruz gets up, wipes her eyes, and sits down in the middle section on a chair that is closest to Eus's. Porfiria sits down farther back. Cruz's face is very dark in the shadow of her *rebozo.* Not a muscle of her face is moving; she is totally frozen still.

Barrera comes back, goes up on the altar, and his first comment, almost in a hush, is, "Let God have mercy on all of us and on all those who truly repent."

Again there is an upsurge of voices from the *casa pastoral,* perfectly in tune with, and in counterpoint to, the events in the church.

Barrera continues that sometimes it pleases God to surprise people—never for material ends, but so that His name can be glorified. There is a powerful answer in prayer and glossolalia from the congregation. He takes up the subject that in baptism there is a chance to receive the forgiveness of sin. He then addresses Porfiria, saying that she has listened to the Word of God for a long time and that this is probably her last opportunity to become baptized. If she is baptized tomorrow, she will have to resolve to serve Christ from now on until the end of what days she may have left.

Barrera turns to the young man kneeling next to Porfiria. Is he aware that there is only one God, and not three? He nods. Does he realize that if he does go through with the baptism, the things of the world are no longer for him? No smoking, no drinking, no bad company? That from then on, his way leads only from his home to the church? That there is no more reading of *cuentos,* but only the Bible? The young man assents. Then Barrera mentions something that had not been alluded to in any of the *doctrinas* I had attended last year, demonstrating how, even under these extraordinary circumstances, financial matters are never far from his mind. He says:

"God's word says clearly that those who are truly the children of God possess everything in common. If one has a peso, and it is needed for God's work, he will have to give it. No one may be egotistical, much less avaricious. The Scripture says clearly that if we surrender to Christ, then, both within the phrasing and the spirit of the Word of God, everything we own must also be surrendered if God needs it for his sacred and blessed work."

Antonio goes out. Since the young man voices no objection, he is told that there will be one more *doctrina* in the water tomorrow, and if he still wants it, they will baptize him.

Barrera then turns to Cruz, who has her eyes fixed on her lap. "Hermana Cruz, you have received much instruction, not to say more than enough instruction," he begins. He points out the significance of the baptismal event and the need for complete repentance. "All old matters have already passed and have now been made new. You must have no thought except to serve Christ faithfully." If she has any other thought, the baptism will not be valid.

"*Ud. ya entendi, Hermana, que nada mas Jesucristo es Dios?* [Do you understand, Hermana, that only Jesus Christ is God?]"

Cruz continues to look down on her lap.

"*Conteste, Hermana* [Answer, Hermana]."

Silence.

"*He comprendido que solamente Jesucristo es Dios?* [Do you understand that only Christ is God?]"

Silence. He switches to Maya.

"*Leti, wa ma?* [Yes or no?]"

Eus leans over to her and putting her hand on her arm says quietly in Maya, "Answer the *hermano,* Cruz." No reaction.

"*Leti, ciic?* [Yes, (older) sister]?"[5]

No answer.

Antonio comes back from outside and kneels down at the altar to pray.

"Do you want to be baptized, Hermana, in the name of Jesus Christ? Do you?"

A hardly perceivable nod.

Barrera sighs. "*Muy bien* . . . [All right]. But remember, from now on, you cannot fight with your husband anymore. You will be completely under the commands of God. Under no conditions may you ever oppose your husband again." He outlines the significance of the baptism once more. "The pact is between you and God; I will not be responsible for the blood that will fall on your head if you don't fulfill what you promise. You will have to go wherever God may send you. Remember, none of us is his own master; we are under the orders of the Holy Spirit. Everything that it orders must be accepted."

Antonio rises from his knees before the altar, fillips the dust off his white peasant pants, and goes back to his seat in the men's section while Barrera announces that there are now a total of eighteen candidates to be baptized tomorrow. The prayer in the *casa pastoral* once more rises high, Rosa's glossolalia and that of one man clearly audible.

Barrera concludes the service and announces a prayer for the sick. Angela comes to the altar and kneels down. Barrera and Mariano place their hands on her head; she is in glossolalia, so is Alfredo behind her. Rhythmically, Mariano begins to pat the nape of her neck. My tape has come to an end, and admitting that I cannot take any more, I close my tape-recorder, and, climbing over two of Gregoria's sleeping children, I make it to the exit. Once more, I was told, some people stayed in the temple to pray through the night.

Since my departure from Utzpak was scheduled for the following day, I could not attend the baptism. But I did take the time to say good-by to Barrera the morning after the service, and with the trance having evaporated during the night, he was his amiable self once more. Too bad that I could not be at the baptism, they had hoped that I could make it, he said.

Eus accompanies me to Merida. Our conversation in the bus naturally revolves around the events in the temple and Cruz's coercion into baptism. Did she think that Cruz went into prostitution because of money, or because she enjoyed it? "She must enjoy it," Eus says. "Most of us are poor, but we don't do it." Of course, Barrera's financial dealings are still on Eus's mind, only now they receive a different interpretation. It seems to her that Barrera's actions proved that the Devil could also make use of a pastor. That the Demon possessed Antonio in the church was a clear indication that he could enter even the temple. Obliquely, this seemed also her way of coming to terms with Barrera's attack on her and Nina during that service. Was he really giving voice to what the Holy Spirit was telling him, or was it the presence of Satan?

We spend the day with Eus's brother and wife and go to Luis L.'s church on Sunday. Before Luis L. lets me see what there is in the way of an archive, I get a brief private sermon about the necessity to believe in the eternity of the soul. He hopes that I have taken something of spiritual value from my experiences in Utzpak. "Yesterday," he said, "sixteen candidates were baptized in Santa Clara; it was a marvelous fiesta of the Spirit. Afterward, when I came back here to hold a service, I really felt the presence of the Lord."

After the Escuela Dominical, we stand around and talk with Valentin, who has come from Temax with his wife to help with construction at the Merida church, where Luis L. wants a community meeting room. "We don't get paid," he says, "but at least we get our food." Luis L. also planned to build a larger temple, but the Holy Spirit revealed that no new temple should be built in Merida; the Second Coming was too close. "They don't need one anyway," is Eus's matter-of-fact comment to me. According to Valentin, the temple in Temax is deserted now because the Holy Spirit is sending the *hermanos* elsewhere to preach. "Anyway," Valentin says, "we are too poor to support an *hermano.*" Eus nods. "It is because of the *henequen.* In Utzpak, *hay povres, pero povre povres no hay* [we have poor people, but there are no really poor ones]."

Licha joins the conversation. As everyone else is, she is familiar with the visions of Antonio and of Jose. "Tell us what wonders you saw," she says, "all those outpourings of the Holy Spirit." When I hesitate, Valentin—I had forgotten that he had been there too—answers in my stead, telling that Rosa had said that certain people had to surrender to Jesus, such as Nina, and Eus, and the husband of Reyes. Why the husband of Reyes? "*El es muy rebelde en las cosas de Dios* [He is very rebellious in the matters of the Lord]." "And how do you know that what Rosa said was *algo de arriba* [something from up on high]?" "Because she was in a faint when she spoke." Enthusiastically, he continues telling her about all the marvelous gifts received from the Holy Spirit, especially Pedro's newfound ability to interpret what was being said in tongues.

Interlude

When I left Utzpak at the beginning of August, and given the somewhat calmer atmosphere of the last service I had attended, I fully expected that things would return to normal after the baptism on August 1, 1970. Just to be on the safe side, however, I left Eus some envelopes, stamped and addressed to me, in case there was anything she thought I ought to know. Still, I was at a loss how to interpret a letter I received from her, dated September 16, 1970, that had been dictated to Nina. After the customary blessings and good wishes concerning my health as well as that of my family and of those surrounding me, and a few personal remarks, she continued:

> I have many other new matters for you, everything that happened in the temple concerning the manifestations as we had discussed it. All the *hermanos* believed it. Satan, our Adversary, robbed them of their senses [*les fue sacada la mente*]. When you left, the manifestations had already begun. All of August, the most horrible things happened in the church. If I would tell you everything, it would fill a whole notebook. I hope to tell you all when we meet again face to face; that is, if God will accord us life and health.

Then in a subsequent letter, dated October 12, 1970, there was the following remark: "When there were those events of Satan in the temple, the book (with the names of those newly baptized) was lost."

During Denison's so-called January term I had the good fortune to be assigned as one of the faculty chaperons for a group of our students who were taken on a guided tour of Mexico. While other faculty members were in charge of their stay in Mexico City, I went ahead to Merida, rented a hotel room, and invited Eus and Nina to be my guests there so they could help me reconstruct the events that Eus had referred to in her letters. I knew from experience how unimpeachable the memories of these two women were; besides, this was only four months later. But we also had a most valuable aid in notes that Nina had made of the events, containing entries for August 13, 20, 22, and 23, 1970. Initially, Nina jotted these notes down in the church, but Barrera objected, saying that this was not school, so why was she writing in church? She then recorded the events at home. This was a considerable accomplishment, for she only had two years of elementary school training. I had never asked her to do this, nor had I trained her in any way. I think she did it, on the one hand, out of an interest in intellectual activity. For years, she had taken notes on sermons (which she had showed me), recorded quotations from the Bible, and made a collection of new hymns. On the other hand, she knew that her mother and I were close friends, and she wanted to do me a favor. She and her mother were very close. She gave direct quotations of what to her were the most striking statements in any given situation, together with the dates. After our sessions in Merida, where I recorded all our conversations, I visited in Utzpak and spoke with a number of women, whose statements confirmed everything that I already knew from Eus and Nina. I also had a long conversation with one of the daughters of Valuch. While we were talking of the events of August, she had a strong nervous tic that shook her entire body. It stopped as soon as we touched on everyday matters. Nina said that this young woman was among those who had been possessed by the Devil. All in all I am confident that the following account gives a reliable and accurate account of what transpired. It is, of course, a composite of my reconstruction and the accounts given by Nina and Eus.

On August 1, 1970, as mentioned above, there was a baptism at the seaport of Santa Clara, and sixteen men and women were baptized.

> Nina: There were some persons there in bathing suits, and they were
> disrupting the baptism, standing around, watching, and generally
> being in the way. Barrera then called Mariano and asked him to pray,
> so that the people who were disturbing the baptism would go away.
> Mariano started praying, and one by one the people who were dis-

turbing us left. And all the *hermanos* were aware of what was happening and it was considered a work of God.

Eus: When I returned from Merida after taking you to the airport, Gregoria and Joaquina acted as if they did not see me. I said, "What's the matter, Hermanas, do you have something in your eyes?" They would not talk to me.

The day after the baptism, nine men went to preach in other villages. They were Isauro, Ernesto, Antonio, Chan Candelario, Alfredo, Iminio, Jose Dz., Pedro, and Alvio. Barrera tried to talk other men into going also, but they refused on the grounds that if everyone went there would be none left to earn the money to take care of the children.

The wives of the evangelists went to live at the temple. Eus did not join them, since Nohoch Felix did not go out to evangelize. Also, she felt that it was unjust that the men earned the money for their own families, and then the *hermanas,* who in her opinion were not entitled to it, went ahead and spent it. She even left the Dorcas and did not join them again.

The women slept in the temple and cooked there even for the *hermanos* who stopped by, such as Luis L., who, according to Eus, was severely attacked. Isauro sold twelve of his steers before leaving for his work "in the field," netting 12,000 pesos. Of this sum, he gave 1,000 pesos as his tithe. Half of it Lorenzo kept as his share by the rules of the church organization, and the other half was earmarked for supporting the *hermanas* and the children at the church. Barrera also brought some merchandise from Merida and sold it in Utzpak, and that money was added to what the women spent on necessities in the church.

Eus: Hermana Gregoria was in charge of preparing the food. Barrera gave her money and she went out to do the shopping, to buy food, to buy maize, all that. They had of everything, of beans, of rice, just everything. But the *hermanas* tell that Gregoria went and bought meat for herself. Then, before the other *hermanas* came home to eat from such errands as evangelizing, she would already be done with eating. When the others arrive, there is hardly any food. She has already eaten, she has eaten meat, and to the others she gives beans, that's all she gives them. She is the one in charge, therefore she eats well. She buys soap and a plastic bag of Fab [one of those bags that costs 1 peso and 50 centavos]; to the *hermanas* she gives a little Fab and a bit of soap, and she has the entire bag and the cake of soap. You know who told me all this? Cruz, the wife of Antonio.

Pues, bit by bit, the *hermanas* began going home. It was the Devil that caused the *hermanas* to fight with each other. The wife of Chan

Candelario went first. Her children are crying, they want salt crackers, but there is no money to buy any. The last one to stay on was Gregoria. She was ashamed to go home because the people were talking about her, saying that she had an affair with Barrera. Somebody was said to have come to the *casa pastoral,* found Gregoria in the hammock, and there was Barrera with his pants down. There was nothing to it, it was all gossip, but she was ashamed anyway. But finally, she also went home again. By the end of August, none of them was left at the church.

In the second week of August, Cruz had her baby in the shower corner of the *casa pastoral.* It was a little girl. One of the *hermanas* took care of her. When the baby was two days old, Cruz went home.

The *hermanos* who had gone to the various villages had a number of problems, too. The first one to come back was Pedro, who had gone out as the associate of Alvio. He said that one evening he saw from the outside of a house how Alvio was preaching inside. He grabbed a stone and wanted to throw it at Alvio. He did not do it, but he came back to Utzpak right away. He told Barrera that he felt that he had sinned against the Holy Spirit and could not go on evangelizing. Soon after that Chan Candelario also returned. In the village where he was preaching, a girl fell in love with him. He left and went to Tizimin, where Isauro had taken over a congregation that was already a going concern. However, Chan Candelario was unhappy there also and went home.

The others in the field held out a little longer, but they had not learned how to obtain support from a local congregation and, receiving no financial support from Utzpak, were near starvation. Alvio lived on 50 centavos' worth of tortillas a day and a bit of butter. The other *hermanos* finally joined Alvio in Cantamayec, and they did not even have the bus fare to return. No one knew how they made it back home, but they appeared one day, so thin that they could hardly keep their pants up.

After the baptism, the life of the congregation lost what little structure had still been preserved. There were meetings every evening, but no regular services were held, only prayer sessions. Moreover, as soon as anyone would kneel down, he or she would go into trance.

> Nina: And they would speak, prophesying like Isaiah and saying that Christ would come soon and everybody should be baptized. At this time, they said nothing bad against anybody else as yet.

> Eus: They would pray awfully long, sometimes until 11 o'clock at night. They did not speak in tongues, but just screamed, and then the *hermanos* would take the *hermanas* to the hammocks in the *casa*

pastoral, for they could not walk, they were as if drunk. And even in the hammocks, they would continue screaming. Some, like Mila, would walk around with eyes wide open, breathing heavily and saying, "If you don't believe in God, you will lose your soul."

And sometimes they would kneel down and they'd start looking around to see who isn't praying. I can see what they are doing because I don't close my eyes. When they look at me, I close my eyes, then I look again. And Rosa would say, "Hermana Cruz isn't praying," or "Tola isn't." And the *hermanos* would come up to us and say, "Pray, *hermanas,* pray!"

Pedro lived in the church, and the *hermanas* cooked for him and made him his bath.

> Eus: He was attacked very strongly and the evil spirits did not leave him so soon, it took a whole month before he was free of them again. As soon as he would kneel down to pray, he would begin to cry, and then his brain would begin to hurt at the base of his skull. He would throw himself down on the ground and would know nothing of himself. He said it felt like *aire* [in Latin American folk medicine, the cause of many illnesses], like a pain going through him. During prayer, he never said anything.
>
> He was attacked by the evil spirits even in the *monte,* and when he was this way attacked, he always wanted to go places. He would go to Merida, or just anywhere. And since he couldn't find his way back, some *hermana* would have to go out and find him again.

Once Pedro left, Hermano Luis L., who was in Utzpak at the time, was angry and said, "He is *hermano* no longer." Luis L. said that also about the *hermanas.* If an *hermana* left, he would right away say, "She is *hermana* no longer."

The same restlessness took hold of other members of the congregation too. Barrera, for one, kept going back and forth between Utzpak and Luis L.'s congregation in Merida. After returning home, he would sit in the church and speak to no one, giving no sermons.

> Eus: His hair was messy, he was staring around, and seemed angry with us, who knows why? But he was this way all the time. This is why all those bad things happened.

Epi was similarly afflicted and kept on the move between Merida and Utzpak. When in the church, he would pray for extended periods, an hour or more at a stretch, while continually hitting his head with his hands. He was the only one who did that. He seemed to be in a perpetual low-level trance.

Eus: Epi was attacked all the time. He would go back and forth between Utzpak and Merida, and when he wasn't praying, he would say what everybody should be doing, and what was right and what was wrong.

Nina: Epi would say to those who were fasting that it was good. And if God forgave someone, Epi would be the one to tell him that it was so. And the people believed him because they thought that he was possessed by the Spirit of God.

All these goings-on did not, of course, go unnoticed by the rest of the village population.

Eus: Dona Juanita's husband, they say, shot into the church, into the roof, because the congregation made so much noise. I never heard the shot, so I don't know.

The people also said that the young girls were virgins no longer, that Luis L. took them, and all the *hermanos* did too, because they heard them scream, and they knew that the *hermanos* took them to their hammocks.

All in all they said that the *hermanos* were mad, shouting and praying all night.

Nina: When the Senores Cristianos would go out to evangelize in the village, the people would not listen to them. They said, "How can you go out and evangelize? You don't even know if you are worshiping God or whether devils are possessing you."

In the second week of August, Barrera brought Lucrecia back from Campeche. She would pray long and hard, hitting the floor with her hands. She did not do this every day, having small children to take care of. In the meantime, the church became very dirty, so dirty that one could kneel on the floor no longer.

Eus: The children urinated on the floor, and no one wiped it up. Alvio had a cold and spit out everywhere. It was as if the people were blind, they didn't see the dirt. They even spread the covers on the tables and on the rostrum backward and did not turn them right side up until a week later when Hermano Luis L. came from Merida.

At this time, a new elaboration appeared. Since it was thought that everything said by those possessed was the word of the Holy Spirit, those *hermanos* who knew how to write would go from person to person and write down what they were saying. They said that they would send these notes "far away," but no one seemed to know where or even if it was ever done. Later on, an exchange of such notes developed between the Utzpak congregation and that of Luis L. in Merida.

Then, under 13 August, Nina has the following entry:

> Mila said, "Where is Don Goyo? He should be here so he can hear this. If he will not consecrate himself to the Lord, he will die, both in the flesh and in the spirit, and he will go to hell with all his riches." Then she said, "I'm not going home, the Devil is there." And that made her mother very angry.

Mila's attack on Don Goyo, the husband of Valuch, ushered in a period of mutual recrimination, mostly assuming the form of an attack on the outsiders, the noncommittal, the doubters. At first it was couched in decrees that these particular members should engage in extended fasting. Again the teenagers took the lead. According to Nina, Pilar ordered "ten days of fasting for Nina, fifteen days' fasting for Cruz, fifteen days' fasting for Eus, and thirty days' fasting for Nohoch Felix, all from six to six. She also mentioned others."

They certainly picked their targets well. Don Goyo, mentioned for the first time in a direct attack, was one of the oldest members in terms of years of membership in the congregation, one of the first to be baptized by Oscar Hill. He and his wife, Valuch, kept wavering, sometimes taking the pronouncements by the various young *hermanas* seriously, sometimes not. Nohoch Felix paid no attention to either the attacks or the fasts decreed. In fact, he hardly even believed that the Holy Spirit was involved in the events at the church. Both Nina and her mother definitely qualified as wavering converts. As Nina said, "Sometimes I believed [that it was the Holy Spirit that was possessing the congregation], sometimes I didn't. The more they told me that I had to believe, the less I believed."

As to the fasting, Cruz did not do it at all—after all, she was nursing a newborn—and neither did Nohoch Felix. Nina resorted to eating a hefty meal before six in the morning and then fasting until six at night. Gregoria fasted for fourteen days, got very thin, and eventually became sick. Pedro overdid it so thoroughly that he could not fasten his trousers anymore. Paula and her daughter were supposed to fast for three days, and they did. Eus persisted for six days.

> Eus: I could see that Gregoria fasted, for she was heavy before and now she got very thin. I am thin, so you cannot see if I fast or not. I did it for six days and felt that I was dying of hunger. While fasting we stayed in the church all day because at home you might forget

and eat something or take some water. I became so weak, I could not hear anymore, and I could not do my washing. I had no strength. When you fast, you don't feel like working. But all our clothes were dirty, so on Saturday, I said, "I'll eat." And I did, and then I did my washing.

Meanwhile, matters also came to a head in the congregation in Merida. As mentioned above, the events in Utzpak of late July were discussed in that congregation with some interest on August 1 when I visited there on my way home to the United States. Subsequently, as a result of the restless peregrinations of Epi, Mariano, and Pedro, the Merida congregation became totally involved. Luis L. kept weeping, saying, "You must believe, you must believe, this is the Holy Spirit!" And he would bring water to those who were overcome by their trance and hold them so that they would not fall off their chairs.

Probably on August 18, a member of the Merida congregation, a 19-year-old girl, a student at the University of Yucatan and here called Olga, proclaimed that the Holy Spirit wanted everything shiny—such as eyeglasses, ballpoint pens, and buttons—to be discarded. Everyone I talked to later, including members of the Merida congregation, agreed that this was not a vision, merely a communication from what Olga thought was the Holy Spirit. She also said that all colors other than white would have to be eliminated; this pertained especially to the Bibles because of the red edges of the pages. The members of the congregation as a result threw their Bibles into the courtyard, and there were also other elaborations of this same suggestion. For example, Epi and Mariano, who happened to be at the Merida temple at the time, said that they could see the Devil with his horns in the rose design woven into the red brocade curtain that covered the wall behind the altar there. They were acutely distressed and suggested that the curtain be burned. There were also other trance manifestations. Epi and Mariano told a woman whom they did not know how many months ago she had left her husband. They knew the exact date. The woman was so impressed that she said, "Truly, this is the Spirit of God, and I'll dedicate myself to his service." And Mariano had visions, seeing a white cross on the chest of some believers. A large black moth called in Maya *mahanay* strayed into the church. Everyone likes the *mahanay*, for it is said that it announces the coming of rain. It does not like to get wet and so *busca casa* [looks for shelter]. But now Olga cried out that it was Satan, that she could see him, and that the monster should be killed.

Making everything white and burning offensive objects were the two suggestions taken up most ardently. After the service in which Olga had made her pronouncements, she and her mother went home and burned the family television set. This action so upset the father of the family, who was not a member of the congregation, that he beat his wife and their three daughters and left them.

When Barrera arrived in the Merida congregation on August 20, the red curtain of the church had in fact been burned. The Bibles had been collected from the churchyard and their edges had been painted black. Then a certain Hermano Pedro started giving orders. He climbed up on the *albarrada* and shouted, "Hermanos, Jesus Christ is already here." From the church, the people answered, "*Gloria a Dios, alleluya!*" Then, conscious of what the neighbors might think, they cautioned him, "Don't shout so loud." He answered, "I give orders here. I am the Father, yes or no?" And they replied, "Yes, we accept it." One *hermano* added, "Father, you have already come!"

Hermano Pedro then ordered a tin washtub to be brought and filled with water. The *hermanos* were to bathe each other's feet in it. It had rained and their feet were muddy. Yet no one objected when afterward Pedro ordered them to drink of the water, calling it the water of life. They all drank of it. Then they asked him, "Father, what do you want, purified water or the water of life?" It was told with some amusement later that Hermano Pedro asked for purified water for himself.

In Utzpak, these incidents were apparently recounted on the same or the next day, for on August 20, Nina recorded similar behaviors there also. In addition, Mila engaged in some unimaginably sacrilegious cursing in church, which even in secular context would have been an entirely unthinkable demeanor for a Maya peasant woman.

> Nina: Thursday, August 20, Mila says, "Throw out everything that is red. Throw out the bibles."
> Mila says, "Nina, take off your colored dress. It disturbs me." And she says to Pilar, "Pilar, take off your colored dress, and then you can put on my [white] uniform." And Pilar answered, "Let's do that."
> Pilar then said, "Throw out everything that is red. Throw out everything that has colors in it, throw out the books, the tables, the rostrum." And Mila sat on the altar, her legs apart, and kept swearing, saying, "*Puta, puta* [prostitute]." Then they prayed very hard, as if prophesying again.
> And Gregoria asked Rosa, "Hermana Rosa, how can I save my younger sister?" And Rosa was also prophesying and she said, "You can't do it, Hermana Gregoria, she is going to be lost, and also your brother Juan and the other one, I don't know his name, oh yes, he is called Placido, and it is the *cura* who is deceiving them, yes, he is deceiving the entire village." And they continued praying and proph-

esying. And I was kneeling and praying and also doubting. And Rosa said, "Nina, you will be lost because of that diabolical woman. Ever since she came, you were lost." That is what she said to me.

There was once more great fear of Satan. Mila had a vision: she saw an eagle overhead, and it was shrieking. "That," she said, "is Satan." Later, Mila had yet another vision, of the tail of Satan.

Nina: "Here is its tail," Mila said. "Close the windows and don't allow anyone to open the door. No one should go outside." And she was standing at the door with some others, pushing against it, as if there were someone outside trying to force his way in. And there were noises heard, as if the plastic chandeliers were being moved by the Demons, which of course, they were. So the chandeliers were thrown out into the yard. Mila began to cry, "For a long time now he has wanted to fetch me." And she begged that the door be kept closed and also all the windows.

Eus: And they threw out everything, even the guitar and the *marimbol* and the flower vases. The children played with them, and everything stayed out in the yard all night. They also tried to throw out the rostrum, but it was too heavy.

On August 21, Nina reported:

I went into the *casa pastoral,* and Mila was there in her hammock. She was thoroughly possessed and was praying and crying. When I came in, she said to me, "Nina, kneel down and pray." "I only pray to God," I answered and knelt down to start praying. Mila said, "The Demon has left you." At that moment Lucrecia came in and Mila said, "Now the Demon will attack Lucrecia." Thereupon Lucrecia fell down screaming. Barrera, Epi, Pedro, and two other *hermanos* came rushing in to pray over her, but she lay there on the floor kicking them, and she was stronger than the five of them. Finally they put her into her hammock, and there she fell asleep, and that way the condition passed. Then Luis L. came to Utzpak to take the place of Barrera, and he and Lucrecia went to Merida, and there the demons attacked her again. She had something like a seizure, and she moved with tremendous force.

Simultaneously, the assaults on the outgroup continued in Utzpak. On August 20, Leidi, another one of Rodolfa's daughters, said to Nina, "Nina, consecrate yourself. Jesus Christ wants you to consecrate yourself." Whereupon

Nina, perceiving that this often-repeated demand discredited her religious integrity, answered, "Yes. I am already doing that, I am consecrating myself. But how about you? Didn't Jesus Christ tell you to let the hems out of your dresses and sew sleeves into them?" When Leidi admitted to these charges, Nina asked, "And didn't he tell you that you chose the wrong boyfriend because he has not been baptized?" "Yes," Leidi said, "he did tell me that."

On August 22, these divisive tendencies came to a head. Although it was now Luis L. who was in charge of the services, there was no structure at all to the meeting that evening. At the outset, Rosa began immediately with making demands.

> Nina: "Throw out Hermano Goyo," Rosa says, "because his laughter kills me."
>
> "Glory to God," counters Goyo, "but you won't throw me out of here."
>
> "He is laughing," persists Rosa, "throw him out!"
>
> Luis L. was at the rostrum and asked the congregation to pray that Hermano Goyo would leave. He was sitting toward the back, and no matter how much the congregation prayed, he would not leave. Finally, Luis L. came down from the podium and asked Goyo to leave. He did, saying, "The spirit of Satan is in the church." My mother agreed with him. "Yes, Hermano Goyo," she said, "Satan is here."
>
> The wife of Goyo, Hermana Valuch, was also at the church with her sons. When she saw that her husband was being expelled, she also wanted to leave. Before going, she called to her son, Jorge. But he would not go. Rather, he wanted to listen to Rosa. When Rosa heard that they were calling Jorge, she said, "No, you mustn't take Jorge with you. His father will go to perdition with all his wealth, and if Hermana Valuch won't consecrate herself, she will go to hell, and if Jorge won't consecrate himself, he will also go to hell. And throw out Angel, too."
>
> This Angel was a young man who had just begun to come to the church. And they did throw him out. Then she demanded, "Throw out Pablo [the husband of the street vendor Cecilia]; he is only coming to laugh at us. And you, Nina," she continued, "consecrate yourself."

At this point, Eus advised her friend Valuch that she had better leave. "They are *tercos* [pigheaded]," she said.

After this incident, Luis L. officially informed the congregation about the revelation that the Lord wanted everything red or colored to be eliminated and that everything should be white. He then told Eus, "Hermana, you will have to put seams into your ʔipil so that the flowers won't show, for the Lord wants no colors. And you must go and find a white mantilla to put on your head." "Hermano," Eus answered, "If a woman has money, she buys one. It is not found in the street."

The next day, August 23, was a Sunday. The congregation arrived early in the morning, but there was no Sunday school. Instead they were told that, according to the revelation, the Holy Spirit had given them two weeks to burn everything they owned that was not white. They were all sent home to carry out these instructions.

> Eus: I saw Rosa and Mila talking together, so I went close to listen, and they were saying, "This evening we'll see who did it and who didn't."
>
> We went home, my husband, Nina, and I, and we were not quite sure whether to believe it or not that these were truly the orders of the Holy Spirit. In a way, we believed it. So we took all the calendars with their pictures from the walls because they had red in them, and we burned them. Nohoch Felix had a red handkerchief, and I said to him, "I won't burn it. I'll save it." And I hid it away. In the church they had said that nothing red was to remain in the house. So I took my pink dish that has the shape of a shell, put it into a bag, and hid that too outside. We burned no clothes, but we did take the casing off the radio because it had colors on it, and we burned that.
>
> Other people went home and, being as poor as we are, they did not burn anything either, like Elide and Rodolfa, for instance. But Leidi burned four dresses, and so did the daughter of Lupe. Paula went home and burned her radio, and they burned some dresses belonging to herself and to her daughter Rosa. They also burned a good blanket. Now that it has gotten cold [this account was recorded in January], she had to sell one of her turkeys to buy another blanket. Many others also burned their dresses.
>
> While we were doing all this, those left at the temple threw out everything—Bibles, the embroidered covers for the tables and the rostrum, books, papers, pictures. They burned many papers and also wanted to burn the marimbol. Nohoch Felix had paid 60 pesos for that. They poured gasoline on it, but it escaped. Nobody knows why it did not burn. What could not be burned, they painted white—the rostrum and also the tar paper they had bought for the roof of the new casa pastoral.
>
> When we got back to the temple, I saw among the embroidered

covers the one that I had bought, and I had paid 60 pesos for it. When I saw that, I picked it up. Gregoria saw me do it and said, "What do you want that for? This is to be burned." I said, "I need it. I'll put it on my table." So I took it home, washed and ironed it, and put it away. Later in the month, Lucrecia asked me, "Where is the large mantel? Did you take it to your house?" "Yes, it is in my house." I didn't say I took it, or anything. So I brought it back and when I prayed, I put it, folded up small, into the inside corner of the rostrum, out of sight. Who knows when they found it, but finally they put it up again.

In the afternoon, the *hermanas* borrowed an electric sewing machine and set it up in the temple. They sewed white dresses, even for Cruz, although Cruz wears no dresses, only the *ʔipil,* and she refused to put it on. I decided to continue in the temple, but I won't buy anything. I have no money for a white dress and white shoes like they buy. And I told Nina, "If they want to give you white material to make your white dress, you won't accept it, not one half meter!"

Nina: When the evening came, most everybody was barefoot and had white dresses on. But there were some who did not come in white, and they were sent home to change. Then the entire congregation formed a prayer circle and they were once more severely attacked by the Adversary. Especially this was true of Angela. "Eus is doubting," she said. "She answered Hermano Luis L. in an evil way [about the white mantilla]. She should not have answered that way. She is doubting." She was crying and she was like drunk with the Spirit. Then Angela continued, "Hermanos, it is not two weeks that we have for burning everything: we only have three days! All shoes should be burned," she said.

Then Hermano Alvio, possessed by the same evil spirit, demanded the shoes of those who had come with shoes on. He put them into a sack, but since there was no gasoline, he could not burn them. Many *hermanos* went and hid their shoes and the next day painted them white.

Eus: Alvio also wanted to burn Nohoch Felix's *alpargatas* [sandals]. He said, "Come on, burn them. I'll also burn my new shoes." But I say to him, "You are young, you can still get new ones. Felix is old, where is he going to get new ones? He doesn't make much money." So we put all our shoes into a bag, and Nina took them and watched them.

Nina: That Sunday when all that was not white was burned, I had a blue dress on, and my blue purse was on the chair. When we were in a circle praying, Mila took my purse. Its color made her angry, and she hit a little boy with it. Luis L. took it and threw it out the window. If I would have been possessed by the Evil One, I would have gone out, gotten it, and hit them with it because I was very angry. But I went on praying. Sometime later that evening, I saw a dark shape near the altar. Still later I realized that it was the mother of Mila praying there.

All this time, Luis L. went around in the church sometimes crying, sometimes not, and saying that it was the Holy Spirit that was doing all of this, that we must believe it. However, he rarely prayed, just helped others who were *agonizando* [in trance], holding them so that they would not fall off their chair, giving them water, supporting them so that they would not suffocate. When they were in this way attacked, all the windows and the doors were closed. And when Mariano went out to get some drinking water, the *hermanas* prayed that nothing would happen to him. They would not let anybody enter from the outside. "*Son misterios* [these are mysteries]," they would say, but they wouldn't explain.

Luis L. also wrote down everything that the *hermanos* were saying, telling the congregation that these were things that the Holy Spirit was telling them. "*El Espiritu lo dice, el Espiritu lo dice*," he would say. Later, he took these notes to Merida, so they would know there also about the messages of the Holy Spirit.

In the meantime, other congregations also burned their belongings, not only those in Merida, but also those in Tizimin, Chetumal, Cuarenta y Dos, and Bacalar. But as Eus pointed out, there was some doubt about the accuracy of this list because subsequently the *hermanos* were ashamed and would not talk about what went on in the other congregations.

When Barrera arrived in Merida, the events took another turn: some of the members of the congregation were married in the church, although they had not as yet been baptized. They were not married by the magistrate, either, an action strictly against the rules governing the Apostolic Church.

Hermana Victoria, of the Merida congregation, with whom I had the opportunity to speak later, gave her version of these events:

Hermano Barrera arrived from Utzpak, and he had this thing of the Evil One. Of course no one knew that it was the Evil One at the time. He told us to pray and to fast. The red curtain was burned. Then the Evil One married some of the people in the church, although they were not baptized. He knew all the names, and he called them out. It was the mouth of Hermano Pedro that he used. Olga was one of the girls that they married with her boyfriend who was not baptized and then two other couples, by using a text from Genesis about how the world began. They even fetched veils, and they embraced and kissed in church. [These marriages, however, were never consummated.]

Then there were two *hermanas,* one of them the sister-in-law of Hermano Manuel. They began to pray, and they decided to have a drawing for Hermano Luis L. and determine by lot which one of them should have him. They asked for guidance on the matter and the Evil One answered, again through Pedro, that this was the way it should be done. When Barrera returned to Utzpak, they told him to inform Luis L. that the two girls wanted to marry him. But when he came back to Merida, he did not get married. They say that in Utzpak he laughed about them. Soon afterward, Juan L. came with an *hermano* from the church office in Villahermosa, and that *hermano* told them that it was Satan and not the Holy Spirit that was making them do all those things.

Speaking about these events in January 1971, both Eus and Nina agreed that after the burning of colored objects, "the evil was beginning to pass." In the week of August 23, 1970, one of the members of the Merida congregation, Hermana Carmen, was accused in the church by her own sons of being unfaithful to the Lord and told that she should fast and repent or she would be expelled from the congregation. Now this woman was one of the very earliest members of the Apostolic Church in Yucatan and one of the first converts of Oscar Hill. She was also extremely devout, one of those who had successfully maintained her glossolalia behavior while others usually lost it after a few years. She occasionally had visions and often spoke in tongues in church.

Convinced by her personal distress that the events in the church could not have been divinely inspired—because they were so obviously wrong in her case—Carmen traveled to Villahermosa, to the regional headquarters of the Apostolic Church. She reported what was going on and spoke to Don Victor, who was highly revered and, as I mentioned before, was thought to have total knowledge of the Bible as a result of divine inspiration. He traveled with her to Chetumal, to the congregation of Juan L., which was also involved in the millenarian events. He convinced Juan L. that it was not the Holy Spirit that was possessing the congregations; quite the contrary. Together, they then traveled to Merida, whence, in the company of Luis L., they went on to Utzpak, arriving on September 10, 1970. A baptism was scheduled on that day for five new members at the seaport of Santa Clara. There they spoke with Epi and told him that it had not been the Holy Spirit, but rather Satan, that had possessed the congregation. Epi wept bitterly, saying, "And that I should have been one of those who thought that it was the Spirit of God!"

After the baptism, there was a service at the temple in Utzpak.

> Nina: When Hermano Victor came to Utzpak in the middle of September, all was already quiet. He gave a sermon in which he said that the congregation should know the Bible better and that this had not been the Holy Spirit acting in them. They should no longer pray by shouting and screaming, for the Lord was not deaf. He also said that this had to happen to the congregation because the Adversary knew that theirs was the right religion, and so he was attacking them first of all. And those that had been the most active in these things were ashamed, like Rosa and Mila; previously, they had always sat in front, now they went to the back and stayed there, and did not sit in the front anymore.

Taking into consideration the heartbreak and frustration that the events in the congregation had brought to Eus, one should forgive her, I think, if she availed herself of the presence of Hermano Victor, her friend of many years, to obtain a bit of personal satisfaction.

> Eus: Alvio was the one who burned the shoes. So when Don Victor comes, I talk with him, and when Alvio comes by, I say, "Here, Hermano, is the *maestro de quemar los zapatos* [the master of shoe-burning]." So Alvio does not want to let that pass and says to Don Victor, "Hermano, how many masters are there?" And Don Victor says, "There are only two, the Evil One and the Lord." Alvio was angry at me for a long time, but now he has started talking to me again.

An interesting late repercussion in the larger community might be worth mentioning here because it demonstrates how the visionary experience, in the same manner as glossolalia, may on occasion be acquired spontaneously by a soi-disant bystander. According to Eus, a man called Emerijildo, who was a member of the Presbyterian church down the street, had a vision in late October which he took to mean that he should speak the truth in his church and should preach what was actually in the Bible, such as speaking in tongues. He tried to do that, but the other members of this very conservative group would not listen to him. So instead he joined the Apostolic congregation and was baptized there with his wife on November 17, 1970.

Trying to make sense in January 1971 of what had happened to the congregation, Eus reiterated the official position:

The *hermanos* say that those things had to happen because this is the right religion. In other religions, people go to picture shows, they go to dances, even right after a service. It was not the *hermanos* who did all those things: it was Satan that made them throw out the Bibles. But I think it became possible because the *hermanos* in the church hated each other. Many still do.

Nina adds her version:

The Evil One had so confused, so emptied the minds of, the *hermanos* that they did not recognize that the hour had arrived when God wanted to test them. Because when they started throwing out the Bibles, they should have realized that this was the weapon for defeating the enemy. But they had no such insight.

When the Presbyterians, however, gloat that the Apostolics were attacked by Satan and they were not, the congregation has a favorite reply: "That is because the Devil is already sure of you!"

Discussion

Predictions about the end of the world have been part of human history for a very long time. Of the various types of societies from which humans have evolved, it was the horticulturalists (societies that in addition to hunting also planted small gardens) who were the first to formulate such expectations. Although the Hopi prophecy is better known in this country, one of the most dramatic ones was recorded by the German anthropologist Curt Nimuendajú, who spent nearly a decade at the beginning of the twentieth century with groups of Guarani Indians of Brazil:

When Nanderuvucu [First Man] decides on the end of the world, to put an end to the suffering of the earth, he will awaken the bat demons that hang from the rafters of his house and will send them out to devour the sun and the moon.

Then he will order the blue tiger lying under his hammock to attack humanity. Singing, the blue tiger will descend from the heavens, and no one will escape his voraciousness. Finally, Nanderuvucu will pull away the eternal wooden cross that supports the earth in the east. Simultaneously, starting at the western edge of the earth, the world will burn below the surface. Farther ahead, the flames will break through the surface, and the piece behind them will crash into the precipice with a thunderous noise. Slowly at first, then ever faster, the destruction will progress, until the earth sinks down into the eternal night. (Nimuendajú 1944)

The reason for the cataclysm is quite clear: First Man can no longer tolerate the suffering of the Mother Earth, caused by the activity of humans, who
with their gardens violated her, forcing her to yield more than she could voluntarily produce.

The predictions about the end of the world take on a different character
when they are formulated by agriculturalist societies. The earth is no longer the
mother, it is the environment to be exploited, and the end of the world is
moved from the natural to the social world. This process is facilitated by the
fact that while the ethics of the horticulturalists are based on appropriateness,
reality is cleaved into good and evil for the agriculturalists. While in the view
of the horticulturalists, all humans opened the door to perdition, in the social
world of the agriculturalists, it is only the evil ones who promulgate destruction, while the good part of humanity upholds order. Logically, then, dreams
about a perfect world, always in the future, involve the destruction of the evil
part of humanity and the survival of the good ones. As Norman Cohn puts it:

> That there will shortly be a marvelous consummation, when good will be
> finally victorious over evil and forever reduce it to nullity; that the human
> agents of evil will either be physically annihilated or otherwise disposed of;
> that the elect will thereafter live collectively, unanimous and without con-
> flict, on a transformed and purified earth—this expectation has had a long
> history in our civilization. (1993, 1)

"Our civilization" is based on the agriculturalists' worldview, and indeed,
Cohn describes such apocalyptic expectations for the Egyptians, the Mesopo-
tamians, the Vedic Indians, and the Zoroastrians, all agriculturalists. What is
less known is that agriculturalists of the Far East equally shared such visions.
As the China specialist Kenneth S. Cohen points out:

> The key text for apocalyptic visions in Tao is "The Annals of the Sage to
> Come," a text transcribed by Taoist mediums in the 4th century A.D., which
> predicted the end of the world in 512 A.D. The Taoists expected a conflagra-
> tion of plagues, war, floods, in which the only survivors would be those
> who lived pure, natural lives, and who had prepared themselves with vari-
> ous meditations and propitiatory rites. At the end of the world the Taoist
> "Messiah" would return, a deified Lao Tzu, known as T'ai Shang Lao Chun,
> "the Most High Lord Lao." (Personal communication; see also Welch and
> Seidel 1979, 153–154)

The Christian apocalyptic tradition is based on the Book of Revelation, the
last book of the New Testament, quoted so frequently by Barrera in the foregoing account. It announces that God revealed to Jesus how the end of the
world was to come about, involving a struggle between good and evil of cos-

mic proportions, and who in turn conveyed the message to "his servant John," who wrote it down. Good will win out, and, eventually, only the good will rule in a purified world.

The Book of Revelation gives no indication about when the world will come to an end, other than that "it will happen soon" and that it will be presaged by various catastrophes, earthquakes, plagues, wars, and so forth. Given the fact that such catastrophes have accompanied the history of humankind through the ages, there have always been individual leaders who were convinced that now, indeed, the moment was at hand and were able to convince their followers to act accordingly, thus initiating apocalyptic movements, often termed "millennial" because of the thousand years of happy life expected after the defeat of the evil empire.

There exists a great deal of literature about apocalyptic movements and no dearth of speculations about why they arise. Historical, economic, political, psychological factors are all cited, and various authors (see Goodman 1974a) have constructed extremely complex models to account for their initiation and evolution. However, behind it all, a single basic process seems to be operating, and that includes the predictions we have from the horticulturalists: the contest between order and chaos. As known from chaos theory, in a chaotic system minute differences in starting conditions can lead to very different outcomes. Both horticulturalists and agriculturalists start out from the same basic observation: the existence of the cosmos is predicated on a balancing act between order and chaos. The minute difference in starting conditions may well be that in the view of the horticulturalists, there is only appropriateness, no good versus evil, but pessimistically, they postulate that eventually chaos will win out and the earth will be destroyed. The starting point of agriculturalists is equally the pre-existence of chaos and order, but since for them, reality is cleaved into good and evil with order being good and chaos evil, they are set to do battle and optimistically predict that order—the good—will win, while chaos—evil—is condemned to eternal perdition. It is ironic to note that ideally, the lifestyle of horticulturalists tends to maintain the balance between chaos and order, and that of agriculturalists has put us on a slippery slope toward ultimate chaos.

The question then is, Why do apocalyptic disturbances arise? This happens, I think, when for a multitude of different reasons the perception of the impending victory of chaos becomes so overwhelming for a particular group that the prediction of the end of the world seems to be the only logical conclusion. Simultaneously, however, a neurophysiological defense mechanism also kicks in, and the community experiences a group trance, affording access to the alternate reality. Consequently, the actions the community resorts to in order to fend off chaos and bring about the end of the world, which to them is synonymous, are the result not of ordinary-reality reasoning, but derive from an entirely different domain. The Jonestown congregation commits suicide, thus escaping chaos altogether in the safety of the alternate reality. The Branch Davidians lay in a massive stock of arms as a defense against chaos. In Utzpak, the community, in addition to a frenzy of missionizing effort, institutes a total change in lifestyle and divine worship.

In an interplay between ordinary and non-ordinary reality, however, the neurophysiological process runs its course. It rises to a peak that is clearly recognizable in the Utzpak congregation because in this case we have the details. During a trance, the pupil of the eye becomes distended, allowing more light to enter. When this continues over a certain length of time, as it did for a week or more in Utzpak, it leads to a near-intolerable irritation. Thus the congregation began to rid itself of everything that might add to the discomfort: all shiny or colored objects were discarded or burned. These experiences were of course interpreted within the available religious framework. Eventually, the arousal of the trance began to attenuate. Don Victor's interference, guiding the congregation back to ordinary consciousness, was successful because the trance had by that time run its course. At the point in time when Representative Leo Ryan visited the Jonestown congregation in Guyana, the group trance was at its peak. He was, to their minds, the representative of chaos, the confirmation of its attack. Had he gone two weeks later, the mass suicide might not have happened. Had the authorities left the Branch Davidians alone, the fiery end could have been avoided.

After the trance dissolves, the entire apocalyptic episode is suppressed or forgotten, as we shall see in Utzpak. On the other hand, if historical conditions are right, it may become "routinized" in a new religious movement, as it happened in the case of Christianity. Had economic and social circumstances been as desperate as they were in 1995 for the Maya peasant majority in Chiapas, Mexico, the episode might have become the starting point for a militant uprising. This is what happened in the middle of the nineteenth century, when the Maya peasantry of Yucatan underwent an apocalyptic disturbance, known in history as the Cult of the Talking Cross. It led to the Caste War, a struggle of the suppressed Maya population against the Mexican state, which continued into the second decade of the twentieth century (Reed 1964).

As far as Utzpak is concerned, an interesting vista opens up there if we examine the story of the contest between order and chaos from the point of view of the alternate-reality protagonists, God and Satan, not in their well-known representation in Revelation, but as they appeared as dramatis personae, as actors on the stage in the Apostolic congregation of Utzpak. Although the congregation accepted the unitary aspect of the Trinity as doctrine, on the experiential level, with the sole exception of one vision of Jesus at the height of the disturbance, interaction of the congregation was solely with the Holy Spirit. This point is of significance, because in traditional theology the Holy Spirit is a puzzlingly scintillating being, playing only a minor role, a "curious god," as the Viennese Catholic theologian Adolf Holl puts it:

> It is striking that although the Holy Spirit is part of the basic Christian system of symbols, yet it is rarely awarded a direct address. Since earliest times prayers are directed mainly to God the Father, for instance in the formula, "Almighty God." God the Son is addressed more rarely, and the Holy Spirit occurs only in the standardized conclusion of the Roman Catholic Liturgy, "Through our Lord Jesus Christ, thy son, who lives with Thee and rules in the unity of the Holy Spirit, God forever and ever, Amen." In addition there are two hymns celebrating the Pentecost that address the Holy Spirit directly ["Veni Sancte Spiritus," "Veni Creator Spiritus"]. And one might finally mention the so-called epiclesis, where during a Eucharistic service the Holy Spirit is invoked to bring about transubstantiation.
> (Letter, January 17, 1994)

By contrast, in the Utzpak congregation—as in the Pentecostal movement generally—it was the Holy Spirit that occupied center stage, and certainly possession was experienced not by God the Father, nor by God the Son, but only by the Holy Spirit. The sole exception at the height of the apocalyptic disturbance, where an *hermano* was possessed by God the Father in the Merida congregation, was reported by the members as being odd, not quite believable, and it did not persist. The Holy Spirit was also experienced as a personalized entity, a divine being that was easily upset, whose loyalty seemed inconsistent, who for unknown reasons on occasion simply no longer possessed a certain supplicant. As usual during possession, this divine being took over, manipulated the supplicant, using his or her tongue and uttering vacuous syllables. However, unexpectedly, at the height of the disturbance, this Spirit switched from vacuous syllables to the vernacular and "used the bodies of the *hermanos* to give instructions." Then Mila began screaming obscenities, the well-known "coprolalia" during demonic possession. The congregation became totally confused, no longer knowing whether at any given moment it was the Holy Spirit that was present or Satan. As, with tragic poignancy, Epi said on the seashore after all was over, "Here I thought it was the Holy Spirit that gave orders, and in reality it was Satan." And he wept.

The question is, How was it possible for the congregation to be confused in this manner? I think the reason was that the events described developed while the congregation was in the religious trance, in fact, possibly in two variants thereof (Goodman 1990). The role of the religious trance as a neurophysiological event remains unrecognized in the literature about apocalyptic disturbances, although the Book of Revelation was clearly written while its writer John was in trance: "On the Lord's Day I was caught up in ecstasy, and I heard behind me a piercing voice like the sound of a trumpet" (Revelation 1:10).

Under certain circumstances, such as the prolonged group trance in the temple congregation, there is a switch to a related but somewhat more powerful trance, which makes possible instead of the relatively mild experience of possession by the Holy Spirit, the overwhelming exit into the alternate reality. The problem for Christianity was that alternate reality rarely conformed to the dogma of the Church. Recently, a German historian reconstructed the tragic story of an Alpine shepherd who at the end of the 1500s made a pact with his friend (Behringer 1994). Whichever would die first would reveal to the other what the world beyond the line was like. When the man began telling about his spirit journeys that he undertook with the help of his dead friend and his encounters with the spirits of the dead, with fairies, and witches—that is with sacred beings that the Church had banished long ago—and even exhibited extraordinary healing powers since these experiences, he and many of his followers were burned at the stake. In fact, his case ushered in one of the most extensive witch-hunts of the century.

Something of this order may also have happened to the congregation of Utzpak. Judging from what the members of the congregation reported, on their accidentally experienced sojourn in the alternate reality they apparently encountered a being whom they had great difficulty recognizing. Sometimes it appeared as the Holy Spirit in white light, prophesying the end of the world and the dawn of the millennium, and then they implored it fervently to come and enter. Sometimes it switched on them and was Satan, complete with red glow and tail, spouting obscenities and demanding a woman for its own, clattering on the roof and causing dissension, and they had to lean against the door and shutter the windows so it would stay outside. No wonder that faced with this terrifying turn of events, Antonio, the visionary, wanted to commit suicide.

Taking the Bible as their guide, the congregation was convinced that they were dealing with two separate beings. But were they? What if instead, in that unknown alternate reality into which they had accidentally exited, it was one and the same being playing its alternate reality game with them? The alternate reality is inhabited by sacred, very ancient beings, as we know from Native American traditions, for example, and among them one that represents both order and chaos simultaneously, namely the Trickster:

> He combines in one personage no less than two and sometimes three or
> more seemingly different and contrary roles. Oftentimes he is the maker of
> the earth and/or he is the one who changes the chaotic myth-world into the

ordered creation of today; he is the slayer of monsters, the thief of daylight, fire, water, and the like for the benefit of man; he is the teacher of cultural skills and customs; but he is also a prankster, who is grossly erotic, insatiably hungry, inordinately vain, deceitful, and cunning toward friends as well as foes. (Ricketts 1969, 327)

Turning the argument on its head, we may indeed speculate that the Holy Spirit, "that curious god," in fact the Trickster, may have slipped into Christianity through the back door, which may account for the ambivalence with which it is treated in the ritual and the literature.

As for the social, political, psychological, and economic factors identified by various authors as playing a role in apocalyptic disturbances, they were all present, individual strands twisted into one rope.

Let us take the minister Barrera as the first strand. His own psychological equilibrium was shaken because as an urbanite he could not cope with the grinding poverty taken for granted by the villagers. He wanted to be allowed to return to Campeche, where he could make a good living, but the church authorities refused to grant his petition. He was infuriated by the resistance of the congregation to his continual raiding of the church funds, and he saw this resistance as coming mainly from the women. As a Latin American urban male, he was conditioned to the view that women are supposed to submit meekly to his authority. Two factors mitigate against this "natural" order. One is the traditional independence of Maya peasant women. The other was the obligation of the minister to organize a women's group, the Dorcas which, unintended by him, provided the women with the structure within which to assert their power. His aggressive reaction to the women illustrated how, for him, chaos was at the door.

As for church dogma, Barrera was committed to the teachings of the Bible, of which the Book of Revelation is an integral part. Initially, it did not play a big role in his church activities. He was more interested in assuring the admittance of the members of the congregation to heaven by teaching them how to speak in tongues. He felt safe as far as apocalypse was concerned—something interesting to preach about, predicted, but not immediate—when unexpectedly, in the visions of Antonio, an event postulated merely as a theoretical possibility all of a sudden became brutally real: the end of the world was going to occur within the next few weeks. It was a fearful shock. But it also seemed a way out. All his problems would vanish, and he would come out victorious. "The world will be destroyed," Barrera shouted from the podium, "won't that be wonderful!" He had introduced the members of the congregation to the trance experience. With his considerable intelligence and energy, Barrera now drove the congregation into ever-higher peaks of trance, along with himself, never realizing that by doing so, he was instrumental in destroying the ritual structure of the worship service, thus opening the door to chaos. By the time the events peaked, he was disheveled and brooding, and he had basically surrendered leadership.

The men, the next strand, had their own, different, schedule. They were involved in the events leading to the outbreak of the disturbance in a variety of ways: Antonio had the visions that triggered it, and Epi, with divine sanction, changed the ritual of the prayer for the sick—it seemed obvious that they were favored by divine guidance. Yet there seemed to be no pleasing Barrera, the one man who had been their guide from the start. Instead of supporting them, approving of them, he cut himself off from them, spatially as well as in behavior. The world was no longer a safe and ordered place to these men who had joined the congregation precisely because it had helped them to overcome their deep anxieties. So they took off on their own. At the peak of the disturbance, they and their companions were the ones who had the important visions, not Barrera. Jesus appeared; they were the ones who received the instructions transmitted from the alternate reality through their bodies. Antonio was said to be possessed by Satan. And it was Epi, who at the end, gave expression to the crushing realization that the prophecy of the end of the world had failed.

Curiously, however, it was not the men who were driving the events. This role does not fall to the adult women, either, our next strand. In fact, the women's position was quite ambiguous. They failed early on, when their communal enterprise (living at the temple, which could have become a model) collapsed. The failure was due not only to only the financial demands which they could not cope with but also because they had no tradition for that lifestyle. Some of them burned their colored belongings and made white dresses, but Eus, with her "sometimes I believed, sometimes I did not" attitude, was not alone. There was also Valuch and Rodolfa, who were not sure either. And during the peak, the mature women did no more than follow along.

Upon close inspection of the data, the strongest strand in the twisted coil, or, to use a different metaphor, the true engine driving the apocalyptic disturbance, turned out to be the young women. They started going into trance in the fall and winter of 1969. From the beginning, they showed a pattern of prolonged glossolalia and a delayed return, and quite possibly Barrera was responsible for the difficulty. Initially, they were clearly infatuated with the suave and fascinating city man who also paid special attention to them. As Valuch said, Barrera raised his eyebrows when he spoke with them, but not when he spoke with her. Soon there was gossip within the village, rumors of seduction, fueled by what the neighborhood of the temple saw but of course misunderstood. Finding no outlet for their feelings, the young women replaced sex with religion. As Barrera began withdrawing from the congregation generally, they were the hardest hit. Speaking in tongues will release tension, but, as indicated by their delayed return, they apparently were unable to achieve a complete discharge of the accumulated tension. I recall a scene from the July 30, 1970, service, where Rosa, already on the descending line of her trance behavior, went into a very steep recovery of her energy with extremely loud glossolalia when Barrera, with the express intent of calming her and helping her to awaken, placed his hand on her head. By the way, the one young woman who did not experience the delayed return was Nina, who had a number of personal disagreements with Barrera and was highly critical of him.

The attacks of the young women against the older men may have been part of their adolescent revolt. Due to longer school attendance and more extensive contact with the lifestyle of Merida, Rosa and her companions were oriented more toward the city than were their mothers. In their perception, the older men were in their way. So their attack was directed against them, especially against Goyo, a man of above-average means. We recall Mila's comment that she did not want to go home because Satan, meaning her father, was there. On the other hand, Barrera was beyond their reach. Caught in what might truly be called an existential bind, it was the young women who, with their most intense trance experience, drove the congregation to the peak. As the trance dissolved, so did their role in the congregation.

Quite generally then, on the basis of this event in the Yucatan, we might propose that apocalyptic disturbances arise when groups respond to the threat of being overwhelmed by chaos by switching into the religious trance.

4. 1971 to 1975

January

After completing our work on the reconstruction of the events of the apocalyptic disturbance at the Apostolic congregation in Utzpak, Eus, Nina, and I travel back to the village. I have been especially curious about how the members of the congregation coped with the fact that the prophecy had failed, that the end of the world did not occur at the beginning of September 1970, and I ask a number of people about that. There are apparently various opinions. Rodolfa is quoted as saying that the *hermanos* had simply miscalculated. She, for one, is going to continue watching for signs. And Barrera maintains that indeed the world has come to an end, but invisibly, and it has emerged cleansed. Many people continue believing that it will still happen "very soon"; to my surprise, even Eus. "Next week, very soon," she says, "*ma? tu shaantahi* [it will not tarry]." And Nina adds, "Previously, I didn't feel this way about it. But now, it seems, I can think of nothing else. And I remember all those people in the city and how sad it is that there are not enough workers to convert them." And what about Satan, I want to know? Nina shrugs, "He cannot be very powerful. He tempted the *hermanos,* then gave up and left."

As the two women told me in Merida, there have been a number of changes in the congregation. Nina is no longer in charge of the section of the young people; she has surrendered that position to Rosa. A number of the members have resigned because they felt Rosa was ineffectual. No money is being saved, Eus knows all the details, and so the plans to build a church out of cinder blocks had to be put on hold. In fact, most of the money that the sections were earning by *talento,* as well as the membership dues, went to pay for Barrera's frequent trips. He seems to have used the congregation mainly as a source of income since the disturbance. He would come, "borrow" the money that had accumulated, ask for an offering for his next trip, and leave again. He did not even spend Christmas with the congregation, but went to Campeche instead to attend the wedding of his wife's sister. In disgust, Mariano resigned as treasurer of the Senores Cristianos and no longer came to the services. Eus and Cruz left the Dorcas, although they continued attending the services. Valuch and her husband Goyo changed over to the services of the Pentecostals. They said they would come back when Barrera was gone.

When I attend the services on January 19, 1971, I find the temple clean once more. The plastic chandeliers have not been replaced, but there are some new religious prints on the wall. The public address system and the record-player are nowhere in sight. "Broken," Eus says. The front of the rostrum is still white, a lingering reminder of past events. By knocking out the wall separating the church from the *casa pastoral,* the meeting space has been enlarged. For the pastor and his family, a new dwelling has been constructed farther back on the property, mud-and-wattle with a palm-frond roof, but square, a hybrid of village and city dwellings.

After the first hymn, Barrera greets me as a visitor, as is customary, and things feel very much like they had before the disturbance. Even Barrera no longer barricades himself from the congregation and instead sits on a small bench beside the men when playing the guitar to accompany the singing. But the congregation seems different. I miss the children running around or sleeping at their mothers' feet. As one of the few innovations left over from the disturbance, Antonio was entrusted with teaching them in the *solar* while the service was in progress. Also, looking around, I cannot see a single one of the men who had been important in the apocalyptic disturbance. One reason might be that the bean harvest is in progress, but Barrera seems to think otherwise because he asks for a prayer for the *hermanos* who are absent, saying, "Who knows why they attend so rarely and what their problem might be?" He is still soliciting offerings for the building of the new temple, and I contribute 200 pesos. I am not sure whether he notices. But when I ask him whether I can take some pictures, he is as polite as ever. Eus, however, tells me that some of the *hermanas* are saying behind my back that the only reason I come to visit is to make more films to sell in the United States.

Strikingly, the congregation abstains almost entirely from any trance behavior. Carefully, it seems to me, they stay away from the joyous, fast *coritos* that tended to induce it, and no one speaks in tongues. Although, on the average, people are able to call up glossolalia behavior for about four years, some of them have possibly lost it due to the events of the disturbance. Nina's observation might be to the point: "They thought when those things were going on that every time you knelt down, the Holy Spirit would come. But now it is not that way." Only at the end of the service, when Barrera and Ernesto are praying for the sick, do they each utter a brief phrase.

I had promised my students who had arrived in Merida for the January term that I would organize a trip to the village for them. So Eus and I make big plans. We go all through the village shopping for gourd dishes, we buy cornmeal and rice and sugar, and Eus makes a fine *atole.* The students come in a chartered bus. I take them for a walk down the highway, and in the end they all crowd into Eus's *solar* and we serve them *atole* and soft drinks. I am proud of how beautiful Eus's traditional oval home looks. Although it is the dry season, Eus has kept her flowers blooming and, of course, everything is neatly swept and tidy. So I am quite stunned when on the way back to Merida, I overhear the remark of the father of one of the students who had come along for the excursion: "How shocking. That woman has to live under more miserable conditions than our cub scouts on an outing."

Keeping in Touch

Until my next visit in July 1971, I received a number of letters from the Yucatan. One was from Chan Felix. He wanted to invest in a business and asked me to help him with a gift of 700 pesos. I did. Another one came from Eus's daughter, Wilma. She asked for a small loan so she could pay someone to weed her *col*. I sent that, too. I also started sending Eus a small monthly stipend. The most important letters, though, were from Nina, who conscientiously kept me up to date on developments in Utzpak. It seems that Barrera became more and more disinterested in keeping the congregation going. In his absence, Nestor, and even Mariano, held services, but they were deemed "very cold," and many members stayed away. Finally, Don Victor took over and conditions improved. But disputes developed between him, Barrera, and Luis L. of Merida, so he left, and in his stead, Barrera asked Nicolas to take over. This caused a great deal of dissension. In the established hierarchy of pastor, minister, deacon, and worker, he did not even occupy the lowest rung, and still he presumed to mount the podium to preach. In Eus's view, Barrera appointed him only so that he could continue being in charge. Nicolas kept hanging on, even though he was unpopular, because he and his family had moved to Utzpak with all their belongings. His wife, Lola, told Eus that they had a lot of moving expenses; they even brought her sewing machine. She made clothes to help with expenses, for they had five boys, the smallest only 1 year old.

Satan, in the meantime, continued in the vicinity. According to Nina's letter of May 16, 1971, Juan, the husband of Oda, one of the daughters of Old Candil, wanted to commit suicide. It was not known why, but the attempt failed. Then Juan went to the *monte* to cut cottonwood branches for his horse. As he told the story, the first tree he found had no leaves. Neither did the next one. He finally encountered one with leaves. So he climbed up to cut some branches, and the devils attacked him. One was on his back, the other at his throat, and the third one pulled him. He fell off the tree. His neck was twisted, but not broken, and he was paralyzed. His son found him at ten that night and took him home. Candil asked the *hermanos* to pray for Juan, and Antonio, who had come to visit his wife, went along. But in the meantime, Antonio had fallen from grace, he had gone back to dancing, cursing, and drinking. When Juan saw him, he said, "Don't pray for me. The Devil has already taken you." Antonio sat down in the back and wept.

Later that day, the family took Juan to the hospital in Merida. When they came back, the *hermanos* organized a service at his house, and it was said that he heard the entire service in his hospital bed in Merida. He decided that if he got well, he would be baptized.

According to a letter dated June 20, 1971, Paula began speaking in tongues once more, then switched over to singing in trance. "I have never heard anything that beautiful," wrote Nina. Generally, however, there was little glossolalia and no more praying for the manifestation of the Holy Spirit on Sundays.

June: Return to Yucatan

Eus waits for me at the Merida airport on June 28, 1971, and we take the bus to the depot. There is not enough time before leaving for Utzpak, so instead of going to see Peregrina, we visit Hermana Maria, whose home is close by. Her daughter Blanca has just begun speaking in tongues. It happened quite unexpectedly, she said. "With Hermano Luis L., we went to my cousin's house to pray. They are not yet converted. That was where it happened. Hermano Luis L. said that I should train myself to control it, so I don't do it in the presence of people who have not as yet been converted."

Somebody mentions that Luis L. wanted to preach over the radio, but half an hour costs 300 pesos, so he decided against it. "We can always go out into the street," he said, "there is no charge for that."

There is only one oblique reference to the apocalyptic disturbances of the previous summer. Blanca tells that she heard of a dream that Consuelo of the Merida congregation had. She was in a church and saw a minister. She thought it was Luis L., but she was not sure. He wore black clothes and was holding a Bible with blank white pages. And Eus adds that Jose, the minister of Chetumal, had a dream in which he saw Juan L. in a deep well. He tried to get out but kept slipping back. Then smoke came up from the well. Despite the obvious references to the apocalyptic events, the women merely nod, and no one has any comment.

There is a pastor's meeting going on in Merida at the time, and Maria says that she has heard that there is a lot of dispute about the nature of the soul. Is it in the breath or in the blood? Does man have only a soul, or also a spirit? Is that spirit the spirit of God? With no answer in sight, the conversation of the women turns to the wedding of Chan Felix. In transit, he often stayed at Maria's house, and apparently the foster parents of Ysaura, his fiancée, who live in Las Choapas, demanded that he buy seventeen turkeys for the wedding and also the napkins. He said that he might as well do it. Money even for napkins? So the business he wanted to invest in was his wedding? Wilma and I laugh about the clever ruse later; she said he often got money out of her the same way, but Eus was not amused. "I say if someone wants to get married, he should work for his expenses. When Chan Felix got converted, he stopped working with his father in the *monte*. He still worked some, but not like before."

Back in Utzpak, I once more stay with Reina and spend most of my time with Eus, as before. I am very low on funds, but although I had sent Eus her monthly stipend, I pay her 100 pesos for my food and her work. She said that was fair and that she would buy *canamo* with it and two ends of material for dresses for Wilma's oldest daughter, Consuelo, who is living with her, to help with her work. We are quickly back to our old pattern of her doing her chores, plucking a chicken, making tortillas, while I ask questions.

The first person I inquire about after getting down on paper the usual litany about Barrera's financial dealings is Antonio. Back in Columbus, I discovered by going through my field notes that his visions had passed through a sequence of first being glowingly white.[1] That was what had caught my attention first, his contention that the demons he had seen were white: I expected them to be red, as described in Central European folklore. Then came that vision about the candles about to be extinguished, which played such an important role in the apocalyptic disturbance. The predominant color there was gold or orange. After that he had seen the priests in the Merida cathedral wearing demonic masks; in other words, a vision was superimposed on an ordinary-reality scene, and with that the visions came to an end. What he experienced during the peak period of the disturbance was no longer vision, but rather possession. The whole visionary episode had lasted about forty days, perhaps a biological constant, for I was able to calculate the same length of time for the visions of Peregrina, Luis L.'s mother, and that same time period was also reported in the Acts of the Apostles as the period between Christ's resurrection and his ascension. So did Antonio have any more visions since September of last year? Apparently not. Instead he had continued on an entirely *mundano* path, working as a barber and having problems with his wife Cruz.

As Eus told the story, at night after work Antonio used to go to the *monte* with his dogs to catch armadillos:

> He catches five, or maybe three. In the daytime he works as a barber. One night he goes to the *monte* and a man comes and pushes against the door. Cruz says, "Go away, my husband might hear you." "Your husband has gone to the *monte*, I saw him." "Go away." He continues pushing against the door. A boy from the neighborhood sees him. He only clears his throat and the man leaves. Next day Antonio asks Cruz if anything happened. She says no. But Antonio hears it from the boy. This was at the beginning of May. He starts swearing at Cruz, using really foul language (*"insultos muy feos, muy graves"*), and she shouts back at him, and there is a big fight. Their oldest

daughter runs to Hermano Paulino for help. "My father wants to kill my mother," she says. So he and Hermano Victor and Hermano Epi go to Antonio's house and Don Victor begins counseling them. Antonio keeps saying, "I'll kill her, I'll kill her!" And Don Victor said, "Then what's going to happen to the little girls?" "Then I'll kill them too." And he would have if the *hermanos* had not been there. This is what Paulino told Nohoch Felix. I was in my hammock and over-heard the entire story.

They continued fighting all night, until about three in the morning. Then Antonio calmed down. A week later everything started all over again. This was mainly because every time he went to the plaza, the men kept goading him, "*Leti hermana tun chuuk yetel le macoob* [That *hermana* is doing those sweet things with the men]," they said. So he left and went to Villahermosa to work as a barber.

With no income to feed her four little girls, Cruz went to her mother for help, but she would not keep her, saying she should go to her husband. So Cruz sought out her mother-in-law, who let her stay and gave her some corn and beans. But out of necessity Cruz eventually drifted back into prostitution.

The Congregation

On June 29, 1971, Eus and I attend the service together. The rostrum has been repainted in silver and shows the words "*Dios es Amor*" [God is love] in bold letters. A drawing by Valentin with the emblem of the Apostolic Church adorns the wall. As a new feature, there is a modest blackboard on a stand with some biblical quotations written on it, but no reference to speaking in tongues.

For a weekday evening, the service is rather well attended, twelve women and nine men. The children are back; after Antonio left there was no other volunteer to do a separate service for them. Somehow, however, the texture of the service is different. As Eus points out:

> There is something wrong with the *hermanos*. They stay for the songs, but during the prayers and especially during the sermon, they go to the well, or out into the street. I think they are holding their own services there. [She laughs.] They continually go back and forth like that. Epi does it, and Pedro too, and even some of the girls.

During the same service, Barrera announces that he is moving to Merida to establish a second congregation there. He is sad that the congregation cannot afford a new cinder-block temple. "We'll have to build it in heaven," he quips. His place will be taken by Nicolas, helped by Hermano Victor. Nicolas then asks for an offering for Barrera's trip to Merida, but very few came forward to contribute. Perhaps he has finally exhausted their patience.

After the service on July 1, 1971, we are still standing around in the street when Barrera comes to say good-by. I remember that I was there when he started his stint in Utzpak and now here I am when it is ending. Of course we do not mention what has happened in between. I thought that was our final good-by, but early on July 2, 1971 he comes by with Nicolas, and for some reason that is not quite clear, he brings me a written note that says that I had always been ready to help and so they hope that I would help them with the present change of pastors. I tell them I have no money at present but will be glad to send them some when I get home. Who should I send it to? To Nicolas. We have a brief chat about doctrinal matters, and Barrera repeats what I heard him say the summer before; at the Second Coming, God will not destroy heaven and earth, only clean it. Clearly, he still needs some rationalization for why prophecy has failed. Nina and Eus, though, have apparently put the matter behind them.

After Barrera leaves, Nina comments on Barrera's plans for Merida. He wants to start a congregation near the depot, where Luis L., in anticipation of such an expansion of the work in Merida had some time ago built a small *casa pastoral*. That is where he wants to live with his family, but Nina does not think that will work out because it is occupied by an *hermana* with her small children whose husband left her because she converted.

I am already in my hammock at Reina's place when at about eight, in the dark, Nicolas's wife Lola comes by to rest with four of her five sons: her oldest is staying with his grandmother. Her youngest, Isaia, is a chubby baby and weighs a ton; it must have been very hard for her to lug him all through the village for half a day, for that is what she has done. She had bought some remnants and sewed dresses from them and had started out in the heat of the midday to sell. But she has not sold a single one. This is a bad time to sell—last year's corn is gone, and people have to buy expensive corn from the merchants. There is little money for anything else. Santiago gives her a *luuch* full of beans, which puts him about two notches above zero, where my estimation of him usually hovers.

The next morning I go over to see her. I find her busy making breakfast for her sons. She has sent one of them to Dona Juana with some slop for her pigs, and he comes back with a few cookies. She divides them between the children, but when she turns her back, the older boy snatches some from his brother's plate. I have gone to her to buy one of her dresses to help out, but they are quite poorly sewn so I buy only one, to her obvious disappointment. Also, she has told Reina that she is selling them for 6 pesos, and she charges me 6 and a half. I do not begrudge her the extra 50 centavos; I just do not like the attitude.

During subsequent services that Eus and I attend there is practically no speaking in tongues. There is an early morning service on Sunday, July 4, 1971, but not specifically for receiving the manifestation of the Holy Spirit. Only as a side issue does Nicolas mention that if you have not received it yet, you should ask for it "with all your heart," but there is no effort invested in teaching the technique, and Chan Felix's sermons of the day do not allude to the experience.

All along I have been wondering if Antonio will show up again. Then, two days before I am scheduled to leave, Eus hears that he has returned to Utzpak because his wife sent him a letter that their youngest daughter was very ill with diarrhea. According to Eus, it started when Antonio left, which affected Cruz's milk. But Cruz was in Dzoncahuich. So Antonio went there and brought her back. I send Eus to her with 25 pesos so she can buy medicine. Antonio attends the evening service of July 6, 1971, although according to what he has told Nina, he is very upset with Barrera who, he says, is dividing the church. He comes to the front to shake hands with me. He is tanned, hoarse, and sweaty, and his pudginess has given way to tough muscles. During the altar call, he utters a few brief phrases of glossolalia, then during the testimony, he asks for the prayers of the congregation because he is going to take his family to Isla Arena, Tabasco, to work in the sugar plantations. I am not to see him again for another fifteen years.

At Eus's Place

In the afternoons I usually go to see Eus. This time, Nohoch Felix has gone with Chan Felix to Baca to see one of Eus's older half-brothers. Chan Felix wants to borrow money from him rather than from a bank, where he would have to pay interest. But his uncle will give it to him only if Nohoch Felix also signs for it. Chan Felix needs the money for his wedding. In addition to the 700 pesos he has received from me, he tells Eus, he has to have at least another 1,000 pesos to pay for the wedding dress, which he had made in Merida and which alone cost 350 pesos, and then there are the shoes and other accessories. He has a good income whenever he works in Merida as a salesman for aluminum cookware, Eus says, 60 or 50 pesos a day, but it is not a steady job.

Later that afternoon, Isauro's wife Juanita comes to visit, bringing along her two sisters. Isauro left this morning to preach in Tizimin and is not expected back for another month. The men really spend very little time at home. If they are not out missionizing somewhere, they work on the ranches, and the women have to rely on their own network of relatives and friends. Juanita does not go along to Tizimin with her husband because there are always mosquitoes in Tizimin and her sons refuse to sleep under a mosquito net. I recall that last year when Juanita wept so much during glossolalia, Eus remarked that she was sad because her two sisters were *muy adulteras* [living in adultery]. So here they were, two very pretty, bosomy, young women, exuding an appealing sexuality, especially the younger one. Eus mentioned later that the older one had been deserted by her husband and now had no *esposo fijo* [steady husband], only boyfriends. When one of her men friends laid down beside her young daughter in her hammock, the child got up and went to her grandfather. "He is not my father," she told him, and her grandfather let her stay. The younger woman, also without an *esposo fijo*, has her 6-month-old baby boy with her. She keeps nursing him, then plays with him in the hammock that Eus has let down for her, and subtly, she is projecting a sex game.

There is very fast chitchat in Maya going on, which I have to get used to again. I do catch a reference to a Don Genaro's wife having a baby, but I had no idea why that was funny until I could ask Eus after the women left. She then explains that Don Genaro had been gone on a trading expedition and that simple arithmetic showed that the child could not be his. Besides, he is a homosexual and goes on his trips accompanied by his young boyfriend. When, upon returning, he found his wife with a baby, he said, "What is in my *solar* is mine," and there was no problem. There are about five adult homosexual men in Utzpak that Eus knows about, and they usually associate with very young men. Some paint their eyes, and they get along well with girls. "They are different from small boyhood up," Eus says. "I have seen it. They prefer sex plays with boys, and from the girls they just want company."

Shuttling back and forth between Eus's and Reina's home, I am once more struck by the rich vegetation of Eus's *solar*. One morning, with Eus's help, I make an inventory of what she is growing. She has various citrus fruit bushes, tropical fruit trees such as papaya, *saramuyo*, and *anona;* a huge avocado tree; and annual plants such as tomato, various chiles, and cilantro. All in all there are thirty-two plants and ten different perennial flowering bushes. Occasionally, there are medicinal implications, such as that you could boil the granada leaves for treating warts in children.

At Reina's Place

The principal attraction at Reina's for me is Lupita, now 3 years old. She remembers me, although I have been away for almost ten months. She likes going shopping with me, and we eat together and she takes it for granted that I will share my cheese, *frances*, or soft drink with her. She sits down in her hammock and then, like an adult, extends the other side for me to sit down in, forming a love seat. Of course she is also a naughty little girl. She refuses to call Dona Andrea, Don Eduardo's wife, her *chichi*, her grandmother; we cannot figure out why. Her father has bought a tom turkey for resale and is weighing it on the scale suspended from the ceiling. She keeps hitting the bird on its wing, and the bird finally pecks her on her hand, drawing blood. "And who provoked the turkey?" Santiago asks. Quite properly, she receives no sympathy.

Several young men come to do business with Santiago, and once more I note how different the rules are as compared to when the visitors are women. At Eus's place, women visitors are always invited to sit in a hammock. I had asked Reina before: If a young man comes courting a girl, in which hammock would he sit? "On a chair," Reina had said. "And if he comes to talk business with Santiago?" "Santiago takes him out into the street." Four men come to buy shirts from him for this evening's dance. Two sit on the threshold; the third stands inside. A fourth one sits down in a hammock but instantly gets up again, although Reina jokes with them, making it a quasi-social occasion. "With your new shirts," she says, "you might snare a girl tonight, or maybe even two."

My stay is short this time because I also want to attend the wedding in Tabasco of Chan Felix and Ysaura with Eus and Nohoch Felix. Even so, Reina decides that we should have a farewell party. I supply the money and she the labor; she makes *vaporcitos* and we send Santiago to buy some bottles of *horchata* [a drink made of oatmeal or rice flour; it was brought by the Spanish and was originally made from almonds]. We invite the women of the corner and Eus comes with Nina and Wilma's daughter Consuelo, and everyone expresses regrets about my leaving with the conventional phrase: "*Ya nos acostumbramos* [We had already gotten used to you]."

The Wedding in Las Choapas, Tabasco

We go by train, the filthiest I had ever seen, first to Tancochapa, Veracruz, then we change to Las Choapas. But the landscape is beautiful, getting hilly, which prompts Nohoch Felix to remark what a miracle it is that God could have created that all in seven days. "*Que obra,*" he keeps saying, what a job.

Does Eus expect anyone of her side of the family to come to the wedding? She thinks her brother Anastasio might; he is Chan Felix's godfather.

Eus does not know her future daughter-in-law. Chan Felix met her at a pastoral meeting in Merida. There had been girls in Utzpak who were interested in him, such as the seamstress down the street from the temple. But Chan Felix found out that she had also talked with Armin, his younger brother, and so lost interest in her. Ysaura was the daughter of a rancher who had four other daughters. The couple whom she called parents, Hermana Tina and Hermano Gonzalo, were the people she had worked for in Las Choapas from the time she was 12. Does Ysaura speak in tongues? Eus does not know. "Chan Felix does not do it very often either," I observe. "I for one have never heard it." Eus agrees, then she reminisces:

> When Chan Felix was converted, there was no temple. The services were held in Don Eduardo's house. When he first spoke in tongues, he fell over to one side as he was kneeling and he spoke and spoke. Now he does it mainly in his sleep. I can hear him, it sounds exactly like it did that first time. It is not Spanish and it is not Maya. In the morning I ask him, "Did you dream?" He says that he didn't.

Chan Felix, with two other young men, meet us at the Las Choapas train station and, taking charge of our baggage, guides us to the bride's house, over clean streets that could have been anywhere in rural Mexico. There are peasant women in colorful embroidered costumes and long skirts offering fruit and vegetables for sale, beautifully arranged on handcarts. Eus and Nohoch Felix remark about the forest of TV antennae, indicative of the affluence of this community where the men have good-paying jobs in the oil fields. But what really interests them is the way cocoa leaves have apparently been woven together to form rainproof roofs. And Nohoch Felix admires the hard, round rocks in the streets, so different from the limestone at home. "Did you ever see stones like that?" he keeps saying, picking one up.

The house of our hosts appears quite affluent and has a number of rooms. We could have slept inside, on beds or a mat on the floor, but we preferred tying our hammocks to the beams of the roofed-over terrace. We must have been quite a sight, Nohoch Felix in his white peasant garb, Eus and I in ʔipiles, "the natives straight out of the jungle," swinging in our hammocks.

We finally meet Ysaura, a slender young woman with an indifferent figure. But I can see why Chan Felix is attracted to her: she has light brown wavy hair and white skin. All over Mexico a light complexion is considered a mark of beauty. Unfortunately, she has very bad teeth and whenever she smiles she covers her mouth with her hand.

At first glance, Chan Felix seems an indifferent suitor. "As romantic as a fish," I write in my notes. He settles down in his hammock next to ours and reads the Bible, while the girl leans against the sink of the outdoor kitchen across the courtyard, watching him. I remember scenes in the house of my relatives in Mexico City in which the groom indicated with intense and unmistakable body language that he could hardly wait to deflower his fiancée. But perhaps Chan Felix's indifference is transmitting the same message, only with different behavioral signals: my fiancée is a virgin and I do not as yet have access to her.

Not having lived in Eus's house, I had not seen much of her interaction with Nohoch Felix before, who was usually at work when I was there. Now it was a pleasure to watch the tenderness between them. But when at nightfall Nohoch

Felix, obviously kidding, asks whether Eus wants to sleep *loch* with him, she says she doesn't like to do that, not even with her children. Besides, she says, his bones are too hard. When I ask what *loch* is, they demonstrate it by lying down in the hammock with a great deal of laughter, with Nohoch Felix placing his arm under Eus's neck and his cheek beside hers. Laughter grows to hilarity when I say that I should have had my camera handy. So instead it is Eus and I who sleep in the same hammock that night, not doing *loch,* but where one sleeper's head is next to the other's toes, the weave of the hammock naturally folding up into a barrier. Of course, we also have a bath after arrival, a Yucatecan one, which is so easy to manage anywhere, requiring only a makeshift curtain and a bucket of water. We cannot tell if the members of our host family also bathe regularly the way we do—they certainly do not rinse out their mouth after eating, as is proper—and that and our baths make us feel distinctly superior.

The following morning, I help Ysaura peel potatoes, and then we work on her floor-length white wedding gown. She needs a new zipper (the one on the dress does not work), and she has other complaints: the dress has some spots, perhaps because Chan Felix packed it in a dirty box, and the shoes do not fit. To help with the expenses, she has found a sponsor, a *madrina,* for the wedding cake, and one for the special pumps she is to wear to the civil ceremony, and one for her perfume, so actually he has to pay only for the food. She says nothing about the wedding gown. When she met Chan Felix, she had a boyfriend, but she broke up with him because he also had another girlfriend. Besides, he did not want to get married. But Chan Felix spoke to her parents and to her uncles about marrying her, and they told her to think it over and she agreed. However, during the year and a half that they have been engaged, he has only come to see her twice. He said it was because of his work. "They call that love," she sighs, "but then that is a woman's fate, she has to be *muy sufrida* [long-suffering]." Where are they going to live after the wedding? She does not know; Chan Felix has not discussed it with her.

Chan Felix in the meantime is running around, doing Hermana Tina's bidding. He is supposed to provide seventeen turkeys but has paid for only ten. They cost three times more than in Utzpak, and he brought three from home but is still short. He is to go buy 10 kilograms of ground beef at 16 pesos a kilo for the filling—could I perhaps help with that?—and eight large cans of green peas. Eus shakes her head: what kind of a turkey filling is that going to be? What you need are hard-boiled eggs and burned chili and *masa.* But she says nothing to the hostess, of course. Nohoch Felix, seeing the problems of his son, offers "a small contribution" to Hermano Gonzalo for the expenses, but he magnanimously refuses, saying all has already been paid for. Maybe he had not consulted with wife Tina.

Various callers start coming by: Juan L. all the way from Chetumal, and Hermano Bernardillo C., whom Eus remembers from his visits to Utzpak years ago before his retirement, when he was still bishop of the Southwest Section of the Apostolic Church. He is going to marry Ysaura and Chan Felix. Eus is clearly pleased that the church hierarchy is doing her son all this honor.

In the course of the day, there will be repeated questions of Nohoch Felix and also Chan Felix about whether the turkeys have been killed yet. I am struck by the special tone of those questions and remember that I had heard an archaeologist say that turkeys in classical Maya times were often substituted for human sacrifices. The turkeys have been placed in a small fenced-in enclosure, and I watch them for a while, feeling their fate as captives soon to be sacrificed. So that morning I film them in their contemptuous splendor. One tom has mounted a hen; she accepts his attentions demurely as he occasionally, between thrusts, preens her feathers and strokes her with his strong feet. Later in the afternoon, they are hung by their legs from a post and their throats are cut, but I cannot bring myself to be witness to that.

Guests begin arriving, first Ysaura's mother with three very shy young daughters, all like Ysaura, with light brown hair and fair skin. There is no expression of affection between Ysaura and her family; Ysaura simply takes hold of the two turkeys that her mother has brought and they are executed with the rest.

We are still sitting at the lunch table after having eaten when there is a knock on the front door and a booming voice asks whether people speak Maya around here. Eus smiles, "*In wiitsin* [my younger brother]," as the visitor is ushered in. Don Anastasio, who has brought his 14-year-old daughter along, and Eus are two peas from the same pod, a very striking resemblance. Eus tells later that she, Anastasio, her Merida brother Agapito, and another sister who died in childbirth when Eus was 20 are children of the same mother, a woman their father took as his third wife when he was 42 years old.

Ysaura serves Don Anastasio lunch, so Eus and I want to withdraw, for in Yucatan, guests customarily eat alone. But Don Anastasio insists that we stay. "*Kulen*," he says, sit down. So we pull up our chairs. "How did you find the house?" Eus asks. It is as if I am hearing Hermano Goyo all over again: "*Pues,* see, we got out of the train, here in this town of Las Choapas, and there stood this man, and I went up to him, and I said, 'Senor,' I say, 'I will pose this question to you.' 'Say it,' he said. 'You see, Senor, the matter is this. I come from . . .'" In fact, he turns out to be as gifted a storyteller as Eus and Agapito, churning out tale after embroidered tale as he goes along, like the one I especially liked about a scribe who was to deliver a letter from the bishop of Sotuta to the padre in a neighboring village but was given an obstreperous horse that merely lifted up its tail, and sailing he went. He and Eus reminisce about their father, who had twenty-nine children and an inexhaustible stock of tales. He was a wonderful storyteller, Eus says, and it was from him that they had learned their story-telling style. The four of them—Anastasio, Agapito, she, and their late sister—together with their father would often spend the evening by going to a neighbor's house and doing nothing but tell stories. In fact, he enjoyed doing that clear until the end of his days. At 95, he sowed some *shpelum*. He harvested them and was going to sell them on the market the next day, but there was a sudden downpour. He was soaked through and came down with a high temperature. Three days later, he was dead.

Don Anastasio is clearly intent on impressing the stranger. "No need for a spoon," he waves away Ysaura. With bravado, he tears a piece off his tortilla, forms a small scoop and eats his soup with that. Then he realizes that we are talking Maya. "*Ud. habla la Maya?*" and it becomes clear that the similarity between Don Anastasio and Eus is not merely one of appearance. They also share their love of language. You have to be respectful of whatever language a person is speaking, he says. Here, he observes, people in town speak only Spanish, although the villages around Las Choapas speak Zapotec. He wonders why that is. Anyway, you have to express that respect toward your own language by speaking it properly. Now his sister here, she is truly the queen of "la Maya." She is not mixing the two languages. It is not, "*in mama* [my mother]," but "*in na?*," for instance. Of course, languages do change; he has observed that. Some expressions his father used were no longer understood, and in Sotuta, the young men substitute a glottal stop for the "p" in *shiipa* [girl]. But it is too bad that "la Maya" is becoming *mestizado* [contaminated with Spanish]. When I point out that languages always change when there is a conquest, he becomes even more animated. *Tu haahil*, indeed? Well, he has always been interested in history. His eyes, green as Eus's, sparkle. Would I write him a letter and tell him more about that? He still possesses the history book that he used in grade school. He had wanted to continue his schooling, and he and his father had talked about that with his grade-school teacher. But a complete education for him and his brother would have cost 900 pesos, and his father began adding up how many loads of corn and fruit and how many chickens and eggs they would have had to sell to come up with such an astronomical sum. At prices one-tenth of what they are today, he had had to give up on the idea.

Eus says something about my being *una doctora*, and he wants to know what the Ph.D. stands for. What is philosophy? Are there books about that? Are they illustrated? That leads to Plato and Descartes, and to dinosaurs 30 million years old that he has heard about from a radio station in Costa Rica. It turns into a very long afternoon of talking, with Nohoch Felix and Eus and Chan Felix (between shopping forays) fascinated listeners.

The next day is the civil ceremony at the courthouse; then the following day the wedding at the church, a large well-kept building; and afterward the banquet in the courtyard, which friends and relatives of the host had labored hard to cover with a leafy roof. Eus and I nod to each other: indeed, the precious turkeys had been lamentably spoiled by a filling of potatoes, carrots, and green peas. We cannot talk; the hymns being piped in over a loudspeaker are much too loud. But Hermana Tina tells Eus the next day when we leave that it had been a fine wedding, actually quite similar to one that a friend had seen in an American movie, and her neighbors remark about the fact that an American woman had filmed it all.

"Did my brother really say that the dinosaurs were 30 million years old?" Eus asks the next day as we are waiting along the highway for the Paralelo bus that is to take us to Villahermosa and on to Merida.

A week later, before my return home, we go to visit Don Anastasio in H., where he is the supervisor of the *henequen* workers. While his wife and daughters are busy preparing a turkey in our honor, we are treated to a very detailed lecture about bees. Going back into antiquity, he says, Yucatan had always been famous for its honey, but that was coming to an end. There was a large variety of bees on the Peninsula, bees that looked like houseflies, black bees, white bees, and bees that had a small yellow spot on their backs, but in contrast to the local wasps, Yucatan bees were all stingless, and that was their undoing. About maybe forty years ago, an aggressive stinging bee arrived on the scene— he called it "*americana*"—and proceeded to exterminate the bees of Yucatan. As a result of their attack, there were fewer bees around every year. The only bee to escape the destruction was a very tiny one with a beehive no larger than a baseball. The *americana* did not recognize it as a bee, apparently. I do not realize the significance of Don Anastasio's report about this *americana* until decades later, when the alarm about the "killer bee" began appearing in the American press.

Developments in the Congregation until July 1972

Following Chan Felix's wedding, Nina continued keeping me abreast of developments in the congregation with her letters. The impression that she transmits is one of a decided decrease in enthusiasm. Nicolas went on holding services, and attendance hovered around thirty, but Nina noted that all was pretty dispirited. There was no speaking in tongues, and fewer and fewer people volunteered to offer special hymns "for the honor and glory of God," as Nohoch Felix liked to say. She actually provided a numerical breakdown. Even Nicolas would wander in and out when one or the other of the men took over a particular part of the service.

Once again, financial matters came to the fore, this time in the more affluent environment of Chetumal. In early September, Nicolas received a letter from Barrera, and Nina recorded the following summary of its content:

The *hermanos* of the congregation in Chetumal had collected money to support evangelizing. Each one of them also, over a period of time, had contributed 5 pesos every week toward this purpose. But when Hermano Juan L. saw all that money accumulating, which by then amounted to about 12,000 pesos, he asked the treasurer of the congregation to lend it to him for the construction of a masonry temple. Instead of a temple, however, he used it to build a new *casa pastoral*. So all the money was spent. The new *casa pastoral* was not completed, there was no masonry temple either, and in disgust, thirty *hermanos* left, and Juan L. had only eight *hermanos* left in his congregation.

It happened that Barrera arrived in Chetumal just at that time with Don Victor. Barrera made contact with the dissatisfied *hermanos* and together with Don Victor held a service with them in a private home, although Juan L. had warned them not to do that, for they were divisionists. When Juan L. realized that he was losing the congregation, he humbled himself before those thirty *hermanos*. He begged their forgiveness, he even wept, saying that Don Victor was right in what he was teaching and that all should learn the spiritual matters of the Lord. This reconciled the *hermanos*.

On September 21, 1971, there was another pastors' meeting, this time in Villahermosa, and a new minister, Manuel H. from Tabasco, was assigned to the Utzpak congregation. Clearly the Church administration was unaware of the strong ethnic consciousness of the Yucatecan congregations. A few years later they would pay dearly for this neglect of Maya sensitivities. Very soon, the placement of a *wacho* [an outsider] in the position of authority into this Maya village congregation had unanticipated consequences. Although Manuel was able to keep the membership more or less stable, he had increasing problems with discipline during the services. The *hermanos,* for instance, simply no longer testified at all, not offering as much as a biblical quotation. Angrily, he admonished them, imperiously interrupting the sermon of a local *hermano,* to whom he had passed:

> Hermanos, I have seen that at the time of the testimonies, none of you rose to give thanks to the Lord for what he had done for you, not even quoting a biblical passage or anything. That is not good, it might lead to bad habits among us. (Nina, November 20, 1971)

There were other signs that could be read as possibly unconscious acts of sabotage. Nina's record of November 13, 1971, reads as follows:

> Mila kneels down to pray, but she does not pray, she chats with the other girls; then she gets up and goes out into the street. Before the end of the

altar call, she comes back in, kneels down once more and says, "Let us pray, Hermanos!" She closes her eyes to pray, but opens them again, and this is how the altar call ended, and she finished and had not prayed.

On December 13, 1971, Manuel left Utzpak, ostensibly because one of his brothers had an accident and he wanted to attend to him. He did not come back. As a result, although Nina did not make that connection in her letters, the diagnostic features of offering personal hymns and testimonies reverted to normal. Unexpectedly, however, a new element entered the scene, once more carried by Barrera. He came two days after Manuel's departure, opened the temple with the key he still carried, and started holding services. To everyone's surprise, he offered a totally new approach.

Enter the William Branham Mission

Characteristically, Barrera aimed his first thrust at the manner, sanctioned by the Church administration, of handling money. He argued that the tithing as practiced by the Apostolic Church had no foundation in the New Testament. No one should demand tithing from the *hermanos,* also the congregations should not be required to send their tithe to the district office, and no share of their offerings was to be surrendered to the central headquarters in Mexico City. And there was more. In Campeche, he and Don Victor had come in contact with representatives of a group originating in the United States that preached the doctrines of a "famous evangelist" named William Branham.[2] Barrera received a tape-recorder from them and two tapes of sermons of William Branham translated into Spanish. According to Nina, who had heard the tapes, the Branham sermons proclaimed that he who listened to them would learn to walk in the wisdom of the God. Jesus was really Lord, and he who said "Jehovah" was actually saying "Satan." Christian churches were bad, the church organizations were bad, and the baptisms performed by other churches were invalid. They had to be done over again using the formula, "I baptize you in the name of the Lord Jesus." In their services, they did not speak in tongues, the women did not cover their heads, and the customary greeting of "*Paz de Cristo*" was no longer used. It was also said, and this of course spoke directly to a congregation that was still smarting from the failed prophecy about the end of the world, that William Branham predicted that the end of the world was indeed imminent, but first San Francisco would be destroyed by an earthquake, then the Third World War would break out, and the Second Coming would come soon after that.

On December 23, 1971, Luis L. and his wife came to visit the service at Utzpak and there was a passionate disputation between him and Barrera. Luis L. announced that Don Victor and Barrera had been expelled from the Apostolic Church because they were preaching an erroneous doctrine. But for the time being the congregation stuck with their own minister. Gregoria had been saying among the women that Barrera was teaching the wisdom of the Lord. Barrera offered a hymn about his being willing to suffer everything because Christ would give him eternal life, and there was no end to the *"Amens"* and *"Aleluyas."* When Luis L. and his wife also offered a hymn, it seemed to Nina that the congregation "abhorred their voices."

Despite the official edict of expulsion, Barrera continued regarding the Utzpak congregation as his own and held services there. And of course he reverted to his old habit of borrowing money from the congregation's milk-can treasury. It was he who married Nina and her fiancé, Desi, the younger brother of Joaquina, in January of 1972. Their marriage tied Eus's family to that of Isauro, for Joaquina was the wife of Ernesto, the brother of Isauro. Soon after her wedding, Nina moved to Chetumal with her husband, temporarily cutting off an important source of information for me.

To clarify matters, a pastors' convention was called for February 15–18, 1972, in Villahermosa, to which Barrera and Don Victor were also invited. Various pastors got up and talked, but when they called on Barrera, he had left, and so had Don Victor. So no congregation was assigned to them. Barrera was reported to have said, "If you give us no church, we'll go someplace else, even under a tree, but we must preach." Any further activity on their part, the convention decided, would not be considered to be on behalf of the Apostolic Church. However, Barrera continued with his visits to Utzpak, and at one time even Joaquin, who also had a key to the church, came along and borrowed from the milk can.

In April 1971, Barrera and Don Victor held a baptism in Tizimin. The two men baptized each other, then Don Victor ordained himself bishop and Barrera became pastor. Alvio, one of Barrera's faithfuls in Utzpak, together with a nephew of Don Victor, were declared initiates. They named their church the Invisible Apostolic Church and proceeded to recruit converts among the Apostolic congregations which had participated in the apocalyptic disturbance.

The Schism of Don Victor

By May 1972, however, Don Victor had second thoughts about the biblical foundation of what the Branham tapes preached. Sometime in the middle of the month he had a revelation. It was maintained in the congregation that the revelation concerned the fact that the Second Coming would take place six months from then. Mainly, however, he began expressing some ideas about theological issues that were at variance with the accepted doctrines of the Apostolic Church. A theologian was sent to Yucatan from the Biblical Institute in Tepic, Nayarit, to debate these issues with him, but they could come to no agreement, and he was expelled from the church. As he put it, "I did not desert the Apostolics: they separated themselves from me." He called his own church La Iglesia Original de Cristo and dissolved his relationship with Barrera and the Branhamists. Instead, he began developing his own following, using his extended family as a base. He and his wife possessed a large homestead in Chetumal, home to three sons and their wives, four daughters and their husbands, and sixteen grandchildren. According to Nina, one of his sons actually wanted to kill Juan L. to avenge his opposition to his father, and Don Victor had had a hard time dissuading him. They even prepared their food together "and never had a quarrel."

In fact, then, the congregation had split into three sections, that of the Apostolics proper, that of the Branhamists, and that of Don Victor. This split was reflected all across Yucatan; the members decided their allegiance mainly on the basis of kinship or personal preferences rather than on doctrinal lines. Barrera, for instance, introduced his Branhamist friend, a Mexican named Tagre, to the Temax congregation. Everyone wanted to hear him preach, "but they came only once, he made no converts, and the people despised him," reported Nina. At this time the temple and the property were in Luis L.'s name. The members of the congregation wanted to found an association and have it put in its name in order to secure their base, but the transfer would have cost 1,000 pesos. So they gave up on the idea for the time being.

July 1972: Return to Utzpak

I arrived in Utzpak on July 1, 1972, to a crop of new babies. According to Reina, Ysaura had a newborn daughter and Gregoria another son. She herself was heavier and had a gorgeous, roly-poly new baby girl, whom she called Concha. She had been born in her *sabana*, her sheet, that is, with her amniotic sac still intact. Dona Raquel grabbed it, tore it open, slapped the baby, and poured cold water into her mouth, which made her cry. "She is very good at things like that, Dona Raquel," Reina said gratefully.

Reina also had a new tiled floor of *retrasos*, odd pieces left over from sets used elsewhere, and she was very happy with it. Too bad her walls could not also be tiled. Their cracks continued to be home to a burgeoning population of the giant cockroaches, and as a welcome, one crawled out of my bag that I had hung against the wall on a rusty screwdriver and ran along my naked arm. Lupita recognized me right away (Reina said from my scream because of the cockroach); she had become quite a talker, while little Cilia did not speak at all yet. The family called her *palomita* [little pigeon] because of the cooing sounds she made.

On the corner there was animated talk about Reina and Santiago no longer attending the services at the temple and about Don Eduardo and his wife's decision to go to the services of the Pentecostals. And then there was the sensation that a man down the street had been bitten by a rattlesnake. It was Don Erme who had cured him. He closed all the windows and gave instructions that no pregnant woman should pass the house and no recently married one either. He cut the bite, sucked out the poison, then put on some herbs, and in a week, the man was cured. But they say that the treatment is only effective if it is done immediately.

At Eus's house my first questions, as usual, are about the congregation. Who is still coming? It is hard to say; some come, then they stay away. Mariano has sided with Barrera, and so did his wife, who said that she would never return to the temple, but they refuse to undergo another baptism. "I think they will stay home and pray to their God there," says Nohoch Felix. Of the women, Old Candil's wife Rodolfa comes sometimes, but usually late. Paula rarely comes anymore; Eus says that she is pregnant again and usually attends the services of the Pentecostals.

And the girls who had basically carried the apocalyptic uprising along? Interestingly, almost the entire group dropped out of the temple's activities. Paula's daughter Rosa married Pedro, who did not even bother to get a divorce from his former wife before marrying her, and she no longer attended the services. Mila went to relatives in Merida because her mother would not let her return home unless she brought a certificate that she was still a virgin. Eventually, her mother relented and accepted her back without such official certification, and she worked at one of the *tortillerias* in Utzpak. She no longer attended the services. Leidi, Rodolfa's daughter, ran away with "a white man," (i.e., from Tabasco), a younger brother of Manuel H. Eus, never loath to point out an interesting connection, reminds us that when Manuel left the congregation because of the accident of one of his brothers, he borrowed the temple's entire cash reserve and never paid it back. "So one brother robbed the money, the other the girl." Dolores, the niece of Juana, the wife of Isauro, was in love with one of the Villanueva boys, who wanted to marry her but only in a civil ceremony. So Juana and Isauro took her with them to Dziuche to prevent her from marrying him. There was talk that she would run away with him, but, according to Eus, "she did not want to lose her soul that way." Reyes, a daughter of Rodolfa, was living in the house of her father-in-law. Her husband, Maximo, got baptized with Don Victor and beat her severely because she would not be baptized also. But she continued to refuse and occasionally came to a service at the temple. Mela, the daughter of Agustin V., now attended Don Victor's services in her father's house. Rodolfa's daughter Angela, who now had a 1-year-old daughter, was the only one of the entire group who was still a regular member of the congregation.

No one speaks in tongues anymore, Eus says. How about the Second Coming? Does he preach about that? I ask Chan Felix, who has dropped by. "The *hermanos ya se fastidiaron* [they got tired of that subject]." Besides, there were many other topics in the Bible. And is there still a Escuela Dominical on Sundays? "The custom simply got lost," he said. Upon my question about how the juvenile section that had been so important the previous year was doing, he maintains that they had all gotten married.

July 1, 1972: Saturday Evening Service

As always, Eus picks me up for the service, and I am startled to see that the brightly painted metal sheet on the entrance door with its happy *"Dios es Amor"* is gone. Inside, the temple now has three new drawings by Valentin on the wall and a poster urging the young people to join the church. There is only one small table in front of the rostrum.

Isauro has been transferred to Dziuche, supposedly so he will not be tempted to join Barrera, and Chan Felix has taken his place. Barrera had attempted to recruit Chan Felix for his side, trying to prove to him that Branham was right, but Ysaura told Eus that she talked her husband out of joining the Branhamists.

The attendance is small, six men and six women; of the leading men there are only Chan Felix, Epi, and Old Candil. Of the young women prominent in the events of 1970, I see only Joaquina. She sits with Teresa, who played a minor role in the apocalyptic disturbance but seems to have become more important recently. Eus dislikes her intensely, saying that she is a malicious gossip. "I have peace in my heart," Eus quotes her as saying. "Too bad it never comes out," is Eus's pointed comment.

That the division in the congregation casts a long shadow becomes obvious when Old Candil says during testimony time, "Let us pray for those who are separated from us. Someday, we'll be of one thought." He has refused overtures from either Barrera or Don Victor and is quoted as saying, "How could I possibly leave my temple? This is where I came to know God's word, this is where I received the Holy Spirit. I will never leave my temple unless services are no longer held here."

Chan Felix and Ysaura offer a hymn together. Chan Felix still has a good voice, but it has lost its youthful, golden smoothness and has become somewhat raspy. He accompanies himself on his guitar, his face tired and drawn. Ysaura's hair is sticky; she is pale with brown blotches on her skin. She carries her newborn on her arm, but the long-limbed infant does not look well and Eus says she has an infected navel. Besides, Ysaura did not nurse her; her nipples did not protrude, so the baby could not get hold of them and Ysaura fed her with a bottle.

Tomorrow will be the Day of the Pastors, Chan Felix reminds the congregation, and if they do not want to bring a gift, that is all right, they can give him a gift of money at his home. That is how it is done in Villahermosa. But his request falls flat and his sermon is uninspired. There is a pervasive feeling of hurt and loss, and no one speaks in tongues.

The mood is no better at the Sunday evening service either, although it is sponsored by the Senores Cristianos, who are usually upbeat. Epi does not join their procession. He stays in his seat instead and spends most of his time outside talking business with Chucho, Teresa's husband, who trades in lumber. At least the attendance is better, ten women and five men. Chan Felix receives one small package as a gift and an envelope with some money from his parents. But there is no prayer for the sick. Instead, during the last communal prayer, Chan Felix lets his voice rise above the others, saying, "If anybody is sick, please, Lord, heal them."

During his sermon, Chan Felix announces that he will go to Tizimin to work and will be back the following Saturday. I have heard from Nohoch Felix that the men of the congregation are not happy about their pastor spending so much time elsewhere and have asked him to write a letter to Luis L. in Merida, asking him to send another pastor. But Nohoch Felix refused, arguing that the congregation could not support Chan Felix and his family, so he had to go and work. He was working as a door-to-door salesman in Tizimin.

Illness of Dona Filipa

There are visitors at Reina's when we get there after the service. Raquel and her son and daughter, and even Santiago, join in the conversation. It seems that Dona Filipa, Santiago's aunt, the older sister of Don Eduardo, had wanted to purge herself, but instead of the prescribed one envelope of the laxative, she had taken three and had nearly died. She was a Catholic, and so the family sent a message to the *cura* for help. But he gave his benediction "from here," that is, his home, and never bothered to come. Given the fact that those assembled were all Protestants, Presbyterians, or Apostolics, it would not have surprised the *cura* to hear their comments. To the hilarity of everyone, Santiago imitated his giving his benediction, drawn out and pompous. "*Cura,*" Raquel says, but he does not cure, and Eus adds that he preaches celibacy, but everyone knows that the priests have women, and that was adultery, and Reina opines that probably those priests no longer even believed in the sanctity of the pope.

As to Dona Filipa, she became incoherent, and Don Eduardo and Dona Andrea stayed with her for two nights, and her grandchildren also came and spoon-fed her some chicken broth. Reina went to help and so did Tomasita, the midwife, and by last night she seemed a bit better and even started speaking coherently again. But when her husband came to inquire how she was, she said, "Go away, Juan, I don't want to see you. Go away." Reina says that he had been very bad to her, getting drunk all the time. She took in washing and made *vaporcitos* for sale to feed her children. Then she had a relapse and once more could not talk. "If you lift her arm," Raquel says, "it falls back down again."

Two days later she seemed to have recovered, though. According to Dona Andrea, she is obviously getting stronger because she has begun cursing again.

The conversation drifts to the topic of healing, and Eus says that there is an *hermana* in Merida who gives flower baths for 25 pesos. She buys the flowers and put them into the bath water. It is supposed to make men fall in love with the woman. Several *hermanas* in Merida had taken the flower bath, even Olga, who took care of Ysaura during her confinement.

Making the Rounds

The following morning Eus and I go to visit some *hermanas*. As we cross the market, a woman's voice comes over the loudspeaker of the Catholic church, admonishing people to pray, and we overhear a man saying to his companion that they should not worship God, but the "god of rain." They mean San Isidro el Labrador, Eus remarks, the saint of cultivators. There is a statue of him in the church, so we go in and I take a picture of him. In New Mexico, he drove an oxcart and was dressed like a Hispanic peasant, but this appealing figure wears traditional Maya garb (a jacket and short pants), has a *sabucan* and a bottle gourd slung over his chest, carries a planting stick, wears a sombrero, and is accompanied by a slender, light-brown dog. If the rains do not arrive at the proper time at the end of May, according to Eus, the people put up a table for an altar on the plaza, decorated with flowers. They bring chickens and even a turkey sometimes and tie them under the table. They are later killed and eaten in San Isidro's honor. He is taken out of the church and placed on that altar, and in the evening prayers are recited and there is a lot of guitar and flute music. After the ritual, he is taken back into the church. This year, there was no such celebration because the rains came on time.

We go to Paula's house first but are told by a neighbor that she has gone to Merida with all her children to visit Rosa in the hospital. Rosa is five months' pregnant and has an infection of some kind. It was said that she needed a blood transfusion, but none of the *hermanos* volunteered to donate blood because Teresa had warned that if you gave blood, you died.

At Rodolfa's the big news is still that her daughter Leidi has been "robbed" and that they still have not received any letter from her.

Angela is at her mother's home with her small daughter. Her husband is in the hammock next to the child and looks startlingly like a Yanomamo right out of the rain forest. Eus says that he sometimes accompanies the family to the temple but never comes inside.

I have brought a bunch of pictures I had taken the year before and am given three eggs in return and offered some *macal,* which I am not familiar with. It looks like boiled potatoes and tastes a little like chestnuts, very delicious, and is eaten with some honey. I keep taking more, which is my undoing, for the next day, it gives me a frightful diarrhea, and I even have to leave the church and go out to vomit copiously. "Of *macal,* we eat very sparingly," said Eus unfeelingly, but she had not warned me. It is a pretty plant; the root, which is what is eaten, is about 2 inches in diameter. It creeps along the ground and it sprouts up shoots a foot apart that look like miniature palm trees.

Of course, there is also talk about the Second Coming. Does she still believe that it will come very soon? Rodolfa asks Eus. She laughs. "*Pues,* when he comes, I'll see him. Maybe I'll be in the temple, or maybe I'll be at home in my hammock, sleeping." Rodolfa is more definite. It will happen because it is written in the Bible. But not even the angels know when.

A Trip to Merida

Eus and I were going to go to Merida on July 5, but El Negro, with whom we had made reservations, forgot us. He has had a lot of trouble recently, Eus says. Pedrito, the dwarf, whom he always took to Merida for free so he could go begging there, used to sit crowded against the right front door of the old Dodge. Suddenly, the lock gave way on a curve and Pedrito was spilled out. He died the same day and El Negro had to pay for the funeral.

I had spent the night at Eus's place in anticipation of the trip, and I am grateful that we do not go that day because the diarrhea of the *macal* started early that morning. Eus says, "*Dios u tsʔaah,*" the Lord did it to save me the embarrassment of an attack in the car. After washing my soiled clothes, I settle back in the hammock, watching the early dawn's brightness of the stars and the brilliant crescent of the moon through the wide-open door, listening to the waking sounds—the roosters crowing and the chickens chirping, the creaking of Eus's rope around the wheel of the well as she drew water, and Nohoch Felix snoring in his hammock next to mine—and smelling Eus's hearth fire beyond the wattle.

A woman's voice calls from the *albarrada*. I see Eus stepping up to the opening in the wall, shaking her head and saying, "We worship only one God."

"What was that about?" Nohoch Felix asks from his hammock.

"She had her *dios* in her *sabucan* and was collecting money for making his fiesta."

"You should have said, 'I don't have anything right now.'"

Eus shakes her head. "No way, then she would only come back."

In the afternoon, Emerijildo comes to start blasting a hole in the backyard rock for an outhouse. I had suggested to Eus that perhaps her chickens would not die all the time if they did not eat human excrement, but she was ahead of me, as always. She had seen an outhouse in Chetumal and immediately thought that I might like to have one, so she had made arrangements with Hermano Emerijildo. He maintained that the fumes of the dynamite were affecting his head and therefore he wanted 20 pesos a day for the work. But Eus was a hard bargainer. Not even the rich people paid that much for a day. So he had to be satisfied with 15 pesos. I filmed the adventure, but when Emerijildo's dynamite revealed a layer of *sascab,* white earth, highly prized for many different purposes, the blasting stopped; neighbors came to buy it by the bucketful, and the outhouse was not completed until the following year.

Two days later El Negro does take us to Merida, and with poor Pedrito's accident in mind, I take a critical look at the dashboard of the car. The fuel gauge shows empty, the oil-pressure gauge is permanently on thirty, the temperature (with the windows open in the tropical heat) is stuck on cold, and the speedometer is out. But there is supernatural insurance for safe passage: a straw cross below the rearview mirror and above it a small picture of the Virgin de Guadalupe. The conversation among the men in the car is about their discontent with the present *presidente municipal,* the mayor. One man suggests that they should simply throw him out. But several others disagree. The state authorities will only bring in an outsider, and that would be worse. El Negro agrees. "There will be no pardon then; he will punish friend and foe alike. It is bad to have a stranger in that office."

The trip through the countryside is pretty with the verdant sisal fields, but as we approach the city, we pass a stinking, smoldering dump, and a row of small black vultures have settled on the advertisement next to it of a housing development called Vista Alegre.

We reach Agapito's. His new house has been completed, and they have a refrigerator, which, in addition to the potted plants Agapito raises, forms the basis of their economic well-being. All day long, people from the neighborhood come by to buy cooled soft drinks. Sylvia makes scrambled eggs and tortillas, which we dunk into a common plate of ground chile in water.

A Private Service

On July 7, there is a private service at Agustin V.'s house to celebrate his son's birthday. It is conducted by E. N. of Bacalar. Although he says not a word about the manifestation of the Holy Spirit, his sermon is quite reminiscent of those of "the good old days" when the Second Coming was still a happy promise and not a frightening imminent reality, and his preaching style is a combination of folksiness and rapture, like Barrera's in his heyday. He explains that he has come to visit his sick father-in-law and that Teresa has invited him to hold the service. He is happy to do it because that way he will be gaining treasures in heaven:

> You here in Utzpak cannot possibly see the greatness of the work of the Lord because it is in the process of developing. But I want to tell you things that you will find interesting. In Chetumal, everyone suffered great pain because some of the *hermanos* left, but by the power of prayer, the congregation became united again. In the congregation of Cuarenta y Dos, the same thing happened, but the *hermanos* prayed and fasted, and most of those lost returned. Others got lost when the storm came.
>
> That was what happened in Utzpak also, *verdad?* There used to be eighty members, then the storm came and split the congregation, and some members were lost completely. But as the Bible says, there will be sad days, times of peril, and that should make us happy because it means that Christ will come soon. But let me warn you: don't let anyone deceive you! Do not be tempted to drink or to smoke, to go to picture shows or dances, or to attend fiestas. If we do not keep faith, then who will? Perhaps those sinners of the street? We are in the last days, *hermanos;* all the world is covered with evil! The Evil One is trying to lead us astray, but he has no good gifts, he promises no eternal life, only diversions. But we have the forgiveness of sins. We will travel the path of righteousness!

Last year, Eus complained about these private services. Now she leans over to me, saying, "Isn't it wonderful?" And when the time comes to sing the birthday song and pin a bill on the boy's shirt, she is the first one.

The pleasant mood in the congregation does not last long, however. At the evening service on July 8, E. N. and Ernesto have a theological disputation about resurrection and whether we will have a visible body right away, even though it will have no blood and bones. Ernesto maintains that that will come later, for Paul spoke of a mortal body being resurrected, and things became so contentious that the two men refuse to sit next to each other. The conflict has of course been noted, so that as the service is being passed from one man to the next, and with Chan Felix still away, no one bothers to introduce E. N. as a guest, as is the custom. Finally, it is Nohoch Felix's turn and he introduces both E. N. and his wife. The old man always has a fine feeling for what is proper in a given situation. Unfortunately, E. N. has an oversize ego. For instance, he has two of his sons with him and Old Candil remarks that the boys look like him, and he says, "Yes, all my seven children *llevan mi cara* [carry my face]." He apparently feels that he has not been treated with proper respect and so does not return to the temple, although he stays in Utzpak for several more days.

By the way, I thought it quite remarkable that these men, without even a trained *obrero* around, are able to put together such a disciplined service, even if their sermons are simply reformulations of the biblical text, which regularly puts Eus to sleep. It is the best sleep she has all day, she used to say.

Family Matters

During this same week, Nina came back to Utzpak because Desi could find no work in Chetumal. Desi is a gentle young man with an Olmec face; it is difficult to reconcile that image with the violence in his family. It is told that there was a man who kept pursuing Desi's mother, one of those tiny women one sees so often in Yucatan, much to the annoyance of Desi's father. When Desi was about 14, the quarrel between the two men came to a head. The suitor was working on a ranch and was fixing his food when Desi's father caught up with him. He hit the suitor on the neck with his machete and killed him. He then fled to Utzpak with his family, where he had many relatives. The brother of the murdered man complained to the municipal authorities, but Desi's father had already fled, so they locked up his wife and children in his place. Thereupon, he gave himself up and was sentenced to four years in prison. While there, he learned to weave hammocks. The family sold me one; it had a beautiful ornate edge.

Early this year, Desi's father and another man were looking for some land for making a *col* near Chetumal and they got lost. They were without food or water for three days. Finally, they shot a small rodent, and Desi's father drank its blood. The other man refused and almost died. They finally reached a ranch, and there were given very little food and water so that they would not die from eating quickly after their ordeal. Eus thinks that this misfortune was God's punishment because Desi's father had killed a man.

While Chan Felix is away, Eus sleeps at Ysaura's place so she will not be alone. I go over to keep her company for a while, which gives me a chance to catch up on what is going on in Merida. Ysaura, having recently come from there, is of course conversant with all the gossip. Luis L. had a girlfriend in

Tepic and kept taking her lots of presents all the time, but then in Merida, he met Blanca. Blanca was pregnant at the time, it was one of those accidents. The boy came with his parents and wanted to marry her but she refused, and after the child was born, Luis L. married her and adopted the little girl. She got married in a white wedding dress and a crown and veil with her infant by another man on her arm. The *hermanos* were scandalized, and now Luis L.'s church was almost empty and he was preaching in Chetumal. Ysaura and Eus agree: the men had no business staying away from the services just for that, for after all they themselves did not take the rules of the Church all too seriously. As an example, Eus cites the fact that the men often still insist on having a second wife like in the old days and try to get away with it even in the congregation, although that is a mortal sin. Her sister's stepdaughter got married; the young husband's mother and siblings came to the wedding. Afterward, he took her to Veracruz, and established her in a rented house. It did not take her long to discover that he had a second wife in another part of town. So she went to Merida and complained to his father. "Does he maintain you?" he asked. She admitted that he gave her 25 pesos a day. "Then what are you complaining about?"

Teresa comes by and joined in the conversation, which quickly turns to "those things that happened at the temple." "Nothing bad like that ever happens to the Presbyterians or the Pentecostals," says Teresa. Ysaura knows why: "That those things happened shows that ours is the true church of God. It says in the Bible that there must be suffering and visitations. When that is fulfilled, then God will come."

Teresa has recently visited the temple in Temax and is full of admiration for how well equipped their temple was. "Everything they want, they get," she says. They have tiles on the wall three-fourths of the way to the ceiling; their altar is also tiled. They have an electric guitar and even a public address system. Ysaura can see where that is admirable, but on the other hand, she is convinced that the fact that things are going so badly around here is a sign that this is the right church.

Her baby begins to cry and will not be pacified with a bottle, which prompts Ysaura's question, "When do you think children begin to feel sin?" Teresa has the answer: "You can see that from the way they behave when the congregation sings and prays. If they cry then, or if they cry when in the church the people sing *cumple anos* [the birthday song] for them, that means that they feel sin. Rodolfa's children never cry on such occasions, so they have a hard heart."

Ysaura puts the crying infant unceremoniously back into the hammock. "I want my daughter to be a queen in heaven. I would rather have God take her now than let her turn away from the religion later." Teresa sighs. "You are right. It is such a pleasure to be in the religion. I wonder if after a while one gets bored with the Lord's path. It has not happened to me; I found it three years ago, but I always feel the same way about it. I simply cannot understand some women. They are supposed to leave their husband if he refuses to be converted. They do it for a while, but then they return to their husband." Ysaura has the right example handy. "Like Elide did. She no longer comes to the services either."

Stories of Witchcraft

JULY 13, 1972

The service opens late and with only a skeleton attendance. In her testimony, Ysaura asks for prayers for her health. She is sobbing, saying that a pastor's wife has to suffer a great deal. "*Cheechona* [whiner]," Eus says contemptuously. "None of my children were like that." But she also criticizes her son. He is in Tizimin most of the time, so why isn't he taking her with him?

The circus comes to town the next day. Eus and I go to the corner with other neighbors to see it arrive, driving down the highway in the oppressive heat, looking dusty and bedraggled. Kimba Internacional, it is called. It has two dwarfs, one gorilla, and four lions. They set up their tent on the plaza, and Rodolfa and her entire family go to see their performance. Eus disapproves, saying that going to the circus is just as sinful as going to a picture show.

The service is canceled that evening, for hardly anybody shows up. The music of the circus may have been too enticing. Eus and I sweep the temple and she brings some flowers "so it would not look so sad," she says, but to no avail. Epi and a few of his friends stand around in front of the temple for awhile. "They are having their service in the street," laughs Eus. Nohoch Felix sits in the temple by himself reading his Bible and is less charitable. "Satan has settled in their hearts," he says in disgust.

So Eus and I go to see her friend Dona Ugulina. She had gone to the session of some *espiritistas* in Merida and speaks animatedly about how one of the men appeared as if dead, then a physician spoke from his mouth, but you had to write down everything because he did not know himself what he said.

Did Dona Ugulina think that man was a *brujo* [a witch]? No? *Pues,* sometimes people make mistakes. Nohoch Felix once shot a female peccary and brought home her two piglets. One of them kept wandering around in the neighborhood, and since everyone knew that there were people who changed themselves into animals, the neighbor woman thought the piglet was one of those *brujos* and hit it in the eye, blinding it.

Warming to the subject, Eus then tells that when she was still in Tibolom, she went to a *waa?y*, a witch's, house and asked her to teach her witchcraft. She wanted to find out what the woman knew. But she told her that she knew nothing of witchcraft. Maybe she was only pretending ignorance, though. She had a lover who later fell in love with a young girl. He became ill and suspected witchcraft because when he came home one evening, he saw a candle burning in his sombrero.

One day the woman who was thought to be a witch disappeared. Her husband found her *nixtamal* in her kitchen, unused. He did not go to look for her because he said that she probably got tired of working and left on her own accord. However, it was said that her lover and some other men, five in all, abducted her, took her to the *monte,* killed her, and threw her body into a cenote.

And then, of course, did I see the house across the street from Dona Ugulina? It used to have a tavern in it, but this year it is all locked up because it is haunted. At night, you can hear strange sounds in it, so no renter would take it. It used to belong to a woman who was a witch. She died years ago. She often changed into an animal, a goat, and one night she was shot in another village. But witches must come home to die. So she came home, and she died, right there in her house.

A Women's Quarrel

Chan Felix did not return from Tizimin; he stayed away another week. Ysaura says that she told him to do that, and Eus wondered aloud *quien manda* [who was in charge]. She is not particularly enthusiastic about her daughter-in-law. Ysaura does not like to cook, she says, so she buys chicken soup at the market, which is thin and not filling. Chan Felix should buy beans and make her prepare her own meals, Eus thinks. And she also notices that Ysaura likes to get up late and does not do her washing early in the morning every day. No wonder the baby's clothes always look soiled. One time when we come in the middle of the day, Ysaura is washing and splashing water against the mud wall, a definite no-no. "You are washing now? Why?" Eus asks. Ysaura does not even get the point.

Eus continues sleeping at Ysaura's house dutifully, though. But a few days later, when she and I have done some shopping and stop in to say *Paz de Cristo,* Ysaura does not let a hammock down for us to sit, and the visit turns into a very uncomfortable occasion. Eus is getting tired and, in the tremendous heat, the perspiration runs down my back and legs in heavy drops. Eus becomes very angry at Ysaura and at noon she goes back without me and asks her why she behaved so badly. "You told someone that I was lazy," was her argument. Eus wants to know who said it, but Ysaura will not come clean and threatens that all will come out when Chan Felix comes back. Apparently a shouting match ensued with heavy cursing on both sides, according to Eus, and so that evening,

Eus fetches her hammock and no longer sleeps in Ysaura's house. "What do I care?" she shrugs, but her eyes are wet when she adds, "Who knows how Chan Felix will feel toward me after all this?"

The fact that Eus is not sleeping at Ysaura's house does not, of course, go unnoticed. Dona Raquel comes to Reina's house with the intelligence, and when Reina does not know why and I do not provide any information either, she decides to go over to see "if anything ate her up." "Maybe the *cuatro narices*," Reina jokes.

But soon the jokes end. When I am with Eus, Reina comes with her children, crying. Santiago had beaten her with his belt, quite badly; she had big black and blue bruises on her legs and back. He happened to go by Ysaura's house and Ysaura complained that Reina had been going around the neighborhood saying that she was lazy. And here she had even given her some beans, Reina sobbed, and then that woman said, "Don't you also have some tortillas?" And she behaved that way also toward Dona Andrea. So Reina went over to Ysaura and threw the rubber duck at her head and the baby clothes that she and Chan Felix had given her when little Concha was born. "That *wacha* with her blood of *atole* [squared to fight] cannot measure up to me," she said, "I am evil when I am aroused! I told her that tapeworm of a daughter of hers can play with the stuff; I don't want it. And I said that I would complain to Chan Felix about her when he came back, but it probably wouldn't do any good, because I was sure that in her house, Chan Felix did not mount her, she mounted him." "*Lo viste?* [Did you see it?]," she said. "I don't have to see it, I know her kind."

All day long Reina went around wiping her eyes, Dona Raquel says in the evening, and by that time, even Reina laughs with us. And Santiago, apparently, was not so sure of himself either as the day wore on. When he finds me alone in the house the next morning, he asks,

"Did the senora come yesterday?"

"Yes, she did come to the temple."

"No, I mean to Dona Eus's house."

"Yes, she did."

"What did she say?"

"That you behaved very badly, and she cried."

"I had warned her. I don't do justice for nothing. There must be no malicious gossip around here. That is how we do things here." I am not going to let him get away with that. After all, he started the conversation. So I say,

"We don't even know whether Ysaura spoke the truth. She also said that Dona Eus went about gossiping about her, and I know for a fact that it isn't true, because I was with her every hour of the day." Santiago concedes defeat.

"Look," he says, pointing to his new floor, "that tile is wiggling. I'll have the man put in some more cement."

In the meantime Ysaura apparently has become worried about what her husband might say about her conflict with his mother, and when she does not see Eus in church, she asks Nina if she came. Eus has started making it a habit of arriving late so that she will not run into her daughter-in-law.

In the end, Ysaura does not dare to complain to her husband about his mother, and, perhaps at Eus's prompting, he takes her with him to Tizimin the next time he goes. She is happier there; Tizimin is a small town, not a village—more like Las Choapas where she came from. And the women of the congregation often bring her prepared food, chile, beans, tortillas, so she does not have to cook. And in August, Nohoch Felix wrote that Ysaura had made peace with them and came to visit. She promised not to pay attention to gossip anymore.

August 1972–Summer 1973: The Congregation

After I left Utzpak toward the end of July 1972, it was mainly Nohoch Felix who kept me informed about what was going on with the congregation. When I return the following June, I am able to flesh out the account, principally with Nina's help, who had come to visit from Chetumal with her husband Desi and her infant son Freddy. This was actually her second son; the first one died at a few months old of boils that covered his entire body. "She wants you to be the *hetsmec madrina* for her son," Eus warns me when she picks me up at the airport in Merida. "His grandmother wants a *madrina* who is *poloc* [fat] so his legs will grow straight, and you qualify," she teases, not without reason. So we carry out the little ceremony at Eus's house soon after my arrival; we have him grab money, a pen, some paper, and a book at his mother's insistence, and later I buy him a new outfit at La Elegancia.

There is the usual gossip, of course. Rosa had a boy, Paula's paralyzed Pedrito never did learn how to walk, and her husband went back to drink. And then there was Joaquin. He married a widow of some means in Chetumal, with two children, who can maintain him. "He was sick when he got married, so now he must be dying!" Nina quips, who has provided the item. "Probably married life is too hard on him," Eus laughs, obviously happy to apply a stab to her erstwhile irritating renter.

The number of those who have divorced themselves entirely from the Apostolic Church continues to grow. They either join the Pentecostals or go "to the plaza," that is, became completely disinterested in a religious affiliation. Reina does not come at all anymore. Because Santiago's business activities never yield enough for his family to subsist on, she now weaves hammocks for an added income. The government sent a woman to the villages to aid with economic development. She brought *canamo* and paid the women for the finished hammocks. She always weighed the finished hammock to make sure that the women kept no *canamo* for themselves, which was humiliating. Besides, she paid a very low wage, so now the women provide their own thread and weave only the body of the hammock for the government program. Eus does not think that Reina is going to stick with this work. It is poorly paid, and standing in front of the loom and weaving all day makes her back and shoulders hurt. "Weaving a hammock is fun," Eus says, "but not if you have to do it all the time."

As to the congregations, the three-way split has apparently continued in the interim. Barrera has established his headquarters in Chetumal. Lucrecia has had another child, this time a girl. His congregation consists of the Branhamist evangelist from Mexico and his family, a family from Tizimin, and Alvio, his wife Gregoria, and their children. Together they have salvaged a semblance of the communal life established during the apocalyptic disturbance. They live on the same lot in adjoining rented houses and have put up a sign which Nina copied, saying, "Entrance forbidden because Christians live here. No man dressed as a woman and no woman dressed as a man may enter." The women wear dresses well below the knee but no mantilla, for according to Branham, a mantilla is worn "only by whores." The women are instructed to wear a pearl necklace with a cross. "That is a sin," Eus exclaims. "Besides, how can they pay for that?" They also need a wedding ring. Nina has to explain that one to Eus, for such rings are not customary in the Maya villages or even in the urban lower class. As a rationale, they are told that "otherwise a man might fall in love with a woman he meets in church, not knowing that she was married." "How come they don't know who is married to whom?" Eus wonders. Then in her characteristic ironic way, she adds, "Maybe by following this Branham, a man acquires some sort of magic, so that when he shakes hands with a woman, she falls in love with him. That's why she needs the ring. It is for protection."

Eus and Nohoch Felix are also skeptical about other claims of the Branham sect. Branham was said to have performed many healings and miracles. Praying in his name was said to change the weather. For instance, a storm came up in Chetumal. The congregation prayed in his name and no rain came.

According to Nina, the Branhamist congregation in Chetumal held services every evening, using the hymnal of the Apostolic Church. During prayer, there was continual reference to "*nuestro precioso* Hermano William, *nuestro preciosisimo* Hermano William." No one spoke in tongues, and preaching was based not on the Bible but on Branhamist tracts. Branham was considered the Lord's Prophet, the last of a line of prophets including Jesus. His most-often-quoted prophecies concerned the end of the world, which would come after a series of seven catastrophes, the last one being World War III.

Early in 1973, Barrera abandoned the commune in Chetumal and moved his family to Campeche but remained unsuccessful in his missionizing there, although he continued to be popular in the surrounding villages.

Eus adds what information she has about the activities of Don Victor, who has remained a friend of her family despite doctrinal differences. He concentrates his missionizing efforts on the villages. His followers considered themselves Apostolics but insist that those joining them be rebaptized, which cost them converts among the Apostolics. His attraction seems to have been his insistence on the imminent end of the world, a point abandoned by the Apostolics, although he emphasized that God's time was not man's time and refused to stipulate an exact date for the time being, at least, for this hoped-for event. "The last time he predicted the end of the world was for January 4, 1973," Eus recalls, not without some sarcasm. "I wonder what he is telling his followers now?" He travels from village to village, picking up converts not only among the disaffected Apostolics but also among disgruntled Catholics. He usually preaches in some home, writing out lengthy Bible quotations in longhand on pieces of white cardboard which are then placed on the walls as decorations. His congregations do not speak in tongues. He used to, but he abandoned the practice. "Since I don't understand what I am saying," Eus quotes him, "I am afraid that I might utter a blasphemy."

In Chetumal, the communal enterprise connected with the temple has also been dissolved. Only Luis L., who is still pastor there, and his wife Blanca live at the temple, and Juan L. continues as a businessman but does not employ any *hermanos*. But their cohesion is still sufficiently strong that neither the Branhamists nor Don Victor have garnered a single convert there.

Generally, it seems, those Apostolic village congregations that have not been affected by the apocalyptic disturbance remain the most stable, while those disoriented by the failed prophecy keep searching for preachers who will reassure them that the end of the world has been only temporarily postponed.

A New Minister in Utzpak

The condition of the temple in Utzpak demonstrates the same disinterest that Eus and her family complained about the previous year. There are no pictures or posters on the walls, only a calendar with an indifferent landscape. The blackboard has nothing written on it. There are no flowers on the podium, and one evening it is Eus who throws out the putrid water from the vases. The services in which I participate in June are very poorly attended. Only those held in private homes, usually occasioned by the birthday of a child, are somewhat more popular. The new minister is an Hermano Alf, sent by Luis L., who does not speak in tongues. He says that he did years ago, but now he can no longer do it. He has problems remembering the sequence of the various rituals of the service, and the fact that he can remember no names is often remarked about. His wife speaks no Spanish and, perhaps to accommodate her, he sometimes preaches in Maya. She may be a bit slow; she told Eus how after marrying Alf, she was beginning to feel sick, she could not understand what was the matter, she was always tired and wanted to eat all the time. Finally, a neighbor woman told her that she was probably pregnant. And the neighbor was right, Eus laughs. One time Nohoch Felix invited Alf to come and eat at his house, expecting him to come alone. But he brought his entire family, and one of his young daughters even carried a small bucket, saying, "And how am I to fill this bucket?"

Alf's one enthusiasm concerned the plan of replacing the present temple with one made of cinder blocks. It would be cleaner and tarantulas could not enter, which was more likely to please the Lord. Besides, the roof on the present one had rotted out again. He never fails to ask for an offering for more and more blocks. His preaching consists mostly of a shouted exegesis, simply reformulating the biblical text, which is usually quite disjointed.

It is obvious that the congregation is bored. Adding to the problem is the fact that he is often late, which is interpreted as indifference. When one evening Eus and I arrive for the service, we think we are tardy, but he is still taking his bath and his wife is busy making tortillas. Often he does not come at all and leaves the service to the *hermanos,* to Ernesto, Old Candil, and Nohoch Felix. The general membership has dropped; that of the Dorcas is down to two. Sometimes Eus joins them out of loyalty, just to fill out the ranks. And no one goes out to "talk to the souls," trying to recruit new members.

During the services, no one claps in rhythm to the *coritos,* no rattles are used, and no one speaks in tongues. The latter fact tends to puzzle visitors who come from other congregations to preach in Utzpak, knowing nothing about the apocalyptic disturbance, or at most, having heard oblique references to the time "when some *hermanos* thought they had some special wisdom." Their exhortations to the congregation that they should let the Holy Spirit use them, that "even the young daughter of Hermano X was able to speak in tongues," so why not them, falls on deaf ears. The confusion of the outsiders is compounded by the fact that on occasion some of the *hermanos* of the Utzpak congregation do speak in tongues—when they are not in the home temple. Nohoch Felix tells of a very emotional occasion in Tibolom, where eight women decided to be baptized. Unexpectedly, he spoke in tongues and, indicative of his high arousal, he had a vision involving Eus, who was not present. He saw hail falling on her, "larger than hen's eggs."

One evening, Hermana Pola, Old Candil's mother, invited the congregation to a service at her house, and Alf promised to come. While we waited, I handed out the pictures I had taken the year before and some hair baubles for the little girls. There was conversation about the Branham mission and that one had better stick strictly to the Bible, not to some tracts, or all would be lost. Very late, even Epi dropped in, but Alf did not come, so we all left. It was said the following day that he had been too tired, and Eus did not hide her disgust.

Another time we waited in the temple until past 9 o'clock and then went to the plaza when he did not come. Nohoch Felix was sitting on a bench under a live oak tree, and as we passed, he playfully grabbed Eus's arm, saying, "*Ola*—don't you want to have your *liquado?*" I suddenly could see behind the 70-year-old the young man with whom Eus fell in love, a charming rogue, full of fun, music, and lovemaking. So we had a *liquado*, a fruit drink, and Nohoch Felix talked with the men, while El Negro joked with Eus and myself—he loved to get me to speak Maya—and there was music from a tavern nearby. We were still sitting there when who should come by but Alf with his wife and daughters, his guitar on his shoulder. He had done a private service, he explained. It was past ten by then, and we did not go with him when he said that he would now do a service in the temple.

A Baptism in Merida

On June 10, 1973, it is announced that the Merida congregation will hold a baptism in the port city of Progreso, and although no one is going to be baptized from Utzpak, Eus and I decide to go, together with Nina and Desi and her infant son. I get up at four in the morning in Reina's house; I am pretty drowsy because there was a dance in the municipal palace and all night long there had been loud music interspersed with fireworks. When I leave Reina's house, the band is playing "Las mañanitas" for someone's birthday. The highway to Eus's place is dotted by the casualties of the celebration, drunks weaving along, hugging each other and talking boisterously. I wonder whether I should be afraid, but then figure that drunks are not very steady on their feet and I can hit harder and run faster. Luckily, I do not have to test my valence. They are involved in their own world and I pass as if invisible. Eus tells that once a drunk accosted her, but she hit him with her flashlight and he let go of her.

By the time I get to Eus, she has everything prepared: a bottle of boiled drinking water, *frances* with fried eggs, talcum for the comfort of all, and a bottle of milk for Nina's little Freddy. Nina does not have much milk and can nurse him only in the morning. We have chocolate and *embotonados* [soft-boiled eggs] for breakfast. It is the last nice thing that happens that day. Instead of the good fellowship of the congregation, all in one truck as it had been at the Utzpak baptism in 1969, we—that is, Alf and his family and Teresa with her children—catch the public bus at the corner of the cemetery, which is full of strangers. Matters became more congenial when in Merida we change into the bus for Progreso and meet up with members of the Merida congregation, but Eus is disappointed that there is only one baptismal candidate from Tibolom. The ritual on the public beach is disturbed by curious bystanders. The weather is overcast, so filming is difficult; the waves are high; and the saltwater ruins my camera for good. And I get such a sunburn that the next day Eus says my back looks like somebody has scalded me with boiling water. After the baptism, the Meridians embrace each other Mexican style, which makes the Utzpak villagers feel odd, and then the Merida congregation brings fried fish on the market and crowds into a restaurant for soft drinks, and nobody invites us to sit with them or even share a tortilla. To top it off, Freddy's milk spoils; he is hungry and cries nonstop. We miss the Utzpak bus out of Merida, there is a torrential downpour, we have to rent a cab that has no windows, and we arrive back home in the middle of the night thoroughly drenched. I spend the night at Eus's, totaling up all my physical and psychological pains.

Of course, the excursion has not been without gain. All through those weeks I had been puzzling over the question of what keeps this small congregation together, despite the disappointment about the end of the world, their dread of the trance experience, indifferent ministers, and bungling lay preachers. Suddenly, I became conscious of what I had intuited all along, ever since I had begun as early as 1969 to trace everyone's family connections and had found that the members represented, in the main, only three extended families. This was not in the urban sense a congregation, it was a kind of extended family, an overreaching superfamily. So they gossiped, they shared information, they were cruel to each other, they ostracized some and forgave others, and the core held together not necessarily because of a shared belief system but because of shared life.

Back in Utzpak

Eus brings a bunch of *limonero* branches for the altar for the service on the 17th, and their fragrance fills the entire temple. The mood is festive for a change, with an initial attendance of six men and six women that keeps increasing, for Isauro and his wife have come for a visit. Old Candil's voice vibrates with emotion when he greets them during testimony time: the family is coming together again. And even Alf seems happy, for Isauro noticed that he has collected almost 100 cement blocks in the church yard, which shows that he has real enthusiasm for the Lord's work. As for Isauro, he has just spent the happiest year of his life, he says, being the minister of a congregation.

When I get home to Reina that evening, Santiago arrives very drunk. He goes to Lupita's hammock and demands a kiss. She gives it, stiff with fear. "No drinking, no smoking . . . " Too bad he lost interest in the Apostolics.

Reina is considering giving up on the weaving of hammocks, as Eus had predicted, and has made inquiries about raising hogs for the state. The government, she says, is distributing sows, also the feed. Of the piglets, half go to the caretaker, but upon raising them, he can sell them only to the government. Violators go to the *peni*. The caretaker has to build a sty with a cement floor at his own expense. "They are to live better than we do," she complains. The pigs are *americanos*, very delicate. Their food has to be served in a trough, and they have to be bathed several times a day, and every day you are also supposed to wash down their sty. The caretaker can do no other work all day. The project is perhaps manageable if you have a water pump, but with only a well, it is impossible. So she is going to stick to her small local pigs. They need no sty; they eat from the ground and find some of their own food in the street. And she can dispose of them as she pleases.

Our gossip corner is disrupted because the authorities have the street torn up in preparation for putting down pipes for drinking water. But no pipes appear. "When they come into office," Reina says, "they do something, then they stop. Maybe we'll get potable water when the next municipal president takes office."

The entire family—Eus, Nina and Desi, and little Freddy—accompany me to Merida on June 21, 1973, to see me off at the airport. This day, however, is going to be dedicated to shopping. We leave our bags at the hotel of Luis L.'s father-in-law and we go to the market. I send Eus to buy me some ?*ipiles*, a strategy designed to keep the price down, and I go to find a chocolate beater and some amaranth candy. For Eus, going to the market is visiting family, and in short succession we meet all three of her sons that work there. Nina insists that we also go to the Centenario, a zoo, so Freddy can see the animals, and Armin comes along. When I maintain that the coyote is the cousin of the dog, they counter that the flamingo is Armin's uncle, for he is tall and thin, and the hippopotamus is Joaquina's grandmother because she is small and fat. For a while, we sit to rest on the plaza, and Eus and Armin step up to the pole of the electric streetlight, where they note a swarm of insects flying around that I take for flies. But they have immediately registered the characteristic white spot on their backs: these are the kind of bees that Don Anastasio had spoken of. They open a small flap on the lamppost, and there is the rest of the swarm, with their hive securely hidden at the bottom inside the lamppost.

First Encounter with Don Victor

We go back to the hotel and I am packing our purchases when Desi knocks and says that Don Victor is talking with Nina and if I want to speak with him, I should hurry and come. I am speechless. Fragmented reports about this evangelist and his doings had been floating around ever since I had come to Yucatan in 1969, but one way or another, I had always missed him. It seems that while I was packing, Nina was sitting with Desi and Freddy in the entrance hall of the hotel. All of a sudden, at quite a distance, she saw a man passing in front of the bus terminal whom she took to be Don Victor. She rushed over and invited him to come and see us.

So there he was. I look him over curiously: an elderly man in simple worker's clothes, a battered sombrero, a classical Maya profile familiar from a hundred ancient stone carvings. He was carrying a Bible in his *sabucan* and, as I note later, also a good-sized dictionary of the Spanish language. "*Paz de Cristo,* Hermano," Eus greets him. "*Amen,* Hermana," he nods, as he settles down.

I am impatient. I tell him that I had wanted to see him for a long time, that Hermano Jose of Chetumal had told me about him. And what a happy accident that we should meet now, the day before I am going to fly home to the United States. He is polite and noncommittal. My name? Was I vacationing in Yucatan? Did I like the people of Yucatan? And the question heard a thousand times: How do you see Yucatan? Yes, there is nothing like Yucatan anywhere. This was pride in the homeland. Of course, one should never forget one's true home, religion. And automatically, as a natural part of the conversation, there came a mini-sermon, complete with chapter and verse, in flawless, erudite Spanish and an amazingly rich vocabulary.

I use a pause for breath: I am interested in the history of the Apostolic Church in Yucatan and I understood that Barrera, whom I know quite well, has also separated from the Apostolic Church. Would he care to talk about that? And would he allow me to tape our conversation? No, he does not mind. In fact, the question puts him at ease. Now he is on familiar territory. There are certain important questions, mainly about the relationship between organization and belief, which have never been answered. Eventually, all became clear to him in a vision. The vision! All sorts of rumors have been circulating about Don Victor's vision, but no one seems clear about the details. What kind of vision? Voices? Pictures? An understanding? He nods. Actually, it was all of that.

> I was in Chetumal and went to the Apostolic church and came to sit next to Hermano Rufino. We did not know each other, but we started talking, and I said that I would like to cooperate with him in

the work of the Lord. He said that we could do that. And right off, he said, "We do not believe in the Trinity." So I say, Hermano, I am going to put this question to you. What does St. Paul mean when he says in his letter . . . and so it went. And I began to study. I had been a Unitarian, and I spent three months in Chetumal and my mind really hurt, and when I returned to Merida, I was in a great deal of doubt. After praying day and night for three weeks and being in severe mental torment, I could not sleep, and thinking about all these matters, at about one or two in the morning, I saw all of a sudden an enormous abyss opening up under my feet. I trembled for fear, but the Divinity came and began pulling me up. "What are you doing in that abyss?" he asked. Then he spoke to me of many things, and I began to understand how every part of the Scripture was there to give support to the mind so that it might understand what was the nature of creation and the creator. Since then for me the Bible has become as if transparent. No matter what I read in it, it always has this marvelous clarity about it.

The problem with the *hermanos,* he thought, was that they did not study the Bible earnestly enough. That is why they often ask questions without actually thinking about them, like what is the creation? And about Adam and Eve. And about whether the dead can call to God. And about the soul. "Here comes Hermano Alvio, and he has his tape-recorder, and he says, 'Hermano,' he says, 'tell me about the soul. What is the soul?'" For the next two hours, we are regaled with examples of such questions, in a series of capsule sermons that demonstrate his impressive biblical knowledge. On the other hand, he is not much interested in practical questions. Does he have any groups? Yes, in Cuarenta y Dos, in Chibul, in Peto, a few others, also on some of the ranches. And do his converts come only from the Apostolics, or are there also Catholics interested? *Pues,* there are many different kinds.

Finally he needs to catch his bus. He leads us in a lengthy prayer, during which we kneel next to our chairs, and I express the hope that I will see him again next year in Utzpak.

June 1974

Shortly before leaving for Yucatan that summer, I receive a rather cryptic letter from Chan Felix.

> The purpose of this paper is to report that the brothers Luis L. and Juan L. attended a ministerial meeting in Villahermosa, Tabasco, and there they met the ministers and the bishops.

They called this meeting because they no longer wanted to continue serving the Iglesia Apostolica de Fe en Cristo Jesus. They were revolting, and in order to stop the dispute, they had to leave the meeting. There were six of them who declared their separation: Luis L. and Juan L., Isauro B., Nicolas L., Manuel Ch., Valentin X., Florensio Ch. of the Cuarenta y Dos, and Gongora Ch. and Alfonso Ch. of Tizimin.

Bueno.

Then the Hermano Luis L. arrived here in Utzpak in order to tell the *hermanos* that they no longer belonged to the Iglesia Apostolica de la Fe en Cristo Jesus. He encountered the two ministers at present in Utzpak, Hermano Rufino and Hermano Felix, who knew what his plans were. And Hermano Luis L. had to leave, for Hermano Rufino would not allow him to address the congregation. . . .

At present the false prophets are continuing to doubt. They are going to all the pueblos deceiving all the souls that are in their churches, maintaining that they had their reunion and that in reality they had not separated from the Church, and they go about with their record-player and their music spreading doubt in all the villages. Because they go about promising that they will pay a salary to each minister, that they will earn 200 pesos. And when they hear that they will earn some money, they all follow the L. brothers.

The Situation in Merida

I arrive in Merida on June 11, 1974, very curious about what exactly is going on. As always, Eus waits for me at the airport. The pilot had insisted that the temperature in Merida was 75 degrees, but by the time we get into town, I am sure it is double that, and I am once again hit by the vague nausea that always plagues me when the tropical temperature and humidity first hit me. Returning to Yucatan is like giving birth again: you don't remember the misery until it is once more upon you. We take the bus to town, and Eus confirms what I have already learned from the letter of Chan Felix: all the Yucatecan ministers except Chan Felix have ceded from the Apostolic Church. It is all Satan's doing, Eus thinks. At the time "when those things were happening," Luis L. intended to marry a girl way below his station. But the Holy Spirit suggested that he should rather marry someone his equal. So he chose Blanca. But Satan disagreed and said, "In two years, I'll come for you." The two years were up now, and Satan's work was evident: Luis L. had left the Church.

In Merida, we take a room in the hotel of Luis L.'s father-in-law. I am appalled at the price; everything seems to have doubled since last year. We shower and then go downstairs for a soft drink and there happen on Luis L., polite and effervescent as always. What about this splitting from the Church I am hearing about, I ask? He pulls out a paper on which he and his fellow ministers have detailed all their grievances which the administration of the Church in Mexico City would not address. Foremost among them was the fact that the ministers that rose from the congregations in Yucatan were sent out into the Republic and strangers were sent here who were unfamiliar with Yucatecan customs and especially with the Maya language. There were many villages where no Spanish was spoken at all. Second, they did not want the Church authorities to decide over the internal matters of the congregations. That should be exclusively a matter of the participating ministers. But when I ask him if I can copy the paper, he refuses, saying that he would have to consult with "others involved." They did not create an administrative center, and they have not elected a bishop. "There are only a few of us, just a group of *hermanos*." They kept the name of Iglesia Apostolica de la Fe en Cristo Jesus, for their quarrel was not with the doctrine, only with the organization. He would continue with the congregation in Chetumal, and his brother, Juan L., would take over the one in Merida.

Reaction from Mexico City

Actually, the fact that Luis L. refused to let me have their secession statement was less of a loss than it appeared at the time. Some time later, I received from Eus's son-in-law Ruben, who was minister in Tibolom at the time, the copy of a ten-page Message to the Churches of the Southeastern District by Manuel J. Gaxiola, Presiding Bishop, dated June 15, 1974.

> Dear Hermanos, May the peace of Christ reside in the hearts of each one of you, Amen.
>
> A few days ago there arrived in my office a document signed by the *hermanos* Juan L., Luis L., Nicolas Li., and other workers who represent three churches in the state of Yucatan and the territory of Quintana Roo and another church in Tabasco, in which they resign from the ministry of the Iglesia Apostolica de la Fe en Cristo Jesus and from membership in said Church. They list three reasons for their decision:
>
> 1) One reason that can be interpreted as a disagreement with the decisions of the Southeastern District concerning pastoral changes adopted during the recent convention, resulting in what according to them resulted in "pulling" some workers out of the Peninsula and sending workers from Tabasco to replace them, who, again according to them, do not sufficiently love the word of God.
>
> 2) The second reason is the supposed concentration of authority in

the governing authority of the Church and the District, which according to them is causing problems such as their secession. They contend that those not in agreement with the regulation issued are being threatened and are being excluded from the programs, being told, "You are going to go to hell if you do not do as I say," although they do not present proof for this statement.

3) They declare that they do not agree with the present economic system of the Church, saying that it causes chaos and nonconformity among them.

The above *hermanos* state that they do not intend to cause harm or damage to the Church, although they give notice that they will keep the temples, real estate, houses of the pastors, the ministers and the *hermanos* that belong to their organization (the name of which they did not communicate to me).

After expressing his regret that he cannot personally come to Villahermaso to take care of matters because of various important trips and preparations for the upcoming general convention of the Church, the Bishop quickly proceeds to attack the secessionists. One of them was even guilty of adultery, but at the time no action was taken. The Church had always been interested in Yucatan and Quintana Roo, even financing the missionary activities of Oscar Hill. And the financial arrangements were entirely fair; only those who mismanaged the money were complaining. Then, as a faint echo of the apocalyptic disturbances of four years previously, obviously scrambling events in Merida and in Utzpak, he says:

1) For some time now the work in Yucatan and in Quintana Roo has suffered from difficult problems, given the special circumstances of the region. When the *hermano* Juan L. was elder with residence in Merida, scandalous events took place in the church there, provoked by the actions of a supposed prophet who said that his name was Jehovah, and who ordered that the *hermanos* live in the temple for several days without being allowed to leave either by day or by night. They took communion and washed each other's feet, subsequently using the water as "holy water" for drinking, he married various couples, even children, and he transferred workers to certain localities, and the supposed Jehovah designated them as evangelists. And the said Hermano L. tolerated this situation.

Returning repeatedly to the worrisome problem of the offerings, the bishop calls Juan L.'s attitudes immature, and complains that when he was minister in La Venta, Tabasco, he equally surrendered much too little.

Turning to the issue of the region's Maya character, he dismisses the differences as being of no consequence. After all, he maintains, even bishops are rarely at home in the district that they govern, and this is the essence of missionizing activity. Besides, people in such social situations are hampered by being tied into their culture, and it is important for the ministers to act as agents of change.

Much of the rest of the document concerns details of the political machinations, maneuvering, and deception during the elections, about which Isauro would have much to say when I had the opportunity to talk with him. The document concludes with an appeal for unity and reconciliation. We will see how fascinatingly all of this played out locally in Utzpak.

In Merida, in the meantime, the difficulty for Juan L. was that the church building in Merida was legally the property of the Apostolic Church and, consequently, he was denied access to it. Eus was told that as a solution they were going to enlarge Peregrina's house with money they received from their sister as her tithe.

Eus suggests that we take the bus to the Colonia Esperanza to see what is going on at the temple. After all, she keeps emphasizing, she is still a member of the "legitimate" Church, like her son. When we get there, after a hellishly hot bus ride, we encounter Rufino, who occasionally has conducted services in Utzpak. He is from Tabasco, and at the time I am unaware of the reasons why he has showed up in a Maya church. I have heard him preach a few times but found him frightfully difficult to understand, as did the congregation. He speaks very fast, runs his words together, and also "eats his s's," as people said here, that is, he drops the "s" in the middle and at the end of the word. Luckily, this time his wife is with him, whose speech is easier for me, and she is anxious to make clear to us women what to her mind is going on.

It is obvious that she is very upset that the Yucatecans are accusing those from Tabasco of wanting to take charge in Yucatan. That is not the case. "When those things happened, the Church administration begged my husband to come here and straighten things out. I did not want to come. We are well established in Tabasco. The way they do things there, they bring to the pastor whatever they grow, they bring corn, and beans, and even milk. Why would I want to leave? But the Church keeps insisting. After all, they only sent five ministers here from Tabasco. And they offered two congregations of Tabasco to the Yucatecans. To Hermano Juan L., they offered the congregation in La Venta; that is a very good congregation, so that is a fair exchange."

Rufino seems very angry. He has just received a letter from Bishop Manuel Gaxiola from Mexico City, he says, asking about the extent of the damage to the Merida congregation caused by the separatists. He wrote back that sixteen *hermanos* joined the movement of Luis L. and Juan L. "A family living close by here decided to come to the service," his wife tried to reassure him, "and there is talk of two other families from a different *colonia* that also want to come."

"There is a larger issue though," Rufino asserts. "Hermano Juan L. wanted to become bishop. But becoming bishop is not a matter of politics. First, all the ministers vote, and then two names, of those who received the largest number of votes, are presented to the assembly, and there is another vote." I wonder privately why he thinks that is not politics. "Hermano Juan L. lost the vote, and because he saw his ambition foiled, he decided to leave the Church. They have planned that for years. They do not want any authority above them. Besides, they want to use all the money for themselves that comes in from the congregations. The Church has done great things with the offerings. They are sending out missionaries, and each missionary gets 1,000 pesos per month while in the field. So clearly the Church needs money."

I ask whether now that he has had to cope with a loss of members the Church will help him out financially, but he does not answer. His wife is more forthcoming. "That," she says, "never happens."

How about Don Victor? "He keeps getting baptized," Rufino shrugs, "I think it has now been seven times, Catholic, Presbyterian, Baptist, Jehovah's Witnesses, Pentecostal, Apostolic, and Branhamist. He says he will seek for a baptism even if it is twenty times, until he finds the right one. Not many people will go along with that."

My skin burns with the heat, and I am beginning to feel faint. Besides, Eus and I are famished. So we go to a small grocery store on the next corner. I buy a can of salsa, one of small sausages, some salt crackers and some eggs, and the *hermana* allows us to use her kitchen. Then she strings a hammock in the church for us, which Eus and I share. An electric fan lazily circles under the ceiling, and I think that I might yet survive.

In the late afternoon, we go across the street to visit Gregorio and his wife. He is not home, but we find his wife lying in her hammock, embroidering an *?ipil* for sale. It is hardly light enough to read, but she maintains that she has no trouble seeing the small cross-stitches she is working on. She is a tiny woman with a very delicate face. Her knees so crippled with arthritis that she can hardly walk; that is why, she says, she is working lying down. Eus tells her that Nina has just given birth to a girl, and she feels sorry for her. One needs sons to help when one gets old; daughters can do nothing for you. She had one son, but he died.

The home of Eus's son Enrique and his wife Petronila is down the street from the temple. Eus spent the night there and wants to pick up her things. They live in a shack belonging to a cousin of Eus's and pay no rent. Enrique sells fingernail polish on the market and Eus says that he spends most of his money on drink. He usually is not home, preferring to spend his time with his other wife, who sells eggs on the market. We open the rickety gate on a filthy lot that has excrement and dirty paper and soiled clothes scattered about on the ground and unwashed dishes in the wash trough. A curly-headed 2-year-old girl is scooting around in the mud. Petronila, who Eus says has four older children, has a gaunt face and is wrapped in a colorless dress that hardly accommodates her pregnant body. "I don't know how this happened to me," she sighs. She has a tiny, very pretty boy on her arms with blue eyes and curly brown hair, skinny arms and legs, and the distended abdomen of a severely undernourished child. Filliping the taut belly playfully, Petronila laughs and stuffs the nipple of a bottle with sugar water into his mouth. "I was sick when I had this one, I had rheumatism all through my body, my shoulders, my back, and only nursed him for two months." She could buy no milk powder (it cost too much), beans had gone from 2.50 to 7 pesos since last year, and the price of corn had also nearly doubled.

Before the evening service Rufino, Eus, and I go to visit an *hermana* who is sick. They say she has sinusitis and, for unspecified reasons, has just had a blood transfusion. After the prayer, we stay for a bit, sitting on chairs in front of her one-room house. The doctor has done the transfusion for 20 pesos because some friends of her family donated blood. He says that she needs an operation, but it will cost 1,500 pesos, which they, of course, do not have. Her husband works for an engineering firm, but he has just started there, and there is no insurance. There was no health insurance at the firm where he worked before, either. So she could only trust the Lord. I remember seeing a story in the day's paper at the hotel which seemed to illustrate the problems of employees in the factories. It was about a university student by the name of Efrain Calderon Lara who had been found murdered. Apparently, he had tried to better the working conditions of the laborers in one of the Merida factories, which cost him his life, and now there are student demonstrations against the governor, who was blamed for the murder.

With only three men and three women present at the evening service, Luis L.'s church looks abandoned and very large. Rufino conducts it with the help of a Gorgonio V., who, judging from his language, is also from Tabasco. He makes it brief; a hymn, a prayer, another hymn, a short sermon in which he announces that the congregation is to pray for the success of the national meeting of the Church to be held soon. No one speaks in tongues.

After an hour on the bus and an indifferent meal at a restaurant, we finally end up in our room, desperate to sleep. Eus is very tired. At Enrique's place, one of the small children had vomited and cried all night, and she got little sleep. I am equally exhausted. But the room is frightfully hot, and although we strip to our half-slips, we find no relief. Eus has brought no hammock, so we have to use the bed, which has cockroaches on it, under it, and in it. Eus soon snores, but the bloodthirsty mosquitoes from the ceiling land on me in droves. At 3 o'clock, I can stand it no longer. Eus wakes up, too, and counts thirty larger and countless smaller bites on my naked back. So we shower, pack, go to the bus station across the street, catch the 5:30 A.M. bus and gratefully arrive in Utzpak four hours later. I spend the whole afternoon in Eus's hammock, trying to recover from Merida.

The View from Utzpak

It is evening before I gather enough strength to walk to Reina's house. Her three little girls are darling. Curiously, they have grown very little since last year. In order to forestall a fight between them, I have brought three identical dolls, and three identical everything else also, toothbrushes, hairbrushes, ribbons, balls. Reina is not well; it has been too hard on her to weave hammocks day in and day out. "I wish we could move to Merida," she sighs. "I am tired of this *cochino pueblo* [dirty village]." But mainly, she has a severe case of *los nervios,* the specifically female health problem of Latin America, a general condition of malaise and depression. At her request, I bought her a year's supply of the birth control pill before leaving last year, and she said that was what caused it. She may have been right; I saw some research later that women of certain blood groups could not tolerate the pill, although Eus had a different theory. She saw a definite correlation between a new house—that is, urban aspirations, which caused women to sell their chickens instead of eating them, causing malnutrition—and *los nervios.*

I buy a hammock from Reina's mother (for which she definitely overcharges me), Dona Andrea loans me a mosquito net, and after a cool night, I am finally back to my old self.

Reina wants to know if I believe in *suerte* [fortune-telling]. Apparently, she and Santiago went to the market together, and when they came back, Santiago's watch was gone. They looked for it everywhere but did not find it. Somebody must definitely have come into the house and taken it. Then, two weeks ago, there was a similar problem. A cousin of Reina's mother invited them to her wedding:

> Santiago says, "Let's go! Why should you always stay here? That is why you are sick *de los nervios* and have a headache." So we all went, and the house was left unguarded. Next day, when we looked at our money that we had saved, there were only 400 pesos, not the 500 that Santiago had put aside to pay to his father for our house. We were terribly unhappy. So yesterday we went to Temax. There is a woman there, she is very good at *la suerte.* She looked at her cards and what came out, she said, was that the person who took what we lost was a woman. It was not a man, a burglar, because a burglar takes every-

thing. It was a woman, a light-skinned one, a neighbor. She is envious of us, and she took what she took for that reason, not because she needed it. But already she is crying bitterly because she has a bad conscience. Things will go ill with her because her husband will discover what she did, and perhaps for that reason she may return everything: she is very much bothered by her conscience.

What you must do, she said, is this. This is not witchcraft, we don't want to make her sick or anything like that, only to make her feel so terrible that she will want to return everything, to press her together and draw it out of her. So at twelve noon today, I am to light four candles and pray a credo for each candle. That will do it.

We figure it must be Dona Ravel. She always wants to borrow money. She even borrowed money from poor old Tomasita, her mother, and never paid it back. She borrowed 75 pesos two years ago and has paid back only 15. She is also into politics. It must be her.

Reina did light her four candles that noon when I was not home and prayed the four credos. She chased out the children and closed the door, for no one must see it, or else it will not be effective.

Reina is a great believer in candles. And obviously she is not going to let any Apostolic dogma get in her way. Repent? No need. You can take some candles, light them, stay with them until they are burned down, and all your sins are forgiven. Pray for healing? You go to the Catholic Church, and instead of kissing the saint, you kiss the candle and take it home and rub yourself over with it, especially your feet, for good health. There are some complications, though. If there are several saints in a church, such as the Three Kings in Tizimin, you have to take three candles and go on a pilgrimage three times, or they will get angry and punish you, perhaps by death or by an accident, such as breaking a leg or an arm. Lighting a candle to recover stolen goods, therefore, is bound to work.

After I retire to my hammock that evening, Reina goes to the Presbyterian service with Ravel. She says she does it to please Tomasita because when she was so sick with the pill, Tomasita often came and prayed with her.

Isauro's Version

The Utzpak temple is still legally registered in Luis L.'s name. So, in contrast to the situation in Merida, here the "separatists" are in and the "loyalists" out. I am curious to see how the situation plays out locally and decide to call on Isauro. As I pass the door of the temple, I see that the old inscription about this being an Apostolic Church has been removed, but no new one has been put in its place. So perhaps a discussion about a change of name is taking place after all.

Juana, pregnant with her fourth child, and Isauro receive me in the most friendly manner. I apologize that due to my friendship with Eus, I cannot come to his services at present, and he agrees. He says that Eus and Nohoch Felix really have no other choice, since Chan Felix, the only Yucatecan minister to do so, refuses to join the separatist movement. He thinks it is a matter of character. Chan Felix is almost like a Tabasqueno:

"If they tell him that he is an infidel because he cannot come up with all that money the Church is demanding, he says, *Amen, Hermano.* If they tell him that he must work harder, he says, *Amen, Hermano.* No wonder that he married a Tabasquena. If he wants to stay where he is, that's fine. Nobody is going to be angry with him."

What happened, Isauro says, was that late in 1973, the Yucatan section of the Apostolic Church became independent as "Section Eight." The Yucatecan ministers had hoped that Juan L. would be elected bishop. With him as the head of the administration of the new section, it would have been possible to develop the work of the Church independently, adjusting to the poverty and the cultural separateness of Yucatan. But the Yucatecan contingent was outvoted. There were only eight of them against fifty-five ministers from Tabasco. Juan L. said that was all right with him; after all, as an elder and then a bishop, he would not have had much time to give to his congregation because he would have had to travel a great deal.

Then, however, there were two threatening developments. There were rumors that all the Yucatecan ministers were to be pulled out of the state and replaced by Tabasquenos. Confirming the rumor, Rufino arrived one day in Utzpak with a Tabasqueno and introduced him as the new elder who eventually would become the bishop of Section Eight.

> So we knew that we needed to act. It isn't that we want no ministers
> from elsewhere to come here. But the Tabasquenos don't know
> Yucatan. Tabasco is a province of plenty, we are poor. They cannot
> even make ends meet here in the agricultural region, and the *hene-*
> *quen* areas are even poorer. They don't know how to gain a bit here
> and there, how to grow a little food. Rufino, for instance, hardly ever
> came to visit. He says he couldn't do it because the congregation
> does not give him enough to pay for his ticket from Merida and
> back. The congregation complains that nobody comes to see them,
> there are no visitors, there is no joy. The Tabasquenos expect the
> members of the congregation to feed them, but here there is not
> even enough to feed the family. So what happens when the ministers

are from Tabasco and not from Yucatan is that one poor congregation after the other gets abandoned. We do not want that to happen.
The people want their church services, they want to sing their
hymns, they want to go to the temples. So we are going to attend to
them. Hermano Rufino does not understand what this is about. He
says that one must submit to the yoke. But we Yucatecos are not
good at submitting to the yoke. The Tabasquenos are.

We have appointed a treasurer, the people will tithe, and we will
make it work. We ministers will receive a small salary from Juan and
Luis L., 200 pesos a month, and Nicolas will receive 300 pesos, because he has so many children. We say to the congregation, this is a
request for a special offering for such-and-such a purpose, there will
be no other request. The national administration keeps putting
intolerable burdens on us. Right now, there are fourteen different
items that we are supposed to pay for. We cannot do that.

Isauro is a mild-mannered man and I always thought of him as one of few
words. But he is angry.

Hermana, I will tell you something. For the last ministerial meeting
in Villahermosa, Hermano Juan rented a fine house for Bishop
Manuel Gaxiola and the others from the national administration. It
even had furniture in it, a cabinet and all that, like we cannot afford,
there were beds, and there was a ceiling fan. He did the best he
could. They took one look at the house and said they would go to a
hotel. And there they spent thousands. When a lot of money gets
collected, it will be misused.

I am curious about how Barrera fits into all of this. Isauro says that Barrera
is still with the Branhamists. In January 1973, they predicted the end of the
world, and once more, they put on their white clothing and waited. So now
they say that it will be in 1977. Both Isauro and Juana think this is funny. "There
was a time when we thought something like that too, but now we have more
experience," Isauro said. Barrera no longer has that *gracia* that he used to have
when he preached. There is no preaching among the Branhamists; they only
read or listen to Branham's sermons. They do not even speak of Jesus anymore,
only about Branham, "the Lord's last prophet." Isauro saw some of the
Branhamist leaflets, and they had Barrera's name on them with a Campeche
address. It is said that he works as a salesman in Campeche and is not much
interested in religion anymore. Isauro says that after all, Barrera has sinned, he
has committed adultery, so that was it. His wife, Lucrecia, had her hair cut

short and she wears a wedding ring. Alvio has come back to Utzpak with his family; they have a house not too far away from the temple.

I ask him about his own financial situation. It seems that in the Territory of Quintana Roo[3] nobody can work a *col* without being a member of the *ejido*, and the raising of cattle is strictly regulated. But here in Yucatan anybody can go and ask for some land and for a small fee can make a *col*, and the cattle used to graze freely on *ejido* land. But there was conflict between those planting a *col*, the *milperos*, and the cattle owners, and on the basis of already existing laws—Isauro called it executive conspiracy—they forced the cattle holders to fence in their cattle, an expense they could not afford. Besides, what little grass there was in a fenced lot was soon gone. Isauro's father, thereupon, sold most of his own and his son's cattle. Isauro "earns a little here and there" to maintain his family. Of course, the increase in prices hurts, but not as badly as in the *henequen* country.

So that is why I had seen striking *henequen* workers along the highway on the way here. It brought to mind the newspaper story about Efrain Calderon Lara I had seen in Merida. Does he know anything about him? He certainly does. He was a student who was trying to organize a union and so the factory owners had him murdered. It seems that the students of the University of Yucatan in Merida formed an organization which they call the United Front of Students, Peasants, and Laborers. They come into the villages, distribute typewritten leaflets and try to collect money for the expenses of their activity. "People here keep passing those leaflets on and save them carefully," Isauro maintains. Efrain was a member of this organization, and he went to visit factories to see what the working conditions were. In a shop where skins were being cured, he suggested, for instance, that a separate room be placed at the disposal of the laborers so they could eat away from the stench of the curing. "He was a *bachillero*, he had a B.A., and the rich hated him because he was for the poor people. So they had him killed."

According to the students, the murder was one of utter bestiality. There was to be a meeting of some kind on February 14, and the governor wanted to prevent Efrain from speaking there. So he sent two of his henchmen and had Efrain dragged into a new car. They gave him two shots to prevent him from screaming, but he screamed anyway. They drove him around, all the way to Chetumal, broke his fingers, tore out his fingernails, castrated him, and finally, near Bacalar, they threw him out of the car. He was still not dead, so they killed him with pistol shots. Three days later, some *milperos* found him. He was nearly unrecognizable, but as a child he had broken his arm and had a platinum pin in it. This is how his mother identified him. The murderers burned the car and scattered the pieces so it would not be identified. But they were discovered anyway and were now in prison with light sentences. The students will not let the matter rest and want to force the governor to resign.

An Excursion to Izamal

On June 13, Eus and I go to Izamal together. I had been sending her monthly allowance by postal money order, assuming that it would be delivered in Utzpak, but that was not so. First, she had to pick up the money in Merida, then in Motul, and for the past few months they made her travel to Izamal. I had mailed the May payment early that month, but it just arrived now. There was only one bus a day to Izamal, so we have to spend the night there, but Eus says reassuringly that we can stay with her cousin. "Before I did not remember her, but now, I immediately do," she laughs. I want to put on a not-so-good ʔipil for the trip; I have my premonitions about the kind of back-country bus we will have to travel in. But she insists that I put on the new one she made for me. "We are going to a town!" is her argument. The bus is one of those "I'll-try-to-make-it-to-the-next-stop-but-I-am-not-sure" kind that keeps skidding dangerously on the wet highway, but the land is lush and green, and we have plenty of time to talk, of course, about the separation of the Yucatecan congregations from the central administration. On doctrinal grounds, Eus argues that it is wrong, a grievous sin. "Not an iota is to be rubbed out," she says. But as far as economics are concerned, she agrees with Isauro. Chan Felix is getting some financial assistance from the Church, so of course he can hardly join the insurrection. "Also, the Tabasquenos want us to feed them," she says, "but the families do not even have enough food to feed themselves. Think of Emerijildo's house, for instance. There are ten persons there, three adults and seven children. Hermana Teresa buys one-half pound of meat and 1 kilogram of beans; that is all she can afford. So for the noonday meal everyone gets one small piece of meat and some broth with the beans and the tortillas. In the evening, there is nothing to eat."

At one of the stops, Valentin boards the bus with his family. Rosa has three children now, which starts Eus talking about birth control. The pill made many women sick, like it did Reina. After she stopped taking it, one woman gave birth to triplets. According to Rosa, one of her cousins was given an IUD four months after the delivery of a baby, which made her hemorrhage. She has been sick ever since, wants to sleep all the time, and does not want to do any work. Eus suggests that the solution is that the men should be "more careful," which earns her general laughter. There is this man in Utzpak, Eus tells, who had to go away for a while. So the woman took a lover. In order to avoid conception, the man used a condom. But it got stuck in the woman and had to be removed by a physician. Of course, the husband found out, and since he never used any condoms, he divorced her. Rosa shrugs. "I'll just have to leave it to the Lord," she says, "and take as many children as he will want me to have."

The couple is on their way to Izamal to see Valentin's grandfather. Rosa has a severe backache, and Valentin's grandfather is a famous *curahuesos*, a "bone healer." We walk with them to his house, which is a traditional oval mud-and-wattle structure in mint condition, surrounded by a yard full of flowers. The old gentleman of 84 years has a splendid physique and classical Maya features. I ache to take a picture of him, but he refuses.

Eus often went to Izamal for fiestas when she was young, so she knows her way around. The town has a beautiful church and convent complex, newly refurbished for the tourist trade. We go to see the Virgin worshipped there, Our Lady of Izamal, but Eus calls her Concha. In the convent garden, exotic bushes are in full bloom and, deftly, Eus breaks some small branches off to plant at home. "Concha won't mind," she says. When Reina heard that I was going to Izamal, she said that there were *cerros* [hills] there. I was sure she had to be wrong. It turns out that she meant pyramids, and indeed, we see two rather small ones, one of them on the plaza.

We spend a mosquito-infested night at Eus's cousin's place. I am apparently feeding the entire mosquito population of the Peninsula. By four in the morning neither one of us can sleep anymore, and we spend the time talking until the bus leaves, mainly about prices and the present inflation and how in the old days, people made all the objects they needed themselves, and so they were independent of money.

Weekday Interludes

JUNE 15, 1974

Rufino had promised Eus and Nohoch Felix that he would come to Utzpak to rent a house where they could hold the services, since the temple is no longer available to him. Eus does not want the services at her place because there are always children that come along who destroy her many plants that she is raising for income. Vicente Ch., the father of the only other family that did not join the insurrection, also refuses, arguing that his house is full; he has his son-in-law living with him. But Rufino does not come. In fact, Eus has counseled him not to. "Why would you want to come, Hermano?" I heard her say. "Nobody can feed you, no one can give you the money for the trip." She feels, of course, that with all the money that the Merida congregation has, they could easily spend some on Rufino's trip, so why don't they? Anyway, the renting has to be postponed, and we go to the *monte* instead. Its scrub vegetation is an important source of firewood for the village. We collect and bundle the dry branches that Nohoch Felix cut from the low-growing trees and listen to the many birds. From afar, there comes the drilling of a woodpecker. Eus says that the woodpecker puts his ear against the tree to hear where the worms are, then he starts pecking at that spot. I brush against an innocent-looking little plant with serrated leaves and get burned as if from a stinging nettle, but ten times worse. Eus says that some of the *cols* are full of it. As if to console me, she describes a larger variety with pinkish leaves, she calls it *chac p'ooposh*, which stings much worse.

At home again, it is another evening without a service. I can see how deprived Eus is feeling. She obviously misses the excitement of getting ready, of putting on a special *'ipil*, of getting powdered and perfumed, of putting the hymnal and the flashlight into the *sabucan*, of locking the door and walking down the highway toward the temple in the dusk. As Isauro had remarked about the abandoned congregations, she also longs for the hymns, for the contact with the other *hermanos*, even for the sermons, although she sleeps through most of them. An entire dimension of her life has dropped out. Both she and Nohoch Felix can of course see the failings on both sides, the corruption in money matters, the political games, but they cannot grasp the distinction between dogma and organization that Luis L. is trying to make clear. That the sign has been taken down from the temple door is of tremendous significance to them: it is a violation of loyalties, and it is no longer their church, their religion. I try to coax them back to the services by arguing that we will only be watching, that I need to know what is going on, but they say that the neighbors know anyway what is happening, they can find out from them, and Nohoch Felix will write it all down for me and send it to me when he confirms the arrival of their monthly stipend.

So after supper, Eus and I sit in front of her main house next to the orange bush and enjoy the coolness of the evening, and I begin asking about those members of the congregation who had left after "those things in the temple." How about Paula, who had started going to the Pentecostals last I knew? Dona Andrea had said that the Pentecostal church in Utzpak had dissolved, so what was she doing now? Paula, whose husband had gone back to drink, is no longer interested in religion; neither is her daughter Rosa. We ran into her in the street the other day and she pretended not to know us. Paula had a number of men friends, foremost among them the son of Don Ch., one of the rich men in town. A man Eus knows saw her get into the car with him, and he followed them on his bicycle. They drove to the end of the village, then turned into a side street and parked. Paula and her husband are building a large house of cement blocks on their lot now, and people say that the money came from Don Ch.'s son.

And Dona Valuch and her husband? They do not attend any services either anymore, and Valuch no longer comes to visit Eus. Her young daughter ran away with a boy, and now the young couple lives with Valuch. The boy's parents told him to get married, but he argued that he had no money. So they provided a chicken, Valuch provided another one, and with only two chickens, they had a fiesta and the boy married her in a civil ceremony.

A man comes hurriedly by on the side street, half hidden by Eus's high *albarrada,* escorting two women. I see a flurry of pink dresses, black hair, golden earrings. Noting my questioning glance, Eus nods, "*Las putas* [the prostitutes]." They are said to be from Tizimin. The pimp, Eus says, collects 1 peso per customer; the dark-skinned girls get 20 pesos per trick, the light-skinned ones 25 pesos. "Who knows how many tricks they have per night?," Eus says. They must be *muy potente* [very strong], she speculates, to take that kind of abuse. The phrase stands out in her Maya discourse and it makes us both laugh. "At 60, those women won't even be able to walk. They do it because they don't want to work, but this is hard, they never get any rest."

Soon a procession of men follows. The house is at the end of the side street, and Eus has watched the goings-on often, whenever there is no service. The men rarely come alone. Most of the time, they arrive in pairs, or even in threes. We see Santiago's *companero,* his work partner, pass by with a friend, obviously tipsy. Usually, though, the pimp allows no drunks to enter. "After all," Eus laughs, "what can a drunk do?" One time, a boy not more than 12 came calling; he had only 18 pesos. "That's all right," he was told, "we can do it for 18." Boys, they say, are the fastest customers, old men and drunks the slowest.

I see Eus raising her eyebrows: "Santiago!" And there he comes around the curve on his bicycle. He comes often. Reina does not know it but may suspect something, for she told Eus, "It's all right with me if he goes to other women. That way he doesn't bother me." One time he came by on his bicycle and Eus saw him standing there, looking down the street. She called to him, "No need to look. The women aren't there." He laughed and left. "He knows I don't tell Reina."

JUNE 16, 1974

There is a three-day "institute" going on at the Presbyterian church. Old Tomasita, her daughters Raquel and Luz, and Reina, with Santiago and the little girls, are all attending and want me to come along. But I am way behind in typing my field notes, so I decline. So does Eus. "*Hach helaan tin wu?uyic* [I see it as very foreign]," she says. I do help the family get dolled up, though. Reina is very careful with the little girls' dresses. What I bring is kept for special occasions. This time they are wearing what I gave them last year. To my surprise, Reina carefully makes up her face. "That is why she likes the Presbyterians," Eus says, "they allow the women to paint their faces. Or rather, they say they shouldn't, but nobody takes that seriously." Raquel is made up, too. Her sister Luz works for an American Baptist missionary family in Merida; that is where Raquel learned it.

There is a service in the Apostolic temple, but Eus insists that we go shopping instead. On the way back, we stop at Dona Ugulina's house. One of her grandsons is a university student and he tells her that the governor had another student murdered. His henchmen had been aiming for the president of the Student Front, but they got the secretary instead. The governor is afraid of the students and had a number of them arrested. He also mobilized two army divisions.

When I get home, the service is still going on. I can hear the sermon clearly when I "go to talk to the pigs" on the patio. The style is that of Luis L., but not the voice. It is frustrating that I cannot just go and look. In the morning, Reina says that the preacher was Pedro N. The name rings a bell. When in Merida years ago, I copied from the Church records the names of those baptized by Oscar Hill. A Pedro N. was among the first to be baptized from Utzpak. As usual, Eus knows all the details. Apparently, he was given a congregation early in the history of the Apostolic Church here. But when, after a while, the *hermanos* from Merida came to visit him, the congregation dissolved and he took his family to Sonora and joined the Baptists there because they had promised him clothes and money. Now he had come back, according to Hermano Gorgono, Rufino's assistant, whom Nohoch Felix had heard talk about it. He said that he was an Apostolic minister; he presented a list of pastors, and he was on it. He wanted to preach, but he had no letter of recommendation, which a minister needs to have if he wants to preach to a congregation not his own. But last night they let him preach here anyway because they are interested in "attracting souls."

"They disregarded their own rules," Nohoch Felix says contemptuously.

Once More Barrera

All morning long, Eus is in a hurry. She goes shopping early before I arrive from Reina's, takes care of her animals, does her washing, and kills and prepares a duck. Shortly before twelve, I am given my meal. Immediately afterward, she gets my bath. Usually I don't bathe until 4:00 in the afternoon or after. But rather imperiously, she says, "*Taac a wichci?* [You want to take your bath?]" *Pues,* who am I? I trot obediently to take my bath. Then it comes out; we are going *shimbah,* for a walk, to see Caduch. Dear Eus. She has obviously been mulling over the question of how I can get some more information about the congregation without attending the services, and Caduch is an excellent choice. She is somewhat of an outsider. She goes to the temple but also engages in prostitution. Her husband knows it, but he says, "What am I to do?" She takes her men to a house belonging to her cousin, or they go out into the bush close by. Eus disapproves, but on the other hand, she excuses her. Caduch, she says, is supporting her aged parents with her earnings. Later, on our walk, Eus points out the old couple, looking quite ailing and wrinkled.

I want to pick up some handmade nails at the smith on the way to Caduch, so we take a rather unusual direction. Suddenly, Eus draws in her breath: "Tagre," Barrera's Mexican sidekick, whom I have never met. He sits in the shade, neat and cool, a slender mustachioed man in a blue patterned shirt, and next to him is Barrera, fat but not paunchy, wearing a blue shirt, a white buttoned undershirt, ballpoint pen and leaflets in his shirt pocket. They are supervising some building activity: Alvio, Mariano, and several teenage boys are busily constructing the tied roof of a square mud-and-wattle house on Mariano's lot. Alvio and Mariano just nod; no "*Paz de Cristo*"—it must seem awkward to them. The last time we saw each other, they were devoted Apostolics; now they are obviously engaged in a Branhamist building party. Only Barrera keeps his cool. He gets up, comes out into the street and greets me with an "*olah*," ostentatiously ignoring Eus. I ask about Lucrecia—fine—how many children—four, and here the tension we are all apparently feeling spills out: "*Tres ninos y un baron* [Three boys and a boy]!" We all laugh, but Eus remarks later that the slip showed that there must be something wrong in his head; he does not think well.

"So you are still walking around the Peninsula doing your studies?" Barrera wants to know. "And Dona Eus here is your interpreter?" It seems to be for the benefit of Tagre. So I take advantage of the opportunity. After all, nobody actually knows how exactly he encountered the Branhamists. Here is my chance to do some questioning of my own. Where exactly did he come to know the Branhamists?

"Actually, in Tizimin, quite by accident. A very simple man, there on a street, showed me a leaflet. I read it, became interested, and wanted to know more." Apparently, this is a significant movement, for there are addresses on the leaflet from Puerto Rico and from Venezuela. He attended some meetings and learned more about Branham. He even saw photographs with a "fire," a halo, over Branham's head. He also heard tapes with Branham's own voice and tapes with a Spanish translation of a number of his sermons. Eventually, he went to a larger meeting. He understood that it was true that Christ was, is, and ever shall be, and that was why he could now appear again in Branham. In July 1933, Branham had seven visions, six of which have come true. He predicted Mussolini's entrance into Ethiopia, for instance, Hitler's takeover, and the death of many American soldiers at the Siegfried line. All of that came true. "How about the end of the world?" He saw the United States enveloped in smoke, covered by craters. That, he said, must mean the end of the world and the start of the millennium. It would occur in 1977. "Of course, there are many things we don't understand. But then we come together, we meditate, pray, think, and then we understand." "And speaking in tongues?" "We believe in all the gifts of the Holy Spirit. They are given to people under special circumstances." The tongues, Barrera maintains, are known languages, but they need to be interpreted, since here people do not understand them. Mariano had the gift of interpretation "at a time when you were not here, and there arose a need for it. At that time, here in Yucatan, we thought we had some special revelation. But it did not work out. Now we have certainty, and the gift of tongues and its interpretation are no longer needed."

This certainty, Barrera implies, came from Branham's message, which is spreading far and wide—in Puerto Rico, in South America, but especially in Yucatan. Right now, they are building a chapel here to spread the message in Utzpak. They just came from a meeting in Tizimin, *puro mayero* [pure Maya], about twenty men, from villages of which he did not even know the name. Since Barrera speaks no Maya, Mariano was his interpreter, "the way Dona Eus is for you." He knows that I love science, but he is not interested in that. It is more important to know of spiritual matters. As Eus comments later, they called their church The Church of Knowledge. Barrera gives me a pamphlet entitled "Odiadores de Mujeres" [Those Who Hate Women], writes his Campeche address on it, and explains patronizingly that the title refers to the prophets who hated women of ill repute. Turning to leave, he says good-by with a hurried phrase of benediction, ignoring Eus, who with her special, cool dignity remains discretely in the background. Mariano gives us a wordless, weak smile, and Alvio remains invisible.

"How things have changed," muses Eus. "Before, how friendly everyone was. Now, nothing. Not even Alvio. They do not even invite you to their service."

Finally, on our way to Caduch, I tell Eus that I have published the account of the apocalyptic disturbances of 1970. I do not have anybody's true name in it, or the name of the village. In view of the oblique references to "those events" we had just heard from Barrera, she thinks that is funny. "He doesn't know that we told you the details!" But as to the names, she does not seem to worry one way or the other.

We find Caduch, pretty and ready to laugh as always, nursing her 7-month-old baby. She has six daughters. Her oldest, about 12, is weaving a hammock at the upright loom by the door. Caduch says that she had not even noticed that the sign above the door of the temple had been removed. It was her husband who called her attention to it. The two women reminisce about the "good old times," how they all did *talento* to buy chairs for the temple, how they embroidered the covers for the rostrum and the tables, and how they contributed money for the cement blocks that Hermano Alf wanted so badly for a new temple. Eus contributed 20 pesos, and Caduch even gave him 30. "My husband didn't know about that," Caduch laughs. "She got that money from her men," Eus says later, "that is why her husband knows nothing about it." Both women seem to feel that as a result of the separation, Luis L. and Juan L. have declared the temple to be their personal property, to their advantage. As to the present activities in the congregation, Eus is right: what Caduch had to report we already knew from the neighborhood network (confirming its reliability), about the questionable credentials of Pedro N., and that Isauro had gone to Dziuche with his family to transfer the congregation there to Valentin in preparation of his taking over in Utzpak.

We have ranged far, and the streets are unfamiliar to Eus, who is navigating by cardinal direction only at this point. Finally, she recognizes a landmark: Lulu's house. Lulu is the sister of Old Candil. I had seen her occasionally at the services, and Eus knows that the living room in her modern cement-block house served as a meeting place for Don Victor's Utzpak group. I wrote him a letter when I first arrived this year, inviting him to Utzpak with all expenses paid, but I received no answer. Then Nohoch Felix also wrote an invitation and sent various messages, but to no avail. Nobody seems to know where the man is; Lulu does not know either, although she has heard that he wants to talk with me again. She invites us to sit, and quickly she and Eus are in the thick of it. Since the camp followers of Don Victor consider themselves Apostolics, although disinherited ones, the two women have a lot of anger in common. They certainly want no Tabasquenos here. They agree that the financial management has always been questionable. Eus does not fail to mention that Old Candil borrowed 600 pesos from the treasury when Rodolfa was sick and never returned it. That was at least eight years ago, but as Eus remarks later, "I say that so Lulu will tell her brother that we have not forgotten."

Lulu's husband and her teenage son are constructing a mud-and-wattle house in the corner of their lot. Eus thinks they should have built it somewhere in the back of the lot, where it would look beautiful, not here next to the modern house. For the first time I see how such a traditional oval house is constructed. The slender sticks of the wattle are already in place, forming a firm weave around anchored uprights. The father is tearing corn husks into neat, even ribbons, while the boy is mixing soil, water, and the corn-leaf strips in a hole in the center of the structure. Then they apply the mud cover on the wattle from the inside, smoothing it on by hand.

When I get home to Reina's place that evening, I find the house locked. Dona Raquel says that the family went to Merida and will probably be back with the evening bus, and she invites me to wait in her house. She is putting her grandson to sleep, rocking in her hammock and cuddling him tight. Later, she will sleep in the same hammock; small children apparently never sleep alone. I overheard Santiago wishing that his youngest daughter would get old enough so he could finally have his hammock to himself again.

When Reina does not come back with the late bus, I ask Dona Andrea to open the house for me. Raquel comes along. Impatiently, Dona Andrea asks her to stay outside, which makes her angry. "Thank you for calling me *una ladrona* [a thief]," Raquel says and leaves. Dona Andrea defends herself by saying that all she wanted to do was to light the kerosene lamp, and after all, she is responsible for the house in Reina's absence. Both women seem to work with the knowledge that Dona Raquel is suspected of having stolen Reina's money.

The night goes by without Reina returning. I have a hard time sleeping; the mice are making merry in Santiago's corn sacks, and outside the pigs are grunting from hunger. A cold wind keeps blowing through the cracks and I am shivering under my towel, my only cover, chewing aspirin. I have no warm clothes with me. Whoever heard of feeling cold in Yucatan in June? Eus makes me lie down in her hammock under a warm cotton blanket the next morning and revives me with hot chocolate, then goes to the mill to have her corn ground. She comes back with the news that a cyclone hit Morelos. That is why we are having such cold, drizzly weather. "I love cyclones," she says. "Too bad it is that far away. There is a lot of excitement. Nohoch Felix takes his thickest *henequen* rope, ties it to a tree root, slings it over the roof and ties it into a root on the other side. I prepare extra food; we take it into the house and we tell stories. "Years ago, a cyclone uprooted a big avocado tree, but we never had any damage to the house." I can see why—for the roof is elastic, the crossbeams and struts are tied together at the joints with liana, and the whole structure rests securely, again without being nailed down, in the forks of the corner posts. Years later, I see an identical tied construction in a straw-thatched traditional Japanese house.

Eus's hot chocolate has breathed new life into me, and I am sitting comfortably under a blanket roof Nohoch Felix has constructed for me from tree to tree, typing at a table he had the village carpenter make for me of some scrap wood they had lying around. Eus is washing at the *batea;* all is well with the world. Suddenly, Eus says under her breath, never taking her eyes off her wash, "*He cu bin Barrera* [Here comes Barrera]."

There are three men, Barrera, Tagre, and a young man they introduce as Alfredo G. Tagre looks pretty unpleasant from close up, his upper teeth cracked and jutting out. Nohoch Felix brings chairs and Barrera asks if I would translate a part of Branham's sermon about marriage and divorce for them. It is a rambling sermon, transcribed from a tape made of a radio broadcast. Many sentences are incomplete, in idiomatic Appalachian English, difficult to translate into understandable Spanish. For over an hour I hunch over Alfredo's battered tape-recorder, translating all about how a woman is not part of original creation, she is only a by-product. She has no morals, is lower than a bitch or a sow. That is why sin entered into life; it was through her. Polygamy came after the original creation. In the future world, there will be no sexual desire; the world will be repopulated by creating people out of clay and water.

I am thankful when Alfredo runs out of tape. Tagre says, "Hermano Barrera always talks about you. When you came, I recognized you right away. I said, here comes Hermana Felicitas." I am thinking, I, a by-product of creation? But I mind my manners.

Barrera wants to know what I am writing on my typewriter. I say, mainly letters. And how is he making a living? He is now a mason. Eus's comment later: he has four children, you learn a trade fast that way. Tagre sells potatoes and onions in a store in Chetumal, and Alfredo is a radio technician and has studied some English. But he has great difficulties with these sermons. Many of the words are not in his dictionary. I recommend that he look at dictionaries at the university library in Merida and then order one in a bookstore. How about their worship services? They have services every night, with hymns, prayers, and mediation upon the words of Branham.

The three men apparently want more information about me. Barrera writes down his address for me and asks for mine. I should come and visit them in Campeche. Eus stands beside me some of the time, especially during the conversation, and they involve her also. She knows Alfredo's parents in Tibolom. Finally, they leave, well past noon.

Reina does not return, so I spent the night in Eus's house, under her warm blanket. Much of our conversation is about Don Victor. There is no way of knowing where he might be because he keeps passing from group to group. So we will have to wait. Too bad, because I have only four more days left.

With Reina still not back, I sleep another night with Eus, and lucky too because it is still drizzly and cold, and Reina's *mamposteria* house is moist and drafty. Nohoch Felix has worked that day and has gone to collect his pay, so for a while we are by ourselves, swinging lightly in our hammocks in the dark. Eus wants to know how I gave birth, and I tell how my first delivery took twenty-four hours. "*Maachis,* my goodness, that's bad!" she says sympathetically. She gave birth very easily. After the pains started, it usually took only two hours for the baby to emerge. Three times she gave birth without anybody being with her. By the time her *comadrona* [her birth helper] arrived, she only had to cut the umbilical cord and wash the hammock and the floor. "It is because I don't like anybody to come near my hammock when I give birth," she says. Then she prepared the food and Nohoch Felix went to work; he did not stay home.

"He always did wage labor?"

"He worked, but *otsil maac* [the poor man], he did not even have a house when we got together. We lived with his sister. But I sewed, and I took eggs to town to sell, and within a year, we had our own house in Tibolom."

The next morning, Eus brings a fat rooster from the neighbors. She butchers it expertly, hanging it by its feet from the branch of a tree and cutting its throat. "This is how those students wanted to kill the murderers of Efrain, hanging them on the trees. But the government took them to the safety of Chetumal." As she proceeds to dip the bird into hot water and then pluck it, she recalls a related memory. In 1917, when she was a small girl, the soldiers hung many men from the trees; some of them lived three days before they died. Others, the soldiers drowned. Her mother's brother and several more men died that way. "They" came, grabbed the men, stripped their clothes off, tied their hands and their feet and threw them into a cenote. One of the men managed to loosen the ties on his hands. He escaped and that was how the village knew how the men had died.

Nohoch Felix has gone to work; he was glad that the call for workers went out again. When he weeds on the ranch, he earns 5 pesos per *mecate,* and if he works hard, he can get a whole *mecate* done in an hour. The ranch is two *leguas,* about 8 kilometers away. This he has to walk; there in the morning, back in the evening. There is no bus. But he is admirably fit. After that kind of work and that kind of commuting, he still likes to go into the village to gossip with friends, not always men either. Eus comes to fetch me at Reina's house, where I went after supper. We go to Dona Rosario, who sells soft drinks in her living room that opens to the street. When we get there, Nohoch Felix is sitting on the curb with Dona Lidia. I think she is pretty, but when I say that to Eus, she snorts, "*Baash ciʔichpam?* [What do you mean pretty?] She has a wrinkled face and gray hair!" Contrary to her usual custom, where we would sit for a while and gossip with Dona Rosario, this time Eus marches right to the cooler. "You will have a *soldado de chocolate.*" "I will?" OK, so I'll have that. I am used to obeying her. She takes one for herself, too. We chat, we laugh, nothing unusual about anything. Until it comes to paying and I recall that Nohoch Felix has offered to invite us. Now he comes to Eus: could she give him 3 pesos? She says, "So you don't have enough?" He seems ill at ease. Later she tells me and seems to think it a huge joke. She must have known exactly how much he had on him. He had invited Lidia to a soft drink, so instead of a Pepsi or something of the same price, she chose the chocolate drink for us, which costs quite a bit more. Neatly, she had driven him into a corner. Because of our extravagance, he had to come and ask her for money in front of Lidia. She laughs about it for a long time. What a chess player she would make!

Finally, Don Victor

I hear Reina and Santiago make love last night, and this morning, Reina complains about a bellyache, dizziness, and *los nervios*. She cries loudly, "My poor daughters, you have a very sick mother . . . " I put Lupita's warm jacket on her abdomen, suggest positive thinking, and offer aspirin. I leave, convinced that she will recover. Maybe Santiago had better continue his excursions to the ladies down our street.

For a comfortable morning chat, I have taken a chair to the *batea*, where Eus is doing her daily laundry, when she interrupts me, "*He cu bin Don Victor,*" here he comes. Finally. He easily negotiates the high threshold of Eus's *albarrada*, saying "*Paz de Cristo,*" and we exchange a limp handshake. Eus brings another chair.

He had been on a trip, he says. When he got home, his son brought him all the letters from his post office box, also the ones from Nohoch Felix and me. So he took the bus to Merida, where he arrived during the night, and changed into the 5:30 A.M. to Utzpak. Eus offers a hammock, but he would rather talk. Immediately, Eus launches into her favorite topic—the division in the Apostolic Church. "The Apostolic Church is the Church," he says, but the Church is both spiritual and "literal," and the problems arose with the latter. He tries to elucidate his view with a simile:

> A seed, when it is placed into the earth, it begins to bud, the plant breaks through the soil, and its body begins to grow. It grows and grows, forms its cane, forms its leaves and then its spike. The fruit begins to form. Bueno. [He laughs, a kind of paragraph marker he uses all the time.] Then comes the time of the harvest; the fruit is cut, then the leaves are separated from the cob; that is, the shuck is separated from the corn. But if you want to eat the maize, there has to be another separation. The corn has to be rubbed off the cob. Then, when the corn is soaked, the skin is taken off, another separation, until you reach what gives life. The present Church is concerned too much with what has been separated, and not enough with what gives life.

Usually, however, his view is not this harmonious one of the "literal" church enfolding spiritual knowledge. Rather, over and over again he sets up the opposition, the struggle between the two aspects, often with the image of the church fornicating with the world and the believers ending up as the stepchildren of this unholy alliance. "This is what is happening with the Apostolic Church now. It is fornicating with Satan. I am with my father, and I certainly do not want my mother to cohabit with the Demon. If God will grant them insight, then we shall be at the same location. If not, then may God be with them."

Eus has prepared a chicken soup with tortillas, which we eat, as is the custom, singly and in succession, first Don Victor as the guest, then I, then Eus. She always stands on ceremony: "When the children were small, they were never allowed to approach their father when he was eating. There are parents nowadays who do not educate their children properly." Afterward, I manage to ask a few personal questions, anxious to get them in before the flow of his theological disquisition once more prohibits any break. Where was he born? In Ac?il, near Oxcuscab. He was the oldest of three boys and also had two sisters. He attended two years of grade school, that was all. How about his parents? They were from the same area, peasants, "the poorest of the poor."

> For fifteen years, my father was a slave in T?uul, on a sugar plantation. In those times, the *patrones* had clever ways for trapping the poor. They obtained an authorization from the state and then talked them into agreeing to their servitude. A poor man might say, "Senor, I cannot go." Then they would say, "What do you mean, look, even the patron is going, and there is pay," and there he was, he had already sold himself. Then, if he needed anything, he received it, clothes, whatever, and then he always owed something and there was never any escape. The *patrones* had chapels built on the ranches; there they could go and confess, but if they tried to escape, the priests knew them by name and turned them in.
>
> Then came the freeing of the slaves after the Revolution, but the *patrones* would not let them go. Some men were so desperate they hanged themselves. But liberty had been proclaimed. Finally, the *patrones* said, "All right, you can go, you owe me nothing, you can go to your own village." This was what my father told me.

Things were not right even now, though, he felt. Slavery continues, "under water," as it were, under cover.

> The *patrones* work scientifically, but the poor know nothing about that. The value of their work does not increase. They work a lot and earn very little. We see it, we know it, but we can do nothing to remedy the situation. But we see it. What I tell the *hermanos* is that soon all the human systems will be destroyed anyway. First will come the persecution. That is what it also says on those leaflets of the students.

I really have to admire how seamlessly he has built the expectation of the end of the world into his perception of the societal situation.

His first contact with Protestantism was through the Presbyterians. He was about 18 then. But they preached in Spanish, which at that time he did not know very well. However, there was one preacher who was a Maya and always preached in Maya. From him, he learned a lot. Then there was a conflict because they never knelt in prayer, not even the minister, and he had read in the Bible that one should kneel. When he argued about it, they kicked him out.

As he began reading the Bible more, he also started having visions of many different kinds; they gave him great pleasure, but he did not understand them until he had his revelation that he had told me about in 1973. "Did they talk about visions at the ministerial meetings?" No, those were only about money. What they would do was to rank the congregations according to how much money they sent and ration the services accordingly, such as sending illustrated leaflets or other teaching material. Utzpak always ranked at the bottom; that was why this congregation received no help at all from the administration in Villahermosa.

Don Victor's visit eventually turns into a two-day theological marathon session. Eus is fascinated and listens in whenever her chores allow it, often asking for explanations in Maya, which he enthusiastically supplies. But he is not really interested in answering questions. I am simply to listen. A woman, he says at one point, is to humiliate herself before God, the bridegroom. But it is not clear whether he means me or the Church. Occasionally, I do get in a question about topics such as the apocalyptic disturbances:

> What happened there was that they [the *hermanos*] did not have enough strength to carry out the work. They were praying and they saw a vision, it was not a dream, and they saw an eagle circling above the temple, but it did not alight and it flew on. Then it flew on to Chetumal and then to Cuarenta y Dos, and it was seen there also, but it did not alight and then it left. It was actually announcing that knowledge, that wisdom, should alight in this church, but no one wanted it. That was what the eagle represented, the Holy Spirit.

On the afternoon of the second day, I finally sense that Don Victor is talked out. We have filled ten 90-minute tapes. He stretches, saying, "*Hach yah tulaca in wincli!* [All my body hurts badly!]" He is also anxious to get to his tiny congregation here to teach them about the *sabiduria*. Money is awfully tight and he can no longer afford much traveling. Since I have also paid for his bus fare, he wants to make good use of the opportunity. In conclusion, we go into Eus's house to pray. He asks lengthily for blessings on my work, for my enlighten-ment, and for a crown in heaven for me. He gives thanks to the Lord for my companionship and my friendship, and for a very brief moment, he utters a glossolalia phrase. Out of respect for the occasion, I do not record the prayer.

After he leaves, Eus tells, "While he was praying, I felt that something was tugging at my dress. It was so strong that I thought it was one of the dogs. I looked down and the tugging stopped. There was nothing there. I even looked toward the door: nothing. I think this may be a sign that I will die soon."

June 23, 1974, a Sunday, is my last day. Eus and Nohoch Felix spend happy hours listening to Don Victor's tapes. It is still raining. I wonder what is more unpleasant: Yucatan cool and wet, or Yucatan hot and wet? Besides, I have a terrible diarrhea. Nohoch Felix gets me some streptomycin from the drugstore, and he earnestly decrees that I will have to spend the night at their place. We look to the sky to send sufficient water to justify my staying without hurting Reina's feelings, who with her bouts of *los nervios* has become very clingy re-cently. I am to entertain her, she says.

We are lazing in the hammock after yet another cloudburst. Suddenly Eus says, "If we plant my chile seedlings now, they won't die." It is amazing how quickly that kind of plan makes her glow. Nohoch Felix gets out his pickaxe to loosen some stones to locate a bit of soil, Eus plants, and I film, although it is really too dark. Finally, she has one pot of seedlings left. "No room for these," she says regretfully. Hurriedly, they get back into the house: "Here comes an-other cloudburst!" How do they know? "We hear it." They laugh because I do not seem to be able to tune in on that band of sound.

Summer 1974–July 1975: The Congregation

True to his word, Nohoch Felix wrote a number of letters after I left. Chan Felix was given a small congregation in Tabasco, he reported, in a gov-ernment project near Villahermosa. The state put up a church building there for the joint use of a number of denominations, and Chan Felix also did some work on the ranches, where they had three yearly harvests. All is not perfect, though, for a thief stole all of Isaura's hens, which brought on a serious case of *los nervios.* Eus has problems with her stomach. And a destructive hurricane hit Chetumal and blew Nina's house away. They had built it only three weeks previously, actually a shack out of cardboard and some scrap lumber, good enough for the tropical climate, but it offered no resistance to the fury of the storm. In fact, all of the squatter settlement where she lived was destroyed, but no lives were lost because the government had all the inhabitants move into a large, heavily built school. "We were safe," Nina said with a grim sense of hu-mor, "but I saw my house blow past the window."

Nohoch Felix also took some notes about the activities at the temple. Isauro continued to conduct the services. Occasionally Juan L. came to visit the congregation, and the *hermanos* offered their individual hymns. Eus did not attend these services, but Ruben had moved his family to a ranch near Utzpak. He was now conducting services in Don Eduardo's house, and Eus attended those. Alvio invited Nohoch Felix to a service of the Branham group, but he disliked the fact that they did not preach on the basis of the Bible, so he did not go again.

Back in Utzpak

I arrive in Yucatan on July 14, 1975. Eus picks me up at the airport as usual, and we take the bus into town. The bus tickets have increased from 40 to 75 centavos. There is a frightful drought, which, for Utzpak, finally broke on June 3, but it was so bad that Eus's seedlings died on her, although she kept watering them. She would water them in the morning and by afternoon they would be dead. She finally gave up, for hauling that much water from the well was too hard for her.

The happy news is that her sow gave birth to seven piglets. The boar was an American breed; Don Vicente had acquired it, and crossing it with the local pigs made the offspring larger while still preserving the hardiness of the locals. They paid 100 pesos for having their sow serviced, and Don Vicente also closed the umbilical cord of the piglets and gave them the necessary inoculation.

And of course there is the all-important gossip. Juan L.'s wife gave birth to a frightfully deformed child. The baby boy had his intestines in his chest cavity. Juan L. would not consent to an operation; he said it was God's will. And Luis L.'s daughter lost an eye; she was injured by flying glass and the eye had to be removed. "It is God's punishment because they left the Lord's Church," Eus maintains. And Dona Andrea told her that Reina had a noisy quarrel in the street with another woman, who accused her of trying to steal her husband. Reina is pregnant, so what would she want another man for? Santiago is not doing real work, only buying and selling. Grinning mischievously, Eus says that he is too fat to work in the *col*; his balls rub against his legs. Then she demonstrates, taking a few steps, her legs apart, seeming to throw his "eggs" from side to side.

Bad luck also pursued Mariano. His wife developed tuberculosis, and she and her two small children were taken to Merida. No one knew when they might be able to come back. The Branhamist chapel was no longer used for services. Alvio kept some of his animals in it.

Eus has made arrangements with El Negro for the trip to Utzpak, so we have plenty of time to go to the market. I am wearing an ʔ*ipil* and am deeply tanned from working on my land in New Mexico, and, to our amusement, I blend in so well that a shirt salesman takes me for a "mestiza" and, touching my sleeve, asks, "*Y una huayabera no quieres llevarte, mamacita?* [And don't you want to buy a *huayabera, mamacita?*]"

We go to Enrique's space. He is very drunk and proclaims in a stentorian voice to the entire market that there is no other woman like me. Furiously, Eus tells him off. We walk all over the market, shopping for bananas, apples, a watermelon, and a pair of sandals with tire soles for me, which last longer than leather. Prices have more than doubled since last year. Even the midwives charge more for delivery, Eus says. Boys and girls now cost 100 pesos, and the prostitutes get 30 pesos per trick. Santiago, by the way, is still a frequent customer.

We arrived at the appointed corner five minutes before the limousine is to leave. I wonder how Eus accomplishes that; she never asks me the time.

Soon, I ease back into my accustomed pattern, spending most of my day at Eus's house. In consideration of the increase in prices, I now pay her 25 pesos for my daily meals; she insists that that is enough. When I point out the price of meat, she maintains that she raises her chickens with the help of the monthly allowance I send her, and so we should eat them when I am here. My nights I spend at Reina's.

Reina is indeed pregnant and back to her cheerful self, with hardly a trace of *los nervios*. Animatedly, she talks about the *telenovela*, the soap opera she is watching every day on the new television set of Dona Juana, who has electricity in her house. She only charges 30 centavos and the children can watch for free. I am very unhappy about the advent of television. It disrupts our congenial gossip corner, and instead of the intelligence about the doings of the neighborhood, conversation often drifts to the bloated adventures of some soap opera character. I do hear, though, that the lumberjack's vivacious wife died of the measles. "I am burning up, I am burning up," she kept crying, but no one could help her. Her children were distributed among relatives.

No doubt the fact that she has become something of an entrepreneur is contributing to Reina's well-being. She is no longer weaving the hammocks; she now has several young girls weaving for her. Then she puts on the *brazos*, the supporting strands. After the death of Reina's father, her mother went to live in Merida with her unmarried son and Reina spent several days with her off and on, taking her little girls with her. She sold the hammocks on the market, and Santiago, "since he is a man," went to the factories, such as the Pepsi-Cola bottling plant. The men received their wages on Saturdays and then often bought hammocks. Those that were left her mother sold to neighbors on an installment plan.

Much of the gossip is about Don Eduardo. As I already know from Eus, who heard it from Dona Andrea, he is in grave financial trouble. Five years ago he sold his ranch because he was too tired to work it; he had a pain in his back and also in his abdomen when he walked. He gave each of his children money or land as their inheritance, and he had lived on the remainder of the sales price ever since. Supposedly, he had a mere 200 pesos left. His only remaining asset was his house, but if he sold that, where would he live? Jorge, his older son, was unmarried, but he could not go there because Jorge hated his stepmother, and if he went alone, his money would soon give out paying for services such as washing and cooking. His daughter in Merida refused to accept Dona Andrea, and the one in Utzpak had a bunch of children and a small house, so there was no room for him there. And Reina did not want him either, because although she did not actively dislike Dona Andrea, she said that she ate too much. Dona Andrea asked her daughter if she would like to take them in, but was told "for that you found yourself a donkey to maintain you. I am not going to do it."

When I mention Don Eduardo's problem to Eus, who of course, knows all about it, she maintains that things did not need to go that way. For instance, there was the grandfather, father of Ernesto and Isauro, close to 90. To be sure, he was richer than Don Eduardo to begin with, but he was also wiser in the arrangements that he made. He gave each of his children some land but kept enough land and cattle to live on. His sons were willing to work his land for him because there was harmony among them. Besides, he also compensated them. In Don Eduardo's family, there was never any harmony, and gossip had it that his sons were also stealing from him because he had his money hidden in the *baul*, where everyone could get to it. Besides, Don Eduardo could have held on to some of his grazing land. A man might put his herd there, and then half of the new calves would go to the landowner. Don Eduardo, she felt, was simply lazy; he loved lying in his hammock and staying home.

"It is hard to get old, isn't it?" I remark in a rhetorical way. Eus disagrees. Living is wonderful, she says, and if your strength no longer permits you to do something, then you should not waste time bemoaning the fact. Her friend Dona Ugulina kept complaining all the time that she was getting older and that she really wanted to die. "I say," Eus says, "if that is what you want, why wait? It can be done well and fast with a rope." And apparently she got no sympathy from her daughter either. According to Eus, Chucha added, "But better go to Merida for that. They've got a pretty cemetery, it's like a hotel, and people even come to eat lunch there."

There is quite a bit of kidding between Eus and Nohoch Felix about the same subject. Nohoch Felix had decided to stay home for the time that I was there, running Eus's errands. He had gone to the store the third time in the blazing heat because he kept forgetting things, and he complained about being tired. "Don't believe him," Eus says, "he is not really tired. He just wants to stay home and take it easy." Not to be outdone, Nohoch Felix counters, "And how about her? She goes to the market once, and she right away says that she cannot take it anymore. She is not good for anything anymore." In the same vein, he points out that he had planted thirty-eight *mecates* of corn this season on his *ejido* land, and to show him up, she also planted some corn in the *solar* using the dibble, and right away she was exhausted. Then they both laugh and there is a glance of real affection between them.

The Death of Mam Dosa

One afternoon, Eus and I sort through my *ʔipiles*. The *ʔipiles* are not merely dresses, they are personal creations. Every woman follows a style characteristic of her village and also has her own personal technique and patterns, by which her *ʔipil* is recognized. Fondly, we recalled that this one was embroidered by the wife of Don Goyo in Merida, these three we bought on the market, this one Eus made for me, and this one was embroidered by the daughter of Dona Rosario. We come across a small one, very delicately embroidered with flowers. "This one is by Mam Pola," Eus says, "nobody else did these blossoms." Had I heard that Mam [an honorific, perhaps derived from the French madame] Pola died? She died only a month after her daughter, Mam Dosa, the wife of Don Antonio, the owner of the general store. Eus keeps talking, and a whole life begins to unfold.

Mam Pola, who with her husband ran a small grocery store on the corner of the main street, not too far from Don Antonio's, did not want Dosa to marry Don Antonio. Eus asked Dosa for the reason, but all she would say was that her mother kept warning her that Antonio was *puerco* [crude, a pig]. After they got married, Mam Pola did not speak with her daughter for eight years, although they lived only a few houses apart. Dosa kept having miscarriages. Once when she was pregnant, she very badly wanted to eat a certain kind of sausage that only her mother had in her store. She sent a friend to buy some for her, but when Mam Pola found out that it was for Dosa, she refused to sell it, and Dosa was so upset, she aborted again. She finally gave birth to the only child she carried to full term, a boy, who now owned a haberdashery next to his father's store. The marriage was not a happy one. Don Antonio soon took a second wife, and that ate away at Dosa, although she never put up a fight about it. She died of unknown causes. The physician said she simply dried up. Her son told Eus it was his mother's fault; she died of stupidity, she should have stood up for her rights. She did fight for one thing, though. She told Antonio on her deathbed that if he did not leave the store, the house, and everything else to their son, she was going to come and fetch him. It was said in the village that Don Antonio did not dare to cross her on that.

When Mam Pola heard of her daughter's death, she said, "*Ma tin shaanta, tin taal shan* [I won't tarry, I will follow her too]." A month later, she was dead.

Next time, when Eus and I go shopping at Don Antonio's, I express my condolences. He says something conventional, like it was sad, but after all, it was a path that all of us would have to follow. Eus's comment? "He is really glad to be rid of Mam Dosa. After all, he's got the other woman."

Some News of the Congregation

After supper, I go back to Reina's house, and in the cool of the evening Eus comes to fetch me and we go to Dona Rosario's for a soft drink. The soft drink business is suffering because of the rise in prices and that has given Dona Rosario a severe case of *los nervios*. She broke out in a bad rash on her arms, and her worried son took her to the doctor in Merida, where they gave her some tranquilizers. "She is so sick," mocks Nohoch Felix, "that she cannot give you the right change anymore."

As we walk down the street, we meet Cecilia, the mother of Nicolas. "*Hach cada ano vienes* [You come almost every year]," she says, and the mixed Maya-Spanish phrase amuses Eus to no end. She keeps repeating it over and over again. Then we run into Alvio, who invites us to come and see his new house and *solar.* The Branhamists had predicted that the world would come to an end on January 4, 1973, so Alvio sold his house in Chetumal; some friends of his deserted theirs on the *ejido,* and they all came to Utzpak to await the end. "When Christ comes, we won't need any house anymore," was the argument.

Nohoch Felix worked on the ranch with the brother of Alvio's wife Gregoria. The man told him that one evening he came home, a bit drunk, and became upset to find his sister there with her five children. So he told her, "You stupidly sold your house, and now you are here, bothering our mother. Go find yourself a house to sleep in!" Alvio had an affluent brother, and with his help he bought a new house, and Gregoria was so upset with her family, she did not return to her mother's house until January of 1975, when she had another baby. Alvio had Mariano's tape-recorder and said that Barrera had not been seen in Utzpak for the past five months. Whatever Branhamist activity was left now took place in Alvio's house. He asserted that the predictions of the Bible about the end of the world would not come true, but those of Branham would. Don Victor, he said, had also once more predicted the end of the world, and when it did not happen, he had to give up his congregation in Dziuche because nobody believed him anymore.

Alvio has a large *solar,* and he is growing corn on it and selling corn on the cob. He is irrigating it with the help of an electric pump attached to his well. Astutely, Eus asks whether his well is not giving out with that much use, but

Alvio assures her that although it occasionally runs dry, the water will eventually seep back in.

On the way home, we also meet Epi. He no longer attends Isauro's services because his children and those of Antonio always fight. In other words, Antonio is back in Utzpak and has sided with Juan L. and Luis L.

The Drought

The weather has been very dry this season, and many people did not do any sowing, and now it is getting too late. Beautiful rain clouds come up, then the wind starts and carries them away. Perhaps because of the drought, there is considerable damage from caterpillars. Every morning, Eus walks around her *solar,* opens up the leaves of her corn and picks them off. She comes with an apron full of caterpillars to feed to the chickens, and the next morning, she starts all over again.

The Arrival of Wilma

This evening, Wilma comes to visit. She comes regularly every two weeks, bringing her own food, and Nohoch Felix has constructed a small bath house attached to the main house for her three older sons. She is very pregnant; she expects the new baby, her eighth, within the month. Husband Ruben has found work as a caretaker of a ranch close to Utzpak. They consider themselves lucky to have found work. In Tibolom there is no work at all. Most of the men are forced to work in Cancun, where the government is developing a summer resort. They come home only every two weeks, and Tibolom has become a village of women and children. The men earn well in Cancun, but they also have to spend a lot because food and lodging are very high. Besides, life is dangerous there; many *wachos* stream in from outside the Peninsula, and violent quarrels and murders are the order of the day.

We go for a walk on the plaza in the cool of the evening and sit on a bench for awhile. The plaza is literally trembling from a cacophony of sounds—the musical advertisement of a circus announcing its imminent arrival, the soundtrack of the local movie, and the loudspeaker mounted on top of the Catholic church, which broadcasts the event of "forty hours of prayer" accompanied by a hymn, "Ven a mi, senor, ven a mi" [Come to me, oh Lord, come to me], to the melody of Joan Baez's "Kumbaya."

Wilma tells her mother about the condition of Nohoch Felix's *col* that is close to the ranch—no caterpillar damage there—but Don Sh.'s corn was nearly destroyed. Don Sh. is an evil man, so this is clearly a punishment of the Lord. Divine punishment is also manifested in Merida, where an *hermana* who had joined Juan L. and Luis L. had an accident with her car and broke three ribs and subsequently returned to the temple.

Wilma has come a week early this time because she wants to tell me about how the Holy Spirit came to Tibolom. This happened earlier, but she had no opportunity to talk to me during my 1974 visit. The following is a translation of her taped account:

The Holy Spirit in Tibolom[4]

This happened in September 1973. We had scheduled an evening service, a private service of thanksgiving in the house of Hermana Ana. When I arrived, I saw Hermana Vidalia, the wife of Hermano Pedro, kneeling on the floor, shivering and shaking. Quite unexpectedly, she began praying in tongues. Soon, everybody else was also kneeling down and praying in tongues, about twenty of us, men and women, myself included. We were all praying and singing and sobbing, all in tongues. Only it was not the Holy Spirit that was possessing us but *el Cʔaas*, the Evil One. I knew it had to be the Evil One because even very small children down to the size of Elias [her own 2-year-old] were attacked, they prayed and sang and sobbed too.

This went on all night. When morning came, no one went home, we all remained in the house of Hermana Ana, continuing to pray and sing in tongues. Finally, at about four in the afternoon, I said to myself, I had better go home and see what my children are doing, although I knew that Consuelo [her oldest daughter] would take care of them. When I got home, Ruben was very angry. He said, "You did not come home to take care of the children, you stayed out all night, who knows what you were all doing?" I got so angry, I took the bucket full of *cʔeyem* [soaked corn] and poured it out to the chickens. After all, everybody knew where we had been and what we had been doing, only he had been sleeping, he was not interested in the words of the Lord at the time, and now he was jealous. I remained at home, but in the evening, another *hermana* came, and she said, "Let's go see what they are doing, what is happening to them." And we went, and Ruben also came with us, and as soon as we entered the house, the Evil One attacked him too. He sang and spoke in tongues, and so did everyone else, even down to the smallest children, who prayed and sobbed until they were totally exhausted. Only then did they stop. The Evil One possessed us all, and no one ate or drank anything, and no one slept.

Another day, the third one, dawned and things went on as before. No one went to his home; everyone stayed at the temple, nobody went even as far as the street. On this day, Gilberta picked up a Bible. Now we all knew that she could not read, not a single letter. Yet when she opened the Bible, she began to read. I stood behind her to see what she was reading, and she had the book open at the chapter that she said she was reading. And to think, she had never learned to read at all.

For four days and for four nights, not one of us had slept. The people were ordered by the Spirit not to sleep and not to eat or drink. On this fourth day, the mother-in-law of Gilberta came and said, "Look at your small children, they are starving, they will become sick, they must be taken care of." And she took the children with her. But Gilberta continued reading from the Bible. She was sitting on a chair, and we could see that she was getting very weak. So we took hold of her and lifted her so she could lie down. For four days the Evil Spirit had possessed her; she had not eaten, slept, or drunk, and neither had the rest of us. How could we continue that way?

Finally we decided to send Hermano Filomeno to Merida with the message that the *hermanos* in our village were attacked and that they should send someone to help. But at that, Gilberta revived and said that there was no need for anyone to go to Merida. Chan Felix, she said, was already on his way, and in a little while he would arrive. Of course, it was the Evil Spirit that made her say that. She also said that the *hermanos* should go out into the street, onto the highway, all the way to Merida, and they should enter every house and should preach and sing. She said that it was the Holy Spirit that wanted them to do that, but it was really the Evil Spirit that was possessing her. She kept saying, "Yes, Father, I'll obey you. I will do what you say." And when the Evil One heard that she wanted to obey him, he possessed her even more strongly. This *hermana* is a very humble woman, that is why the Evil One attacked her so strongly.

Once more, night fell, and Chan Felix had not arrived. By this time, we were all worried. If help did not arrive soon, one of us might die. After all, it had now been more than four days and nights that we had not eaten, drunk, or slept. The Evil One would get hold of an *hermano*, throw him to the floor, and there he would writhe, squealing shrilly like a pig. Then we would say, "We must pray for him," and all of us would start again, singing and praying in tongues once more. So we decided that one of the men should go to Merida and fetch the minister. Filomeno volunteered to go, but the Evil One did not want him to get to Merida. On the path through the *monte* it attacked him. Filomeno saw how it approached him, horns on its head, almost like a steer. But looking closer, he also thought that it seemed to have the shape of a man. Filomeno ventured closer and, approaching the shape, he said, "In the name of Jesus Christ." And when he got to the spot where he had seen the shape, it had disappeared. At about the same time, Jose [her 15-year-old son] went for a walk and saw snakes all over the path. But when he looked, they were gone.

After walking the 9 kilometers from Tibolom to Holcah, Filomeno took the bus to Merida and found Luis L. and Juan L. at home, and there were also two *hermanos* from Tabasco. All four of them decided to come to help. They arrived the same evening because they had found a truck that was delivering merchandise to Tibolom. They immediately came to the house where the people were still being attacked. Many neighbors who were not believers were beginning to crowd around the door to see what was going on. They had heard that there was a woman who did not know how to read, yet she was reading. They also heard that there was singing and speaking in tongues. When the Evil Spirit was possessing an *hermano,* he would tell all the sins he had committed and would start cursing. And the people watching said, "Let us leave because this sort of thing might happen to us too," for they were also beginning to be possessed. This was true because by this time the Evil One was starting to leave and then come back again. Like one time, Ruben was standing by the door, and the Evil Spirit went into a boy, and he fell down as if dead. Ruben said that he could feel how the Evil One passed by him, very cold, and entered the child. The other *hermanos* were praying; that was why they did not see it right away. There was also a young *hermana* called Anita, the last child of her parents. The Evil Spirit prompted her to demand over and over again that she go and live in the house of Hermano Filomeno for a month and learn to play the guitar. He knows how to play it because he is preparing for the ministry. She had been a good girl until then, and now she was forward, demanding bad things. I was still singing in tongues, but I also listened to what others were saying. Gilberta, the one who had been reading although she did not know how, noticed what I was doing, and she reproached me, saying, "You are not praying at all. Only I am praying."

The *hermanos* from Merida immediately came to where we were and asked Gilberta to read for them, but she could not do it. They held a regular service, and at 9 o'clock they sent everyone home.

They said that if they stayed at that house, the Evil One would probably attack them again. That is why they sent them home. The
neighbors were happy because all that noise and commotion
stopped, and this was how the affair came to an end. When we got
home, we all drank some water and we went to sleep. Only Gilberta
did not sleep because the Evil One was still in her. She lay down in
her hammock, but soon she got up again and started praying in
tongues. Her mother-in-law scolded her, telling her to go back to
sleep, but she was doing what the Evil One was telling her to do.
When her father heard about all of this, he got very upset and
blamed his son-in-law, saying, "If my daughter dies, I'll see to it that
Pedro ends up in the penitentiary." For her parents could see that she
was sick, that she did not recover, that she was not sleeping, not
eating even a single tortilla, and drinking only a bit of water occasionally. She continued speaking in tongues, and they were afraid
that she was going to stay that way all the rest of her life. Of course it
was the Evil One that was making her do all that, possessing her that
way. This lasted for about eight days, but even after that, she would
have fainting spells. Her husband took her to Tabasco, and then out
to the ranch. She was well there, but when she comes back to the
village to visit, she is sick again. The other day she came, and she had
three fainting spells in one night.

Anita has also continued being bad. Before these things happened,
she was a good girl. She was strongly attacked during those days, and
looking at her now, it is clear that it was an evil spirit that attacked
her. Her mother guards her well, so she did not go to live in Pedro's
house to learn to play the guitar. But she acts up during worship
services. She pulls on her mother's *rebozo* and tells her what hymns
are to be sung, although her mother is the president of the Dorcas.
When the *hermanos* from Tabasco come to hold a service, she says
nasty things about them in Maya. They cannot understand her because they only speak Spanish. Since both her parents are members
of the congregation, they keep bringing her, but she does not stay
put during the services. Instead, she keeps going out to talk with
boys, and although nothing may happen, still, what will the people
say? She has no *novio*, no steady boyfriend, but runs around with
fifteen different boys. Nothing happens; she only deceives them. One
of the *hermanos* from Tabasco, a young minister, fell in love with her
but lost interest when he saw how evil she was. When her sister got
married, they were going to play hymns on the record-player, but
instead, she put on records with *puro porqueria* [offensive texts]. She

was baptized both by water and by the Holy Spirit, but all the *hermanos* hate her because she always gives trouble. One time, she brought a bottle of perfume to church, and afterward everything smelled of the perfume, even the temple.

When I ask why she thinks all these things happened in Tibolom, she contends that the reason was that at the time only one of the *hermanos* had been baptized. With that, the Holy Spirit had arrived in Tibolom, and the Adversary came to contest its takeover. It was clear that it was not the Holy Spirit that was responsible for what had happened, since even small children were attacked and kept crying and crying. And if it had not been for the *hermanos* coming from Merida, somebody would surely have died. When all was over, everyone who was involved got baptized, including herself and Ruben. Nobody participated in the various splits that involved the Apostolic Church in Yucatan, and there were no millenarian expectations.

A Service in Don Eduardo's House

For a while, the services of the "loyalists" are held in Eus's garden. But Don Eduardo went to Merida and there heard that some *hermanos* are planning to come to Utzpak to conduct a service. It is going to be a big party, Hermano Gorgono and his wife, also his mother and another *hermana*, so Don Eduardo offers his home for the service. Eus told me about this Hermano Gorgono, who in the intervening time had occasionally conducted a service in Utzpak. When he comes to Utzpak, he demands the red-carpet treatment— soap for his bath, sugar in his *atole* [corn gruel], even toothpaste. All from Eus, of course, since everyone else seceded from the "legitimate" church.

In the end, the Merida party does not come, but we have the service in Don Eduardo's house anyway. The poor old man goes about borrowing chairs for two hours beforehand. It is an intimate occasion, only Don Eduardo and Dona Andrea, Eus and Nohoch Felix, Wilma and Ruben and six of their children, and myself. Jose, to the chagrin of his parents, usually absents himself. Nohoch Felix comes in with a flourish, carrying the congregation's guitar. He says that when the *hermanos* separated from the Church, he went to the temple and took it. When Antonio objected, he countered that the guitar belonged to the Church, and since they no longer professed to belong to it and he did, he had the right to remove it.

Ruben conducts the service along traditional lines. As we sing the first hymn, the congregation in the temple next door also starts singing, and Ruben, the only powerful singer in our group, gets pretty hoarse trying to outshout them. Wilma and her daughters offer a hymn; so do Don Eduardo and Andrea.

I had heard them practice it when I was in Reina's house. Don Eduardo is holding a candle so they can read the text, and his hand trembles so badly that Andrea takes the candle from him impatiently. During the prayer, Ruben utters a brief glossolalia. Ruben preaches very simply, but at least, as Eus points out, he does not say "*hermano*" after every second word, as inexperienced preachers are wont to do. He speaks of the Devil, "also called Satan," who always stands ready to attack people.

Visit to the Rancho San Jorge

Wilma invites us to the ranch where Ruben is the caretaker. I had always wanted to see a ranch. These isolated homesteads gave the Spanish a lot of trouble when they first invaded Yucatan, and it is still the favorite way to live for most rural families. Reina promised to take me some day when I came the first year, but then it never happened. "Too many mosquitoes," was her excuse.

I sleep at Eus's house the night before we leave and, with Wilma's family also spending the night, it is pretty crowded. In fact, with ten hammocks strung every which way, the scene reminds me of a Hungarian attic on washday. Eus keeps a light on, a rag wick burning in a small bottle of kerosene. It gives enough illumination to make out what everyone is doing. Eus and Wilma have this trick of keeping one *ʔipil* on while slipping into another one. I was never quite able to duplicate that. I either got stuck in an armhole that was where it was not supposed to be or, in desperation, I ripped something.

I sleep in the same hammock with Eus, but with all this humanity around, I am awake quite a bit, listening to the noises of the night. Outside, the sow grunts at an obstreperous piglet. Uproariously, the dogs go in pursuit of an opossum, called *zorro* [fox] around here. Birds chirp, and at intervals some disconsolate cattle low at the butcher's station next door. Inside, an indistinct shadow urinates into the family chamber pot. Eus gives me one all to myself, but I try very hard to use it as little as possible. At about four, a child stirs, and Eus asks sleepily, "What is it?" "*Taitac saasta, ʔbuela* [It is almost dawning, grandmother]," came the answer from one of the boys. Despite this momentous observation, everyone still tries to catch a few winks, until 2-year-old Elias lets go in his hammock and the urine sloshes noisily on the floor. There is also a curious purring sound, and when I ask about it, Wilma calls me over and holds out a little blue bag made from the pocket of a discarded pair of pants, and in it the kids' pet squirrel is purring because it is cold.

While we wait for the truck, I ask Wilma how they are making a living on the ranch. Ruben, she explains, earns 40 pesos a day (about $3.00 U.S.) weeding, watching over the cattle, cutting down trees, repairing the fences, and turning the irrigation pump on and off. Jose does the same kind of work and earns the same wage. In addition, they are permitted to keep their own livestock there. They have a house rent free (the children keep saying, "It even has a floor!"), the use of a kitchen, and a large *solar* where she can keep her chickens and is at liberty to plant what she needs.

Finally, Don Placido, the owner of the ranch, arrives with his truck. He looks every inch a Maya peasant, but one who made it: he owns two ranches. Everyone piles in the back, and there would have been room enough also for Eus and me, but Eus insists that we two should be riding in the cabin. There is already a passenger there, a young woman with her small child, so Eus and I squeeze in beside her. We drive the length of the village, picking up and discharging passengers, then turn onto a paved highway, which soon turns into a country road that becomes more and more rutted as we progress toward the ranch, finally becoming merely a narrow jungle path. At one point, Don Placido stops, gets out and picks up a turtle. With a larger one that he had picked up earlier, it will make a fine meal, he tells Eus. The low trees grow close to the path now; one branching across the path had an orchid sitting on it like a deserted bird's nest.

Finally, we arrive at the ranch. We drive into a wide, almost circular clearing with a few buildings on either side, an *albarrada* all around it, and a tall wooden gate on either end. We unpack by the main house, Wilma's daughters give the floor a quick scrubbing, the hammocks are strung, and with the day's heat intense, we women soon take advantage of them while the boys go out adventuring. Soon Jose comes back with two birds whose black feathers have a bluish hue, which he had killed with his slingshot. He hands them to me, obviously proud of himself. "Why did you kill them?" I ask. "They are *pich*, Hermana, crows, they eat corn." That obviously is sufficient justification. The incident foreshadows what increasingly spoiled the outing for me. There is no living thing that these children do not kill. It is like a reflex action for them. When I do not accept the crows, Jose gives them to little Elias. He tries feeding beans to them, pushing them against their closed beaks, then he drags them out outside.

Wilma lays exhausted in her hammock, her oval, delicate face drawn, her over-slender hands with long fingernails resting on the edge of her hammock. This will be her ninth delivery. She tells of eighteen years of nearly continuous pregnancy, lactation, and miscarriages. One child would not grow, a little girl so delicate that she looked like a tiny baby doll in her hammock, until one day, in her eighth month, she died. Did she ever think of birth control pills? She had heard of them, but did not seem to want to try them. "And certainly I would not take anything that might hurt something that was already alive in me."

It is getting even hotter, and one of the girls brings in a large plastic washbowl with water for Elias to bathe in. The little boy stands in the water and patiently lets her rinse off his chocolate-colored body. Then he steps out of the water and makes footprints on the dry cement floor. "*Wai,*" he says with his tiny voice, pointing to the footprints, "*wai.*" "*Tuush cu man wai?*" his mother repeats for him, where did the changing witch go? His sister put a woman's blouse on him, he gathers it up around him and starts taking a few little dance steps, humming with his high little voice, then cracks a funny little smile with his eyes winking rapidly to the call of his sisters, "*He cu cheo, he cu cheo!* [He is smiling, he is smiling!]" His sisters place a *sabucan* on his head. Now he is a *wai,* and the others pretend to be afraid of him. Tiring of the game, he finds a small rubber doll, and sitting on the floor, he presses it against his nipple. "*Chuuch,*" he coos, "*chuuch,*" nursing. All the children speak Maya with each other and with their mother, and only their father breaks into Spanish occasionally.

Wilma's younger daughter, Marjelia, goes to the kitchen to start grinding the soaked corn for making tortillas. Eus follows her to make a meal for the two of us. She simply places three rocks on the mud floor at some distance from where the girls are cooking and that way has her own hearth. Then two of Wilma's boys come rushing in: the cattle are coming! It is a daily occurrence. They push through the gate; it is a majestic sight, the large herd, Brahman hump-backed bulls, longhorns, all of a sudden materializing against the backdrop of the lush green of the bush. They are really scrub cattle, and because there is so little to graze on, their ribs are showing, their udders hanging limp. They want to cross over to the pasture on the opposite side, but their path is barred, for that part of the range has recently been burned over and, due to the drought, the fresh green shoots are slow in coming. They eat what supplemental food is thrown to them, mainly top shoots of sugarcane. But at 1,000 pesos a load, there is not much of that. Even that is a luxury, but cattle owners who cannot afford it lose their animals. Then the cattle just stand around, lowing, ruminating, sometimes menacing each other with their heads down, the cows nursing their young calves. Then, about five, they meander out again.

We intend to leave the following day, but the truck does not come. The children quote Placido as saying that if he got too drunk he would only drive to Motul, and not all the way out to the ranch. And his nephew Chito, who makes regular runs out to the ranch, is drunk so regularly that he cannot be counted on. And indeed, he does not show up either. To spend the time, Wilma, Eus, and I, with all the children except Jose, who had to work, go for a walk to the neighboring ranch. It is a beautiful walk, and both Wilma and Eus, almost as a reflex movement, pick up and throw to one side any twig or small branch that is obstructing the jungle path.

The ranch has the same layout as ours. The lady of the house is shelling corn and tells about the sudden illness of her 2-year-old, a peaked little girl who was still nursing. She woke up well in the morning, then developed a high fever and would surely have died had it not been for her father, who took her to the children's clinic in Temax for some shots.

She shows us around the *solar* with its beautiful trees of various kinds of oranges, limes, avocados, *luuch,* and *wayum* (a small green fruit with a pleasant, slightly sour taste). She had been expecting a good fruit harvest, but three days ago the pump broke down, and if either the repairman or the rain do not show up soon, much of it will be lost.

On the way home, there is big excitement: the kids locate an iguana high up in a tree. We can clearly see its flat reptilian head, dull gray body with some green and yellow patches, and long tapering tail. Nine-year-old Joaquin climbs up fast as a monkey by using a slender neighboring tree for added security. Three-quarters of the way up, he begins to shake the tree. The kids below, as well as Eus and Wilma, begin shouting; the dogs yelp. Then, there is a triumphant cry as the iguana loses its foothold and falls to the ground. Almost simultaneously, the kids excite the dogs with a "*Hale, hale!*," which drives the dogs to a frenzy. They pounce on the iguana and bite it nearly to death, but not entirely. Six-year-old Oscar grabs hold of its tail and drags it behind, then hits its head against a stone to kill it. "Will we eat it?" I ask. "We could, but this one is for the dogs."

Suddenly, the kids get excited again. We are almost at the gate when they spot a second iguana on the path. The dogs are driven into action, Oscar drops his prey, and Eus picks it up by its tail. It is smaller than the first one, and more yellowish. "Why don't the dogs get them now?" I want to know. "Because they won't eat them raw," Eus explains patiently. "*Tac*" is the word she uses. I remember her telling me that the reason cats first play with their prey is to prepare them for eating because they won't eat it *tac.*

Watching the killing has made me nauseous, so I head for my hammock. On the way there I notice a gorgeous green, orange, and black caterpillar crawling around on the small tree where the children have hung the bag with their pet squirrel. I keep mum about it, but soon after I settle in the hammock, a shout goes up outside that I have come to dread: something else is going to die. They call me and I go to see the little squirrel munching on the caterpillar, its green gut oozing out the other end. The kids think that great fun and go hunting for more caterpillars. They also bring butterflies, but it does not like butterflies, so they pull out their wings to make them more appealing.

I have not eaten all day, and in spite of all of this unpleasant killing, I am finally getting hungry. Eus calls me to the kitchen, and I sit down on the footstool next to the round tortilla table. She has made some broth; she says she prepared it because she saw that I liked it in the restaurant by the bus station in Merida, and she is happy that apparently it stays down. Then the door flies open, and in comes Oscar with both iguanas and throws them on Eus's open fire. By this time, my will to live has taken over. I am determined to eat. A delicate stomach will get you nowhere. Soon one of the iguanas begins to smoke, and Oscar wants to pull it out. Indignantly, Eus gets up. "*Tonto!* [Stupid!]," she says, and begins turning the two reptiles expertly over the coals. While doing that, she tells me about how they are prepared for human consumption, how you take the intestines out and cut off the head, and slice the body into portions, just like you would a chicken. "Does it taste good?" "I don't know," she laughs, "I can prepare them, but I don't eat them." Oscar throws them to the dogs and they nearly kill each other: there are three dogs and only two iguanas. So Eus picks them up and hacks them into pieces, and peace is restored.

Eus and Wilma strike up another conversation about how bad things are getting in Tibolom. A chicken will bring only 5 pesos there, while in Utzpak you can get 20 pesos for it. And if the harvest fails on your *col,* that is it; you cannot make it up. I am puzzled about this dependence on cash income from other sources. After all, harvests have failed before, and people have managed.

"That is correct," Eus says, "but in earlier times men did not work only the *col* close by, as they do now. When I was a girl," she continues, "the men got up at three, took their tortillas and corn gruel, walked two or three *leguas* [10–15 kilometers], and then stayed in the *col* until they were done. No one does that anymore. They go only as far as the bus will take them, and they want to be back for supper in the evening. Anyway, people used to walk more. I used to know a man who would walk all the way from Holcah to Merida to go to the market. For food on the way, he would take some eggs. It would take him two weeks."

The children are happy: they have found a brilliantly green *sacuchero,* a dung beetle. Oscar ties a string around its middle, and the beetle zooms around at the end of the string. Jacinto has constructed an oval *albarrada* and has sowed some corn. "Are there any caterpillars?" Eus asks the children that have trudged along. "None," the kids assure her. "*Ba'ash mina'an?* [What do you mean none?]" she taunts them. "I bet you did not look carefully enough. See all the droppings?" And for half an hour, Eus and her three grandchildren pick caterpillars off Jacinto's planting, crushing their heads with their fingertips or with a stone. Now, I can of course see the utility of all that—if you want to eat corn, you cannot let the caterpillars do their thing—but I feel this urgent need to put some distance between myself and yet another creature's death. But no such luck: Jose comes back from the evening hunt and triumphantly brings three baby birds and places them in my hand. They are still blind and their tailfeathers are barely sprouting; very quietly they quiver in my hand. "They have to die," Jose says in his strident way. "Why?" "They dig up the corn after it has been planted and eat it." Gleefully, he grabs the little creatures and carries them away. All the kids follow him out, and a little while later a shout goes up. He comes back in, saying, "They are dead." But I already know.

That same evening, Oscar comes into the kitchen and demands a second supper from his big sister Chelo. She is a quiet, cheerful, efficient girl going on 18 who practically runs Wilma's household. She is impatient. "What are you, a dog, that you can't get filled up with one supper?" Her father overhears it and beats her with a thick *henequen* rope. I hear her cry, and ask Eus what that was about. Eus explains that Chelo was so angry, she picked up her purse and said she would leave. Later that evening, when the kids get me to tell stories again, like we had done every evening in the old days, she stands by the entrance door of the house, still sobbing occasionally. But she does not leave.

The next morning Jose rushes into the house to get his father's shotgun: something is frightening the hen with her six chicks in the palm-frond shelter on the other side of the *albarrada*. There is a shot, and then the word comes back: a snake. The men have gathered at hearing a shot so close to the house: two handymen who were working at the pump on the cenote some way off in the bush, Ruben, the carpenters busy repairing one of the gates, and two men on horseback who materialize from the bush on the other side. The children and we women also walk over, picking our way through the mud and the cow dung. Jose has hit the snake in the middle, creating a tear in the abdominal wall of a boa that is only about 1 millimeter long. He has brought it out of the shed, where it had killed one of the chicks, and it is still contorting this way and that, writhing in the dung. I mourn; I have always found snakes exceedingly beautiful, but of course I say nothing. Finally, Ruben crushes its head and takes it out into the bush. For a while, there is worried talk about whether its companion is still around, for Wilma's sow is about to drop her litter, and when the chickens on the other side of the house kick up a storm of cackling, Ruben rushes out with his shotgun. But it is a false alarm.

If, for the children, all animal life is there to be killed, they behave quite differently toward plants. Oscar had found a curious kind of grass with heavy seedpods where the horses are usually tethered. They all rush out to see it and badger their grandmother to tell them what it is and ask if she can get them seed for it. They do not pull it up.

Finally, on the morning of the third day, two trucks come in. One brings family members to the neighbor woman, the other one an extra contingent of carpenters, who will repair the cattle ramp. So now we have a way home.

We take a bath in preparation for our departure, and I contemplate the dismal choice between two *ʔipiles* equally sweaty, soiled with dust, food stains, and mud. But as I am drying myself behind the small curtain, there comes a hand with a clean *ʔipil*. I knew Eus had an extra one stashed away in a plastic bag hanging from the corner post, not ironed, but oh so clean, but I did not ask for it because I knew it did not fit me, for my arms are so much thicker than hers. But sensing the emergency, she has simply ripped open the seam under the armholes, and there it is, the one and only, the dry, the gorgeous, the clean *?ipil*.

For the trip home, Chito is only mildly tipsy. He supervises the loading on the truck of an enormously heavy load of cedar trunks, then he perches the son of one of the carpenters on top of the load. This boy is in charge of a sack of corn for the pigs at home. With his one eye (he lost the other one in a childhood accident), Chito carefully scans the jungle path as he eases the truck along. But once we are on the highway, all caution is thrown to the wind. He sings all the way home, taking his battered vehicle up to 100 kilometers an hour. I am hoping to slow him down by telling Eus as loudly as I can about the progression of the speedometer. "Where do you see that?" she wants to know. I point to it, but that deters Chito in no way. I shudder to think what will happen if some driver unexpectedly emerges from a side road. With his heavy load and the probable deplorable condition of his brakes, we would kiss sweet life good-by. But it is nearly six by then, and there is practically no traffic anymore. Squeezed, sweaty, hungry, but relieved, we finally do make it home by seven, as darkness falls.

Early next morning, Eus scurries around her household, happy and eager like a young girl. Poor Nohoch Felix, she sees all his failings. He did not water her pots evenly and some of her chili peppers have fallen off the plants because of lack of water, the piglets have not been fed enough greens, and the watermelons are overgrown with weeds, so an angry torrent of "*Ma ta wilic?* [Don't you see?]" rains down on his guilty head. He takes it good-naturedly and while Eus is sweeping up leaves from her flowerbeds and heaping them against the *albarrada* "to make more soil," Nohoch Felix settles down to clean a bag of black beans. The mites have gotten into them, and he mixed them with lime last night, which kills them more efficiently than the Lindane that Don Antonio sells.

Eus starts up her fire on her hearth and cleans her wattle kitchen from top to bottom. How lucky she is, she says, that she still has firewood. The *monte* around the village is public land and you cannot legally cut any of the wood there. The women go out very early to gather some for the family hearth; the authorities look the other way if it is only this kind of small-scale pillaging. Nohoch Felix gets their wood from the ranch where he works, at 2 pesos a bundle. When the new school was being built, Reina and Raquel collected a lot of wood where the machines had cleared it, not only for themselves but also for sale. The man in charge of forestry surprised them and asked them to stand still; he wanted to take their picture for the Diaro, a mimeographed information sheet put out by the Cuartel, the administration. But, Eus tells laughingly, they did not want their picture in the Diario in the act of pillaging wood, so they scurried home without their loot. Santiago was stealing wood close to where Eus lives, and Eus warned him, "The *presidente* will see you!" He shrugged off the matter, but three days later he was caught, exactly as Eus had predicted, and was ordered to appear before the Cuartel. He was fined 80 pesos, or maybe 100; Eus did not know, and Santiago wasn't talking.

The school that Eus is talking about is a new government trade school. Reina says that after initial enthusiastic participation, some parents decided to take their girls out again. The school has a farm where agricultural subjects are taught, and the students watched the birth of piglets. The parents did not like that. "Why? They can see that on their own *solar* any day!" Reina's explanation: "The parents objected because the girls watched it in the presence of the boys."

There are also other problems. Maria, one of Dona Ugulina's granddaughters, developed a crush on one of the teachers. The teacher, Eus says, was also at fault, for he liked the girl and often came to the family home, supposedly to teach her. The teacher was married and had several children. One night the girl's mother woke up and Maria was not in her hammock. She looked all over for her. Finally, about three in the morning, she went to the teacher's house. His wife and children were away visiting and there was Maria in his room. Her mother grabbed Maria and made a terrible fuss, waking up everybody and accusing the teacher of seducing her daughter. She kept screaming, "Return my daughter to me!" The matter became so ugly that the parents took it up with the school administration. The teacher's defense was that the girl had followed him around. The school administration apparently believed him and expelled the girl. Dona Ugulina told Eus that Maria's mother did manage to blackmail the teacher into giving her the money for a physical examination for the girl, and it was found that nothing had happened to her. The teacher left for the summer vacation, and for a while the girl stayed inside, but now she was beginning to go out again.

When I finally get home to Reina's, I ask whether she had worried when I had not come home on Tuesday, as I had said I would. "No, I saw Don Felix buying tortillas, so I knew that you had not come back yet." Everybody keeps track of where everybody else is. No wonder there is so little crime in Utzpak.

An Excursion to Chetumal

Nina has two small children now. It would be hard for her to come to Utzpak, so Eus and I decide to go see her instead. The highway that used to end on the outskirts of Utzpak has been extended, so we do not have to go to

Merida to travel to Chetumal but can go directly from Utzpak to Tizimin and then on from there. In Tizimin, we have to wait in the bus station for several hours. There is not much of a crowd, and we notice a man sitting not too far from us who is carefully wrapping the stump of his right leg to a wooden peg. He notices us too, and his task accomplished, he comes over to us, asking where we are going. He keeps on talking to Eus, and wants to know whether I am her *yiitsin* [her younger sister], and when she (with a straight face) says yes, he says that there are beautiful white women in his family also—with a toothy smile for me. Actually, he has a handsome, regular face and unusually large, sad eyes. Eus asks him how long he has been a cripple, and he says only about two years. His leg was blown off with dynamite when he was blasting for a well. But he has plenty of money, he contends, cattle, a house, and work whenever he wants it. When he hears that we want to get to Chetumal, he suggests that instead of waiting for the bus, we should rent a cab to Valladolid, where there are many buses to Chetumal. It would not be any more expensive, and we would be more comfortable. So Eus goes out and finds one charging only 2 pesos more than the bus. It already holds six passengers, but the driver squeezes us in, so the matter of comfort is not quite relevant. On the way out of town, he picks up one more, so he has to drive practically hanging out of the window. It prompts irrepressible Eus to remark in Spanish Maya for all to hear, "*Pero ahora contento?o, chuup u co?oche* [But now he is happy, his car is full]."

I am amazed how many ruins of small pyramids we pass on the way and am expecting great things of Valladolid since it played such an important part in the Caste War and before. But it is just another small, colonial-type market town, like Tizimin, at least the part that we see as we pull into the bus station. And as for bus connections, there are only two, one early in the morning, the other at 5 P.M. We are immobilized by our heavy bags, so we are stuck. Eus has a picnic lunch for us, but it is hard to eat because of the stench of the toilets. There is very little water due to the long drought, and so the attendant comes every two hours and flushes, once. Then he gives up altogether and locks las Damas [women's restroom]. With little compassion, we observe a rather portly woman in a flowery ?*ipil* trying the door over and over again. "*Taac u wish, taac u ta?, pero mina?an tuush* [She wants to piss, she wants to shit, but there is no place]," Eus laughs. The phrase has a rhythm to it, a certain ring, so we recite it a number of times. We also repeat some Maya stories to each other from a collection I found in a Merida bookstore. Eus finds some of them amusing, like the one where two vagrants offered to pray at a Maya wake in exchange for the fiesta food and recited a string of Spanish profanities for the unsuspecting mourners. I go out and buy some soft drinks, but the hours crawl by ever so slowly until finally the bus leaves at 5 o'clock.

Nina meets us at the Chetumal bus station. She is pitifully thin, but very cheerful. Desi stayed at home because little Teresita had diarrhea. When Eus asks whether there is another baby on the way, she says that they cured her at the clinic where Teresita was born, they put in one of those little things. That way, what Desi might earn for six, two could eat. I hire a cab, which is expensive because it is late and the squatter settlement where Nina lives is far. We cannot see much, only the indistinct shapes of many small houses. The children are still up, Freddy with his big smile and Teresita stiff with fright. Our hammocks are strung in the middle of the house, and all through the night I keep hearing, even in my sleep, the wind rustling through the dry leaves of the banana trees in the back.

The next morning, I see that the house is rectangular but built with the technique of a mud-and-wattle structure: heavy limestone fragments form the two-foot foundation, holding uprights at three-feet intervals. Instead of wattle, tar paper is fastened on to them with wire through bottle caps, which is whitewashed. Desi, who has a job in Chetumal as an apprentice mason, did all the work himself, and he has even bought some cement for a floor. The lot was his; he bought it from his father, who planted the bananas. The hurricane which blew away their first house embedded seeds of wild chili peppers and saltwort in the dry and powdery soil, which did not grow there before. Nina has a small fenced-in area shaded by tar paper, where she keeps her two chickens and two turkeys, and an eating section on the other side with a table, a chair, and a high chair. Her hearth is outside, surrounded halfway by a low *albarrada,* but making tortillas there is laborious (she has to use charcoal because there is no firewood), so she usually buys them from a nearby *tortilleria.* There is also a small grocery store and a store for soft drinks.

Actually, the city recognizes the squatter settlement as a subdivision. The street has a name, the houses are numbered, and down a ways there is a tap for drinking water. Three times a week, although not always reliably, the city sends in a truck with water for washing and bathing. Nina keeps her supply in a covered oil drum. Her "patio" is a curtained-off corner among the bananas with a hole dug in the middle for excrement. She has a tin can in it that she found at the dump. When it is full, she places it in the sun to dry and substitutes an empty one. When the excrement is dry, she shakes it out on the street and re-uses the can. Most probably there is a connection between the saturation of the air with the dust of excrement and the constant illness of her children. Regularly, they come down with diarrhea, vomiting, and high temperatures, and part of Desi's income inevitably goes for medicine. Things would be better for the children in Utzpak, Eus thinks, but there is no work there for Desi. Besides, Nina does not get along well with Desi's relatives, who all live there.

On Saturday morning, we go downtown to do some shopping. I need vitamins with iron for Wilma, who according to her doctor is severely anemic, and

I have provided some money for clothes for the children. "There is money for food, but not for clothes," Eus had said, and happily, Nina picked out several outfits. Then, we go to the Puntos de Estrella, where a section with a lovely marble floor is portioned off for a dance later in the evening. Both women like to watch "rock-and-roll" because the partners do not touch. Whenever I describe a dance I have seen, their question is always, "*Tu machcabao?ob?* [Do they grab hold of each other?]"

And how about worship services? The situation is complex. The temple belonged to the Apostolic Church, and an *hermano* from Tabasco is conducting the services there. Luis L. lives in Chetumal and now has a new temple. Some *hermanos* are holding services in their own homes. Nina has not been to church in four months but goes with Desi to hear a Branhamist service, sometimes held by Barrera, who comes over from Campeche for that purpose. They are obviously still shopping abroad, and in the meanwhile, Desi, who has always been bored in church, has reverted from the Bible to lighter fare: the local scandal sheet with stories of prostitutes, pimps, and murderers.

On Sunday afternoon Desi takes us over to Don Victor's compound, close to the *tortilleria.* From the street, it looks like four large, square houses, the cement floors rising a foot or more above street level, and the kitchen apparently in the back. The houses seem connected, so that only the roofs mark them as separate structures. There is an enclosed porch in front, where a number of teenagers and smaller children are playing with a ball. Desi goes ahead while we women wait farther back, but we can hear him ask if Don Victor is in. A man in his 30s steps up and answers that Don Victor is on a trip, but we are welcome to come in. Desi turns to us to ask if we want to, or what he should say. So I step forward and, giving my name, I say that I am sorry not to encounter Don Victor and hand him the snapshot I took of him last year. He immediately brightens, saying that Don Victor took his family on a round trip to visit his congregations, progressing toward Campeche and then north toward Merida. At Escarcega he sent them home, and he went on to Merida and is now staying with an *hermano* there. He introduces himself with the usual formula, *para servile* [at your service], and says that Don Victor had often spoken of me, worrying, "Did she understand everything I said?" and saying, "I have so much more to tell her."

On Monday morning, we leave Chetumal. Our farewell is mainly concerned with the children. They are the ones that we hug and give kisses to. Eus's last words to Nina are, "*Calant a chan pa?ala* [Take care of the little children]."

On the way home, the driver stops several times to buy meat on the way. At one point, in a village near Valladolid, there are two men selling meat by the roadside. The bloody skin of the steer and its intestines are spread on the street next to the stand. We also carry a group of customs officials, and farther on, one of them asks the driver to stop, for there is meat for sale down the street. He is a giant of a man by Yucatecan standards and has a badly deformed left arm. It looks like it was mangled when he was a child and then put back together again by the village butcher. He reboards the bus with the wildest-looking piece of meat I have ever seen; it is hairy and looks as if it has been roasted over an open fire. "*Ke?*" somebody remarks behind us. Eus shakes her head. "*Kitam* [peccary]," she says. That kind of meat is never sold on the market. Too bad; Nohoch Felix often brings *kitam* home from a hunt and it is very tasty. But they have become quite rare in recent years.

When we have to change in Tizimin, we encounter a first-class bus on its way to Merida. The driver agrees to stop in Utzpak, and I sit next to a woman who is clearly from Yucatan but apparently of the affluent class. She wears a white ?*ipil* embroidered in white silk, no *rebozo*, and her traditional jewelry is obviously gold. I wonder which way the diffusion went, from the village to the rich, or the other way around? I am at a loss about how to formulate this question, so I never ask Eus about it.

The Home Turf

I sleep the first night after our return at Eus's place because, once more, Reina is in Merida with the children. She maintains that the children love to be there and always cry when they have to leave. Next time I have the chance, I ask the three little girls why they want to stay in Merida. They shrug. Is it because they like playing with their cousin Mechito? No, that is not important. Then one evening, while Reina is on her shopping tour, I overhear them talking about what Mariana is doing now. Mariana, I know from Mexico City, is a soap opera character. Cilia, the youngest one, then begins to tell an involved story about a monkey stealing some medicine, and how they track him down. Is that on *Mariana* too, I ask? No, that is another program. And then there is *Hawaii Five-O* and *Tarzan*. The list goes on. When Reina comes home, I say, "The little girls really know their television." Reina is quite proud. "That's right. In the *tele*, the children really learn something. My brother's house is next to my mother's, and the girls sit there all day in the hammocks and watch. They adore it."

Returning the following evening, I find Reina distraught: her piglets did not come home. By this time they are always home to eat their corn. Where could they be? She rushes off, scouting the streets where she knows from experience that her piglets like to forage. Last year, she bought a piglet from Eus and later had to sell it at a loss when it was fattened up because it turned out to have trichinosis. It could still be turned into sausage, she maintained. I tell her that the disease is spread by the pigs eating intestines and other remnants of infected animals. But she still wants to let them roam the streets because that way they get fatter so much faster. Tomasita, I point out, always keeps her piglets locked up and goes to the outskirts of town to cut weeds for them. As I say it, I realize how urban Reina actually is: I cannot imagine her walking down the street, the short sickle in hand, a bag over her shoulder, in search of weeds. Neither, apparently, can she.

Reina spends a restless night, getting up several times to check if the piglets have returned. I sleep poorly too, feeling sorry for her. Clearly, she is also afraid of what Santiago will say if the piglets are lost. At three months, they represent some value.

At the crack of dawn, Reina is off again, telling Lupita, still groggy with sleep, that she should go hunt for them too. In an hour, while the little girls help themselves to coffee and animal crackers, their usual breakfast instead of the "old-fashioned" black beans, she comes back: still no piglets.

Finally, when I get home in the evening, the piglets are back. A man Reina knows told her that his wife heard that somebody had seen the piglets wander into a *solar* near the new school. And that is where she found them. But she is glum: the man told her that her piglets destroyed some of his corn and demanded 20 pesos for damages. I can see that she is pondering how she can get out of paying.

"Couldn't you have avoided the problem" I ask, "by having the priest announce over the church loudspeaker that your piglets were missing before they caused all that damage?"

"He charges 10 pesos for such an announcement."

"Could it happen that somebody's pigs are stolen this way?"

"Not really. Somebody is bound to see it; you can't hide pigs that way, and the owner would hear about it."

"What if no one knows who the pigs belong to?"

"Then they are taken to the cartel, and they charge 10 pesos per night per pig."

"What would happen if you refused to pay the man?"

"Then he would complain to the cartel, and they would make me pay."

What a neat system.

July 30, 1975

I have never seen a *pib,* an earth oven, used. So Eus brings some banana leaves from Nina's place (the ones in Utzpak are too small because of the drought), and she kills a duck. We have duck soup, and then she smokes the meat over the hearth fire to make it keep until the following day. When I get there in the morning, she is working on the preparation of the food that is to go into the *pib* that Nohoch Felix has dug in the backyard. I get to film the entire sequence, how Nohoch Felix lights the sticks and loads them into the pit together with fist-size stones, how he spreads raw *henequen* fiber harvested from his plant in the back over the hot stones, and how he places *abana* leaves over the fiber, forming a star.

Eus, meanwhile, fashions five pots from the thick *masa*, fills them with a mixture of cooked shredded duck meat, chopped onions, and coriander and pours a gravy over the filling, also made from *masa* and colored brownish-red with *achiote*. Then she places a lid of *masa* on each pot and glazes it with the gravy. The pots are packed into banana leaves loaded on a board and carried with great ceremony to the pit. Gently, she and Nohoch Felix place the packages on the hot stones. Nohoch Felix puts freshly cut green branches on top, then a piece of corrugated tin plate, and on top of that, the soil that had been dug up. "In an hour," he says enthusiastically, "the *pibil waʔ* [the earth-oven bread] will be done." Actually, it is more like an hour and a half later that he opens the pit. To Eus's consternation, there is a "*pibil* lizard" in the limp green branches. "*Otsil* [poor thing]," she says. It must have been hiding in the branches and paid with its life.

The *pibil waʔ* comes out shiny and bronzed, very appetizing. I am given a big hunk, of which, to Eus's disappointment, I can only eat about one-third. It smells great but tastes rather bland, and it is just about the heaviest food I have ever eaten. It sits on my stomach like a stone, but at least it does not give me any diarrhea.

As we are eating, Reina's three little girls come to visit. "The night you went to Chetumal," Lupita says, "there came a *tuʔucho*." "What is a *tuʔucho*?" "It is a *tawai*, a changing witch; it is white, with claws, big like a bear. I woke up, but my mother was not home, so I closed the door to the kitchen, and I also closed the window with a latch. But the *tuʔucho* wanted in; he kept scratching on the window, but he could not get in." Little Cilia, saucer-eyed, nods in confirmation. "Our papa says that a *tuʔucho* eats little girls." I am happy to record that TV does not, after all, reign supreme.

When I ask Eus about the *tuʔucho* or *tawai* later, after the little girls have left, she maintains that they are not all that rare. In fact, a *tawai* might have been involved in trying to dig up Venunciana. She is the lumberjack's wife whose death from the measles was the talk of our corner when I first arrived. Eus is not sure it was the measles that killed her. Her husband might have to be blamed because she took sick on the day that Don Panza, the local tanner's son, died of touching a high-tension wire on the highway out of Chetumal. Venunciana's husband went to the *velorio*, the wake, and that was careless, for death was contagious. If you went to a dead person and then home to someone who was sick, that person would die. Finally, getting to the *tawai*, she adds, "I was coming from the mill and stopped to talk to the *camposero* [the cemetery warden], who was weeding the road in front of the cemetery. He said that the week after Venunciana died, something or somebody had tried to dig her up. There was such a big hole next to her [temporary] coffin that the stench of her decaying body was all over. It might have been a dog, or perhaps a *tawai*; they eat the dead, you know." Then she continues, "There was also a child that died recently. The *camposero* found its coffin dug up also. It may have been a *wai*, too, a person who can change himself into an animal." Later, she adds as an afterthought, "By the way, Venunciana's husband did not remember her very long. A week after she was buried, I saw him go to the girls down the road."

JULY 31

Dona Andrea comes to buy some *waya* from Eus, a small green fruit that grows in bunches on a tall tree on her *solar*. Actually, such small purchases are usually undertaken more to have a reason to visit than for the merchandise and are strictly ritualized. First comes the very extensive exchange of information, and then the brief commercial affair. Eus never hesitates to tell the details of Dona Andrea's wasteful lifestyle, and no doubt Dona Andrea has stories ready about Eus, but all that is par for the course, and the two women consider each other friends. And so Dona Andrea immediately launches into an extensive complaint about Don Eduardo, how for a while he was really nasty to her. Things got so bad that she went down on her knees in the kitchen, "and you can see how hard that is for me," she says, pointing to her ample folds and fat legs, "and I asked the Lord for help in my affliction." She finally threatened to go home to Temax if things did not improve. Now Don Eduardo is nicer to her.

Perhaps the whole performance is a political move, countering the rumors that she is going to return to Temax if Don Eduardo's money runs out, also repeated by Eus. She has three married daughters in Temax, but that is not much help. Her misfortune is that her two sons died in infancy. Asking a woman if she has any sons is equivalent to saying, "Don't you have anybody else to take care of you?" The other day an old woman came to Eus's *albarrada* asking for *caridad*. She had on an *ʔipil* stitched together from a flour sack. Eus knew her: she had no sons.

In the end, Dona Andrea asks for a peso's worth of *waya*. Eus brings her a small bunch and does not take the money. Neither of us could know that we had heard the beginning of the end of Don Eduardo's sad story.

Another Visit by Don Victor

Dona Andrea has just left and I have settled down under my blanket sunroof to do some more typing, when I see a blue-shirted man appear in the opening of the *albarrada:* Don Victor. Without stopping off at Utzpak, he had returned to Chetumal, where he heard from his family that I had asked about him, and now he has come all the way back to Utzpak.

He ends up spending the day, reiterating many of the things he had touched on last year. But there is added urgency now, for he feels that we are talking with each other for the last time. We will not see each other again next year, for the end will be upon us, and since it has to come, let us hope that it will come fast. He is telling all his followers that they need to fight for themselves, for the doors are already being locked. As is done by many millenarian groups, who adjust their reasoning about the end of the world to events in present-day Israel, he warns that he has heard on the radio that the Jews have signed a peace treaty and that is the sign. But there will be many disasters before the end. War will come with stealth, as predicted. It will come under a sky of metal and on a soil of iron, as was said about Babylon in Deuteronomy. Eus and Nohoch Felix, who are listening in much of the time, keep nodding when he points to the drought and the plague of caterpillars and ants as other indications that the end is near.

He keeps bringing up many different topics, as though anxious that I should have a review before that final event is upon us. Next year, he says, there will be a world congress convened by the Pope, who is the Antichrist. Following that, there will be a general interdiction: no one would be allowed to preach unless he accepts the papal doctrines or at least is the member of some other recognized faith. Turning to more local concerns, he reminds us that the Apostolics have a presiding bishop. If we accept that Christ is the head of the Church, then that office is Christ's, not of a worldly administrator. The modern Apostolic Church was founded by men, not by God. Religion does not save men, Christ does. We should ask Christ for forgiveness and not pay attention to what others do, such as curse or fornicate.

"Although we live far from each other, I want us all to be united in spirit, as in one container, which will be as the ark."

The Apostolic Church, he continues, was not of Rome, it was of Jerusalem. Moses came for the Jews, and Elias was in charge of the gentiles. Moses did not die, he was guarded for the "wedding." There were thus two temporal churches with one spiritual head, which was Christ, two cherubim and one head, and the spiritual church was called the wedding. Quite generally, Don Victor seems much more at home in the Hebrew Bible than in the New Testament, and I record his idea about Moses "not dying" as simply another one of his rather out-of-the-ordinary ideas. It was a big surprise when I came across a reference to a book entitled *Like unto Moses* (Indiana University Press, 1995) in which James Nohrnberg, a literary critic and teacher of English at Harvard and at Yale, maintains that "the Moses of the Bible . . . is a creation of Israelite literary and scriptural tradition, an ideological construct." With only a second grade education, but guided by his visionary insights, my old friend had intuited something very similar about that famous figure.

The entire Bible, Don Victor continues, has only two words: the origin and the end, just as there are only two principles: the good and the bad. The bad confirms the good, and the good cannot exist without the bad. God's love shows in man being bad. If it were not for the authorities, people would fall upon each other (*"el mundo se comiera"*). The Church is administered by men and subject to men's laws, and that actually constitutes an adulterous relationship. Eventually, according to the Bible, all churches will unite in the Spirit. "I don't want to destroy any groups, I only want all of them to know God. On the promised day, all Gentiles will be together, while all the Jews will be awaiting Elias in Jerusalem. Then will come the single body of Christ."

After a break for the noonday meal, the conversation turns to practical matters. He has been homesteading on *ejido* land near Cuarenta y Dos, but there is a lot of infighting; that is why he has built the home for his extended family in Chetumal. The hurricane blew it away, so he instructed his sons to rebuild it, not even of cement blocks, but of large stones. Those are the kind of buildings that withstand the hurricanes.

He sees things becoming bad in the congregation in Chetumal, too. In 1972, many *hermanos* started smoking pot and deserting the Church. Even Manuel H. was no longer minister. Juan L. and Luis L. have congregations in Chetumal, Dziuche, and Merida. Eus adds that at one time Luis L. came to Utzpak to preach and did not even salute Nohoch Felix, *leti nohoch maac* [the old man]. It was a weighty charge because in Maya, "*nohoch*" does not just mean old, it is also an honorific. "It is a sign that the end is near," is Don Victor's comment, "that there is no tranquillity in the churches. All churches are divided among themselves."

His own groups are located in Chetumal, in Cuarenta y Dos, Chibul, Campeche, Santarita, Uman, Merida, and Utzpak. In Peto, the *hermanos* object to tithing, calling it robbery, although he explained that he needed money to defray the expenses of his travels. So he left them.

He does a lot of preaching by standing on the plaza of a village and using a loudspeaker. One day a young man came up to him and said that he had never heard any preaching of that kind. He was the member of a *pandilla* [a gang] in Mexico City. His kind was everywhere, he said. They would walk up to a man who was dressed well, take all his clothes, and kill him if he offered any resistance. He was not afraid of being shot, and he had many scars to prove it. But he wanted to learn what he, Don Victor, had to say. He had a quick mind and soon knew almost as much as Don Victor's own sons. He was not shy. In Chetumal on Sunday mornings, he would dress well, pick up his Bible, go to a store where maybe they were selling soft drinks, and start preaching. Don

Victor wanted to keep him around, but after two months, the young man said that it was God's will that he should return to Mexico City and preach there.

In Chetumal, Don Victor was holding services in his own home. He also baptized people, for there was no one else to do it "in the name of Jesus Christ because this is how the Apostles did it."

I ask about speaking in tongues. Don Victor has worked out a theory of his own. He thinks that speaking in tongues really means that after being baptized, people should speak in a new manner, for their old language is not capable of expressing spiritual matters. If he has the urge to speak in tongues, he suppresses it by becoming silent, for the Evil One might use him at that moment, for he would not know what he was saying. When the urge passes, he resumes talking.

In one instance, a man told me, "At a service, I spoke in tongues. Next day, I was riding on horseback through the *monte*, when I had the feeling that I should jump, that I could fly." Just think, if he had done it, he would have gotten hurt. It must be the Evil One suggesting such things. It might be an evil spirit of a lower order that might enter a person under such circumstances, sent by Lucifer and acting like the Holy Spirit.

I ask whether he has had any more visions. He says no, only sudden flashes of insight. But sometimes there are disturbing dreams. During one of them, he says, he fell in with a party of marijuana smokers. They were about to kill him so that he would not betray them. When they were about to kill him with a machete, he woke up. In another one, he was walking along and there came a train, and he was afraid that the train would run him over. In still another one, he was standing in front of a line of soldiers, and he was about to be killed. The officer lifted his knife, "but I don't know whether he killed me or not."

We come to the end of the day, and he repeats a suggestion that he had first mentioned last year. He needed someone, he said at the time, perhaps someone like me, who would be able to put all his ideas in writing and make them known to the entire world. Now, he feels, there is added urgency, for the end is so near. He makes it very concrete: "You know where my house is. You are invited to come to my house, I long to unite with you in the spirit."

I realize that this might have been the real reason why he sought me out in such a hurry and try to ward him off as gently as I can, arguing, "The end may not be as near as you think. After all, as you say, God's time is not man's time, and you may have made an error in interpreting the signs. Also, the world is very big, a large part of humanity is not Christian. You would need a man to help you, not a woman."

He sighs, and I am touched by the poetic quality of his rejoinder: "Here I speak in obscurity, and my voice rises only to the trees."

We go into the house for a prayer, and he offers a lengthy oration, asking for a blessing for the house and its inhabitants, for health and enlightenment for Eus and Nohoch Felix, and (very fervently) for my spiritual progress, for an aura of light and a crown of glory. For an irreverent moment I wonder whether he realizes that beneath the cloak of his message, he is wooing a woman?

It looks like there might be a downpour, so for a while after the prayer, he waits around. But the wind carries the clouds away once more. I give him his bus fare, which he has not asked for but gratefully accepts. Eus invites him to come back tomorrow, but we know he will not come. He has said what he had wanted to say; it is time to move on. Soon he will be on the bus again, a peasant among peasants, but instead of going to the market and being invisible to the dominant society, he will continue on his errand of capturing souls, debating some theological point, and warning about the end of the world.

Some Diary Entries—1975

As we get ready to pray with Don Victor, Eus comes into the house looking rather strained. When I go for my *rebozo* to cover my head, I ask her what is wrong.

"*Taak in ta?*," she whispers, I have to shit. She does hold out through the long prayer and disappears afterward. Actually, Nohoch Felix had gone out three times before it had hit her. Both of them are miserable the rest of the day. What had happened apparently is that there was still a little left over from the *pibil wa?*, and they had had that for breakfast. She offered me some too and was rather hurt when I refused. But I always tried my best not to eat anything left over from the previous day. So now, for the first time in history, I am well, and they have themselves economy-size super-diarrhea, which they try to cure alternately with Alka-Selzer and Balsamo de Dr. Castro (ingredients not given). Eus is incredulous. "It could not have been the *pibil wa?!* It was not even sour yet."

AUGUST 1, FRIDAY

Last night I went to the *quincenera* [fifteen-years] celebration, a kind of coming-out party, for a young girl down the street, held in the Presbyterian church. Raquel had invited me and so had her mother, Tomasita, who wanted me to be there because her grandson, San, was going to be *chambelan*, one of the attendants. Eus did not want to go but helped me dress for the occasion. She chose the *?ipil*—wear this new one, I want people to see that you don't have just old ones—pulled the *pici* [the half-slip] down so that the eyelet embroidery showed at the proper length, and draped the *booch* over my shoulders in a graceful arc. Tomasita and I walked down the three blocks to the church because it was cooler there and sat on some stones until the service started. An old gentleman in the white baggy clothes of a peasant, his baby grandson on his arms, joined us, and Eus had done such an expert job of camouflaging me that in the twilight he mistook me for the real thing, especially since I also used all the right polite formulas and projected my voice up to the proper Maya pitch. My triumph was complete when he wanted to know whether I had learned any Spanish yet. Vanity of vanities.

It struck me how urban the ceremony was, a carbon copy of the one I had been invited to in a Catholic church in Mexico City. Only some of older women wore an *ʔipil*. The girl had on a fancy lace hat, a yellow floor-length dress, and long-sleeved gloves. She was sitting in front of the rostrum, flanked by her *padrino* and *madrina,* her sponsors. Her parents and grandfather were ranked proudly on the benches on the right. Six girls in their early teens—all dressed in floor-length blue dresses, their black hair piled in formal curls on their heads and decorated with white artificial flowers with sparkling outlines—and six boys (San the tallest) in white shirts and trousers, were her attendants. They held up sprigs of white gladiolus to form an arch for the processional in and out of the *quincenera* and her party, while one of the church members picked out "Glory, Glory, Hallelujah" on the harmonium. The congregation had no minister of its own, but the parents invited a minister in from Merida, who gave a convoluted, lengthy sermon, mainly about girls having to obey their parents and be grateful. There were prayers spoken, hymns sung, and a singing group from Progreso—a man, a woman in a fancy *ʔipil,* and a girl—performed various musical numbers. At the end, pictures were taken and everyone was invited to a party at the girl's home, but I slipped into Reina's house: I did not trust anybody else's tacos.

AUGUST 2, SATURDAY

I have to go to the village telephone center, located in the bakery, to confirm my flight out of Merida. Offices in Merida do not open before ten, so I have to trudge down the highway at a temperature of 120 degrees plus, when no sensible person would be anyplace but in a hammock in the shade. It gives me a terrible headache, which does not improve when toward noon, Wilma arrives with her brood of seven, who promptly descend on Eus's *waya* tree because they see a bird's nest in it. It is a perfect nest, fit as a model for an illustration in a children's book, complete with baby birds, woven of small twigs a bit hastily, but soft and cozy inside. They knock it down and Jacinto dangles it triumphantly before his grandmother. "Look, *ʔbuela,* what we found!" She nods approvingly, and the children throw the fledglings to the ducks, which eagerly gobble up the babies. I can stand it no longer. "Why do those children kill the birds?" I ask Eus. "But Hermana," she says, exasperated, as though she had read my thoughts on all those other occasions, when I secretly objected to the killings, "those are not nice birds, not like songbirds. They are *pich,* and *ts?el,* and *ca?o,* birds that eat corn." There is no arguing with her. Of course, it occurs to me, as I am stewing in my hammock, don't I insist on the execution of every cockroach in sight? And the other day, when I was exceptionally hungry, didn't I keep mentally slicing up her innocent, appealing, rust-colored pig into juicy portions of expertly smoked Westphalian ham?

I go back to Reina's that afternoon a bit earlier than usual, before the little girls come back from the *telenovela,* because I want to say good-by to Isauro. They have made some changes. There is a new sign above the church door, reading, "Iglesia Apostolica de Jesus Cristo," leaving out the "de la fe en." Eus told me that they used the cement blocks that we helped collect to build an outhouse when Hermano Alf was minister, which irked her no end.

Both Isauro and his wife are at home. Juanita is combing the hair of one of her daughters, then she goes out and brings in some *waya.* "Offer some to the Hermana, too," she says to her husband. I figure I had some at Eus's, but a few more certainly won't hurt me.

Freely, Isauro answers all my questions. Yes, Luis L. is still paying all his pastors. Of course it is not enough; he himself works as a day laborer at whatever jobs he can find. Eduardo N. is no longer a minister but has a good income as a collection agent for a firm in Chetumal; he is giving Nicolas L. money to help support his family of seven. Attendance in Utzpak is irregular, sometimes one (family) group comes, then another. Their biggest handicap is that they do not have enough ministers.

August 3, Sunday

Well, this time the *waya* does do me in. I hardly make it from Reina's to Eus's chamber pot, cutely called in Maya "the peeking through the trees." Wilma surveys my limp form in the hammock, remarking sympathetically, "*Mina?an muuc tech* [You don't have much energy]." That gets me back to the typewriter, but when she notes that I can hardly finish a sentence before running again, she wants to know, "*Ba?ash ts?aac a wucic?* [What medicine are you drinking?]" What indeed? Dr. Castro's Balsamo, peppermint tea, streptomycin, Lomotil, and that last resort of Mexicanists, enterobioformate. Finally, at noon, all systems stop. I hope that they will not resume until I am back home three days later.

There has been no rain in the area since July 24, an impossible situation for the rainy season. A brief shower will not do it. The soil is too porous; the water has to stay on it for a while for it to absorb the moisture. Eus talks darkly about this being a punishment of God visited on humanity and says that according to Don Victor, this is a sign that the end is near. Then this afternoon we are hit by a beautiful, prolonged downpour. When it first starts, we all rush out to carry things in: Eus spreads her nearly dry wash on the beams and No-hoch Felix brings in his freshly washed hammock. Nothing is worse than sleeping in a moist hammock. After that we all settle in the house. Eus sits by the door and counts out bunches of *wayum* for sale. Oscar is practicing his sales pitch, snapping his fingers and calling out, "*Wayum, caballeros, wayum!,*" but the rain is still too heavy for him to go out and sell on the baseball field across the road. Wilma is resting in a hammock, Eus and I in another one. Nohoch Felix sits in his, strumming a hymn on his guitar. Wilma strums along while Eus dozes off. Naked little Elias sits on a footstool. He grabs his grandfather's harmonica and blows delicate little sounds. Adela and Marjelia, 15 and 13, have spread a burlap sack on the floor to lie on and are whispering to each other. Jacinto sleeps in the dark shadows of the oval end of the house, while Oscar jumps around with a cardboard box on his head. Elias thinks that looks like great fun and screams until he gets it from him. He soon gets tired of bumping into bundled forms in hammocks, so he steps out into the rain on the high threshold to catch some of it in his box as it drips off the palm-frond roof. Consuelo hands him a plastic cup when the box begins to come apart, and with big gulps, Elias drinks the rainwater. Wilma asks for a Bible, but it is too dark to read and she gives up. A leak develops in the roof. Nohoch Felix places a burlap sack under the drip at the height of the beams to protect the hammocks. There is a lull in the cloudburst and the children all gather at the door to watch the ducks splashing in the puddles and the baby piglets burrowing in the fresh mud.

The rain has almost stopped and the boys are impatient to go and sell the *wayum.* Eus practices with them. A bunch costs 25 centavos, so if you sell three bunches, how much do you charge? If they give you a peso, how much change do you have to give back? Soon they have it down pat and rush off. It is the only arithmetic they get right now; with Ruben working on the ranch, they have no way to get to school. But arithmetic is difficult for adults, too. There is the curious custom of the women buying something, paying for it, and then buying the next item. Saves on addition. Nohoch Felix cannot do any addition in writing either. It has become a regular ritual that he brings me a list of the items he bought on his daily shopping trip for Eus and asks me to add it up for him. If he does not have the right change, Eus makes outrageous fun of him, saying that this *nino* [this little boy] can always be cheated. He comes back at her by countering that she could do her own shopping and that if he is not going to be given any better treatment, he is going to go and work his *col* tomorrow. They laugh together, and he slaps her back.

A bare twenty minutes later, Jacinto comes back waving 4 pesos and calling "*ʔBuela, ʔbuela,* look!" He has sold all the *wayum* to the ballplayers and their spectators. Proudly, he hands Eus the money.

In the afternoon, I go to Reina's place to do some packing, then stretch out in my hammock to rest. My present hammock is the best I have ever had. When I arrived, Eus had said, "You don't have a hammock." "I don't?" "No, you don't. I sold it." "You did?" By now I know that something good is coming. "I sold it and made you a new one. I know you like color, so I took all the many leftovers I had, and I wove it very tightly, *hach pim*, not like the ones that Reina sells in Merida, where the eyes are so wide you can fall through."

And *pim* it was. I could pass my hand over it and it gave the feeling of a soft, very resilient cloth. I was once more enjoying it, luxuriating in its feel, stretching this way and that, lying first lengthwise and then diagonally and finally straight across. Tired from my intestinal upset, I must have dropped off to sleep, for seemingly from afar, and then more closely, I heard Reina's very loud voice, saying, "No, you can't come in, Santiago is not home. Go to your place, just go down the street, you can't come in." A man's rather thick voice says, rather tipsily, "Where is Santiago? In Chetumal?" "No, he went to Merida. Now go on, you can't come in." Then she comes in. That was Santiago's *companero*, she explains; he gets drunk all the time, then he comes in and talks with Santiago, and Santiago will talk with him and calm him down. Good thing that Santiago was in Merida selling hammocks, or he would be right there with him getting drunk too.

Eus, Wilma, and the children arrive at Reina's place. Elias is asleep in Consuelo's arms. We go to Don Eduardo's for a service. Little Elias is placed in a hammock, and Ruben conducts the service. He also briefly speaks in tongues.

After the service, Andrea begins talking to Eus very excitedly. It seems that before I woke up, there was a conversation between Reina and Santiago's *companero* out in the street that Andrea overheard. He wanted to come into the house to Reina, and he pulled her hand confidentially like this (Andrea demonstrated), and Reina kept saying, "No, you can't come in because Chichi Felix [that is what her children call me] is there." Now I also understand the scene we saw from a distance as we entered for the late morning service, when about a block away, the wife of Santiago's *companero* was screaming at him, saying that he should get the hell out of her house, that she was not going to tolerate his running around to other women's houses anymore. According to Eus, Reina told her that that woman was insanely jealous, she had called her a *quita esposos* [a husband snatcher] when all she had done was feed their pigs when they were gone, and that in Santiago's company.

There is another rain in the afternoon, but Eus does not come into the main house. Instead, she is busy ironing in the kitchen. She wants me to take all my *ʔipiles* home dry and well ironed. I sit on a footstool beside her and we talk. She has a nice new flatiron, which is breaking at the handle. She noticed it lying on the ground in front of one of the houses as she was going to the market. She observed it for several days, but no one picked it up, so she assumed that whoever had owned it no longer wanted it. "Perhaps she has an electric one now." So she picked it up and brought it home. We talk about the various embroidery patterns while she busily walks back and forth between her fireplace and the table, using one flatiron while the other one is heating up on the *comal,* and each time applying some stearine to the ironing surface to make it slide better. My *ʔipiles* represent nearly ten years, and we note that each successive year the embroidery has become looser, the stitches larger and fewer. I have one that I bought on the market in Merida in 1966, when I was just a visitor to the world of the Maya, not yet a fieldworker. Eus wants Consuelo to copy the pattern, but the girl will not do it. "Look at all those stitches," she said. Wilma can start a cross-stitch pattern going around the neck and the bottom edge of a *ʔipil* at nine in the morning, when it is too hot to do anything else, and by the time the day has cooled, about 4 o'clock, she has it ready for sale. It is the tourist trade, Eus says. It is the same thing with the hammocks. The more they are traded, the looser they get. The tourists, after all, do not know any better. She quotes Reina as saying that she sometimes tells a customer that it is a hammock of five sections, when in reality it is only one of four. Another way to save on thread when making a hammock for sale is to make it shorter. Reina's have become about as short as the trade will bear. That way either your head or your feet rest on the unwoven section, which makes the hammock uncomfortable and also less durable. By the way, I am amazed at how early kids learn to weave. Lupita has made a hammock for her doll using the legs of the table as the upright loom, and now she is helping her mother weave, as long as the weave has not gone up too high.

In the afternoon, there is another rain, so we get to Reina's house rather late for the *despedida* [my farewell party]. We had talked about whom to invite, Andrea, Tomasita, maybe Raquel and her sister Luz. The latter is one of Reina's favorites because she is so citified, having grown up in Merida. I once asked Tomasita how that came about.

> *Pues,* she said, as you know, I had a number of daughters, and one of them, Raquel, was already able to make tortillas. [She must have been about 8 years old at the time, judging by that.] My husband's mother lived alone in Merida, and she asked him to let her have one of the girls, since we had three at the time, so she would have a companion. So my husband came home and said we would give Raquel to his mother. So we did.
>
> About a month later, my husband went to Merida to visit his mother, and Raquel said that she wanted to come home and see her mother. Her grandmother got angry. She said, "Here I have accus-

tomed myself with this girl, and now she wants to go home. *Pues,* if that is what she wants to do, then I don't want her to come back. Give me another one of your daughters." That is how I came to send Luz. Luz liked it in Merida and did not want to come back to Utzpak, even when her grandmother died. By that time she was already a senorita, and she went to live with one of her aunts, and later she got married in Merida.

On the way over, I buy a large bag of cookies and ten soft drinks and am amazed when we arrive to find that Reina has invited the entire neighborhood and an untold number of kids I have never seen before. My supplies are of course woefully inadequate, especially since Reina's little girls grab at the cookies as if they haven't eaten all day, dunking them into their soft drinks. "Haven't these children eaten yet?" I ask, half in jest, but get no answer.

After the service in Don Eduardo's house, there is a lengthy good-by from the little girls at Reina's before I go to Eus for the night. They remind me for then umpteenth time not to forget their dolls. I usually bring some, but this year I thought panties and dresses would be more important. "I want one with rose-colored clothes," says Lupita. "I with red clothes," calls Cilia, my squeaky little *hetsmec* daughter. And energetic saucer-eyed Fidelita, the youngest, wants a doll *"con un vestidito mollado [morado], con pantaletitas molladas y con calcetines mollados."* I am not sure if I can find everything in lilac—little dress, little panties, little socks—but I know that I had better try.

Eus's house is still crowded with Wilma's family. Wilma has been looking for a house to rent in Utzpak. Eus does not have enough room for her, and she wants to stay in the village, since the clinic has facilities for delivery, charging only 100 pesos. Besides, she wants to be with her mother for the event, as is the custom generally. Ruben has found one, close to the market but it has not been vacated yet, for 150 pesos a month, three times what it would have cost in 1969. An hour after we have settled down in the hammocks and I am halfway to dreamland, Ruben comes and says, "We can get more in." There is a scurry and a flurry as nine people try to find their belongings by the dim, smoky light of the kerosene bottle lamp. Adela cannot be roused and is picked up bodily together with little Elias, who is sleeping with her. The truck Ruben has found is tooting outside. There is a clatter of powdered-milk cans, sacks of corn are dragged along the floor, hammocks are untied and wrapped, and firewood is loaded. Finally all is quiet and I stretch into that wonderful diagonal position that makes me fall asleep instantly. However, within what seems like minutes, there is another commotion. Jose has been on some adventure or other in the village, together with his cousin Samuel, one of Enrique's sons. He arrived from Merida yesterday to pick up a gun his father loaned to Nohoch Felix. Jose can locate nothing and nobody and is finally shooed out to go find his family and his home hammock, while Samuel gets invited into his grandfather's hammock. After the briefest of snoring intervals, there is another alarm: Ruben comes with my *sabucan* containing my new hammock. One of the children had taken it along, and he was sure that by now I was frantic trying to find it. Not having missed it and limp with fatigue, I turn to the other side, which is not easy to do in a swinging hammock. And just as I close my eyes, the family rooster, positioned, I swear, at the exact spot outside the wall where my head is located inside, crows in a bugle voice, "*Tsʔuuuuuuuuu sasta* [It has dawned]." And I, the avowed foe of all killing, am ready and willing to ring his neck and personally expedite him to the stewpot.

Discussion

In the course of the period covered in this section, that is, from 1971 to 1975, the fracturing of the Apostolic congregation became permanent. One element was the continued search for someone who would give a creditable date for the end of the world and the dawning of the millennium, thus the attraction to William Branham and, to a lesser extent, to Don Victor, who garnered only a minimal following due to his strongly intellectual approach and his insistence on divine *sabiduria,* on religious wisdom or science. Another element was the powerful Maya ethnic pride of the Yucatecan ministers, who were offended by the representatives of the regional authority of the Apostolic Church riding roughshod over them and supporting the dominance of the Tabasqueno majority with its ruthless monetary policies.

During the worship services of the various factions, the trance behavior, specifically the speaking in tongues, was not overtly discouraged but rather tacitly abstained from, to the consternation of outside visitors, who knew nothing of "those things that happened at the temple." When away from their home grounds, as when Nohoch Felix visited Tibolom, the need to engage in the behavior immediately asserted itself. As we shall see later, when the opportunity presented itself, this subliminal need would powerfully reassert itself.

The group trance disturbance in Tibolom that Wilma reported requires special consideration. At first glance, we might think of it simply as a kind of copycat event, following in the footsteps of the apocalyptic disturbance in Utzpak. That interpretation, however, will not hold up. The Utzpak congregation was deeply embarrassed about these events and would not even discuss them among themselves. As we know from the official pronouncements of Bishop Gaxiola, quoted above, he was aware only of the brief incident in Merida, where one of the *hermanos* was possessed by God the Father. Even Wilma was only dimly aware of the Utzpak events and no one of the Tibolom

Apostolic congregation knew anything at all about them. Besides, the events in Tibolom came fully three years after those in Utzpak. A comparison of the two disturbances yields a number of significant differences. In Tibolom, it was not triggered by visions capable of being interpreted as indicating the approach of the end of the world and the millennium; there was no suggestion of any date for that event and certainly, there was no charismatic leader giving shape and direction to the behavior.

Yet, very strikingly, there are a number of detailed resemblances. The trance behavior spread through the group and quickly became uncontrollable; a timid teenage girl turned assertive; as a startling paranormal phenomenon, an illiterate woman considered "humble" and ignorant could suddenly read—in Utzpak hearing knocking on the roof may fit into the same category—and began to attack those apparently not devout enough; Satan appeared in the shape of a horned being; and a man began confessing past sins and started by "cursing." In other words, what is termed "coprolalia" made its appearance, as it did in Utzpak.

So what happened? The service at which the events took place was in a private home, and as usual, such services are attended not only by members of the congregation but also by neighbors who are curious about the Apostolics but shun attending a regular service in the temple because that might be interpreted as a more serious interest. Usually, the uninitiated are in the majority. Trance behavior is a genetically transmitted ability; it is very easily "awakened," which gives the impression that it is "contagious." Wilma suggested that once more, as in Utzpak, there was an attack of the "Adversary," which was successful because none of those present had been baptized. I think her suggestion has merit in the sense that trance behavior needs to be ritually channeled, which process had not yet been internalized by most of those present.

The puzzlement, however, is all of those striking details which the two events have in common. As I noted very early on in my research (see Goodman 1972a), trance behavior is internally structured, just as any other biopsychological process are. It is not haphazard; the similarities I have pointed out are built in, and we would know more about them if there were more reliable eyewitness reports such as Wilma's available in the literature on these spontaneously occurring disturbances.

5. January 1977

Arrival

After suffering with attacks of insects and excessive heat and moisture for a number of fieldwork seasons, I decide that I will try the Yucatan in the dry season. So instead of returning to the Yucatan in June or July of 1976, I return in January 1977, making for an absence of a year and a half. I gather various gifts to take, such as packages of needles (which always rust in the hot and wet climate) for Eus, Vaseline for Nohoch Felix, aspirin for both of them, baby dolls for Reina's little girls, and, since I planned also to go to Chetumal and visit Nina there, a package of little trucks for her oldest son, Freddy.

Now I once more assemble cotton panties, ʔipiles of many different designs, tried-and-true sandals, and "camphophenic," a tried-and-true medicine against insect bites. I am not quite sure whether Yucatan is as free of insects in January as I have been led to believe. It is like getting together the pieces of an old, well-beloved uniform. On top of the pile I place my comb, a gift from Eus. It was given to her by her son Enrique. He sells combs, nail polish, and other small articles on the market in Merida. Touching the comb carries with it a gentle joy, though tinged with worry. In the handful of letters that I've received in the intervening time, remarks about Eus not being well are a constant refrain. Nina came to Utzpak from Chetumal to give birth. Her new little daughter was given the name Isabel.

The letters have been written both by Nohoch Felix and by Reina. Apparently, the conflict between Eus's extended family and the congregation in the fold of the L. brothers continues. On June 30, 1976, the L. brothers organized a ministerial retreat in Utzpak. Nohoch Felix had always enjoyed taking part in such events, but his only remark now was that the L. camp followed a false doctrine. Instead of going to the temple for the services, Eus's family apparently organized their own rituals in Don Eduardo's house. Late in August, Wilma and her husband bought a house in Utzpak, and from then on the family held their services there.

Two tragic events held center stage in many of the letters. Reina wrote in September 1976:

> I experienced a terrible blow. My little girl is no longer alive. She had an awful pain, and being as tiny as she was, she was not able to resist the illness. It was so rapid a disease that overcame her; she could not cope with it. God took her away. But perhaps he will give me another little girl. After the

death of my father-in-law, in January, losing the child was a fearful double blow.

Nohoch Felix also reported Don Eduardo's death, giving the date as January 21, 1976. Dona Andrea, he wrote, left him and he died because of a broken heart.

As I leave Columbus today, the temperature is well below zero degrees. From the plane I see the land covered by snow all the way to Atlanta. It is so beautiful how the mountains are etched in black and white. I have on a woolen turtleneck, sweater, and slacks. My lighter clothes are in my Japanese handbag, which the man at Aviateca insisted on checking through to Yucatan. I must somehow accomplish changing into a dress before seeing Eus, for she might be shocked to see me in pants.

In New Orleans, I change to a flight on Guatemalan Airlines. This gate area is really steerage, with worn seats and linoleum tiles that are not even swept. The "Pink Panther" jet, a kind of bus that circulates between New Orleans, Merida, Guatemala City, and Mexico City and back to New Orleans, is painted pink. Our flight is an hour late. Once at the airport in Merida, I do not see Eus. I have her paged twice, but no result. I walk through the airport and ask if anyone has seen her, but no one has noticed any mestiza, which is not surprising because the passengers are city people who make it a habit of not "seeing" the peasants.

It is hot and muggy. How come? It is supposed to be hot and dry right now. I go to the ladies' room and change into an ʔipil. Finally, I give up and take a cab to the Hotel Margarita, my usual stopover.

Before going to bed, I reach Nohoch Felix by telephone, in the village. Eus came to the airport and, not encountering me, is spending the night with Don Agapito, her brother. Nohoch Felix will come for me in the morning.

Poor Eus, she must be as exasperated as I am. Here I am alone in this small hotel room with its dirty walls and clammy bed, humid and cold, instead of lolling in a comfortable hammock someplace talking with Eus.

JANUARY 13, THURSDAY
Shortly after 9:00 A.M., Nohoch Felix arrives, all smiles, *abrazos* and a peck on the cheek. He has a horse-drawn buggy waiting for me. He knows I love that. Eus will not let me use them because she thinks they are too expensive.

We go to the new market which the government has had built in an old convent school. It is cool and picturesque with its arches and is shaded by live oak trees. There is Eus at the market, and everyone laughs affectionately about our joyous reunion. I cannot help being worried, though, because she looks so gaunt and she tells me that she has trouble swallowing her food and keeps bringing up phlegm. But soon we talk of other things.

Nohoch Felix takes us to where the Utzpak taxi is waiting for passengers. El Negro is not the driver because he was tragically drowned with his wife, 15-year-old daughter, son, and two grandsons. "*Otzil maac* [poor man]," Eus keeps saying. "Remember how he used to like to tease you, calling out long Maya phrases and laughing if you couldn't think of the right answer?" It seems El Negro and his family went out from the port at Izamal in a small boat and got out of the boat to swim. His brother warned him not to go out that day but El Negro kept saying, "*Cosh shimbah* [Let's have fun]." They got into an eddy current and were all dead within minutes. It was the daughter's celebration of her fifteenth birthday and a kind of coming-out fiesta was to be the next day. They said she went back into the water after escaping the current to rescue her mother and then drowned. There was talk about the fact that before this tragedy happened, a neighbor had a vision. He saw many people and cars around El Negro's house. But then when he went to see what was going on, there was nothing there. El Negro left two surviving sons, an adult one, who now operates his father's thriving taxi business, and an 8-year-old. The latter now lives in Merida with his mother's sister because his older brother's wife refused to feed him.

Other stories of drowning are recalled in connection with the tragedy of El Negro's family. Eus recalls a drunk who went to the cenote and jumped in. He jumped in and then came back up again. Then he jumped in and bobbed up again. Then he said, "Alright, this is the last time." So he jumped in again and it was the last time. He did not come back up again. Several days later, his putrefying body bobbed to the surface of the cenote.

Death of Don Eduardo

We begin our journey to Utzpak. On the way, I mention that Reina wrote about the death of her baby. Eus is unsympathetic; "She was too busy sewing clothes and neglected the baby. That is why it died." Then, Eus asks me whether it is true that I am sending money to Reina. I say that I never have and can see no reason why I should. She tells me that Reina is spreading it around that I had sent them the money with which they built the addition to their house. It was my room, she quoted her saying, and whenever I would come to the village, they would take their hammocks out of it and I could move in. My conjecture is that Reina and Santiago had a source for funds that they did not want to reveal and that I served as the convenient explanation. I had intended to go that same evening to see Reina, but decide against it. She can wait. Once at Eus's house, I am home, and I do not want to interrupt the mood.

After we have had our bath and something to eat, Wilma comes visiting with all of her children (except Jose, who is away working), including her little one,

Rebecca. Rebecca is homely, like her father, but coy and cuddly. Nohoch Felix gets out his harmonica and starts playing for her and she begins to dance; everyone claps for her and laughs.

JANUARY 14, FRIDAY

Eus gives me further details of Don Eduardo's death, which happened a year ago next week. It all had to do with money. She says that in 1974, Don Eduardo found that the money he had left from selling his ranch had suddenly dwindled alarmingly in his *baul*. Someone was stealing from him.

Toward the end of the dry season in 1975, Don Eduardo and Dona Andrea went to Merida to see his sister. She had been sick for several weeks and was not expected to recover. When they came home, Don Eduardo saw a powdered-milk can in the street that he thought looked familiar. He rushed to the place where he had buried half of his money and found it was dug up and his can was gone. He went to Santiago to confront him. "The pigs must have rooted it out," Santiago shrugged, "you know how hungry they are in the dry season."

"But the money. Where is all the money?" asked Don Eduardo.

"Of course the pigs ate it," said Reina. "What else?"

Don Eduardo and Dona Andrea searched all over the *solar* and the street, but found not a single shred of any peso bill. The only money Don Eduardo had left was 200 pesos.

Eus felt that from the start, Don Eduardo had mismanaged his affairs. He should not have sold his ranch.

Where could Don Eduardo have gone at that point? I ask Eus.

Eus responds, "He could not have gone to his older son, because they had quarreled. Besides this son hardly made enough to feed himself, since he was not married and had to pay for his tortillas and for his washing. Santiago said that he would give his father food but he would not take care of Dona Andrea. She ate too much. Dona Andrea had two sons, but both of them died as babies. So she had no one to go to. She did ask her married daughter in Temax, but she said, 'For that you found yourself a donkey, so he can support you. I certainly won't do it.' And of course she was right, because only the sons have an obligation to take care of their parents." I recalled the constant refrain of Dona Anita, who regularly came to Eus's gate and asked for *caridad*. Eus often invited her into the *solar* and gave her some soup. If only I had a son, she would say.

"What would you do if something like this happened to you?"

"In the first place, Nohoch Felix and I both work. He still goes to the ranches, although he is too old to do his own *col*. I have my animals, my chickens and my ducks, and I go to the highway and find used cans and plant many seeds, and Nohoch Felix knows how to graft fruit trees. We have much nursery stock to sell. Unless you are blind and lame, you can always do something like that. And if I need cash, I go to Merida and my three sons. They know how hard we worked to raise them. I knock on their door, and I say, "I have come to collect." They laugh and never let me go empty-handed. The oldest son gives me money and he does not care if his wife sees it. The second one is the same way. And the third one does it when the woman he lives with is not looking."

In 1973, Santiago went to his father and said that he wanted to stay in the house on Don Eduardo's property. He liked living in a *mamposteria* house and on that building lot, but all he could hope to build was a mud-and-wattle hut with a tar-paper roof. He would pay for the house, if Don Eduardo was agreeable. Don Eduardo was quite relieved because it meant that instead of money always going out, something would be coming in also. Santiago paid 400 pesos down. Reina was making some money then weaving hammocks for a woman the government had sent to stimulate this cottage industry in Yucatan. So that was why Santiago was able to pay something on the house. But after that he kept dragging his feet. He said he would pay the other 500 pesos later, maybe next year. However, when 1974 came around, he still had not paid it. He said times were bad, that Reina's shoulders hurt from all the weaving, that the government was paying only 20 pesos for each hammock body. How was he going to feed his family on that? He had been reduced to cutting firewood in the *monte* for sale. This was stupid; the government had forbidden such cutting, except for household use. He was caught and had to pay a fine. How was anybody going to get ahead that way?

Soon afterward, however, Santiago bought a truckload of tile and had his dirt floor covered with a tiled one. Where did the money come from, the neighbors asked among themselves? At the same time Don Eduardo found that his money had suddenly dwindled alarmingly in his *baul*. Someone was stealing from him. Santiago maintained that the same thing had happened to him also. He had the 500 pesos ready to give to his father because he had been able to sell a number of hammocks in Cancun, the new tourist playground on the Yucatan coast. The tourists paid good prices; they were easy to cheat because they had no idea what anything was worth. But then one day he had come home and there were only 400 pesos in the wardrobe. They asked a woman in Temax to read the cards for them. She said the thief was a neighbor of theirs, a fair-skinned woman living on the same street. She was being consumed by her bad conscience right now and was about to return the money. All that was needed was for Reina to light four candles and to pray four Lord's Prayers. Reina did that, with her door wide open, so that everyone could see it, but no money was ever returned. (This is a slightly different version of the story Reina told me about this incident.)

Don Eduardo by this time had gotten somewhat tired of the soft life. He played with Santiago's children, but they did not come often. Reina quarreled with Dona Andrea over the use of the well. Dona Andrea maintained that Reina would take her bucket for water and not return it. So Don Eduardo built an *albarrada* between his *solar* and Santiago's section, and Santiago had to have a well blasted on his side. Again the neighbors wondered aloud about the fact that the rim for Santiago's well was of cement, much more expensive than the usual limestone wall other people had. No wonder, they said, that Don Eduardo kept complaining about someone stealing from him. It was obvious who was the culprit.

Tired of going hungry all the time, Don Eduardo decided to move to Temax with Dona Andrea and go to work weeding on a ranch. But he was too old for that, so he got fired. At a loss for what to do, he came back to Utzpak alone. Eus says he was not really sick when he came back from Temax, just weak. He came by her home to ask if Ruben, Wilma's husband, would hold a church service in his home. Ruben could not do it because he usually came home from working on the ranch very late.

The next evening, Dona Juanita happened to see Don Eduardo lying in his *solar*, naked and unconscious. The neighbors took him back into his house and told Reina. He was very sick. Santiago sent word to Dona Andrea that he was just a little sick, so she did not come to see him. The next day, Don Eduardo was visibly sinking, and Santiago took him to the Seguro Social Hospital in Cascahcab. "In that clinic," Eus said, "they don't do anything for people. They just wait till they die." The day after being taken there, Don Eduardo died. When news came of his death, Santiago bought a coffin in Utzpak and paid for it out of the money that he got for a pig. "He spent the money on the funeral instead of spending it on medicine for his father," Eus said. Santiago rented a pickup truck and, with his *companero*, brought his father's body home.

Wilma helped with the funeral and said that when they opened the casket so the children could kiss their grandfather, she noticed that he was wrapped in a white shroud held together with safety pins. She thought they had probably done an autopsy in Cansahcab without telling anybody.

When, a week later, Wilma had to go to Temax to see the doctor, she also dropped in to tell Dona Andrea that Don Eduardo had died. By that time, he had already been buried. No one had bothered to notify her. According to Reina, said Wilma, Don Eduardo left Temax because Dona Andrea had moved to her daughter's home and told Don Eduardo that he should go to his. His illness came very suddenly and had something to do with his heart. And when Dona Andrea came to Utzpak to get the few things she had left behind, Reina would not allow her to enter the house and even refused to allow her to pick up the pictures of herself and Don Eduardo.

Dona Andrea related that Santiago had come to her and had her sign a paper ceding Don Eduardo's house to him. He promised to pay her a small sum for it but never did. She also recalled that Don Eduardo was in the habit of taking sleeping pills. If he still could not sleep, he would take more. Maybe he had taken too many, she thought.

Visit at Reina's House

The morning after my arrival, I finally get it together to walk over to Reina's house. I have hesitated because I know that Reina wants me to move in with her again, as I have done before, and I can no longer see the utility of it. Her circle of friends is no longer recruited from the congregation. I will be socially cut off from information about the developments there. But I don't quite know how to broach the subject without causing Reina undue distress.

When we arrive at Reina's house, I can see another indication that my decision is the right one. There stands Santiago in front of the house with a heavy, gold-plated chain and cross on top of his T-shirt. The Apostolics adamantly opposed the wearing of all jewelry, and he would not have done that as long as Don Eduardo was alive.

I go with Eus, and Reina greets us in a very friendly way and proceeds to take us through her newly refurbished home. Her house is painted pink and her windows are barred. Instead of the lean-to she formerly had for a kitchen, there is now a large airy room with a corrugated tar-paper roof. She now has a butane gas cooking stove and above it a set of shiny aluminum cookware of the kind that the *hermanos* sell on installment. There is also now a separate cabin for showering. The sow is ready to drop her piglets and, as before, the yard is bare. Not a single flower, only a scrawny set of banana bushes of a poor variety because the pigs keep rooting them out since they like to munch on the sweet stalks. Reina has become very heavy; she is nearly bursting out of her dress, which has plastic beads sown around the neck and is dusty with talcum powder.

Reina lets down a hammock for Eus and myself to sit in and once more we talk about the death of the child. She says that the child cried all of the time and the doctors said it was bronchial pneumonia. She seems pretty matter-of-fact about it and I recall Wilma telling me that Reina remarked to the neighbors that it was all right that the baby was dead. "At least now I have more time to work," she said. She weaves two hammocks a week, and she has other women work for her. She puts on the edges only. Santiago goes to Cancun to sell the hammocks there.

The little girls are happy with the dolls and dresses that I brought for them, especially the youngest one, who is very pretty with enormous dark eyes, heavy eyelashes, and the dark complexion and soft rounded features of her father. However, to my horror, I discover that all three of them have the mumps. Reina laughs when I exclaim, "Goodness child, don't rub against me! I have never had the mumps." I don't think it is all that funny. However, one good thing comes from this situation—I now can tell Reina with equanimity that I know mumps is highly contagious and since I have never had it before, I had better stay in Eus's house. To my relief, Reina does not put up any fight.

Keeping Warm

Eus's place in the dry season is wonderful. Eus has acquired a length of garden hose and, with a tub which she and Nohoch Felix keep filling from the well, she waters all of the various plantings of the *sala*, including all their nursery stock. That way her area is as lush now as it is in the rainy season. It is such a relief not to be attacked by the multitude of blood-sucking insects, and even the cockroaches are in short supply. One problem I had not anticipated, however, is the cold nights. The few frigid nights that I had occasionally experienced at Reina's place in years past were of no consequence. Reina would shutter the window and close the two doors. The air would soon smell like warmed-up three-day-old tortillas, but it would be warm and comfortable. But although on the second day at Eus's place the temperature, as always, was a comfortable 90 to 95 degrees, unexpectedly it began to drop soon after sundown. It probably does not go much below 60, but with the wind blowing through all of the cracks and crevices it began to feel like the North Pole. Startled, I put on just about everything I had in my suitcase in the way of warm clothes, but when I get into the hammock I feel it isn't enough. Every strand of the hammock feels as if it were woven from wires of ice. Nohoch Felix has placed a frying pan with glowing embers from the kitchen fire under his hammock, but by 12 o'clock when I wake up icy and with a full bladder, he is shivering as badly as I am and Eus is moaning in her hammock. From then on, I sleep very little, have to use the family chamber pot twice more, and end up putting on even my woolen slacks and turtleneck, which under the circumstances affords little additional comfort. I do, however, make one useful discovery—Eus always gives me "my" pillow, which she calls my companion. She made it for me herself the first year I was here when she noticed how uncomfortable I was in the hammock without something to put my head on. I have long since stopped using the pillow for that purpose. I have gotten used to sleeping in the hammock diagonally as everyone else does and the pillow now gives me a crick in the neck. However, I always accept it anyway to please her. During this night, I end up stuffing it under my butt and that center of my anatomy, now properly insulated from the cold radiation of the cement floor, stays warm throughout the remainder of the night. It is, in fact, the only part of me that is content.

After two more nights of suffering, I finally eat crow and observe what I should have done in the first place, how it is that Eus is not cold. I discover that she does not just cover herself the way I have been doing it. She swaddles herself, as it were. In other words, she puts one corner of her square cotton blanket on her head and folds the other two corners around herself, so that the diameter of the blanket is in her middle,, and then she steps into the hammock. Not only that, Eus also has her own special refinement; she lines the blanket with a freshly washed sheet. That is, she first wraps herself in the sheet, then in the blanket. In that way, in the hammock, the sheet is against her hands and face. I am awkward about it as I try to imitate her, but she helps tuck me in and, swaddled that way and still wearing my turtleneck, sweater, and flannel pajamas, I do not wake up until the new municipal clock strikes three. Even then, I am not really suffering.

Wilma's Place

For quite a while, Wilma had been wanting to move from the ranch, where her husband Ruben was working, to the village. She wanted her children to attend the school in Utzpak and also she wanted to be closer to her mother. She tried to find something to rent but could not find a suitable place for her large family. Then a lawsuit made the move possible. As Nohoch Felix explained, for several years now, the legal daily wage had been 40 pesos for a full day's work on the ranch. Pancho E., Ruben's employer, continued to pay him only 30 pesos and would not increase the wage despite complaints from Ruben. Finally, Ruben went to Licha, a member of the Apostolic congregation in Merida. She worked for a lawyer who, for a considerable fee, set up a legal complaint for him. Pancho E. was drunk and was quite cocky when he went to the law court. He had a silver peso in his pocket. He drew it out and said, "He is not going to get more, not even this peso, than I am paying him." Now, however, under whatever pressure the courts applied to him in Merida, he buckled under. Nohoch Felix did not know the details, but at any rate, Pancho E. was forced not only to pay the legal wage from then on, but also to make restitution for wages lost. The sum was sufficient to pay for a good-sized homestead with three mud-and-wattle houses and a good well. Pancho E. did not fire Ruben, not only because efficient cattle handlers are hard to find but also because he badly wanted to marry Wilma's oldest daughter, Consuelo. Neither Wilma nor Ruben were in favor of this match, though it would have been wonderful for Consuelo, getting her out of poverty and into an affluent household. But Pancho E. drank heavily and Ruben thought it best if Consuelo was no longer on the ranch.

On Friday afternoon, Eus decided that we would go to visit Wilma. She says,

"Wilma lives only two corners away, which, however, will take us nearly an hour to walk." It is a lovely walk; the wide avenues are edged by white *albarradas* and with the rain we have been having, there is a profusion of wildflowers growing in between the smooth backs of the limestone outcroppings. A path, not even a foot wide, has been worn through the vegetation skirting the hunchback stones. Eus walks ahead of me, humming a tune and picking flowers to see how many different ones she can find. I help her locate others, and all the while I ache because of her emaciated condition. The afternoon sun paints light spots on the road through the leaves of the trees.

Wilma's place exhibits her mother's style. There are many well-tended flowers, a cleanly swept yard, a multitude of the useful plants—tomatoes, at least nine different kinds of chili, clumps of bananas, coriander, yucca, a small tree-like plant with leaves reminiscent of mimosa and a long brown root which is edible. It looks like boiled potatoes and is eaten with honey but is hard to digest. I remember what a diarrhea it gave me a few years ago when I ate too much of it. There are also limes, *zeremuyo* and *wayum* (both fruits, the former grows on a tall bush and the latter on a tall spreading tree), and much more. Wilma brings out the *ʔipil* which she has embroidered for me in the intervening time. It is lovely, but she will allow me to pay only 140 pesos for it and even that she thinks is too much, but she excuses the price by noting that embroidery floss has also risen in cost. Wilma and her two daughters, Consuelo and Marjelia, keep the three houses clean and tidy. Chairs are brought out, and while Eus settles in a hammock close to the entrance, we sit outside the front door. Little Rebecca vents her baby anger at me because I don't want to surrender Eus's bouquet to her. Giving up, she sits on a stool and "reads" in the hymnal. Then she comes up to her mother and wants to suck. Wilma still nurses her. "It keeps another one from coming too soon," she laughs, which brings up the topic of contraceptives. Wilma cannot tolerate the pill and they gave her an IUD, which she finds uncomfortable. Nina also received one at the clinic in Chetumal after the birth of her third child but it fell out, so she became pregnant again, mainly to please Desi. Eus disapproves of Nina having another child because living expenses are going up. "Desi wants to prove that he is potent," she teases. Then she quips, "He is potent for making children, but not potent for taking care of them." After a brief orange dusk, the darkness of the tropical night takes over. The girls light the Coleman and Wilma and her son Jacinto begin singing hymns. I am asked to record. "You can play the tape to the *hermanos* in your hometown," Wilma suggests. Her voice and Jacinto's blend in beautiful harmonies. Rebecca has settled in Consuelo's arms. Consuelo is so much a second mother to the little girl that when she went to be with Nina in Chetumal to earn some money Rebecca fell ill out of homesickness for her, and so Consuelo had to come home.

Finally it is time for us to go home and the children take us the short way through the village. Consuelo lights the way with the Coleman, and Marjelia carries the baby. We have to climb the *albarrada* in the back, and at that point Jose arrives from work on the ranch. He makes a man's wages now and at 18 is a tall and handsome youth. He reminds me of Michelangelo's David, with his curly hair over a low brow and his muscular body. He greets me with a peck on the cheek. When I make a remark about how strong and handsome he is, Eus tells of how he has taken up with the homosexuals in the village who pay him with beer. She thinks he plays the woman's part for them. He leads a wild and roving life, getting drunk and staying out late at night, but he does show up for work in the morning, for Wilma says she will throw him out if he does not work. He likes women, too, though, and would perhaps get married except that Wilma does not want him to marry a *mundana*, a woman of the world; that is, a woman who is not a member of the congregation. With the congregation shrinking to only three families, that means a rather narrow range of choices for Jose.

Visit to the Doctor

All night long the procession of noisy men continued down the street toward the cathouse. This morning, we see the girls leave. One of them is rather blonde; she has a blue bandana on her head and pulls the corner of it over her face, looking rather like an American coed. The other one is very much a Yucatecan girl, curvy everywhere, long black hair. A few steps behind them there is the *padrote* (the pimp). Eus remarks, "1,120 pesos per trick is not a bad income. It should be enough for beans." She laughs.

There is a gentle rain this morning. You can hear it on the thatch of the roof. When I go out to the outhouse, there is a heavy brown fog. It is not at all typical of the dry season. Ruben is not going to have a service for us this morning, so we are in no hurry to get done. There is light-hearted banter between Eus and Nohoch Felix. Eus wants him to irrigate the tomatoes, the trees, and the many chile plants. Instead, he sits on the threshold reading the Bible and whittling his toenails. I tell them about a former student of mine by the name of Chuck who I have invited to Cuyamungue to work for me, for moderate pay, of course. The best working time in New Mexico is from about sunup to about 9 A.M. in the summer. After that, it gets too hot to do anything outside. In theory, Chuck was completely willing to work on the roof at that time. In practice, however, he always worked on his pimples instead until 9. "I have this fetish about my face," he would say. And then, of course, he wanted to have breakfast. Eus immediately picks up on it. "So where is the kid?" she says. "Probably putting cream on his face like Chaak." Nohoch hears us talking, so he comes to the open door and Eus tauntingly repeats what she has said and slaps his bare chest playfully with a wet towel she is about to hang out to dry. We decide to go to see the doctor about Eus's condition. We finally start for the doctor at 10:30 in the morning. He works in the government clinic in Temax, but he also has a large private clientele and is said to be quite good. However, the house where he sees patients is still closed, so we go across to settle in with one of Eus's friends who sells soft drinks. She wants me to tell her about my work in the United States, about prices there, and about my children. She has a small haberdashery and we buy some elastic, so she gives us a present of some soft drinks, some *camotes,* and a Mexican candy bar. Finally, we go to sit on a bench in the park. When the new town clock strikes 12, we go back to the office of the physician. A man we don't know is sweeping out the empty room, which is divided in half by a curtain. He looks like a butcher and I hope fervently that he is not the physician. A small tarantula crawls out from under the curtain and the only other patient, an old woman, tells him imperiously to sweep that out too. It is dangerous. Since he complies, I guess he is not the physician. She is the first one to disappear behind the curtain. We are called in. That part of the room is bare also, except for an old desk and a cot to one side. I stand toward the back to be inconspicuous. The doctor is a ladino of sallow complexion. He is a glob of blubber, making a strong contrast with the local Mayas, with a huge diamond ring on his right ring finger above the wedding band. He seems quite competent, judging from his questions. He rules out an ulcer, but apparently he is not aware of the linguistic difficulties. He has the usual irritating condescension for the Maya villagers, which is evident in his questions. It bothers me, but Eus does not even seem to notice. "Does she note any signs of faulty digestion in her excrement?" he wants to know. It sounds like a textbook quotation. I should like to translate the question into Maya. It seems so simple to say it that way: *Bish a wilic a tal*—how do you see your shit? But I don't want to irritate him. So she answers with the stereotypical, "*Pues,* regular." I'm sure she did not know what he was talking about. But he does let her tell him about her complaints. His diagnosis is reassuring. He thinks that since her teeth are in deplorable condition, this has caused an infection and irritation in her esophagus and stomach. She should have her teeth pulled, what is left of them. This, he thinks, will take care of the problem. He prescribes an antispasmodic, some Vitamin C, and six ampules of an antibiotic. The visit with the physician does not cost anything—it is paid for by the government— but we pay for the medication. Eus is not worried about the antibiotic shots. "Consuelo has learned to give shots," she says. I note in passing that no physician is considered to be competent unless he prescribes some shots. We buy the medication from the doctor's assistant, who carefully enters Eus's name and the medications into a ledger. The prescription costs close to 100 pesos. We go over to the dentist, who also has office hours on Sundays. He is young and personable, says he took over the practice from his father, and at least dispenses with the irritating (to me) way of the city dwellers in their treatment of the peasants. He agrees to pull Eus's teeth and make her a denture for 3,400 pesos (approximately $170), which I agree to take care of. I leave a down payment, and in return, he pulls two of Eus's teeth without any anesthetic. She is terribly brave about it.

We rest for a bit on the bench in the plaza and Eus takes one of the antispasmodic pills. It immediately gives her relief. She says, "I was really sure that I was going to die." And then she starts teasing, "You would come to the Yucatan and you would go to the cemetery and cry." But I remember from past visits to the cemetery that the bones of the dearly beloved are cleaned and stored in a cardboard detergent box. I tell her I would rather postpone the romantic event.

The medication that the doctor gave Eus makes her feel better very quickly, and so we decide to go to the cabinetmaker. Nohoch Felix had gotten some samples of wood from him that I wanted. He has lovely lumber from the Peten, the rainforest to the south of here, with intricate color. Some of it is pink, some brown on the outside, the inner layers lemon yellow or marbled black and gray or chocolate brown. The cabinetmaker had given the pieces to Nohoch Felix for free but had asked to have his picture taken in return. We ask in the *tortilleria* located in front of the homestead on the street if he wants to have his picture taken now. We are told by the women of his household who work there that he is drinking with his friends and cannot be disturbed. We see him through the back door of the *tortilleria;* he is sitting with some other men around a table in the yard, surrounded by tools, tree trunks, saws, and assorted pieces of lumber. In the afternoon, we are finally admitted to the presence of the cabinetmaker and I take the pictures of him and his wife and some of the other members of the family.

Fragmentation of the Congregation

Sunday does not seem right without going to the service, I remark that evening. Eus's answer points out the problems the fragmentation of the congregation represented for her. "Wilma took her children to Tizimin," she said. "The congregation there remained loyal. But to whose service could I go here?"

"How about Pedro N.?" I asked. This preacher, a cabinetmaker by trade, had attracted quite a following at the north end of the village, where he held open-air services. His attitude toward the insurrection was unknown.

"Besides," Eus said, "I would not go to his service anyway. He mistreats his children and beats his wife." According to the old rules, he was not even qualified to preach, having been promoted only to *obrero,* or worker. It was also known that he did not conform to the orders of the (central) church in Villahermosa. They decreed that he was not qualified to baptize, but he said he would do it anyway.

One of Pedro N.'s followers was a woman by the name of Julia. She had some money because she and her husband had owned a small ranch. The two of them held a service in Don Fulgencio's house; Pedro N. and Julia collected the offerings. But Ruben and Nohoch Felix decided not to attend.

In January of 1976, Nohoch Felix noted in his copybook that Pedro N. had had a big problem. Julia had stolen a turkey and invited everybody to a service; she served the turkey afterward. Lots of people came to the service but did not know that the turkey was stolen. They all ate it. Later, Pedro N. found out it was stolen. Some man saw the feathers and recognized that it was his turkey. They all had to appear before the *presidente municipal,* even Don Fulgencio. "Even you steal turkeys, Don Fulgencio?" the *presidente* asked him. "*Ay carrajo,*" said Don Fulgencio. He was hugely embarrassed. They had to repay the turkey's price in three installments.

In addition to such homegrown efforts, disparate missionizing efforts from the outside targeted the village. Sometimes the source was not obvious. Thus, Eus told of a faith healer sent by Luis L. to attract people to the temple. He "came from Guadalajara in a mini-bus. He cured by the laying on of hands. He stayed for three days." Reina went just to see what he was doing.

"She wanted to know if I had gone too, but I did not, for Barrera and his Branhamists also dropped in for evangelizing visits. They preached for four nights and offered communion. Their temple was at Alvio's house. No one from Utzpak attended their services, only outsiders," Eus said. According to Nohoch Felix, they maintained that they needed no bishops. Damning their services, they did not testify to the Lord, nor did they sing any hymns. "And they had no joy," said Nohoch Felix. I had written to the Branham missionary organization in Jefferson, Indiana, concerning their work in the Yucatan and was told, to my bemusement, that they ministered "principally only to the Spanish."

Despite all of these distractions, the faction of Luis L. continued to be stable. According to the records of Nohoch Felix, Luis L. came to Utzpak repeatedly to discuss the matters of the congregation with Isauro, who was still in charge, but he did not hold a service. On April 7, 1976, Ruben, Nohoch Felix, and Chan Felix went to a reunion in Villahermosa, Tabasco. There were about eighty people present, and there were four days of services, with Rufina de la Cruz, the Merida minister (of the central church) officiating. Then, on June 26, 1976, Luis L. also convened a ministerial reunion to be held at his power base in Utzpak. In his chronicle, Nohoch Felix enumerated the doctrinal aberrations of the independents. "They have no faith," he maintained. "How do you know?" I asked. "It is obvious: they left that word out of their new name! They have no peace to greet each other with—'*Paz de Cristo*,' Christ's peace. They simply say '*Ola*, Hermano' like ordinary people do. And now they dance!" When I pressed him further on this startling point, he knew no details. "You'll have to ask Wilma," he said.

And Now They Dance

Nohoch Felix is very proud of the fact that he kept a record of church events in my absence. In Merida, he says, Luis L. now holds services in his mother's home. It is always full. Occasionally, he comes to Utzpak to talk to Isauro and to bring him his pay.

And of course, Wilma knows more of the dancing. "It was Luis L.," she tells, "who brought the innovation, the dance, to the congregation in Utzpak from Guatemala."

> They came to B. to hold a service and they danced all night, forming a circle. They kept repeating a particular *coro* [a longer hymn than a *corito*]:
>
> *Yo le alavo con el corazon,*
> *Yo le alavo con mi voz.*
> *Y si me falta la boca,*
> *Yo le alavo conlos pies,*
> *Y si me faltan los pies,*
> *Yo le alavo con los manos.*
> *Y si me faltan los manos,*
> *Yo le alavo con el almal*
> *Y si me falta el alma,*
> *Es que ya me fui con el.*
>
> I will praise him with my heart,
> I will praise him with my voice.
> And if my mouth fails me,
> I will praise him with my feet.
> If my feet fail me,
> I will praise him with my hands.
> If my hands fail me,
> I will praise him with my soul.
> And if my soul fails me,
> It is because I am already with him.

Chetumal Once More

Eus's sister-in-law, Sylvia, likes to travel, and when Eus and I decide to visit Eus's daughter Nina in Chetumal, I invite her to come along. She is so excited about the trip that she takes the 3 A.M. bus out of Merida and arrives at Eus's homestead just as we are finishing breakfast. Eus hears the scraping of the boards barricading the opening in the *albarrada* and walks down the path to help Sylvia, who with her tiny stature—she is barely 4 feet, as are so many Maya women—has problems negotiating the high steps of the entrance. Besides, her *sabucan* is heavy with her hammock, several fresh *ʔipiles,* and a rusty tin can with a bright bougainvillea from Don Agapito's nursery for Eus's garden. Sylvia hits the ground talking. She got a letter from her daughter, who works as a seamstress in Los Angeles. "That American pays her very little, but what can you do when you are there illegally?" Her son Pedro has brought home an excellent report card, and she suspects that Agapito has another girlfriend. She found "one of those little rubber shirts in the trash can, you know what I mean?"

Wilma joins us, bringing along her two youngest, Elias and Rebecca. Eus sends Nohoch Felix to catch her fat hen, an American breed described as double-chested, *doble pechuga,* that she wants to prepare for the trip. "And you still have not shaved!" she scolds. Nohoch Felix calls from the barnyard that the pig has gotten loose. Everyone crosses through the house in pursuit of the pig, which keeps eluding him, until one of Nohoch Felix's hunting dogs hangs on to its hind legs, but not before it bites the head off one of Eus's small ducks. Then everyone settles down. Nohoch Felix kills the chicken, which Eus proceeds to scald and pluck, while Wilma prepares the duck for Rebecca, and Sylvia picks and peels oranges.

At noon, we go to the plaza, a whole procession of us: Wilma and the kids, Eus, me, and Nohoch Felix, huffing under the baggage. Near the *tortilleria* we happen on Reina. She is carrying a bucket of *masa.* She says she wanted to invite me, too bad we are not going to be here. They are going to have a service for Don Eduardo, for the anniversary of his death. She is still wearing the dress I saw her in the day after I arrived. It fits like a bathing suit. In the sunshine, you can see that many of the white plastic beads on the bodice are missing or hanging loose, and there is a layer of several days' talcum around the neck and on the back of the dress. When I remark to Eus about the fact that Reina has not changed dresses since I came, she says, "It saves on washing, you cannot see the dirt." Wilma is miffed because Reina did not also invite her to the service for Don Eduardo. After all, she helped with the funeral.

As we wait for the bus, Lupita comes by, carrying a small package of meat. The child looks wan and is dressed in several layers of dirty clothes—a skirt, blouse, and a once-white T-shirt on top of that. Alicia, her cousin, is with her. This is Librada's child, Santiago's sister, with whom Reina had so much trouble when she was first married. Now they are good friends. Alicia is 16, and she has a boyfriend, Wilma says. The girl is decked out in a fashionable dress, she has a permanent, her lips are painted, she is wearing platform shoes, and her fingernails and toenails are lacquered. Two days ago she had to be taken to the doctor in Temax at 2 A.M.—Santiago rented a car—because she had an attack with convulsions and screaming. The doctor gave her a sedative. The family thinks that the reason is that although she has a permanent *novio* [fiancé], the neighbor girl of the same age keeps losing hers. So this girl and her mother keep saying all sorts of frightening things to her, like they will break them up.

Wilma says that Reina keeps feeding Lupita vitamins to make her grow faster. Looks to me like she needs a square meal more.

The bus comes at 1:30. There is a casual farewell between Wilma and her 15-year-old Marjelia, who is going with us so she can earn some money in Chetumal, where domestic servants are well paid. I am paying for her trip down; she'll earn her way back. We buy the tickets in Tizimin, there change into the Valladolid bus, and have to wait only an hour for the one to take us to Chetumal. I recognize the driver from the summer of 1975. His nervous sidekick is gone, though; instead, his son, about 11, helps him, collecting the fares and opening the door. The noise of the bus engine is excruciatingly augmented by music from a tape-deck, which is beamed into the bus by several loudspeakers. We leave Valladolid to the strains of *La Traviata*. I do manage to sleep, though, and don't even wake up for the stop at Bacalar.

Nina and a friend, who is also her little daughter Chavelita's *madrina* (a Catholic who gave Chavelita earrings), expect us at the station. She has her hair loose, wears a plastic flower in it, and reeks of cheap perfume.

We take a cab to Nina's home, but he takes us only to the corner of her street, which opens up to a large thoroughfare of the squatter settlement: the stones of the road would do damage to his car. I see no change in her home; the only new item is a set of aluminum pots on the wall. They show no stains; they are a prestige item, just as they are in Reina's house. It is Hermano Pepe who collects the weekly installments on them, and this gives Nina an opportunity to talk with him about church matters. Desi has taken care of the two little girls and Freddy, my godson, was at the bus station and greeted me with his lovely big grin. We settle down to sleep, five hammocks accommodating nine of us. It is decidedly warmer than in Utzpak.

The little boys, as I had observed especially last year, are subjected to a constant pattern of teasing by the men and are rewarded by laughter and approval when they react. It apparently produces a very fast flashpoint. No wonder the women consider their men violent. My *ahijado* Freddy has learned his lesson well. I was lying in my hammock, with my glasses on my lap, relaxing. He was trying to get hold of my glasses. We told him not to, but he did anyway. Eus said that she would spank him, whereupon he picked up one of my shoes from under my hammock and threw it at her. I happened to be positioned in such a way that I could reach him and gave him a whack on his little behind. Furiously, in a flash, he turned, grabbed my other shoe, and hit me squarely between the eyes. It really hurt, too. His mother spanked him, he cried for a while, and now Eus is putting little pieces of wet paper on my forehead so it won't swell up.

She says that when Nina was with her mother-in-law in Dziuche to wait for the birth of Chavelita, he went at his grandmother with a machete. Another time, he wanted to eat chicken. They did not have any, so he went out into the yard, and a few minutes later came back with a dead chick: he had killed it with a stone.

The next day is a cloudy day with occasional showers. The squatter settlement is like a refugee camp of peasants; the sounds of animals are all about, of chickens, turkeys, pigs, even horses. The women have their *sembrados* [places to plant and sell seeds], although of course they are smaller than they are in the village. Nina has a number of large clumps of bananas; the children look healthy and munch on bananas all day long. The men work in Chetumal; that is the attraction for all these people. They say half of Utzpak is here because there is wage labor. The government is building several new subdivisions.

Luis L. and his brother have a larger temple here and have lots of followers. Not all of them dance, but the dancing does continue, according to Nina. (I am writing this in semi-darkness, lying in the hammock. It's warmer and more comfortable: my tail hurts from sitting for hours on end in Nina's hard straight chair.) Nina says that the way the dance is carried out is that each person walks or hops in his own little circle with a movement (she demonstrates) as if he were playing a guitar. They endlessly sing the *coro* Wilma recorded for me. The *coro* ends not on a bass note, but on the third, so that it easily carries you into the next repetition.

Nina tells of an odd incident in March and April of 1976. A young man came from the village of Setenta-y-Uno and sought out Luis L. He said he could eat only apples. So the *hermanos* of Luis L.'s church went to the market and came back saying that there were no apples. So he said he could do with bananas. They went back to the market and, finding no bananas either, they bought pears, though they were more expensive and they had to take up a special offering in order to pay for them. He stayed for a week and said that he was Christ and could forgive sins. Chan Chulin heard about it, went to Luis L.'s temple, and prayed over him. Thereupon Satan, who was possessing him, left. Despite the conflict between Luis L. and Chan Chulin, Luis L.'s brother did not ask him to leave. (It seems to me that possibly the incident stimulated Joaquin K.: according to Nohoch Felix's entry, the reunion where the latter was possessed by Christ was in June, that is, only a month or so after the above occurrence.)

Again, I observe the women working together. Nina is cleaning up Teresita. (It seems to me that the child has not grown at all in the year and a half since I last saw her; they say she is going to be just as small as Desi's mother, who is not even as tall as Sylvia.) Eus has Chavelita in her arms and is peeling an orange for Freddy: the peel is cut away only to the white part underneath, then the orange is cut and sucked out. Sylvia washes the clothes. Marjelia is cleaning the vegetables for the soup. Nina is happy that Marjelia came. She will baby-sit for her so she can go shopping, maybe taking only Freddy along.

Freddy, at four, still does not understand the principle of counting. His speech is quite indistinct, and Teresita, at three, speaks hardly at all. Yet neither of the children acts retarded; Freddy plays, is toilet trained, and lords it over his playmates from next door. Teresita is also toilet trained, a bright, competent, and contented child. Only their linguistic performance seems to lag if I compare them to my own children.

Desi sticks to the traditional order in which the family eats: last night I saw him eat supper, hunched over the small bench that serves as a table in the small lean-to that is Nina's kitchen, constructed against the back wall of her pole-and-cardboard house. Assuming the same posture, his son Freddy was sitting beside him, being served together with his father, as it is done in the village.

Since I was last here, Desi has blasted a deep hole in the rock of the backyard for a latrine. It is covered with a simple zigzag of thin poles and broken lathes. The family squats at the edge for elimination. For us guests, there is a little cleared space between the bushes. It has an old blanket draped hip-high over a pole for entrance, with a chamber pot behind it. Teresita uses the banana thicket.

I am watching Freddy and Teresita play. He has loaded the toy trucks I bought him on a "car," a contraption consisting of two wheels, a seat, and a long handle. He sits on the seat and Teresita pulls him around. There are stones in the path in the yard; he has her clearing them away so she can make a turn. He tires of the game, gathers up his trucks, and vanishes in the direction of the neighbor's yard. Teresita picks up a dirty piece of paper and begins methodically to scrub the "car," going over each part several times.

Desi stays at home with the children while we go for a walk, so there is time for some real, uninhibited women's talk. We go for a walk through Chetumal to show Sylvia the sights, Eus, Nina, Sylvia, Marjelia, and I. Eus was anxious for her to see the lovely palm-frond (*huano*) roof that one of the restaurants has. There are two lovely playgrounds on the seashore with concrete vividly painted with wild animals, still in good condition (this was supposed to have been the gift of the wife of President Echeverria to the children of Mexico), not mauled, worn down, and vandalized as it would be in Mexico City. Nina is sinewy and slim like her mother and moves like a boy. She and Marjelia—free of the kids— play like two happy children, climbing through the big tube, running around a *caracol* (a structure of concrete in the shape of a snail's house), and climbing the tall play watchtower. Even Eus, Sylvia, and I go swinging, although we do not fly quite as high as the girls.

We talk about birth control. There is a rumor—I first heard it from Reina— that the government intends to tax every parent for each child beyond three. How many children there are in a family often boils down to a contest between the women and the men, with the women trying to restrict the number. Sylvia tells that her son complains that his wife cheated him. After only two sons (one of whom died as a result of neglect, according to Sylvia), she had an IUD put in without first consulting him. Salvador also wants another one, since the fourth one died, though Reina is now 40. She says publicly that she does want one, but the consensus is that she just pretends. Wilma has tried the pill but is allergic to it. She has had nine live births and two miscarriages, and Ruben is certainly not doing anything to prevent another pregnancy.

Sylvia talks a great deal about bewitching. Once, she even went to a doctor to find out whether a man she knew was really bewitched. The physician told her the man had a liver ailment. *Tin hoosa in suerte* [I have someone tell my fortune] is a regular part of her life. The fortune-teller—always a woman— does it with playing cards. "If you know how to read, you can do it yourself; the cards and also the *oruaculo* are sold in the stores. Or the fortune-teller takes three, six, and nine grains of corn, throws them on the cards, and tells your fortune that way."

She talks continually, often repeating the same story several times, which is good for my Maya. To listen to her is to understand the prodigious efforts on the part of women of her generation who lived through the change from village to city. Don Agapito had saved 1,000 pesos in Tibilom and wanted to go to Sotuta to start a market stand there. She was to stay in Tibilom, but she said that she was neither a widow nor a divorced woman and that she would go with him. Then, after years of work and saving in Sotuta, they made the jump to Merida. She often worked in the market, came home, made food, washed the clothing, ironed, went to bed at 12 or 1 o'clock, and got up again at 3 or 4 A.M. She kept telling her children, "Study, it is not for us, there is nothing to be done for us, I can't even read or write, but for you." And they did.

She has five children: her oldest son works in a bathroom supply store, Sylvia is a seamstress in Los Angeles, Socorro and Agapito teach school, and Pepe, now 17, attends school in Cordoba, where his sister Socorro teaches. For a while Agapito, her husband, could not work because he had to have a bladder operation. He is better now, and they have a stand on the pretty new market in the convent where her daughters used to attend school. She raises the plants they sell in her backyard: chives, for instance—a bunch of rooted plants sells for 5 pesos, she just sold 100 of those; and all sorts of flowers, especially roses right now, where each pot sells for 40 pesos. She also still carries on a trade with Tibilom. Despite the fact that she has a number of illnesses (she is a diabetic and has a big hernia that should be operated on, but she does not want to have it done because her daughters have no time to come to her house and take care of her after the operation; she has stomach trouble; and she has glaucoma), she projects great strength. She is much coarser in her habits than Eus and uses a lot of swear words, while at the same time condemning people who *pooch* [swear]. *Cabron, puta,* and *chinga tu madre* [bastard (actually billy goat), prostitute, and f— your mother] are constant constituents of her vocabulary. Strange that she and Eus came from the same village. She has successfully made it in the city, but she was lucky, for none of her sons drink. Perhaps her luck was in being the wife of Eus's brother. Eus's sons seem to have a harder time of it, possibly because they did not have a father pulling in their direction. Erme, Armin, and Chan Felix have to some extent overcome their handicap now—none of them has any schooling; they lived in the village or on the ranch during their adolescence. I saw the former two in Merida. But when I arrived in Merida this time, Enrique had been on a drunken binge for a fortnight, financed by the money he received when he sold half his building lot in Merida. His wife Petronila thereupon left him, taking all her children with her except Samuel, who stayed with his father. But he said he would also leave— he is now 15—and go to work for his uncle, who has some sort of trade. Eus visited him the day before I arrived—he has always been her favorite—and the house was, as always, in hideous condition—food on the floor, paper strewn about, pots on the floor. Petronila had even left her washing soaking in the tub, where it lay rotting.

Eus says that in Utzpak an old man wanted to try the girls, too. He went, but *udzu chilikba* [it remained lying down]. So he couldn't do anything, but paid anyway. As to her own sex life, she says she won't have Nohoch Felix in her hammock. She tells him she is sick, he should look for another woman. He stays away for long periods when he goes shopping for her. She says who knows where he might be going.

The next day at about 5:00 P.M., Don Victor's record-player begins broadcasting hymns over a really good public address system. His house is only a few blocks from here. We decide to go to his service that is being announced between the music. After supper, we go: Nina carrying Chavelita (6 months old), Eus, Sylvia, Marjelia, and I. The main street of the settlement has been cleared of man-high rocks that used to obstruct it and it is rather passable now. However, when we turn toward the left, in the direction of Don Victor's house, we nearly fall in a deep hole full of rainwater and have to pick our way around boulders and over ruts by the waning light of Desi's flashlight. All the way over, I feel happy, anticipating Don Victor's surprise.

We enter like the delegation of a foreign power, all with our heads covered, except Nina, who did not bother to bring a mantilla. Eus is quite upset about her and says that Nina is endangering her salvation; she even had Chavelita's ears pierced. The meeting room is actually the entrance hall to Don Victor's complex homestead. Its walls are painted blue, and there are colored paper decorations hanging from the ceiling and around the *vigas* [roof beams], left over from Christmas. Some men are seated on a bench against the right wall. One holds a guitar; with his chiseled aquiline profile, he is clearly Don Victor's son. In the middle toward the back there is a table, covered with a plastic table-cloth, decorated with a vase full of red roses. One end of it is occupied by the record-player and a pile of records. Behind the table there is another narrow bench. A young man (according to Nina, one of Don Victor's nephews) is giving a prayer as we enter. He is clearly in a low-level trance, rhythmically and compulsively moving with the prosody of his own words. On another small bench to the left there sits Don Victor. He has his eyes half-closed; his white hair is longer than I had last seen him wear it, which emphasizes his age. Beside his bench there is a sewing machine; a teenage boy is sitting beside it, the guitarist's son. On the first one of the benches, facing this setup, sits Don Victor's wife Justa, plump and pleasing, wearing an ʔipil, but a mantilla, no *rebozo.* Two large rooms open to the left, clean and entirely empty, an electric lightbulb dangling from the ceiling. A little girl hurriedly carries a baby out of sight. There is a feeling of depth about the place, and I long to sink into its allure. But there was a time some years ago when Don Victor invited me to spend a week in his house so that he could fully instruct me in his theology. I heard him pray for me, and the sexual imagery was all too clear. Also, Eus says that Don Victor shook hands with Rodolfa and followed her hand and arm up until his hand found her breast. Too bad; there are some fieldwork assignments I will have to let be. An *hermano* invites us to take our seats on the benches. As we sit down, a very old woman passes in front of us: Don Victor's mother-in-law. In a whispered question, she asks Nina who I am. Don Victor looks up and recognizes us. Gravely, he comes over and shakes hands with each of us, greeting each by name. Then the service resumes.

During this service, which takes the form, more or less, of an Apostolic one, Don Victor acts as a kind of supervisor, occasionally answering aloud a rhetorical question put by the old *hermano* who preaches, smiling to himself as he does so. The sermon is a straight exegesis of a passage from Song of Solomon. During the sermon, Don Victor's nephew kneels by the bench in the back, his back turned toward us, hymnal in hand, swaying back and forth until I expect him to burst into a peak of some kind; suddenly he stops—he must have expressed it in some way not discernable to me.

After the sermon, Don Victor gives a short prayer, asking for a special blessing for us, the visitors, and anointing me, and asking for a crown, and placing an open mantle on my shoulders.

As the meeting breaks up, he comes over to talk. How are things in our country? He knows that Carter has received the baptism of the Holy Spirit and worries that he may become the target of assassination attempts, just like Kennedy. He feels that the end of the world is very near; he sees the "seals" everywhere and fears what might be coming. "If we only make it through it all safely," he says, accompanying his words with the typical Maya gesture for "going through" or "away," left hand remaining in front of the stomach, the other, palm inward, describing a path slanting upward and out, "from then on, all will be well."

I ask about the dancing. He maintains it came to Yucatan from Sinoloa, carried by a woman by the name of Mareli. He and his son went to see it here in Chetumal, and his son fasted and had visions about it:

1) There was a little devil under the table in the temple, struggling with a man. The man was trying to pull him out, but no matter how hard he tried, he could not.

2) He saw the earth open and a snake rose up, its head reaching to the sky, with its forked tongue playing upward like a flame (he makes the movement with his hands; apparently he does not know the Spanish word for it, and the dictionary has no good English term for it, either; the German, very graphically, calls it *zuengeln*).

He interpreted the two visions for his son as meaning that the dancing was a temptation, not something they would want to adopt. As for the preacher, he said that he was a Presbyterian. He had discovered in the Bible that women should cover their heads in church and demanded that in his church they do so. They kicked him out instead. "He is not very knowledgeable yet," Don Victor says, "but he is learning." I have the impression that the old man really wants to be the big fish in Don Victor's little pond. There is some question about when to hold Sunday school tomorrow, and he wants to make the decision. Don Victor cuts him short: "It will be at 9 o'clock." And that is that. The old man yields smoothly, but he may not the next time. However, Don Victor has kept his own extended family under his fist for a lifetime. He is practiced at the game. It will be an uneven contest.

By the way, Eus and Nina thought the visions of Don Victor's son funny. They laughed all the way home about the small devil under the table.

The Dancers at Chetumal

We had been to Calderitas, a small recreation area at the ocean shore, a long way from the squatter town. It was a beautiful, hot, sunny day, the ocean gray and wide. We ate some oranges and took some pictures. On the way back, a rather drunk man sat on the floor of the bus behind the driver. Two boys boarded the bus, 9 or 10 years old, real slum kids. They knew their way around; they spat pepita seeds and kidded the drunk. I was thinking then: Nina can probably keep hold of her two daughters. But Freddy is 4 now; three or four years more and he will probably be like that, aggressive, slick, a product of the Colonia Adolfo Lopez Hateos. Interestingly, she does not send him to the Sunday school of Don Victor or to any other—there are various ones close by—and she herself is not associated with any congregation. She says it is because of the children, but Desi never goes out in the evening, so she has an effective baby-sitter.

I want to see the dancing of the *hermanos* of Chetumal, so Nina agrees to take us. She has not been there before, and we have a hard time finding the temple. Someone tells us to walk down that street there, and we are now guided by the high-amplitude public address system that carries a familiar hymn. The temple sits on a rather large lot, is constructed of wood, and is painted blue. It carries the inscription:

Templo Bet-el
Iglesia Universal Cristiana

There is an entrance hall; people are coming and going and a multitude of children are running around. Luis L. is praying into a microphone on the rostrum as we come in. Although we all have *rebozos* except Marjelia, who wears a mantilla, and Nina, who wears nothing, he recognizes us and lifts his hand in greeting. He then calls for a *corito,* which leads into the one about praising the Lord with one's feet; he shouts, "The Holy Spirit is here, it has arrived," into the *coro.* The first one I notice going into an altered state of consciousness is a teenage boy in front of the rostrum. He goes round and round, lifting his feet rhythmically, holding his arms high. To my left, there are four teenage girls also dancing, as well as a rather stout woman. One of the girls, very slender, is in a deeply altered state of consciousness, trembling violently, her head bobbing back and forth, her leg movements uncertain while she tries to keep the rhythm of the dance. In front of the rostrum, a woman is also in an altered state of consciousness, trembling, her hands held high. Soon her hands assume an irregular flutter. On the rostrum, Luis L. is also dancing, that is, performing a small hop, holding onto his microphone, singing, while many in the congregation follow his movements with shouted singing and vivid clapping. Sometimes he goes round and round, singing at the top of his voice. The slender girl does not come out of her altered state of consciousness when, after twenty minutes of this activity, Luis L. begins slowing down and shouts "*Aleluya!*" at a very slow pace. She trembles, and his dance is now a kind of back-and-forth shuffle. Luis L. calls for the reading of the Bible verse that talks about David dancing (I miss the biblical citation). She holds the book and cannot stop trembling. She finally calms down somewhat, but when Luis L. reads about David, she starts trembling again, attempts to brush the ends of her mantilla from the book, and is hardly able to hold onto it. Luis L. reads the biblical passage, then says "This is not of the Devil." The stout woman, her arms raised high, starts shouting glossolalia, and then goes into altered-state-of-consciousness singing, very slowly, in the middle registers. Luis L. continues, "There are seven visitors who came maybe to judge us, but they should know that this is of the Holy Spirit." He makes the usual pitch for the *hermanos* to get baptized, then calls us by name, starting with Nina, Eus, and me, even giving Sylvia's full name—Sylvia P. from the market in Merida. I am given Hermana Felicitas, I think, from the United States. (Later we laugh a lot about this.) He asks the congregation to rise and greet us. The only person he does not recognize is Marjelia. While he is talking, there are still some very small boys, they cannot be more than 4, still trembling and dancing in front of the rostrum. He asks for a prayer for an *hermano* who fell from a tree while cutting *chicle.* His name is Ts'ul. He asks for any offering to enlarge the temple, and a number of people get up and I see bills—not small cash, as in Utzpak— gathered on the trays when I go up and give him a five. He shakes my hand and laughs. "You look very Yucatecan," he says. But there is no opportunity to talk. There is another prayer for some *hermanos* who brought them some food (i.e., to Luis L. and his family; I saw his wife Blanca, very pregnant again) in the fulfillment of a promise (*una primisa*). It is like old times; we attend a service, but Eus and I make eye contact and she calls my attention to the teenagers in an altered state of consciousness.

Luis L. gets ready for a sermon. He asks for control of the children, who are a noisy nuisance. His sermon is a very mild one, on Jesus talking with the Samaritan woman. The disciples are surprised, they had not seen him talk with a woman before. What is he doing? How come he is talking with her alone? Well, of course, he is evangelizing her. In the end, he converts her, along with the other Samaritan. He then calls for those people who want to have their sins forgiven to come up front as an indication that they want to be baptized. About ten go—quite a number. He prays for them, placing his left hand in turn on the head of each person, while holding the microphone in his right hand. This prayer is also very low-key, and after the baptismal candidates get up, he calls on everyone to say good-by to each other, in accordance with Apostolic custom.

Looking at the structure of the service as a whole, then, the introductory phase leading up to the dance as the high point is the shorter one. When we arrived, I was struck by the obvious fidgety excitement of everybody around. There was clearly an air of expectancy. There was another *hermano* (in other words, not Luis L.) shouting a prayer into the mike involving many repetitions from the same formulas. As we were looking for a place to sit—some *hermanos* brought in two benches and placed them on the right, because on the left, where the women sit traditionally, there was no more room—Luis L. took over the mike, suggesting a quickening of the pace. Luis L. skillfully drove the congregation from this point on, asking such questions as, "Is everybody happy to be here?" and "Who wants to praise the Lord?" He was aided by the noise level and the constant commotion in the large room. By the time he called for the *corito* that led to the *coro* accompanying the dancing, he had everyone in high excitement, sitting, as it were, on the edge of their chairs. For the *corito,* the people stood up so that passing into the dance behavior was very easy. After the dance, twenty or more minutes later, everything was designed to let the excitement attenuate. Actually, when we first came in, there was such a palpable sense of excitement that for a while I was afraid to get out my notebook, thinking, "They'll tear me limb from limb." But then the fear of not being able to reconstruct the details got the better of me. I started writing and nobody paid any attention to me, although Eus did say that the woman next to us on the right seemed to observe what I was doing. Afterward, when we talked matters over, and I suggested that an upheaval like the one in Utzpak is a distinct possibility, Nina agreed, saying, "*Son muy calientes ellos* [They are very "hot"]." After all, she added astutely, the practice of everyone dancing was new, relatively speaking.

Whenever we pass through the street here, somebody is bound to call to Eus, asking for his family members or telling her a message to take back to Utzpak. (The grammar of this sentence is misleading; only women do this.) Not only can the men find work here, the labor market for the women is better as well. In Utzpak, a woman can earn 150 pesos a week for doing housework for such affluent households as that of Dona Bartola. Here, a woman can make 30–40 pesos per day. Marjelia just earned 10 pesos for washing a neighbor lady's floor. There are also other ways for women to earn something here, a pattern brought from the village.

When we get home, Marjelia takes her bath first, contrary to the usual custom, where I, as the guest, am asked to go first. (Bath, of course, is the Yucatecan kind, a bucket behind a curtain, both doors closed, so you wash in semidarkness. Also, we have to be very careful with the water; there is very little water in the settlement. For household purposes, there is a pump now put in by the city, but it is several blocks away; drinking water is still brought in by a truck once or twice a week, also by the city.) She puts on her clean red dress and combs her hair; she really looks neat and pretty. Nina gives her some change and sends her off to sell fruit. I admire her courage. It takes her just 15 minutes to sell her load, all to strangers: she encountered no one from Utzpak on this round.

On our final day in Chetumal we go shopping. While waiting for the foreign exchange quotation, I go to the drugstore to get some medication for Eus. Luckily, most everything can be bought without prescription. For Wilma, I get some vitamins with iron. When she was carrying Rebecca, she was so weak with anemia that she could hardly move. It is much better now, but she is still nursing the child, so I thought more vitamins would be a good idea.

We have no particular trouble getting out of Chetumal. For a while, the customs officials were quite strict, trying to cut down on illegal traffic of merchandise from the duty-free harbor into the Peninsula. Now they are more interested in the passengers to and from Cancun.

Our bus is waved on. Sylvia is the one who is most worried because she has done quite a bit of buying, deodorants for the men in her family and all sorts of textiles, but even at the second *caja fiscal* (the station for collecting internal revenue), the official just comes in, touches some of the bags in the overhead net, and leaves. Eus and I have much less. Eus's bag is mostly full with banana shoots—the bushes are propagated vegetatively—that Nina traded her for some *shpelum*, which is hard to get in Chetumal.

Eus and I resemble each other in a certain cheerful austerity; on trips, we eat what little we take along, and that's it. The same goes for drinking: Eus always has a bottle of boiled water with her, mainly for me. Not so with Sylvia. In the half hour that we must wait for our bus in Tizimin, she eats with us—we have some *frances* with cheese—then goes to buy freshly baked pastry and soft drinks, which she shares with us. Then she gets up again to search for a vendor of peeled oranges. "*Bey paala,*" Eus quips; just like a child, she always has to snack. When we are finished with sucking out the fruit she has bought, she gets up again. "Perhaps I can find some Popsicles." Eus and I burst out laughing—we are really quite uncontrolled in our mirth. Sylvia is startled until Eus explains that we had talked about her unquenchable appetite. She would have gone looking anyway, but the Utzpak bus comes at that point.

Utzpak Once More

When we get home, we all enjoy a plentiful bath, a great big bucket full of lukewarm water each; not like Chetumal, where we tried to leave something over when Nina gave us each a quarter bucket. Here, we say, it is much better. There is all the water we want; all we have to do is draw it from the well, and that is only about 30 feet away from the kitchen.

When we return we hear about Pedro N. Wilma tells that Julia, her three sons, and two daughters-in-law were baptized by Pedro N. in San Felipe (near Tizimin). Wilma's children observed that Julia bought all sorts of articles for the wedding of her two sons (who had to marry their wives to gain permission for being baptized). She and her husband have now sold their ranch.

As the conversation drifts on, Wilma says that she had a vision, lying in the hammock, "but I was not asleep."

First she saw many large white stars. Then pigeons flew by, a bright orange color (she points the color out on my hammock). Then there was a cenote, with lots of animals coming out of it—toads and a big monkey that waved to her. Then there were lots of people who walked along as though they were drunk.

Rereading this account many years later, I was struck by a coincidence. It was in the summer of 1977 that I discovered the role of ritual body postures in shaping the visions during trance. Animal spirits played a significant role in these visions, and the intense ecstatic trance that I and my colleagues experienced during those initial investigations could well have looked like being drunk to an outsider.

Reina comes to call. Conversation first turns around the service for Don Eduardo. It was held in his house. Isauro was going to hold it, but unexpectedly, the brother of Luis L. arrived in his car with two young *hermanos* that were unknown to Reina, and he held the service. They left immediately afterward. The tempo of the conversation picks up when her sister-in-law Librada is mentioned. Reina feels that all the trouble Librada's daughter is having now with her envious neighbor is really retribution for her mother's meanness, although this should really not be visited on the innocent child. Reina recalls the details of the rough time Librada gave her when she was still living in Don Eduardo's house. We recall with gusto all the conversations we had about that when I was here in 1969, and that knock-down, drag-out fight Santiago had with his brother that same summer. Reina thoroughly enjoys that part of the conversation. Earlier she kept wanting to leave, but now she is her former talkative self. Before, she kept saying that her daughter, who was with her, really wanted to go home. Now the child keeps tugging at her dress, and she says, "Soon, soon," and goes on talking.

Wilma tells of her neighbors, a young married couple. The girl was 13, the boy 15 when they got married; she is now 15. They have no water on their *solar* and asked to be permitted to share Wilma's. Wilma gave them permission, but now they share Wilma's well, her rope, and her buckets, and Wilma's family has to wait while they draw water. Wilma suggested that they buy their own— you can use two ropes in one well—but the girl became angry and now walks all the way to her father-in-law's house to get water. The boy makes good wages and they go to all the fiestas in the neighborhood, but they won't buy a bucket and a rope. Her father-in-law has ten children, who often do not have anything to eat. The school-age children often go to school without having eaten any breakfast. Wilma has observed them digging up some soil and eating it before leaving for school. What they do is they steal a little sugar from their mother and mix it with the soil to make it more palatable. Of course, they suffer from stomachaches all the time. Yet their parents and two oldest sisters have money to spend. They go to the picture shows every weekend, at 4 pesos per person. The girls work in the *tortilleria,* so they can buy platform shoes, which cost 240 pesos a pair, which only last a few weeks on the stones around here.

This calls to mind a talk Wilma and I had later about Pedro N. He says that he wants to be like King David, whose seed was too numerous to count. "With one woman?" I ask. It seems he tried to do it with several in Sonora and that was the reason he had to leave there eventually, although he had a good job there as a carpenter. Here, he has only his wife for that ambition, who has had thirteen children in as many years. Wilma once went over to his house to ask him whether he would hold a service for Eduardo and saw him beat her. There is very little in the house, for Pedro makes very little. He sells some produce from his *solar* and occasionally he makes stools or chairs and takes them to Xbek, a community about six miles from Utzpak, for sale. His father is quite well-to-do, but the two men do not get along, and so Pedro gets no help from him, not even a little corn for his children. He beats his children mercilessly, pulling their ears or lifting them up by one leg and slapping their behind. They don't have a single hammock; all sleep on the floor. "I wonder how the poor woman does it when she has to deliver a child?" Wilma asks. (Delivery is done in a hammock.) In addition to Pedro's family, Pedro's sister also lives with them, and she has five children. Her husband was killed as he was guarding his father-in-law's *col* (*milpa*). Somebody saw what he thought was an animal moving through the corn—he had laid down with his head resting on a stone—and shot him right through the head. His widow gets some help from her father because her husband was killed while working for him, but it is very little. She has to make *vaporcitos* (an enchilada in banana leaves) to make ends meet.

January 27, Thursday

I go to reconfirm my flight with Aviateca. It is such a small outfit that it does not even have an office, just a girl working for someone else and taking messages.

At noon, after lunch, Wilma comes to help make the *vaporcitos* for the afternoon. I wanted to invite the neighbors—Reina, Raquel and her old mother —but Raquel is in Merida for the treatment of a skin ailment, and her mother (Dona Tomasita) went to see her.

In the afternoon, I write down the recipe for *vaporcitos,* and Nohoch Felix goes shopping for *horchata.* It always takes him an eternity to get back, so Reina and her three daughters come when the *vaporcitos* are ready but the beverage is still tarrying someplace in the village. The little girls have their dolls with them, still unsoiled, which means that Reina must have locked them away and trotted them out just to please me. The *vaporcitos* are delicious. Wilma's children eat their fill, and Eus sends a portion to their house for Ruben and Jose. Reina asks about the medicine against diarrhea which she has written to me for. But, according to my physician, that kind of sulfa tablet is no longer available: the doctors prescribe antibiotics instead. I get the impression that she does not believe me. I think she is sore that I did not stay with her and jealous that I am with Eus all the time.

After she leaves—her children want to see the soap opera on the neighbor's TV—we take down the hammock stand. This matter of the hammock, more than anything else, demonstrates how sick Eus is. Usually, she is an enthusiastic companion in any enterprise at all that I might suggest. This time, she was dragging her feet. When I arrived, I explained to her that we wanted to make a film on how to weave a hammock. We discussed how we would have to put the upright loom up outside because it would be too dark in the house. We bought the boiled cotton thread and there the matter stood. I let it rest for a while but then became worried. Dennison had paid for the film cartridges; I did want to take something home. When I pressured her, it finally came out: she did not think she could stand that long, for weaving is done in an upright position. So we agreed that I would pay Consuelo (Wilma's oldest daughter) to do the weaving; Eus would only start the hammock, which Consuelo does not know how to do. "And I will also do some weaving," Nohoch Felix volunteered, to everyone's merriment, for at the loom he is all thumbs. By this time, of course, it was much too late to produce a complete hammock. So I filmed the start, then Consuelo worked for a day on it, then we got out a hammock and showed the various designs, then Eus put on the *brazos,* the strands that are attached to the woven body, and demonstrated how to make the *muneca,* that solid, tightly wound loop that gathers the *brazos* into which the ropes are tied. The thread had gotten very expensive; the price for a good, tightly woven hammock had gone up to 300 pesos and more in the village. In Cancun, tourists are charged 600 pesos and are made fun of, because in their ignorance of Peninsula prices, they pay it. Eus shakes her head; she thinks that kind of cheating the customer is immoral.

Little Rebecca is getting restless. She's had some *vaporcito* and drunk her fill at her mother's breast but still wants to suck. Eus, who now has her in her arms, teases her: "So, you want your *chuuch*? All right, here it is." She lowers the neck of her *ʔipil* and pulls out her breast with its nipple standing upright and almost black with pigment, just like Wilma's. The child sucks and then lets go, disappointed. Laughing, Eus hands her to me. "Here, try the *hermana*." I had felt rather detached up to now about reports I had read from the Amazonian rain forest, where kinswomen suckle a restless infant even if they have no milk anymore, just to please it. But now I had a wriggling girl in my arms who was grabbing for my breast. So I pulled it out and offered it to her—and as she was grappling with it, I realized that my nipple, small and buttonlike, was so different from her mother's and her grandmother's, which were nearly an inch long and cone-shaped, that she would probably not be able to get hold of it. Well, she did try, but then threw back her head and squirmed out of my arms as a wave of disappointment swept over me. For a long time afterward, I could feel the touch of her cool lips on my nipple.

When all things are cleared away—the loom, the dishes, the glasses—we all sit outside around my table. It is getting dark and soon the moon comes up, full and clear. The fire in Eus's kitchen burns brightly; the yellow flames, shining through the gaps between the poles, throw them into bold relief. We begin telling stories, and Wilma encourages her children to sing. Even little Elias produces a ditty about a little pig who gets its belly scratched. In the soft light of the hearth fire and the moon, we are all one—people, trees, shadows, and the shirring insects.

The boys come back from having taken the *vaporcitos* home and bring the Coleman along. It is lit and assiduously pumped to burn brightly, and suddenly, we are no longer part of everything: the light builds a wall around us, and I ache for what we have lost. At Eus's prompting, Nohoch Felix brings out his guitar. They had wanted Ruben to hold a service on this my last evening in Utzpak, but he declined, saying he was too tired after fourteen hours in the fields. So Nohoch Felix brings out the hymnal too, and while Oscar, Adela, and Elias play hide-and-go-seek around the yard, Jacinto and Wilma begin singing a hymn, something about the end of the world. Jacinto has a strong, clear voice and knows all the melodies securely. Wilma lets him start, then joins his, harmonizing a third lower. Hymn follows hymn; they are indefatigable.

Consuelo comes from the house where she has put Rebecca to sleep in the hammock. She stands behind her brother and joins in the singing. The Coleman begins to attract insects—little flies, mosquitoes, and especially the enormous flying cockroaches, usually in hiding during the dry season. It is getting toward 9 o'clock. Wilma gathers up her kids, and they all leave, saying a friendly good-by. For the last time this year, Eus helps me with the blanket, and I snuggle into the hammock.

As we get ready in the pink dawn, there are noises from the Utzpak fiesta preparations; music and the gunshots from the church signaling the start. Nohoch Felix stands by the well, looking toward the athletic field, where the bullring catches the first rays of the sun. "Will you go to see the fiesta?" I ask. His usually jolly face turns solemn. "All of that has long been forgotten," he says. "It is all of the world, the work of Satan."

We take the coach to Merida, driven by El Negro's surviving son, who has taken over the business. Eus calls my attention to the fact that Agosto is sitting in the front seat beside the driver. I want to greet him, but he turns only briefly, as though he does not even know me. Too late I remember that in the coach, I don't know why, there is this rule that the women do not talk to the men.

We shop all day in Merida, with Eus obstinately tagging along, although she is burning with fever. In the evening, while she snores in her hammock, her brother Agapito talks about some childhood memories from the time of the Mexican Revolution, which in Yucatan did not abate until 1924. When he was about 5 (i.e., in 1919), some soldiers came to Libre Union. They were *liberates,* and Libre Union had just chased out its own *liberates* and gone over to the conservative side. Agapito was interested in the soldiers' weapons, and one of them showed him how a gun was fired. They also let him try the shiny trumpet. In the course of the morning, the soldiers went from house to house, arresting the men, including Agapito's father. They put them all into the jail at the municipal building. Old Zapata, Agapito's father, was worried that the soldiers would kill them all. So he suggested to the young men who were arrested with him that they make a break for it. "They may kill one of us as they shoot after us, but if we stay, we will all get killed." He thought they had a chance since their jail had an unbarred window and the *monte* was only a few hundred feet away. But his companions did not want to take the risk. They did not really believe that anything would happen to them. So old Zapata decided on a different strategy. He called to the soldier guarding them and told him "Let me talk to your commander." After some hesitation, the soldier let him out so he could talk to the commander of the troop. What he told him, basically, was that he was an old man who had a little store and who had never shown any partisanship to anyone—who sold to both sides and had always tried to help everybody who needed any help. The commander asked the other prisoners "Is it true what this old man is saying?" They all confirmed that it was so. So the commander said, "So you have a store? You would not by any chance have something to eat?" Eagerly, the old man said, "Of course I do. I have some corn, and there are chickens in the yard, and even a piglet, you can have it all." "And how about some money?" "*Pues*, I am a poor man, but I do have a little saved for an emergency. Why don't you come to my place and we'll see." So they went to his house and he gave him what food stores he had and he dug up a little pot with gold pieces and he gave those to him also. The commander said, "I can see that you are a kind and friendly old man. Don't worry, nothing will happen to you." In the meantime, the men at the jail had gotten worried, and three of them had tried to make a break. The soldiers fired after them and killed one, but the other two escaped. In addition to old Zapata, they were the only ones who did. The others were executed before the liberals left the village. Old Zapata did not hurt too much, because he had dug up only his small pot with gold pieces. His larger pot was safe in another hiding place, and when things became calmer and the Revolution was over, he started his store once more.

While out shopping, I had asked to buy some *arepa*, a crumbly confection baked with *masa*. We could not find any; besides, Sylvia maintained that what you get in the streets is not all that good anyway. So after Eus slept a few hours and seemed a bit better, the three of us sat in Sylvia's kitchen and she showed us how to make them.

Don Agapito and Eus took me to the airport. Eus was very sick, bringing up a lot of mucus as we were waiting for the plane. As I turned once more to wave in the long hallway that leads to the planes, she looked bent and emaciated.

The Aviateca flying bus was full to the last seat.

The author, 1969

Don Fulgencio, 1969

The temple, 1969

The preacher Barrera

Inside the temple

Speaking in tongues

The new temple, 1980

Reina and her children

Yucatecan shower

Eus, 1969

Eus's home

Nohoch Felix

Eus at the mill

Eus harvesting *anona*, 1980

Anona harvest

Eus with grandchild

Eus's sister-in-law Sylvia

Marci, 1985

Wilma (ABOVE)
Eus (LEFT), 1986

The author, 1986

6. April–August 1977

Various Services but None for Easter

This is the Holy Week, with childhood memories claiming their mood-space all week long. I have been expecting that somehow this fact would be recognized in the services or sermons. But nothing. Yesterday was Good Friday. There were prayers broadcast from the steeple of the Catholic Church, and the feeling of the finality of an execution pending hung palpably in the air. Eus and I both expected an evening service not usually offered on Fridays. We really primped for it, putting on our best ʔipiles. Eus remarks that Joaquina and Teresa are really conceited, *se creen,* because of the variety of dresses they are now wearing. They have always worn dresses, not the ʔipil grande of the kind Eus has given me as a present. The ones I have brought along (*alta seda*—high silk) now cost 800 pesos or more. With a lot of laughter we envision, as we walk down the highway, how we are going to go down to the front to pray, even if the service has already begun. "*La gran entrada*" [the great entry] I call it. But when we get to the temple, it is closed. Isauro is apparently still in Celestun. Besides, he always maintains that nobody actually knows on what day Jesus was born or executed, and he refuses to celebrate either event. We don't want to be like the *mundanos* [the worldly ones].

Our disappointment is acute, and it is not alleviated by Reina's admiration for my ʔipil and that of her crowd—Dona Juanita, Dona Rach, and others—sitting in front of Dona Juanita's house, or that of Dona Rosario, where we end up drinking a Pepsi.

We talk about Isauro on the way home. He wants to be changed to another temple and was offered Temax. But there are no *hermanos* there, so he let Valentin K. have it. Most of the time, he is in Celestun, as he is just now. Apparently, he is building up his own congregation there. Perhaps it is economically better on the coast, although with Pedro N.'s congregation joining his congregation here, he is quite well off right here in Utzpak. Everyone speaks of Juana, his wife, because she is so jealous. If *hermanos* come to visit them and greet only him and not her, she is jealous. Then they start fighting.

More gossip: Don Victor came to preach in Hermano Antonio B.'s temple. They passed the service to Antonio C., but not to Don Victor, although he had his Bible prepared. So he got miffed and did not come again.

There is also a healer who keeps coming back. His name is Miguel Montiel, and he is said to be an *espiritista.* The way he does his faith healing is to line up the sick. Then he lifts his arms three times, saying "*En el nombre de Cristo* [In the name of Christ]," and he lays on his hands. The person then swoons backward. Afterward, the patient is expected to say that his pain is gone. Pedro N. learned the method from him. Then he says, "I did not heal you, God did." He might say, "I was given to understand by the Holy Spirit that there is someone who has a hernia here—*que pase* let him come forward." Then he prays over him in the above way. Eus says that Chan Felix got cured of his hernia that way. Miguel M. keeps saying that what the Church needs is a revival—*avivamiento de la iglesia*. (He is the pastor at the Apostolic church at Guamuchil, Sinaloa, the biggest of the Apostolic congregations. It even has a *conjunto* [orchestra] in church. He has been a friend of Juan and Luis L. since before secession.)

Speaking of the dance episode in the church, Eus later told me how one time Luis L. and Juan L. came to Utzpak and also the *hermano* from Madrazo. As many as twenty-eight *hermanos* danced; they threw the chairs out of the window, and Isidro E. swept everything off the table, breaking the vases. Isauro kept saying, "*Cristo ya pronto viene,*" for everything was being destroyed. But Pancho N. maintained that the Evil One had taken him by the hand, that is why he danced and jumped like he did. At a later service he said that he had done everything—gotten drunk, smoked (Eus: "I don't know what other sins")— and now he was happy to be back in the temple. He wanted to offer a special hymn, but Isauro would not let him. Pancho N. got so angry that he has not been back to the temple since. (They stopped dancing in Utzpak in 1979.)

Eus has a lot of fun stored up in her. We are talking about some people changing denomination quite often, getting baptized each time over again. "They must enjoy taking a bath," she says, a standard joke of hers. She also tells about a Catholic girl who was going to get married in the Catholic Church. She bore her mother's name. The priest asked "Doesn't she have a father?" Mother: "Of course she does. *No Brota el huevo si no hay gallo*—the egg does not hatch without a rooster."

Down the street from Eus there is the house of a crippled woman whom I had not met before. Her husband left her years ago, and her only son pretends that she is not his mother and never comes to see her. About two years ago a man came to live with her. I imagine he had no other place to go. He is a skinny guy with a few hairs sprouting from his chin. She keeps both of them fed by begging. He pushes her around in a wheelchair, but the side street that Eus's house is on is very bumpy, and once she had a bad spill. So now he leaves a folding chair in Eus's yard next to the entrance to her *solar* and, when necessary, places that chair halfway between the two houses. He then lifts her from the wheelchair, carries her to the folding chair, rests a while, and then takes her the rest of the way. She has spindly legs, frighteningly deformed hands, and fingers like claws. She is also incontinent. She calls Eus "*hermana*" and says she is also *evangelica*, and Eus always chats with her. This particular day she tells

Eus that begging has been good and she has been able to buy a piglet with her earnings. She cannot move her body at all now, except for one of her arms. Wilma maintains that she has not always been this immobile, that this came as a result of arthritis, about twenty-eight years ago. "People say that in a previous life, she killed as many people as the number of years this condition will last," she says, with a shrug that indicates that she half believes it. (Actually, the only way a woman would be able to kill that many people would be by witchcraft.) I watch as Eus talks with her. She has a wonderfully strong face, looking like a younger sister of Margaret Mead. The way her hair is bobbed reinforces the impression. There is humor, compassion, and a great capacity for love in her face.

She comes by today. Eus says that her sister-in-law did "it" (witchcraft) to her. Thirty years ago she was still normal; she even had a son. She calls herself *hermana,* but sharp-eyed Eus sees a sliver of a palm leaf tied to the strap of her shoulder bag. "*Bendido por el padre* [Blessed by the priest]," said Eus with some emphasis.

Last night a young woman came, a small boy at her hand. She stopped at the *albarrada* and called out to us. Eus said under her breath, "*Es una blanca* [It's quite a woman]." She went up to the *albarrada,* and I heard her ask "Does Felicitas de Goodman live here?" She introduced herself as Patricia Fortuney of the anthropology department of the University of Yucatan in Merida. She knew me from the article I had contributed to the volume about the Mesa Rodonda (Goodman 1972b), also from Prof. Medina of Mexico, who had told her that I was still working in the area. They are working on a project about the distribution of sects in Yucatan. She went to Isauro and he told her that I was with Eus. She is young, white, petite, and Mexican. (I was tremendously inhibited while talking with her. My "cover" had been blown, so to speak. She wants my books and articles for her project, and I'll send them, of course). She invited me to talk to her group on Tuesday. I told her of my worries about protecting my informants when later I saw her alone at the hotel. I don't know if she understood the import of what I was saying; she seems quite inexperienced in fieldwork. She is looking for a place to stay in Utzpak.

In a way I am glad that the University of Yucatan is going to sponsor some research here. After all, it is a remarkable social phenomenon that without the support of any kind of hierarchy or outside funds, these Indian villagers, barely literate, should on their own get together to worship and create a viable organization, build their own temple, and insist on their own interpretation of what the Word of God was about.

I took Patty over to La Elegancia and had her buy a kerchief for her head. Later she came to fetch us by car, for we were going to an *accion de gracia* at

Hermana Juana's house, which was quite far away, on the other end of Utzpak. It was somebody's birthday, and there was a cake. However, Eus's appearance in the car generated just about as much excitement as the prospect of a treat.

Before the service started, Nestor asks us to come and pray for a Hermana Christina. We stumble over an unbelievably stony side street in pitch darkness to the small traditional house. Hermana Christina sits on her hammock, a towel wrapped around her head. We leave after a short prayer and return to Juana's house.

Patty's entrance causes another stir. I cannot help noticing the smiles of greeting of Isauro and Nestor for her. Of course; here comes upper-class Mexico to pay attention. It is not just that they now see another observer, something they had come to know from my presence. This visit had a social edge to it, and it pleases them. I was wondering how that might tilt the data in a different direction than my presence had. Can we ever delete our personal and social effects?

I look around at the congregation. Reyes is here with her small daughter, her only child. Genaro and Augustin have come with their guitars. The service is conducted by Nestor. Eus has her usual observational acuteness. "What do you say?" she whispers. "Hermana Juana calls for *una accion de gracia,* and all her daughters come in pregnant." I had noticed the pregnancies, but was unaware of which family the young women represented.

Some individual hymns are offered by two women and then by two girls. The guitarists try in vain to pick up their nonexistent melodies. Then comes Joaquina.

Finally, Isauro appears behind Nestor at the open door. Suddenly I remember him as he appeared at another door, ten years ago, at just such a service, announcing that they were going to stay up all night so they would not miss the end of the world. Eus has fallen asleep. I think it's okay to let Patricia be bored to death for a while. Why should I be the only one?

A Bible text is read, some letter of Paul's. It has nothing to do with Easter. There is a hymn, then another one, calling for the offering. The entire room is full, just as Eus has predicted it would be—there are always a lot of people if there are refreshments. Rodolfa's deaf-mute daughter has just taken her offering to the table. She has blossomed into a lovely young woman.

Communal prayer, then Nestor preaches. He intersperses his none-too-meaningful sermon with many "*Glorias*" and speaks of Lazarus dying and being awakened from the dead. "Not only the world needs more faith, but even we here also." Behind me, a child is vomiting. Isidro explains why they have called an *accion de gracia.* It is his birthday, but he doesn't say so. Now he comes out with it: it is his twenty-ninth. There is a double-tiered cake on a homemade wooden stand, a creditable likeness of some magazine illustration of a wedding cake.

Finally the service winds down and everyone can get to the cake. To Eus and Nohoch Felix's consternation, no one congratulates Isidro, and they do not sing the birthday song. Isidro is one of the two brothers who were dancing the last time I was here. The other one is in Merida. Rumor has it that he is the lover of Elide, who is working there as a washerwoman. She is said to have had a child by him, which she gave up for adoption: *lo regalo*.

Eus has killed another chicken for the Sunday meal, and we chat as she plucks it and carefully scrubs it with wood ash. She complains about the women of Pedro N.'s congregation,, who have basically taken over the old congregation of the temple. "They will not get up if someone needs a seat; not even a wind can move them," she says. "They let their children sleep on the chairs and don't let the guests sit down."

Eus has a nice relationship going with her neighbor, Don Antonio, although she disapproves of the way he and his wife treat their children. Don Antonio's wife sends the children over with samples of food, such as *chaya* in egg batter, marinated onions and beans, or, today, she sent them some *relleno negro* [black filling] that she had made with the chicken.

We have a visitor, Don Diego. He used to work in the *col*, but now he is too old for that. So he goes begging. He says that his *yilip*, his daughter-in-law, is a very good (meaning efficient) witch. She makes others sick by introducing something into their body. In the case of one woman, they afterward found a zipper under her lower rib when they dug her up to rebury her bones. Eus recalls that Hermano Felipe's wife came home from Motul one day with some mangoes and gave one to her husband, saying, "This one is for you." From that mango, he became very sick, almost dying [*se paso a morir*]. His wife had bewitched him. The man's son is married to Felipe's daughter. His wife did not like this match; that is why she made him sick.

There was no service this morning because some of the men from the congregation went to Bek to preach. Nohoch Felix went along and came jubilantly home close to three: they had found a very receptive audience.

EVENING SERVICE

We are late getting out of the house and arrive when the testimonies are about to begin. Nestor is in charge and there are two guitarists. There are nineteen men and twenty-eight women at the outset and only a few children; some are playing outside. All the chairs are taken, but Candil notices us and brings two, for Eus and myself. After the testimonies, they sing "Andar con Cristo" and pass to the altar to pray. Patty is here too, standing by the window and taking notes.

I hear Teresa's glossolalia above the prayer of the women. On the men's side there is Isidro with his vocalization "*cristia, cristia, cris, cris . . . ,*" very loud. He is holding his right arm up, his hand slightly bent over his head. The dancing *corito* is intoned, but no one dances.

The service passes on to Emerijildo. He calls for special hymns. A man and a boy sing. Eus says he is the son of Reyes. As they sing, I try to take down some of the things Eus has told me. For instance, she complains that Nohoch Felix has changed, and she is right. We are sitting in the back row and just now he comes by, but there is no smile (which used to be so characteristic of him); he is just looking for his bag. With obvious anger, he lifts Eus's, which hangs on the back of the chair in front of her; he does not find his but Eus's falls down. He does not apologize, pick it up, or look at us; he just goes on.

The next are two teenage girls, who usually come forth, then Pancha (Rodolfa's younger sister) and Joaquina, then two more women. The entire sequence, in other words, is that of women. Somehow, they string along together, although Isauro has no organizations in his congregation. "*Sociedad—suciedad*" he is reported as quipping. Nor does he want any shared food on festive occasions, because he says that some might eat more than they contributed, or maybe they might eat without contributing any food.

There is an offering, and a number of girls present hymns, but nowhere is there any reference to Easter. They pray without going to the altar, then Emerijildo gives a brief sermon and passes to Isauro.

Isauro calls for the hymn, "Yo me gozo el lunes" [I am happy on Monday, Tuesday, and on . . .], then continues with other hymns and *coritas* in the tradition of the dancing phase. Only nobody is dancing, they just stand there and clap indifferently, except for Reyes, who claps with an involvement of her entire body. She is standing beside two of the Violets, who are wearing demure identical dresses of contrasting color.[1] I look for Rodolfa, but she must be in the back. I remember that she has told me once again that "everyone" is worried about new signs that the world is now really coming to an end.

Isauro preaches without much of an outline; he merely rambles on. We have changed from childhood. We were reborn with water, which washes away the sins. Now we have reached maturity. On and on. I glance at Eus, who has primped so nicely and is now taking her usual nap. She has on a freshly ironed ʔipil, a crisp, well-ironed *piki* (underskirt), and scrubbed shoes. The nape of her neck is powdered, and her hair is freshly washed and shiny with a bit of Brilliantine she scrubbed into it.

Isauro: We should always listen to the word of God because we are like newborn babies. The word of God is *la leche espiritual* [the spiritual milk]; we want it for salvation. In the back, a baby is crying and children are playing catch. We should learn to appreciate the spiritual milk. We must expect the day when Christ will come back. Then on about the spiritual milk. I asked Eus if there is ever any communion service. She maintains there is, but rarely.

Isauro announces that there will be a baptism in Campeche, and everyone is invited. He calls for the hymn, "Gracias Cristo," and has them repeat the chorus many times. Patty has stayed to the end, and Eus remarks how Teresa watched her as she stood by the window taking notes.

APRIL 7

I love swinging in my hammock in the yard, singing and talking and watching. Eus has a brood of fluffy yellow ducklings which were hatched by a hen. She worries about them because the hen has not taught them to go into the water, which they need to learn for survival. So she puts them with some larger ducklings hatched by a duck. But the mother duck goes after the little strangers with vicious pecks, and Eus has to tie her to a tree.

I keep asking Nohoch Felix for some *jarana* songs (Spanish dance tunes) on his harmonica—no, not hymns, please. He gets upset with me. "Why would you want to hear *mundane* Maya songs? You, an *hermana*." I have never really led him on; in fact I have explained several times that I am a Lutheran. It has even caused some amusing discussion, because he has thought I was speaking of San Martin. But that was a long time ago, and I am now firmly associated with the temple congregation, at least in his mind.

He is adamant about Maya songs—I wonder why; they must really represent the allure of a world he has left for good. But he finally consents to play "Dios me va a castigar"—"God will punish me," he says, only half in jest. Later he squats down to watch his young dogs fight with a rooster. A hen pecks his arm and draws blood. "See, God punished me," he says. Eus is not sympathetic. "It is a good thing you bled," she laughs. "You've got too much blood in you head."

Eus is irrigating with Nohoch Felix. Or rather, Nohoch Felix is irrigating and Eus is directing. She sounds like a football coach urging on the players. Mostly it is "*Baash ca beetik—ma ta wilic?*"—"What in the world are you doing now?" and "Can't you see?"

Later, we go to have the corn ground for tortillas. The corn has soaked overnight and is now *huuch,* and it is very heavy, but she insists on carrying it. She also takes a bunch of *anonas* with her. Some she sells to the women waiting their turn at the mill. One she gives as a present to Dona Ugulina, who is back in Utzpak. She says she does not like living in Merida. All the neighbors there keep their doors locked, and there is no one to talk to. Here she has her friends, and her daughter sends over her food. For her daily bath, she puts a bucket of water out on the sidewalk in front of her house, and the sun warms it.

We get there early enough so that I can watch the people—and gossip a little. I remember that they say that Isauro believes that the congregation will dissolve because the women gossip too much. I notice Balaam is speaking with his mother. Both mother and son have very delicate features, which remind me of the findings at the Bonampak site, and they are extremely dark; chocolate powdered with charcoal. I wonder if the Maya priests (*balaam* means priest) looked like that?

There are nineteen women and twelve men. Isauro has taken up a guitar. I did not know that he could play it. I can see now that he can. A man I don't know opens the service. There is a hymn; Isauro tries his luck with the guitar, then gives up. During the testimonies, Teresa says that she has been feeling sick and had decided that she was going to go and see a physician. But during her prayer, God told her that she would be well, and she now feels healed. Mostly, the women merely read some small text from the Bible as their "testimony." The man who opened the service does, too—barely. There is an altar call, but no glossolalia. Eus said that she was tired but that she would postpone sleeping until we got to church. She sure did. I am surprised that she does not fall off the chair.

Emerijildo takes his turn in conducting the service. He calls for special hymns. Two girls come forward, then one of Emerijildo's sons. Another man, two women, a woman, and a man called Angel. Then there is the hymn accompanying the offerings. Eus maintains that after Juan and Luis L. separated from the central church, they proclaimed that they would collect no offerings. Now, however, if one day there is no service, it is promptly *doble ofrenda* [double offering] the next day. But it is still better than with the Presbyterians, who are said to demand 35 percent of a person's wages in the name of tithing.

After some more Bible passages and a prayer with people standing in their places, the service passes to Isauro. Nohoch Felix has singled him out also for displeasure. He was reading the Bible at home and pointed out a passage from II Thessalonians 3: "If anyone will not work, let him not eat. For we hear that some of you are living in idleness, mere busybodies, not doing any work. Now such persons we command and exhort in the Lord Jesus Christ to do their work in quietness and to earn their own living." "The *hermanos*," he said, "don't like this section. Isauro goes out and all he does is sell suiting [*cortes*]. That's not work."

Isauro preaches on the topic of spiritual laziness:

> We are spiritually asleep. The day of salvation is approaching. And before that day arrives, we will have to achieve piety and sanctity. Let us not fall into evil ways; they smell bad. We are preparing for Christ's arrival. In

the world as it is today, there is no justice. Everything must be put in order before we go "to that place." We can reach purity and should thank the Lord for his teachings and exhortation. It is terrible to be against the Lord.

APRIL 8

There has been a terrible accident with the Merida bus. Eleven people died; four from Utzpak. Others were injured, some seriously. In Utzpak one man was told that his wife was killed. His comment: "*Por su gusto murio* [She died by her own choice]." He begged her to stay home and said that he would give her money, whatever she wanted. He was a fisherman, had his own boat, and made enough. They also had a ranch and cattle. But she would not listen. What she enjoyed was buying and selling. So she continued going to Merida.

Reina and Santiago come by with all their girls so I can take a picture of them with their car. Reina has six seamstresses working for her, she says. Sometimes she gives Eus small pieces of leftover material, and Eus makes aprons out of it. After I take the pictures, they buy some limes from Eus.

I look at one of those polyester aprons on Eus and reflect on the relative merits of cotton and this slinky, plastic stuff. A cotton ʔipil dies slowly and gracefully. Its material becomes soft and gentle with wear. It acquires little tears here and there, they spread, and in the end, the woman cuts off the embroidery and the skirt becomes an apron, or perhaps a diaper. Eventually, it yields rags to tie up a wound or wash a pot. In the end, it returns to the dust from which it came. A synthetic dress turns ugly with age, like a wrecked car; the seams start gaping and the color gets an ashy hue. It cannot be torn, and it absorbs nothing. When it becomes too unsightly, it is thrown out, the dogs drag it about, and it remains scattered about forever prevented from resting like a cursed soul.

Lecture at the University of Yucatan

Eus and I take the bus to Merida. Nohoch Felix is staying behind with the chickens and the ducks. In Merida, Eus stays at Don Agapito's house, while I take the bus to the university.

Patty has invited all of the participants in the religion project to my lecture. It involves the census of all protestant denominations on the Peninsula.

For the lecture, we go to a room with air conditioning. Outside, it is hotter than blazes, which I am used to, but which of course makes me perspire. During my talk, I am hit directly by the stream of very cold air. By the time I am done, I have no voice left. Back in Columbus, it takes me a week to recover it.

I speak mainly about glossolalia and find the young people interested and eager questioners. Some of them promise to write, but none of them have done so.

Interval 1977: A Boy's Story

As usual, I had left a dozen airmail envelopes with Nohoch Felix, exhausting Don Antonio's entire supply. Nohoch Felix mainly used them to confirm the arrival of my monthly money orders and the vicissitudes of cashing them. Utzpak had no bank, so Eus traveled to Izamal to get her money, where she had assorted relatives and she could spend the night.

Usually, Nohoch Felix's communications also contained brief news flashes. Eus had had her teeth pulled, as the Temax physician had suggested. After a few problems, the dentures I had paid for fit. But being able to chew did not improve her health. With difficulty, she could eat at most five tortillas, but she could hardly keep any water down. She quit going to the doctor in Merida; he was too expensive. Nothing could be done about her illness; it was a visitation by God. As for Nina, she was still living in Chetumal; she had problems with her husband Desi. He was getting drunk and had another woman. Maybe he wanted to get a divorce.

In April, Luis L. brought a group from his Merida congregation to visit Isauro's congregation in Utzpak. They spoke in tongues and danced, but Isauro's flock did not dance along. Nohoch Felix and his family continued to stay away from the services. The members of Luis L.'s congregation were false prophets and they were possessed. If Ruben cannot hold a service, they go to the Pentecostals, or they travel to Temax or to Dzilam Gonzales.

In a letter at the beginning of June, Nohoch Felix apologized that his writing was so poor, but he could no longer see the lines. And at the end of the month, there was the brief mention that Wilma's son Joaquin would record the events at the congregation for me (Joaquin was 11 at this time). With his careful schoolboy letters, he chronicled the events at Isauro's services, the way he had seen me do it. While the adults of Eus's family no longer attended Isauro's services, no one apparently paid attention to Joaquin, who even insinuated himself into the baptismal rituals at the seashore, all the while recording "the story of the Devil" in his thick copybook.

The following is the somewhat abbreviated account of the events in the congregation from June to October 1977:

History of the Devil

JUNE 6

The ministers Luis L. and Miguel M. came to the village of Utzpak for an evangelizing campaign. With them came also the Devil and two young girls, the sister-in-law of Luis L. and Marina. The daughter of Hermano M. Hermana Marina prayed in tongues, and the sister-in-law of Luis L. understood what Marina was saying. They sang hymns and *coritos* while dancing and continued dancing on and on; they danced even worse than before. And the Hermano M. preached concerning the dancing. And the Hermanos M. and L. did not dance, but they were observing who was not dancing, and Hermano Luis L. got up and said, "Everybody must close his eyes, because if you don't, the Holy Spirit will not enter into you." And he said, "How sad is a soul without Christ." And Luis L.'s sister-in-law did not dance. The Hermano M. put his hand on the head of the younger sister of Hermana Blanca, and they sang that *corito* that has the title, "Yo le alavo con el corazon," and then the sister-in-law of Luis L. became inspired to dance. The Hermana Marina prayed, putting her head close to that of the son of Hermano Dito; they all prayed, and these two, possessed by the evil spirit, came forward to pray, one after the other. They pulled them by their hands, even the daughter and the son of Hermano Pedro N., they prayed over these two. And the Hermana Marina was jumping with all her strength and stepped on the foot of Hito. Melquicedec, the son of Hermano Pedro N. Even Hermana Julia danced, together with her two sons. However, these [Julia and her sons] did not dance; they did the *jarana* [a Yucatecan folk dance]. They grabbed each other by the hand and danced very hard and, gradually, they began getting very hot.

JUNE 9

On the 9th of June, people came to the temple at nine in the morning, many *hermanas* and eight *hermanos*. At 11 o'clock in the morning they went to the port of Santa Clara, and even we went. Hermana Chari did not want to be baptized. When we arrived in Santa Clara, a terrible rainstorm broke upon us. Hermano M. said, "Let us pray so that this rainstorm will stop," and they prayed, scolding the rain. In eight minutes, Hermano M. baptized seven *hermanos*. When they arrived at the seashore, the Hermana Marina said to Chari, "Just look how clever the Devil is; did he tell you not to get baptized?" And the Hermana Chari said, "No, because no." And so they baptized only seven *hermanos*, the two sons of Hermano Dito and the daughter of Hermano Antonio. And the other thing that happened was that they did not even sing the baptismal hymn, and they did not pray. After having been baptized, the son of Hermano Dito did not come out of the sea, but he was swimming. They told him to come out, but he would not come out and laughed. Then Hermano M. said, "Let's go," and we left the seaport.

JUNE 8

Hermano M. and Luis L. prayed over the people. They asked them, "Has the Lord healed you?" and they said, "Glory to God! The Lord Jesus Christ has power! He can save and heal!" And the elders said, "*Amen, amen! Gloria Dios! Aleluya, Aleluya! Gloria Christo!*" And the Hermano M. said, "The Lord Jesus Christ is indicating to me that a certain person is sick. Come forward, come forward, so that we can pray over you. The Lord Jesus Christ is working in me, come forward so that we can pray over you." Many came forward, understanding the message, and they prayed over the sick, saying, "In the name of Jesus of Nazareth, leave this person! Be gone in the name of Jesus of Nazareth! I order you to leave, leave!" And they brought a man to them who could not get up because he had had an accident. He was the last one they prayed over and they said, "In the name of Jesus of Nazareth, rise! In the name of Jesus of Nazareth I order you to rise! Rise, I order you, rise!" And the man did not get up, and the Hermano M. prayed ceaselessly and saw that the man could not get up. And he said to him, "Give me your hand." And the man gave him his hand, and they grabbed his other hand, and they said, "Rise, rise!" and he could not, and they pulled his hands and they lifted him, but he could not get up. They pulled him up, he fell, and they left him without curing him.

June 10

On June 10 they went to the seaport of Dzilam Bravo and they baptized thirteen *hermanos.* These were not believers; it was the first time that they had been to the temple. And there were twenty young girls from the Pentecostal congregation who came along to criticize. They also danced and they said, "We are also going to get baptized," although they had not been taught the doctrine. And they baptized them. The sister-in-law of Hermano Luis L. also came; she said there had been many visions and that the Devil had appeared to her, saying, "I am going to make this pickup truck turn over so that all the *hermanos* will die." It was not she who said that. So the pickup truck started up, and then they had to brake and the daughter of Isauro cut her forehead. And then the daughter-in-law of Hermano Luis L. said, "I saw this in a vision, and the Devil said, 'I am going to turn over this pickup truck and all the *hermanos* will die.' But," she said, "God would not let it happen." They arrived at Utzpak, and held a service in the evening, but we did not go to that service.

After this, they held a service in the house of Hermana Julia. They say that many people were healed, and there was even a wedding. They said to Hermana Socorro, who was not married, that she should come forward so that they could pray over her, but she did not want to do it, and they pulled her by her hand and told her that she should get baptized, but she did not want to. Then they jostled her and told her that she should leave. They were going to have the wedding of Hermana Julia, and she did not want to join in it.

When the day of June 10th broke, the two young girls of the Pentecostal church who were baptized by Hermano M. said that they saw visions that indicated that those who had been baptized were false Christs. As it is written in the sacred writings, before the Lord Jesus Christ would come, there would be false Christs "who are going to come in my name, and who are going to cure many people. And the blind will see and the lame will walk. They are like good shepherds, but inside, they are roaring wolves." And the two girls of the Pentecostal church burned their dresses in which they had been baptized, saying "here is the wind of the false prophets." And they asked forgiveness of the Lord —"Forgive us, Lord, because we did not know what we were doing."

The girls' sister went to fetch their cousins so that they would pray over them, because the girls were jumping and falling on the ground, asking for God's forgiveness for what they had done. But their cousins were not home, only their uncle; their cousins had gone to the service in Cansahcab. And their uncle arrived and they knelt down in front of him as if he were God, asking him for forgiveness. And their uncle said, "It is not I who is going to forgive you, *hijitas* [girls]. God will forgive you." They had no dresses on because they had burned them; they were naked, and their uncle prayed over them, so that the devil would leave them and let them have peace. On the same evening, they went to the service in Temax.

JUNE 11

There was a service in the house of Hermano Tomas M., and while it was going on, young Pedro was attacked; his eyes nearly came out of their sockets. They prayed over him for an hour, and it did not leave him, and he fell under an orange bush. They made a chain of prayer around him and around the house, like children playing. They did this saying that this would make the devil leave him. When they grabbed the boy, he fell into the hearth, and then went outside, running, where he fell. Hermano M. picked him up, and Hermanos Luis L. and Isauro and many other *hermanos* prayed for him. And the Devil did not leave him, because Hermanos M. and L. and many other *hermanos* were in demonic possession, with the Devil and the other devils fighting each other. The one possessing Hermano Pedro did not leave him, because everyone was in demonic possession. In this manner things went on without the devil leaving Pedro. The Hermanos L. and M. and the others were dancing; they were jumping and they danced like crazy, like they were out of their minds, like ballerinas, like performers in a cabaret. They went out of the house, as they could see that they could not perform their buffoonery inside since the house was very small. They danced under the fruit trees, there they sang. Hermano Tomas said that when he passed by where Hermano Pedro fell, he felt afraid.

JUNE 18

We went to a service in the house of Hermano Emerijildo. They sang hymns and *coritos* and danced. There were the two *hermanas* of the Pentecostal temple who had burned their dresses. They were still possessed. They began to pray; one spoke in tongues, the other understood it. Even the Hermana Victoria spoke in tongues. She kept repeating the same words, saying, "*Ma me! Ma me! Sir, siri! Siri!*" And the Hermana Victoria went out with the son of Hermana Julia to discuss what they were going to say; when they came back in, she prayed in tongues, the other one understood her: "There are . . . some . . . *hermanos* . . . who . . . are . . . thinking . . . bad . . ." They continued praying, "There are . . . some . . . of . . . my . . . *hijos* [sons] . . . who . . . only . . . come . . . to criticize . . . my . . . Name. . . . Come . . . to the front . . . so that . . . we pray . . . over them. . . . He who . . . knows . . . that . . . he is . . . thinking . . . something bad . . . *pase* [come to the front] . . . *pase* . . . *pase*. . . . I . . . will . . . not . . . hurt . . . them. . . . *Pase* . . . *pase* . . . *pase* . . ." She said it crying and shouting, and they saw that no one came to the front. Hermano Nestor got up and said, "Hermanos, the Lord Jesus Christ is telling us that there are some among us who are thinking bad things; come to the front, says our Savior, no one is going to get hurt, come to the front so that we can pray over you. Don't be afraid, because the Lord Jesus Christ will not hurt anyone. He saves and heals, and forgives, and if there is anyone who is thinking something bad, come forward, and we will pray over him, so that the Lord Jesus Christ will forgive him tonight."

During the same evening, the Hermano Pedro also said, "There . . . are . . . some . . . of . . . my . . . children . . . who . . . only . . . come . . . to criticize. . . . Come . . . so . . . we . . . can . . . pray . . . over . . . them. . . . *Pase* . . . *pase*. . . . I will not . . . hurt . . . them! . . . I forgive. . . . *Pase*. . . . I . . . will . . . not . . . hurt . . . them." However, nobody came to the front. And the Hermano Nestor rose and said, "Hermanos, the Lord Jesus Christ is telling us that there are some people here who only came to criticize. Come to the front so that we can pray over you, so that the Lord Jesus Christ will forgive you." But no one came, and the Hermano Pedro repeated, "There is someone . . . who only came . . . to . . . criticize. . . . *Pase*. . . . so that . . . I . . . can forgive him. . . . It . . . is . . . someone . . . with a . . . blue . . . shirt . . . with stripes. . . . *Pase* . . . so that . . . we . . . can . . . pray . . . over him. . . . *Pase* . . . *pase* . . . my children . . ." But no one came to the front, and each time they prayed even harder and louder. "*Pase* . . . my children . . . so that . . . I . . . can . . . forgive . . . you. . . . *Pase* . . . *pase*. . . . It is . . . someone . . . with . . . a . . . blue . . . shirt . . . with . . . stripes. . . . He . . . is . . . at the door . . . judging . . ." And no one came to the front. And the Hermano Nestor rose and said, "The Lord Jesus Christ is telling us that there is someone who is doubting, and he has on a blue shirt with stripes; he is at the door. *Pase, pase*, we will not do anything to you, the Lord Jesus Christ says that he is the one who forgives." And many went outside to see that person, but there was only the uncle of the young girls who are possessed by the evil spirit. He had on a blue shirt, but it was not striped. And the Hermano Nestor said, "Let us pray for them," and they prayed, and the service ended. Then the son of Hermano Dito said, "My belly hurts," so they began to pray, saying, "Get out of him, cursed sickness, I know you, get out, for if not, I will destroy you." And, continuing with these words, they spent about ten more minutes, then fifteen, then twenty, then thirty, and an hour passed. At the end of the hour, they finished with this. As if they had been in a river or a cenote, they came out wet with perspiration, and we left, and they also left.

JUNE 24

The Hermano Pedro and his family, and the souls whom they had deceived, held a service in the house where we used to live. It was for the second anniversary of the late Tomas Lizama who died, shot by his hunting companion. They held two services, dancing the way Hermano Luis and Hermano Juan L. dance. All of his children prayed in tongues, and the mother of the children prayed in tongues and then said the prayer in Spanish. She said, "The Antichrist, who, they said, will arrive, they have been saying this for a while, and he is with you beginning today. I am the Antichrist. He is here now, it is I, the Antichrist, he is here already. This is what our Lord Jesus Christ has said, that we will be him, and we are the ones who are fulfilling this. He who wants to come with us should come, for we are the Antichrist, so let those who are here hear it." And all those who were there were afraid and did not come back.

JULY 8

There was a service on July 8 in the house of Hermana Julia. The Hermana Melencia came to the front so that they would pray over her, and she received the evil spirit and fell on the floor, and they prayed for her. The Hermano Montiel said to her that she should get baptized, and she did not want to. There was even some foam that came from her mouth, and she did not continue coming to the services. Rather, she went arm in arm with a *torero*. She has five lovers. The first one left her with two children; the second one also left her with two; the third one left her with no souvenirs; and the fourth one, the *torero*, has no child with her as of yet. They live in Utzpak. The *hermano* who is the false Christ, we now know who that is; it is the Hermano Pedro. They hold their services in the house of the mother of Hermana Melencia, because Melencia has a younger sister who is crippled, and Melencia's mother wants to see if the false Christ (namely, Hermano Pedro) will heal her.

The Hermano Pedro held a service, and a boy of six years received the evil spirit and spoke in tongues, and when he was finished, he was tired. He started crying, and he cried and cried. And they did not come back to the services. And the son of Hermano Pedro prayed in tongues, and when he was done praying, he said, "Mami, I don't have my little chick! Mami, where is my little chick? I don't have it!" And he cried.

JULY 13

On July 13, they held a service in the Apostolic Temple of Jesus Christ. The Hermano Isauro said, "Hermanos, this matter seems to me to be very cold, it seems to me that you are sleeping; we have to consecrate ourselves to the Lord, as it says in the *corito*, 'Spirit of God, allow us to feel you, see how your people is sleeping.' Hermanos, you are sleeping, we have to consecrate ourselves to the Lord. You are getting cold. It is important to become hot. Once more, *hermanos*, we are going to sing a few songs to praise our God." And they began singing, and nobody danced. They began moving very gradually, and the one who started dancing first was Dona Julia, the queen of the ball. They removed the chairs that surrounded her, and she began dancing very hard. She passed toward the center, and ran into the table and knocked against it, and the flower vase fell over. Hermano Isauro stood it up again; the Bible had gotten wet, and also the tablecloth, and the Hermana Juana said to her son that he should clean it up. He wiped it up, and the Hermano Isauro cleaned the table. Only one person danced; this was Dona Julia, and when the dance was finished Hermano Isauro said, "Hermanos, really, you are not singing very well, you are asleep, as the *corito* says. Hermanos, you sang very forced; I cannot do what you are doing, for example, dancing. I don't do that, but some day I will do it. We will have eight days of consecration, so that you will become the way you were. You are not singing enthusiastically, but you will become enthusiastic."

JULY 14

On July 14, they held a service in the temple, and when we arrived, they were dancing. Juana danced with her eyes closed; she saw nothing, and she got to the door and almost went out back. The Hermano Isauro pushed her inside, and that way she entered again into the temple. The sons of Juana were laughing because their mother was dancing. The bell was sounded and everyone knelt down to pray. And as they were praying, the Hermano Isauro collected the pieces of the flower vase; then he gathered up the flowers, and wiped the floor with a rag. While they were praying, he was working with everyday matters.

JULY 20

On July 20, we went to a service in the temple, and they danced like people who want to sleep. We went to the front to sing a hymn. They read the Bible; then Hermano Isauro took over and read the Bible, and he said, "Hermanos, it occurs to me that if the Lord should come, He would leave again because none of you is paying any attention. We announce a prayer session for the afternoon, at 4 o'clock; you come at 5. Instead of praying for an hour, we pray for a quarter of an hour. We announce that there will be a service at 7, and you come at 9, and the service starts at 9:30. Hermanos, none of you pay any attention, you are not doing things well, we have become a bit cold, as food gets on a platter. You are very, very negligent; we have to consecrate ourselves to the Lord Jesus Christ."

JULY 23

On July 23, they held a service in the temple. Some *hermanas* from Merida came, along with others from Vaca. When we arrived, the service had started but they had not yet started to dance. The Hermano Pedro said, "Hermanos, let us sing some *coritos,*" and they started to sing the *corito* "Tengo un hogar en gloria." Dona Peregrina began dancing. The congregation had not danced for three days, and Hermano Isauro said that God communicated with these persons and they came.

Dona Peregrina started off; she was followed by other *hermanas* and *hermanos.* In the end, there were fourteen who danced, so that the earth even shook. Hermano Isauro did not dance, but he said, "Although I do not do what you are doing, I am happy." The Hermano Pedro fell down in a sitting position. He opened his eyes and said, "*Gloria a Dios!*" He quickly got up and continued dancing. Hermana Peregrina did not go into the open space to dance for fear that they might knock her down. She danced at the edge in a cramped position. The two daughters of Emerijildo and the daughter of Teresa were holding hands, like a piece of chain, and these three little girls danced very hard. They bumped into another small girl and nearly knocked her down. Everything was in confusion; they even took the chairs and table away from the center, so that there would be room for the fourteen persons possessed by the devil to dance.

They stopped dancing and began to pray, and two of the visiting girls began going around trying to find those who were not praying. The girls grabbed these persons by the hand and pulled them toward the altar. This happened to Francisco E.; they were pulling him, and he did not want to go, and they shouted at him in tongues. He got up but did not go to the altar. And the girls went to pray, and they knelt down. When they were done with praying, they got up. The girls had hurt their knees, and Dito's daughter hit her lips when they were dancing, and her lips became swollen. And Hermano Isauro began speaking, and he said, "Hermanos, the Lord poured out His power. Last week there was little help. But the Lord returned once more to pour out His power until this day. Hermanos, it is nothing what you have seen here. In the North, they jump very high, I think they even get frightened when they see how they jump very high in their places. The Lord speaks to them a great deal by way of prophecies. One time, the Lord said, 'In such and such a street, such and such a house number, there is a person possessed by the devil, who has been locked up for twenty years. Go there, and I will go with you.' When they arrived there, they knocked, and his mother said, 'What, it has been twenty years that my son has been here behind a locked door; there is not even a key.' But they entered there, and they went around the house seven times, and they prayed. When they finished praying, the door was open, and one of them went in, and they hit the man on the cheek. The others entered; they grabbed the man, and they pushed him back, and he was healed. And the Lord spoke to them later, and He said in prophecy, 'Go once more where you found the one possessed, the demons have returned into him. They won't let you enter, but I am with you.' And they went once more and spoke with the man's mother, and she said, 'No, my son has not been cured, and this is nothing but madness.' But they convinced her, and she allowed them to enter. The Lord told them to pray with their eyes open, and they did so and saw how the lock opened by itself. The door opened, and the demons left the man, and the man was cured. They took him to his mother, and he remains cured to this day. Therefore, what you have seen here, it is really nothing."

In the meantime, the two girls went and each pulled the one who had said he was God. He ran clear to the corner of the street. Teresa spoke in tongues, and she herself interpreted it, and said, "My children, you must obey me." And Dona Peregrina said the same thing in Maya: "Children, you must obey me, because I will come soon, and those who are stubborn, I will not take with me. Earthquakes are going to come, and many will die, but nothing will happen to those who will obey." And all the while the girls went around, gathering those who did not go to the front to pray. Rodolfa said, "If I don't want to go to the front, how are they going to force me? If I don't want to go, nobody is going to force me." And Wilma said, "How are they going to pull me? I don't believe they are going to drag me. If they come, I am going to give it to them; I will say, 'I will pray over you.'" And the one who made himself God said, "If you will come now, I will embrace you; if not, I will hit you." And Wilma said, "Well, I'll go home. These here are badly attacked." And many were murmuring about what was happening, and Isauro said that he should pray, and he was the one who was singing at the time of prayer. And Maximo and his wife left, but we remained until the service was over.

JULY 25

On July 25, they held a service in the temple, and the visiting girls began singing a hymn, the title of which was "Nuestro viaje." They sang it about three times, and Dona Peregrina began dancing immediately. The *hermanos* from

Temax arrived. There were about twenty *hermanos;* the temple was filled. Before they began to sing, they said to the daughter of Emerijildo, "You'll have to dance today." They began singing the hymn that I mentioned, and they continued with many *coritos.* They danced with their eyes closed; some bumped into others. The singing ended and all knelt down at various spots, and they spoke in tongues. They interpreted some words, saying as follows: "Children, give me freedom. Children obey me. Children, give me freedom." No matter who was doing the interpreting, they all said the same words. They finished praying and sang many *coritos* and danced again.

JULY 28

On July 28, they held a service at the temple when Hermana Wilma arrived, and Teresa said, "The *hermano* has not come, he was invited." And Hermano Pedro N. arrived with his congregation; there were about thirty of them. Hardly anybody spoke in tongues, and only Joaquina and Pedro danced. And Hermano Pedro N. said, "Hermanos, we are at present here praising the name of the Lord. We will unite with God. I used to disobey the pastors, but I will now obey them, because I read in the Bible, in Hebrews 13 or 17, 'Obey your pastors.' Let us have a brotherly meeting."

Because when Hermano Isauro was praying in the afternoon, he was told in prophecy that they would have to unite with Hermano Pedro N. Therefore, Hermano Isauro went to Hermano Pedro and told him what he had been told in prophecy. And Hermano Pedro said that it was all right, and he humbled himself. In the evening, they went with his congregation, and he said, "Within a month, we will carry out a brotherly meeting, because all the ministers of Luis L. will know about it." And this evening, Hermano Pedro preached, "Obey your pastors, because they watch over your souls. And the Spirit said that all those who separated from us will unite with us, because this is what God wants. Because when Christ comes, and we are divided, he will not take us with him, because the division was not done for Jesus Christ."

JULY 30 AND 31, AUGUST 1

The first night when we went to attend the campaign in the Cinema Canton, there was an *hermano* who had the gift of healing. He preached, jumping and shouting with all his might. He healed many *hermanos.* He healed Hermana Wilma, whose feet were swollen, but the Hermano Celso prayed over her and healed her. The *hermano* who had asthma was also healed, and a man who had had a headache for three years was cured. They had with them a musical group called "Alpha and Omega." There was a boy of about eleven years who played many percussion instruments; he was in charge of the rhythm section. For two nights in the cinema and one night in the temple there was joy, and eight people were converted. They gave them some New Testaments and prayed for them. When they finished praying, Hermano Celso said, "*Hermanos,* I am very happy because there are those who were reborn today, there are young *hermanos,* and the temple was full." Then the service was concluded, and they showed the film, "The Face of Sin." The Hermano Celso said that there were three new fields, that is, newly started congregations, and that prayers should be said for these (in Dzemul and two other places), because these villages were very stubborn.

OCTOBER 16

Accident and death of Hermano Gorgonio:

On October 6, the Hermano Gorgonio completed the service in the Colonia Bogorques in Merida, and on his way to the temple, he had an accident. He was following a car when the car braked very suddenly because it lost a tire. The Hermano Gorgonio crashed into the car. His motorcycle fell over, and the Hermana Dulce, his wife, fell far from the motorcycle. The motorcycle fell on top of Hermano Gorgonio, and the gasoline tank opened and ignited. Hermano Gorgonio's pants caught on fire, and his feet also burned. They took him to the Hospital Horan, and the physician asked, "Where do you work?" And they answered him. And they took him, and put him into a room, and abandoned him; on October 15, he died. They took him to the temple and in the Iglesia Universal it was said in prophecy that he wore two crowns. They buried him on October 15. . . .

On April 8, we were alone because my mother went to visit my grandmother, Dona Eus. Then came Ana, the daughter-in-law of Dona Eucebia, and she began to insult us. We said, "Bitch, you are trying to pick a quarrel," and she continued shouting insults. She demanded that Marjelia come outside and to fight with her. Marjelia went out, and Ana hid in the back, continuing to shout insults, and we put her to flight with stones. Not a single stone hit her, but even our dogs got into the act and attacked her.

Then Dona Eucebia saw it, and they all came, not quite to our house, but they stood in the doorway of Dona Eli; Dona Eli was there. She heard what they were saying. They said, "They keep bothering us, we should get them out, we who belong here; they are like dogs, we should throw them out." We remained at our house, but when we crossed the street, they shouted insults at us. And they continued saying things to us, but we did not answer. When they saw that we did not answer, they went to Las Cinco Calles to wait for us. At about seven in the evening, we went out to buy kerosene, and there we saw them waiting, and out came Dona Eucebia, who went to the middle of the highway. And she said, "Listen here, XEli ["X" or "sh" before a name denotes extreme disrespect], why do you keep saying things to us?" And she kept on asking this. And Eli answered, "I never said anything to you." Then she turned on my mother and said, "It was you, it was you." Her daughter came and grabbed Marjelia, and her daughter-in-law came and grabbed Consuelo. Veti came and grabbed Dona Eli. I was hitting her with a stone. They hit her in her stomach, and she fell on the ground. I was going to hit her with a stone, but my mother would not let me. They tore her dress from top to bottom. Then came her mother, who said, "Come on, daughter, let it be, let's go." They sprayed chile into Consuelo's eyes. They had bought four packets of ground chile so they could spray it into our eyes. They also carried a rope to hit us with, but they did not hit anybody. Everybody had left the quarrel except Eli and Veti. Veti is a woman who has defeated Eli three times before. But this time, Eli scratched her face, and she was screaming: "Let me go, you *comal* [flat metal plate for baking tortillas], let me go, you bitch!" But Eli would not let go. Marjelia passed by and pinched her, and she screamed. Ana was thrown on her back. Stones were thrown at her, and her aunt started screaming. Then Ana said, "You'll pay for this, Marjelia!" And Ana said, "I'll beat Oscar because he threw a stone at me and hit me in the back." When we left, they remained there and started crying, all of them.

7. 1978

Arrival

In Columbus, we had a wind chill factor of minus 60 degrees Fahrenheit yesterday. This morning the car crawled over the icy streets to the airport. By the time I got to Atlanta, it was 17 degrees. The mountains below, the Ozarks and then the Smokies, were a map etched precisely in black and white. I still am awed, after so many years of flying, that we should be so high above it all; that this is what we get to see. New Orleans greets us with 30 degrees—we are improving. I go to Aviateca on Concourse C, and at the counter there are now three employees—an elderly man, who also takes care of cargo problems, and two uniformed girls. But the waiting area is still on the "lower level," unswept and inhospitable. I note that no one has repaired the plastic seat covers that were torn last year. It is also cold, which I find pleasant with my layers and layers of clothes. (I brought no coat—where would I put it in Utzpak?)

The "Pink Panther" finally rolls in, half an hour late. It is painted yellow this year. There is not a seat left after we have piled in.

Eus and her brother, Don Agapito stand exactly where we had agreed they would stand, after last year's miss. Eus looks gaunt, but more lively than I remember and says she has finally found a physician who is helping her to get better. We take the bus to town, and everything seems satisfyingly familiar. The smell is the same, and all the faces look like my long-lost cousins. Except the bus fare has doubled. *Tulaka ba kohi* [Everything is expensive]. The phrase rings of last year, but the process of prices rising has speeded up.

Agapito's wife Sylvia expects us at home. She makes tortillas with beans cooked with fat pork. We talk and laugh till 9:30. Agapito has a very distinctive way of telling things, like variations on one theme, much repeated. How one has to be careful of spoiled food, and then he tells of experiences with spoiled food. Like when he and his father were invited to eat by some men working the next *milpa*. There was a pot of food and a pile of tortillas, and they all sat on the ground. He was a little boy then, but he sat close to the pot and could see the maggots floating in the broth. "Now, if meat is spoiled, you can still eat it; you can wash it, and broil it over the coals, and you can hardly taste that it was spoiled. But you should not cook it with the maggots." His father kept encouraging him, "Eat, boy, *hac ki?* [very tasty], take some broth with your tortilla." But he just couldn't.

We take my bags to the market area. It is a long bus ride; we pick up crowds of shoppers on the way. Eus takes charge of my bags, while Don Agapito and I walk up the bank to exchange my travelers' checks. While I wait at the cashier's counter, Agapito talks with the policeman acting as guard. "I remember her from last year," the policeman says. Makes me feel like I belong here. Agapito squires me around the market. The authorities have installed a handicraft market on the upper floor of the old market, lovely stuff—rocking chairs of native woods, a profusion of embroidery. Nothing like the spectacular cloth that Sylvia's niece composed for me though. Sylvia mentioned last year that her niece in Tibolom embroidered Christmas tablecloths, with the nativity scene and lots of animals and fruit. I bought some percale in Chetumal, 1 by 2 meters, and told her to ask her niece to make one for me, too. She delivered it a day before I arrived, for 700 pesos. It has the nativity scene in the center, angels above, Walt Disney rabbits at the foot of the manger, flowers and peacocks in the four corners, all in the style of ʔipil work, executed on the treadle machine with shiny, thin thread. A feast of color.

Agapito knows lots of people at the market, of course. He suggests that I buy some *chinas* (small, exceedingly sweet oranges; the outer peeling is cut off, then they are halved and sucked); I ask for five from a stand where he talks with the woman about his daughter who recently married a boy from Tibolom and now lives there. She used to work as a seamstress in Los Angeles. The woman—Agapito introduces her as Alicia P.—puts ten oranges into a plastic bag and some tangerines, then won't let me pay. She says her daughter has been anxious to meet me, and I invite her to come to Agapito's house on the 24th when I'll be on my way back to the United States. Later, she comes by as we all stand in the street, waiting for the car that Eus has located for the drive to Utzpak. I note how hurriedly she waves to us and slips past. Eus supplies the explanation: it is her mother that Eus is supposed to have bewitched. The woman has since died.

Daniel is our driver. He is very friendly, although not in the earthy way that characterized the *difunto, le Boocho,* who drowned last year with his entire family. Daniel's first wife died not too long after they were married, together with the child she was carrying. She was ironing and, thus overheated, she opened her refrigerator door. That gave her pneumonia. Daniel is now married to a schoolteacher, not as pretty as his first wife, says Eus, for she has very thick lips. He likes to speak Maya, and we joke about my wearing the ʔipil. I remember seeing some truly odd women as we were waiting for him, wearing high-heeled shoes, stockings, dark-blue culottes, shirt blouses, kerchiefs on their heads tied to the back, and on top of that, straw hats. Probably tourists.

The road to Utzpak is lovely this time of the year, the air cool and fragrant;

an abundance of yellow flowers lines the highway. The cruel, drying winds don't start up till February. I ask about the harvest. It was very bad around Utzpak this past summer. The *monte* did not dry properly because of untimely rain, and the men could not burn the bush. On Ruben's *milpa* there was nothing but stalk. "There is always something," Eus says. "If it isn't the rain, then it is the sun. And then, sometimes, there are the locusts." "When the locusts ate the *milpa*" is a kind of time marker. It happened in 1940–1941. Eus had Aurora, Enrique, Erme, and Wilma, and was pregnant with Soco. She talks about walking two *leguas* to get to the *milpa* and dig for *camotes* (tubers). They would make a *pib* [an earth oven], bake them, eat some, and take the rest to the children. The *milpas* were all dug up; the people would burrow under the stones, turn them over, and dig again. It was for this reason that Agapito and his family left Tibolom and tried to make a living in the city. Sylvia's youngest son, born when she was 40, is now with his older sister Chucha, going to school in Cardenas, where his sister teaches school. They feed and clothe and house him, and Sylvia and Agapito give him the money for books and supplies. He is getting ready to enter medical school.

At the entrance to Utzpak, not too far down from Eus's place, there is a filling station, the first for Utzpak. It is close to the slaughterhouse, where the vultures sit on the *albarrada* all day, watching for offal. Fittingly, they built the new *caja fiscal* right into its wall. Farther on, down the road from Eus, there is a new bar, a square cement-block building with a fresh, thick palm-frond roof. Eus approves of the roof. As to the beer, she laughs about the claim that it is nutritious.

There is also something new in Eus's house: electricity. She paid for the installation by selling her pig. It gives her light (naked bulbs) in the main house, the kitchen, the front yard, and the back yard. Their monthly electric bill is about 5 pesos (25 cents in U.S. money). Eus says that candles had become so expensive and bad—they kept going out at night—that she no longer bought them. The bottle with kerosene and a rag wick was not very reliable, either. With this year's pig, she wants to buy an electric iron.

Reina's Cottage Industry

Nohoch Felix comes with the news that there will be an evening service at the temple. Eus and Nohoch Felix now attend the services of the temple. They went to the Pentecostals for a while, but then drifted back to their old group. "After all, it's all the same God," Eus says with newfound tolerance. We primp in preparation. I always let Eus decide which ʔipil to wear; there is a definite gradation in patterns and material from everyday to festive, a kind of code that is obvious to her, but which I am just beginning to feel—and to think that this is my tenth year in Utzpak! Eus and I tarry on the way; the start of the service is never on time, and we drop in at Reina's on the way.

Reina still wears the dark blue dress I remember from last year; this time there are more white plastic beads missing. She has switched from hammocks to sewing now, and all her products go to Cancun. Not to the tourists, but to the satellite town that has apparently grown up around the tourist center—all the many people that keep the hotels, bars, restaurants, and shops going. "They have not a single *modista* in Cancun," she says. She buys the material, all shiny jerseys, in Merida and has it edged by someone in Utzpak, which gives the seam a pretty wave, and sews about twenty dresses a week. She and Santiago alternate going to Cancun to sell them. She does not use patterns; she says she just "sews what she sees." Since the material stretches, I suppose she has some latitude for mistakes. What she does not sell she leaves in a store on consignment. "You used to have others weave hammocks for you. Do you now work alone?" I ask. "All alone," she says, "and I work day and night." Her friend Irma, the daughter of Dona Juana down the street from the temple, comes in. The two of them go to Cancun together. Irma also sews dresses. They stay overnight with a friend but never venture on the street at night. There are murders and much robbery in Cancun. One time, Santiago was stopped by two men who got out of a car. They demanded his necklace and his money. He had several hundred pesos on him. He handed everything over. Although he cannot read, he knows numbers and remembered the license number of the car. With that he went to the police. The men who had robbed him were the police who took his complaint. They gave him back what they had taken and told him to get lost.

Irma's son comes in at this point with a huge bag stuffed full of clothes. Both Reina and Irma have another woman sewing for them. They carefully examine the dresses, complaining that they are not as carefully made as their own. One is even missing some buttons, and the boy is sent to Bartola to get some.

All the while we talk, Reina continues sewing, which Eus considers rude. Meanwhile, Santiago lolls in the hammock. Eus tells me he still visits the prostitutes; once she even saw him take some soft drinks to them, which now cost 3–4 pesos per bottle, as against the 60 centavos I paid ten years ago. This weekend, both are going to go sell in Cancun because Reina's aunt agreed to take care of the children. "It is easy to work and go selling when there are no little ones to take care of," remarks Reina. Lupita, , now nearing 11, goes shopping for her, but she has not made her do the washing, which other girls her age have to do. She needs the money she earns for her daughters, she says. She bought them a chiffonier and gives them a peso every day when they go to school so they can buy tostados.

Temax: The Doctor and Dona Andrea

We take the morning bus to Temax; Eus needs more medicine from the doctor. I want to talk to Andrea, to see if she can add anything to the story of Don Eduardo. The physician is the son of Chinese immigrants. They own the store on the town square that burned out a few years ago. We do not find the doctor in: he is at his father's store across the street, weighing out macaroni to a customer. He looks like a kind man, rather slim, none of the infuriating (to me) condescension of the government doctor we saw last year. He addresses Eus with "*usted*" instead of "*tu*" and gives her several samples, so that she only has to pay 40 pesos for the consultation.

It seems that last summer Eus got very sick; she was trembling and was hardly able to walk. Her son Enrique took her to a clinic and there they gave her some intravenous glucose, which got her over that crisis. But she was hardly able to swallow anything, and whatever she did swallow she would throw up, especially if it was coarse. She could not drink any water. It is easy to see how that could have led to the dehydration in the hot season. The clinic sent her to have some X rays taken. They charged her 350 pesos and sent her back to the clinic with them without telling her anything about the results. At the clinic, the bundle of X rays went to a physician, who looked at them, charged her 50 pesos, and sent to her to a specialist. That specialist looked at them, charged her another 50 pesos, and said, "You'll have to go to another specialist." At this point, Eus had no money left: neither the monthly allowance from me, nor the 40 pesos her daughter Aurora had sent her via Eus's youngest sister, nor the gifts from her sons Enrique and Erme. "That's it," she said, "no matter what they say now, there is no money left for medicine." So she went home, and for a fortnight took no medicine at all and went to no other physician. She happened to mention the matter to Dona Rosario, however, who had gone through a similar runaround with her niece. She recommended "El Chino" in Temax; he only charged her niece 40 pesos for the consultation, he charged her nothing for the medicine, and he cured her. So Eus also went to El Chino in Temax. He gave her some medicine, and since then she has been getting steadily better.

We then decide to look for Dona Andrea. We do not know her last name or her address, and trying to find an Andrea just with the information that she is fat is a bit difficult in a big place such as Temax. Eus trusts the biographical approach: she was married to a man in Utzpak, her husband died last year, she is supposed to live with her mother. We are directed to a house where we do find a Dona Andrea, *poloc* [fat], but not the one we want. However, after hearing the life history, she tells us that the Andrea we want has a nephew who lives down the street. We find him sitting in the front room, working on some broken TV sets. He assures us that she lives "very far," no sense going there. Only when Eus won't give up does he finally volunteer the directions.

We find Dona Andrea with her 88-year-old mother in the *solar*. She says she is not married again, but Eus tells me later she counted five hammocks—so who uses those? Andrea's father died when he was 90. She shows us a picture of one of her daughters in *ʔipil*. "Ah, mestiza," Eus comments. "Yes, but a month ago she started wearing a dress." "*Tsʔoki* [It's over]," comments Eus regretfully. "True," says Andrea, "but she does look nice in a dress." It is the first time I hear of a change of this kind. I had the impression that it was something that happens in childhood only, the way Nina never wore an *ʔipil*, perhaps as a result of the family's moving from Tibolom.

Andrea says that Don Eduardo had diabetes; he also had a pain in his heart. Eus had mentioned earlier, and it was also said last year, that he had sleeping pills and may have taken too many. He wanted to go back to Utzpak, but Andrea had no money for the bus fare. She does not know why he wanted to go back. All of a sudden he was gone. Then Santiago came to tell her that Eduardo was sick, "but not very sick." Eus: "They did not want Andrea there—they are very bad." Then Wilma came to Temax to see the doctor with her daughter Adela and also went by Andrea's house. She said, "Don Eduardo is dead." Andrea said, "What, dead? When did he die?" She had not been informed of his death. She signed what Eduardo's children wanted her to sign, namely papers so that she would have no claim to any property. "Why have a fight about it?" she shrugs. Santiago would not even let her take the pictures that I had taken of her and Don Eduardo, which she had framed. She was married to him for eight years. I promised to have new prints made for her.

Andrea's mother has a big lot around the house with lovely tall trees, *wayum*, avocado, *chinas*, and others. They have an outside faucet for drinking water. She is a lively old lady who likes to make tortillas under a roof in the yard, where she allows me to take her picture. "And did you see how many tortillas Andrea's mother made? A big pile. Andrea does not live alone," says Eus later. She gives us each a fresh, warm tortilla. We go back to the plaza and miss the 11 o'clock bus by a nose. As we wait around, Andrea's nephew comes by on a bicycle. "Did you find her?" "Yes, but we missed the bus," I say. "There is another one at one." Eus tells him, "*A abuela tu pakʔach* [Your grandmother was making tortillas]," but it goes by him entirely. Maybe it is the Maya. But perhaps he is too citified to participate in the pattern of uninterrupted information flow that constitutes the fabric of village life.

Later, as we approach the plaza again for the return trip, we hear a bus pulling up. It must be the one to Dzilam, Eus thinks. It also stops at Utzpak. We hurry toward the stop, and overtake a man dressed for work on the *col* but hobbling along on crutches, his right leg missing. You see so much of that in Yucatan. These men are usually victims of blasting accidents. We stand in line to buy our tickets and I recognize the driver as the one who years ago took us to Izamal. He is a short man, not much over 4 feet, with small eyes and full lips, a short stocky neck, broad chest, and long arms ending in large, muscular hands. He owns his bus, Eus says, and also carries cargo. As we board, I see blocks of ice stored in the back.

The passengers are mainly men going to work on their *col* or on the ranches, getting on and off, machetes girded on their sides like swords, *henequen* bags slung over their shoulders; some carry rifles. There is a lot of joking among the men, raucous calls back and forth. No participation by the women, who have buckets of *huuch* [*masa*] standing next to them, perhaps because they are going to the ranches where there are no mills to grind the corn.

Excursion to Chetumal

Sunday morning we get ready for the trip to Chetumal. Actually, we had done most of our packing on Saturday. Eus thought we should go this early during my stay, even though this way we could not send word to Nina that we were coming, because they had sent a letter to Wilma via Chan Felix. Eus and I both did our packing at the same time, without even talking about it: we seem to run on a similar internal schedule. We have an early lunch, with Eus prompting me, "Eat a lot, so you won't be hungry on the trip." She tries to follow her injunction, but every bite causes her trouble, and tears sometimes come to her eyes; she does not say if it is from the effort or from the pain. The bus is supposed to leave at 1:00, but Nohoch Felix is apprehensive that we might miss it, so we leave home at 12. You cannot hide any activity in Utzpak: it is like walking down the main street preceded by a sound truck. Of course, the bus does not roll in until 1:00, as Eus had said all along. A group of teenagers comes running down the street, both boys and girls, the girls in sepia-colored uniform dresses, a boy carrying something like an Olympic torch. Nohoch Felix makes some derogatory remark: Apostolics do not believe in sports. Then the family of Old Candil arrives, a sign that Sunday school is over. There is Rodolfa with her two youngest, her daughter Angela with a small baby, Reyes with a child, and two teenage girls. Joaquina is also with her two boys, and there is Manuela C., whose husband is a Chan, and Old Candil himself. I show them some of the snapshots of my children I brought from home. Eus thinks that's good politics; they always ask her whether I am really married and whether I have any children. Eventually, they move on, but Candil still talks with Nohoch Felix. He does not know how many ministers the Iglesia Universal Christiana (the name Juan and Luis L. now give their group) now has. At the last meeting of ministers, there were nineteen, nearly double the number during the time of the secession. No money is ever sent to Juan and Felix by the individual congregations. It all remains for the needs of the local temple and the minister. If some congregation has an unexpected need, the word is passed on, and a special offering is taken. Eus tells me that when there are plans for a ministerial gathering, money is collected ahead of time for the expenses, and then all that money is spent on food, and everybody eats his fill. Last time, Wilma went along with all her children; so did Isauro with his six, and Nicolas Lizama brought his six. They all ate a lot, even meat. The Apostolics, now dominated entirely by the Tabasquenos, also collect money for their ministerial gatherings, but then hardly give the people any food at all.

As for other expenses, Chito, Wilma's son-in-law, loaned the temple 2,000 pesos with which to buy cement, and Isauro saved 1,000 pesos from the offerings, so they think that they will have the temple completed soon.

As we wait, the talk turns to that quarrel between Wilma and the neighbors again; Eli is rather gaunt now, which makes her swarthy face look like that of a Navajo. She has had lots of fights with her husband, who keeps leaving her. She went to the hospital to learn how to sew. Her husband came home and found that she had not cooked anything. He got very angry, beat her, and then left her again. She lives alone now. Her father gave her her inheritance, a building lot, and she has her own house now.

Finally the bus comes; it is very full. We have to stand all the way to Tizimin. A girl has her window open. When I ask if it could be closed, she says no. I am sure it could be closed but don't want to make a fuss. She apparently likes the wind in her face, but for me, standing up and getting it full force, it is cruelly cold, and the *rebozo* gives scant protection. I finally work my way farther back and stand behind some men, who act as a windbreak.

From Tizimin to Valladolid, in another bus, we stand again. "*Wata, wata,*" Eus grumbles, standing, standing. The drivers are tired and churlish, the windows are open, and the wind is cold.

We have to change again, into the Valladolid–Puerto Carrillo bus; Puerto Carrillo, the old Chan Santa Cruz, the headquarters of the Cruzoob—the People of the Talking Cross, Maya revolutionaries who fought for the independence of Yucatan against the Mexicans beginning in 1849 until the struggle petered out, without a peace treaty, more than half a century later, about 1912. In Valladolid I can get no information about buses to Chetumal. All schedules have changed to accommodate the tourists going to Cancun. I stand in line for half an hour, only to find out when I finally get to the ticket agent that the next bus to Chetumal will leave tomorrow morning. No other way? Yes, to Puerto Carrillo, and then take another bus from there to Chetumal. We barely make it to the last one going in that direction for the day. They sell no numbered tickets, which means that we have to stand again in the bus and pay in transit. We stand next to a young couple dressed in peninsular elegance, the girl in clingy blue dress, lots of jewelry, U.S. overnight case, he in white slacks, white *huayabera*, white embroidery. They quarrel, she goes to the front to escape, and Eus can at least sit down. I crouch on the armrest beside her. In Carrillo Puerto, we have to wait for an hour for the bus to Chetumal. The sun goes down at six, so it is pretty dark by now. We stand again and get to Chetumal at 10:00. We take a taxi to Nina's street corner; the taxis do not enter those streets, they are too bumpy. We start hunting for Number 527. It is nearly 11, not a soul about, dogs barking furiously. I can see the headlines—"Dos Senoras Muertas en la Colonia Lopez Mateos—Asalto y Robo" [Two Ladies Dead in the Colonia Lopez Mateos—Assault and Robbery.] We are lost in the 400s with our heavy bags getting heavier and heavier. Eus had insisted on warm clothing for the night. Unaccountably, the 400s keep getting lower instead of higher as they should. We cross the highway again, now going in the opposite direction. I slow down because I can see some men in the street lights—after all, caution is the better part of valor. A being, we cannot see which gender, wrapped in a blanket comes out of a house, perhaps to relieve himself. His house? Number 481. Number 527? Oh, farther down thataway. The street is unreal; stones like on a Cyclop's playground; a ditch, perhaps for drinking water; little light. We finally find our way to something that looks like Nina's house, although it no longer has the gate I remember from last year, and the number is 525, not 527. A new stone house next door is 527. Does Nina maybe have a new house? Eus says no. So I suggest that she go and call at the door of 525. "Does Nina live here?" she calls in Maya. Again she calls. I wonder who is going to come out, or what? But there is an answer from inside: we are at the right place! The numbering of the houses had been changed recently. Nina says she dreamt a few nights ago that she went to the depot and we arrived, and she asked, "Why didn't you write?"

Nina is fully dressed because of the cold. I put on everything that provident Eus has made me bring, and still it is no use. The walls of the house are constructed of sticks and cardboard; it's like being outside without a tent and not much of a sleeping bag. I feel icy to the bones. In my misery, I remember having read that we tremble when cold because that increases the temperature of the body. I try moving, kind of rocking in intense, small movements, in the hammock. There is a pleasant heatflush all over and I fall asleep. After a while, I wake up because I have not kept up the mock trembling while asleep. So I have to start all over again. It is a long night.

Nina and Desi are on an even keel. "They don't fight," is Eus's assessment. Nina still refuses to have another child; I don't know what method of birth control she uses. Desi began drinking with the neighbor, but Nina told him to his face that she did not want to have him come back. Then he went drinking with his friend in a tavern. Nina got together with his wife and the two of them went to the police, charging nonsupport. The police locked the men up for five days. That put a stop to Desi's drinking bouts; he only drinks a beer now and then.

There are a number of nice cement-block houses going up in the *colonia,* and the government has begun to work on the drinking-water line. In the meantime, it has put up huge round tanks which are filled every day with drinking water. Nina's household is the same as last year; she has a wardrobe with shelves on one side of the general Yucatecan design now, and on top of it, a plastic Christmas tree without ornaments or lights. When the little girls don't play with their dolls, the dolls are placed out of reach under that bare tree.

Desi now makes 600 pesos per week. It sounds good, but food has doubled in price since last year, the cost of bus tickets has tripled, and clothes are nearly out of reach. Yesterday, the price of bus tickets for intercity traffic went up all over Yucatan. A man comes to Nina's door; he is from Tikʔin, a community about 80 kilometers from Chetumal. Nina buys clothes on the installment plan from him, and he has come by to collect. He also sells ʔipiles. He fears that soon it will not be worth his while to continue his business because fares will be higher than his profit.

The next evening we go to Don Victor's home. He now has a small temple next to his home, but we cannot see it, it is locked; somebody from his family says he has just gone to the center to do some shopping. There is no service tonight. Nina leaves word, asking that he come to see us at her house. She says he comes quite often and sits to chat with her. As we turn to leave, we hear someone preaching over a loudspeaker. It is almost like Luis L.'s style, so we go to find out. We trace the sound to a private home jam-packed with people— about five men (some more outside standing by the window), at least twelve women, and lots of children. There is a microphone attached to the loudspeaker outside. A woman, identified as the wife of the preacher, by her style and manner not a Yucatecan, teaches the children religious hymns. They sing something like "marching for Jesus," with the children mimicking a trumpet during the refrain. "Let's go in," says Nina. We are politely offered chairs. The preacher has taken over the microphone. I wonder where he is from; it appears to be the Valle de Mexico—he is clearly unfamiliar with the Maya version of Spanish. He preaches with tremendous exertion, and his phonology involves lots of trilled r's. He wants his audience to be enthusiastic about the Segunda Iglesia's [Second Church's] decision to buy a building lot for a temple in the neighborhood. There is a prayer for the sick after the sermon, during which a woman is fanned with a towel in the back. She may be the one I heard singing during the prayer. It sounded like she was singing in trance but with intelligible phrases. All three of us have the impression that this is a congregation that speaks in tongues but holds back because of strangers crowding at the door and the windows, ourselves included. It is a curing service, we are told, for the woman of the house. According to the sermon, it is the Devil that sends illness and sin; Jesus is there to defend the people against this onslaught. There is a kind of electric enthusiasm about it all, which I don't think the preacher could have created without some base in trance. A rather somber man by the name of Fuentes, again not Yucatecan, accompanies the singing with a pair of Mexican maracas; that is their only music. The preacher fumbles for a piece of paper in his folder containing the *corito* he has announced. We leave after the general hand-shaking. None of us has ever heard about a Second Church. Maybe it is another one of the many Pentecostal sects springing up all over.

JANUARY 17, TUESDAY

The night is not as cold as the previous one. Nina changes into a cotton dress to sleep in. When Desi comes home from work he takes a bath; changes into clean, good clothes; eats; and lies down in his hammock. The children pile on top of him. "That is how they keep warm," he says.

Don Victor comes by the next morning around ten, looking fit and virile. I want to find out from him how he has taught his son to have visions. First of all you meditate, he says. There is no particular procedure; wherever you are, whatever you do. Then you kneel and pray, trunk upright, arms lifted, hands turned forward with fingers curled, eyes closed. His son Daniel could have had more visions, but he stopped praying. As to the church of Juan and Luis L., the dancing was really wild in the beginning, with people staggering, falling on the floor, and writhing. But in October a man by the name of Juan Castillo came from the States and told them that what they were doing was wrong. He also objected to the fact that when the people were speaking in prophecy, they identified with God, talking to "*mis hijos*" [my children]. He took Juan, Luis, Nicolas Li., and Jose G. (Don Victor's nephew) to the States with him for a visit. What happened there, Don Victor does not know. Even this is only hearsay, for Jose G. hates his uncle and will not tell him anything.

Don Victor still has a group in Utzpak. He and Eus gossip a bit. There have been intimations of adultery between Alvio and Lulu, the wife of Augustin. Augustin is supposed to have complained against Alvio to the authorities in Valladolid. Eus says maybe it isn't true that anything has happened between them; maybe Alvio just came to the house to rest. But Rodolfa says that, yes indeed, they were seen in the hammock together, "wrestling." Rodolfa is the enemy of Lulu, says Don Victor. According to the Bible, he says, if there are adulterous relations between a consenting couple, both should die; if the man violates the woman, the man should die.

He has few followers—"We progress slowly." According to Eus, there is no one outside the family in Utzpak, and according to Nina, it is just his family here in Chetumal. "People don't want to study," is Eus's comment. That is about right: Don Victor is interested purely in theological disputations. The pieces of cardboard on which he wrote so much of what he found meaningful in the Bible have long been removed from the walls of the temple in Utzpak. He has not heard of the Segunda Iglesia, either. When we tell him about the preacher saying that illness comes from the Devil, he shakes his head. "Why don't those young men come and talk with me?" Presumably, to be enlightened. He still avers that the gift of interpretation is not available anyplace in Mexico, although I have seen it in Utzpak. He is clearly out of touch.

As for Nina, she is not connected with any congregation. She says it is too difficult to take the children. Two girls come by and leave again when they see that she has guests. Nina says they are Jehovah's Witnesses, and they are "studying" with her.

January 17, in the Evening

I would love to ask Luis L. a few questions, but when Eus, Nina, and I arrive at his Templo Bet-El, Iglesia Universal Cristiana the next day, he is not in. He has gone to hold a service in a temple near Belize. We are asked our whos and wherefroms and are greeted very kindly. The service is as usual; I am curious to see if they will drive the congregation into a trance by way of the *corito* rite as they do in Utzpak and what else might be general for all of the churches of Juan and Luis L. Once the *coritos* have started, a woman in the front row begins to become agitated; I can see the muscles of her buttocks moving under her tight dress, she is subdividing the rhythm the way the small girls do in Utzpak, giving two eighth notes to each quarter note. She starts moving toward the rostrum in steps that look like Joaquina's. But since she is so lively, her mantilla slips off her head. There are two men on the right who are getting very restless also, when the *hermano* in charge cuts off the sequence of *coritos*. It is obvious that this takes the woman by surprise; she has difficulty coming out of the trance. Her movements—I see her from the back only—have become disoriented. Finally she angles for her mantilla and goes to her seat. I think the dance was aborted because of our presence. No other sequence of *coritos* is initiated, and eventually, after an abysmally boring sermon, the service is concluded.

Outside, we see Joaquin C. He has put on weight, which with his thin frame makes him loom like a stuffed sausage. He still works as a housepainter. When

Jose, Wilma's oldest son, was here trying to find a job, he worked with Joaquin for a while. But Joaquin was mean and surly, fighting and quarreling with Jose. Jose finally went home again to his parents.

JANUARY 18, WEDNESDAY

The trip home was considerably more pleasant. I was able to buy tickets in Chetumal for as far as Valladolid, so we had numbered seats, and even after we changed buses, we did not have to stand. In Valladolid we ran into the daughter-in-law of Don Agostin. His son left her with four children, and since he did not pay her any alimony for a year, she finally had him put in jail in Valladolid, where he and his new wife worked. The judge did not let him out until he paid her what he had accumulated.

By the time we get home, I am very hungry. So I let myself be tempted by a plateful of very hard black beans that Nohoch Felix had sitting on the fire. Eus hesitated, but I threw caution to the winds. I paid the next morning with a miserable diarrhea.

Wilma's Visit

In Chetumal, we had a tin can with a wire for a handle for our body waste, which Desi occasionally emptied out on the street. I thought, well, we in Utzpak have an honest-to-goodness outhouse! So first thing when we get home I go to the highly prized facility. As I come back to the house door, I am hit from behind by what feels like a big branch with thorns on it. I turn around, surprised, and there is a large rooster, a brilliantly plumed package of fury, trying to assert his regal rights over the yard. As I hurriedly slam the door, he crows victoriously. When I tell of my adventure, both Eus and Nohoch Felix laugh. "We forgot to tell you—he attacks everybody." Great.

Next time, I take a branch and try to intimidate him with it. We join in a battle royal; I hit his legs and his wings, but this makes him all the more enthusiastic. "Hit his head," Eus calls from the benches. She and Nohoch Felix are having a great time watching. I hit his comb, almost reluctantly, but my branch is no match for his strength; it begins to splinter, and he manages to score a direct hit with his spur on the back of my hand (which remains blue after five days). Eus finally comes in on my side, and he beats a hesitant retreat, crowing victoriously. Nohoch Felix suggests that next time I take the implement, a kind of mop, which they use to wipe water from their floor. It has a long handle and ends in a transverse piece of wood that has a strip of tire nailed to it. The rooster is supposed to be afraid of that. Not so. He jumps on the transverse section and tries to get to me that way. "How about the whip?" Eus asks, but I am battle-weary, and to the amusement of Eus, and especially of Nohoch Felix, who always tries to prove to me—in his affectionate way—that I really know nothing and don't understand anything, I now call for my bodyguard. "Hermano Felix, *le tˀeelo!* [the rooster is coming!]" He takes the whip to it, then throws stones, without much success. He refuses to let Eus kill the rooster; he thinks it's funny that the bird should be so malicious.

At this point, Wilma arrives. She is pregnant with her tenth child and very beautiful. She is lugging a monstrously heavy suitcase with samples of all the bounty of Tabasco where she now lives, much of it strange to her parents—cocoa still in its pericary, plantain, and sweet corn and pieces of sugar cane for her father, who likes to chew and suck it. Ruben and Jose are cutting sugar cane. It is hard work; they are not used to it, but at least they earn enough to feed the family. Also, there is much fruit around because there are three harvests per year, and the members of Ruben's congregation give the children bananas and other things to eat.

At La Mina, where the family now lives, the women prayed for a year that the officers of their church in Villahermosa would send them a new pastor to replace the one who had left. Finally, they sent Ruben. When he and his family arrived, the congregation had dwindled to four adults. Now it was back to twenty-five members and still growing. Ruben and Wilma taught them all the hymns and *coritos* sung in Utzpak. Their previous pastor, a Tabasqueno, severely exploited the congregation, demanding their best food and fattest chickens as gifts. Since there was no other pastor, they had to put up with him. "If a pastor demanded one of my chickens," remarks Eus, "I would kill it and eat it myself first." When an offering was collected, the *hermanos* were told what they had to pay—100 pesos per man per week, 50 pesos per woman, and 20 pesos for each child. Gonzalez also told them that he had the power to throw out anybody who did not promptly pay all that was allotted. Eventually, the *hermanos* could take it no longer and started drifting away. Gonzalez lost interest in the unprofitable congregation and concentrated instead on two other ones, coming only occasionally to extort more money. What he would do was read a biblical passage, give a brief sermon, and that was it.

Under Ruben's guidance, the congregation has started to get "hot" again—that is, speak in tongues—and the attendance keeps increasing. As to the offerings, Ruben asks only for 5 pesos per week, and only if they can afford it. And he does not send the offerings to Villahermosa, as is demanded by the church authorities. If they try to force him to do that, Ruben has said that he will join Juan and Luis L.'s organization.

Wilma also brings other news. Nicolas L. has a congregation in Nicolas Bravo. Everyone danced when Ruben and Wilma visited that congregation. The temple was trembling, they danced so hard. Some fifteen students from the nearby technical college also danced and sang, although they did not know the *coritos*. They even started falling down, and Ruben watched them and helped so that they would not hurt themselves. In prophecy, one *hermana* said that God would punish them if they did not also speak in tongues. The students became scared and asked the congregation to pray over them, and many did receive the baptism of the Holy Spirit.

When a congregation, Wilma observes, does a lot of dancing, there tends to be a lot of speaking in tongues, along with interpretation and dreams and visions. One *hermana* saw in a vision a huge black pot that was breaking apart. In a dream, an *hermano* received the interpretation that the pot breaking meant that they had defeated the devil. Precognition is also reported. Wilma, for instance, knew beforehand (and told Eus about it) that Gorgonio, a Tabasqueno preacher living in Merida, would have a motorcycle accident. His wife, Dulce, Wilma says, still has not gotten over it. She just lies in her hammock and can hardly take care of her small son. It seems that she is also pregnant again. I am wondering about all these reports of prophecies. Does it have something to do with the special quality of the trance introduced by the dance? Wilma certainly makes that connection.

The woman who was the president of the Dorcas in the congregation that Ruben took over continued to hand over to Gonzalez all of the money she collected from membership dues and *talentos*, even after Ruben became pastor. The congregation thereupon elected another woman as president of the Dorcas. The previous president, the woman, protested against this election in church. She became louder and louder and more and more abusive. So Ruben had the congregation pray over her to stop the altercation. Then the Holy Spirit started to manifest itself. There was also a healing in Ruben's congregation when the *hermanas* prayed over a sick little girl. Wilma thinks that it happened because the praying *hermanas* believed that it would. Gonzalez, on the other hand, says that if a person puts his hand on another person's head to heal him, it is the Devil's work.

Wilma has also come to do some shopping in Utzpak, and the next day the three of us create quite a stir as we walk down the street in our immaculate *ʔipiles*. The information comes from Nohoch Felix, who makes a habit of reporting the men's reaction to us. It is the time of day when women, wearing a faded *rebozo* or a Turkish towel, usually go to the mill in clothes rumpled from having been slept in overnight.

Wilma buys some plastic shoes for Rebecca. In La Mina, people walk barefoot in the soft mud; her older children have adapted to that, but Rebecca still needs some protection. I bought a doll for her, which I had promised but had forgotten: it was not in my notes. I also bought some slacks for Joaquin to match the shirt I brought him. Wilma had tried to borrow some money from Chito, her son-in-law. He gave her the price of her bus ticket, but not more. He was out of cash because he was paying on his new truck.

Wilma, by the way, also shows signs of picking up words of the local language in La Mina. I don't know what indigenous language is there, and neither does she. Characteristically—she has a sensitive ear—she is beginning to drop her final "s" sound, a phonological rule not applied to Spanish in Yucatan, but apparently in force in Tabasco.

The Services

When we arrive at the temple, the service is already in progress. The old mud-and-wattle structure is no longer visible; the cement blocks rise around it like a new skin. To the right and left of the temple, there are half-finished walls of cement block. Luis L.'s sister, who owns a grocery store, gave the congregation a gift of 2,000 blocks. The congregation rented a truck to bring them to Utzpak, and Isauro and his younger brother are building the new temple. When we enter, I see on the rostrum a bag of cement. I privately mourn the imminent demise of the cozy little mud-and-wattle temple, home of so many memories, but I admire the stubborn persistence of the congregation.

The day before, Wilma and I visited Isauro because Wilma wanted to deliver a letter from Ruben. Isauro and his family live behind the temple in the *casa pastoral.* The walls of this building are of mud and wattle with some cardboard nailed against it. The usual invitation to enter answers our knock. Juanita is in a hammock, nursing her youngest, about a year and a half old. A hen wanders in and out, pecking in the refuse on the cardboard floor. Isauro, a Bible in his hand, rises from a wide, flat frame bed made of poles and covered with Mexican *petates* [reed mats]. I know from Eus that all the children sleep on it, for the family is so poor, they have only one hammock. There are some ends of rope strung overhead, with an assortment of *cortes* [material for pants] that Isauro sells.

We are offered chairs, and Wilma tells about the problems in La Mina. Isauro comments that it is the same all around the country. The Apostolics want to have nothing to do with the Holy Spirit. He knows of a book about the history of the Apostolic Church in Mexico entitled *The Serpent and the Dove* (Gaxiola 1970). "The Dove is tired," he jokes. "In fact, it is dead." Juan and Luis L. went around to various meetings in the country, and also to Tepic, Nayarit, to the Biblical Institute there, listening to what others were reporting. They heard that with the dance came many manifestations of the Holy Spirit. Only the Apostolics do not want this. Hermano Montiel even went to the authorities in Mexico City to find out whether anyone could be forbidden to dance in church. He was told that Mexico had religious freedom, and that included dancing. People want the Holy Spirit, and if the *hermanos* in the temples no longer want that, then people will hold services in private homes and the ministers will be left as caretakers of temples without congregations. This is what is happening. Juan and Luis L. have congregations even outside of Yucatan; for example, in Belize. "Too bad," Isauro says, "that not many *hermanos* dance in the temple in Utzpak. Perhaps they are shy about it." (When we tell Nohoch Felix about the conversation later, he scoffs—"He [Isauro] does not dance either," he says.) As to the financial abuse, Isauro says, there are people who now talk about the Apostolic Mafia. They collect as much money as they can. They pass the high offices around within a small circle of friends and relatives, just as it is done in worldly politics, maintaining that only they are capable of running the organization properly. All is for profit.

Wilma finally hands Isauro the letter. He opens it and reads it, nodding. "It is the same development everywhere," he says, without reading it aloud. He assumes, I suppose, that Wilma knows what Ruben has written. On the way home I ask Wilma about Ruben's letter to Luis L. "I'll take it to Peregrina's house when I am in Merida," she says.

I often recalled this conversation with Isauro as I observed the services. True, as Nohoch Felix had observed, Isauro did not dance. But clearly, he had assumed a different, equally important role and was loyal to his commitment to keep the dove alive. In a most sophisticated way he was employing a sequence of *coritos* to "drive" the congregation into the dance and, subsequently, to facilitate the manifestation of the Holy Spirit.

This is my first service after my arrival:

My initial impression is that the congregation consists of many new faces with a sprinkling of the old ones until I start identifying people with Eus's help in a whispered conversation. Then the revelation hits me. I had determined quite early on that recruitment to the congregation proceeded along kinship lines. That had now continued into the second generation! The sea of unknown faces were the small children, now grown into early adulthood—after all, girls marry at 13 or 14 and boys at 16 or earlier. There was still the large family of old Candil; Isauro was represented by six children, two of them boys in their early teens; there were Teresa's children; and to my total surprise, there were Hermano Antonio B.'s wife and two of his daughters, who previously were not churchgoers. Some members had become more prominent: Eli, only marginal ten years ago, is now very active. Her oldest daughter is an important dancer, as are the two daughters of Antonio, while it seems that her sister Goya and husband Alvio are still with the Branhamists. Joaquina is more prominent in the service. Teresa's oldest daughter is an active dancer. The only important blocs that have dropped out are that of Goyo and Valuch and of Rosa and her mother Paula. And some formerly insignificant ones are now in the front row: Emerijildo's daughter Aurelia is central. His mother and wife are important, and he was too, until a few days ago, when he had a motorcycle accident while riding with Juan L. The latter suffered only minor injuries, but Emerijildo broke a leg. After the accident, he was taken to a hospital. They made him wait for twenty-four hours, although it was quite obvious that his leg was broken, with bone fragments sticking out of his flesh and his foot turned sideways. The doctors and nurses would just go by and look at him, but they did nothing for him. Finally, Juan and Luis took him to a clinic, where his leg was set and put into a cast. He prayed all the while he was waiting in the hospital, and he felt no pain.

During the service I hear a lot of glossolalia. Perhaps due to Isauro's efforts, some members of the congregation who had not spoken in tongues now do, as, for instance, Rodolfa. Occasionally, the behavior blossoms into unusual forms, such as when Pancho N. and Emerijildo's 11-year-old daughter engage in a glossolalia duet, very beautiful.

After the sermon, Pancho N. stands next to the table. He says that after danc-ing he saw the moon at three cardinal directions, but not in the south. A week ago, there was a service in the house of Fuana. After the dance there, he says, he had a vision in which a man came who was very tall. Then another one came. They put chewing gum into his mouth, then took it out again. This Pancho N., the husband of Rodolfa's sister, also makes up his own songs. He writes the text into his notebook and then sings. Nohoch Felix and the guitarist try to dress it up as he sings. "He keeps forgetting his own melodies," Nohoch Felix remarks, rather amused.

As to the dance, it is a kind of shuffle step. Joaquina is standing next to me, her eyes closed, hands folded on her chest in prayer. Then she begins to dance, back and forth. But since she takes a larger step with her right foot, she begins to move forward. A woman sitting in the row in front of me motions to some girls obstructing the aisle to move out of the way, managing the scene so Joaquina can go forward. Others simply clap and shuffle in place.

The next evening service is to be held at the house of Felipe N. It is to be a *confraternidad*, a joint service of Isauro's and Pedro N.'s congregations. Pedro N., says Nohoch Felix, keeps refusing to bring his group into the temple. "No man is going to tell me what to do," he is quoted as saying. The N. house is quite far, at the outskirts of Utzpak. We, that is Eus, Wilma, and I, go to Chelo's house first and there pile into the cabin of Chito's truck, packed as tightly as sardines, with Chelo next to Chito and Wilma squeezed against the door. There is some joking about me being fat, and Chito asks, "How much *do* you weigh?

Eighty kilos?" I indignantly deny it, which they think is funny because being *poloc* [fat] is actually a Maya attribute of beauty.

I had been debating whether I should ask Isauro for permission to film the dancing. Now I see that it was good that I did not bring up the issue, because we are going to have the service in the courtyard and there would not have been enough light. There would not have been any room to film either, for quite a crowd gathers under the trees. There is an electric light on the side of the house illuminating the table with the flowers and the dish for the offering and another bulb to the left in the back, strung on a tree.

Eli arrives, very friendly. There is a certain restlessness in the crowd. I cannot count how many there are, but it must be around 100 if we include the many children. Teresa, who sits in the first row close to the table (we are behind her in the second row), begins to intone a *corito;* many join in, as a kind of rehearsal.

Pedro N. arrives. He has a cattle truck now; his father gave him some of his inheritance so he could pay for it. The truck disgorges at least twenty people, among them the Four Violets. Today three of them have white lace mantillas; the fourth wears a dark blue kerchief tied back on her head. Wilma tells me later that the girl with the dark kerchief is Pedro N.'s daughter. Pedro N. is a swarthy-looking man, rather stocky, with an aquiline nose. He goes over to Isauro to greet him.

Isauro opens the service and asks for a *corito.* They actually sing three and then stop. A woman calls out, "*Ya se acabo?* [It's over already?]" There is some laughter, and two guitarists, one from Isauro's group and the other from Pedro N.'s group, restlessly pluck cords. Isauro intones the rousing "Yo quiero mas y mas de Cristo" [I want more of Christ]. At first the two groups sing in different rhythms, but by the second *corito* they begin to adjust to each other. The singing of various *coritos* lasts over twenty minutes.

Dancing begins very soon after the start of the *corito* rite. It is dramatic when the movement of the dancers begins after a few beats of the *corito.* There is a rhythmic agitation of the women's buttocks and shoulders; then the steps begin. Julia from our congregation goes first; then the girls around her; the Violets from Pedro N.'s group follow; and then some women here and there in the crowd. Then Isauro calls for prayer. The dancers fall on their knees and there is glossolalia, loudest from Aurelia. She soon passes into intelligible speech, which then loses its trance-produced intonation and becomes a stereotyped prayer with conventional phrases. Then she returns into trance and glossolalia. She continues this alternation. Nahuat keeps in the background; later he offers a brief testimony. There is a duet emerging between Aurelia and the Violets, who speak one at a time. Again the communal prayer becomes hushed, making the glossolalia and the alternating "prophecy" stand out in bold relief.

The communal prayer becomes louder as Aurelia briefly descends into a barely audible phrase. She gets her second wind, and once more the communal prayer recedes. "*Aminiseriba, aminiseriba,*" is her glossolalia phrase; then, "*ah mis hijos . . . esta noche . . . yo quiero . . .* " "Oh, my children," she says, " . . . tonight . . . I want . . . " There are many "*Gloria a Dios,*" "*Aleluyas,*" and "*Amens*" from the congregation, then the communal prayer is over. Isauro calls for an ascent to his *Gloria a Dios,* and it comes, a loud shout: "*Amen! Gloria a Dios, Amen!*" He then asks for a hymn that has as its refrain "*Hermano, da mi la mano* [Brother, give me your hand]." He asks that instead of shaking hands, everyone give the person next to him an *abrazo* [embrace]. The entire congregation starts milling around, women among women, men among men, never losing the strands of the hymn. "After all," says Isauro, "some of those present are already charged, as if by an electric current, and others are, well, a bit discharged. If you put a lot of effort into this *abrazo,* possibly some of that charge will be transmitted." We are all caught up in this embracing. Women I have never seen before, from Pedro N.'s group, many of them in faded *rebozos* and wrinkled *?ipiles,* embrace me, some with tears in their eyes. I can see Wilma and Elide in each other's arms; Teresa puts her arms around Eus, her erstwhile foe; and we also hug each other, that is Chelo, Wilma, Eus, and I. Joaquina comes, and Rodolfa, and I try to note who joins in the embracing and who does not. In a conversation the next day I realize that I was not the only one doing that. When I ask if anybody saw Hermano Antonio B.'s wife, Eus says, "She was there, but didn't you see that she did not come to give us an *abrazo?*" "She still is not reconciled," adds Wilma. Everyone continually reads the social map. The next hymn, "*Que gozo es, que gozo es estar aqui*" [What a pleasure it is to be here], which ends in "give me your hand, Hermano," goes on and on.

Finally, Isauro calls for another hymn, of somewhat lower key; "Amenonos de corazon" [Let us love each other]. Testimonies follow. I can see Chito, hands in his pants pockets, leaning immobile against the corner of the house, close to the entrance. Nohoch Felix is by him. Isauro passes into another, shorter series of *coritos,* capped off by a communal prayer. I can hear Teresa and Joaquina in glossolalia, but what becomes very prominent is the glossolalia of the Four Violets. Their syllable inventory is somewhat different from that prevailing in Isauro's congregation. Again, the prayer is hushed as the Four Violets become stronger. I now see that they represent a ritual unit: the three, wearing the white mantillas, utter glossolalia phrases, while the fourth one, Pedro N.'s daughter, wearing the dark blue kerchief, is the interpreter. Teresa is also in glossolalia, but she keeps her vocalization barely audible. Pedro N. stands in front of the kneeling Violets, holding his hand over them. His daughter has her right hand behind her back, her left arm raised. The other three have their arms down, weaving back and forth to the rhythm of their glossolalia. I am amazed at the sophisticated performance aspect. Isauro also takes note; he is turned toward them, although standing further away, turning his uplifted hand toward them, his arm raised. The Four Violets go on and on with their glossolalia. They don't run out of steam; apparently they know how to husband their energy by alternating their glossolalia—quite a remarkable feat. However, their interpreter does tire. Both Isauro and Pedro N. drop their arms. The Violets are still weaving sideways in synchronization, uttering glossolalia. Their syllables become very simple: "*adifa, adifa,*" a pause, then "*hariba, ba . . . ba . . .*" and out.

Wilma whispers to me, "The prophecy has been that the service will last till 12, and anyone who leaves before then will be punished." So while I was trying to understand the ritual structure, she was listening for "the message." Wilma is right. Isauro now repeats the same statement. "I imagine," he says, "there will still be people who will want to leave. That is the reason why not everybody will enter the kingdom of heaven." He then asks, Is there anybody present who has never experienced the presence of the Holy Spirit? No one comes forth. He waits a moment, then says, rather ironically, "The prophecy says that a number of you have not. You mean to tell me that the Lord made a mistake?" "Those who have never experienced it should now come forth and kneel here," Isauro continues, pointing to the area around the table. About thirty men and women come forth, rather hesitantly, and kneel down on the cold and stony ground. Isauro instructs them to say "*gloria, gloria,*" assuring them that soon their tongue will change, indicating the presence of the Holy Spirit. Both he and Pedro N. "drive" the seekers, clapping, Pedro N. speaking in glossolalia. They move from seeker to seeker, placing their hand on the heads of likely candidates. A small woman standing to my left is in a lengthy glossolalia.

Finally, Isauro steps back and intones a melodious "*Aleluya, aleluya . . .*" Against that background of chanting, Teresa starts a glossolalia utterance which blends in beautifully. Upstaging her, however, the Four Violets begin again, with glossolalia and interpretation. "I am sad," the interpreter says, "because there are still doubters here. My sisters Librada, and Reyes, and [I don't catch the next two names], you should all come forth, pray, and surrender yourselves." The glossolalia of three of the Violets is nearly exhausted, but the interpreter is still going strong. She is on her knees, as are the other three, and she rocks up and down.

Teresa and the small woman next to me now take up the glossolalia strand. There are still quite a number of people praying at the table, now spurred to renewed effort. Isauro repeats that they should say, "*Gloria, gloria.*" Teresa and the woman next to her are in glossolalia, which is also acting on the supplicants. From the direction of the table I can hear a high "*rirtriririri,*" which soon is drowned out. It is 9:45; the service started at 7:30, and some people are beginning to leave. Isauro is clearly aware that his congregation is fraying at the edges. So he tries to calm the assembly by starting on a slow hymn—Alavanos . . . let us praise the Lord. . . . But his move is futile. The principal actors follow their own trajectory. The Four Violets are in vivid glossolalia, pulling along Julia's son Lorenzo. Teresa jubilates in a gloriously pulsating glossolalia song. The congregation follows along. In the row of the seats to the left, I see Roldolfa's deaf-mute daughter Imelda. She is holding on to the back of the chair in front of her, rocking back and forth, suddenly uttering a hoarse but audible glossolalia. The hymn has long run out; Eus and I sit down and, despite the cold, Eus drops off to sleep. Then Isauro begins to speak. "Despite these beautiful manifestations," he says, "let us remain humble. Many have experienced a manifestation. Does anyone want to tell what he felt?" After some hesitation, a teenage boy comes to the table and says that he was in a white light; he did not know where he was.

Pancho N. steps up to the table and says that while he was praying he saw the Lord, who was wearing a white belt hanging down to the floor on the side and had some letters on the palm of his hand, and there was a white horse.

A man comes to the table and says that he wants to be baptized, but to do that he will have to get married by registry; he asks that one of the ministers accompany him to the registrar's office, for "I want to marry my wife."

The man kneeling at the table now gets up and steps to the edge of the table. His hair is tousled; he is past middle age. He apologizes for making his statement in Maya. He is greeted with a lot of enthusiastic *aleluyas* and *amens*. He says he cannot read, and it is hard for him to tell of his experience. He saw a white arc, and he was standing under it, and it filled him with indescribable joy. "Many of us cannot say what we have experienced, it is so overwhelming," comments Isauro.

It is now 10:35. Isauro suggests that there should be some special hymns, three from each congregation. The first to offer a hymn are Teresa and Juana, in lovely harmony. Then come the two sons of Juana, Lorenzo and Fausto. They can't sing, but they are well intentioned. After the two daughters of Rodolfa with Elide, it is the turn of Antonio's wife. Then we have the Four Violets, together with another girl who has also done some interpreting, harmonizing beautifully, leaning on each other as they sing. Next are six women from N.'s congregation, and then the Violet who did the interpreting, then another woman, and then the guitarist. I learn later that they are N.'s wife, daughter, and son. Again, the offering is very pleasing musically.

It is 11:00. All those hymns have innumerable verses, and Isauro passes to Elias Li., the son-in-law of Valuch, who reads from the Bible and calls for the *ofrenda*. Isauro tries to stem the tide of people leaving by saying that it doesn't matter how cold it is or how late; the Lord wants everyone to stay.

Elias passes to Pedro N., who also reads a text from the Bible. He opines that if the whole world would be Christian, there would no longer be any wars. Everyone must be involved in the work of conversion. It is now 11:20. Pedro N. calls for a *corito*, then for a communal prayer. He asks that a special offering be given for Elias Li., whose funds are now exhausted and who wants to "work the field" in Temax. Pedro passes to Isauro, who announces that there is a visitor, Wilma, who now lives in Tabasco. He then reads the letter of Ruben. Ruben says that the congregation to which he was sent in La Mina was in shambles, but that now most of the families are once more attending the services. The ministers there no longer love the Holy Spirit and he has decided that he will appeal to Juan and Luis L. to "take the people home." It is a strongly and simply worded letter. I cast a sideways look at Eus to see if she is taking it amiss that Wilma has kept the knowledge of the letter from her. But her face is entirely immobile.

(Later, at home, I gather that Eus approves of Ruben's letter. But Nohoch Felix, always the conservative, insisting on proper form, objects: "Ruben should have waited to see whether his bishops will really forbid him to do the things he is doing. It would have been time enough then to apply to Juan and Luis L. Of course they will rush and take over that congregation.")

We give the special offering for Elias Li. Then there is another prayer, and I am surprised to see how many people there still are, sticking it out. It is now 11:45. Another communal prayer follows, and by the time Isauro gives his closing remarks, the municipal clock strikes twelve. "You see," Wilma says to me, "the service did last till midnight, just as the prophecy foretold." As we get ready to leave, a woman approaches Pedro N. She has a toddler asleep on her arms and looks up at him, half-smiling: "He has a temperature." "We'll pray for him," promises Pedro N.. Others join her as she kneels down by the table: they all want to be prayed over. But we pile into the cab of Chito's truck instead and he takes us home.

There is a lot of conversation about the service the following morning. Wilma needs to leave at the crack of dawn, but as she gets ready, we talk back and forth from hammock to hammock. Nohoch Felix says that Pedro N.'s congregation is very small. "I know because I used to go to the services with him."

"Then where did all those people come from?" we ask.

"He just goes around and invites them."

But Wilma disagrees. "Pedro's group is larger than Isauro's," she insists. Nohoch Felix is probably talking about an earlier time. This in fact was the situation last January, but in the meantime, the dancing got started, the glossolalia picked up again, and more people joined.

I remark about Antonio's wife attending and say that I did not see her husband, Antonio B. Everybody knows the complicated explanation. Valuch and her family were living in Chetumal; her husband Goyo and Elias Li. used to go drinking together. Finally Valuch got tired of all that drinking and insisted that they move back to Utzpak. Because of "those things that happened at the temple" and the later fractioning of the congregation, they were at a loss as to what congregation to join. Then their cousin Antonio C. came up with the idea that they should form a congregation of their own. Epi joined, and he prayed, and when he got up from his knees, he said that he had had a vision that he should baptize. So he baptized Antonio C. According to Eus and Nohoch Felix, the group consists of Antonio C. in addition to Valuch and Goyo, Antonio B., Paulino, Epi, and some others. Antonio C. and Antonio B. act as ministers. They play the guitar and hold a service just like the ones at the Apostolic temple, except that no one speaks in tongues. Cruz disappeared and went to Pedro N.'s group instead.

We continue lingering in the hammocks for a while after Wilma leaves. We were absolutely frozen stiff when we got home last night. The temperature could not have been much above 40 degrees Fahrenheit, and we were all dressed in our light ʔipiles and silk rebozos. My field notes about the service are dotted with, "I'm cold up to my stomach"; "I wish I were in my hammock over some glowing charcoal"; "Oh, for my long johns"; and, in utter desperation, "I wish I were in my bed in Columbus." When we arrived home, Eus scurried around, giving everybody his own pan of glowing charcoal before she went to her hammock. Despite such activity, she says she did not thaw out all night, although I urged my lamb's-wool sweater on her. "Last night I nearly died," she says. "Another service like that will kill me."

Isauro announced that there would be three more services "at this location." I am torn between my dedication to fieldwork and the dread of another five hours like those last night. Eventually, Eus simply decides the matter. "Since we are not going to the service, what would you like to do today?"

I ask if we could go and see Valuch. So that is what we are going to do this afternoon.

Visit to Valuch and Other Final Images

It is a long way to Valuch's place; there is plenty of time to gossip. Eus was there once before, when they came back from Chetumal. Valuch and her husband Goyo sold the property they had close to the market in Utzpak and bought another holding on the edge of the village. From the difference in the sale and buying price, they built a new cement-block house with several rooms and a tile floor. The front room they made into a grocery store.

We enter the store, and there is the long ringing of a bell. Shelves filled with canned goods cover the walls from floor to ceiling and a medium-sized refrigerator occupies one side, the heart of all these small stores, providing a steady modest income from the sale of trays of ice, cold soft drinks, and eggs.

Valuch enters from the back, sallow-faced, wearing a faded dress, and even skinnier than I remember from years ago. In addition to the store, they also have a ranch and some cattle, where Goyo goes to take care of things every second day. Elias Li. is lazy, Valuch complains; he has a place here in Utzpak, where he occasionally works a little, but he still has no house on it. We see her daughter and her grandchildren, a little boy who is extremely cross-eyed and a curly-headed girl about two and a half. They are living in Valuch's house until their own home is built. Elias is trying to find a job, but there is no work in Utzpak, not even for construction workers. I remark to Eus later that Valuch is probably paying for the children's food and milk powder; the latter is always a worrisome and expensive item. But Eus says that both Valuch and Goyo are very stingy and she is sure that they do no such thing.

Valuch offers to show us their temple. "Maybe Elias could make a living as a preacher," she speculates on the way over. After all, he was told in a prophecy in Chetumal that his sins were forgiven and that he should seek a field to work. He chose Temax, where the missionizing efforts of the Apostolics have flourished and then repeatedly failed during the past ten years. There is no congregation there at the moment, but he hopes to restart one by going to various previously interested people and inviting them to a service.

The temple of the two Antonios was constructed on the basis of a vision. It is a *casa de paja* [a straw house] of pleasing proportions, square, with a mud-and-stone foundation. The wattle is parallel to the ground instead of vertical, as in the oval traditional homes, and there is a palm-frond roof. It has a large entrance and large window openings. A gradually ascending ramp along the side wall leads to the podium, a feature revealed in the vision. Valuch complains bitterly that the authorities have decided to run the road through the plot in such a way that the temple will have practically no grounds. They will not accord any consideration to the matters of the Holy Spirit, she says.

We come by the N. homestead on the way home. Some people are sweeping the courtyard in preparation for the evening's services. I recall how during last night's interminable service, members of his family kept going in and out. There was light inside his house, and as the door opened, there was the tantalizing smell of freshly beaten chocolate drink. It made me very hungry.

The sun goes down at 6:00, and it is quite dark as we approach the Catholic church. A man comes toward us whom Eus recognizes as Don Fulgencio. In the distance, we can hear the loudspeakers of the Pentecostals as we stop to talk with him. Don Fulgencio says that the Pentecostals are having a campaign and that he and his wife are going to attend it. "Do come along," he invites us. "I'll present you to the missionary." Eus is tempted; she had actually suggested it even before we met Don Fulgencio, but I feel ill. I don't know what is wrong, but I am nauseated and somewhat dizzy and would rather go home. I suggest that we could get dressed in warm clothes and then return, but Eus says it's too far, and we had better stay home.

At home I cannot eat at all. The *frances,* usually my favorite, taste like chalk.

Nohoch Felix goes to the service. Eus and I are in the hammock trying to stay awake—the hammock usually makes me fall asleep instantly. We talk about Eus's children. Erme gives her 100 pesos whenever she comes to Merida, and Enrique usually gives her a can of Dutch cheese, the kind he sells on the market. Armin lives with a woman who has a house. He works at a parking lot and has a little boy by her. She has other children but maintains that this one is the prettiest because it resembles Armin. Eus says he is quite fair and has his father's curly hair. Enrique's son Samuel, the oldest, will not work with his father. He hardly works at all. He sniffs glue and passes out in the street; he was taken to a correctional institution for several months, but that did nothing for him. He often does not even come home, but sleeps in the street. I remember the boy, exceptionally handsome. He came to visit his grandparents, and when I pointed out to him how beautiful his grandmother's *solar* was, he retorted emphatically that he would never come to live *in ese pueblo* [in this village].

After a while, Chito and Chelo come by. Eus told me about their wedding. Chelo was married in November. Chito attended Isauro's services for two weeks and they baptized him, although he was known to drink a lot. That is why Ruben did not like the match and refused to sign the consent form demanded by the registrar's office until almost the last minute. Privately, Chito said that until he was baptized and married, he would do as he was told, even stay off the booze. After he was married, *he* was boss; the *hermanos* would have no say any more. The wedding took place at Eus's *solar;* Juan L. even had his microphone and loudspeaker along. They killed seven turkeys. When I ask if Chelo is happy, Eus says, "Of course she is. When Chito and she got engaged, he took her to the store, bought her clothes, perfumes, a wristwatch. There is always enough to eat. His mother is still alive, so she has company." Although Chito started drinking again soon after they got married, he does not beat her when he is drunk. Wilma is also very happy about the match. "I know her, she is happy because Chito has money," says Eus, and since Chito is more than twenty years older than Chelo, she can look forward to being a rich widow: he has thousands of cattle grazing on his ranch. I saw the two of them at the service, and Chito looked very distinguished in his freshly washed and ironed *huayabera.* Before he was married he always looked grubby. He is essentially a self-made man; he inherited the ranch from his father but no cattle, and he likes to list all the many jobs he has worked, always investing the money in cattle. He has been blind in one eye since birth. It is nice to see the two of them together; they obviously care for each other. When I say this to Eus, she quips, "Of course: *tumben,* they are still new to each other."

Chito is tipsy. It is nice to see how Chelo teases him, just enough to make it interesting, not enough to get him angry. He wants me to sing him a song about love, and moves comically to the German folksong I sing. He seems an okay guy, even when drunk. As Rosario says, he drinks, but he does not fall down. He is clearly in love with Chelo, who has blossomed, her shyness turning into womanly pleasantness. Chito obviously enjoys playing at being a young lover (he is over 40), taking Chelo to the circus that is playing in town right now and checking twice beforehand to see when there will be a performance. He wants me to sing another song, in which a man dedicates himself to love. I know the style of the Mexican love song, which is what he has in mind, but I don't know such a song. So he has to settle for another German one. Eventually we get away from singing because Chelo wants him to leave the truck parked at Eus's place. He should not drive when he is drunk. He maintains that whatever happens to him is his fate and cannot be avoided at any rate. He teases Chelo into kissing him, and after much hesitation she plants a kiss on his cheek. It occurs to me that this is the very first time I have ever seen anybody kiss here, even within the family circle. And they do drive home. "There isn't much traffic," Eus says, "and it is only two corners." But she is clearly as worried as I am.

A woman comes to buy a bundle of firewood. Laughing, Eus camouflages the spot from where she took the wood with some rags and a rope. "I'll hide it so Nohoch Felix won't see it's gone, and I'll keep the 8 pesos." We laugh together about the deception. There is a base of affection between the two, although Eus is continually on her husband's back for not doing the work in the homestead that he is supposed to do. He no longer goes to work on the ranch. He is too weak and cannot see well enough. At home, he feeds his dogs carefully but forgets about Eus's chicks, and he does not water the plants sufficiently. He may have his own reasons for feeling resentful. "For two years, I have not felt like it," Eus says. "I don't know why. *Mish soots, mish meek* [neither kissing nor hugging]."

Soon, we can no longer resist the hypnotic effect of the hammock, but at this point, Nohoch Felix comes home. He says he could see that it was going to be another lengthy service just like the one in Felipe N.'s yard, and he did not stay. Apparently he does not savor a revival meeting Yucatecan style either.

About midnight, I am attacked by a terrible diarrhea. Luckily, it isn't cold, the rooster is locked up, and the dogs keep me company as I trudge to the outhouse. I cannot bring myself to use the family chamber pot in the house. After six excursions and a near accident in the hammock, I decide that I had better take some antibiotics. Eus is awake by then and we go to the kitchen. She stirs up the fire and makes me some peppermint tea from leaves picked fresh from the yard. She fills a pan with glowing charcoal and we go back to our hammocks to sleep some more. The diarrhea stops as if by magic, but there is still a very unpleasant heartburn.

I start packing some things; the bucket made of the bark of a rain forest tree that Nohoch Felix has crafted for me, and some of the fancy *rodeas,* 4-inch rings for under the *jicaras,* made of dried *henequen* fiber and tree bark. Eus ordered them for me from a woman in Dzoncahuich, and she also bought some for herself. She has them hanging from a stick fastened diagonally in the corner over the table, which is decorated with a few Christmas-tree garlands. She has her best dishes on them: her painted little milk pitcher and her clay sugar bowl. On the third one, she has the fancy plastic talcum-powder box that I brought her some years ago. When Wilma saw the arrangement, she said, "Look at that! That is how we always put up the food for the dead." Eus had never mentioned that to me. My packing prompts Eus to sigh, "*Kaapʔe kʔiin mas de alegria, y dzʔooki* [Two more days of joy, and then finished]."

We take it easy. Eus does some washing, then goes to borrow the electric iron from her neighbor. After a while she comes back. "It was taken far away; she loaned it to her daughter." She is clearly disappointed. Heating her flatirons on the *comal* is such a tedious chore. I hope that the little runt of a pig that Wilma gave her as a present before she left for Tabasco grows up fast so Eus can buy that iron. The antibiotic continues to work, but I can feel that I am not up to par. I don't even feel like writing, a serious symptom for me. And I pick at my food like a bird, most atypical.

As the afternoon wears on, I begin to feel a little better. Chelo comes to show me how to finish the *hiit-puuts,* that lace-like edging that Eus also knows, done with a sewing needle. Eus says that Chelo does it better. Eus learned it from her mother, but she says that her mother did real fancy work, with loops on top of the edging that Chelo teaches me.

I start packing again. "You used to stay for a month," Eus says reproachfully.

I am packing the *henequen* bag for the *jicaras.* Eus ordered them from Tibolom. I need to record some final images that come crowding in before parting; unsystematic, but still precious. Like the birthday celebration for one of Isauro's sons:

Isauro calls an end to the prayer. The people go back to their seats, and Isauro speaks of his third son, Hermano Pablo, whose sixth birthday is today. He hopes that he will be *humilde y obediente.* We sing the church's birthday song; the child stands in front of the table in his ill-fitting white shirt. Everyone, even some of the men who have just come to gawk, pass by and give him money. I slip him 20 pesos. Afterward, Isauro's children pass out bits of *camote* boiled in sugarcane juice to the congregation. I nibble on my piece but find it much too sweet. So does Eus. So we pass our portion on to Nohoch Felix. And I recall how we knelt to pray in a circle because Aurelia had the vision of a wheel.

I recall also how Eus and I went to the bank, newly established in Utzpak, to open an account for her in order to save her the expensive bus ride she takes to cash the monthly check I send her. I ask the girl who takes care of me at the Banco de Comercio where she was trained. She attended school here in Utzpak, then in Motul. Eus later tells me that her mother is the woman who once gave me some food that made me sick. For the life of me, I can't remember who that was, or the food, either. The bank even changed my last travelers' checks. The dollar stands at 22.49 pesos at the moment. Eus's neighbor, Don Chucho, comes in to deposit money. It again amazes me how Eus can sit someplace, looking for all the world like she is either half asleep or dumb and passive, and afterward know every detail of what went on. She even knew the amount that Don Chucho deposited, although that was said in a rather low voice. Don Chucho, by the way, no longer speaks to her or to Nohoch Felix. He had been emptying the refuse from his sties into the street between his property and theirs. Nohoch Felix asked him to stop it, but Chucho said that the street belonged to everybody. Nohoch Felix finally went to the municipal president and complained that the excrement was threatening his well. They sent someone to clean up the mess and made Don Chucho pay for it. Since then the street is clean and relations are frosty.

There is also the matter of prostitution. The girls no longer use the house down the street from Eus. There was a dispute between the owner of the house and the procurer, Don O., about the profits. So for a while, there were no girls coming to the village. The men got so angry, they went to Don O.'s house and broke down his door by throwing stones against it. Wilma saw the stones, bigger than a fist. Eus does not know if now there is another house available.

Then I remember that I need to say good-by to Dona Rosario. Her speech is not very clear; she has dentures, but finds them uncomfortable and does not wear them. Occasionally, she does not feel well, but that is her age, she says—she is 76 now. I always thought she was in her 60s! Her father lives with her and is now 97. Her husband, Don Amado, is a good friend of Nohoch Felix. We see them gossiping together, sitting on the curb or on the threshold of his house. Nohoch Felix reports that Don Amado thinks that I look like a 20-year-old in my ?ipil. But when Eus and I visit with Dona Rosario, he pretends that we are both invisible.

New images intrude into the familiar ones:

In the afternoon, Nohoch Felix says that there has been a prophecy that the next service should be held in Temax and that people are beginning to board Chito's truck. I would not mind going, but Eus has tamale on the fire—*masa* mixed with meat and wrapped in banana leaves which she brought from Chetumal for this purpose. Besides, tomorrow morning early we have to leave for Merida. So we decide not to join the congregation for the trip. After a while, we hear the truck going by, with people clapping and singing the dancing *corito*. So after the tamale supper, we go to say good-by to Reina. As always, she is sewing, rather listlessly, it seems. Salvador is playing with blinking Christmas lights that are hanging over the doorway to the new room: one section won't light up, and he is trying to discover which bulb needs to be replaced.

I give Reina some addressed envelopes so she can write to me, and I hug the little girls. The temple down the street is dark.

We have two places reserved with Daniel for the trip to Merida, and he has told Nohoch Felix that he will leave punctually at 6:00. At 3:00 A.M. Nohoch Felix startles us, telling us in a stentorian voice that "it is 5:00, you'll have to get up!" He gets some razzing from both of us, but we can no longer sleep after that. Now it is 5:20; Eus and I have eaten breakfast and have gone back into the house. Nohoch Felix is curled tightly into his hammock, hidden entirely under his blanket. Eus tears off a little toilet paper. "*Taakʔin taʔ* [I have to go shit]," she says. It is a joke between us. It was one of the first complete Maya phrases I learned without benefit of the textbook. Nohoch Felix pokes his head out: "So go, already!" We laugh uproariously.

Daniel toots his horn at 5:30! Good thing we got ready so early, thanks to Nohoch Felix. We arrive in Merida at the unprecedented hour of 7:30. Daniel takes us directly to Silvia's *barrio* for an extra 10 pesos and even carries my heavy suitcase to the house: the street is too bumpy for his cab to enter. Don Agapito is sweeping the area in front of the house. It always looks like an extra room, it is so immaculate. Silvia has some coffee for us and we settle down in her parlor, the only room with chairs. The others are given over to a refrigerator, hammocks, and a wardrobe. A neighbor lady comes to visit; her daughter lives in Mexico City, and I am to visit her there. Don Agapito has left to fetch some manure for his backyard nursery and misses a caller, an elderly man with his young, deaf-mute wife and 6-month-old baby girl. The young woman tries to strike up a conversation with me. She makes crude but rather effective signs. With the help of her husband, she tells how they went to *sacar el nombre* to register the birth of her baby, and she had to sign the document with her thumbprint. The man came to ask Don Agapito to accompany him to the city hospital and morgue, for his brother, who lives in a rented room close by, has been missing for a month. Later Silvia says, "That man is a very bad person. His wife told me that he beats her if she won't accept him from behind." He is one of those compulsive missionary types—tells me that he has studied the Bible for ten years, quoting passages at me ad nauseam, finally pulling a Bible out to read to me. I am saved by Don Agapito and his supplier, who have arrived on a tricycle, bringing soil and manure. The soil is red with iron oxide. I wonder where it comes from here in Merida. While Don Agapito washes up, his helper and I stand in the front room and talk politics. Don Agapito explains later that this man, heavy and tall for a Yucatecan, is his business partner. He owns the tricycle, and together he and Don Agapito also go to the dump to collect tin cans for the plants. With the tricycle they make the rounds of the *colonia*, selling nursery stock. He is training the man about how to sell and what the prices are. You always have to ask for cash payment, because some people will swear that they will pay later and then they either won't or can't. Like that woman around the corner who has owed him 40 pesos for months. But there is much sickness in her family, because she does not give her children any nourishing food and lets them run around naked. He saw the little boy the other day, going to the store naked. "I told him, 'Look at that, your eggs are showing' to make him ashamed, so he will demand that his mother put some clothes on him." The children keep catching cold now that the mornings and nights are so fresh.

I had asked Eus about going shopping. I would love to go right away; the morning is inviting, with bright sun and a cool wind. "*Caʔacat ʔe,*" she says, in a little while. But after Don Agapito and the family of the deaf-mute leave, Silvia goes shopping. Then Eus helps Silvia with preparing lunch. Then we eat. The food is great, pork steaks marinated with peppercorns, oregano, garlic, and sour orange juice; fresh tortillas; fried plantains; and bean paste, which I refuse with a shudder. There are also crisply fried cracklings. Silvia, who is diabetic, has a soft drink but puts a little salt into it. "That way it is not sweet," she says. Then Don Agapito comes and tells of the search for the missing brother. Eus and Silvia had both seen him in the area until about a month ago. He walks with a tremor—Silvia imitates it—and they say he has pellagra. Eus asks me about the cause of that disease, but when I attribute it to vitamin deficiency, she is doubtful. She says she knows a woman in Tibolom who had it and eventually died of it. She woke up one night and wanted to urinate. Angling for the pot in the dark, she accidentally put her hand into a tub full of very cold water. That was when the disease started. She eventually went out of her mind and ran into the *monte*, and her family found her the next morning, nearly dead from the cold.

I still worry about my shopping trip. I tell myself that the women surely know how long the stands are open on the market. Besides, Eus is aware of all the many things I want to shop for and will see to it that we leave at the right time. So I don't ask about the matter again. Finally, we leave about 2:30, when it is beastly hot. Due to the kind of things I want to buy, such as a small bottle gourd, a round *comal* for baking tortillas on an open fire, flour sacks for a blouse, and hammock ropes, we go to the old, unfashionable part of the market, where the peasants who come in from the outlying villages shop. There the alleys are only 2 feet wide: turkeys and hens, their legs tied, pant on the cracked pavement; shoemakers sit next to the sale stalls, working at their treadle machines, sewing stacks of precut shoe parts together; and their youthful apprentices whittle soles from old tires. There are small piles of smoked and salted fish, and nearby an almost bald old woman is reading in the ragged *cuento* books that she has for sale.

We find all the items I want, although at appalling prices—20 pesos for the hammock ropes, which used to cost 6 pesos; 20 pesos for the gourd that used to fetch 2 or 3; and so forth. It is getting late; many stalls are being closed. We buy the gourd from a man who hands it out to us through a 2 by 2–foot opening in his metal shutters.

Blouses are not a traditional item. For those we have to go to the new section. I choose them at a stand that gives me a good price because Silvia buys the man's merchandise by the dozens when she goes on her trading trips. At the next stand, Eus greets a young man who is visiting with an elderly couple who have rather drab blouses for sale. They are all of Juan L.'s church and eagerly write its address down for us: Calle 80 #529, 69x65 A, Iglesia Universal Cristiana. "Come by all means," the young man says. "Great things are going on. We have been praying and fasting for a fortnight. There is a prayer service at four, and an evening service from seven to ten." Eus asks the young man about his job. "I gave that up," he says, waving his Bible. "*Me estoy dedicando completamente a lo espiritual* [I am dedicating myself completely to spiritual matters]." I wonder how he eats.

As the market closes up all around us, we go to buy beans for Silvia and Eus at a dark store, housed in one of those Spanish-looking houses with tremendously high ceilings and crumbling paint. On the wall, there are the now-obsolete price lists the government has issued: Lista Primera, Lista Segunda. While I wait, I observe the manager making a telephone call in that breathless, extremely fast jargon that is the trademark of the merchants. Then we go and see Silvia's son Gum, whose business has moved into new and more spacious quarters, exhibiting the washbasins, commodes, lighting fixtures, and Mexican ceramic tiles to better advantage. She tells him proudly that her grandson in Tabasco invited her to the fiesta of his sixth namesday.

On the way home, the buses are crowded to the roof. Eventually, Silvia, who managed to grab a seat, makes me sit down. The woman next to me is her neighbor, Dona Lola, portly and pleasant, wearing the ʔipil. Silvia brags, loudly enough for everybody within ten seats in either direction to hear, that I can make tortillas. "*Masima a pakʔach* [Isn't it true that you can make tortillas?]" she shouts above the din as I, somewhat embarrassed, sit down. Dona Lola and I have a nice conversation. I work hard at avoiding the many pitfalls of Maya grammar by using phrases that ring in my ear after two weeks of practice at home. Dona Lola has a little corner store, full to the brim with what looks like a baker's dozen of children, and we buy *frances* there before going on home.

Don Agapito and Eus take me to the airport early the next day. We chat away the two hours before departure. I remind Eus about the X ray I want her to have done and talk about the eye operation Nohoch Felix will be needing. Finally, I must leave. They go with me to the entrance where the passports are checked, and I can see by the reaction of the official that he thinks that the small gentleman in his broad-rimmed hat and white *huayabera* and the emaciated old woman in her *?ipil* are my relatives who are loath to let me go. I think I have been here so often now that in posture and gait I give a cultural message that people pick up as unconsciously as I send it. Like that man at Juan and Luis L.'s temple in Chetumal, who asked us whether we were sisters. For fun, we said yes. "*Haa,*" he nodded, "I can certainly see some family resemblance."

I get to Columbus at midnight, beating the "worst blizzard in Ohio history" by only a few hours.

8. 1982

Arrival and Settling In

In the air, jetting our way toward Miami, I get some last-minute jitters. What if Eus did not get my telegrams? I have had to postpone the trip twice. But the case of the nerves passes. After all, I am a "local" now. I know my way around Merida and if Eus is not at the airport, I'll take a bus to the terminal and go to Utzpak alone.

We pass over the Everglades, and for the first time in my life I see from the air what I already knew from photographs: the stone desert of the Florida peninsula. The violation makes my heart contract.

In Miami, I almost miss my plane. When I check in, the AeroMexico counter clerk does not know the gate yet. So quite casually, I sit down at some distance, opposite the counter, and eat the sandwich I have brought with me from home. Everyone around me speaks Spanish. There is an elegant lady with two children fresh from the bandbox. She is dressed in white fluff and lace, which sets off her dark skin to perfection. Her gesture and language marks her as a *capitulena*. In a most animated fashion she tells of the accident that caused her swollen ankle. Next to me on the other side are two young Hispanic women in uniform, which identifies them as members of an investigative unit. I wonder what it is they are investigating. They flirt with the Hispanic janitors who come and sit with them for a while. All this time, the gate does not materialize on the board. At 2:50, about 30 minutes before the plane is scheduled to leave, I finally become restless and get up to investigate, only to discover that all along I have been staring at the wrong spot. Then, getting to Gate E30 proves complicated, involving an endless corridor, a narrow escalator where I nearly get stuck with my carry-on luggage, and a ride in a train with tinted windows that obscure the station signs. Luckily, my fellow travelers, airport officials who talk about a flight to Guatemala being canceled, know their way around, so I leave the train at the correct stop. With twenty minutes to spare, I arrive at E30. I sit down for a few minutes to catch my breath—boarding is five minutes away—and see a cockroach, as breathless as I, trying to reach my baggage for a free ride to Yucatan. I feel very uncharitable toward cockroaches and get a perverse pleasure out of acting the executioner.

The AeroMexico plane leaves on the dot—we were half an hour late getting out of Columbus—and we are soon over the Gulf. It is at first hidden under a thick, fluffy blanket of clouds, but soon we get to see the mottled bottom under the transparent waters. We are served a delicious meal with a delicate pastry, seafood, and a miniature salad and are offered champagne. Afraid that Eus might smell it on my breath, I decline, probably a superfluous precaution. The pilot tells us that the temperature is now 85 degrees. We left Columbus at 31 degrees. I take out my earrings and hide them in my key purse as we start the descent. No time to change out of my warm clothes.

Customs waves me through, and after miles of familiar corridors I finally see the glass door and Eus behind it, wearing her glasses so she will not miss seeing me. I find her immeasurably improved. She says that on occasion she still has problems with her stomach, but most of the time she can eat, and it shows. We are as happy about our reunion as two high school kids, laughingly waving aside a disappointed cabby, and taking the bus to the city. With only carry-on baggage it is not bad at all. We skip from topic to topic. She did not receive my first telegram and waited until the evening of March 11. But the second one was delivered, so here she is.

I have on a cotton blouse, an undershirt, and wool slacks, and the temperature is definitely more than 85 degrees. I could feel my clothes getting wetter by the minute. To Eus's amazement, I leave a wet spot on the bench. We laughed outrageously on how some people might interpret that as we wait for two-and-a-half hours for the bus to Utzpak to arrive. I show her pictures to pass the time, of her and hers two years ago and of my family.

Finally, the bus. A big one, no longer the old model held together with baling wire and started with a screwdriver. It has intact red plastic upholstery, a powerful but (unhappily) also roaring engine, and a good radio set at top volume. The windows are open and as we speed through the countryside in the pitch dark, the wind blows on my perspiring head and neck. My ears and head still hurt from the changing cabin pressures because of the severe upper respiratory infection I had taken on board with me. I cover my head with a scarf but feel that my body will just not take any more punishment. Eventually, however, I relax. The bus gets us to Utzpak in a record one hour and twenty minutes. I wonder how many speed limits the driver broke in the dark. No wonder there have been a number of serious accidents on this route. But no matter, we made it, and the driver lets us off close to the new filling station, which is now more of an accepted landmark than the cemetery.

In the light of the streetlamp, we see Nohoch Felix standing on the highway. On his way home from the church service, he saw the bus coming and waited, hoping we would be on it. He takes my bag, and I note some new features on the way. They have a gate now to close the gap in the wall, the entrance to their property, no longer simply a corroding piece of corrugated tin. In front of the kitchen shed, Nohoch Felix has constructed a roof so I will have shade when I sit there. A hammock is waiting, tied into a bundle, fastened to a tree. There is the usual banter, with Eus saying that he constructed it but it was about to fall down and that she has done a lot of work to shore it up. Nohoch Felix shines his light on a cardboard sign he is very proud of. Nailed against a tree, it says in his inimitable orthography, "Bien. Benido La. Her. Fes.," "Welcome Hermana Felicitas." Eus is proud of her gas range with two burners, which Nina gave to her. It uses bottled gas, which is cheap even with the present 30 percent inflation rate. She makes it for about $45 for six weeks and has developed a mixed method of using her range and her open hearth. I am thirsty, and Eus brings me a cup of water. She has *agua potable* [drinking water] for me this year. She gets it from a neighbor lady for me, while she and Nohoch Felix continue drinking the water from their well. They say it tastes fresher. Where they live, the water line does not reach beyond the cemetery. I am so thirsty I drink close to half a gallon. It tastes so much better than the boiled water she used to have to prepare for me. The drinking water also made me independent of the now very expensive soft drinks. Eus makes me *agua de tamaridno* and later orange juice from a bush of the fruit they reserve for me. Eus makes me some chocolate while I take the most wonderful of all Yucatecan inventions, a tepid bath. Then I unpack my presents. A huge can of Vaseline and Band-Aids, a safety razor and blades for Nohoch Felix, and as a special treat, a pocket radio. For Eus, eyelet embroidery for an underskirt (*pikʔi*), perfume, soap, and a thick cotton terrycloth towel which in the cold time of year serves also as a shawl. Nohoch Felix immediately turns on his radio. We hear Reagan saying "a freeze of nuclear weapons is unrealistic. . . ." I am glad when he goes to another station. For just a few days, if I can, I want to forget the insanity of the superpowers and the annihilation of Utzpak, among other places.

In the morning, we settle down, or rather I settle down, under the new sunroof to work, while Eus plucks a young rooster, the first of a series of victims to my visit. I ask about the members of the congregation. Even in this first conversation of my 1982 stay, two pivotal issues immediately pop up: Miguel, the new minister who has taken Isauro's place, and the women's cottage industry.

Old Candil has gone back to making *col*. That is what he liked to do best, though he was a good tailor. But some of the women of his family are now sewing clothes for sale, so he can afford the luxury of being a full-time peasant. I might add here that in the second week of my stay, Candil had to go to a doctor because he had a strange diarrhea, mostly water. It turned out he had a gall-bladder condition. The medication he was given provided enough relief so that he could go back to working in his fields. He also has problems with the new minister, Miguel. This minister wants everyone to come to a prayer meeting every afternoon from 4:00 to 5:00, except Fridays, and Candil cannot do that. Miguel scolds everyone who does not come and Candil does not like that. But "Where else could he go?"—a refrain I hear from both Eus and Wilma.

Speaking of Old Candil reminds Eus of the women of his family. There is my good friend, Rodolfa, always late at the services. But to everyone's surprise, she spoke in tongues for the first time. This was during the big revival meeting Juan and Luis L. organized in February of this year. I see her deaf-mute daughter during the service that evening, Imelda. She has grown into an engaging, slender young woman and when I see her for the first time this year, she has a little daughter about 18 months old at her breast, an adorable toddler. She is married to Ilario B., thus joining in marriage two extended families of the congregation.

Candil's daughter, Reyes, so important during the upheaval, no longer attends the services. She came to the temple service last September during a well-attended revival meeting when Juan and Luis L. were there, as were *hermanos* from Chetumal and even as far away as Carlos Madrazo. She asked for a gift, a *caridad*, because her husband was sick. She was given 7,000 pesos supposedly. Her husband stayed in the back when this request was made. He never came to the front or sat down in the men's section. She never even thanked the congregation properly and has not been back for the services since.

Teresa comes to the services regularly; her husband and she are generous contributors to the *ofrenda*. At the evening service that day, she brings along her daughter Rosalinda, whom I remember as a cross-eyed toddler. Teresa would like to see an alliance between her daughter and Isauro's oldest son. After the service, she takes them out together, buying soft drinks for them. Teresa is said to be ill—"too much salt," they say. She is very heavy. Derisively, behind her back, Eus's family calls her a bag of salt.

How about Joaquina? She is the sister of Desi (who is the husband of Eus's daughter Nina) and the wife of Nestor. Nestor has become middle aged, not the slender youngish man anymore, graying at the temples. Joaquina does not come to the services very often; she is too busy sewing dresses. She has become quite heavy; Wilma's crowd calls her *la banqueta* for her wide derriere. She is only about 4'2", so the weight shows. Nestor is still one of the preachers of the congregation. Eus says he has only three topics, the prodigal son, Sodom and Gomorrah, and wise and foolish virgins. Eus is heartily bored with him.

Among those newly baptized, Eus mentions one in particular, an Alexandro N., who was apparently quite a ladies' man. He had two wives, but then he repented and lived with his first wife, badly, it is said; he spent a lot of time with his second wife. With his first wife, he had six children. He supported them, but by his second wife he had three children, whom he also supported. She finally moved into his house. There was a great deal of quarreling in his house. At the revival meeting in February this year, she became converted. She withdrew from Alexandro and asked for forgiveness from his first wife. During the baptism at Santa Clara, Alexandro knelt in front of the *hermanos* and said that he repented, that he was tired of sinning against the Lord. And everyone cried, Wilma said.

Actually, Eus had already told me an abbreviated version of the Alexandro story while we were waiting for the bus in the Merida depot. It seems that when his first wife decided to become a member of the congregation, he decided to marry her and then be baptized. For the first time in many years, Eus decided to go along and she really enjoyed it. "Both Miguel and Isauro talked to him," she recalled, "telling him that he must sin no more." His first wife was also baptized. Alexandro has a large house, and his daughters live with him. When he got home from the baptism, he told them that from now on, that there would be nothing worldly in this house, only the Bible, that they would have to get rid of their TV set and their *cuentos*. They obeyed him. Wilma said, "What could they do? If you are poor, you cannot go and build yourself another house. It was either obey or have no place to live."

Problems continue with Dona Julia. She has stopped coming to the temple. Only her one son, El Gordo, still attends. He is married to Sauri, who has it rough; she had two children, then a set of twins. El Gordo still speaks in tongues occasionally. Dona Julia may have to sell the family property. El Gordo's brothers went on a binge of breaking and entering as far as Merida and beyond, and their father sold what they robbed—bicycle parts, tape-recorders, TV sets. Dona Julia is trying to get them out of jail, but she has to pay huge fines. So that is why she will have to sell their house and land.

Pedro N.'s son Solomon N. is a schoolteacher in the local grade school. Wilma's little daughter is in his class. She is as outspoken and sharp as her mother. "Solomon," she is quoted as saying to him, "don't you see the kids are pulling my hair? You are supposed to take care of me." The superintendent told him that he was not to call any member of the congregation "*hermano*." Eus: "Satan made the superintendent say that to Solomon." He occasionally attends services at the temple.

Understandably, much conversation concerns Miguel, the new minister, about whom I am quite curious. I realize later that I should have paid him an "official" visit immediately upon arrival. Failing to do that put us both in an awkward position, and his resentment was palpable until the end of my stay.

With Eus's help, I try to assemble a new list of the presently active congregations. They are scattered all over the Peninsula like a swarm of fireflies, some suddenly extinguished, others lighting up in unexpected corners. The group in Celestun has shriveled to five members, leaving Isauro without a flock. It is said that he is very homesick and is now preaching in Tizimin. The congregation in Temax is gone. Others appear in settlements not mentioned before, such as Nicolas Bravo, Dziuche, and even Belize. Only Juan and Luis L. seem to have a solid hold of their congregations in Merida, Chetumal, Tizimin, and they have a solid alliance with Utzpak.

As to other congregations at one time or another historically related to the Iglesia Universal of Juan and Luis L., Antonio B. has started drinking. He and his companion, Antonio C., still have their small congregation and hold occasional services. They are said to be Branhamistas, "the party of Luis del Valle." Mariano C. also has his own little temple now, built right next to his house; he has about five members, including the wife of Alvio E. They are also thought to be Branhamistas, but they do not seem to have any connection to the Antonio B. group. Of Barrera, their founder, there seems to be no news. As to Don Victor, who also used to have his own small congregation in Utzpak, there seems to be no news. Nohoch Felix repeats the story I had heard a few years ago, how he came to the temple, Bible in hand, ready to preach. But they paid no attention to him, just let him sit there. So he left and did not come back.

Since I have been gone for two years and can stay only briefly, I ask Wilma to let me tape some of our conversations when she comes to visit on my second day. Here are some of her (abbreviated) remarks, together with lively additions by Eus and Nohoch Felix.

Montiel, a well-known healer from the congregation in Guadalajara, told the congregation that he was no longer interested in speaking in tongues. He now heals by simply praying over people. Wilma maintains later that in fact, he can no longer do it, and that recently he has not been able to heal anyone. He no longer has the gift of healing.

Dancing (in trance or as an induction into trance) is no longer done at the temple. Sometimes people feel like doing it, but then they move in their seats. Reyes, for example, the mother of the B.'s and Imelda C.'s mother-in-law, does it in her seat. They say that she is sick with cancer. "She is quite pale already," Eus says. "In the temple they asked for offerings for her to take to Merida. Miguel said [and this is repeated in a tone of voice that suggests it is considered bragging] that 'Whatever the operation costs, we will pay for it.' They will have to operate on her; she is in pain."

In the temple there is a prayer for the Holy Spirit every afternoon. But it is simply a prayer, and nobody speaks in tongues. Miguel never mentions it. Nohoch Felix says, "One time, Nestor asked, 'Let's see, who has the Holy Spirit? Raise your hand.' He knows there is no one, and they paid no attention to him. Nobody lifted his hand. Of course, Candil knows how."

Eus says, "Miguel tries to force people to do things the way he wants to have them done, by saying, for example 'If you don't come to the altar to pray, then why don't you just go home?' So I went home. It is too difficult for me to kneel for a lengthy period on the hard concrete floor. Even Nestor went home."

Wilma says, "Isauro would like to come back to Utzpak. He was the one who asked to be transferred, but now he wants the congregation back. First he was in Celestun, but the congregation wasn't doing well. Now he is in Tizimin, facing the same problem. His wife remained in Utzpak. But Miguel won't give up the Utzpak congregation; he says this is where he is going to stay until he dies."

Eus says, "Don Fulgencio died. He stayed in his hammock, he was well past 80, and in that way he became paralyzed. His daughter did not want him to go begging. He stayed home and that is how he became paralyzed. In that way you quickly come to your end. I also find it difficult to do much walking anymore."

Wilma says, "The new temple has doors and windows. The windows can be opened by pushing them up, and they are opened for the services. That way, the building is protected. No one can get in. The windows were put in when Isauro was still minister in Utzpak. He did not tell anyone how much they cost."

I say, "But when Isauro wanted to tell the *hermanos* how much money was collected and how it was spent, no one was interested."

Eus says, "But Hermana, we know that an American sent 150,000 pesos for the support of poor people. Nobody ever talks about what happened to that money. I was in the *casa pastoral* when Tagre asked, 'Whatever happened to the money the American sent?' And Luis L. said, 'Some of it was spent on the temple in Merida, some of it was used in Progreso, some of it in Merida.' He said Merida twice!" [Both Eus and Nohoch Felix laugh about this often-remembered incident.]

I ask, "How come that cooperative enterprise failed that Juan L. had going in Chetumal, that the two of us visited years ago?"

Eus replies, "Who knows? The *hermanos* did not stay; the merchandise that was bought with the money of the American was all sold."

I say, "Chan Felix was here to visit about a year ago. He also spoke with Juan L."

Eus says, "It had nothing to do with the temple. When he visits the L. brothers, they ask him to preach, but he remains with the Apostolics."

A remark about Miguel's frigidity in interacting with his children leads Eus into teasing Nohoch Felix. When he was young, he never picked them up or played with them. "That is how old roosters behave. Now he does it with his grandchildren, just like an old rooster."

Eus says, "When the *hermanos* were here for the revival in February, Wilma helped with the preparation of the food, and she went and bought ice. Then

Miguel's wife said to those who had helped and now wanted to eat with the out-of-town visitors that they were not allowed to do that. And she put the lids on the pots. I don't know what sort of food there was, but by evening, the food was still there. Who was going to eat it then? Wilma was angry; she had contributed, and she said, 'I am not going to eat there. They put the lid on. Who is going to go and take some?' I think this was done on the order of Miguel; I think he told his wife to do that. The idea probably was that if the lid was on the food, it would be left for them. It is evil what this *hermano* does. He should take what food he wants and then invite everyone else to eat. The first time at the revival, they prepared the food; they even slaughtered a pig. Miguel was the one who gave the orders. Then his wife took a lot of food out for herself, a lot of meat. For other people there were just some tiny pieces. Juanita, the wife of Isauro, came with her pot. She waited until the cracklings rose in the grease, and she filled her pot with cracklings and left it standing there, so she could pick it up the next day. Next morning, when she came for her pot [Eus thinks this is hilarious], it was empty. The cracklings were all gone. It is not right for the cooks to take much food for themselves, all the meat. Miguel's children came and watched as the cracklings rose in the grease. There they were, eating cracklings. It is bad what they do. I contributed a large hen, but I won't do that again. If I want to eat chicken, I will kill it here. If I kill one that big, it is enough for us for two days."

Nohoch Felix says, "Miguel says to Wilma she should testify, but she answers, 'Hermano, if I am full of evil, how can I?' This *hermano* wants to humiliate people."

I ask, "Was there a celebration of Christmas?"

Nohoch Felix, "No, nothing. They don't understand these things. They say Christmas is not in the Bible."

There is a joyous interruption in Maya from the backyard. Eus has found another egg; she now has four for her brooding hen. She usually keeps a batch of about fifteen.

My discussants are getting tired. Besides, there is work to do and everyday subsistence places greater demands on everyone than before.

Eus and Nohoch Felix have discovered a new source of income. About 2:30 or 3:00 in the morning, when the screaming of the pigs indicates that they are about to be slaughtered, one of them goes to the slaughterhouse. The butchers used to sell the pig intestines but it became too bothersome, so now they simply throw them away or give them to those who ask for them. Eus and Nohoch Felix clean them and rinse them. With infinite patience, Eus strips the fat off the small intestines and rinses it several times, then renders it. It gives much cleaner-tasting lard than what you can buy at Don Antonio's. Besides, the commercially available lard is often adulterated with vegetable oil. Some of Eus's neighbors buy it from her; a small jar goes for 35 pesos. Eus does not tell them where she gets it. If somebody asks, she tells them she gets it in Merida. That is where she used to buy it before she discovered that the intestines were available. The dogs and cats get the cleaned large intestine and that is why the animals look so sleek and well fed. They are so spoiled now that they won't even touch a tortilla.

Nohoch Felix has put up a hammock for me under the sunroof that he constructed for me in front of the kitchen. He is tired, for he runs all the errands for her, shopping for a constant supply of fruit, ice, tortillas, more ice, maize for the chickens and ducks, and other groceries, and he gets nothing but ribbing for his pains and more than that if he cannot remember how much change he was given. Now he is relaxing in his hammock with his favorite book, a gift from Nina, an illustrated version of *My Favorite Bible Stories*. Eus says, "This is what a lady said, 'I have a rooster, but he does not sing.'"

Family Gossip

MARCH 25, THURSDAY

We go to see Wilma today. She does not have to pay rent on the house in which they now live, a blessing considering the low wages that Ruben makes as a farmhand. Eus found the house for her; a man who lives on his ranch most of the time needed a housesitter. Her children have grown a great deal since last I saw them. Joaquin is very skinny, thin as a rail; he wins all sorts of prizes in school for orthography, poetry, and stories. The stories "just rise from my head," he says. But the superintendent is jealous and says that Joaquin must have learned his stories from his grandmother. The entire family laughs about that, for Wilma told the man that his grandmother (Ruben's mother) is dead.

Chelo no longer gives money to Eus, as she used to when she was first married, but she does send some food over occasionally. All of Eus's children and grandchildren give her presents, usually small amounts of money, although she never asks for it.

Marjelia is still unmarried. There was a man from Tabasco who wanted her and even came to Utzpak to visit her. She met him in the market and talked with him. The family does not know what went on, but he left. She makes money sewing dresses, but right now, dresses are hard to sell. Some people who take 100 dresses to sell come back without having sold even a single one. There is too much competition; even some of the men are sewing now. The market seems to be glutted. Marjelia has her own sewing machine, which needs to be paid off, but Wilma is raising a pig for that. From the leftover swatches, Wilma sews clothes for her little boys.

Wilma, now 46, has given birth to two more children since I last saw her,

Daniel and Huancho. When, later during my visit, we talk to her about having her tubes tied, something the local clinic will do for free, she likes the idea. She has been pregnant fourteen times, losing only three infants. But a woman has to have her husband's consent, and when she asks Ruben about it, he says, "*Pa que?* [What for?]" "And he does not even have a house," Wilma says reproachfully.

Jose is a good-for-nothing, just like he was when he lived with Eus and Nohoch Felix, losing one job after another. While he was living with Norma, Nico's mother, in Tabasco, he also had a lover, a 15-year-old girl. When the girl went into labor, her family sent several messages that Jose should come, but he ignored them. Wilma was afraid to go, for you have to have a license to help a woman give birth, which she, of course, did not have. Finally, toward evening, she went over. She found that the little boy had been born in the early morning hours and no one had come to attend them. Wilma cut the navel cord, got rid of the placenta, and washed and cleaned both mother and child. Jose did not contribute even talcum to this new son of his. People in Tabasco do not bathe infants; they say it will kill them. The parents of the girl finally agreed to keep the baby.

Jose still lives in Tabasco. He has a common-law wife, Norma, and he had a son by her two years ago. His parents neglected the little boy outrageously, not feeding him, not bathing him. There was also constant fighting between Jose and his wife. Finally, they took the little boy to Norma's grandmother, who is said to be a witch. She was the one who raised Norma, who may be the child of an incestuous relationship between her mother and her mother's brother. This grandmother used to hit Norma on the head with a slab of firewood. Wilma thinks this is why she has headaches all the time and thinks her psychological problems may also have been caused by her treatment in childhood. "Norma," Wilma says perceptively, "cannot be happy unless someone has mistreated her. After Jose has beaten her, she is happy." The grandmother mistreated Jose's little son Nico the same way she had Norma. Finally, Wilma appealed to the authorities and was given custody of the little boy, a darling chocolate-covered curlyhead. While Wilma was busy with the legal wrangling to get custody of Nico, Jose offered him up for adoption and got 3,000 pesos from one couple. But these prospective parents gave up the little boy when she showed them the legal documents. She showed me the statement of the authorities that the boy was severely malnourished, infested with intestinal parasites. She took him to the doctor for medication and also cured him with herbs. Wilma spent thousands on medication for him. "If Jose ever wants to have him back, he will have to pay me for all of that. Nico is in hock," she jokes. They brought him to Utzpak when they moved back and the children occasionally tease him, saying "Here comes Norma" or "Who is your mother?" Then the poor little tike pulls up his shoulders and says, "*Cui-a-o* [*Cuidado*—Be careful]." Little Nico flashes his big smile at me. I play peek-a-boo with him for a while. Then he runs very fast on his short little legs. For a 3-year-old, his speech is still poor, indistinct; yet he seems so bright. But most children here seem to be late talkers. He calls Wilma mama and recognizes his father from pictures.

Wilma experienced Tabasco as a frightening place. One day she saw men fighting with machetes, four against one. They discarded their victim in the dump, among broken bottles. She heard him plead for help, but no one dared to go in among the broken glass. She finally went in. His one arm had been nearly cut off. Every time he spoke, the blood pulsed from the open wound. His head was split open from the crown to his neck, clear down to the bone, and he had wounds all over his chest and shoulders. Wilma and family arranged to have him taken to the hospital and there he lay unattended. No physician would treat him until his family came forth to pay for it. He wanted his arm back and the physicians joked with him that they would glue it back on, but they had already buried it. He recovered and, some months later, with only his one hand, he killed a man with his machete.

Eus talks about family members in Merida. Her son Enrique's wife, Petronila, gave birth to her twelfth child. Ten of them are living. "She should have had an operation," I suggest. But Eus replies, "Petronila doesn't need that. If she doesn't want Enrique to come near her, she simply does not take a bath." This is a big joke in the family, for Petronila rarely takes a bath, an oddity in bath-conscious Yucatan.

Enrique's son, Samuel, gets drunk alongside his father, presaging the gruesome fate that would overtake him later. But Elias, his younger brother, does not. Elias likes to work. He helped build a wall around their property in Merida, where their house is located.

Eus's son Erme separated from his wife, Clara. Clara was left without any income at all to raise her four children. Eus counseled her to seek help from the authorities. They told him he had to pay 1,500 pesos a week for their upkeep or they would put him in jail. Now Clara is very nice to Eus, because she took her part in the domestic quarrel.

Chan Felix is still in Tabasco. He now has five daughters and one son, and his wife, Ysaura, had her tubes tied, so there will be no more children. She does washing for the physicians in the hospital and Wilma told me that one of those men was Ysaura's lover. Eus heard about it when she was visiting there but did not tell me.

Wilma complains about her daughter Adela, now 13. All she does is watch TV at Chelo's house. If she cannot avoid a chore, she does it as fast as she can and then she rushes back to the TV. She does not play with the little ones, which she is supposed to do after coming home from school. "I think she bites them," Chelo told Eus. "Then they cry and I have to take over. It is not TV, it is *cuentos!*"

Chelo has become a very nice-looking young matron. I enjoy watching her ripe young womanhood. Her little boy, the spitting image of his father, has been in the hospital twice in his four months of life. She says she got dizzy nursing him, so she quit and then had problems with his formula. He nearly died. "And very soon there will be another one," says Wilma, referring to the relationship between nursing and pregnancy.

The eyes of one of the little girls is suppurating. Chelo puts some very caustic ointment on it and the girl keeps crying. Wilma suggests we go to the drugstore and get the proper medication. But when we all see each other at Eus's house again that evening, she still has not done it.

There is lots of laughter about the pictures I took of everybody last year. Chito is a bit tipsy—as he often is—and says that he is looking for a second wife, someone like me. To everyone's delight, I start dancing with him. Then he begins singing, composing as he goes along, about his love for his wife, that a mother-in-law is kinder to a man than a father-in-law. I record his second selection. He says he wants to say how nice I am but that would be dangerous, it might get him in bad with my husband. A good thing that he does not know of my divorce. Eus knows, of course, but in her loyalty does not spread it around.

After the family, there is also the congregation as a favorite topic of gossip. Eus is as good at this as Wilma. She is rewarded with an enthusiastic round of laughter when she says, "Both Joaquina and Teresa have gotten very fat. The size of their bottom needs to be taken into consideration when they build that outhouse for the temple. Five meters square for their seat!"

"Maria, the sister of Isauro's wife, got married," says Wilma. Eus says, "She hoped that in that way she would no longer have to work. But as it turned out, she had to contribute to the household expenses, so she took in washing. At least her health improved. Getting married, that was the doctor."

I asked about Elide, who got baptized with her sister Goya in 1969. We had been talking about Dona Julia, who used to bring beautiful flowers to the temple. But she stopped coming because Isauro accused her of being gossipy. It seems that Dona Julia met Elide. "Where are you going?" "To the drugstore to buy pills." "What do you need pills for?" "*Hayveces se descuide uno* [Sometimes one tends to be careless]." Elide was having an affair with Dona Julia's married son at the time. She went to work in Merida and kept meeting him there. They say she became pregnant by him and had a child that she gave up for adoption. Eus says, "Poor Elide. She has no man. She cannot get married because she cannot get a divorce from her husband. No matter how many times she goes to Campeche to try to find him, she never catches up with him."

Evening Services and the New Minister

"How about the new pastor?" I ask after all important matters, kin and affines, have been settled. From Nohoch Felix's letters, I only know his name. Eus says, "*Pues,* Miguel and his wife Clementina maintain that Wilma has the devil in her." The occasion was a money-raising project for "the work of the Lord," in this case building an outhouse for the temple. Some of the *hermanas* made *talento,* that is they asked for the donation of ingredients and then made food for sale. But those who made it also ate most of it. Wilma criticized them, saying, "That is not what *talento* is about." So Miguel said she was full of the devil, and although she continues to attend the services, she does not go to the altar to pray or offer special hymns. She says, "I have the devil in me and as long as that is the case, I am not going to the front to pray or sing."

"Where does he come from?" I ask. Wilma replies, "They say he had a congregation in Dziuche. Before then, he lived on a ranch and knew only a few people." Then Eus adds an observation that is much on everyone's mind: "He does not work. He sleeps till ten every day and riles against the *hermanos* because they do not give him gifts of clothes for *dia de pastores.* His wife Clementina does not work either. They have seven children and they send the oldest out to sell Popsicles. But they do not approve of the fact that he goes into the Catholic churchyard and also sells them there. What everybody is upset about is that his kids play ball in front of the temple, even during the services, and the other day their ball hit a Presbyterian *hermano* and also a woman walking by. People complain about the disrespectful behavior of the pastor's children, but he does nothing about it. Reina's brother-in-law also complained that they threw stones against his door. He now lives in Don Eduardo's house and sells dresses for Reina. But when he complained to Miguel about it, all he got was 'You play with them, it is your fault.'"

Eus: "He said in a sermon that he does not understand how children can be misbehaving, going out to play in the street while the service is going on. 'My children do not do things like that.' That is bad. How can he say things like that in the temple? Wilma told him that his children misbehave, playing ball in front of the temple during services, hitting people with their ball. Besides, he never picks up his children or plays with them."

The topic is inexhaustible. Eus says, "This *hermano* does not work, although it says in the Bible, St. Paul says it, that he who does not work does not eat. He gets up at ten and does not work at all. The *hermanos* built a house of cement blocks for him (the previous house was of mud and wattle) but he never touched a block. If they put a block down, there it remained. They are in the process of building the bath (an enclosure with a curtain for taking a bucket bath), but they ran out of building materials for right now."

"How did he make a living before?" I ask. "He and his brothers owned a number of trucks. They drove around the ranches and bought honey and sold it. When Miguel converted, they took everything away from him and kicked him out."

Eus and I are still primping when Nohoch Felix leaves for the service. He says he wants to tell Hermano Miguel that I have arrived so that he can officially greet me, as is the custom. As it turns out, this does not happen.

On the way to the temple, Eus recalls, "When the politicians came, asking people to vote, all the *hermanos* went to the plaza. There was Candil, waving his little flag. Only I did not go. The politicians said, 'Let us know what you want. Just write it down, give the paper to us and we will try to get it for you.' Many did. Afterward, Miguel asked in the temple, 'whoever was there, raise your arm,' but nobody did. He knew, of course, because he was there too and saw them. He says that people should not be going out [participating in something other than the events at the temple, I guess].

Eus tells me that many young people in Utzpak are getting their degrees as grade school and high school teachers, but then there are no jobs for them. Or they are sent to jobs outside the Yucatan. The daughter of Dona Reyes was given a job in Puebla. Did I know Puebla? I tell her of the marvelous pyramid near there, in Cholula, close to the Universidad de las Americas. I tell her of the probable voluntary labor in the service of the gods. Eus: "Now, people won't do things like that. Miguel says 'This Sunday there will be no service; the *hermanos* should come and work on the bath and the outhouse at the temple.' But nobody comes. And if some people do come to work, Miguel just sits there and watches. He has never lifted a single cement block. Not like Luis L., who even went to the *monte* with the men and cut stems for the roof."

As we approach the temple we hear the opening hymn; we are late, as usual.

The service runs its usual course. There are about seventeen women and six men. Balam, of the former congregation of Pedro N., is in charge. As we sit down, Balam calls for special hymns. The first group of women consists of Clementina, Joaquina, Nazaria, and Licha. The new temple has the Mexican-style, metal-framed windows that can be opened like louvers. Over the altar platform there is a picture of an open book and above it the inscription, "*Mi casa casa de oracion sera llamada*" [My house will be a house of prayer]. All the lettering was done by Valentin K. On the table are some plastic flowers. When Chelo was married, Chito bought two vases for the table, but they broke when two *hermanos* were dancing. Eus gave Miguel two large potted plants for the temple, but his turkeys ate them. The old rostrum is different, too. It has been stripped of its blue paint and now displays its basic brown wood.

The next group of women to sing consists of Wilma, Joaquina, and Teresa. During biblical reading, Balam reads so-so, stumbling over not more than every third word. The women who answer are much better readers. Isauro is here, and he preaches. It is said that he has a very small congregation in Tizimin, that he left his Celestun congregation because he could not make a go of it, and that he would like to return here. In a pause, I have to sneeze fortissimo and, as in a surrealistic movie, Teresa, her daughter, and Joaquina, who sit side by side farther toward the front, all turn around simultaneously and seem to have distorted faces and large grinning mouths. Isauro speaks about how to pray, but of course he makes no mention of the Lord's Prayer, which is never said in the temple. He is as tedious as ever, and because it is my first full day here, I am getting terribly sleepy. Eus is blissfully asleep, as she always is during sermons.

Eus wakes briefly and looks toward the front where some *hermanas* have moved and briefly nods. Miguel is a small, swarthy man in a huge white *huayabera*. As Isauro preaches, he keeps nodding his head in agreement.

I have brought my tape-recorder, as always. Some children come by to gawk at it. I do not find out until later that Miguel, apparently in agreement with the other ministers, had forbidden tape-recording and picture-taking in the temple. It is supposed to be against the commandment about graven images. Nobody came to me about it, but I did not bring it again. I just made a drawing of the inside of the temple and took photos of the outside. The list of all the things that were now forbidden kept growing during my stay. Had I come to do my initial fieldwork in 1982 instead of 1969, I would have gotten a very different picture.

To my joy, the public address system is out of order, so I am not blasted out of my seat. Adela, Wilma's daughter, comes to hug me, a charming teenager, pretty as her mother.

I notice the first day that the air is no longer cluttered with the endless litany issuing from the public address system of the Catholic church on the plaza. In answer to my question, Eus says that the local priest was transferred and the new one does not believe in crowding the air. She overheard some women angrily complaining that he was also against the carnivals. He will no longer give permission for the local double celebration, maintaining that all carnivals are the devil's work. Miguel has a brother under the skin!

I remark that I want to take a picture of the interior of the temple. That is forbidden because of the prohibition against worshipping graven images. "I do not intend to worship a picture of the temple," I reply.

Wilma says, "They have even forbidden pictures at weddings. They are studying the Bible to see exactly what can be allowed. Miguel also forbade the recording of hymns in the temple." I ask, "Is that by the order of Juan and Luis L.?" There is no information on that.

Eus: "Birthday celebrations are now also forbidden, even in private homes.

The birthday hymn is no longer sung, either in the home or the temple. But they still distribute sandwiches at such occasions. *No desprecian la comida* [They don't despise their food]."

Wilma: "But they did celebrate the fifteenth birthday of Teresa's daughter. I saw it. Miguel went with his wife and children but they hid it from the congregation."

Neither is there any presentation of a child to the congregation, and they no longer want any church weddings. They say that the state takes care of it so there is no need to do it in church. The couple sits down, presumably in front (though that is not stated), a Bible passage is read, and they are finished.

Isauro passes to Miguel, who keeps saying "*Aleluya*" until Balam has adjusted the public address system to its highest possible level of screeching. He then starts preaching, introducing his sermon with a number of questions that nobody answers. The distortion is so complete that I have only the faintest notion of what the man is talking about. He apparently derides science, then he passes on to Solomon and David. The gist seems to be that Solomon got to messing around with all sorts of strangers. God didn't want that—although of course God wants everybody to get along. But Solomon was to have nothing to do with their gods. He keeps throwing the word "*social*" in, which is obviously intended to impress his listeners with his erudition. I keep wondering where he got his vocabulary. Also, he does not stumble over the difficult or unusual words in his text, not even over the formal grammar. That cannot have come from the ranch.

Solomon, he continues, allowed his women to continue worshipping their own gods, which displeased God. Miguel goes on and on, flailing and jumping, perspiring.

After the service, quite a number of *hermanos* come to greet me, among them a very dark-skinned, serious young man. Rodolfa tells me that he is Solomon, son of Pedro N., the grade school teacher. I can't help remembering earlier times when the minister made sure all the guests were made to feel welcome; they were mentioned from the pulpit, who they were and where they came from, and traditionally were asked to say a few words. That geniality has disappeared also; it was actually no longer a custom two years ago. Nohoch Felix tried to revive it for my sake, but apparently his attempt failed.

At the next service, during the altar call, Wilma also goes to the front. I assume she has decided on a temporary armistice. Or, more likely, she has gotten hold of some money to pay for the participation. Miguel prays into the microphone. I hear a glossolalia consisting of a number of utterance units and a beautiful final attenuation. The speaker is Nazaria, of the former congregation of Pedro N., slender, middle-aged, wearing an *ʔipil*. The next section, one of individual hymns, is always very trying for me, with singer and accompanist blissfully unaware of each other and the hymns, lamentably, consisting of twenty verses or more. Of course, they are singing not for me, but for the honor and the glory of the Lord. Besides, I should remember what this performance means to the people involved, what a precious privilege it is to them to be standing up for all to see and hear.

Then it is Licho's turn. I have to admire the forbearance of the *hermanos*. His performance must be difficult to bear even for them. Then he begins to preach, and without a word, although it is out of turn, they let him do that, too. Eus tells me he has been retarded from birth. He earns a living by making *albarradas* and is supposed to be very good at it. He found a woman and brought her home to his father's house, where he lives, and he fed them both. But because he had a woman, Licho no longer went to work, for all he wanted to do was to be on his woman. So his father kicked them both out and his woman left him, for she got tired of him. Luckily, she had no child by him. We are talking about retardation and Nohoch Felix said that it was not the fault of father or mother, that God does it to show his power.

Licho passes to Nestor, who reads the Bible, many verses, alternating with the congregation. We are standing and my legs are swollen and hurt. While this is going on, a young mother is beating her 3-year-old because she cannot go to sleep in the cacophony of noise reverberating from the walls. But now she is picking lice for her.

Nestor passes to Miguel, who fires a number of rhetorical questions at his audience, which I cannot understand because of the distortion through the public address system and which no one bothers to answer. He then proceeds to talk about Elias and the word of the Lord coming over him. There is another Bible reading, a prayer, then more preaching, then some history of some story of the Hebrew Bible. Eus never wakes up, so she misses this exegesis of the Old Testament, which never used to be of interest to this congregation. I don't get the impression that it is now. I think there ought to be a law—no sermon longer than ten minutes. At the most.

As I listen to Miguel, it becomes clear to me that he is painstakingly avoiding the topic of speaking in tongues. It can be forgiven, of course, that he does not recognize "the word of the Lord comes over Elias" as a reference to speaking in tongues. However, he himself never lapses into the behavior while preaching, only perhaps becoming "weepy" as the result of an arousal, as Wilma describes it. So I ask, "Does Miguel ever speak in tongues?" Wilma says that he told her he never did. He was baptized at the "77" (a village). "He was thrown to the floor but did not speak in tongues, only lay there as if dead, and all the *hermanos* prayed for him. The *hermanos* thought this was punishment from God for being so headstrong." Wilma remembers another odd instance. It seems that in 1979, there was a revival meeting organized by Luis L. in

Andreas, a village near Dziuche, when Miguel was the pastor there. The way Wilma, who was present, tells it, several girls started prophesying and when they were done, the devil got hold of Miguel. He fell down as if asleep and an animal attacked him, as large as a horse. He started throwing stones at it and even broke the door. And then he woke up and said he could remember nothing, but he did remember fighting with that animal. As for speaking in tongues by the parishioners, Miguel seems quite inconsistent. Teresa and Joaquina used to sing in tongues, very beautifully, the *hermanos* said, until one day Miguel forbade it, saying it was only vanity. In others he tolerates it. But certainly he does not teach it, encourage it, or even preach about it.

There are constant mutterings against Miguel in the congregation because he is very selfish. Luis L. handles things very differently. He refuses to take any more than others and insists upon feeding the children first, no matter how dirty a child might be. Miguel is also continually after money, making inventive use of his every opportunity. Miguel has reinstated the church organizations, such as the Dorcas, that Isauro abolished, but now it is just a money-making proposition for Miguel. Each week, each organization marches to the front for a hymn and pays 10 pesos for the privilege. Ten pesos is no longer the money that it used to be; Mexico had a 30 percent inflation rate last year and the dollar costs 45.58 pesos now. But tortillas, with government support, are still only 5.58 pesos per kilo, so 10 pesos is still quite a sacrifice. Wilma paid it for a few weeks, but after that, she simply could no longer afford it.

MARCH 26, FRIDAY

Eus suggests that we skip the next service. I am happy to escape the painful noise pollution. But I was never one to derive much pleasure from playing hooky. Basically, neither does Eus. We go shopping in the cool of the night, sit for a few minutes under the trees of the plaza on a stone bench, and then go home, knocking about like two peas in an empty pod. As could be predicted, we end up in our hammocks: gossip time.

The daughter of Emerijildo got married here. Rosa, the sister of Luis L., was *madrina*; the bridegroom did everything in the proper fashion. He bought the right clothes for the girl and the food for the wedding party. But afterward, her family would not give him his wife for a whole month, until Miguel got around to doing the prayers for them in the temple. Luis L. allows engaged couples to sit together in the temple; they may even kiss. But when Luis L. tried to intercede on behalf of the couple, Miguel told him that this was his temple and he could do as he pleased.

When Miguel preaches, he always scolds people, like he railed against those who tried to get his children to behave in the truck to and from the baptism in Santa Clara. People should help him and pray for him, not criticize him. He says that nobody is forcing anyone to go on a trip and that he for one is not going to bother getting a truck again; they can go as they please, by car, train, bus, or airplane. Miguel also says that the reason Wilma's small son Danu cries so much is because he is possessed by the devil.

Eus paid the 10 pesos for participation for three weeks in the singing of the special hymns before the altar, then she stopped paying, so she can no longer go and sing. Miguel also objects to people coming to church only on Saturdays, although a number of the men are not even home during the week, saying that he wants no "Sabatistas" (Seventh-Day Adventists). Miguel also objects to people clapping along with the special hymns offered at the altar.

When Nohoch Felix finally returns from the service, we eagerly pump him for the details of the service: who preached, what did they say, who offered hymns, did anyone speak in tongues. "Why didn't you go?" he finally grumbles as he settles in his hammock and pulls the blanket over his head.

MARCH 27, SATURDAY

There is going to be a revival meeting in Tizimin and Wilma very much wants to go, so I give her the money she needs. The congregation is making preparations for the trip. They will take their beloved public address system with them in the truck. I try to suppress my evil wishes concerning that devil's invention. Maybe just a teensy-weensy mechanical failure? Enough to put it out of commission until Monday, when I leave for Merida?

Reina and the Cottage Industry

We stop by Reina's house on the way home from Wilma's. Her neighbor Raquel is also there, and Reina brings out some chairs. It is a pleasant, cool evening. We chat in front of the house while Reina's children watch television.

The gloomy picture Marjelia painted of the dressmaking industry is not in evidence here. While we are there, some women come to pick up huge bundles of dresses to sell. She is clearly keeping a careful book on who gets what and how many. Yes, some days are bad, but she still sells well despite the competition, because she concentrates on small sizes, which not many do. A young man comes by and picks up a pile of polyester material. He embroiders by machine, cuts out dresses, and sews them "better than many women, because he used to sell and knows what appeals to customers." Perhaps Marjelia just does not have the right connections. She sews for a woman who is not a member of the congregation. Certainly Teresa is successful, distributing a considerable volume to the traveling men. So are Rodolfa and her daughters. Even the L. brothers have gotten into the act, selling fabric, as do the grandsons of Don Fulgencio. Some men are also said to be sewing, but the women do not seem to know anything about their networks. Occasionally, sewing cuts into attendance at the worship services, apparently with no remorse attached.

In the course of the evening, I slip into the house and give the little girls necklaces and rings that I brought. I see the girls several times later but do not see them wear their trinkets. They are now affluent, and the gifts I bring them do not mean much. Santiago is not home, but I see him pass us on the highway some days later. He was no longer in the VW bug but was in a larger one with fringed edging decorating the windshield. Reina was sitting next to him and both of them waved to us. He is still up to his old tricks. I hear from neighbors that one evening, after the service, Reina came lugging her hammock and asked to hide in the temple. She was trembling and said that Santiago was drunk and was threatening her. To think that Reina is actually making all the money for the family and that he is just an adjunct! He no longer even sells dresses for her.

The remnants, little swatches, mainly are used in the family and by others to make children's clothes. All of a sudden, these little girls are no longer ragamuffins, but cute and well-dressed, for their mothers have a knack for combining different pieces into little skirts, blouses, and ruffles. Eus says that part of the loss in sales that people complain about is not for lack of money on the part of the public. Some dresses are made better and prettier than others. Because of the volume of dresses, the buyer now has a choice.

The conversation keeps coming back to the matter of dresses, which is now the mainstay of many of the households in Utzpak. I keep asking over and over, who sells and who sews, hoping to uncover a pattern whereby the economic network coincides with the membership in the temple, but it does not. Some of this sewing activity, in addition, is not dictated by economic necessity, but by the joy of learning a new skill. Chelo also sews, but not for sale. "What would people say—she does not need the money." So she sews for her children and even helps Marjelia, who does it for a living.

Selling is now done in the neighboring pueblos, such as Temax, Xbek, and others. I hear from Reina that there is now a problem with the merchants in Merida. They don't want the dress competition from the outside. A discussion is being planned between the village salespeople and the Merida authorities. A threat to the far-flung Utzpak enterprises has arisen quite unexpectedly as a result of a natural disaster.

Apparently there was a tremendous volcanic eruption in Chiapas, and details are beginning to be reported in the village by some men who were that far afield selling dresses made in Utzpak. Thus, the younger brother of Manuela C., her husband, and a third man told that the day turned to night as a terrible rain of sand and gravel began falling. All public transportation stopped, and people had to flee on foot. They were picked up by a Yucatecan coming from

Mexico City, but they nearly landed in a ditch since the lights of the car did not penetrate the darkness.

Wilma comes to call. We listen to the news together. There is talk of twenty-one villages destroyed and 64,000 head of livestock displaced; many refugee centers have been opened by the government, at least ten in Villahermosa alone. One general is quoted as saying that he has never seen fireworks the likes of this eruption. The eruption is on everyone's mind. Many have relatives in the affected area—Chan Felix is there, as is one of Sylvia's daughters and many people from Utzpak.

Life with Eus

The night is terribly cold. I wake up shivering, and Eus notices it and gets me a cotton blanket. This morning, everything is very beautiful. The sky is clear, the sun is bright, birds are calling, a yellow butterfly is sampling the flowers. The sun's rays light up a small red tree until it glows as if from inside. Eus has tomatoes, onions, and coriander growing. She waters it all attentively —"I don't consider that work"—and all is lush and inviting. She no longer borrows the neighbor's pump, because the neighbor's children considered that to be something for which she had to reciprocate and continually came with demands for food. She cannot afford that. One day, they asked her for a whole jar of *minsa* (tortilla flour). So she now waters her garden with the help of water accumulated in the tub on the rim of the garden wall. To fill it takes six buckets of water. Even for Nohoch Felix, but especially for her, the small buckets (she has switched from the large ones of the old days) are too heavy. I will definitely have to get her a pump now that they have electricity to run it. Nohoch Felix does help with the watering, but he is not very good at it. "He just sort of urinates at the plants," mocks Eus.

MARCH 28, SUNDAY

I wake up with a bellyache. I never last longer here than six days. I take two charcoal tablets and a Lomotil. The pain stops after evacuation. It may be a reaction to the lard Eus uses. I cook with oil and am no longer used to it. I am sitting under the sunroof, writing. Eus has just knocked a scorpion off my back, a nasty-looking little bugger with reddish legs and a swollen yellow belly. It must have fallen off my lovely sunroof. Its sting is painful, but actually I am more afraid of the cockroaches. I thought that maybe my memory had been playing tricks on me and exaggerated their size—until the real McCoy appeared in black armor, 2 inches long or more and very, very threatening.

Nohoch Felix is happy with his new radio I bought him. He proudly displays it to his grandsons, Joaquin and Oscar. To think that he is so opposed to everything *mundano,* but the radio does not fit into that category. Just a cute little noisebox. "The gentle folk never recognize the devil," said Mephisto to Faust.

Joaquin came over to show me his story about Maya antiquity, a little love story, nicely composed. He called it "Nicte-Haʔ," the name of a paper company, and also "The Water Flower," but his teacher, who knows no Maya, would not give him a prize for it because of the Maya in it: "That must not be an original story. It must have come from your grandmother." When I first came to know Joaquin as a little boy in Tibolom, he knew not a word of Spanish.

Rodolfa comes to see us with her small son Miguel to tell a complicated story of witchcraft. It seems that her son-in-law Ilario bought some land from his father which his sisters considered their own inheritance. So these women went to Temax and bought "something" from a person to put into Ilario's food. "This is for you," his sisters said, "something special only for you." He ate it and became deathly ill; he swelled up and felt pain all over his body. He consulted various physicians, but they could not help him. Finally, they took him to a woman, an *espiritista.* She went into a trance and the spirit of the person who sold the women the poison for 6,000 pesos possessed her.

The *espiritista,* or rather the spirit possessing her, said that Ilario could be cured. They had done a "33," a powerful witchcraft strategy, against him. She then woke up and was possessed by his sisters. Ilario recognized his sister's voices. They laughed about him and, upon being asked, admitted they made him sick because he was taking away their inheritance. He was cured with the medicine the medium gave him, which was a liquid in bottles.

While Rodolfa was still talking about the witchcraft, Chito came driving up and brought the entire family, his own and Wilma's (except for Ruben, who had drifted in earlier). Wilma brought food for her kids and a huge watermelon that Chelo had bought. Adela had carried it and had fallen down with it. I did a lot of picture-taking, joking about Nohoch Felix getting in the way. "I have more back of the *hermano* in my pictures than anything else," I complained.

I asked about the history of that congregation that Ruben took over in Tabasco. First there was a Tabesqueno named Samuel G. He demanded a great deal of money from the congregation and the *hermanos* did not want him. They knew Chan Felix and they said they wanted a Yucatecan one, one that did not demand so much money. Samuel went to work on an oil rig and is no longer pastor. Then came Ruben, sent by the Apostolics. Ruben and Wilma told about how the *hermanos* were prophesying in the Iglesia Universal. They started praying in tongues and dancing. So the *hermanos* asked for Juan L. or Luis L. to come and talk to them. The Apostolics expelled Ruben and they brought in Elias J., who also demanded large financial aid from the congregation and who fought with Ruben. The Apostolics then gave Elias another congregation and brought in Manuel H., but he started a love affair with a 14-year-old girl, so finally the Apostolics closed the church and transferred Manuel to La 71 (Nicolas Bravo), a village near Chetumal.

Rufino de la C. sued to be pastor in Merida. Then he became bishop in Villa-hermosa. Now he would like to join the L. brothers. His three years as bishop were up at the time Ruben was expelled.

I also checked up on the strange incident that I know about from Joaquin's written account of 1980, in which some girls got undressed in trance. They were two Pentecostal girls who knew that at the Apostolics people spoke in tongues. So they came to the temple. But their mother was very angry about this and scolded them furiously. As a result, it was said, Satan entered into them. They became crazy and their cure turned out to be very expensive; they took them to *espiritistas.* They remained Pentecostals, Wilma said, confirming the account. Juan Tʔuul did not get them, she added. Seeing my questioning gaze, she explained that Juan Tʔuul was really a name for the devil. In the desolate region mentioned earlier, if men go out at night, Juan Tʔuul will teach them to be bullfighters. They become very good at it, but when they die, the devil gets their soul. I asked if that was what Don Fulgencio had done, but no one seemed to remember that that was being said about him when I first came to Utzpak.

Wilma gives Huancho a bath in Eus's washtub under the tree. He does not have the Mongolian spot. But Chelo's little baby boy has a pronounced one. I love to watch her children. Her two little girls are antebellum dolls, Yucatecan edition, her little boy a miniature Maya warrior.

Sometime at the hour of the noonday meal, two ladies, not of the congregation, come to buy some chicks from Eus. One is very pregnant, the other considerably older. The older is a most enthusiastic talker. Eus offers them seats, and all of us are the audience. The older woman speaks of everything from the two pigs, this high, which were slaughtered for her son's wedding, to the *relleno negro* and *relleno blanco* prepared for the same occasion to the virtues, or lack thereof, of her husband. Once again, I see the familiar pattern of a very long conversation followed by a hurried commercial transaction, in this case for two of Eus's plants, and for the younger of the callers, the payment of the chicks and a debt to Eus.

In fact, there are two kinds of sales transactions. One kind, which we had just seen, favored by the women, is the one where you come in, have a very long conversation, and at the end take care of the transaction very quickly, almost like an afterthought. The other one is allowed if you do not want to make the buying of something a social occasion. In that case, you stay outside the gate at the street, shout what you want, and wait, no matter how long it takes to fill your order. Like just now, a man waited for fifteen minutes while Eus and No-hoch Felix picked the thirty limes he wanted.

I am getting extremely hungry. Finally, with the callers gone, we all get to eat. The small ones and I eat first, then I have a bath, a triumph of organization with so many needing it also. The children bathe outside in the yard, Danu protesting when he has to get in the bath and Huancho protesting when he has to leave the bath. Eventually, we all get done and changed into fresh clothes.

Eus and I and all the many small and large family members, except Ruben, walk to the temple together. On the corner by the new drugstore, we meet Valentin K., who is taking the bus home to Temax. They now have seven children. A walk is always also visiting.

The authorities closed the cathouse down our street, and the pimp had to find other work. Sometimes, women from other villages would come and work for a few hours, unbeknownst to their husbands. "Or their husbands sent them," said Nohoch Felix.

When we get to the plaza, the celebration has just started. There are ten lovely couples in fine Yucatecan costumes dancing various *jaranas,* Yucatecan-Spanish folk dances. I assume that Eus and Nohoch Felix will turn their backs on something as worldly as that, and then I will not get to see it either. But instead, they watch knowledgeably and enthusiastically, commenting to each other about the various numbers. I remember that Nohoch Felix once told me that Eus would eagerly gather eggs from her hens, then go out and sell them so they could go and dance. That was when he made the lovely tape for me with the *jaranas,* playing the mouth organ. The girls wear gorgeous double-tiered ?*ipiles,* flowers in their hair, fancy combs and barrettes; the young men wear sombreros, white suits, and *huayaberas* buttoned to the neck. They dance various pretty numbers, one on top of boxes, another one with bottles on their heads, all very well rehearsed. Another dance is around a sort of maypole; as they dance, the ribbons of many colors, which are attached to the pole, became braided around the pole and then unbraided again. Wilma says that she taught the children at the school how to do that, and Eus says, "We just happened to arrive at the right moment," with obvious satisfaction. But, a few days later, she apparently repented of her enjoyment of the dances, and said pointedly, "It was Satan who made all that appear so beautiful." Wilma showed no remorse.

On the way back from the plaza, Eus and I sit talking with Dona Ugulina for a while. She is now past 80. She speaks animatedly about her various illnesses, but she still has a youngish charm about her that never ceases to amaze me. Her friend, several years older than she, has unkempt gray hair and a booming voice; she presses words out with effort (she may have bad teeth or a speech impediment) and is angular in all her movements. Yet she has a nice sense of humor, and the two old ladies laugh heartily at each other's jokes. I heard later that she is called "Professora" and still has a sort of preschool for well-paying Utzpak families. Reina's daughter was her student for a while.

Last night, there was no service. We missed the one on Thursday. It was rather far away, in a private home. Eus says that, anyway, there are numerous times when she does not go. If they have the public address system on, one cannot understand anything, not even the hymns. So why go? And all Miguel does is exhort the congregation.

Eus has killed her third rooster since I got here. "There are too many roosters anyway," she says when I worry about the depletion of her barnyard. Nohoch Felix encourages me to eat. "It's all yours," he says. When we add up expenses for my food, Eus will not let me pay for anything that they grow themselves, including expensive poultry.

She now has twenty new chicks. One sells for 20 pesos (about 40 U.S. cents), but she wants to keep this batch. Two of her hens are brooding now. She will sell those chicks. On the day I arrived, twenty-one chicks hatched. Eus does not do it only for the income. "It is as if a child is born. You love to watch them. When you have a new baby, you go to see how it is doing, and you enjoy that. This is how I feel about the little chicks. I watch them and love to take care of them."

MARCH 29, MONDAY

Wake up with diarrhea again. Back to the charcoal and Lomotil that kept me going all day yesterday. During the night, a cockroach landed audibly in my hammock. I called out briefly, more like a gasp, but there was Eus, awake instantly. "*Baash*, Hermana? [What is it?]" I would like to report that I answered "*Untul shnaats*," but in my horror, only the Spanish word occurred to me. She found the monster, killed it, and threw it out to the chickens.

Wilma comes, as she does every morning. It seems that Ruben has lost his job. The farmer has work but no money to pay his farmhands. "Do many men still go to work in Chetumal?" I ask.

"Not only to Chetumal," Eus says, "but also to Merida, to Cancun, and to other places. They go Mondays and come back on Saturdays. Their women and children stay here. Sometimes, the men find other women where they work. That is the way it happened with Cochinito X. He has a house here and his own land. Yet he left all of it and went to stay with the other woman."

There is a lot of conversation about the witchcraft done to Maximo, the son-in-law of Rodolfa. His sisters were afraid he would come and live with his father and the house would pass to him instead of to them. To pay for the *espiritista*, his father sold all his land to Wilma's landlord (who wanted it for his number-two wife). The medicine made Maximo vomit. What came out of him was a ball of hair, well tied together, so that he even bled when he vomited it out. It contained some old wood with a centipede in it, also worms with black hair, and fragments of butterflies. The *espiritista* said Maximo had only two more days to live, for those creatures were eating him from the inside out. That was the illness he had when his wife Reyes came to the temple and asked for a donation for her husband. Now that the old man has sold all his land, his daughters hate him. They will not even give him anything to eat.

Although wearing the ʔipil, those fast-talking (and by village standards elegant) women who came on Sunday to buy plants from Eus were different from the women in the congregation. But the differences are hard to pinpoint, as difficult as it is to discern their source. They remind me more of lower-class city women, such as live in the Colonia Moctezuma in Mexico City. I think of economics. What do their husbands do? They sell clothes. What sort of house do they have? *Mamposteria*. Do people in the temple have *mamposteria* houses? Yes. So economics is apparently not it, although at present there are few in the temple who could be classed as affluent. Teresa perhaps, but she projects a different image. Eus proposes that the difference is lifestyle. Those women like to dance, drink beer, lace their conversation with vulgarities. We come to no conclusion.

Eus describes how the harvest used to be brought in from the *col* in the old days. The men started out in Sotuta, each with five or six horses, and came back with two sacks loaded on each horse. The corn was threshed with large slabs of wood. With all that corn, her father fed forty pigs of all sizes. If lard was needed, they killed one. The meat was salted and smoked and cooked with beans. There was deer and pheasant, pheasant so big that the meat filled a bucket. In the *col, makal* (a root, long and slender, with small tree-like shoots sprouting up at intervals, its fingered leaves like those of *rhicinus*) grew, as well as chile. "We will never see life like that again."

When she was 10, she started her own garden, surrounding it with a stone wall against the chickens and sowing herbs, such as *ruda* (peppermint) and *yerba buena*. "Today, the girls run around in the street; they no longer like to do things." A long time ago, the boys went to school for maybe two years. At 10, they started helping their father or earning something. Now, their father has to support them for many more years of study. And nobody can tell whether all that schooling is really helpful. After all, Eus's sons Enrique and Erme make good money selling, but their lives could be even better if only they did not drink.

I am eating when I hear Eus draw water from the well and then she says, "*Chispa* (little neighbor boy), look, what is down there? One of your chicks maybe?" So I go out to see what is up. Eus is holding a soaked, bedraggled-looking white hen, which the boy has retrieved from the well. Eus had seen a beak and an eye in the depth, but wasn't sure whose chicken it was. Apparently, the hen had left her eggs and for some reason had fallen into the well but was able to save herself from drowning; the wall of the well is uneven and has some depressions in it. Still, something like this had never happened before. "And how nice that Chispa was there to get down into the well." Eus is easily made glad.

By now, the hen is dry, has eaten maize and drunk water, and Eus thinks that she will live. It was because of her disappearance that Eus had had to find a new brooder.

On the way home from the service, we pass a shuttered, closed house. Nohoch Felix calls out, "Samuel?" "*Haa*," from the inside. "*Wenech?* [Are you asleep?]" "*Haa.* [Yes.]" To be at home that way!

April 1, Thursday

My diarrhea (or dysentery?) has become intractable despite charcoal tablets. So I break down and buy some enterobioforma from Dona Bartola, who swears by it. (I saw in a German article later this year that the stuff may cause neurological damage, not specified. So I won't use it again.) I take one tablet in the evening. I have to use the chamber pot about 3:00 a.m., then have a thorough evacuation in the morning. I feel just fine right now, but I wonder how long this recovery will last.

Eus's neighbor, the crippled woman's man, has bought some land and built a home on it of sticks and cardboard boxes. He comes by to leave his well rope for safekeeping and comes by a second time with his radio. They are going on a *caridad* trip and he can "not leave anything in the house because Pablo would break in and steal everything." Pablo is their neighbor, the pimp who was recently put out of business by the municipal authorities. The neighbor no longer carries the woman along the street because Pablo "spreads powder [witchcraft] on the street," which make the woman's feet itch terribly.

I did not realize that Pablo was someone that I knew, but Eus reminds me that he was the one who came by to ask for some English instruction a few years ago. Amazing that she should remember!

The crippled woman's man also asks if Eus would like to keep his duck in her *solar*. They could go halves on her eggs. He brings a very pretty bird, black and white with an undercoat of green. One of Eus's drakes immediately mounts her. She looks like a shy, delicate teenager among Eus's large, gruff, white drakes.

Later, we go to see how the congregation got off to Tizimin. They were to leave at 3:30, but when Eus and I get there at 5:00, they are still waiting. So we go to Reina's, where we are welcomed by Salvador and Reina. Occasionally, one or the other of Reina's children peeks in—we are sitting in the open door—and reports that they are not leaving yet. We talk mainly about the volcanic eruption in Chiapas. Nobody wants to go and sell dresses there, since no one knows what the conditions are like there.

Reina sends out for *refrescos,* a sign of her affluence and an historic first (before, it was always I who paid for them), and we also talk about drunk driving. Reina is emphatic about not letting Salvador drive while he is under the influence. The son of an old lady I used to know just ran his truck into a house. The old lady comes by as we are sitting there, but she will not stop since she is on her way to see her son at the *calabozo.*

They say that the police often strip the men naked to keep them from hanging themselves.

We see the policeman—in sombrero—drive the truck in question home just around the corner from Reina's house, the frightened bunch of children and the wife of the man crowded around him in the cab of the truck. In response to this problem of drunken driving, the police have now ordered that there will not be any sale of liquor on Sundays. But from what I have seen in Utzpak, the locals are not listening. I read later in a Merida paper that in Tizimin the order is not followed either. Eus comments, "What good would that do anyway? They'll buy the stuff on Saturdays, and by Sunday it will be nice and cold in the refrigerator." (Reina has a big one now.)

The drinking of the men is much on the minds of the women. Another woman comes to buy chicks from Eus and says that her husband is almost an *hermano,* for he reads the Bible all the time. But her mother said what kind of *hermano* was that, when he still continued drinking?

Finally, at 6:00, the truck leaves. We stay at Reina's for a while longer. I go to take pictures of the temple, which looks so different now, a hulking cement-block box instead of the gentle lines of the mud-and-wattle building. Too bad there are no pictures allowed inside. I'll have to try to draw it instead. They have not forbidden note-taking yet. It probably does not happen all that often.

On the way home, we meet Pipo and Concha—I finally find out the names of the crippled woman and her man—in a most extraordinary getup. She is in her wheelchair and has a hat fastened on her head by a rubber band circling her double chin. He has on his head some indefinable gray covering, perhaps part of an old felt hat without a rim. He is carrying his radio and a bag. In his bag are two cooking pots with a messy-looking roasted chicken. On his back, a bag of clothing. Concha clutches a handbag stuffed with something. A whole household on the move, assembled around a wheelchair.

We stopped a moment for a chat and Concha asks for a kiss. "You want one from me?" I ask. "No, I want to give you one." So I bend over, humbled by her kindness, and she plants one on my cheek, saying "*Dios le bendiga.*" I answer, "You, too." It somehow seems more appropriate than the typical, "*Amen, Hermana.*"

When we get home, we find Nohoch Felix living the life of Riley. He is sprawled in his hammock, reading his Bible stories. The little radio is blaring away, propped up against a glass on a little table beside him. Eus tells him in three pithy Maya sentences what he has neglected to do while she was away. By then, as he points out, it is too dark to do any chores.

April 2, Friday

On occasion, I had asked Nohoch Felix whether he could sing any Maya songs for me. All he would produce would be a Christian hymn in translation. But on this day, the world of the grandfathers suddenly broke through the crust, showing how thin the crust actually was.

It seems that at the ranch where Ruben works, which is very far away in a deserted area, something is scaring the cattle. The ranch owners finally decided to arrange for a *reso* [a prayer]. They killed a steer and chickens and went hunting for deer. Today will be the ceremony. Nohoch Felix demonstrates how a very large gourd will be filled with soup and pieces of meat and the officiating priest will put it on his head. Dancing will invite the "Lords" to eat. Then everyone will eat; there will be thick tortillas and lots of meat and other food. The men will then have to drink hard liquor all night. Wilma, who joins us later, adds that there is a region where *munecos* [classical Maya figurines] are buried. *Alush* [little people or spirits] make their home there. "Sometimes during the night, one can hear a man screaming. That is the Devil."

It must be 110 degrees in the shade. My diarrhea is under control, although I could not sleep from 2:00 A.M. on with abdominal pains, for fear that I would not reach the chamber pot in time and would mess up the hammock. The badge of honor of an anthropologist doing fieldwork in the tropics must certainly be mounted on a roll of toilet paper.

I keep Eus company as she is readying a chicken for the noonday meal. We are talking about small children and their perception of external sex organs. Eus: "There was a man who lived with his only son, a teenager. A neighbor asked if he could not send his son over to guard the house and his wife while he was away on a trip. Getting into her hammock, the woman was careless and the young man became worried—was she wounded? No, she explained, this is the house for the little ones. It is there that they enter and leave. And that is how he learned about it."

Wilma returns from the revival meeting. There was only one service at Tizimin, and they sang hymns all the way back, Nazaria in glossolalia. Wilma did not join in, because when she sings, her lungs hurt.

To my surprise, Salvador shows up to invite Eus and me to see the ʔonoot [well] and the fishery being built around it. Since Reina is not going and there is room in the car, he lets Wilma come along with Danu and Huancho. I do not think I will survive the ride. But the ʔonoot is exceptionally lovely, very deep— a student drowned in it the other day—and despite many delays, the construction of the fishery seems about three-quarters finished, with a complex of basins to hold the fry and, eventually, the adult fish.

When we get back home, I collapse in the hammock. Later, we have some fried fish from the market. Eus is convinced it is fresh, and I eat it with no ill effects. I have a bath and Eus makes me some *anona* water. She mixes the soft, sweet pulp of the fruit, almost the consistency of pudding, and adds a bit of milk powder, sugar, and ice. Eus and Nohoch Felix have *pozole* with ground coconut, exquisite but too rough for me. So I have only a spoonful to taste. But I do drink the cocoa water, a gift from Rodolfa, very refreshing.

APRIL 2, FRIDAY

Next day, Eus's chicks are ready to hatch. She lets me listen to the chick chirping in the egg. A lovely little miracle I have never experienced before. Eus says, "When chicks hatch, I am happy. It is like a child being born. Even if you have several, you still go to see it over and over again." The ones that are hatching now are for sale. The twenty-one that hatched the day I arrived she will keep. She also has a batch of half-grown ones.

The following day, two eggs are still left unhatched. One shell is cracked. "Should I open it?" ponders Eus. "Maybe it would not be right, like performing a cesarian section on a woman," I suggest, thinking of infection for a chick not quite developed. So she does not open it and the chick dies. It has its head tucked under one wing, that was why it could not hatch. "I am to be blamed," I say. But Eus consoles me that there are always some that do not hatch and that die—"*Es su suerte* [It is their fate]." She glories in the twelve that did hatch. Two seem to feel cold, so she tucks them back under the hen. The rest are in a box; the hen tends to step on them and then they die. She puts another batch to hatch under a hen.

I feel better today; no diarrhea this morning and I had a wonderful night. But as the heat gets worse, my buoyant spirit flags. Just a few more days and then home again.

A young man comes to the *albarrada* to offer half a cleaned *habali*, a large Central American rodent, for sale. I buy it, 3.5 kilograms for 420 pesos. Part of it Nohoch Felix fixes in the earth oven with fragrant leaves over it. The result must be tasted to be believed; a roasted meat that, while still tasting like meat, smells like flowers. I never ate anything like it. Eus and Wilma have a field day preparing the meat, making a kind of meat salad with part of it; they debone and shred the meat and mix it with onions, chile, and tomatoes. The few larger sections Eus fixes for me in the form of small steaks.

As I watch all this preparation, it occurs to me how much fits into this tiny room, circumscribed by its wattle walls: three brooding hens in their old washbowls or cardboard boxes, a box with twelve chicks, a bucket of pig's intestines, a long bench loaded down with water and dishes, a large plastic container with my drinking water, a table with two gas burners on it, three cats (one of them pregnant), and a box with four recently born kittens in it. Then there is Eus cooking, Wilma getting food ready for the kids, and around the low table, the little ones. All in the space of about 6 by 8 feet.

April 3, Saturday

My last day. We meet Wilma and her brood on the plaza. We go to the ETA, the new junior high-cum-agricultural school, while it is still cool but then encounter a couple selling yard goods in front of the Catholic church. Eus and Wilma are both enthusiastic because there are white remnants, appropriate for making ʔipiles. It is past 9:00 by the time we start for the school and it must be 110 degrees. As we walk on, I get progressively weaker. I am not all that enthusiastic about agricultural schools, preferring animals in their natural settings or in settings like Eus's, where she takes care of her baby chicks at home, instead of the brutal handling of injured birds in the egg-producing concentration camp. Afterward, I feel bad because Wilma is excited and I should have shown more interest.

On the way back, we stop on the plaza and I buy saburines, a kind of Popsicle in a plastic pouch, for all of us, ten in all. Danu and Nico have been fighting the whole time. I had bought each of the little boys a plastic truck—they had not a single toy—and Danu had left his at home and was trying to take Nico's away. When I mentioned the matter to Eus, she scoffed and said, "I bought a ball for them, but they threw it in the neighbor's yard and we could not get it back for them. They are careless about everything."

Then we go to shop for eyelet embroidery—easier to get here, where it is used for making ʔipiles, than in Columbus, where it is not fashionable at the moment. The owner now has a pocket calculator and also a huge color TV, where we see some special reports on another eruption of the Chichonal, even larger than the one before. Rodolfa and Eus feel that these catastrophes indicate the Second Coming is finally close at hand. With a rather strange relish, Eus quotes the prophecies, how the wells will run dry and disease will consume the people and animals will die. "I would not want to be alive when that happens," I say. But Eus shrugs, "I would. I would want to see it all, for nothing will happen to me. I believe in God." I try to tell myself that it is not Eus who is callous but the teachings she holds to be true.

We look in at Chelo's house, still a peasant home but with obvious signs of affluence, such as a bed, a refrigerator, a mixer, a large TV, a record-player. She is playing hymns and she shows me the cover of the one she has just put on. It has a surprise for me. On the back, the singer, Juan Miranda, is described as having starred in many movies, with such all-time Mexican greats as Jorge Negrete and Pedro Infante. Then there is a paragraph written by Miranda himself. He tells that he was converted in 1977, in "*a caberet de la ciudad de Mexico llamado, 'El Social,' donde Dios mando un siervo suyo llamado Enrique Portes Gil, y un otro Eduardo Huerta . . . ,*" [in a cabaret in Mexico City, called 'El Social,' where God sent his servant Enrique Portes Gil and another one Eduardo Huerta. . . .] So here, unexpectedly, is the full name of the elusive missionary from Guadalajara who started the Apostolic movement in Yucatan and whose name no one knew how to spell when they first told me about him in 1969. Obviously, he had gone on to greener pastures, from Bishop Gaxiola's gutters all the way to the nightclubs of the capital city.

Chelo has two Yucatecan deer tied up in the backyard, caught in the *monte* with the help of the hunting dogs. I go to the smaller one. I don't remember seeing one so close to its sleek, coffee-colored coat, delicate black hoofs, and black, shiny nose. I feel sorry for its terrible fate in captivity, reduced to domestic boredom, prevented from running free among the trees. It comes closer and begins to lick my fingers. I assume it likes the salt from perspiration.

After lunch at home and hammock, Eus and I go to the *tortilleria,* still in heinous heat, fit only for mad dogs and Englishmen. I am supposed to take a picture of the owner and her husband, the cabinetmaker. Nohoch Felix made the promise and I'll have to honor it, heat or no heat. She rushes into the house to change from her grubby apron into one of the Utzpak dresses, which sets off even her crooked figure to advantage. Someplace in the yard—it is not neat like Eus's, but strewn with refuse and trash—I gouge a hole in my calf and it bleeds profusely. I let it bleed for a while before putting pressure and a Band-Aid on it, and it heals with no sign of infection.

Later, Wilma and her family come over to say good-by. Two women come to buy Eus's youngest chicks, all eleven of them.

Finally, we are alone and I am almost too weary to pack my things. Luckily, I travel light.

April 4, Sunday

The next morning, Eus and I miss the early bus out of Utzpak. We have not tried very hard to make it. We wait endlessly across from Don Chucho for another one. One is full and passes by without stopping. At 8:30 another one stops, also very full. The driver's helper opens the back door and pushes us in. We stand all the way to Merida.

We take a cab to Agapito. Eus gasps in dismay at the price of 250 pesos (6 dollars at the exchange rate of the day), but with three shopping bags and my three bags, it would have been torture to go by bus. We are very kindly received by Agapito and Sylvia, who are still working as mini-distributors, their refrigerators full of soft drinks and their backyard resplendent with truly magnificent nursery stock. We laze around—mostly I laze around while Eus kills and dresses the rooster we have brought. We have a lovely meal and go to the market for a bit of last-minute shopping. We get home under an evening sky, due to the eruptions, the likes of which we had never seen. It is as if the gates of hell had opened; its dome appears carbon-black at the horizon, passing into an angry flaming red and then dusty orange up to its zenith. Don Agapito scolds us for returning so late; there are lots of bandits about and we could have been robbed.

April 5, Monday

Don Agapito gets us a ride to the airport with a neighbor for 200 pesos. We arrive there hours too early but I thought there might be problems with the flight out due to the volcanic activity. There are none, and we spend three restful hours in the cool of the airport, talking and laughing away. Eus goes upstairs with me, where we say good-by at the immigration counter. The last I see of her, she is looking out over the airport, her frail and slender frame leaning against the casement.

9. August–September 1983

Arrival and a Revival Meeting

We approach Merida via Cancun, and bits and pieces of letters from Nohoch Felix start bobbing up. Eus's health? Passable. Wilma sends cordial greetings. Nina is selling Utzpak dresses in Chetumal. Chelo left her husband and hired a lawyer. Too much booze, *aguardiente*. Very sad. Nearing Merida, there is a reception committee of fluffy gray clouds crowding around a black one. As the plane drops, they dissolve into raindrops splashing against the windowpanes. Then all is blue sky as we walk down the stairway upon landing.

Passport control is expeditious, and baggage inspection nil. Lugging my two small bags, I enter the main hall, and there, looking the other way, is Eus. She really looks well, I think with relief, and her welcoming smile (once I step in front of her) is as bright as ever.

We take the bus to the bus depot, and I stand in line for the tickets.

Eus says that a three-day revival meeting is going on right now. There are lots of people attending; Luis L. has organized it.

At 3:15 the bus leaves. The air is cool and the window in front of me to the left is open. I am sweaty and getting colder by the minute. I finally borrow an end of Eus's *rebozo* and drape it over my head for protection.

We get to Utzpak at 6:00. We are tired, and I am dripping with perspiration. Eus sets out a bath for me in record time. I join her as she prepares an omelet for supper, while I entertain her with the description of the airplane breakfast and lunch without much taste and in quantity designed for the appetite of an undersized dwarf.

Nohoch Felix has left for church decked out in a gleaming white shirt, white slacks, and a new white sombrero. "People have come from many places," he said, repeating what he had written in a tablet, "from many towns and many villages." Eus and I ate comfortably. I fully expect a relaxed chat in the hammock and an early Paz de Cristo for a good night. No such luck. If we hurried, Eus said, we might still catch most of tonight's revival meeting.

So we dress with care, ʔ*ipil grande* and all. By 7:30 we are walking down the familiar highway to the temple.

Apparently, the service has not started yet. We are greeted by a joyous scene, the brightly lit temple courtyard, kids playing, women and young people chatting. There is Imelda, nursing a new infant. "Esbaron," it is a boy, says proud grandmother Rodolfa, who comes to greet us with a bright, welcoming smile. "How wonderful that you should arrive in time for this fiesta," she gushes.

I drape my head with my new white mantilla. Rodolfa finds us two seats in the back, which is difficult, for the temple is crowded to the rafters.

Someone opens the service. I cannot see who it is, and his voice is drowned out by a cacophony of shouts of *aleluyas* and *glorias* and by countless children crying. A hymn is intoned; three guitarists are keeping the rhythm and everyone is clapping and shouting. There are many verses, then another one, on and on, for close to half an hour. There is a scripture reading, the rest is obliterated by the noise, then another hymn. As it winds down, Eus closes her eyes. A sermon: nap time. Then a sonorous voice cuts sharply through the din. Eus opens her eyes and looks at me. I nod: Luis L. No sleeping now.

Luis L.'s sermons are always worth listening to because of his verve, his enthusiasm, his imagery, but today, perhaps stimulated by the shouting crowd, he is on fire. When he is too loud, the public address system chases him and makes his words ricochet from wall to wall. Something about humans succumbing to temptation. Then a rhetorical question: "Is it the head that is to be blamed, or is it the heart? The heart, of course," he shouts, "of course the heart!" Then dropping unexpectedly into a lower level, he continues: "There was once a piglet, a very pretty little piglet, un *cochinito muy bonito.* And it belonged to a *princessa.* She loved the little piglet very much. She would wash it, rub it down with body lotion, and scrub it with laundry detergent. One day she took it for a walk. Suddenly, the piglet saw a mud puddle. No sooner did that piglet see that mud puddle, it wriggled out of the arms of the *princessa* and *uuuuuh,* it jumped into that mud puddle. The *princessa* cried. '*Que voy hacer?* [What am I going to do?]' So she took it home, washed it, put lotion on it, and once more she had a pretty little piglet, *un cachinito muy bonito.* But after a while, she took it for a walk again. *Y que paso,* what happened? There was another mud puddle, and *unnnh;* in jumped the piglet. The *princessa* was desperate. She started crying. '*Ma que voy haca?* [What am I to do?]' Just at that very moment, a lamb died. So what did they do? They opened the lamb, took out its heart and exchanged the piglet's heart for that of the lamb. Instantly, there was the changed piglet. It now was perfect. The mud puddle no longer was any temptation."

Tempestuous shouts and much laughter followed the successful resolution of the story of the *cochini to bonito,* the pretty piglet. And during the lengthy exegesis of the edifying tale my only regret was that I had had no instrument to record it. As it turned out, however, Wilma's teenagers had borrowed Chelo's tape-recorder for the special occasion. The next day, I copied that part of the service. Not having a scratch tape, I did it by audio, and very fittingly, the story of the miraculous piglet was saved for posterity accompanied by the bucolic sounds of Eus's barnyard.

When after a very lengthy exegesis Luis L. finally ran out of steam, I went up to the podium in the ensuing pause to greet him. He motioned for me to wait, then jumped down to shake hands. His dark face streaked with perspiration only inches from mine, he said, "Hermana Felicitas, the world is slipping more and more into sin, *verdad* [right]?" Since Christ would be coming soon, we would have to convert the world. Everyone needed to be baptized by water and by the Holy Spirit. "You do believe in the resurrection, right?" I assented. He was clearly still in trance. In fact, he had obviously been in trance at least since he had embarked on his story. I had noticed a special way of moving while he preached, dancing as it were, as he preached into his tightly held microphone in small mincing steps, almost on tiptoes. It reminded me of a report I had read about St. Francis of Assisi preaching to the bishops who were upset about his contention that Jesus was poor. He had also "danced in small steps on tiptoes" while delivering his sermon. There were still other surprises during this service. I was startled to see that the dance was still being practiced. While Luis L. was in trance—tripping on the rostrum in his light, rhythmic pattern—there was a small portly *hermana* in *ʔipil* and *rebozo* dancing and turning around her own axis. In front of the men's section to our right, two slender brown arms were raised, their owner obviously in trance. At one point, a jubilating glossolalia utterance arose above the shouts reverberating from the walls.

Such good will was generated by all that joyous celebration that at the end of the service even old adversaries were mollified, and Teresa and Joaquina came to greet Eus and myself with unaccustomed kindness.

Life with Eus

Soon after returning to Ohio last year, I made arrangements for a pump for Eus's well. It cost us $250 including installation. The relief it brought them was palpable in Nohoch Felix's first few letters. They told about the crops they were now able to water—tomatoes, chile, coriander, black beans—and how they had planted some banana trees.

Eus shows off bundles of bananas they have just harvested and some huge oranges. "*Gracias a Dios y gracious a. Hermana F.,*" she says; with her new pump she can now irrigate.

A horrible night started soon after falling asleep. I woke up with the need to defecate. Weaving my way around Eus's *pavellon* [her mosquito net] and Nohoch Felix's hammock (I have his mosquito net), I just make it out the front door. I thought this would happen every hour on the hour, but it was more frequent. The excrement had a hideous smell, so I finally broke down and took a new type of pill, some sort of new antibiotic. I burped and brought up something that smelled and tasted like fermentation. I had previously taken Lomotil, and that (possibly by preventing evacuation) caused the accumulated food to ferment: Who knows? Eus said I did not wake her, neither did Nohoch Felix hear me. The trouble lasted into the morning, then all of a sudden it was over. I just ate some rolled oats, a *frances,* and drank.

I confronted Nohoch Felix: "You loaned me your *pavellon.* Such a sacrifice! How can I thank you?" His answer: "Yes, you can't. After you're gone, I will have no blood left. But then, when I hear them singing—tink-e-tink, tank-e-tank— I'll pull my blanket over my head, and they can't sting through that."

The streets of Utzpak are being leveled, with the adjoining householders being assessed by the municipality for the cost. "For you, no more swollen ankles," says Eus. Nohoch Felix and Eus have paid their share, but their neighbor Don Churcho still owes for his. For the electric cables, the government wants to install concrete posts, more durable than the wooden ones. The householder who does not pay for the change gets his electricity discontinued.

My condition is still not stable, so Eus makes me a medicinal drink of mint, orange peel, and *siisim,* an herb I don't recognize. It has a smooth texture and a disagreeable taste, but as Nohoch Felix comments, "*Sale la panza masiso*"— apparently, it stops the diarrhea.

AUGUST 31, 1983

I slept most of yesterday and most of the night, until Nohoch Felix got up to go to the slaughterhouse next door for pig intestines. But it was not even 4 A.M., so I went back to sleep. When I told Eus upon waking that all was well, she embraced and kissed me with relief. I even dared to eat an egg. She told Nohoch Felix not to sell even a single one because I "drank" them.

Now I am sitting at the new table they bought. The sun is sifting through the lush vegetation; it is cool and lovely. Eus is cleaning the pig intestines and stripping them of fat for rendering. The cats are watching and getting their share.

We talk about dogs. Nohoch Felix's two dogs keep the neighbors' dogs out, even Wilma's. How Nohoch Felix's sister, who lived in Hofcah, gave him a hunting dog, very good at scaring up deer. One day, it was gone. It arrived at his sister's door. Sternly, she told him, "I will give you food, but only this once and no more. Then you return, you know where." And he did. Nina was asleep at the time at home and let him in. He had been gone three days.

One of Nohoch Felix's dogs got into a dogfight with a pack out in the street and was badly mauled. The wounds got infected and infested with maggots. Nohoch Felix got medicine for 80 pesos and cleaned out the wounds, but they were still open when I arrived.

As for firewood, there is very little *monte* left. People used to collect only dry wood, but now they also cut the green wood and take that home and dry it, further destroying the *monte.*

There was a *tumba,* a clearing out of the *monte* to make room for *sacatal* [pasture]. The director of the new school had it done at the school's expense.

Then he brought his own cattle to graze there. When it had grown to the proper size, he sold it and pocketed the money. Since then, no one has been weeding it, and it *se echo a perder* [it went to waste].

The students do all the work at the new school, even the girls; they sell all the produce, and no one knows who gets the money or what it is needed for.

Don Felipe comes to visit Nohoch Felix. While he has only us women for company, he tells of a case of miraculous healing, judged to be of special interest to us women. It seems that a woman's husband had a quarrel with an acquaintance. The couple invited the acquaintance to eat and fed him some poisoned food. He became violently ill. They called in the priest, but his prayers gave him no relief. Then they appealed to Hermano Montiel, a known healer, who happened to be in the area. He prayed, and smoke rose from the poison, healing the man. The priest then had to admit that Hermano Montiel had more power than he. As a result, the woman joined the *hermanos*.

Nohoch Felix arrives and now the two men are discussing what "sin" it is (i.e., adultery, murder, lying) which prevents one from entering heaven. Felipe refers to his little pocket Bible. They are like two scientists debating a fine point of quantum mechanics. And how triumphant they are when making a fine point! The true message is that only he who does not have a hard heart understands truly what the Word of God is. Their discussion is half in Maya, half in Spanish, and they chuckle in their pride and certainty. And, of course, the sinner is not resurrected until the Second Coming, only to be condemned again!

After Don Felipe leaves, the air of male superiority still pervades, reminding me of rural Japan. So I tell about a somewhat apocryphal head of household, who said "No" to everything. So Nohoch Felix goes around all afternoon, impersonating the admirable model with all the obstreperous females of his household, myself included.

I ask Nohoch Felix for a new twine for my drinking gourd. My old one is all frayed. I watch him cut some of those huge leaves from their *henequen* plant in the back of the barnyard and strip off the fleshy pulp of the leaves, using a U-shaped, wooden implement that leaves behind a bundle of long, slender, light-green fiber, which he flings on the thatched roof to dry. Tomorrow, he will drape a piece of leather on his right knee for protection and then will roll the fiber with a practiced motion, shaping it to the requisite thickness.

It started raining hard at three, and Eus is lolling in the hammock and talking in the dark. Hermano Genaro is supposed to have had an affair with Chucha, the widow of a man killed in a hunting accident. People went to complain to Miguel, but he said there was nothing he could do, that after all Genaro does what is expected of him. He recites his Bible passages, he sings his songs. (This is not only a privilege, but also expected as obligation.)

Seven P.M., still raining. In the kitchen the mosquitoes have ample supper on my legs, which are burning from knee to toe. Eus reminisces about her father. He had two wives and at least two lovers, plus a young girl to work at the house. He liked her, too. A total of twenty-eight children—Eus thinks that Marjelia's suitor may have a similar lifestyle in mind. After all, he is not from here. He comes from Falisco, or anyway from someplace far away. He probably left a wife and is now trying to deceive another one. He seems very pushy, not at all like people around here. He entered into the temple with the women, which is not the proper way.

With all this rain, the house is alive with non-human beings. Dung beetles fly around, a huge spider lugs her bag of eggs on the hammock beam, then a tarantula falls from the rafters and lumbers across the floor until Nohoch Felix kills her.

I always am amazed at the absence of passion in all this killing. Nohoch Felix fetches a rooster for today's soup from the barnyard. "*Shotuca!* [Cut its throat!]" says Eus casually. Nohoch Felix with equal equanimity brings the knife and does it. Like picking an orange.

Another large black spider falls from above. Eus immediately jumps into action, pulling off her sandal and killing her. Then she energetically rubs it over the floor to kill also her offspring that are invisible to me. I assume she is poisonous.

Another dung beetle flies through the air, a black cricket crawls into a crack between the wattles. Then Eus discovers a tarantula warming itself in the ashes of the hearth—and so to bed.

We awaken to a thoroughly soaked world. In Merida, Nohoch Felix's radio says, the sewers have overflowed and the streets are under 20 centimeters of water. Eus wants to wash my laundry. I wonder how anything could possibly dry. At least it will not stink—only mildew.

Eus says she does not have to go to the temple. (She is miffed because Nohoch Felix does not wait for her.) After all, she can hear some recorded hymns at home and knows the sermons by heart, and if she is sleepy, she can shut the tape off and go lie in her hammock. She also likes the (apparently fundamentalist) services that she hears on their radio from Guatemala.

Eus has a bellyache. She tries to be agreeable, but it makes her extremely irritable and she snaps, vaguely, at me, when I ask a question. Oh, well, nobody is perfect. It is a comfort to know that the rule even applies to Eus, such a paragon of virtue most of the time.

Is it all the unwelcome creepy-crawlies that bring to mind Marjelia's suitor? While Eus is peeling and slicing plantain to fry for lunch, "Nohoch Felix dislikes him," she intimates. His name is Victor, but Nohoch Felix calls him Margarina, supposedly because of his "soft" way of singing. Eus gave him a hammock, "old but still usable."

Ruben is railing against Marjelia's suitor. Basically, he wants to keep Marjelia's earnings in the family. Eus's comment: "And when he is dead and she is old, who will take care of her, no children, no husband!"

We talk of food. When she was a child, she tells, they went to steal *zapotes* (a type of fruit) from a lot where the owner did not live. Then they made a *pib*, an earth oven, starting with a big hole in the ground. They heaped dry leaves and other trash in it and ignited it. Then they cleaned the ashes out and repeated the process, and when the fire was out, they put in the *zapotes*. Her father then showed them the most important part; namely, how to reduce the opening of the cover of the *pib* to only about a span across. In three hours the fruit was done, and it tasted delicious.[1]

Although it is still raining, Nohoch Felix goes out into the soggy world, steadfastly refusing an umbrella, to reserve two seats in a cab for us for the trip to Merida. Finally, the gardens dry out and Eus and Nohoch Felix pick oranges and *chinas* as a gift for Sylvia tomorrow. Eus is on top of a tall stool, Nohoch Felix holding her. "I grabbed something that I had forgotten," he quips, smiling broadly.

Services

On the way to the evening services, we pass Reina's house. There seems to be a prayer meeting going on. About ten women standing in a circle, all *de vestido*. I had heard that Reina became an active member of the Presbyterian congregation, whose church is further down the street, past the temple of the Iglesia Universal. The block has all *mamposteria* houses now, so the new cement-block temple fits right in with its half-finished block garden wall. It still has a work-in-progress look, a reminder of the fact that it is a project assembled with admirable dedication, centavo by centavo and brick by brick.

The inside has much that is familiar. The table in front of the rostrum is covered by an embroidered mantel, Eus's handiwork. What is new is a light-blue curtain covering the wall behind the rostrum. "Wilma bought it," says Eus when she sees me admiring it. Its soft folds disguise the cement blocks. It also mercifully cuts down on the echoes produced by the public address system and magnified by Miguel's electric guitar.

With the excitement of the revival meeting soon fading into memory, I find the boredom engendered by the daily services more and more difficult to tolerate. Eus, whose reaction is similar, escapes into sleep, I into fieldwork.

On one occasion, Miguel invited Don Victor to preach. Despite doctrinal differences, Juan and Luis L. are using him as evangelist, financing his trips. The sparseness of the "*Glorias*" and "*Aleluyas*" was an indication that his sermon was mainly over their heads, filled with his erudite arguments against the virgin birth and other "Catholic errors." After the service Don Victor came to the back, and we stood for a while chatting. He greeted me with just the right mixture of kindness and dignity; I could imagine a Maya priest of old in that role. He had a word for everyone—Eus, Nohoch Felix, Wilma, also Candil. He joked that I could "fly home on butterfly wings." Turning serious, he concluded that the earth belongs to God, and we should ask for permission to walk on it.

Licho, it is said, tried to attend the meetings of Jehovah's Witnesses, but they sent a message to his father that they would put an electric wire across the entrance if he tried to come again. If he touched it, it would kill him, so he no longer goes there. When he tries to sing in front, he sometimes cries and scratches his wrist or his chest. He is never aggressive, although interested in the girls, smiling at them across the aisle. When he sings, the *hermanas* call out a lot of "*Aleluyas*." I am touched by their compassion.

The *hermanos* may forbid jewelry, but apparently they have not yet figured out how to react to, or forbid, the dress parade at the services. Every evening, there is a lovely and impressive display of the most varied cute patterns, laces, mantillas, which are either large and embroidered or are lovely pieces edged in lace (perhaps remnants). At every service a different dress; also children so nicely dressed.

Eus and I stayed home last night because I was not well, so Nohoch Felix went by himself. He said that at the service, Miguel used the opportunity to scold the congregation, especially Wilma, although not mentioning any names in the celebrated affair of the *molino* [hand-operated grinder]. It seems that some men had a *molino*, which was loaned to them by the *rancheros* so they could grind their corn to make tortillas. They stay to work during the week, returning home only on weekends. Ruben says one of the men took it and sold it (although it wasn't his). The buyer: Miguel. Wilma heard it from Ruben and did not hesitate to spread the tale. The details were told in the presence of three witnesses: Emerijildo, Nestor, and Candil. The matter was also discussed when Victor was here. Wilma thinks that although Miguel bought it unknowingly, something should be done about it. Instead, Miguel keeps riling against her. As she never fails to point out, his children never come to the service, playing in the street instead or trying to seduce little girls.

Wilma's Children

Wilma comes by daily to visit Eus, carrying Dawn on her hip, with Rebecca trudging behind her, hugging her youngest brother. Much conversation is about money. She has to buy school uniforms for 100 pesos (U.S. $7.30) each, also shoes and books; a large sum of money, with Ruben earning little and sometimes nothing at all. She and Marjelia sew dresses for Reina. Reina has not increased what she pays for a dress for an entire year, giving her only 40 pesos per dress, although the price of the thread, which the seamstress has to supply, has gone up. When Wilma complains, Reina says, "If you don't like it, there are many others who do." She makes money hand over fist, just distributing to sellers. So I loan Wilma money to buy some fabric. She hopes that Nina will sell their dresses in Chetumal; Marjelia will make them with sleeves, because many *hermanas* buy dresses from her, and they want them with sleeves.

Norma just came; Jose's wife, a beauty fit for Gauguin's brush. She has the smoothest brown skin and regular features and is obviously a *macha* [a stranger], not a Maya bloodline Yucatan. Jose went to work, leaving her not a penny to buy her food. Little Nico is still sick. He became ill when Jose came home raging drunk. He does not eat, does not even want the Coca-Cola that Joaquin gave him money for. I suggest that she go to the local clinic. They treat children free of charge. She never tries, of course. Fear of having to pay may have something to do with it, but, I am afraid, indifference to the child also has something to do with it. Eus says she would just as soon see him die. They say that the children in Wilma's house all got sick when Jose came home raving drunk that time.

Wilma tells about traditions in Chito's family. When they celebrated the one-year anniversary of the death of Chito's father, they put a white sheet into the *batea* [the wash trough] as if the dead person were in it. If the plates on the dinner table are *brillan* [shiny], then the spirit is present. On All Soul's Day, they put *jicaras* filled with frothy chocolate or other food for each dead person on the table. It is called *pis-han* [spirit food].

The trouble between Chelo and Chito that Nohoch Felix alluded to in his letter and which led to their separation started with a *pochero* [a one-dish meal] which Chelo had prepared and which Chito said was no food. He was very drunk at the time. He started beating her and threw her on the floor. Her brothers, Oscar and Joaquin, pulled him off of her, and all three of them beat him in return. For three nights afterward Chelo slept in Eus's house with her children. I saw Chelo at the service the other day. She had her small son on her arm. She was very beautiful. I wonder how Chito feels about being separated from her. She says she will only return to him if he stops drinking.

Chito would not give Chelo part of the house to live in. So Chelo came to Wilma's to live. She threatened on Wilma's advice that if Chito would give her no place to live, she would go to Merida to work and give the children up for adoption. So Chito gave in and gave her the large kitchen in his house. Chito has to pay child support to the municipality and Chelo gets it there. He also buys food for her at the market. He has his drinking companions in his house all the time and says he cannot be without drinking. Since he married Chelo, he has been evacuating blood. One time, he went to the judges here and said that he had a million pesos in his house and it was stolen. They even asked Chelo to come before them under suspicion, but at their separation, he changed all the locks, so she could not have entered. They were going to lock her up, but Wilma said she would go in her stead, because Chelo had small children to take care of. So they locked up neither.

Demonic Possession

In one of his letters this spring, Nohoch Felix wrote about an attack suffered by Miguel. The *hermanos* had been on an evangelizing trip. During the night, he became completely paralyzed in his hammock. They brought him home in his hammock. He was as stiff as a stick. The group thought he was drunk. Nohoch Felix did a bloodletting on his forehead. His blood was very dark, not bright red at all. The treatment brought him out of his condition. He told that just before he became paralyzed, he heard someone walking around. The *hermanos* came to believe that he had been attacked by demons.

The last time there had been any demonic possession in the congregation was during the apocalyptic events in 1970. It was therefore a considerable surprise when, in a letter posted in March 1983, Nohoch Felix reported the following:

> Today, on the first day of March, the Hermanos Antonio B. and Antonio C. entered our Iglesia Universal "Cristo Viene" because there were some problems that came about in their church. God can solve problems that arise.

According to Eus, it seems that one of these *tonos parisioners* [congregants of the churches of the "Tonos," the two Antonios], the daughter of Don B., was "attacked." They prayed over her, but to no avail. Then they called in Miguel, who prayed over her for a whole hour. Then the demon said through her mouth to Pancho N., who was also present: "We've been wanting to get you. There were only seven of us. Now we are double that number. Now we'll get you." And Pancho N. became very scared and started coming regularly to the temple.

Wilma confirmed the account. After that prayer session, she saw the girl. She was walking slowly with her arms away from her body.

I thought this would be the end of the demonic possession. I certainly could not foresee that in my subsequent absence, it would be Wilma who would carry out a successful, classical, prolonged ritual of exorcism.

10. January 1985

Arrival and at Home with Eus

A good flight. I love the smells of Merida that greet you just as you leave the plane. As I round the corner of the hallway, I crane to see, catching sight of darling Eus. I am home. She is with Nina, who came to visit her parents-in-law in the neighboring village with three of her five children: my godson Freddy, Miguelito, and four-month-old Nelli. Teresita and Chavelita have stayed with their father in Chetumal. The two boys are darling, slender little fellows.

They have mini-buses here now. It takes us to a new bus station, actually a mere hole in the wall, but at least it does not have the crowds of the main depot. I imagine the fancy one is reserved for the tourists, safely segregated and aseptic.

We wait only an hour for our bus. I buy tickets from the driver. People crowd in, so many that not a pin could have dropped, but the bus is clean and has comfortable seats. And there is a welcome change: instead of the usual four hours, the trip takes us only a little over two.

Eus has a nice new gate; a friendly young man, a neighbor, made it for her. The old three-stone hearth is now outside under the trees. Eus: "I put more shavings on the fire so you'd have a nicer picture of the smoke."

The open space between the range and the house is occupied by a new shed: Eus's son Erme helped them build it and put in a cement floor. It is a lovely, airy space. There has been no rain since September and, although they irrigate, plants do not grow well without some rain as well. I eat a delicious tomato that Eus has saved for me. There are ripe *chinas* [oranges] on two bushes that they have left unharvested for me. However, the bananas are not doing well this year. Eus's pride! She bought three turkey eggs; all three hatched, and two lived. She sold one for 3,000 pesos and kept the other one.

The pig intestines that Eus used to strip for fat are no longer given away for free, for people now buy them as a substitute for meat.

Because of the drought, the bees are dying for lack of flowers.

Eus's son Enrique, she was told in Merida, was drunk yesterday. His son was attacked by three men. His brother Elias went at them with a pistol. Now Samuel is in the hospital, wounded, and Elias is in jail. He has no permit to carry a pistol.

Teresa's matchmaking efforts were successful: her daughter Rosalind recently married Isauro's son in a ceremony in the temple. She wore a white wedding dress with a train and a veil. Of course, Isauro had to pay for all of it. They killed many turkeys. Eus teased everyone, saying, "You are hungry? Go eat at Teresa's; they killed fourteen turkeys." Miguel allowed the fancy wedding to be celebrated in the temple, but when the daughter of Nazaria wanted to be married in the same way in the temple, he forbade it. His decision was puzzling, because her bridegroom was from Celestun, but of the temple there; that is, not a *mundano*. As a result, Nazaria does not attend the services in the temple. But she says her mother is ill and she does not want to leave her alone.

I have settled down to the daily chore of writing. Eus thoughtfully has padded my chair with my Mexican *rebozo* and I am happy with the air, the twittering of the birds, the smells of the street, the smoke of the cooking fire. Little Danu and Rebecca come visiting in the afternoon; I give Rebecca the doll I had brought her and to Danu a small car.

There is a little rain, finally, but then a wind comes up, and we all watch as it blows the clouds away. Chelo comes to call with her children, then Wilma with the rest of hers. We have fun looking at the photos I brought, and the boys play with the small model car I had for them. Then Norma comes with her new baby, a long-legged brown little girl, and Jose, who is on his best behavior.

Finally, it does rain—a gentle "female" rain, and we all crowd into the new room. Only Norma stays in the house with her new baby. Nohoch Felix joins us; he brings his guitar and his harmonica. We start singing hymns, then he plays *jaranas* on his harmonica, and little Rebecca and I dance. After a while I get tired of dancing, so I sit down, but the children have become very excited. They crowd around me, all those black heads. So I invent a game: I guess (from the presence or absence of barrettes) whether a head is of a boy or a girl.

They cannot get enough of it, because I dramatize the game by closing my eyes. There is a tremendous laugh when Wilma joins in without my knowing it. It is quite a crowd: three of Chelo's, five of Wilma's, and Nico all in the same age group. Then Wilma takes my hand further down on the little boy's crotch: "You can find out there, too!" she says. More laughter. I say: "Just so no bigger ones join in!" Finally everyone leaves, and since it is continuing to rain, there is no service. So there is no need to hurry, and we have a leisurely supper.

Expecting it to turn cold during the night, I put on almost all the clothes I have brought along. Eus contributes her thickest towel, and I fall asleep happily. My bliss lasts until about 3 A.M., when I wake up gradually because "things" begin crawling all over me. I think of bugs, then briefly of spiders or possibly scorpions. Finally, I need to use the chamber pot and I get out of my hammock. I try to find it in the dark but get confused because the hammocks do not seem to be hanging in the accustomed relation to each other. Then Nohoch Felix feels me bump his hammock and turns on his flashlight. "What are you looking for?" "The *vasinilla*. Where is it?" It turns out that something had been eating him also, so he had changed the location of his hammock, throwing my orientation off.

I try to go back to sleep, but things soon go from bad to awful, so I finally softly speak to Eus, trying to raise her. She is up instantly. She lets down a reserve hammock perpendicular to mine. I get into it, and we spend half an hour picking ants out of my blanket, the nice one that Eus bought "the year that the mountain erupted." She finally settles me in the other hammock. She has a way of wrapping me tightly like a babe. I get into the hammock, but I cannot fall asleep again because I imagine I can hear the tiny rustle of the ants in the *huano*. But Eus thinks that what I am hearing has to be another animal, because you cannot hear "those tiny ants!" But all that morning, I kept picking ants out of my hair, and some even crept out of my sleeve.

Nohoch Felix coughs a lot. Eus says the Lord sent the ants and made him sick because he played *jaranas* and we danced. The Lord is responsible for quite a lot around here. I point out that it says in the Bible that God loves a happy heart. I have no idea where that is in the Bible, but luckily Eus does not quiz me on the chapter and verse.

Wilma comes to repay some money I did not remember having loaned to her, and I ask her to keep it as a token of my affection.

In the morning, Nina returns from visiting with her parents-in-law. After her fifth child, she had her tubes tied. She talks happily about their *barrio* in Chetumal: the streets have been paved and there is a park for the children, drinking water, several stores, and a school only three blocks away. Because of all the construction, her husband also has work most of the time.

I do not feel well all day, and toward evening it becomes very cold once more. We gather everything in the way of warm things for the children. Nina has brought one nylon hammock for the two boys. I contribute a woolen *rebozo*. Eus insists that I keep their blanket, which might keep me warm, but it is so cold I am afraid to move for fear of losing my cover.

All night, there is traffic to the chamber pot. Eus has brought in a lid in case I have diarrhea, but luckily nothing happens.

The day dawns mild. I sit between the *batea* and the hearth and a riot of tropical plants and flowers are all around. "Eden," an elderly woman calls it who comes to buy some plants from Eus. Then a girl comes to buy flowers for 30 pesos. When the *hermanos* come to get flowers for the temple, she does not charge anything. Eus composes a bouquet for her: bougainvillea, ferns, red double rose of Sharon, and multi-colored leaves. She calls it *pluma de gallo*, rooster's plumes. The girl wanted to take it as an offering to the Three Kings in Tizimin. Their fiesta was celebrated there this weekend. The girl's arms are covered with warts; she hopes that the Three Kings will cure her. "They will do nothing for her," says Nina contemptuously.

Nina leaves with her children at noon. Freddy, her oldest, is quite a helper for her, carrying the bags, while Miguelito takes charge of the box of chicks Eus has given her; Nina carries the little girl. The younger daughter of Chelo is also visiting. She passes an intestinal parasite. At first, I think it is a very young snake in the chamber pot, but when I look closer, it is more like a rainworm, about 6–7" long. "Everybody has these around here," Chelo says.

JANUARY 7, 1985

This morning I see Eus's dogs rubbing their anuses on the stones, apparently depositing the eggs of their worms. Chelo is right; intestinal parasites are everywhere. I have escaped them because Eus always boils my drinking water and energetically scrubs all plates and pots with Fab.

Eus comes home from shopping; Dona Ugulina is very ill and is in Merida. She is past 90 and fell a second time. Her daughter says she keeps asking for Eus. She left all her property here to her son—her house, her land—and now her son does not want her in his home. He wants her to go to "someplace where they put sick old people." Ugulina laughed it off, saying, "See, how people talk!"

It is very cold in the afternoon, so Eus decides that it is too far to go to Antonio B.'s temple. Instead, we end up with Hermano Miguel again. There is only a skeleton congregation, only some of the old-timers, and Hermano Miguel has even less to say than usual. But Wilma is there and says that Chito's mother fell out of her hammock and broke her arm. Chito took her to Merida to have her treated, and for three days he did not drink. Then he was back on the bottle again.

Because there have been several weddings, the financial burden incurred by the families of the grooms is much on people's minds. Eus: "Teresa sometimes speaks in tongues, but it says in the Bible that by their fruit you shall know them, and when Teresa's daughter married Isauro's son, they demanded that he buy a lot of clothes for Teresa's daughter in addition to the wedding outfit, also a lot of streetwear."

Teresa's husband Chucho owed everybody money because of the wedding, even Wilma. She finally had to go to the authorities a year ago. Originally Chucho and Teresa said they needed a going-away dress for the bride, but later they demanded a fancy wedding dress with a train, veil, and everything.

The day following the wedding, the young couple came to the service in the temple and, to the secret amusement of the women, Teresa kept waking up her daughter, who kept falling asleep after a presumably strenuous wedding night.

We have such a comfortable evening together. Nohoch Felix is reading in his collection of bible stories, occasionally aloud. Eus is ironing and talking with me. We have a good tough laugh at the expense of Hermano F., who had wife trouble. Their pig got loose, so his wife and his *compadre* went looking for it.

She left her little daughter with her husband. He was not to move from the child's side. So the woman and the *compadre* could do what could be imagined.

Jose comes to call, dragging a large iguana, its head bloodied, but still alive. Jose is such a handsome young man, but there is always the smell of brutality about him. He kicked Norma in the abdomen some time ago until she aborted. He had left half a chile and when he wasn't home, she ate it. He beat her savagely for that. Eus and I try to understand why women do not leave their husbands. We come to no conclusion about it. Nohoch Felix and Jose put the iguana on the fire and laugh when its belly breaks open. Their excuse: I guess it's chicken.

When Wilma comes, the ways of men continue as a topic. El Cordo, Dona Julia's son, she said, left the Church. His first wife had no children. So he left her. The second one had five in succession, among them one pair of twins. She had a daughter as the result of a childhood rape. Her husband wanted to rape that daughter, so she gave the child to her sister in Cancun, whose own children were grown.

"Who speaks in tongues?" I often ask. "Rodolfa," Eus says, "speaks in tongues occasionally, but that does not make her morally stricter, because she allows one of her daughters and her boyfriends to neck in front of the temple. Also, Rodolfa and her daughters spend a lot of time playing cards. If her husband Candil is busy sewing, they go to some other woman's house." Considering the fact that Rodolfa plays cards with her daughters, perhaps it is not the Holy Spirit that speaks through her mouth.

Her daughter Imelda is the only one in the family who does not play cards, and she and her husband attend services regularly. Imelda gave birth to a daughter, then to a son. After that delivery she lay in her hammock paralyzed for months. Then she became pregnant again.

Hermano Miguel continues to be the thorn in Eus's side: "Hermano Miguel never works, and he continually badgers the *hermanos* for their tithe. His wife asked one, "Didn't you understand what the *hermano*, my husband, said? You are supposed to bring us some chickens." Of course they know that we have some chickens. But then they are young; they can work. What they should actually do is that they should ask for an offering for the elderly of the congregation. They never do that!" With Nohoch Felix approaching 79 and Eus 75, she certainly has a point.

So I asked, "If Hermano Miguel is bad, if he does not preach well, if Antonio is the only one to whom he gives permission to preach, why do you go?" Eus said, "For a while, I did not go. But I don't want to stay at home all the time. Hermano Miguel is hard to hear with the amplifier going all the time. Often I don't understand what he says. His hymns have no tune. His son's twanging is even worse. Their music [on the electric guitar] is only chinga-ta, chinga-tu

[Eus's whimsical allusion to *chinga tu madre,* f— your mother)] . . . but all in all, it is still better than staying home."

There is a light rain. So we figure that Hermano Miguel will once more cancel the evening service. Nohoch Felix goes to check and comes back: no service. So after supper, it is story time again.

Eus: There was a woman in Tibilom, a fat woman, a cousin of Nohoch Felix. The edge of a local cenote collapsed, so that part of the village had no water. She had money, so she had a well blasted, and she was the only one who had water. She would lock up when she went out, and the poor women of the area had no water for days on end. She became sick, and her entire body got bloated. They kept a chamber pot under her hammock, and urine and water kept dripping from her all the time until she died, they said because she withheld water from those who needed it.

This story of the woman and her well is almost a cautionary tale: exert too much control and you may end up the loser. Another account about a woman, actually a young teenager, that Wilma and I were assembling during that time, surrounded by the fragrance of Eus's flowers, carried the opposite message: defend yourself against external control, and in the end, you will emerge unscathed.

Invitation to the Demons

Soon after my return home in September 1983, I received a letter from Wilma concerning the demonic possession of one of the girls who casually attended the services at the temple:

> The girl who is possessed by spirits does not now come to the temple. She continues having her attacks at home. I asked her mother and she told me this.

After a lengthy hiatus in the correspondence, in July 1984, Nohoch Felix touched on the same topic:

> A woman was possessed by the Evil One. We prayed for her one week. She ran away into the *monte.* She was caught, but the poor woman did not become well. She is 15 years old. Her mother is an *hermana.*

I was aware, of course, that the experience of demonic possession was nothing new to the congregation. It had occurred prominently during the latter part of the 1969–1970 disturbances. It seemed to me at that time that the character of Barrera, the minister in charge, was in some obscure way involved with conjuring up those demonic experiences. But that had been nearly fourteen years ago. So why now? Perhaps, I thought, Barrera and Hermano Miguel had something in common that could be construed as calling forth the experience of demonic possession, more dominantly in the most susceptible part of the congregation, the teenage girls. Clearly, I needed to take a closer look at Hermano Miguel. Hermano Miguel, the new minister, was certainly different from Isauro, the pacific pastor of the congregation for the past nine years. The more I puzzled over him, the clearer it became that I needed first of all to recall some background.

The congregation whose guest I had been now for almost a decade and a half, where I had seen the toddlers grow to adulthood, the men's hair become grizzled at the temples and the women become fat (all except Eus, who continued to be as thin as a rail), was a very small congregation. It usually had an average attendance at services of around twenty adults. Personal conflicts tend to become magnified in such a small group. Furthermore, women always outnumbered men by at least three to one. Also, as I pointed out elsewhere, it was the women who had the power, women who as a matter of course exercised the control. Men of rural backgrounds, such as the always-pacific Isauro, had no problems with this. This was how the world was constituted. Not so with the pastors of Latin-American urban derivation. The battle royal that Barrera fought, foremost with Eus, during the early history of the congregation, eventually resulted in his parting.

After a number of village preachers, the pastor who took over from Isauro, however, was an urbanite, not a corn grower or small rancher. Instead, he had been a merchant, a honey trader. His Spanish vocabulary pointed to city schooling; so did the ease with which he handled difficult biblical grammar and vocabulary. His lifestyle was that of an urban retiree, like his habit of sleeping until ten, which so scandalized the women of his congregation. So did his pronounced preference for affluent parishioners, for whom he had no problem bending the rules of conduct, which he proclaimed as obligatory for the common folk. It did not take him long to transfer the ritual institutions already in place into money-making schemes. He was sitting pretty. However, there was a thorn in his flesh: the women. Perhaps subliminally, he perceived their disapproval. Clearly, they had to be subdued if he was going to have the good life for the next ten or fifteen years, as he had planned. Utzpak was the right kind of place, a *cabezera,* the central community of a region, almost a town. However, for the situation to be perfect, the women had to be pliant. In an irritating way, these *hermanas* were not. Actually, there had been some initial victories. He had cowed Teresa and Joaquina into silence: no more singing in trance—that was only vanity. As for the others, they kept radiating independence, and his gut reaction was to attack them. "He does not preach" was the recurrent refrain in Nohoch Felix's letters, "he only exhorts." "An overblown, screeching little rooster" was my irreverent characterization in my field notes.

Wilma, however, was too tough for him, just as Eus had been for Barrera. After a number of futile skirmishes he decided on a different tactic: Wilma's daughter Marjelia had a suitor, not a local boy. By attacking him, he could get at Wilma. If he blocked the desired match, she would have to acknowledge his importance. However, he completely left out Marjelia in plotting his strategy. A pretty, spunky, independent young woman, Marjelia had all the steely determination of her mother and grandmother.

In October, shortly after returning from Yucatan, I received a letter from Wilma. After a number of other bits of information, she wrote:

> In front of the congregation Hermano Miguel said that they should neither receive nor give food to Victor [Marjelia's suitor], and that they would let him have 15 days to find work. If not, they will give him his bus fare so he could return to his place of residence.

Apparently, Victor let Hermano Miguel's attack roll off his back. For in November, Wilma reported an even more vicious onslaught:

> In the temple, the quarrels continue with Hermano Miguel because of Victor; [Hermano Miguel says] that [Victor] is a prevaricator, which is not true. Hermano Miguel only maintains it because when Victor asked for Marjelia, he did not tell Hermano Miguel about it, and for that reason he hates him. Hermano Miguel said that he would not accept Victor unless he had a letter of recommendation. When Victor came with that letter, he did not accept him even with that letter.
>
> During the ministerial meeting they held in Merida, Luis L. made a statement about Victor from the pulpit. We also went, myself, Chelo, and my father. He said that Victor was a member in good standing of the Merida church, that he participated in everything. Sometimes they had to scold him, but he was always obedient.

That Hermano Miguel was in reality aiming his barbs not at hapless Victor, but at the women supporting him became clear later in Wilma's letter:

> This week Hermano Miguel said that those who were sitting in the back and did not rise when they were supposed to seemed like mummies, and their flesh was stuck to their bones. This is what he said about my mother, about myself, and about Marjelia.

According to a brief note from Teresa some time later, for reasons not mentioned by any of my correspondents, Victor returned to his home in Sinaloa without marrying Marjelia.

This victory produced an instant euphoria in Hermano Miguel. As Nohoch Felix reported in February 1984, "There are services every day now. Hermano Miguel does not exhort anymore as he used to before. We even sing again in front of the pulpit."

Soon, however, the constellation was to change once more. Quite possibly, as Wilma's account indicates, Hermano Miguel was anticipating the pleasure of bludgeoning the girl who had dared to make nuptial plans without asking for his permission. But Marjelia had her own plans.

In June of 1984, Nohoch Felix wrote:

> As far as Marjelia is concerned, she became very rebellious. She says nobody should order her around. She will do what she pleases. And she went to Cardenas, where she had worked before. She wrote to the lady where she had worked before and asked if there was any work, and she answered that there was, and so she went. And her mother said that she should go with God's blessing.

In August, Nohoch Felix wrote that Marjelia came to visit her mother. She revealed that in Cardenas she would marry *un mundano*, that is, not a member of the congregation—without informing Hermano Miguel, of course.

As I heard when I visited once more in January 1985, Hermano Miguel, upon finding it out, fumed for months after.

Whether as a result, or simply coincidentally, the demonic disturbances began soon after Hermano Miguel became the new pastor of the congregation. Wilma, occupied with her affairs, apparently did not notice a child named Marci at the time. Why should she? Less than 12 years old at the time, Marci actually had a number of connections with the congregation. She often came from her home community of Bek only 6 kilometers away to visit her grandmother and her Aunt Nazaria, who was a member of the congregation and took her to the services. Nazaria's husband frequently acted as a faith healer and was known for his own, apparently ecstatic, healing prayers. It seems reasonable to assume that this ambience, together with the brutality of her stepfather and the extreme overt aggressiveness of the strange new pastor, may have all added up eventually to the eruption in Marci of a full-blown, classic case of demonic possession.

As satisfying as this explanation may appear to the social scientist, we should not be tempted to fall victim to our own hubris. For, as in all cases of demonic possession, there remains a residue of the unexplainable, and that is certainly also true of the encounter with the possession of this young teenager from an obscure inland Maya village.

Hermano Miguel Opens the Door

The following field observations were recorded in January 1985, at a time when Marci had already been delivered of her demonic possession. However, it is important in this context to emphasize what is most injurious to those psychologically most vulnerable, namely the inconsistency, the unpredictability of the exercise of power. And that is, I think, what the following fragmentary segments add up to in the manner of a jigsaw puzzle, contributing, I hope, to an understanding of Marci's experience.

For while it was apparently Wilma's impression that the onset of Marci's demonic possession correlated with the assault of her father on her, it seems that there is an even more important, although occult, correlation with Hermano Miguel's comportment.

Evening Service

Wilma had suggested that I continue taking notes unless Hermano Miguel forbade it specifically. So I do. The service proceeds as always, starting out with nine men and twenty women. In his sermon, Hermano Miguel keeps complaining that he does not get enough money from the congregation. Everyone seems bored, so he tries to enliven matters by switching into a Sunday school format. What does the word "*Candearia*" mean? Silence. He keeps leafing through his Bible.

There is lengthy discussion of the value of God's word—then he switches to a sure-fire topic, "When I was young, I enjoyed dances, but that is not a Christian life. . . ." The following day, Nohoch Felix acts as the messenger: "Don't take notes; wait until you get home and then write down what you remember so they will regard you favorably." They? It is not difficult to guess who "they" are. As always, with Hermano Miguel, the issue is control. As far as Hermano Miguel's power game is concerned, I am only of minor significance, an irritant on the sideline.

As Wilma noted, he allowed only Antonio B. and no one else to open the service or carry it on, and he would not let anyone preach, not even Alex, who is a preacher.

One of Hermano Miguel's sermons that I note (obediently from memory) deals with the joy of giving up the body. This is standard biblical fare, but I still wonder how a man who so obviously enjoys food and sex has reconciled his beliefs with his practice. It would be wonderful, he proclaimed, if we could lose the body because with the body there is always the temptation to sin, which prevents people from arriving in heaven. And around the throne of the Lord there are angels singing "*santo, santo . . .*" as we do in the temple. Actually, I had my heart set on Mozart, not on Hermano Miguel's *umpapa*. He then went on to a complicated calculation about the 40,000 who would be resurrected, who were really our forbearers, and he had obvious trouble trying to fit the rest of humankind into that sum. Of course, the sermon included the topic of collecting tithes.

The dearth of eligible marriage partners within the congregation had become critical over the years, and that Hermano Miguel would latch onto it as another source of power was predictable, as was the fact that the girls would not wait until their fathers, or Hermano Miguel, would come up with a solution. Thus, Antonio C.'s daughter ran away with a boy who was not of her father's congregation. Three days later they came back and asked for forgiveness. "I don't know you," was her father's reaction. "You are devils."

Hermano Miguel apparently came to the conclusion that it would add to his stature if he came up with a desirable suitor for the girls of the congregation. The young man he chose for the role was the son of one of the affluent families of the congregation called Daniel.

There is a bit of history about this Daniel. He and his gang bought a boat and sailed up and down the Gulf Coast and plundered vacation homes. When they robbed and raped an elderly English lady during one of these escapades, the authorities stepped in and put them all in prison. His parents had to sell quite a bit of land in order to bail him out. When he was back in Utzpak, his father, as did also the authorities, demanded that he attend the services regularly. That was where I saw him; he was quite a dandy in his tight jeans and long black hair.

Attendance at the services did not improve his moral fiber. Eus: It seems that Daniel's sister was working in Dona Ba'tola's store. Daniel came and asked to buy some shoes on credit. They gave him the shoes. Next day his sister said that he had paid for them.

"Where did you put the money?" she was asked.

"In the cash register."

"How did he pay?"

"In 500-peso bills."

They checked; there were no 500-peso bills in the cash register drawer. They took away her job and let her wash the bed linen of the hotel. But after a while, she quit that job.

Hermano Miguel, it was thought, had promised Daniel's father to get him safely married. Why he thought of Wilma's daughters no one knew, but he actually tried to pressure the family to agree to a marriage of Adela, the younger sister of Marjelia, with Daniel. She, of course, rebuffed his advances. She would not marry a *marijuano*.

Wilma the Exorcist

Eus and I go to visit Wilma. She has a spacious *mamposteria* house, rather high, but the roof leaks like a sieve. When I suggest that she might want to buy some tar paper to fix the holes from the money she has received from me for fieldwork assistance, she argues that that would not be such a good idea, because the neighbors would conclude that she has money.

Perhaps the intended target of the deception is also her husband. However, Ruben won't do any work on the house because it is registered as Wilma's property. He goes to work in Tibolom but does not bring home any money. Wilma threatens that she will divorce him, especially since there are rumors that he has a lover there.

Wilma and her younger daughter Adela also do some sewing and then there are occasional gifts from Chelo, who is still affluent, although separated from her husband. Eus and I go to see what her home is like, now that she has her own section. Actually, she has two rooms, with a lovely tiled floor. In the front room, there are two dusty wardrobes. There are pictures of her and the children on the wall, also a wedding picture. On top of one of the wardrobes there is a scrawny plastic Christmas tree with lights on it. The back room has a big dining-room table and formal chairs. The children have lots of toys, the girls, big dolls.

One night Chito was drunk and tried to get into Chelo's living quarters. So Chelo took her shoe and beat him and kicked him out.

Abigel, one of Chelo's little daughters, complains of a stomachache, so Chelo gives her two spoonfuls of some medicine. Half an hour later the child passes twenty-four worms of the kind I had seen before. Chelo simply throws them out on the patio. I suggest that she might want to burn them, but I don't think that she did.

Of Wilma's sons, Jose is still unemployed. His wife Norma gave birth to a little girl on December 31. Because Jose has no job; they do not have a penny. The newborn needs medicine for her inflamed eyes, but there is no money for that. Jose says that it irritates him when the baby girl cries, so he has been beating her.

In the afternoon, Adela comes by with Norma's baby. She has made her some clothes, like doll clothes, out of remnants. They are going to call her Sofia, for Ruben's mother who lives in Tibolom. They let Rebecca hold her and rock her. Eus and I both get upset when Rebecca nearly drops the baby.

Wilma's next son, Oscar, works as a farmhand, and Eus can't understand why Wilma does not make him help around the house. After all, Eus says, he lives there and even gets his meals from Wilma. But then, the two women do not see eye to eye as far as the training of children goes.

Joaquin, my faithful chronicler, is quite different and helps out when he can. During the vacation months, he worked for an air-conditioning company in Merida. He now attends the *preparatoria,* the high school. He needs three more years till graduation. He wants to take a half a year of English during the coming school year.

During the services, Wilma often sits next to me. She points out people that we have talked about—see, that is Alex . . . and here comes Daniel—and she makes irreverent comments where appropriate. Nestor steps up behind the table to preach. "How come Hermano Miguel lets him do that?" Oh, change of rules. Nestor talks about man being the head of woman, so the woman has to cover her head in the temple. Wilma, in response, takes off her mantilla and places it on the back of the chair in front of me. "Now you can take notes," she whispers. "The *hermano* cannot see you."

The Demonic Possession

Eus and I have been to the bank, and as we come out, we stop to talk with Nazaria. "*Cush Marci?* [And how about Marci?]" Eus asks. "Oh, Hermana," Nazaria takes a deep breath. "It was terrible how that girl attacked me! Not she, but *el demonio* [the demon]. She grabbed my tongue, it tore so I could hardly speak, it was so badly torn. The *hermanos* prayed for her, but only a few stayed with her. Hermano Miguel came only once. '*Dios sabe por que* [God only knows why this is happening to her],' he said. Only Wilma stayed with her when she was raging so."

Something in Nazaria's disjointed account suddenly seems very familiar. In the late 1970s, I had researched a case of demonic possession in Germany. The girl in question was a university student (see Goodman 1981), and the allegation at the time was that she died as a result of the exorcism.

Was this girl still alive? "What is the girl's name?" I asked, "and is she still alive?

"*Buen y sana,* well and healthy. Her name is Marci."

Recalling some salient features of the Anneliese case, I asked, "And did the girl smell bad?"

"Oh, yes. When her mother came to see her at my place, she said, '*Hija,* daughter, what is the horrible smell? Better take me to the house of my relatives. I can't stand this stench.'"

To rid themselves of the frightful odor, Nazaria and her family constructed a small tar-paper shed in the back of the *solar* for Marci. She was made to stay there.

As soon as I saw Wilma again, I asked her to tell me the entire story of Marci's demonic possession on tape. The following is the transcription.[1]

Wilma: "Marci and her mother came here to my mother's place, and Marci was *en demoniada,* possessed by the demons."

Eus: "I had harvested some bananas. Marci tore one off the bunch and ate it without peeling it. I said to her mother, 'Let her do it.' The girl took another one, she stuffed it into her mouth, again without peeling it, and then another one. She tore off a green one, tried to peel it with her teeth, then threw it on the ground. She tore an unripe orange from a bush and grabbed a knife from the table in the open kitchen shed, cut it in half so she could suck it. Her mother would not let her do that, so she turned on her mother, putting her hands on her throat and choking her."

Wilma: "Then she let go of her mother; she started dancing. First she sang a hymn, then a popular song."

Eus: "Then she needed to urinate. She went to the gate of the *albarrada,* pulled down her panties, and pushing her pelvis forward, she urinated in plain view of the men standing on the corner.

On the basis of Wilma's taped account, I later wrote the report of Marci's exorcism, subsequently published in my book, *How about Demons? Possession and Exorcism in the Modern World* (1988b, 108–114). The following, with some minor editing, is that account.

This is the story of Marci:

When Marci was 12 years old, her stepfather, for a considerable sum of money, agreed with an old man to send the girl to him as a permanent sex partner. Earlier, he had successfully concluded a similar bargain involving his somewhat older stepdaughter. Marci, however, refused to go to the old man and stayed home. One day, when her mother had left for work in the family's cornfield, Marci's father prepared a dish of scrambled eggs and let Marci have some, too. Marci's mother later insisted that he had mixed a witching powder into Marci's portion. Such powders are sold openly on the market in Tizimin. For soon after eating of those scrambled eggs, Marci became ill. She was disconsolate, she would cry incessantly, and for hours on end she restlessly ran up and down the Xbek village streets. Her mother took her to the physicians at the government clinic. After examining her, they came to the conclusion that she was suffering from *los nervios.* In Latin America, that is a catch-all diagnosis whenever women complain of depression. No need to worry; it would pass, they said.

Instead, however, Marci's condition grew steadily worse. Her mother took her to *espiritistas* [spiritualist healers] in Tizimin and also in Motul, another provincial town. But Marci was frightened by the skulls she saw in those houses, and the healers could not help her. Marci hardly reacted anymore when anyone tried to talk to her. She stripped before strangers, and once during a visit in Utzpak, she scandalized Eus by going to the gate, pulling down her panties, and, pushing her pelvis forward, urinating while standing, in plain view of the men standing on the corner across the street. She also had numerous convulsive attacks. As Wilma tells the story:

I saw Marci for the first time in the middle of 1983. I was on the market and I noticed her because her entire upper arm was burned. Since I did not know her, I asked a boy selling at a stall, "What happened to that girl?" "They say she fell into the hearth fire, into the food." "And why did she fall?" "They say she suffers from *los nervios,* and she also has attacks," he says.

The next day I saw her once more on the market; she was crouching in the middle of the street. "What is the matter with this girl?" I asked her mother. With a dispirited voice, her mother said, "She is sick. The doctors say it is *los nervios.* She just doesn't get any better. I have been taking her to the doctors for two years now, and they can do nothing for her." So I said to her, "If you believe that God can cure her, we have a temple here and you can go there and we will pray over her, so God will make her well." She just listened to me, but she never came to the temple, they say because she was a Catholic.

About half a year later on the market, I met Nazaria, her mother's sister, who is a member of our congregation. She told me that Marci and her mother had come from Xbek to visit but that Marci was very ill. So I said, "I'll come in the afternoon to see what is wrong with her, what the sickness is that she has, and we'll pray for her." I asked whether we should also tell Hermano Miguel, our preacher, to come. "No," she said, "we asked him, but he came only once and then did not come back. He said that she was possessed by demons, and he does not want to pray for her. He says that if a person such as he is not prepared, the demons will leave the girl and will possess him. Miguel is afraid of the Devil," says Nazaria, "he can't resist him, that is why he doesn't come back." So I asked Hermano Alfredo; he is also a preacher, and by way of his mother he is related to Nazaria.

Alfredo arrived at Nazaria's house first and Marci was so sick that he left again to try to find somebody to help him with the prayer. "Come quickly," he said, "her mother is of no use to me, she has no idea what praying means, and she knows nothing of the Word of God." The girl, he said, was close to death. She was rolling on the floor; the Devil was about to kill her.

So we hurried to Nazaria's house, he on his bicycle, I on foot, and we started to pray. As soon as we began, the Devil attacked her even worse. She writhed on the floor, foam came from her mouth, she had an attack, she could hardly stand it any more, she was close to suffocating and could no longer even scream. We continued to pray, and finally she quieted down and was able to get up from the floor. But she was not healed. She started to insult us in the most obscene way, even Alfredo, and she blasphemed God. Alfredo, who was not prepared for that, grabbed a piece of cane and started to beat her, but I demanded that he stop it. "We are fighting an evil spirit," I said, "and you are thrashing the flesh. It says in the Bible that the Devil can be defeated only with fasting and prayer."

During the following weeks, Wilma and Alfredo, often joined by Wilma's father and Nazaria's son-in-law, came every day after the service in the temple and prayed for Marci for many hours. They tried to take her to the temple also, but Miguel forbade it, because she often had to vomit or spit, although her mother spread some paper on the floor in front of her. When she was awake, she would cry like a small child and beg them, "Let me die, I am burning up. They are torturing me, I am hurting all over, they want to kill me." Or she would say, "Don't pray, when you pray it burns me." Then she would start trembling and go into convulsions and writhe. Frequently Wilma would have to hold her down while Alfredo read from the Bible, especially from the 91st Psalm; prayed in his own words; or laid the Bible on the raging girl. They tried to get her to kneel, but she resisted that. She often retched, as if she were about to vomit up something big. She would bring up quantities of foam, which left a bluish stain on the cement floor, and with that, her attack would stop, only to start over again. Even while she was lying in her hammock, foam would stream from her mouth and stand in puddles on the floor. Sometimes at night those present would hear a noise as if a horse had jumped on the roof. The dishes clattered in the cupboard, and plaster fell from the walls. Then the demons announced themselves.

Wilma: "We recognized the arrival of the Devil, because Marci would begin to curse, and she would urinate. That is why we knew that the Devil had come. Her urine had a terrible stench."

In the beginning, there were a large number of demons; later on only two remained, but they refused to give their names, although Wilma kept asking for them. Marci had practically no schooling; she could neither read nor write, yet the demons sounded highly educated. They named a large number of places where "without using a bus or a plane" they had been roaming for the past 2,000 years, localities in Mexico and in the United States and other places, the names of which Wilma did not recognize. The demons also described disputes in the temple, which Marci had no way of knowing about. When the demons spoke, they never sounded like Marci. They either used a thin, piping voice or the trembling voice of a very old woman or the deep voice of an old man. There was a curious intonation to what they said, a monotonous singsong with an occasional choking glottal cutoff, which the 8-year-old daughter of Wilma, who was often present at the prayers, delighted in imitating and demonstrating for me.

Even when there was no exorcistic prayer, Marci exuded a repulsive stench, so that her grandmother, who lived with the family in their one-room house, asked to be moved to relatives in the village, because she could not stand it. So the family constructed a hut of tar paper and limestone for Marci and her mother some distance away from the house. That almost caused a tragedy. Marci's demons tried to kill her mother. Wilma and a group of visiting women heard shouts: "Come on, help us, we'll kill her!" They arrived in the nick of time: Marci had her mother by the throat and was about to choke her to death.

She caused her family much anguish also in other ways. She kept attacking them with floods of insults and curses. She scandalized them by grabbing the cat and putting it to her breast as if nursing it. If she had an especially severe attack, even her grandmother began to tremble. Hideous creatures invaded the house; enormous tarantulas crawled through a crack in the wall and passed over the floor, and during the night, an owl kept screeching on the garden wall.

Marci also caught some of the chickens of her aunt and even one of her precious turkeys. She killed them by twisting their necks and then tried to tear them apart with her teeth. She tore unripe, bitter bananas from the trees and ate them skins and all and pulled hot chili peppers from the bushes and stuffed them whole into her mouth. She had enormous strength; she would uproot banana trees 9 feet tall or more or pick up large chunks of limestone, the building material of the area, and set them into the middle of the street. She also frequently threw stones at passersby, injuring at least one woman. With her hands as stiff as claws, she grabbed the tongue of her aunt and tore it. Nazaria showed me the gash when I arrived in January. Marci always felt hot and kept begging her family to bathe her.

One day she escaped from her mother and got to a small chapel at the edge of the village, where a farmer had set up statues of the Virgin Mary and of San Isidro, the patron saint of peasants. She threw the statues out into the street, broke them, and then fled into the thorny bushes of an abandoned homestead. Her mother later found her and dragged her out by her hair. Had she stayed there overnight, the enraged owner of the chapel would surely have slain her. At intervals, there were also times when she could not move at all, lying in her hammock as if dead.

The exorcistic prayers did not seem to do her much good. The rainy season passed, and the weather turned dry; it was October, then November. Repeatedly, Miguel said publicly in the temple that what the exorcists were doing was not of God. After all, the Apostles never had to pray for months when they exorcised evil spirits. They expelled them with a single command. It was obvious that the girl could not be cured. Even Marci's family was ready to give up. "I can't take it any longer," her mother complained. "She rages day and night, she can't sleep; not for a moment does she rest. She won't eat anything, she is getting thinner and thinner. She is sure to die on us." The exorcists finally agreed that they should seek medical help once more.

Wilma:

> So we went with her to the government clinic, Alfredo, myself, Nazaria, and her mother. The doctor asked her, "When did your illness start?" because we had told him what had happened. "I am not sick," she said. "For 2,000 years I have been roaming this earth, for 2,000 years I have been plaguing people in this way." "Your mother tells me that you are disrespectful to her, and that you scream a lot." "You never heard me do that, not a single time did you hear me like that," she answered. She talked completely sensibly. "Well," says the doctor, "there is no medicine for this kind of sickness. We can give you the money for the bus fare. I suggest you take her to Merida to the insane asylum."
>
> We discussed the matter among ourselves, and I said, "We are not going to accept the money. After all, there is no way in which you can cure a spirit. All of you know that there are no cures for evil spirits. How could you possibly heal a spirit? It is like the wind. The physicians cannot see it, so how could they tell what is wrong with it? Even this physician, who is a Protestant, doesn't know the Bible well enough. He had no idea what Marci meant when she said, 'I have been roaming this earth for 2,000 years and am tormenting the people.' This sort of thing, after all, didn't start here and now. You heard him ask the girl, 'And why are you doing these things?' And the way she answered: 'Why are you asking me these questions?'"
>
> So Alfredo said, "All right, so let us leave. This physician cannot help us." "We are leaving now," he said to the doctor, "and we want to thank you," for the doctor had not asked us to pay for the consultation. He gave us a few pills, which we were supposed to give to Marci so she would calm down a bit and could rest some. But after she took those, the demon raged even more furiously. I told her mother, "If you believe that your daughter will get well, then she will be cured; you just have to be patient, because we cannot know when God will work his miracles."

So the exorcists continued with their prayers, and occasionally they asked the demons when they would finally decide to leave. The usual answer was, "We'll leave now, but tomorrow morning at five we will be back." And punctually, as soon as the town hall clock struck five, they would return. But one day, about two weeks before Christmas, the demon suddenly said, "In half an hour we'll leave, and we won't come back."

Wilma:

> The next day, it was a Sunday, about eleven in the morning. I met Nazaria in the market, and she said to me, "You know what, Marci has been asleep since yesterday. She won't move, she won't get up, she doesn't wake up, she does nothing at all. She has not eaten any breakfast, either." "Let her be," I said. "I'll come as soon as I can." The family was afraid to wake her, because in the past, she had often struck them when they did that. About four in the afternoon, I went to Nazaria's house. "She still didn't get up," her mother said. "She just lies there under her coverlet and doesn't move. I touched her, and she felt very hot. I tried to feel her pulse, but could not find it." I wondered whether she was having another attack. So I said to her mother, "Make a tea of crushed orange leaves." I tried to lift Marci up but couldn't do it. Tears came streaming from her eyes, but she could not open them. I asked her if she hurt anywhere, but she shook her head. So I lifted her head a bit and gave her the decoction. She drank half a cupful. So I said to her mother, "Make her something to eat." Then with the help of her brother, who is younger than I, we helped her to sit up in the hammock, for if we left her lying there, she was going to die of hunger. She took the food and ate two whole cupfuls. "Better take it away from her now," I said to her mother. "She didn't eat anything yesterday, maybe she should have something again later." Then Marci got out of the hammock, went outside [to urinate], then came back and we started talking. "Why did you lie down yesterday?" I asked her. "I had a bellyache." "Will you come to the service at the temple tonight?" "Yes," she answered, quite normally.
>
> They brought her a bucket of water, so she could take a bath, and in the evening, she came to the service. A different *hermano* conducted the service, not Miguel. We sang many hymns, and the Holy Spirit manifested itself in Marci, and she danced beautifully and it seemed that she was never going to stop. It seems that Marci continues well. The last time I saw her was at the temple the Sunday before I left Yucatan that year. She was kneeling at the altar with her mother among those who had asked to be baptized the following week.

Hauntingly, Marci's story is almost a carbon copy of that of Anneliese Michel, one an illiterate Maya village girl, the other a highly educated German university student. The only difference between them is that Marci lived, while

Anneliese died. Comparing the two case histories, the only difference is the fact during the exorcism Anneliese was treated with massive doses of Tegretol, an anti-seizure medication, and Marci was not. Wilma, very perceptively, noted how "the demons raged even more furiously" when Marci was given a tranquilizer. By not insisting on further medication of that sort, Wilma, I think, saved Marci's life (see Goodman 1988b for further details).

Visit with Marci

Understandably, after assembling the jigsaw picture of Marci's story, I was anxious to put a face to it.

On January 5, at Wilma's suggestion, we went to visit her. The day was convenient because there was usually no service on Fridays. We met at the corner of Wilma's street and the highway—Wilma, Atela, Rebecca and her two little brothers, and Eus and I—decked out in our fanciest ?ipiles. Eus and I were lugging Eus's heavy tape-recorder because, according to Wilma, Marci sometimes sang some hymns, and she wanted to record them. As it turned out, Marci did not sing.

Nazaria's home, where Marci is staying, is very far, all the way on the road to Tizimin.

When we finally get there, we find all the doors of the small *mamposteria* home closed. Wilma knocks on the front door and a woman's voice calls out something that Wilma takes for an invitation. So she opened the door and there is Nazaria with a surprised "*Olah!*" inviting us all in.

The reason all the doors had been closed, Nazaria says, was that the grandmother had just taken her bath and the house is too small to string up the customary curtain. So they closed the doors instead.

I take a step in and look around. Because the room is so small, it seems crowded. In addition to Nazaria, there is an indifferent-looking middle-aged woman whom I take to be Marci's mother; then Marci's grandmother, all bones and shriveled skin, reclining in a hammock; next to her on a rough-hewn stump, a very dignified elderly Maya lady in a pretty ?ipil; and then to the right, a slender teenager in a faded cotton dress, whom I take to be Marci.

"Come in and sit down," Nazaria urges us. Actually, the coming-in part is not easy. Nazaria and her husband make a living by selling tacos and sandwiches on the market, and we have to thread our way through most of the ingredients spread out, while I am occupied trying to kick the live chickens and stepping on the dog and the cat. Eus, always the most astute in sizing up a situation, has made her way to Grandmother in her hammock. It seems Eus knows her from the time when Hermano Hill was missionizing in Utzpak, and she immediately locates her (this a favorite pastime) in her honorable kinship map. The old lady enjoys the conversation with Eus tremendously, and her appreciation even extends to me. When she rises to leave, she assures me that I am *ki?ichpam* [pretty] and gives me a peck on the cheek.

In the meantime, everyone finds a seat except Wilma's two little boys, who keep running in and out. Grandmother scrambles out of her hammock to make room for me. It is the most comfortable place to sit, I am assured, a courtesy one cannot refuse without totally upsetting the social order. Eus settles down on a stool, Adela and the others sit on various stumps, and Wilma with Rebecca on her lap sits near Marci, who apparently feels more comfortable standing.

"Do you still have any perfume?" I hear her ask Wilma.

Wilma had sold it all. Besides, that was not the direction that she wanted the conversation to take. Clearly, she was hoping that Marci would recall some of her spectacular demonic information. But she was to be disappointed.

"The *hermana* comes from Columbus," she tries to prime the pump. Marci smiles, as if to say, "And so what?"

"You have been there, haven't you?" Wilma persists. The same blank reaction. Then, feeling obviously uncomfortable with these unintelligible queries, Marci turns to me and wants to know where I had spent the New Year. The demons have totally vanished from her memory bank.

"In Mexico City," I answered, "and you?"

"At Chelo's. And we had turkey." It was very nice. Eus had made the black filling; it tasted very good.

The conversation turns to family matters. Marci should be sent home, but there was her stepfather. On the other hand, feeding her was a great burden, although Nazaria's two brothers, who work in Los Angeles, do send money home, but that is supposed to cover Grandmother's expenses.

I take some pictures of Marci; one of Marci with her mother, and another one with Wilma.

"You did such a good job exorcising Marci," I reassure Wilma on the way home. "That is why she has forgotten everything."

The Door Closes

While we are visiting with Marci, Nohoch Felix has gone to see the "Tonos" [the two Antonios, Antonio B. and Antonio C.] to consult them about the tile floor they are planning to put into their temple. He comes home with the news that they have invited a Presbyterian *hermano* to preach at their upcoming service.

"It has been decided," Eus informs me. "We are going to the service of the Tonos."

The temple of the Tonos is quite far. Years ago, Eus and Nohoch Felix used to cut firewood there. Now the area is a subdivision of Utzpak. There are even some elegant new homes there, such as the one of Chito's sister, of cement block with lavish wrought-iron gratings and gleaming tile floors.

The temple of the Tonos is a simple rectangular mud-and-wattle building. Antonio B. greets us effusively at the door, and when he notes that I look at the rostrum, which has a ramp leading up to it on both sides, he explains that there are instructions in the Bible according to which the Lord's altar should not be approached on stairs. Actually, Nohoch Felix told me that there had been a vision to that effect, but he did not know whose. Anyone can preach in their temple, Antonio explains. Only a priest who wanted to come and set up his images would be forbidden, because Satan was in those images.

There is something in the simple and unassuming style of the subsequent service that transports me back to the early days of the congregation. There are hymns that are no longer sung in Miguel's services. And then there are faces I have not seen in years—Eus's erstwhile friend, Hermana Valuch, who lives in this area now, and her husband, who opens the service, and there are others who left the temple after the millennial disturbance in 1970. Instead of limiting participation, Antonio C. encourages both the offering of Bible verses and of hymns. Proudly, Nohoch Felix offers his hymn, with a much stronger voice than he has at the temple. We, the visitors, are lined up facing the congregation. It takes me way back when the congregation sings "*Bien ve nidos, Hermanos . . .*" the traditional welcoming song. Then everyone passes to shake hands or for an *abrazo*. I take no notes, although Nohoch Felix says, with considerable emphasis, "You can take your notebook; nothing is forbidden there." But we are sitting in the front row, and I think it might be disturbing.

One total surprise: both Antonio C. and later Hermano Martin, the Presbyterian preacher, instead of ad-libbing a prayer as is customary, rattle off the Lord's Prayer. I had in truth never heard it in Spanish, and the familiar formulas seemed to glitter with Spanish jewels and pearls. This Hermano Martin is relatively young and obviously well trained. But he lacks the lively interaction between preacher and congregation customary among the Apostolics.

Eventually, Eus proceeds to fall asleep, and I, despite Martin's eloquence, proceed to suffer intense boredom trying to contemplate the perfume of prayer rising to the throne of the Almighty. I am also tortured by the slats of the folding chair. However, there is no altar call, and no one speaks in tongues. This is, of course, a disappointment, but all in all, I feel that the essence of the early congregation has actually survived here; perhaps it will later be able to refructify the mother temple.

The following day we go to the service at the temple, and I say good-by to Rodolfa. I see Marci and her mother go to the altar to register their intention to be baptized.

In the afternoon, to my surprise, Old Candil comes to visit. He says he wants to tell me about when he spoke in tongues for the first time. His visit is a melancholy occasion, as though he were saying, "Why do you always pay attention only to the women? After all, we men also have something to say." I don't ask why he never speaks in tongues during the service anymore. I think neither one of us want to bring up the topic of Hermano Miguel.

Sunday, January 13, 1985, is my last day. Eus washes my warm underwear, then kills and prepares a chicken for that day and the next. Morosely, I sit by the hearth and make sure that the cats do not snitch the pieces of chicken—before boiling them, Eus always toasts them over charcoal first. She makes the charcoal herself; charcoal-making folded because there was no more *monte* anymore.

I slept only four hours the night before, waking up at 2 A.M. with another case of diarrhea. I swallowed a massive dose of Lomotil, hoping to suppress it for the trip, and it did work.

We catch the 6 A.M. bus, which is extremely crowded. We finally get some seats at Motul and I promptly fall asleep.

It is on this occasion that I have the vision of Oscar Hill's preaching and see the beautiful tree with the shimmering leaves. As I later mulled over these visions, I finally came to the conclusion that perhaps in their hasty flight, Marci's demons left open a crack of the alternate reality to expose the enchanted small tree with its single silver pearl, Oscar Hill, the ragged preacher with the forgotten Bible in his tattered jacket pocket who started it all.

11. December 1986

Arrival and at Home with Eus

My flight goes to Detroit and changes in Miami, where I change to a Mexican airline that takes me to Cozumel. I meet a woman who teaches history at Central Florida State and works as a travel agent on the side. Basically, we can't compare notes, having access to very different parts of Mexican society.

At the airport, Eus! And Marjelia with her baby girl, and Eus's younger sister, whose guest she was for nearly two months after her operation. Eus's sons brought money for Eus's food. When my $200 check got lost in the mail (the bank eventually refunded it), Eus borrowed from Chelo.

December 5, 1986

Inflation: a first-class seat on the bus costs 1,100 pesos. "*Kinsaa tuush kʔuchuk?* [Who knows where it is going to arrive at?]" Eus remarks as we roar through the night, making no stops at all until Utzpak. Wilma's tribe expects us as the bus stops. All the little ones are reminded to embrace and kiss me. Rebecca and Elias are now "big," Rebecca in the fourth grade, Elias in the sixth, but Huancho, Danu, and Nico are still small. Norma could no longer take Jose's abuse, so she went back to Tabasco, taking baby Sofia, now nearly two, with her. Nico refused to go with her, so Wilma raises him. Jose gives her no money for his keep. Nico is cuddling up to Wilma as we talk on the way home, and she responds by tenderly stroking his head.

Jose occasionally goes fishing. As soon as a prostitute comes to Utzpak, he moves in, spending his money on her.

The motor is still working. Nohoch Felix and Eus irrigate, and Nohoch Felix sells a lot of bananas. What is left they eat and give to Chelo and Wilma.

We talk till nearly 11 P.M. There are hardly any men left in the congregation, only Nohoch Felix and Old Candil and one of his cousins. The *hermanos* say that they will come back when Hermano Miguel leaves.

"Why don't you complain to Luis L.?"

"The people just don't. They are afraid that Hermano Miguel will exhort them."

"But he does that anyway!" Eus just laughs.

On Sundays, there often are only three men and three or four women. A woman brought a chicken to Hermano Miguel. He performed her daughter's wedding ceremony. There was a big meal, people went to attend that, but the young couple never came to the temple again.

Hermano Miguel has ten children now, one born for every year he has been here.

The dress business has declined. The polyester jersey has gotten too expensive. Many sewing machines are idle, and people have gone back to weaving hammocks or buying a few calves and raising them in their *solar.*

All the vultures [*sopilotes*] *chʔoom,* have left Tibolom. Nobody knows why. There are some here because of the slaughterhouse nearby. One circled overhead just now. A few days ago, Nohoch Felix saw close to a thousand crows; they made an enormous racket. Then they left, and now you cannot see a single one.

Eus and Nohoch Felix are listening to a radio program being broadcast in Maya from Chetumal, but it is not clear enough because a Texas station advertising Folger's coffee is drowning it out.

Eus tells about her operation. She had started vomiting also at night. She thought if they operated on her she might die, but without the operation, she would certainly die soon. So from one day to the next, she decided to have it done. The physician said that she was too old. They were greatly impressed with how well it went and how quickly she recovered. "*Como esta la quince añera?* [How is the debutante?]" one of the physicians asked Wilma.

She recalls the help her sons provided her. Erme is burdened with a lot of alimony payments. Enrique no longer drinks, but his son Samuel is drunk all the time. He who does not drink is a *maricon,* a fag, he used to say to his son. Now he is sorry that he said that.

Santiago kept his car, although Reina wanted him to sell it. Then he had six drunks in his car, himself included. He collided with the Tizimin bus, injuring his forehead and totaling his car.

Teresa's daughter, who married Isauro's son, has no children as yet. "I believe he has no seeds," laughs Eus. Isauro's second son, Esteban, is engaged to be married, but Isauro's wife Juana hates the girl because she has no father. "There is no food for the pig of your lover," she told her son. The pig is for the wedding. The girl "has everything already, a refrigerator, a washing machine . . ." When they are married, she says, she and Esteban will go to work someplace else. She won't stay in Espitas, where Isauro is pastor, because Juana is so mean to her.

Teresa's husband has a girlfriend in Cancun. He told Teresa that he was asked to have a nice dress made and to shop for nice matching shoes. So she sewed the dress and chose the shoes, and her husband took them to Cancun.

Teresa found out who the girl was, and when she happened to go sell in Cancun she saw her, and she was wearing the dress and the shoes.

The cathouse has been re-established down the street from Eus. Santiago keeps visiting the establishment, and he is not very subtle about it either, parking his new car at the corner. And because Reina was jealous, he called his car La Celosa, The Jealous One.

As I know from a letter of Nohoch Felix, Hermano Miguel got mad at Ruben for saying that preachers should work, maintaining that it was not in the Bible. He also became very upset when Alex told the *hermanos* about Marci's exorcism and that Wilma helped with it.

While the temple is sparsely visited, many of the *hermanos* fill their need for religious experience by attending the many revival meetings of the area, where, as Wilma says, there is joy, also much speaking in tongues.

Don Antonio comes to see us, which reminds me of a certain custom.

Eus: Don Antonio's mother had just died. She was a *cantinera,* a woman who ran a tavern. Eus and some other women were preparing food for a ministers' meeting. Antonio's mother came to tell Dona Rach that she had a chicken for sale. Dona Rach went to look at it. Later she came back and said that it was too expensive. Later Eus heard from someone who knew both women well that "looking at a chicken" was a signal, indicating that there was a man at the *cantina* who wanted to have sex with her.

Wilma tells about Chito's severe illness. She encountered him shaking and vomiting blood. Wilma went to his sister, but she was not interested. Chelo did not seem to understand the gravity of the situation. Finally, with the help of his brother, she found a cab and took him to the clinic in Merida. He was told there that if he ever drank again, it would be the end. He is now reading Alcoholics Anonymous literature. There is a local chapter.

In the evening, we primped, not for a service (there was none on Fridays) but for the start of the fiesta. We dressed in our best ʔ*ipiles,* and Eus put perfume on me. It was cold, so I cheated a little, putting on white woolen ski pants, German, very thin, under the ʔ*ipil.* I thought no one would notice, but the plaza was brightly lit, and the wife of Don Panza, the tanner, asked Eus what I was wearing, stockings, pants? Eus said she did not know.

It was old home week: people whose name I did not even know came up to say "*Bish a beel* [How is your road]?" or just "*Ola.*" A granddaughter of Don Fulgencio remembered me from her childhood, and there was Rodolfa with her son, who was Miguelito no longer, but nearly as tall as his mother. We greeted Dona Radi. She has a fast food stand that sells double tortillas with bean paste inside and onions and cilantro for seasoning. She also sells warm *atole,* a corn drink. They say that her husband was killed by witchcraft.

I buy cotton candy for the kids, and for a while we watch the traveling *jarana* group dance. I had seen them perform years ago and was struck by their beautiful costuming, the girls in double-tiered *ʔipiles,* the young men in white suits with a red kerchief hanging out of their left pants pocket.

At the evening service on Saturday there are eighteen women, of whom I recognize only Teresa and Joaquina. Among the adult men, in addition to Nohoch Felix, there are only Nestor and Candil, whom Hermano Miguel addresses as *anciano,* an elder of the congregation. As I think of the list of those who no longer attend, I am surprised about tonight's attendance, but then this is the service when the various church organizations present hymns; attendance is always good for those. I notice a few plastic flowers on the table and stuck to the walls, which makes the gray cement blocks look a bit livelier. Wilma says that if she brings live flowers, they throw them out the next day, so she no longer brings any. The music is reduced to the tedious *umpapa* of the electric guitars, as it has been for years. Only we old-timers remember the handmade marimba that now serves as a cover for Eus's pump. The happy jaws ended on the trash heap long ago. There is now a collection for an organ, but I see little enthusiasm for it in the collection plate. Hermano Miguel does not generate much enthusiasm for the end of the world in his sermon, but at least he does not exhort.

Sunday Morning

On my way to the outhouse, the big white rooster flies at me from behind and hacks at me with its talons in a flurry of feathers. I had been warned, but until now it had given me no trouble. He tore my skin through my sweatpants! I thought it all extremely funny and laughed my head off. Eus was not amused and disinfected the scratch with some alcohol.

According to Wilma, Chito has recovered. He wanted to give a big feast to celebrate the occasion, but Chelo objected; that was why there were problems between them again. But Wilma, who apparently can see through the walls, asserts that *kubeetik loch* [they are making love], so things are all right. When Chito was sick, his relatives said that there would not be anything for Chelo; she would leave the way she came. That is why she wants to have nothing to do with them. They came to a big meal at the anniversary of his mother's death. His sister's son started a fight with Chito. He was going to hit him with a bench, but Chito's brother stopped him.

They now want to have a service every evening. "Finally they remember how it used to be," says Eus, "in order to collect money for the organ."

The fiesta is getting to me. There is extremely loud dance music all night. I go in and out of sleep; sometimes I hear it, sometimes I don't.

Ruben comes to call, and Adela brings Chelo's two little girls. Especially the smaller one is ravishingly beautiful with her large slanting eyes in a classical Maya profile, reproduced on countless stelae.

Our attendance at the fiesta stimulates Eus to speak of the fiesta in her childhood in honor of the local saint in her home village of Libre Union. They would kill a pig, then put a loaf of bread into its mouth, and one man would dance with it. They distributed *pinole* made with honey. They called it the vomit of the pig. Next year the person who had danced with the pig would provide the next one. Here in Utzpak they just take a roasted pig to the town hall, food is served, and everyone who eats a plate of food has to provide a chicken next year. Sometimes the person in charge, called the *interesado*, cheats and does not prepare all the chickens brought to him.

Then Nohoch Felix also reminisced about a rain-making ritual. He said there was an extremely old man from Yaxchilan who would contemplate his *canica* [marble]. When I asked what that looked like, Nohoch Felix described it as a crystal ball about 2 inches across. He kept looking at it, then said that the hunters who had gone out to shoot some deer for the ritual would shoot nine deer and one wild turkey. Nobody believed it, but it happened exactly that way.

Although walking is strenuous for Eus, we do go to the evening service. The attendance is mainly the younger generation, including Teresa's married daughter, who, as Eus points out, still has not lost her girlish figure.

After going to the bank on Monday (when the dollar had risen to 877 pesos), we go to see Chelo. She has developed into a very charming, "plump and pleasing" young matron. Chito is there too, very sober. He has caught a cold and is trying to cure it with ice water. There are affectionate smiles between him and Chelo, but sober, he is tight-fisted to the extreme. When drunk, he was the financial aid to Wilma and her family, so that Wilma was able to have a lovely addition built to her house, quite expensive. Chito knew nothing of his role in Wilma's good fortune, and since he has sobered up, there is no longer a penny forthcoming. He has settled nothing on Chelo. She did manage to buy four steers, which were registered in her father's name. She also has some turkeys at Wilma's house that Chito knows nothing about. Wilma thought that Chelo should put her profit in the bank, but I cautioned her against that in view of the present runaway inflation.

Oscar is a student now. To Eus's annoyance, he wears a gold necklace and two gold bracelets, and no one knows where his money comes from. Jose now earns some income from fishing. He never gave his wife any money for food, and continued mistreating her, so she went back to Tabasco, taking her baby daughter with her.

Wilma took very good care of Eus during her illness, and continues to do so and come every day to do her laundry. She is also a fine consultant, understanding what I want to know. Eus has lost nothing of her acuity, but she does not get out much anymore. We spend much time correcting my genealogies and the constantly changing lists of congregations. Nohoch Felix, on the other hand, loves to talk about the recent earthquake. After all, he thinks, it is a sign that the Second Coming is close at hand. It says so in the Bible. Eus is more open to my suggestion that such events are bellyaches of the earth. But to Eus it is important; the end of the world may come any time as a judgment on the evil sinners and the vindication of the true believers.

The large white rooster keeps lying in wait for me, and since I don't want to use the chamber pot in the safe confines of the house, Eus gives me a stick. "Hit him on the head," she says. "If you kill him, it's all right. I have not yet killed a chicken for the day." So I take the hefty stick, and indeed, the bird does come for me. This time though, I do not turn my back. With my stick I catch him on the head in midair. He goes cackling loudly, fleeing toward the back of the barnyard. I am really worried that he is hurt, but after a while, he comes back crowing triumphantly. I thought perhaps my dark blue sweats were irritating him, but he also attacked Eus and Wilma, and they wear ?*ipiles*. So we all go armed with sticks now.

Was it the rooster that reminded me of Hermano Miguel? Anyway, they tell me that he never goes to visit the sick for fear of catching something. One time when Marci had an attack in the temple, the *hermanos* took her to the *casa pastoral*, and afterward, Hermano Miguel had his wife mop the entire floor. When Nohoch Felix goes to the service of the Tonos, they always give him something, money for a *frances* or a soda, but Hermano Miguel never does that. One time, he was invited to go visit the congregation in Maderas Blanca, and he told the congregation that he would only go if there was enough money for the ticket in that day's offering. When Marjelia came home after getting married in Tabasco, they had a big feast for the young couple at Chelo's house. They killed three turkeys. They did not, of course, invite Hermano Miguel. He was furious about it for months.

Marjelia had known the man she was now married to before, but when she went back to Tabasco she did not know whether he was married or not. They met accidentally on the market, and he was still single. It is a good marriage. He treats Marjelia well. When Marjelia is busy, he will even take care of their little girl, giving her her bottle. But when they spend time in Utzpak, he is homesick. When they are at home, his entire extended family, twenty-five people, live at home and even eat together, then leave the dishes to Marjelia to wash. She does not like that. He wants to go home for Christmas, but she does not want to go along. He makes good money repairing heavy truck engines.

We go to visit Reina. She has put on a lot of weight, but as far as the cottage industry is concerned, she confirms what I had also heard from others—

dressmaking is really down. The fabric, but especially the thread, has gone up in price. People spend their money on food, which has gotten much more expensive.

She has had other problems too. Because of Santiago's accident when he crashed his car into the Tizimin bus, he had to pay three days' wages of 17,000 pesos per day to the bus driver. This is a rule of their union. So Santiago had to sell his car. She had to sacrifice her fancy record-player and one of her sewing machines. Poor Reina; her house really looks bare. She is still sewing. Her oldest daughter is getting training for secretarial work.

Reina's neighbor died recently. He had a strange skin disease. I once saw his hands. They were covered with dime-size warts. The physicians could not cure it. They tried for years, and he finally succumbed to it. They said it was inherited. When he was dead, nobody wanted to wash and dress him for burial; all his garments were soaked and covered with blood. The Presbyterian minister, to whose congregation he belonged, finally did it. After his death they plastered and painted the house, and then his mother, Dona Tomasita, the local midwife, moved in. His sister, who also lived near Reina, spent two years in a hospital in Merida, but they could not cure her either. She is back home now and keeps her hands covered with a towel.

I had expressed my admiration for the Presbyterian minister. So Reina takes me over to see their church. He is not home, but his wife opens the church for me. I was expected to take some pictures, which I did. It all felt rather cool.

We go to buy a hammock. Inflation is making its impression everywhere. The weaver no longer uses the Araña thread, which is the strongest and most durable *canamo*. It is not only every expensive but also in short supply. You can also buy hammocks woven of nylon thread, "*Dos Elo fantes*," which are easy to wash, but I hate them; they cut into me.

I am still lying in the hammock after a heavy meal of *empanadas* [fried tortillas filled with bits of meat and fruit] when Eus orders a bath and formal change. Hermano Miguel is away on a trip, leaving Candil in charge of the temple. So the Tonos have decided to invite the orphaned congregation to their service, and that is where we are going.

We have just turned the corner coming out of Eus's place when we come face to face with the circus parade. The circus has set up for only one day on the athletic field across the highway, a really big one: "Hos. Suarez, Fundado en 1872." We watch the poor animals go by—lots of them, lions and tigers in cages, camels, elephants—in an advertising procession through the village.

On the way over to the Tonos we enter the house of Dona Eduarda, the widow of Don Fulgencio, who is frail and nearly blind in her hammock. "I can see, but as if through smoke," she says. Eus seems so young and strong next to her, solicitously talking to her, as does Wilma, who is with us. Eduarda is talking about one of her grandchildren. It seems that one of Eduarda's daughters had no children. One day there was a box in front of her house with a newborn baby girl in it. She raised her as her own. Now she is married and has a child of her own but won't let Eduarda's family fondle and enjoy the child as a grandchild. The Tonos, she says, send her *caridad* even if she cannot go to the service. The mayor will provide a coffin if the family is too poor to pay for it. He gave it for the mother of Candil, who died two months ago. They buried her with her gold teeth, six in the upper jaw and two in the lower one; they must have been very expensive. Because she died of cancer, her body exuded a terrible stench, but they put a lot of talcum and perfume on the body, so they were able to hold the wake.

It is past 7 P.M. and thus pitch dark when we pass Dona Valuda's store. Her husband is working outside, but he comes to the service when it is half over.

During the service, Antonio B. refers to the fact that I have come for so many years and have participated in some important events. He also later prays for me. Actually, I would rather be in a very small hole totally invisible, but if publicity is necessary, it is this mild, well-intentioned kind that is certainly preferable.

Antonio is a fine preacher; what a relief from Hermano Miguel. And his gentle guitar so pleasant without electrical amplification—*aleluya!* I had forgotten, or perhaps did not notice, how delicate this Antonio is. And he is possessed of some actual philosophical insight. Of course, I must not forget that this man at one time actually did have some visions. That makes him a different breed. After all, the 1969–1970 upheaval started with him.

Fascinating, however, that in his sermon, he never makes reference to his own visions as a source of revelation. Instead, his slender brown hand keeps resting on the open pages of the Bible as he keeps lifting the book. Only that revelation is the safe one, which builds the ramparts for him against the open world outside. No wonder he tried to commit suicide.

DECEMBER 12

Good old perceptive Eus. She maintains that I merely say that I like her food, and in reality it is not so. I can't make clear to her that I can "order" myself to relish an unusual or even to me unpleasant food.

I have not seen Joaquin for a while. I had given him some money for tuition at the high school he attended in Merida, but although he was living at the house of one of his maternal uncles, he ran out. Then his father pawned his gun, so we'll see how long that will last.

Oscar attends private classes in bookkeeping here in Utzpak. The teacher charges 1,500 pesos, about $2 a month, but Oscar missed three months already because he did not have the money. Chelo pays for Adela; she has even bought a typewriter for her that Oscar can also use. But she cannot be Santa Claus for everyone, although she tries; and sewing dresses, which Wilma and Adela have relied on, is no longer a profitable business.

With no service tonight, Eus and I go *shimbal,* walking for pleasure. Eus is in a great mood. Animatedly, she tells about walking fourteen miles from Tibolom to Chumayel to see the bullfight. She was only about 18 years old at the time. There was a whole group of young people together. On the first day, they walked to Sotuta and stayed overnight, then to Tiyabo for another night, this time in a ranch. The ranchero allowed them to pick *ciruelas,* and they ate their fill, liberally salted. When they arrived in Chumayel, they climbed into the church tower, which was very high. They went to all the *corridas* [bullfights] and they danced at all the *vaque-rias* [formal dances]. I love to listen to her stories, so full of exuberance and uncontaminated by the fear of Satan.

As usual, we go by Don Antonio's general store to have a soda. We bump into Don Antonio's son, Don Pastor, a plump and comfortable middle-aged man, who is officially in charge of locust control. There has been talk of locusts approaching, but he maintains it is not bad. We would soon find out how wrong he was.

A visit with Don Antonio is usually one-tenth shopping and nine-tenths talking. He watches Mexican TV and loves to demonstrate his knowledge of the big world to someone who will appreciate it, like me. So how about the oil prices? And why did the USA, so big and powerful, insist on picking on little Nicaragua? And how about the dirty business of the armament industry? Eus, I discover, is an interested listener.

Wilma has also recently discovered a source of information outside the Bible: *E Alarma,* a scandal sheet of the caliber of the *National Enquirer,* from which she quotes liberally of such events as the recent birth of male Siamese twins.

We end up on the plaza. Because of the fiesta, there are still various stands up. At one of them, they are raffling off plastic housewares, with a guinea pig choosing the winning numbers.

There was tragedy in the village today. Don Falipan—I did not know him—crashed against a car with his motorcycle. Reina comes by this afternoon as Eus and I are sitting on the street outside the *albarrada,* watching the dense gray clouds of locusts rustling overhead. He broke all but two of his ribs, she says. This evening Wilma is told that he has died. He was a rich man by local standards, but he left no will. His wife died seven years ago in a bus accident. He had asked her not to go on business trips, he would give her all the money she wanted, but she loved her business and did not want to abandon it. They had several children who were members of the Presbyterian congregation.

December 13

This afternoon I see for the first time huge clouds of locusts being whipped by the wind above the village. Don Pastor has called for help and now there are two small airplanes, reminiscent of crop dusters, buzzing the locust clouds. Their dust settles on everything—the dust of death, I think, and I am apparently allergic to it.[1] I begin to itch all over my body. The stuff must also be penetrating the well water, for taking a bath brings no relief.

We attend a last service and I say an affectionate farewell to Rodolfa and Wilma. There is talk of one corn farmer of Utzpak who saw his corn garden, lush and green in the morning, destroyed by noon; the locusts had chewed it down to the roots. He became so distraught that he committed suicide.

Nohoch Felix thinks that fighting locusts is stupid. "*Son cosas de Dios* [They are things of God]," he says. Don't interfere with the signs of the imminent Second Coming.

We catch the 6 o'clock bus out of Utzpak and in Merida take a cab to the home of Eus's younger sister, Felipa. It is a spacious place with a bathroom and everything, but it is extremely hot under a corrugated tin roof. A bath with city water finally relieves the irritation caused by the anti-locust dust.

We attend a service in a cool and neutral Baptist church, among a clearly upwardly mobile lower-middle-class congregation. One of Eus's nephews is an assistant here.

After an extremely long day that includes sight-seeing and a birthday party, I am finally settled in my hammock and falling asleep when suddenly in front of the door I hear a violin and a guitar, then a male voice and a guitar. Struggling up from the depth of sleep, I finally realize that I am being serenaded. The old-fashioned Mexican songs flutter down about me like yellowed nineteenth-century picture postcards. I find out too late that Felipa's husband does serenading for a living. And in the plane on the way to Miami, I still feel terrible that I did not pay him.

Correspondence

March 1985–October 1986

Professional work kept me away from Yucatan for almost two years, from January 1985 until December 1986. As before, my monthly modest stipend remained the stimulation for our correspondence, with Nohoch Felix acting as the conscientious chronicler. Some letters are, of course, merely confirmations of the receipt of the money order. In many instances, however, they also represent a continuation of uncounted conversations, with Eus, no doubt, hovering over her husband, saying "Are you sure you told her?"

So now, I'll turn the story over to Nohoch Felix, with other family members occasionally adding their voice, concentrating, of course, only on the salient information, and skipping the numerous blessings and repetitions.

May 24, 1985

We are happy because the garden is growing well. We have onions, chives, tomatoes, which we already harvested, also limes, oranges, and vegetable corn and seedlings in pots, which we sold. Hermano Miguel is still reproaching Wilma for not telling him about the wedding. So she never goes to the front to sing.

July 16, 1985

There was a ministerial meeting in Chetumal where they decided to move the pastors around, but Hermano Miguel did not move. He said he was going to stay in Utzpak for another ten or fifteen years. If we wanted to lodge a complaint against him, we would have to wait another year. He keeps having a conflict with Wilma.

Eus's condition is unchanged. Sometimes she can eat well, sometimes less so.

Wilma's son Oscar, October 21, 1985

Our grandmother had an accident in her *solar*. We immediately took her to the hospital, a wound of about 5 centimeters; it was sewed. Three days later we took her to the hospital again. The wound had not healed well. Then two days later she fell again, inside her house. She was unconscious for three hours. Wilma nursed her, but her mind is not working well. She converses well, but very quickly she forgets. We are thinking of taking her to Merida. She needs treatment that the local doctors cannot provide. We were going to call my Uncle Felix, but the equipment is out of order.

The cause of this accident was that a turkey hen got lost for three days. Suddenly, it reappeared and my grandmother wanted to catch her. She stumbled on a stone and split her forehead.

It has been six days and the wound has not dried. The doctor said that my grandmother was allergic and that is the reason why the wound won't heal.

P. S. Nohoch Felix: If there is any change, we will let you know. She may need a cataract removed.

Nohoch Felix, November 6, 1985

The Hermana Eus is somewhat better. The wound is drying. It cost us a little money. She is walking well now. She even goes to the kitchen, but she cannot work, she has no strength. Wilma is nursing her while she is in her hammock. Wilma gives her the injections of the medicine, Chelo also gives her injections.

Oscar, undated

We are well, except for my grandmother. Her wound has dried well, but she has no strength to walk. But with the help of the vitamins which she takes and God's help, she should be better in a few days.

My father has problems with Hermano Miguel because my father said that the pastor should not live only off the tithe, as he does. And he became angry and he struck my father from the list of members, also Chelo, my grandmother, and my grandfather. My father said he did not care, for he obeys only God.

Oscar, January 22, 1986

On January 18, my grandmother started having a stomachache. They took her to Merida, where she was examined by specialists. She was found to have gastritis. Wilma took her and her sons took her to the clinic. She will have to return at the beginning of February. The charge was 30,000 pesos. It will be that much again. She also needed to be treated for an eye problem.

Nohoch Felix: They treated her with a tube, Wilma said. They pulled out 1-centimeter-long pieces. They pulled out about five pieces of what was stuck in her stomach. She will return on the 25th.

Oscar, undated

We received the money you sent for my grandmother's treatment. They say she has a stomach ulcer, but she refuses an operation. She says she would not survive it.

Nohoch Felix: Do not worry so much. Perhaps we will meet again.

Nohoch Felix, May 6, 1986

The Hermana Eus is in the clinic in Merida. They operated on her stomach. The operation was extremely expensive. Her sister Felipa was with her.

Oscar, May 22, 1986

My grandmother's operation was successful, but she has some infections and she cannot travel. The operation cost 3 million pesos. She is staying with her sister Felipa.

Nohoch Felix, July 8, 1986

The Hermana Eus is at home, eats and drinks well. The operation was successful and she returned home on July 2. One of these days we will meet again as we used to.

Nohoch Felix, October 25, 1986

Salvador [Reina's husband] had an accident. He was drunk. He ran into a bus with his car and injured his forehead. It was on the way between Temax and here.

Rebecca, daughter of Wilma and now a grade-schooler, adds: "Marjelia lives in Merida with her husband and baby daughter.

Nohoch Felix, November 13, 1986
(In anticipation of my arrival on December 4, Nohoch Felix writes that Eus will come to meet me at the airport. Then follows an exuberant listing of all the food awaiting me, all in Nohoch Felix's idiosyncratic Maya transcription.)
>*Yan* [there is] *cax* [chicken]
>*Yan xan pata* [ducks]
>*Yan xan ulum* [turkey]
>*Tulaca yan*—there is everything!

March 1987–November 1988
Eus and her sister Felipa accompanied me to the airport in December 1986, and the two of them carried on a conversation as animated as two schoolgirls. I left reassured that the operation Eus had undergone had finally brought her lasting recovery. And Nohoch Felix's letters seemed to confirm that impression. Everyone was continuing with the same problems and occasional relief as before.

Nohoch Felix, March 1987
Chito started drinking again. Chelo became angry and worked him over with a slab of wood. Hermano Miguel definitely will not leave; he bought a building lot in Utzpak. He is now conducting services very day. He baptized a couple.
There was an earthquake in Xbek, so Christ is definitely going to come soon.

Nohoch Felix, May 15, 1987
In April, there was an evangelizing campaign. Many people came.
Hermano Miguel made peace with Wilma and Ruben. He even let Ruben teach.
Adela: Chito and Chelo made peace again. Chelo is pregnant. Marjelia is pregnant too.

Nohoch Felix, July 8, 1987
Hermano Miguel is behaving quite well. Jose quarreled with his mother, and moved to Cancun.

Nohoch Felix, August 30, 1987
There is renewed conflict with Hermano Miguel. His wife quarreled with Wilma.

Nohoch Felix, September 30, 1987
Thank you for your kind letter of the 27th of September, and many thanks for your friendship and consideration which you gave us for so many years.

And the Hermana Eus fell down and hurt her arm, but all is healed now.

Nohoch Felix, undated, 1987
The Hermana Eus is a little well. Chelo gave birth to a boy, Marjelia to a girl.

Nohoch Felix, February 20, 1988:
Don Antonio received the photograph of Rommel.[2]

Wilma, March 9, 1988
Adela will graduate and will work as a secretary in Cancun. Joaquin is in Merida, Oscar works as a fisherman, Ruben and Jose on the ranch, Rebecca is in the 4th grade, Danu is in the 2nd grade, Huancho in the 1st grade, Nico in the 2nd grade. Chito is sick, he continues drinking. He is dizzy, has no appetite, and is pale.

(Wilma also reports that she *hace orac ones* [conducts prayer services] in those homes where people ask her to come. Luis L. is no longer pastor in Merida; instead, he visits all the congregations.)

Nohoch Felix, April 15, 1988
Hermano Miguel continues behaving well.

Nohoch Felix, July 18, 1988
The Hermana Eus has some stomach pain. Oscar married a girl from Temax. Chito is worse.

Nohoch Felix, August 6, 1988
Hermano Alejantro bought the harmonica that you had brought. He is pastor in Maderos Blanca and will pay in three payments.

The Hermana Eus complains of rheumatism.

Nohoch Felix, September 7, 1988
The *hermanos* of Maderos Blanca have not paid yet for the harmonica. I am going to remind them in love and friendship.

The Hermana Eus complains of spells of dizziness, but not every day. When she lies down in her hammock, it passes after a while. She also suffers from rheumatism.

Nohoch Felix, October 1, 1988
Here I want to communicate to you that Samuel, the son of my son Enrique, who lives in Merida, had an accident there in Merida. He was drunk, and he

went to lie down on the railroad tracks, and there he fell to sleep. And at 4 A.M. the train arrived in Merida and rolled over him, and they pulled the poor boy out in three pieces. This happened on the 25th day of September.

And also we were hit by a hurricane here in Yucatan and many people died, and all of Yucatan was devastated. Thanks to God my small house was not damaged. But those houses of corrugated plate and of cardboard—hardly a single one remained standing here in Yucatan. The name of the hurricane was Jilberto.

The Hermana Eus, her body is a bit broken. She has no strength anymore to walk the way she used to. This started because of her rheumatism. The doctor just came. He gave her a shot, also some serum in her hand. She seems to be a little better now. This all began in August. Her sons wanted to take her to Merida. And the Hermana Eus is now walking a little, slowly. She makes her food, and she eats a little, and she drinks a little, as much as she can.

Nohoch Felix, October 10, 1988

Here I am communicating to you that the Hermana Eus is very ill. She spent a few days with her son Enrique in Merida. And today Wilma went to bring her mother home. She is going to take her to her house in order to care for her there until she leaves us, for she is seriously ill. But I beg you, do not worry about it. For if perhaps if she is better, I will send you another letter. There is no one like our Lord Jesus. He will support us. And I am sending you greetings, I am alone in my house.

Adelaide, October 30, 1988

As to my grandmother, she is here in my mother's house. She continues being very ill, she cannot get up. She has no strength, that is why she was brought here. They took her to the clinic in Merida, they treated her with a sonde and they X-rayed her, which cost 75,000 pesos; all told they spent half a million, but it did not do any good, because she continues being ill. My Aunt Felipa came from Merida, and the *hermanos* come to see her, so she has lots of visits.

Adelaide, November 1, 1988

The purpose of this letter is to let you know that grandmother Eustaquia died on the 30th of October, at 10 o'clock at night.

My grandfather lives with my mother because he is alone. Many people came for her wake, many *hermanos*, her sister Felipa, her niece and other relatives, the pastors of Merida and of Tizimin. Only my Uncle Felix could not come.

Adelaide, November 16, 1988

My uncle Enrique bought the coffin for my grandmother.

We received the photos that you sent on Saturday, Oct. 29. My grandmother saw them, and on Sunday, Oct. 30, she died, at 9 in the evening. The funeral cost half a million and Chelo contributed 50,000.

After the funeral, my mother and my grandfather both became ill.

Nohoch Felix: Do not grieve so much. Do not think so much about it. The departed begs you. This was Hermano Felix talking to you.

Notes

Preliminary Remarks

1. All persons are identified by first name and, where necessary, the initial of the last name only, except where for various reasons revealing any part of the name might cause harm or embarrassment, in which case the name has been changed. The true name of the community where I did fieldwork is not given for this reason.

1. The Context

1. Sections of the following discussion were published earlier in my "Disturbances in the Apostolic Church: A Trance-Based Upheaval in Yucatan," in Felicitas Goodman, Jeannette H. Henney, and Esther Pressel, *Trance, Healing, and Hallucination: Three Field Studies in Religious Experience* (New York: Wiley Interscience, 1974).

2. For details see Felicitas D. Goodman, *Where the Spirits Ride the Wind: Trance Journeys and Other Ecstatic Experiences* (Bloomington, Indiana University Press, 1990).

3. Felicitas D. Goodman, *Ecstasy, Ritual, and Alternate Reality: Religion in a Pluralistic World* (Bloomington: Indiana University Press, 1988).

4. Felicitas D. Goodman, *How about Demons? Possession and Exorcism in the Modern World* (Bloomington: Indiana University Press, 1988).

5. Felicitas D. Goodman, *Speaking in Tongues: A Cross-Cultural Study of Glossolalia* (Chicago: University of Chicago Press, 1972).

6. All figures cited in this section are taken from the 1970 census, unless otherwise noted.

2. 1969

1. Not its real name.

2. This conversion and a number of the subsequent ones were first reported in my *Speaking in Tongues: A Cross-Cultural Study of Glossolalia* (Chicago: University of Chicago Press, 1972).

3. Barrera's strategy was first described in my *Speaking in Tongues*, p. 91

4. H. Maloney and Samuel Southard, eds., *Handbook of Religious Conversion* (Birmingham, Alabama: Religious Education Press, 1992).

5. This conversion experience was first reported in my "Disturbances in the Apostolic Church: A Trance-Based Upheaval in Yucatan," in *Trance, Healing, and Hallucination: Three Field Studies in Religious Experience*, by Felicitas D. Goodman, Jeannette Henney, and Esther Pressel. (New York: Wiley Interscience, 1974).

6. Peregrina's acute experience lasted about thirty-seven days.

7. Such dramatic stories tend to travel. I heard subsequently that it was supposed to have happened in a village near La Venta, Tabasco.

3. 1970

1. This section is an expanded version of my dissertation, published under the title of "Disturbances in the Apostolic Church: A Trance-Based Upheaval in Yucatan," in *Trance, Healing, and Hallucination: Three Field Studies in Religious Experience*, by Felicitas D. Goodman, Jeannette H. Henney, and Esther Pressel. (New York: Wiley Interscience, 1974), pp. 231–364.

2. Mary R. Haas, "Interlingual Word Taboos," in *Language in Culture and Society*, edited by Dell Hymes (New York: Harper & Row, 1964), pp. 483–494.

3. For details, see Felicitas D. Goodman, "Possible Physiological Mechanisms Accounting for Some Cases of Faith Healing," *Medikon* 3, nos. 6–7 (1974): 39–41.

4. Antonio calls these beings *angeles* [angels], but it is clear from the context that no Christian beings are meant.

5. Barrera's Mayan is quite faulty; in this case, as Eus noted, the question should have been "*beyo,*" not "*leti,*" and "*ciic*" is a kinship term, "sister," not the same as "*hermana,*" which denotes membership in the congregation.

4. 1971 to 1975

1. See my article, "Glossolalia and Hallucination in Pentecostal Congregations," *Psychiatria Clinica* 6 (1973): 97–103.

2. William Branham was a prominent "deliverance evangelist" born in 1909 near Berkesville, Kentucky. "The cornerstone of 'deliverance evangelism' is the belief that just as God wants everyone to be saved from sin, so also does He desire everyone to be well" (Nichol 1966, 221–222). Actually, Branham himself never claimed to have healing powers. Rather, he maintained that he had received two gifts: he could feel in his left hand what illness a person had, and he could discern the thoughts and deeds in the past life of an individual (Lindsay 1950, 79). When confronted with a sick person, he said that he could see if God had already healed him, and he would then proclaim this fact. "She [a small Finnish girl on crutches] looked at me with her baby blue eyes, tears rolling down her cheeks. I saw a vision . . . and I knew that the child was healed. I said, 'Honey, you're healed'" (Lindsay n.d., 43–44). In the evening, Branham allegedly saw the child again and asked that her crutches be removed; she ran up and down the steps and across the platform.

In the late 1940s Branham preached to large "full gospel" meetings. He was invited to speak in the Scandinavian countries and in South Africa. A fellow minister, Gordon Lindsay, published his biography and a collection of sermons. Soon after the South African trip, the two men separated. At issue may have been attempts by Branham to form his own church, which Lindsay may have opposed. "The Lord knew that he [Branham] would never attempt to start another organization of his own," Lindsay (1950, 13) says in the biography of the evangelist. Yet in a personal communication to this author, Lindsay speaks of people who tried to put words into the preacher's mouth, and the same statement also appears in essence in the above-mentioned book (1950, 11). Sermons by Branham were not included in the tapes issued by the Church for the Nations, Inc. organization, of which Lindsay was president. The Spanish-language tracts and tapes of Branham's sermons mentioned by my various consultants were distributed by Spoken Word Publications, Jeffersonville, Indiana. William Branham died on December 24, 1965.

3. Quintana Roo has since been granted state status.

4. The account of the trance disturbance in Tibolom was initially published in "Triggering of Altered States of Consciousness as Group Event: A New Case From Yucatán," *Confinia Psychiatrica* 23 (1980): 26–34.

6. April–August 1977

1. The Violets are four adolescent girls who typically attended services all dressed in long skirts and identical pale violet dresses with a white trim that outlined their small breasts. I thought that their uniform, long-skirted dresses, might have been available because they were *damas* [bridesmaids] at a wedding. But Chelo says, "No, they just dress that way when they come to the service." Since I know neither their names nor whose daughters they are, I call them the Four Violets in my notes.

9. August–September 1983

1. Frank Cushing describes the same kind of earth oven in use among the Zuni in *My Adventures in Zuñi* (Santa Fe, N.M.: The Peripatetic Press, 1941).

10. January 1985

1. The account of this exorcism was first published in my *How about Demons? Possession and Exorcism in the Modern World* (Bloomington: Indiana University Press, 1988).

11. December 1986

1. The anti-locust spray used was BHC 5% HELIOS, manufactured by Helios Laboratories of Hecho en Mexico. According to the product label, its chemical components were Isomero gamma del 1, 2, 3, 4, 5, 6 in a solution of 5 percent Hexacloro ciclohexano and 95 percent diluyentes otros isometres del HCH.

2. During a visit in Germany, I told my brother of a small Maya boy being named for the famous German general whom Hitler had forced to commit suicide. It so happened that my brother knew Rommel's son, at that time mayor of Stuttgart. When he told him the story, the mayor gave him a picture of his father, which I forwarded to Don Antonio.

Bibliography

Behringer, Wolfgang. 1994. *Chonrad Stoeckhlin und die Nachtschar: Eine Geschichte aus der frühen Neuzeit.* München: Piper.

Bourguignon, Erika, ed. 1973. *Religion, Altered States of Consciousness, and Social Change.* Columbus: Ohio State University Press.

Bricker, Victoria Reifler. 1981. *The Indian Christ, the Indian King: The Historical Substrate of Maya Myth and Ritual.* Austin: University of Texas Press.

Cohn, Norman Rufus Colin. 1993. *Cosmos, Chaos, and the World to Come: The Ancient Roots of Apocalyptic Faith.* New Haven, Conn.: Yale University Press.

Cushing, Frank Hamilton. 1941. *My Adventures in Zuñi.* Santa Fe, N.M.: The Peripatetic Press.

Cutten, George Barton. 1927. *Speaking with Tongues, Historically and Psychologically Considered.* New Haven, Conn.: Yale University Press.

Deiros, Pablo A. 1992. *Historia del cristianismo en América Latina.* Buenos Aires: Fraternidad Teológica Latinoamericana.

Gaxiola, Manuel J. 1970. *La serpiente y la paloma: Análisis del crecimiento de la Iglesia Apostólica de la Fe en Cristo Jesús de México.* South Pasadena, Calif.: W. Carey Library.

Goodman, Felicitas. 1969a. "Glossolalia: Speaking in Tongues in Four Cultural Settings." *Confinia Psychiatrica* 12:113–129.

———. 1969b. "Phonetic Analysis of Glossolalia in Four Cultural Settings." *Journal for the Scientific Study of Religion* 8: 227–239.

———. 1972a. *Speaking in Tongues: A Cross-Cultural Study of Glossolalia.* Chicago: University of Chicago Press.

———. 1972b. "Un Culto de Crisis en Yucatan." In *Religion en Mesoamerica XII Mesa Redonda,*" ed. J. Liking and N. C. Tejero.

———. 1973. "Glossolalia and Hallucination in Pentecostal Congregations." *Psychiatria Clinica* 6: 97–103.

———. 1974a. "Disturbances in the Apostolic Church: A Trance-Based Upheaval in Yucatan." In Felicitas Goodman, Jeannette H. Henney, and Esther Pressel, *Trance, Healing, and Hallucination: Three Field Studies in Religious Experience.* New York: Wiley Interscience.

———. 1974b. "Possible Physiological Mechanisms Accounting for Some Cases of Faith Healing." *Medikon* 3: 39–41.

———. 1980. "Triggering of Altered States of Consciousness as Group Event: A New Case From Yucatán." *Confinia Psychiatrica* 23: 26–34.

———. 1981. *The Exorcism of Anneliese Michel.* Garden City, N.Y.: Doubleday.

———. 1988a. *Ecstasy, Ritual, and Alternate Reality: Religion in a Pluralistic World.* Bloomington: Indiana University Press.

———. 1988b. *How about Demons? Possession and Exorcism in the Modern World.* Bloomington: Indiana University Press.

———. 1990. *Where the Spirits Ride the Wind: Trance Journeys and Other Ecstatic Experiences.* Bloomington, Indiana University Press.

Haas. 1964. "Interlingual Word Taboos." In *Language in Culture and Society,* edited by Dell Hymes. New York: Harper & Row.

Hammond, Norman, ed. 1991. *Cuello: An Early Maya Community in Belize.* Cambridge: Cambridge University Press.

Jaquith, James R. 1970. *The Present Status of the Uto-Aztekan Languages of Mexico: An Index of Data Bearing on Their Survival, Geographical Location, and Internal Relationships.* Greeley, Colo.: University of Northern Colorado.

Lalive d'Epinay, Christian. 1969. *Haven of the Masses: A Study of the Pentecostal Movement in Chile.* Trans. Marjorie Sandle. London: Lutterworth P.

Maloney, H. and Samuel Southard, eds. 1992. *Handbook of Religious Conversion.* Birmingham, Ala.: Religious Education Press.

Martin, David, and Peter Mullen, eds. 1984. *Strange Gifts?: A Guide to Charismatic Renewal.* New York: B. Blackwell.

Marty, Martin E. and R. Scott Appleby. 1991. *Fundamentalisms Observed.* Chicago: University of Chicago Press.

Nichol, John Thomas. 1966. *Pentecostalism.* New York: Harper & Row.

Nimeundajú, Curt. 1944. *Leyenda de la creación y juicio final del mundo como fundamento de la religión de los apapokuva-guaraní.* San Pablo, Brazil.

Nohrnberg, James. 1995. *Like unto Moses: The Constituting of an Interruption.* Bloomington: Indiana University Press.

Rambo, Lewis R. 1993. *Understanding Religious Conversion.* New Haven, Conn.: Yale University Press.

Raynaud, Georges, Miguel Angel Asturias, and J. M. González de Mendoza. 1946. *Anales de los xahil: Traducción y notas.* México: Univ. Nacional Autónoma.

Redfield, Robert. 1941 *The Folk Culture of Yucatan.* Chicago: University of Chicago Press.

Reed, Nelson. 1964. *The Caste War of Yucatan.* Stanford, Calif.: Stanford University Press.

Samarin, William J. Field. 1967. *Linguistics: A Guide to Linguistic Field Work.* New York: Holt, Rinehart and Winston.

Sargant, William Walters. 1975. *Battle for the Mind: A Physiology of Conversion and Brainwashing.* 1957. Reprint, Westport, Conn.: Greenwood Press.

Spoerri, Theodor. 1969. *Kompendium der Psychiatrie. Klinik und Therapie für Studierende und Ärzte.* Basel and New York: Karger.

Stoll, David. 1990. *Is Latin America Turning Protestant?: The Politics of Evangelical Growth.* Berkeley: University of California Press.

Welch, Holmes, and Anna Seidel, eds. 1979. *Facets of Taoism: Essays in Chinese Religion.* New Haven, Conn.: Yale University Press.

Index

Chelo (daughter of Wilma), 321, 438, 452;
children of, 455, 514; end of marriage with
Chito, 477, 485–486; marriage to Chito,
436–437, 457
Chetumal (city), xvi, 78, 110, 111, 149; Barrera's
headquarters, 271; congregation of, 124, 227;
Cooperative Church Compound, 182–187;
dancers at, 366–369; excursion to, 323–327,
417–423; farm labor in, 468; ministerial
meeting in, 520; shopping in, 157; trips to,
358–365
Chiapas (Mexican state), 10, 233, 463, 471
Chichen Itza (city), 167
childbirth, 159, 299, 371
children, 22, 29, 47, 116, 154; author's, 38; babies,
161–162; demonic presence and, 146–147;
education level of, 12; inability to conceive,
25–26; number of, 49; nutrition and, 85;
play of, 361; sexuality and, 472
China, apocalyptic visions in, 231
Chino, El (Chinese merchant), 164
Chino, El (doctor), 415
Chito (nephew of Placido), 318, 322, 418, 428;
drinking of, 455, 498, 522, 523; end of marriage with Chelo, 485–486; family of, 485;
illness of, 512; marriage to Chelo, 436–437
Christian Home, The, 123
Christianity, xv, 8, 231–238, 236. See also Catholic Church; Pentecostalism
Christina, Hermana, 393
Chucha (daughter of Sylvia), 413
Chucha (landlady), 47
Chucho (husband of Ester), 86
Chucho (husband of Teresa), 260, 439, 475, 480,
490
Cilia (daughter of Reina), 157, 160, 199, 257–258,
327; hetsmec ceremony for, 200; illness of,
163
circus, as sin, 267
Cisteil (village), 3
civil ceremony marriage, 50, 51, 73
Clementina (wife of Miguel), 456, 457
climate, 27, 116
clothes, 57, 60, 76; dolls', 340; dresses, 308;
gender roles and, 271; at services, 366;
wedding ceremony and, 177, 178
Cochinito X, 468
cockroaches, 38, 63, 373, 444, 468; absence of,
143; author's consternation at, 25
Cohen, Kenneth S., 231
Cohn, Norman, 231
communication, 9
Concha (crippled woman), 471–472
Concha (daughter of Reina), 257, 269
Confinia Psychiatrica (journal), 20
congregations, xv, 11, 448–449; communication
with Holy Spirit, 9; as households, 54;
impermanent nature of, xvi; number of, 10

consciousness, 6–7, 64
Consuelo, of Merida congregation, 242
Consuelo (daughter of Wilma), 175, 243, 337,
339, 353; care of younger siblings, 311; hammock weaving and, 372; marriage prospects
of, 351; women's quarrels and, 410
contraception. See birth control
converts, 17, 78, 98, 125, 200; conversion stories,
33–35, 58–60, 86–88, 107–108, 111–113; domestic troubles of, 245; experience and, 61;
of Oscar Hill, 146; recruitment by public
preaching, xvii; among relatives, 108
coprolalia, 234, 342
Cordo, El (son of Dona Julia), 491
coritos, 36, 41, 105, 195, 405, 406; Bible readings
and, 43, 53; dancing and, 366, 367, 408;
glossolalia and, 44; invocation of fire, 35, 68;
offerings and, 203; request to sing in English, 42
cottage industries, xviii, 413–414, 462–464, 515–
516
Cozumel, island of, 125, 133, 139, 161
crime, 12, 497
Cruz (wife of Antonio), 226, 246, 434; baptism
of, 211, 212, 213; birth of daughter, 217;
domestic problems of, 243–244; Dorcas
(women's organization) and, 239
Cuarenta y Dos (town), 227, 264, 278, 332
culture shock, 64
Cutten, George B., 8

dancing, xix, 53, 81; abandonment of, 108;
filming of, 429; Holy Spirit and, 426–427; as
part of services, 357; during religious services, xviii, 400, 404, 421; sermons against,
188; during services, 391; as sin, 29, 31, 45
Daniel (driver), 412
Danu/Daniel (son of Wilma), 453, 462, 488, 510,
523
Dawn (daughter of Wilma), 484
Day of the Pastors, 260
death, 83, 92, 99
Deiros, Pablo A., 5–6, 8
demonic possession, xvi, 81–82, 201, 215, 360;
chain of prayer and, 402; exorcism and, xix;
killing and, 32; of Marci, 499–507; Miguel
(new minister) and, 486, 492–495; "supernatural" feeling and, 148; in Tibolom, 312–
314. See also Satan
Desi, Hermano, 265, 325, 352, 399, 420
Devil, the. See Satan
Diego, Don, 394
"discerning of the souls," xviii
diseases, 2, 15
Dito, Hermano, 200, 400
divination, xviii
divine punishment, 305, 310–311, 336, 460
divorce, 38, 39, 43

evil eye (*mal ojo*), 163
exorcism, xv, xvi, 201, 486, 499, 503
experience, 7, 61

faith healing. *See* healing, divine
Falipan, Don, 518
fasting, 103, 162, 184, 219, 220
Felipa (sister of Don Eduardo), 127
Felipe, Don, 146, 481
Felipe N., 428
Felipe V., Don, 17–18
Felix S., 101
Fidelita (daughter of Reina), 340
Filipa (sister of Don Eduardo), 260–261
filming, 161–162, 240, 275, 429; of baptism, 119; of children, 198; of glossolalia, 79
Filomeno, Hermano, 312–313
Floriano, Hermano, 170
food, 23, 25, 274, 290, 450–451; ceremonial occasions and, 175; earth oven and, 328–329; *habali* (large rodent), 473–474; "hot" and "cold," 26; meat consumption, 115; preparation of, 50; religious services and, 395; at seashore baptism, 120; spirit food, 485; spoiled, 411; tortillas, 51, 175; *vaporcitos,* 62; at wedding party, 178
Ford Motor Company, 25
fornication, 39, 71, 111, 159
fortune-telling, 285–286, 362
Fortuney, Patricia (anthropologist), 392–393, 394, 396, 398
Four Violets, 429, 430–431, 432, 528:6n1
Francis of Assisi, Saint, 479
Freddy (son of Nina), 270, 274, 275, 276, 325, 487; education of, 366; speech of, 361; violence in upbringing of, 359–360
free will, 22
Fulgencio C., Don, xvii, 15–19, 58, 145, 196, *376,* 435–436; as bullfighter (*torero*), 89–90, 105, 466; chapel of, 104–105, 131; death of, 450; Don Rich and, 18, 19; services in home of, 356
fundamentalism, 8, 17, 24, 102
funerals, 18
furniture, 47–48, 51

gardening, 14
Gaspar, Don, 205, 206
Gaxiola, Bishop Manuel J., xvii, 198, 280, 282, 288, 475
Geertz, Clifford, xx
Genaro, Don, 247, 393, 481
gender, 75–76
Gilberta, 312, 313, 314
Gill, Oscar. *See* Hill, Oscar
girls, 81, 89; loss of virginity, 219; *quincenera* celebrations, 334–335, 345, 459
glossolalia, xviii, 8, 29; analysis of, 135; author's university lecture on, 398–399; body ges-

tures and, 185; ecstatic trance and, 135–137; inducing of, 64; mother tongue and, 148; physical tiredness and, 67; prayer and, 40; spontaneous acquisition of, 201; utterances, 41; vocalization, 124; women and, 73, 78–79, 115, 153, 162, 197. *See also* tongues, speaking in
Goethe, Johann W. von, xix
Gonzales, Gregorio. *See* Duarte, Hermano Goyo
Gonzalez, Hermano, 424, 425
Gonzalo, Hermano, 250
Goodman, Felicitas D., 16, *376, 389*
Gordo, El, 448
Gorgonio, Hermano, 284, 294, 315, 409, 425
gossip, 45, 47, 126, 128, 158, 160; apocalyptic disturbance and, 237; author's caution and, 199; disrupted by television, 306; domestic violence and, 269–270; Eus's family and, 452–455; fate of congregation and, 397; misfortunes, 305; Nohoch Felix and, 300; sermons and, 169
Goya (sister of Elide), 455
Goyo, Don (husband of Valuch), 59, 83, 115, 131, 220, 224; drinking of, 434; Pentecostalism and, 239; young women's attack on, 238
Gregoria (wife of Alvio), 70, 71, 73, 76, 113; children of, 85, 257; evangelizing and, 108; fasting of, 220; in glossolalia, 153, 197, 202, 208, 211; gossip about, 217; level of dedication to church, 200; literacy and, 72; pregnancy of, 143; at seashore baptism, 118–120
Gregorio, Hermano, 205–206, 283
Gregorio A. *See* Goyo, Don
Gregorio D., 159
Guarani Indians, 230
Guatemala, 20, 357, 482
Guerrero, Gonzalo, 2
Gum (son of Silvia), 442

hammocks, 54, 63, 129, 154, 183, 338; storage of, 75; tourist trade and, 339, 347, 372; uses of, 51; visiting rules and, 248; weaving of, 116, 191–192, 265, 270–271
Handbook of Religious Conversion, 60–61
healing, divine, xv, 150, 390–391, 408, 495; William Branham and, 528n2; false Christs and, 402; as "special intent," 52
heaven, 53, 83
Hebrew Bible. *See* Bible
hell, 81, 87–88, 166
henequen belt, 12, 15, 47, 93, 141; and market for *henequen,* 172; poverty of, 287; striking workers of, 289–290; wages in, 48, 75
Hernandez de Cordova, Francisco, 2
Heroes of the Old Testament, 123
highways, 11
Hill, Oscar, xvii, 19, 90, 98, 124, 509; baptisms

Latin America, xv, 8
laying on hands, 102
Leidi (daughter of Rodolfa), 223–224, 225, 258, 262
Librada (sister of Santiago), 359, 370
Libre Union (town), 374, 514
Licha, Hermana, 99, 119, 154, 351, 457; author's farewell and, 134, 135; author's return to Yucatan and, 138, 139
Licho, Hermano, 460, 484
Lidia, Dona, 300
Like unto Moses (Nohrnberg), 331
limestone, 1, 2, 12, 51, 57, 130
limousine drivers, 65–66
linguists, 8
literacy, 29–30, 37, 72, 112
livestock, 141, 317, 318, 327–328, 358; free-roaming pigs, 15; on *solares*, 55
Lizama, Nicolas, 418
Lizama, Tomas, 404
Lola, Dona, 442–443
Lola (wife of Nicolas), 241, 245
Lopez Palma, Sabino, 183
Lorenzo (son of Julia), 432
Lucrecia (Barrera's wife), 147, 148, 166, 187–188, 288–289; children of, 142, 271; demonic possession of, 223; gossip and, 158; illness of, 145; return from Campeche, 219
Lucy (child), 85
Luis del V., 103, 110
Luis L. (preacher), xvi, xviii, 80, 159, 391; author's arrival in Yucatan and, 21, 24; author's farewell and, 134; Barrera and, 33, 255–256; in Chetumal, 326; congregations of, 427; dancing and, xix, 357; defection from Apostolic Church, 279–280; demonic possession and, 224, 227; Epi's conversion and, 86; evangelizing of, 200–201; history of Apostolic congregation and, 15–17; house of, 66, 97; laying on hands and, 102; meets Blanca, 266; Miguel (new minister) and, 461; on ministerial visit, 74–76; pastors of, 336; plan for larger temple and, 214; radio preaching and, 17; revival meeting and, 477, 478–479; at seashore baptism, 119–122; sermons of, 171, 367, 478; temple of, 101, 360–361
Luis P. (deacon), 16
Luisito (son of Barrera), 152–153
Lulu (sister of Old Candil), 297
Lulu (wife of Augustin), 421–422
Lupita (daughter of Reina), 45, 47, 62, 108, 157, 257; attempted weaning of, 84–85; bathing of, 26; growth of, 141; hammock weaving and, 339; method of crawling, 162; mother's anxiety and, 132; at seashore baptism, 118, 120; shopping and, 414; at three years of age, 247–248; toilet training and, 30–31; trip to Chetumal and, 358–359; on witches, 329

Luther, Martin, 29
Luz (sister of Raquel), 339

machetes, 51, 454
machismo, 49
Mam Dosa, death of, 308–309
mamposteria houses, 12, 50–51
Manuel H., 99, 119, 186–187, 228, 254, 466; as Barrera's replacement, 96; departure of, 255; glossolalia and, 102; high rank of, 121; on Holy Spirit, 126
Manuela C., 417
Marci, *387*, 495–496, 499–507, 515; baptism and, 508; exorcism of, 512
Maria (granddaughter of Ugulina), 242, 323, 455
Mariana, Hermana, 327
Mariano, Hermano, 162, 203, 206, 211; bad luck of, 305; gift of interpretation and, 296; in glossolalia, 189–190; visions of, 221
Mariano C., 449
marijuana, 105, 333
Marina, Hermana, 400
Marjelia (daughter of Wilma), 318, 337, 352, 353; earnings of, 368; marriage of, 515; marriage prospects of, 452, 482–483, 494; trip to Chetumal and, 359; women's quarrels and, 409, 410
marriage, 19, 51, 59, 145, 170; Catholic Church and, 50, 86, 391; legal, 164; by magistrate, 227; second-wife custom, xix, 73, 266; wedding ceremonies, 176–178, 285; wedding in Las Choapas, 248–253
Martin, Hermano, 508
Maximo (husband of Reyes), 258–259, 407, 468–469
May, Ricardo. *See* Rich, Don
Maya Cruzoob, 32
Maya Indians: apocalyptic movements among, 233; Caste War and, 32, 130; classical civilization of, 1, 90, 251; kinship range of, 150; Spanish conquest of, 2; standards of beauty among, 429
Maya language, xvi, 1, 20, 27, 54, 190; author's knowledge of, 65, 66, 75, 127, 134, 144, 362, 442–443; comparison with English, 175; comparison with Spanish, 77; defections from Apostolic Church and, 280; expletives in, 165; glossolalia and, 135, 137; glottal stops of, 41; hymns in, 104; learning, 30; New Testament in, 123; preaching in, 273, 303; pride in, 97; radio broadcasts in, 511; in sermons, 36; Spanish influence in, 4, 155, 252; spoken by children, 318; varieties of, 2
McQuown, Professor, 175
Mechito (cousin of Reina), 327
medicine, 46, 52, 68, 104, 126, 372, 415
Medina, Professor, 392
Melencia, Hermana, 404
men, 66, 165, 237; bachelors, 55; biblical role of,

Oda (daughter of Old Candil), 241
Old Candil, 17, 68, 76, 153; children of, 241; Epi's conversion and, 86; glossolalia and, 78; hymns and, 187; money borrowed by, 297; new minister and, 446–447; private service in home of, 169–170; Rodolfa's conversion and, 123
Old Zapata (father of Agapito), 374–375
Olga (university student), 221–222, 261
omens, 163
orthodoxy, xv
Oscar (son of Wilma), 321, 337, 373, 498; as fisherman, 523; iguana and, 319, 320; letters from, 520–521; Maya language and, 4; as student, 514, 517
overpopulation, 14

Pablo (pimp), 470
PAN (Mexican political party), 84
Pancha (sister of Rodolfa), 395
Pancho E. (Ruben's employer), 351
Pancho N., 391, 428, 486
Panza, Don, 329
parasites, 161, 490
pastors. See ministers
Paul, Saint, 54, 61, 79, 278; resurrection doctrine and, 264; on women's dress, 57; on work, 456
Paula (mother of Pedrito), 65, 77, 81, 101, 117, 162; children of, 87, 88; conversion story of, 87–88; fasting of, 220; glossolalia and, 78–79, 202, 242; home of, 261; Pentecostalism and, 292; pregnancy of, 145, 203, 258; at seashore baptism, 117, 120, 121
Paulino, Hermano, 76, 85–86, 113
peasants, 13, 302, 334, 344, 503
Pedrito (child with polio), 65, 77, 79, 81, 113; fate of, 145; first birthday of, 106–107; inability to walk, 270; medical prescription for, 66, 68; Paula's conversion and, 87, 88; prayers for, 68, 69, 105; presentation to congregation, 74; at seashore baptism, 117, 120; at services, 198
Pedrito (dwarf), 262
Pedro: evangelizing and, 202, 216; living in church, 218; marriage of, 258; testimony of, 170; "water of life" and, 222
Pedro N. (preacher), xvii, 294, 297, 355–356, 390; baptisms performed by, 370; Bible readings from, 433; children of, 371; divine healing and, 391; as false Christ, 402–406; Isauro's prophecy and, 408
Pentecostalism, xv, 89, 175–176, 239, 421; conversion experience and, 61; doctrinal distinction from Apostolic Church, 83; Don Victor and, 285; fundamentalist doctrines of, 102–103; Holy Spirit and, 234; prominence in Latin America, 8; Protestantism and, 5; in the Yucatan Peninsula, 10–11. See

also Apostolic Church of Mexico; Christianity
Pepe (son of Sylvia), 362
Peregrina, Dona, dancing of, 406, 407
Peregrina L. (mother of Luis L.), 21, 26, 97–99, 101, 102, 103, 171, 243; author's return to Yucatan and, 138–140; home of, 282; trance song of, 104, 186
Peregrino, Hermano, 180
Petronila (wife of Enrique), 283, 284, 363, 454
Pilar, Dona, 220
Pipo (husband of crippled woman), 471
Placido, Don, 317
plants, 321
Pola, Hermana (mother of Old Candil), 273–274
police, 109, 110, 171, 414, 471
politics, 286
Popul Vuh, 31
Porfiria (mother of Old Candil), 211
prayer, 28, 69, 124, 162, 393; Catholic, 99; embracing and, 430; Holy Spirit and, 32, 40, 78; for sick people, 52–53
pregnancy, 47, 143, 145, 203, 317; inability to conceive, 25–26; multiple, 169; nursing and, 85; out of wedlock, 98
Presbyterians, 17, 90, 140, 193; attitude toward makeup, 293; demonic possession and, 230; Don Fulgencio and, 19, 89; missionizing of, 93; spread of, 108; tithing of, 397; Don Victor and, 283, 303; worldliness and, 86
PRI (longtime ruling party of Mexico), 82, 84
prophecy, xv, 429, 431, 439, 461
prostitutes/prostitution, 140, 207, 294–295, 353, 510; cathouse, 467, 512; dispute over, 439; Eus's comments about, 39, 293, 295; prices for, 306
Protestantism, xv, 5, 15
pyramids, Mayan, 27, 324, 457

Quintana Roo (Mexican state), 4, 10, 183, 281, 289

Rach, Dona, 199, 512
Radi, Dona, 512
radio, preaching on, 17
rainy season, 46, 63
Rambo, Lewis E., 61
ranchers, 13
Rancho San Jorge, 316–323
rape, 49
rapture, 42, 70
Raquel, Dona, 84, 104, 131, 147, 199, 257; author's farewell and, 134; baptism and, 209, 210; firewood collection and, 322–323; home of, 108, 163; quincenera celebration and, 334–335
rats, 53, 63
rattlesnakes, 38, 173, 258
Ravel, Dona (daughter of Tomasita), 286
Rebecca (daughter of Wilma), 346, 352, 358, 373,

FELICITAS D. GOODMAN taught anthropology at Denison University until her retirement. She has written a number of books, including *Speaking in Tongues; The Exorcism of Anneliese Michel; How about Demons?; Ecstasy, Ritual, and Alternate Reality;* and *Where the Spirits Ride the Wind.*